S0-BME-603

WORLD REPORT

2012

EVENTS OF 2011

Copyright © 2012 Human Rights Watch
All rights reserved.
Printed in the United States of America

ISBN-13: 978-1-60980-389-6

Front cover photo: **Egypt** – *Fatma, 16, joins a pro-democracy protest in Tahrir Square, Cairo, on February 8, 2011. President Hosni Mubarak resigned on February 11.*
© 2011 Yuri Kozyrev/NOOR for Time Magazine

Back cover photo: **Kenya** – *Women widowed by clashes between the insurgent Sabaot Land Defence Force and Kenyan government in 2006-2008 have formed a collective to support one another in the aftermath of their husbands' disappearances and deaths.*
© 2011 Brent Stirton/Getty Images for Human Rights Watch

Cover and book design by Rafael Jiménez

www.hrw.org

Human Rights Watch is dedicated to protecting the human rights of people around the world.

We stand with victims and activists to prevent discrimination, to uphold political freedom, to protect people from inhumane conduct in wartime, and to bring offenders to justice.

We investigate and expose human rights violations and hold abusers accountable.

We challenge governments and those who hold power to end abusive practices and respect international human rights law.

We enlist the public and the international community to support the cause of human rights for all.

HUMAN RIGHTS WATCH

Human Rights Watch is one of the world's leading independent organizations dedicated to defending and protecting human rights. By focusing international attention where human rights are violated, we give voice to the oppressed and hold oppressors accountable for their crimes. Our rigorous, objective investigations and strategic, targeted advocacy build intense pressure for action and raise the cost of human rights abuse. For over 30 years, Human Rights Watch has worked tenaciously to lay the legal and moral groundwork for deep-rooted change and has fought to bring greater justice and security to people around the world.

Human Rights Watch began in 1978 with the founding of its Europe and Central Asia division (then known as Helsinki Watch). Today, it also includes divisions covering Africa, the Americas, Asia, and the Middle East and North Africa; a United States program; thematic divisions or programs on arms, business and human rights, children's rights, health and human rights, international justice, lesbian, gay, bisexual and transgender rights, refugees, and women's rights; and an emergencies program. It maintains offices in Amsterdam, Beirut, Berlin, Brussels, Cairo, Chicago, Geneva, Goma, Johannesburg, London, Los Angeles, Moscow, New York, Paris, San Francisco, Tokyo, Toronto, Tunis, Washington DC, and Zurich, and field presences in 20 other locations globally. Human Rights Watch is an independent, nongovernmental organization, supported by contributions from private individuals and foundations worldwide. It accepts no government funds, directly or indirectly.

The staff includes Kenneth Roth, Executive Director; Michele Alexander, Deputy Executive Director, Development and Global Initiatives; Carroll Bogert, Deputy Executive Director, External Relations; Jan Egeland, Deputy Executive Director, Europe; Iain Levine, Deputy Executive Director, Program; Chuck Lustig, Deputy Executive Director, Operations; Walid Ayoub, Information Technology Director; Pierre Bairin, Media Director; Clive Baldwin, Senior Legal Advisor; Emma Daly, Communications Director; Alan Feldstein, Associate General Counsel; Barbara Guglielmo, Acting Operations Director; Peggy Hicks, Global Advocacy Director; Dinah PoKempner, General Counsel; Aisling Reidy, Senior Legal Advisor; James Ross, Legal and Policy Director; Joe Saunders, Deputy Program Director; Frances Sinha, Global Human Resources Director; and Minky Worden, Director of Global Initiatives.

The division directors of Human Rights Watch are Brad Adams, Asia; Joseph Amon, Health and Human Rights; Daniel Bekele, Africa; John Biaggi, International Film Festival; Peter Bouckaert, Emergencies; Richard Dicker, International Justice; Bill Frelick, Refugees; Arvind Ganesan, Business and Human Rights; Liesl Gerntholtz, Women's Rights; Steve Goose, Arms; Alison Parker, United States; Graeme Reid, Lesbian, Gay, Bisexual and Transgender Rights; José Miguel Vivanco, Americas; Lois Whitman, Children's Rights; and Sarah Leah Whitson, Middle East and North Africa; and Hugh Williamson, Europe and Central Asia.

The advocacy directors of Human Rights Watch are Philippe Bolopion, United Nations– New York; Juliette De Rivero, United Nations–Geneva; Kanae Doi, Japan; Jean-Marie Fardeau, Paris; Meenakshi Ganguly, South Asia; Lotte Leicht, European Union; Tom Malinowski, Washington DC; and Wenzel Michalski, Berlin.

The members of the board of directors are James F. Hoge, Chair; Susan Manilow, Vice Chair; Joel Motley, Vice Chair; Sid Sheinberg, Vice Chair; John J. Studzinski, Vice Chair; Hassan Elmasry, Treasurer; Bruce Rabb, Secretary; Karen Ackman; Jorge Castañeda; Tony Elliott; Michael G. Fisch; Michael E. Gellert; Hina Jilani; Betsy Karel; Wendy Keys; Robert Kissane; Oki Matsumoto; Barry Meyer; Pat Mitchell; Aoife O'Brien; Joan R. Platt; Amy Rao; Neil Rimer; Victoria Riskin; Amy L. Robbins; Shelley Rubin; Kevin P. Ryan; Jean-Louis Servan-Schreiber; Javier Solana; Siri Stolt-Nielsen; Darian W. Swig; John R. Taylor; Marie Warburg; and Catherine Zennström.

Emeritus board members are Robert L. Bernstein, Founding Chair, 1979-1997; Jonathan F. Fanton, Chair, 1998-2003; Jane Olson, 2004-2010; Lisa Anderson; David M. Brown; William D. Carmichael; Vartan Gregorian; Alice H. Henkin; Stephen L. Kass; Marina Pinto Kaufman; Bruce Klatsky; Joanne Leedom-Ackerman; Josh Mailman; Samuel K. Murumba; Peter Osnos; Kathleen Peratis; Bruce Rabb; Sigrid Rausing; Orville Schell; Gary Sick; and Malcolm B. Smith.

ACKNOWLEDGMENTS

A compilation of this magnitude requires contribution from a large number of people, including most of the Human Rights Watch staff. The contributors were:

Fred Abrahams, Pema Abrahams, Brad Adams, Maria Aissa de Figueredo, Chris Albin-Lackey, Celina Almeida, Joe Amon, Elizabeth Ashamu, Laetitia Bader, Pierre Bairin, Amanda Bailly, Clive Baldwin, Heather Barr, Shantha Rau Barriga, Noah Beaudette, Nicholas Bequelin, Jo Becker, Daniel Bekele, Eleanor Blatchley, Carroll Bogert, Philippe Bolopion, Amy Braunschweiger, Sebastian Brett, Reed Brody, Jane Buchanan, Wolfgang Buettner, Maria Burnett, Inga Butefisch, Elizabeth Calvin, Anna Chaplin, Grace Choi, Jane Cohen, Adam Coogle, Tanya Cooper, Eva Cosse, Judit Costa, Zama Coursen-Neff, Emma Daly, Philippe Dam, Kiran D'Amico, Sara Darehshori, Juliette de Rivero, Rachel Denber, Boris Dittrich, Corinne Dufka, Mariam Dwedar, Brahim Elansari, Marianna Enamoneta, Amanda Erickson, Jessica Evans, Elizabeth Evenson, Jean-Marie Fardeau, Guillermo Farias, Alice Farmer, Jamie Fellner, Bill Frelick, Arvind Ganesan, Meenakshi Ganguly, Liesl Gerntholtz, Neela Ghoshal, Thomas Gilchrist, Antonio Ginatta, Giorgi Gogia, Eric Goldstein, Steve Goose, Yulia Gorbunova, Laura Graham, Jessie Graham, Amna Guellali, Shilpa Guha, Eric Guttschuss, Danielle Haas, Aloys Habimana, Charlene Harry, Andreas Harsono, Ali Hasan, Jehanne Henry, José Luis Hernández, Peggy Hicks, Nadim Houry, Lindsey Hutchison, Peter Huvos, Claire Ivers, Balkees Jarrah, Rafael Jimenez, Tiseke Kasambala, Aruna Kashyap, Elise Keppler, Nadya Khalife, Viktoriya Kim, Carolyn Kindelan, Juliane Kippenberg, Amanda Klasing, Erica Lally, Adrianne Lapar, Lotte Leicht, Doutje Lettinga, Boryana Levterova, Iain Levine, Diederik Lohman, Tanya Lokshina, Anna Lopriore, Drake Lucas, Ellie Lust, Tom Malinowski, Edmon Marukyan, David Scott Mathieson, Veronica Matushaj, Maria McFarland, Megan McLemore, Amanda McRae, Grace Meng, David Mepham, Lianna Merner, Wenzel Michalski, Darcy Milburn, Kathy Mills, Lisa Misol, Brittany Mitchell, Heba Morayef, Stephanie Morin, Priyanka Motaparthy, Rasha Moumneh, Lewis Mudge, Sahr Muhammedally, Jim Murphy, Samer Muscati, Dipika Nath, Kristi Ng, Stephanie Neider, Agnes Odhiambo, Alison Parker, Diana Parker, Shaivalini Parmar, Elaine Pearson, Rona Peligal, Sunai Phasuk, Laura Pitter, Dinah PoKempner, Tom Porteous, Jyotsna Poudyal, Andrea Prasow, Marina Pravdic, Sasha Rahmonov, Ben Rawlence,

Graeme Reid, Aisling Reidy, Meghan Rhoad, Sophie Richardson, Lisa Rimli, Mihra Rittmann, Phil Robertson, Kathy Rose, James Ross, Kenneth Roth, Faraz Sanei, Joe Saunders, Ida Sawyer, John Sawyer, Rebecca Schleifer, Max Schoening, Jessica Scholes, Birgit Schwarz, Jake Scobey-Thal, David Segall, Kathryn Semogas, Anna Sevortian, Vikram Shah, Ivy Shen, Bede Sheppard, Gerry Simpson, Emma Sinclair-Webb, Param-Preet Singh, Mickey Spiegel, Xabay Spinka, Nik Steinberg, Joe Stork, Judith Sunderland, Steve Swerdlow, Veronika Szente Goldston, Maya Taal, Tamara Taraciuk, Letta Tayler, Carina Tertsakian, Elena Testi, Tej Thapa, Kate Todrys, Bill van Esveld, Gauri van Gulik, Anneke Van Woudenberg, Elena Vanko, Nisha Varia, José Miguel Vivanco, Florentine Vos, Benjamin Ward, Matt Wells, Lois Whitman, Sarah Leah Whitson, Christoph Wilcke, Daniel Wilkinson, Hugh Williamson, and Minky Worden.

Senior Editor Danielle Haas edited the report with assistance from Deputy Program Directors Joe Saunders, Tom Porteous, and Babatunde Olugboji. Publications Director Grace Choi and Graphic Designer Rafael Jiménez oversaw layout and production, in coordination with Creative Manager Anna Lopriore, Creative Director Veronica Matushaj, and Senior Online Editor Jim Murphy. Program Project Manager Brittany Mitchell oversaw and coordinated the report's editing and production process.

The report was proofread by Grant writers Leeam Azulay, Carolyn Kindelan, and Stephanie Neider; Coordinators Maria Aissa de Figueredo and Adrianne Lapar; and Associates Noah Beaudette, Guillermo Farias, Lindsey Hutchison, Scout Katovich, Erica Lally, Paz Petersson, Jake Scobey-Thal, Matthew Rullo, David Segall, Vikram Shah, and José Luis Hernández, who coordinated the proofreading process.

For a full list of Human Rights Watch staff, please go to our website: www.hrw.org/about/info/staff.html.

TABLE OF CONTENTS

Time to Abandon the Autocrats and Embrace Rights:
The International Response to the Arab Spring

By Kenneth Roth

The sad truth is that the dominant Western policy toward the Arab people traditionally has been one of containment. Today many applaud as the people of the region take to the streets to claim their rights, but until recently Western governments frequently acted as if the Arab people were to be feared, hemmed in, controlled. In other regions, democracy spread, but in the Middle East and North Africa, the West seemed content to back an array of Arab autocrats, so long as they in turn supported Western interests. Elsewhere, governments were expected, at least in principle, to serve their people, but the West looked to the monarchs and strongmen of the Arab world to guarantee "stability," to keep the lid on popular demands. The world's promotion of human rights had an Arab exception.

The Arab Spring showed that many people in the region do not share the West's comfortable complacency with autocratic rule. No longer willing to be the passive subjects of self-serving rulers, they began to insist on becoming full citizens of their countries, the proper agents of their fate. In one country after another, an act of repression sparked popular outrage at a regime that had taken one brutal step too many. This time the much discussed but long quiescent Arab Street arose and upended the old order. In finding its collective voice and power, the region's people transformed its politics in a way that will not be easy to turn back.

In Tunisia, the catalyst was the self-immolation of fruit vendor Mohamed Bouazizi after a routine case of humiliation by the police. In Egypt, it was photos of the deformed face of Khaled Said, a young man beaten to death by the police. In Syria, it was the torture of teenagers for scribbling anti-regime graffiti. In Libya, it was the arrest of Fathi Terbil, the lawyer for the victims of the 1996 Abu Salim prison massacre. These quotidian examples of abuse, among countless others, sparked what in essence became a series of human rights revolutions—driven by demands for governments that, finally, would be elected by their people, respectful of their rights, and subject to the rule of law.

The West is still adjusting to this historic transformation. While generally opposing the violent suppression of peaceful demonstrations, many of the world's leading democracies remain reluctant partners of the protesters, worried by the consequences of entrusting these pivotal countries to their citizens.

And if Western governments have been hesitant to abandon autocratic friends, many other countries have shown outright hostility to the rebellions. Dictatorial governments have been predictably terrified by the precedent of people ousting authoritarian regimes. China went to extraordinary lengths to prevent "Jasmine rallies" inspired by Tunisia's Jasmine Revolution. North Korea was so determined to keep its people in the dark about the Arab Spring that it prevented its workers in Libya from returning home. From Zimbabwe to Iran, Sudan to Uzbekistan, Cuba to Russia, Ethiopia to Vietnam, autocrats live in fear of the kind of popular power demonstrated by the Arab Spring.

They are not wrong in their apprehension. The uprisings show that the quest for rights has broad appeal, capable of uniting disparate elements of society and generating a powerful collective force for change. The old tools of repression—the censorship, the arbitrary detention, the torture, the killing—seem only to have emboldened the demonstrators once they gained confidence in their numbers. Rather than instilling fear and grudging acquiescence, the repression showed the autocrats' true colors and highlighted the righteousness of the protesters' cause. That sends a chilling warning to regimes long confident in the assumption that their repressive capacity would always eclipse the public's discontent.

More disappointing in their response to the Arab Spring have been some democratic governments of the global South, such as Brazil, India, and South Africa. They seemed to be guided less by the aspirations of the Arab people than by their commitment to outmoded views of national sovereignty, even when it has meant shielding repressive regimes from urgently needed international pressure. Despite themselves having developed accountable governments and the rule of law, these Southern democracies showed only sporadic interest in helping the people of the Arab world who were struggling to do the same. More often, they pointed to the potential misuse of human rights pressure—the fear that it might serve as a tool of Northern dominance—to justify failing to use their own influence on serious violators of human rights.

This indifference from many quarters to the rights of the region's people must end. Standing firmly with the people of the Middle East and North Africa when they demand their legitimate rights is the best way to exert pressure on their persecutors to stop the bloodshed. A principled insistence on respect for rights is also the best way to help these popular movements steer clear of the intolerance, lawlessness, and summary revenge that are a risk in any revolution and its aftermath.

The Arab Spring is a transformative moment, an historic opportunity for a long-suppressed people to seize control of its destiny. Yet the transformation will not be easy. The people of the region, like everywhere else, deserve the world's support for their rights as they embark on this long-awaited venture. It is time for the Arab exception to end.

The West's Embrace of Arab Autocrats

Western governments allowed the Arab exception because they believed their interests in the region would be better served by authoritarian rulers' illusory promise of "stability" than by the uncertainties of elected government. Five core reasons explain the West's past acceptance of these would-be presidents and monarchs-for-life.

The first was containing any threat to Western interests from political Islam. Western governments and their allies have always had a certain ambivalence toward political Islam—promoting it when seen as a useful foil for a more dreaded enemy (the mujahedeen against the Soviets, Hamas against the Palestine Liberation Organization) or when it aligned with Western interests

(as in Saudi Arabia). But when political Islam challenged friendly governments, the West has been deeply wary.

A major catalyst for this distrust was a non-Arab nation—Iran, as it emerged
after overthrowing the Western-supported Shah. The dread of "another
Khomeini"—of Iran's hostility to the United States, brutality toward its own
people, and support for Hezbollah and Hamas—led many Western governments to distrust political Islam when it took the form of an opposition movement challenging an ally.

The nadir of this distrust came in the early 1990s when, after a brief political
opening in Algeria, the Islamic Salvation Front appeared to be on the verge of
electoral victory. A military coup stopped the electoral process with scant
Western protest. Coup supporters argued that the Islamists' secret agenda
was to allow "one man, one vote, one time."

Many Islamic parties have indeed embraced disturbing positions that would
subjugate the rights of women and restrict religious, personal, and political
freedoms. But so have many of the autocratic regimes that the West props
up. Moreover, Islamic movements are hardly monolithic or implacably
opposed to rights. Yet rather than engage with them to demand respect for
rights, Western governments have often treated them as untouchable.

That distrust made a mockery of occasional Western support in the region for
democracy. For example, in a post-facto attempt to justify his invasion of Iraq
as an act of democracy promotion, US President George W. Bush briefly
pressed for elections elsewhere in the region as well. But that democracy
agenda quickly ended once Hamas prevailed in fair elections in the West
Bank and Gaza in 2006, and the Muslim Brotherhood won most of the seats it
contested in Egypt's parliamentary elections in 2005.

Despite Western caution, political Islam has gained adherents as it has
become a primary mode of expressing discontent with the region's corrupt
and unresponsive rulers. Because the mosque has often been the freest institution in an otherwise suppressed civil society, it has also become a natural
gathering point for dissent. Arab leaders typically have had only to dangle the

threat of hostile Islamists replacing them in order to lock in Western support for crackdowns and defer demands for elections.

A second reason for Western indulgence of Arab strongmen was the perception that they could help to combat the threat of terrorism. Arab extremists by no means hold a monopoly on terrorism, but Western policymakers viewed certain Arab groups as particularly menacing because they murdered civilians not only in their own countries but also in the West. In the name of protecting their citizens, Western governments were willing to promote Arab autocrats who vowed to fight these terrorists. That these autocrats also tortured or repressed their own people was seen as secondary. That this repression often fueled support for violent extremist groups was ignored.

Third, the West trusted Arab autocrats more than the Arab people to reach a *modus vivendi* with Israel—a factor that was particularly important in policy toward Egypt, Jordan, and to some extent Syria and Lebanon. Many Arabs were naturally disturbed by Israel's repression of the Palestinian people, and often protested. The autocrats of the region soon learned that allowing—even encouraging—these protests was a good way to channel discontent away from their own misrule. So long as Arab dictators kept the protests under control, they enjoyed Western support. Those who went further and signed a peace treaty with Israel received massive US aid regardless of their domestic policies.

Fourth, the West saw Arab autocrats as the best way to sustain the flow of oil. Of course, even Ayatollah Ruhollah Khomeini's Iran and Muammar Gaddafi's Libya willingly sold oil to the West. But with markets tight and prices high, revolutionary change, particularly in Saudi Arabia, risked economic turmoil through a disruption of the oil flow. Nor did the West want a hostile Iran to gain control over the vast oil reserves of its neighboring Persian Gulf states. To prevent these scenarios, or any threat to the cozy relationships that developed between Western and Arab business elites, the West preferred the strongmen it knew to the vagaries of popular rule. Meanwhile, often-bountiful oil revenue gave these autocrats the coercive means to retain power without accountability to a tax-paying public.

5

Finally, the West—particularly the European Union—looked to the region's authoritarian governments to help stem migration. Northern Africa is both a source of, and an important transit route for, undocumented migration to Europe. The West relied on pliant governments to help curb it—to prevent migrants from departing their shores and to accept their summary return. The EU, in turn, rewarded these governments with various trade and aid agreements.

The Fallacy of the "Arab Exception"

Despite their self-interested motives, Western governments did not like to admit their preference for Arab authoritarianism. Instead, they proceeded as if the usual convenient mischaracterizations of Arab society were true—that it was politically passive and underdeveloped, that deference to authority was inherent in Arab culture, that some combination of Arab tradition and Islam made the people of the region uninterested in or unsuited for democracy. The uprisings that have shaken the Arab world belie these convenient excuses for accommodating the region's despots.

Ironically, none of the forces most feared by the West lay behind this last year's outburst of popular protest. Political Islam was little in evidence as a spark or sustaining force for the uprisings; it emerged mainly later, when the Islamists' better organization and traditional opposition role gave them a competitive advantage over newer activists and parties. Nor was there any prominent place in the protests for opposition to Israeli policies, support for terrorism, or anti-Western sentiment. The uprisings represented a determination to improve life at home rather than flee to Europe.

The driving force for the rebellions was opposition to autocratic rule itself. Tunisians, Egyptians, Libyans, Bahrainis, Yemenis, Syrians, and others had had enough of the repression, corruption, cronyism, arbitrary rule, and stagnant societies of the autocrats. These were protests of outrage at an out-of-touch, self-serving elite. Much like the revolutions that upended Eastern Europe in 1989, the Arab upheavals were inspired by a vision of freedom, a desire for a voice in one's destiny, and a quest for governments that are accountable to the public rather than captured by a ruling elite.

International Ambivalence

Yet Western governments still at times have been ambivalent about these movements and selective in their response, unsure how to reconcile their comfort with the old autocrats and the growing realization that these despots' days are numbered. The US and EU were most principled and determined in responding to repression by two Arab governments that at various points had been considered antagonists. In Libya, they imposed sanctions and invoked the International Criminal Court (ICC). Several of them forged a rapid military response to what they saw as an impending human rights disaster. In Syria, after some hesitation, they aligned themselves with a peaceful opposition movement and instituted targeted sanctions against President Bashar al-Assad's government.

Elsewhere, however, the Western approach to the region's uprisings has been more tentative and uncertain. The US government was reluctant to challenge Egypt's President Hosni Mubarak, a perceived bulwark of regional "stability," until his fate was virtually sealed, and then was hesitant for too long to press Egypt's ruling military council to subject itself to elected civilian rule. France remained similarly attached to Tunisia's President Zine el-Abidine Ben Ali until his reign had largely ended.

Similarly, Western governments imposed no meaningful consequences for killing protesters on the government of Yemen's President Ali Abdullah Saleh, whom they viewed as a defense against al Qaeda in the Arabian Peninsula. They condemned Bahrain's suppression of its democracy movement, and urged some reforms, but applied no real pressure on the government out of concern for the fate of the US Fifth Fleet's base, as well as deference to Saudi Arabia, which worried about Iranian meddling in that Shia-majority country and feared a democratic model off its shore. Even within the US government, policymakers were divided on Bahrain, with the US Congress blocking an arms sale proposed by President Barack Obama's administration. Meanwhile,

Western governments urged reforms in the region's other monarchies, such as constitutional amendments in Morocco and pledges for change in Jordan, but said little when monarchies have taken anti-democratic actions, such as the adoption of new repressive laws in Saudi Arabia and the imprisonment of five democracy activists in the United Arab Emirates.

Nations outside the West have shown similar inconsistency. Arab League governments historically sought to defend each other from any form of human rights criticism. Now, they have become more constructively engaged, driven to varying degrees by the new post-rebellion governments, regional rivalries (especially with Iran), and an attempt to stay relevant amid the region's pro-democracy movements. In Libya, the Arab League's endorsement of pressure on Gaddafi laid the groundwork for action by the United Nations Security Council. In Syria, the Arab League protested the political killings and crafted a plan for ending the violence to which Syria theoretically agreed. When Syria predictably broke its word, the Arab League suspended its membership and announced sanctions.

By contrast, the African Union has been shamefully complacent. Ostensibly founded to promote democracy, it has acted like a dictator's support club, siding with whichever government happens to be in power regardless of its conduct. As the revolutions proceeded in Tunisia, Egypt, and Libya, the AU was at best irrelevant, at worst unhelpful. Only the AU's independent African Court on Human and Peoples' Rights, in its first substantive case, ordered Gaddafi to end the killing.

Russia and China tolerated international action in Libya only when their political isolation would have made blocking it seem callous. When they had partners in their indifference, as in the case of Syria, they had no qualms about vetoing international action.

Brazil, India, and South Africa—the key Southern democracies on the UN Security Council—endorsed or tolerated international action on Libya, but then cited NATO's alleged overstepping of its protection mandate there as a justification for not endorsing even symbolic Security Council pressure on Syria.

This international ambivalence comes at a time when the Arab Spring revolutions are anything but complete. Idealistic revolutionaries face serious countervailing pressures with no guarantee of victory. Moreover, the revolutionaries themselves have at times violated rights, as in Libyan militias' apparent summary execution of Muammar Gaddafi and his son Muatassim and their persecution of black African migrant workers. The international community could play an important role in countering these threats to the emergence of rights-respecting democracies—from both the old powers and the new revolutionary forces.

Three Groups of Countries in the Region

In considering the region, it is useful to think in terms of three broad groups of countries.

The first, comprising Tunisia, Egypt, and Libya, has overthrown long-time autocrats (though in the case of Egypt, not entrenched military rule) and at this writing is in the difficult process of building a new governmental order. The task is not simple. It is easier to tear down autocratic institutions than to replace them with democratic ones, to build consensus on the need to oust the despot than to forge a common vision of what should replace him. And unlike in Eastern Europe in 1989, there is no lure of prospective European Union membership to encourage the new governments to respect rights (although the EU does have other carrots to offer, such as trade preferences and visa liberalization). Nor are repressive regimes crumbling as quickly as in 1989 or opponents of those regimes as united. Rather, the cautionary tale comes from the dictatorships of post-Soviet Central Asia, where anti-democratic forces prevailed and substituted new repressive regimes for their Communist predecessors.

Fortunately, the countries in this first group are relatively unburdened by the sectarian strife that so poisoned Iraq's post-Saddam Hussein nation building and continues to rear its head in Syria, Bahrain, and Saudi Arabia. However, these countries have their own divides at risk of being inflamed—tribal in Libya, Copt-Muslim in Egypt, coastal-interior in Tunisia. Particularly in times of uncertainty, people are more susceptible to the fear-mongering and provocation that encourage resort to communal identities, and there are always beneficiaries of the old order who are willing to stoke those fears. Moreover, if hard economic times continue, the danger grows of people forsaking democratic ideals for uglier, less tolerant, politics.

At the moment, Tunisia seems best placed to move forward. Old laws restricting association, assembly, speech and political parties have been reformed. After elections for a constituent assembly that were widely seen as free and fair, the Islamic party al Nahda ("The Awakening") gained a plurality of the vote, and its leaders made encouraging pledges about building a broad governing coalition and respecting the rights of all Tunisians. This is a promising beginning, but the pledges, of course, remain to be tested.

In Libya, the transitional authorities repeatedly vowed to respect citizens' rights, to establish control over all militias, and to subject themselves to the rule of law. But fulfilling these pledges will be difficult, particularly in a country that Gaddafi deliberately left bereft of developed government institutions. So far, the new authorities have failed to gain control over the many militias that have power and substantial arms. And despite stated plans to try Saif al-Islam Gaddafi, the former leader's son wanted by the ICC, they have not built a criminal justice system capable of meeting ICC requirements for a fair trial.

Egypt, the region's largest country and long-time leader, must still overcome intense internal divisions among three broad groupings: the military which despite great popular discontent remained in power after replacing Mubarak, the largely secular leftists and liberals who were so prominent during the Tahrir Square uprising, and the Islamists who at key moments joined the demonstrations in large numbers and have emerged as the dominant political force. At various points each group cautiously has seen the others as both potential allies and adversaries.

The military, under pressure to give up power, at times saw the Islamists with their social orientation as less likely than the liberals to impede its autonomy or to scrutinize its massive budget and business interests. The liberals looked (illiberally) to the military to enforce limits on political Islam, while joining with the Islamists in an effort to oust the military. The Islamists, distrustful of the military after decades of suppression, hoped the liberals would help to secure a democratic transition, yet potentially differed from the liberals on a range of social freedoms. And to further complicate matters, the Islamists were divided in their interpretation of Islamic law and the role they see for Islam in governing the country. It remains far from clear how this complicated tug-of-war will be resolved.

The second group of Arab countries—Syria, Yemen and Bahrain—is enmeshed in struggles between abusive governments and oppositions calling for democratic rule. Syrians have shown remarkable bravery, repeatedly taking to the streets despite the omnipresence of security forces that frequently respond with lethal force. Yemen's overwhelmingly peaceful protests have been gradually overshadowed by armed clashes among rival elite factions, and it is too soon to tell whether an exit pact signed by President Saleh is a step toward genuine reform. Bahrain's rulers, backed by security forces led by neighboring Saudi Arabia, have used a panoply of repressive tools—lethal force against peaceful protesters, torture and ill-treatment, unfair trials, abrupt dismissal of workers from jobs and students from universities—but have succeeded only in creating a divided population with many seemingly counting the days until the next opportunity to rise up. The success of the protest movements in these countries remains very much in play.

Finally, there are the region's monarchies which, apart from Bahrain, have largely avoided large-scale uprisings. They enjoy the advantage of being able to diffuse popular discontent by sacking the government—Jordan in particular has seen a revolving door of prime ministers—without jeopardizing the monarchy. Some monarchs—in Morocco, Kuwait, and Qatar—have experimented with granting limited powers to elected parliaments while retaining control over the most important levers of power. Some in the Persian Gulf have tried to buy social peace by showering salary increases and subsidies on disgruntled populations. These tactics, at times coupled with a heavy dose of repression, have mostly diffused large-scale protests.

Yet that social peace may be short-lived. Saudi Arabia, for example, has elements for its own springtime movement: an aging leadership and a young and disenchanted population. (The same can be said of non-monarchial Algeria, which suppressed the limited protests it experienced in 2011.) The Saudi royal family has been savvy so far about preserving its rule—whether by disbursing oil money or whipping up sectarian fears—but that is only buying time.

The Proper Role of the International Community

How should the international community respond to this complex and varied landscape? Before taking up prescriptions, a degree of humility is in order. The revolutions of the Arab Spring have been internally driven—the achievement foremost of those countries' citizens. External forces have had influence, but in most places only around the margins.

That said, the response of external actors can be important, and sometimes decisive. The Arab League's abandonment of Gaddafi as his forces opened fire on protesters in Tripoli and he threatened a massacre in Benghazi laid the groundwork for UN Security Council action to protect civilians. US pressure, reinforced by the leverage of large-scale aid, helped to convince Egypt's military early in the revolution to protect the Tahrir Square demonstrators from attacks by police and Mubarak supporters. Targeted economic sanctions on the Syrian elite provide one of the best chances of convincing its members to part with Assad's brutal strategy of repression.

Looking forward, to promote democratic, rights-respecting governments, the international community should adopt a more principled approach to the region than in the past. That would involve, foremost, clearly siding with democratic reformers even at the expense of abandoning autocratic friends. There is no excuse for any government to tolerate Assad's lethal repression, to close its eyes to Bahrain's systematic crackdown, or to exempt other monarchs from pressure to reform. All autocrats should be dissuaded from using repression to defend their power and privileges.

Such principled support for protesters can also positively influence the outlook of the new governments they seek to form. Revolution can be a heady experience, opening previously unthought-of possibilities for the majority to take control of its fate. But the revolutionaries must also accept the constraints on majoritarian rule that rights require, especially when it comes to the rights of minorities, whether political, religious, ethnic or social.

Revolutionary zeal can lead to summary revenge or a new imposed orthodoxy. Continuing economic hardship can lead to scapegoating and intolerance. International affirmation of the importance of respecting the rights of all citizens can help to ensure the emergence of genuine democracies. Conditioning economic assistance on respect for those rights, just as the EU conditioned accession for Eastern European states, can help to steer new governments in rights-respecting directions.

By the same token, the international community must also come to terms with political Islam when it represents a majority preference. Islamist parties are genuinely popular in much of the Arab world, in part because many Arabs have come to see political Islam as the antithesis of autocratic rule, in part because Islamist parties generally did a good job of distinguishing themselves through social service programs from the corrupt and self-serving state, in part because Islamists enjoyed organizational advantages that long-repressed secular counterparts did not share, and in part because political Islam reflects the conservative and religious ethos of many people in the region. Ignoring that popularity would violate democratic principles.

Rather, wherever Islam-inspired governments emerge, the international community should focus on encouraging, and if need be pressuring, them to respect basic rights—just as the Christian-labeled parties and governments of Europe are expected to do. Embracing political Islam need not mean rejecting human rights, as illustrated by the wide gulf between the restrictive views of some Salafists and the more progressive interpretation of Islam that leaders such as Rashid Ghannouchi, head of Tunisia's Nahdha Party, espouse. It is important to nurture the rights-respecting elements of political Islam while standing firm against repression in its name. So long as freely elected governments respect basic rights, they merit presumptive international support, regardless of their political or religious complexion.

The Quest for Freedom of Expression

The right to freedom of expression also requires consistent defense. The Arab revolutions became possible only as civil society was able to organize itself and, using the internet, build public outrage by circumventing the state's monopoly over the public dissemination of information. Satellite television, represented foremost by Al Jazeera, also played an essential role in galvanizing outrage to the brutal repression that it regularly beamed throughout the region. Just as civil society must continue to be nurtured, so this key medium of communication needs a strong defense, even when its message may be seen as "anti-Western."

The newest frontier for the battle over free expression is social media. Though limited to a wired elite, and surpassed in importance by more prosaic technology such as satellite TV and mobile telephones, social media played an early and important role, allowing seemingly leaderless movements to build momentum gradually, with participants standing up to be counted (for example, by signaling support on Facebook) without necessarily taking to the streets until there was a sufficient sense of safety in numbers. Social media such as Twitter also helped protesters to communicate with each other and the world about police repression and ways to outfox it. Activists used YouTube to post mobile-phone videos recording military and police brutality.

But social media can also be a tool for monitoring and repressing the opposition. That was President Assad's calculation when he invited Facebook and YouTube into Syria at the height of Egypt's revolution. His bet that his secret police could stay a step ahead of proliferating users turned out to be misplaced, but other countries both in the region and beyond are still trying to limit the political threat that social media poses, often using Western technology.

The winner of this cat-and-mouse game between censor and user, the repressive monitor and the freedom-seeking protester, remains in doubt. Strong global standards are needed to better protect the freedom and privacy of internet users. And international companies should be prevented from selling equipment or know-how to governments, in the Arab world or elsewhere, that allows them to spy on or repress ordinary citizens.

Complicity in Torture

Even the tightest controls cannot prevent some whiff of freedom from entering public consciousness, and the region's security forces have all too often responded with torture. In principle, the international community firmly opposes torture, as reflected in numerous treaties outlawing it without exception. Yet the fight against terrorism and political Islam led to growing international tolerance of, and sometimes active complicity in, torture. Following the September 11, 2001 attacks the Bush administration not only used torture itself but, aided by various allies, also sent terrorist suspects for interrogation by the region's security forces despite their pervasive use of torture. That inexcusable complicity set a terrible precedent, reinforcing regional security forces' worst habits, while weakening the credibility of occasional protests from the West.

The Obama administration ordered an end to this complicity in torture but has refused to investigate, let alone prosecute, the US officials who were responsible. The short-term political calculation behind that dereliction of duty risks dangerous long-term consequences by signaling that torture is a policy option rather than a crime. The United Kingdom government has at least authorized an investigation into British complicity in torture overseas, but so far under rules of secrecy and unilateral inquiry that bode poorly for an honest examination.

Western hypocrisy toward torture in the region is best illustrated by the use of "memoranda of understanding," or "diplomatic assurances," to justify sending terrorism suspects to security services that are likely to torture them. CIA documents that Human Rights Watch found in a Libyan intelligence office show how these worked. The US and UK cooperated in sending suspects captured abroad for interrogation by Libyan intelligence services despite their notorious torture record. Yet the CIA dutifully sought assurances from the Libyans that suspects would not be mistreated. These assurances were no more than a fig leaf. Given that the Libyan government was already flouting its legally binding treaty obligations not to torture, as the US government itself regularly reported, there was no reason to expect it to respect a quiet promise between diplomats or intelligence agencies. It would make an enormous contribution to ending torture in the Arab world if the West were to come clean about its own complicity, punish those responsible for the crime of ordering or facilitating torture, and explicitly end use of diplomatic assurances to justify sending suspects to countries where they risk torture.

The Need to End Impunity

Revolutionary movements need help building the governing institutions that the autocrats deliberately left weak and underdeveloped, above all national institutions of justice for holding all representatives of the state subject to the rule of law. Until security forces and government officials have a reasonable expectation that their misconduct will land them in court, the temptation to resort to the former regimes' corruption and abuse will be hard to resist.

Yet at least when it comes to international justice, the international community still sometimes acts as if democratic transitions are best advanced by sweeping past abuses under the rug. As the Arab upheavals have shown, a precedent of impunity is not easily forgotten, increasing the likelihood that bad habits persist. And prosecution is not the impediment to democratic change that is so often assumed.

When the ICC issued arrest warrants for Muammar Gaddafi, his son Saif al-Islam, and his intelligence chief Abdullah Sanussi, some argued that this act of justice would discourage Gaddafi from relinquishing power. Yet in common with most dictators, Gaddafi had already made clear even before the ICC warrants that he intended to stay in power until the bitter end, with his son Saif vowing that they would fight on "to the last man." If anything, the arrest warrants hastened Gaddafi's downfall by signaling to his coterie that they had no political future with him and were better off defecting.

But Gaddafi was a tyrant who was easy to abandon and hold to account. The international community was less principled in the case of Yemen's Saleh. In an initiative launched by the Gulf Cooperation Council (GCC) with no clear disapproval from the UN Security Council, Saleh and other senior officials were offered blanket immunity from prosecution in exchange for stepping down. The perverse effect was that Saleh's government was given a green light to continue killing demonstrators without consequence. Even when Saleh agreed to resign as president, his supporters continued to kill, knowing that if they succeeded in clinging to power, they obviously would not prosecute themselves, and confident that if they failed, the GCC had said they would not face prosecution either.

The international community was no more principled in its approach to justice elsewhere in the region. Russia, China, Brazil, India, and South Africa all refused to support authorizing ICC involvement in Syria, despite levels of killing that far exceeded Libya's at the time of its referral to the ICC. And the West persisted in its usual exemption of Israel from the demands of justice, most recently insisting that if the Palestinian Authority is accepted as a UN observer state it must not seek access to the ICC. The US even opposed a proposed UN Human Rights Council request that the Security Council refer Syria to the ICC for fear that it would set a precedent that might be used against Israel.

The Role of Brazil, India, and South Africa

The international response to the Arab rebellions illustrates the importance of building broad coalitions in defense of human rights. Multilateral pressure for reform reaffirms that the values in question are universal rather than the narrow agenda of a particular region. Quite apart from the much-contested military intervention in Libya, the international community was strongest in putting pressure on Gaddafi when it acted in unison. That Brazil, India, and South Africa, backed by the Arab League, joined the major Western powers in referring Libya to the ICC made it difficult for China or Russia to stand isolated in opposition. The result was historic—unanimous UN Security Council action—sending Gaddafi a powerful message he ignored at his peril.

Sadly, when it came to defending the Syrian people, Brazil, India, and South Africa reverted to their reflexive opposition to human rights pressure and refused to support Security Council action even as the Assad government killed thousands of protesters. Only in the less powerful UN General Assembly did Brazil support a critical resolution on Syria, while India and South Africa abstained. As noted, their main excuse for not supporting Security Council action was NATO's alleged overreaching in Libya—when, they contended, NATO moved beyond the authorized protection of civilians and adopted an agenda of regime change. But no one could have interpreted the mildly worded draft Security Council resolution on Syria that they refused to support as authorizing military force. Instead, they effectively asked the people of Syria to pay the price for NATO's alleged misconduct in Libya. That indifference to Syrians' plight is particularly disappointing coming from countries that enjoy strong democratic governance, and in the past have suffered the indifference of other countries to their own struggle for freedom.

The Role of Turkey

Perhaps the most interesting new presence in the region is Turkey. Despite its distinct history, it remains a powerful example of a country with a religiously conservative elected government that has not used Islam as a pretext to undermine basic rights. Turkey has capitalized on its growing stature by entering the political fray of the Arab world. More vigorously than its Arab neighbors, Turkey denounced the political killing in Syria, championed democratic change in Egypt, and opposed Israel's punitive blockade of Gaza.

Yet Turkey faces several challenges if it is to live up to its enormous potential in the human rights realm. Will it use its growing influence in multilateral arenas to oppose the outdated view of India, Brazil, and South Africa that it is somehow imperialistic to stand with people who are risking their lives to protest repression by their governments? Will Turkey press for democratic change not only among the uprisings of the Arab world but also in Iran, which crushed its Green Revolution in 2009, and the stultified and repressive countries of post-Soviet Central Asia? And will Turkey clean up its worsening human rights record at home—including persistent restrictions on freedom of speech and association, a flawed criminal justice system, and long-term mistreatment of its Kurdish minority—so it can be a less compromised proponent of human rights abroad? Turkey can make a positive difference on human rights in the region—if its leaders take the bold decisions at home and abroad needed to advance this cause.

A Global Responsibility

The past year has seen revolutions in the Arab world that few would have imagined. These uprisings present extraordinary opportunities to heed the pleas of people who so far have benefited little from global human rights advances of the last half-century. Yet given the violent forces resisting progress, it is wrong to leave the fate of the Arab world solely in the hands of the people facing the guns. The international community has an important role to play in assisting the birth of rights-respecting democracies in the region.

So far, that role has been played only equivocally. Short-term parochial interests are still too often allowed to stand in the way of a more principled and helpful response. Ultimately, the international community must decide what it stands for—whether it values the rights and aspirations of the individual over the spoils and promises of the tyrant. As we pass the first anniversary of the initial Arab Spring rebellions, the international community will help to determine whether violent governments prevail over protesters seeking a better life, and whether the protesters' vision includes respect not only for their own rights but also for those of all their fellow citizens. It is a global responsibility to help see a positive conclusion to the Arab people's brave efforts to demand their rights, and to ensure that the toppling of one autocratic regime does not lead to its replacement by another.

The World Report

The World Report is Human Rights Watch's twenty-second annual review of human rights practices around the globe. It summarizes key human rights issues in more than 90 countries and territories worldwide, drawing on events from January through November 2011.

The book is divided into five essays, followed by a photo essay, and country-specific chapters.

In the first essay, Eric Goldstein considers signs of change that human rights workers overlooked before this year's populist revolts ("Before the Arab Spring, the Unseen Thaw"). Rachel Denber sifts through the aftermath of the USSR's collapse 20 years ago in search of lessons ("After the Fall"). Meanwhile, Ben Ward notes that while many European officials see the Arab Spring as "the most thrilling period since the fall of the Berlin Wall," domestic rights policies increasingly are falling short ("Europe's Own Human Rights Crisis").

Next, Shanta Rau Barriga looks at misguided policies that often deprive people with disabilities of the ability to make fundamental choices about their own lives, while claiming to protect them ("From Paternalism to Dignity"). "Good intentions," she notes, "don't always make for good policy."

Finally, Jo Becker and Nisha Varia sound a cautious note of victory, hailing a new International Labour Organization convention that establishes global labor standards for the 50 to 100 million women and girls worldwide who clean, cook, and look after children and the elderly in private homes ("A Landmark Victory for Domestic Workers").

The photo essay that follows—which includes images from the 2011 uprisings in Bahrain, Egypt, Libya, Syria, Tunisia, and Yemen—captures some of the tumult, violence, and also hope seen during the past 11 months.

Each country entry identifies significant human rights issues, examines the freedom of local human rights defenders to conduct their work, and surveys the response of key international actors, such as the United Nations, European Union, Japan, the United States, and various regional and international organizations and institutions.

The report reflects extensive investigative work undertaken in 2011 by the Human Rights Watch research staff, usually in close partnership with human rights activists in the country in question. It also reflects the work of our advocacy team, which monitors policy developments and strives to persuade governments and international institutions to curb abuses and promote human rights. Human Rights Watch publications, issued throughout the year, contain more detailed accounts of many of the issues addressed in the brief summaries in this volume. They can be found on the Human Rights Watch website, www.hrw.org.

As in past years, this report does not include a chapter on every country where Human Rights Watch works, nor does it discuss every issue of importance. Failure to include a particular country or issue often reflects no more than staffing limitations and should not be taken as commentary on the significance of the problem. There are many serious human rights violations that Human Rights Watch simply lacks the capacity to address.

The factors we considered in determining the focus of our work in 2011 (and hence the content of this volume) include the number of people affected and the severity of abuse, access to the country and the availability of information about it, the susceptibility of abusive forces to influence, and the importance of addressing certain thematic concerns and of reinforcing the work of local rights organizations.

The World Report does not have separate chapters addressing our thematic work but instead incorporates such material directly into the country entries. Please consult the Human Rights Watch website for more detailed treatment of our work on children's rights, women's rights, arms and military issues, business and human rights, health and human rights, international justice, terrorism and counterterrorism, refugees and displaced people, and lesbian, gay, bisexual, and transgender people's rights, and for information about our international film festivals.

Kenneth Roth is executive director of Human Rights Watch.

BEFORE THE ARAB SPRING, THE UNSEEN THAW

By Eric Goldstein

Like everyone else, we didn't see it coming.

Even though we human rights workers spent much time scrutinizing the Middle East and North Africa from the bottom up, talking to the disenfranchised, the oppressed, and the stubbornly defiant, the timing and extent of the popular revolts that shook the region in 2011 surprised us as much as they did policy-makers, scholars, diplomats, and journalists.

Why didn't we see the upheavals coming? One reason was because we overestimated the robustness of some of the authoritarian regimes, and underestimated demands for a better life, measured partly in human rights terms. Yes, we heard a lot about the *hogra*, an Algerian term used throughout North Africa to denote the contempt of rulers toward their people. But we failed to see how quickly it could ignite into a region-wide revolt that is, in large part, a struggle for dignity.

It's a concept that is, of course, central to the human rights enterprise. The Universal Declaration of Human Rights leads with the assertion that "recognition of the inherent dignity...." of human beings is the "foundation of freedom, justice and peace in the world." The Koran says that God has "dignified humankind," while contemporary philosophers have reflected on the link between dignity and human rights. Martha Nussbaum, for example, writes that all persons "are of equal dignity and worth." The primary source of these values, she says, is a power of moral choice within them that gives them a fair claim to certain types of treatment from society and politics. "This treatment must ... respect and promote the liberty of choice, and ... respect and promote the equal worth of persons as choosers," she states.

The notion of dignity is so central to human rights that it had—for me at least—become an abstraction until the Arab Spring protests forced me to reflect on its meaning. Long before Tunisian peddler Mohamed Bouazizi set himself ablaze on December 17, 2010, to protest a humiliating run-in that day with local police—igniting unrest that ousted President Zine el-Abidine Ben Ali one month later and spread as far as Syria, Bahrain, and Yemen—there were countless, equally poignant protests against indignity that passed unnoticed. But they added to the pent-up frustrations that gave resonance to Bouazizi's desperate act.

In 2004, for example, Slaheddine Aloui, a Tunisian agricultural engineer recently freed from 14 years in jail for political activity, sat down in a local market holding a sign that offered, with Swiftian irony, to sell his daughters. The Ben Ali government had prevented him from supporting his family by pressuring employers not to hire ex-political prisoners and had imposed a 16-year sentence of post-prison "administrative control" that subjected him to onerous and time-consuming sign-in requirements.

This quest for dignity, including the right to self-governance, was evident throughout Tunisia on election day, October 23, 2011, as more than 80 percent of registered voters joined long lines to vote in the country's first free election, in this case for a constituent assembly that will write a constitution. "It's the first time I've waited on line for three hours for anything and am smiling," one voter told me.

And it was the demand for dignity that propelled a depoliticized Egyptian middle class into action, as Ramez Mohamed, a 26-year-old computer science graduate who works in telecommunications told *The New York Times* in February 2011:

> ... the [government's] websites' blockade and communications blackout on January 28 was one of the main reasons I, and many others, were pushed to the streets.... Imagine sitting at your home, having no single connection with the outer world. I took the decision, "This is nonsense, we are not sheep in their herd." I went down and joined the protests.

For many Libyans, dignity came via a rebellion that showed the world, "We are not Gaddafi"—the leader with whom the country had been synonymous for four decades—but rather a people able to shape its own destiny.

We failed to predict the Arab Spring was because we were more focused on supply than demand when it came to human rights; that is, we were more attuned to the extent to which governments supplied (or did not supply) the chance to exercise basic rights than we were with the pent-up demand of people to exercise those rights, despite the risks involved.

We tended to see mainly the authoritarian governments, whose grip was never in doubt, even when they tolerated a controlled pluralism, cautiously independent print media, and a fragile civil society. What we undervalued were rising expectations on the demand side, which subsequently fired the 2011 upheavals, during which thousands of peaceful demonstrators gave their lives in Tunisia, Egypt, Libya, Syria, Yemen, and Bahrain.

In some sense it was an understandable error in emphasis. After all, at the start of the year most Arab societies had lived under repressive rulers for decades. Less apparent was the human rights activism and economic and political protest that had been slowly growing in many Arab countries during the previous decade.

For example, in Egypt, the *Kefaya* (Enough) movement emerged in 2004, mixing street protests and online activism to oppose a new term for President Hosni Mubarak and the grooming of his son as successor. Labor strife in Egypt intensified; in April 2008, police repression of a textile workers strike in Mahalla al-Kubra killed four people. A Facebook group called the April 6 Youth Movement was formed in solidarity with Mahalla, which grew quickly to tens of thousands of members, many of them young and educated with no history of political activism. The movement was among the key organizers of the Tahrir Square protest that began on January 25, 2011.

It was a similar story in Tunisia, where in 2008 protests convulsed the forlorn Gafsa region, where the poor and unemployed filled the streets to oppose nepotistic hiring by the state mining company. When police responded with mass arrests and torture, a gutsy solidarity network of union, political party, and human rights activists formed to support the Gafsa victims. While President Ben Ali's government ultimately crushed the Gafsa protests and prevented their supporters from gaining steam, the combination of grassroots protest in the disenfranchised inland and the solidarity movement in the north now seems a dress rehearsal for the regime-changing uprising of December 2010 and January 2011.

Following the unification of North and South Yemen in 1990, civil society blossomed and was largely able to resist efforts since 2007 by President Ali Abdullah Saleh, who has ruled since 1978, to clamp down on independent media and associations. In early 2011, civil society leaders had become a key force in the protests calling for the president's exit. (The anti-Saleh movement gained force also from Huthi rebels in the north and separatists in the south, which both allege discrimination by the central government, and from a renegade military brigade and tribal militias).

Even in Syria and Libya—where the governments were among the region's most brutal—human rights contestation picked up during the past decade. In the former, the "Damascus Spring" reform movement and the Committees for the Revival of Civil Society that launched shortly after Bashar al-Assad succeeded his father as president in 2000, as well as the Damascus Declaration of 2005, displayed a new assertiveness by small groups of Syrians demanding basic rights, although many wound up serving long prison terms. And in Libya, families of victims of the 1996 mass killings in Abu Salim prison became the first group in the country to demonstrate regularly in public after a North Benghazi court in 2008 ordered the government to reveal the fate of Abu Salim prisoners who had "disappeared."

In addition to such frontal defiance, subtler strands of opposition were also forming.

In Tunisia, sympathizers with the cause of human rights who had demobilized in the early and mid-1990s under pressure from Ben Ali's government re-emerged in the 2000s. In 2001, for example, we found a journalism professor attending events organized by the Tunisian Human Rights League and briefing foreign visitors on the lack of media freedom; just five years earlier, he had declined to meet with Human Rights Watch because he feared questioning and surveillance by the secret police. Families of political prisoners, who had just a few years earlier shunned contact with international human rights groups fearing reprisals against themselves or their loved ones, now sought out such organizations and strove to publicize the plight of imprisoned relatives.

What had changed?

For the professor it was a newfound sense that civil society had been paralyzed too long and it was time to take a stand. For the families of political prisoners, it was the realization that by remaining silent they had gained nothing and that with their relatives still in prison, there was nothing left to lose. As a result, around the core of diehard activists there formed an outer circle of people willing to take a stand, if somewhat more discreetly, on some human rights issues.

These shifts were reinforced by the spread of new communication technologies that connected activists, in real time and at minimal expense, with domestic and international audiences. Able to exchange information and opinions securely and anonymously, their link to larger networks encouraged activists to persevere despite repression. It also encouraged them to formulate their demands for change in terms of human rights, a universal and nonpartisan framework that their audience could endorse whatever their political orientation.

At the same time, governments started to recognize that they could not ignore their human rights image. Leaders who had once tried to discredit human rights as a Western concept alien to local culture began in the 1990s to create and promote their own human rights commissions.

By 2000 such commissions operated in nearly every country in the region. In practice, most of them put a positive spin on the government's record while trying to divert attention from violations. The point here is not the objectivity of such commissions; rather, the fact that they reflect governments' recognition of human rights as a critical factor by which they were being judged, both domestically and internationally.

Another indicator of human rights awareness in these countries was the remarkably high number of victims or witnesses who agreed to provide evidence to human rights investigators. When seeking people's accounts about, say, torture and unjust imprisonment, our researchers explain that we are preparing a public report to expose abuses and pressure the government to clean up its act. Given how little we can promise victims and witnesses, it is surprising and moving how consistently they agreed to tell their stories. Narrating their experiences gave them a sense of dignity or of honoring victims, reframing what might otherwise be a random, local act of cruelty and injustice as a human rights event that fit an international framework built on treaties their government had committed to respect. Testifying about an unlawful killing also connected families to one other, establishing patterns of abuse that undermined governments' efforts to minimize violations by misrepresenting them as isolated events.

The year's events remind us that asserting one's rights against repressive governments does not mean embracing all rights for all people. Human rights demands may have energized the protests that shook the Middle East and North Africa in 2011. But protecting rights, especially for vulnerable sectors of the population, remains an uphill battle in the countries where authoritarian rulers have toppled, not just in those where they still rule.

In the months since Ben Ali and Mubarak fell from power, for example, women demonstrating in Tunisia and Egypt to demand gender equality have been slapped, groped, or threatened by counter-demonstrators. Protesters in Tunis ransacked a cinema in June and burned a television executive's home in October to protest programming they deemed insulting to Islam. In Libya rebels have mistreated thousands of sub-Saharan African migrant workers on the pretext that they were mercenaries for Muammar Gaddafi. And in Egypt deadly sectarian violence has cast a pall over the Muslim-Christian unity seen during the anti-Mubarak protests.

This newly volatile region is likely to bring more surprises in 2012. Just as rising expectations for a dignified life shook several governments of the region in 2011, they may yet motivate revolts against successor governments, in

Tunisia or elsewhere, should those governments fall short in this regard. We didn't see the Arab Spring coming because we missed signs of the thaw. But we would do well to keep in mind what Arab peoples showed us about the power of the aspiration for dignity, a power that they are unlikely to surrender anytime soon.

Eric Goldstein is deputy director of the Middle East and North Africa Division at Human Rights Watch.

AFTER THE FALL:

HOPES AND LESSONS 20 YEARS AFTER THE COLLAPSE OF THE SOVIET UNION

By Rachel Denber

Twenty years ago, in July 1991, I was poised to start a job researching human rights violations in the Soviet Union. A month later, the failed coup to unseat Communist Party leader Mikhail Gorbachev precipitated rapid political changes that would ultimately lead to the dissolution of the Soviet Union. Watching these events, my family told me I would no longer have a job when the position was to start in September. Like many of us, they assumed that the end of communism would usher in a new era of democracy, rule of law, and human rights protection in the Soviet Union's successor states. I started my new job as planned and it took five minutes to see that such assumptions were wrong.

Now is a good time to take stock of some lessons learned from 20 years of efforts to bring better human rights protections to former Soviet Union countries. Where were our assumptions faulty? What could be done better, or differently, to promote human rights during tectonic societal shifts? It is an exercise worthy in its own right, and one that has relevance beyond the region, particularly given the ongoing historic upheaval in the Middle East and North Africa.

The differences between 1991 and its aftermath and the 2011 Arab uprisings are vast, and the task of comparing these two historic moments is tantalizing but alas beyond the scope of this essay. Still, I hope that these reflections 20 years after the fall of the Soviet Union will be relevant and useful to observers, policymakers, and human rights communities focused on the former Soviet Union and beyond.

1. *There is Nothing Inevitable about Transitions to Democracy*

The first lesson is about heady assumptions. Watching decades of authoritarianism come to an end in Egypt and Tunisia was thrilling; who does not hope that it will usher in a new era of democracy and rule of law? But Soviet Union watchers have seen how the collapse of a repressive, authoritarian regime—while it brings months of euphoria and sets complex political transformations in motion—in no way guarantees the arrival of governments committed to human rights protection. As the dust settles, the historical forces that have shaped the society for decades come again to the fore and, absent deep institutional change, can be accompanied by reemergence of authoritarian rule.

To be sure, the end of communism ushered in freedoms unthinkable during the Soviet era. While circumstances varied widely across the former Soviet Union in the early years after the break-up, people could worship more freely, travel abroad, own property, and express their ethnic identity in ways they could not under communism. There was a vigorous debate about Soviet history and Stalinism, even as the monstrous crimes of the Stalin era remained unpunished.

But in many parts of the region, governments' human rights records have been poor. Year after year, chapters on most former Soviet Union countries in this volume have born grim testament to that. The reasons for this vary, but in several Central Asian countries the leaders and political classes in 1991 had no interest whatsoever in relinquishing power. Rather than commit to a post-Communist transition, many leaders used police, the military, intelligence services, and the criminal justice system to consolidate their personal rule. They worked to neuter alternative political forces demanding more profound change. As a result, the institutional reforms necessary for accountable government, pluralism, and effective rights protection never happened.

A focus on political elites also helps, albeit only partially, to explain why reforms were much more far-reaching in Eastern Europe than in former Soviet Union states. For the most part, Soviet-era political elites in those states, as well as in the Baltic states were swept aside. This left more space for new political actors who were more serious about building strong institutions, instituting checks and balances, and implementing legislative reforms prioritizing due process and human rights protection. But there were certainly other critical factors at work, such as a legacy of pre-World War II democratic government in many cases and a real prospect of European Union membership for most.

The Soviet successor states run the gamut in levels and styles of repression. Uzbekistan and Turkmenistan are surely among the most repressive governments, not only in the region but the world. Their brands of authoritarianism fossilized very early after the 1991 collapse. Turkmenistan is a one-party state that allows no independent civic activism, arbitrarily limits citizens' ability to travel abroad, and blocks virtually all independent human rights monitoring. There is no press freedom, and the authorities imprison stringers for foreign news outlets. In Uzbekistan the government barely tolerates a handful of independent human rights activists, routinely sentencing them to long prison terms on trumped up charges, and the media is heavily censored. Police torture is endemic. The government has also imprisoned, on charges of religious "fundamentalism," thousands of devout Muslims who practice their faith outside state controls or belong to unregistered religious organizations.

Russia itself is no role model. Under Russia's "soft authoritarianism," perfected under eight years of Vladimir Putin's rule, independent civil society is tolerated but whistleblowers have been killed and threatened, and very little is left of the media freedoms that had blossomed during the glasnost era. There is no genuine political competition or public accountability. Putin's announcement in the 20th anniversary year that he would again run for president, conceivably putting him in power for a total of 24 years, prompted parallels to Leonid Brezhnev's 18-year reign.

Many of the region's political elites preside over eye-popping corruption, and have used political power to enrich themselves and their vast patronage networks. It is no surprise that they use authoritarian mechanisms of control—media censorship, repression of critics, phony elections—to cling to power.

Political ouster means not only loss of power but loss of wealth and possibly worse. In countries like Azerbaijan, Russia, Turkmenistan, and Kazakhstan hydrocarbon wealth exponentially increases the stakes.

In much of the region, entrenched, post-Soviet authoritarian leaders allowed for some openings, but held onto power, resulting in political and social stagnation. In Georgia, Ukraine, and Kyrgyzstan this stagnation was broken by a second round of political changes a decade after the fall of the Soviet Union, this time driven by popular uprisings full of hope for meaningful change. In scenes not dissimilar from those we saw in the Arab world in 2011, people in Georgia, Ukraine, and Kyrgyzstan took to the streets demanding fair elections, an end to corruption, and public accountability. But the experience of the so-called colored revolutions of 2003 to 2005 is a sobering reminder that popular uprisings do not automatically or necessarily lead to good human rights outcomes.

Kyrgyzstan's "Tulip Revolution" in 2005 succeeded in ousting then-President Askar Akaev, but hopes for reform under his successor, Kurmanbek Bakiev, were quickly dashed. Bakiev proved far more interested in enriching his family and patronage networks, and within a year his government started harassing human rights activists and independent journalists. His record deteriorated precipitously from then through his violent ouster in April 2010.

In Ukraine's 2004 "Orange Revolution" thousands of Ukrainian citizens peacefully protested the government's manipulation of the presidential election in favor of Viktor Yanukovich. The pro-reform, pro-Western candidate, Viktor Yushchenko, defeated Yanukovich in repeat elections. But Yushchenko's government found itself mired in serial political crises and corruption and unable to deliver on social and economic reform. It was also poorly equipped to deal with Ukraine's myriad human rights problems, including torture and ill-treatment in detention, violations of the rights of migrants and asylum seekers, and violations that fuel the HIV/AIDS epidemic. Yushchenko left office after losing badly at the polls in 2010.

Georgia's 2003 "Rose Revolution" brought Mikheil Saakashvili to the presidency with aspirations of judicial, police, and economic reform. Reforms brought some positive results, but the government's use of excessive force against demonstrators in 2007 suggested the fragility of its commitment to human rights and the rule of law. Today Georgia's human rights record is mixed. Saakashvili is bound by the constitution to leave office in 2013, but because he has dominated the political system there are real doubts about what will come next. Nine years later the Rose Revolution paved the way for a leader who professed a commitment to rights, but it is not clear whether it succeeded in creating a competitive political system that can protect rights.

2. Guard against Misplaced Blame

In the aftermath of political upheaval, many people become disillusioned as they cope with economic, political, and social instability. Many come to blame "democracy" for their suffering. Supporters of human rights and democracy need to fight this misplaced blame. There are surely rocky times ahead in the post-uprising Middle East, so this lesson has relevance there, too.

The end of the Soviet era brought about real and colossal privations for millions who lost their life savings, jobs, and sense of identity. In Russia, for example, corruption was seemingly boundless: privatization programs under Yeltsin favored a handful of Kremlin cronies who bought up the most valuable state assets at bargain-basement prices in exchange for crucial political backing. Unsurprisingly, many blamed their struggles not on the deeply-rooted flaws of the *ancien regime* or the corruption of power, but on "democracy" and human rights movements, seeing them as the handmaiden of chaos. Putin exploited this anger and a growing sense of public nostalgia for the Soviet era to his advantage. His team willfully conflated chaos and democracy to justify reforms in 2004, making it more difficult for opposition parties to gain seats in the Duma, and instituting the appointment, rather than election, of regional governors. After the "colored revolutions" the Kremlin accused NGOs of being fronts for foreign governments that sought to interfere with Russia's internal affairs, and started a campaign of bureaucratic harassment against them. The overall result was the weakening, beyond recognition, of the checks and balances that are inherent in an accountable political system.

A related lesson here is that Western policymakers who care about human rights need to support institutions rather than individual leaders. The enthusiastic support the West at times showed Yeltsin during the chaotic 1990s, or Saakashvili during the early days after the Rose Revolution, backfired in the long run. As popular opinion about the democratic credentials of each soured, so too did popular backing for more far-reaching democratic and human rights reforms.

3. Institutionalize Strong Minority Rights Protections

Both during and after the shattering of the Soviet Union, many parts of the region succumbed to armed conflicts whose roots, for the most part, lay deep in the Soviet past, including regime attempts to manipulate ethnic tensions to its advantage through favoritism and calculated border designations, as well as Soviet policies suppressing national, ethnic, and religious identity.

New governments—in some cases buoyed by national reawakening—clashed with minority or marginalized populations, who felt strongly that the new leadership should recognize the rights and opportunities that the previous regime had long denied them. Toward the end of the Soviet era and after, both the Kremlin and several Soviet successor states responded to new nationalist demands and movements with force. In some cases, such as Abkhazia and the first Chechnya war, governments stumbled into armed conflict. But the consequences in both scenarios were disastrous.

It is beyond the scope of this essay to analyze the causes of secessionist wars in Nagorno Karabakh, South Ossetia, Abkhazia, Chechnya, and Transdnestria, and of devastating communal violence in places like Osh and Ingushetia. (Tajikistan's civil war took place along regional, not ethnic fault lines, but is also worth noting). However, in each case the civilian population bore terrible suffering from serious violations of humanitarian law, and, in some cases, long-term displacement. Twenty years later, some of the conflicts have morphed, some are frozen, and well over a million people remain displaced. The lasting harm of these intractable conflicts should serve as an important warning to governments and civil societies alike in the Middle East about the need to respect minority rights and build tolerance among minority and majority populations.

New governments need to acknowledge and address past minority griev-ances, ensure language and confessional rights, give minorities a place in law enforcement and security agencies, act swiftly to protect minorities from violence, and initiate public discussions that emphasize tangible common interests that transcend interethnic and interconfessional differences. They also need to act quickly to disarm both separatist and pro-state militias, pur-sue accountability for war crimes, and undertake security sector reform.

4. International Institutions Matter

Another lesson is the importance of motivating states in transition to join international institutions and processes that champion human rights. The for-mer Soviet Union is perhaps unique in this regard given the critical role in for-mer Soviet states of the prospect of membership in the EU and Council of Europe. But the lesson is a more general one: the international system now includes a panoply of institutions dedicated to human rights protection and reform of judiciaries, security services, and other government bodies critical to advancing human rights. These institutions should not take at face value regional states' ratification of human rights treaties. It is essential that they become actively involved in supporting democratic and human rights reform in countries "in transition."

As prospective EU member states, many Eastern European countries were motivated to carry out thorough reforms of their political and judicial sys-tems. EU membership was not in the cards for former Soviet countries, apart from the Baltic states. But some—including Russia, Ukraine, and the South Caucasus states—were offered membership in the Council of Europe. They were expected to undertake significant institutional reforms as part of the accession and membership process. For example abolishing the death penal-

ty, overhauling the prosecutor's office to strengthen the courts, and transferring prisons from internal affairs to justice ministries. The impact of these
reforms should not be overstated. For example, the prosecutor's office in
almost all of the post-Soviet Council of Europe member states is still disproportionately powerful, and courts still lack independence. But the reforms
were historic and important.

Most important, membership has given their citizens access to the European
Court of Human Rights (ECtHR), providing them an avenue of justice when
their own deeply flawed justice systems fail them.

At the same time, each of these countries was invited to join prematurely,
before government practices had come close enough to meeting Council of
Europe standards. At the time accession proponents argued that it was better
to bring the states in sooner rather than later, even if they did not meet standards. More would be accomplished, they argued, by continuing to engage on
reform once these states were Council of Europe members. Ten years later,
however, many of the same human rights violations that plagued these states
prior to accession have worsened, and the organization's monitoring procedure has struggled to secure compliance. Azerbaijan, for example, was
admitted in 2000, days after a blatantly manipulated parliamentary vote.
Elections since then have been largely empty exercises and sparked political
violence in 2003 and 2005.

Although Russia was admitted to the Council of Europe in the midst of its first
horrific war in Chechnya, the Parliamentary Assembly of the Council of Europe
(PACE) had the political courage to suspend Russia's voting rights for six
months because of grave violations of humanitarian law during the second
Chechnya conflict. However, PACE restored the voting rights without getting
any guarantees that perpetrators of massacres, torture, and forced disappearances would be held accountable. And 10 years later, they still have not.

The Council of Europe's addition of former Soviet states with poor human
rights records gave millions access to justice through the ECtHR, but it has
also stretched the court's resources. This would not be an insurmountable

problem, if it were not for states' failure to implement the ECtHR's judgments. This failure threatens the court's integrity and floods the court with similar cases. A glaring example is Russia's stubborn failure to implement roughly 170 judgments in which the European Court found Russia responsible for enforced disappearances, torture, executions, and other serious human rights abuses in Chechnya.

5. Establish Concrete Human Rights Benchmarks and Give Them Teeth

Experience in the former Soviet Union region, particularly in Central Asia, highlights the importance of setting out human rights benchmarks as a condition for international engagement and unrelentingly pursuing their implementation.

One of the most disappointing developments in this regard was the EU's failure to hold firm in demanding human rights improvements in Uzbekistan as a condition for dropping sanctions imposed on the government following the May 2005 killings by government forces of hundreds of civilian protesters, most of them unarmed, in the city of Andijan. The sanctions were mild and targeted, a symbolic arms embargo and a visa ban on a handful of government officials. But almost as soon as the sanctions were adopted several EU states set about openly undermining them, sending mixed messages that could not have been lost on the Uzbek government.

The EU had made the release of imprisoned human rights activists a condition for lifting the sanctions but when it ended the sanctions regime in 2009, 12 remained in prison. In a move that could only have encouraged Uzbek government intransigence, the EU justified the lifting of the sanctions by referring to "positive steps" taken by the Uzbek government, such as agreeing to hold harmless but meaningless human rights dialogues with the EU. After two years the dialogues have had absolutely no bearing on the human rights situation in Uzbekistan.

The lesson here is not that sanctions can never work, but that they can work only if states are united in demanding rigorous implementation. Regional officials are no fools. They know when their interlocutors are serious about their rhetoric and when they are not, or when rhetoric will have real consequences and when it will not.

A related lesson is that assigning an abusive government exceptional status in light of its strategic importance sabotages efforts to get it to improve its human rights record. Western policymakers EU policymakers like to point to Kazakhstan as a regional leader in a rough neighborhood. Led by Germany and France, the EU warmly supported Kazakhstan's bid to chair OSCE in 2010 and host an OSCE summit, though Kazakhstan's brand of soft authoritarianism made it an inappropriate choice for an organization with a mandate to promote democracy and human rights.

The gamble that the chairmanship would prod reform turned out to be misguided. It's been a year since the summit and chairmanship year have ended, and Kazakhstan's record has deteriorated. For example, they adopted a new repressive law on religion in October, returned the prison system to Ministry of Internal Affairs jurisdiction, and imprisoned one of the country's top human rights activists.

International actors should also learn from the post-Soviet experience that viewing human rights and security interests as tradeoffs is exactly the false choice repressive leaders want them to make, and that bargaining with dictators over human rights concerns will not lead to a good outcome, almost by definition.

Too often, Western actors resist seeing the leverage they have in relationships with abusive governments. For example, eager to secure alternative routes to Afghanistan to avoid less stable Pakistan, the US has developed the so-called Northern Distribution Network (NDN)—a transit corridor that runs through Russia and Central Asia—which supplies non-lethal cargo to Afghanistan. To sweeten its relationship with Uzbekistan, a pivotal state in the network, the US is waiving restrictions on assistance, including military aid, to the Uzbek government that were established in 2004 over human rights concerns.

What policymakers seem to minimize are the financial and other benefits the NDN brings Uzbekistan, which should be used to stymie bullying by Uzbek officials over rights issues. Instead, by dropping all restrictions on aid— including military aid—without insisting on improvements, the US is creating a huge windfall for an extremely repressive government, and may ultimately create long-term instability in Uzbekistan and Central Asia. It also sends the detrimental message to ordinary Uzbeks that the US is indifferent to their plight.

6. Support a Strong Civil Society

A resoundingly positive lesson of the last 20 years has been the importance of support for civil society in countries in, and beyond, transition. These are the organizations and media outlets that, in the absence of checks and balances in post-Soviet authoritarian regimes, are doing the most to hold their governments accountable, often providing services to help the public access their often opaque governments and exposing government corruption and wrongdoing.

In many countries these communities are now so deeply rooted and vibrant that it is easy to forget that they are in fact quite new. At the same time, no one should take their vitality for granted. The past 10 years have witnessed how one government after another in the region adopted laws restricting NGOs and used an arsenal of bureaucratic tools to harass and overburden them, and, in some countries, imprison them. The creation of civil societies throughout the region was one of the signal achievements of the glasnost era, and policymakers need to support these communities now more than ever.

The differences between the fall of the Soviet Union and today's Arab Spring upheaval are significant. But 20 years of post-Soviet experience should lead policy makers to embrace the opportunity for change in the Middle East, guided not by heady optimism, but by an enduring commitment to universal principles, far-reaching institutional reforms, and strong support for the people who continue to fight for both.

Rachel Denber is deputy director of the Europe and Central Asia division at Human Rights Watch.

Europe's Own Human Rights Crisis

By Benjamin Ward

To many friends of human rights in Europe, the Arab Spring has been the most thrilling period since the fall of the Berlin Wall. Judging from their soaring rhetoric about yearning for freedom among Arab peoples, European Union leaders share that enthusiasm. Today there is an opportunity, the optimists proclaim, to have an arc of human rights-respecting countries around much of the Mediterranean rim.

The reality of human rights policy in Europe itself and toward its Mediterranean perimeter has been far less edifying. Documents discovered in Libya by Human Rights Watch in September 2011 evidenced British complicity in rendition to Libya under Muammar Gaddafi. Italy, which was willing to send African migrants and asylum seekers back to Libya during the Gaddafi era to face abuse and worse, moved quickly to sign a migration cooperation agreement with the transitional authorities there (although at this writing it has yet to resume forced returns). EU governments have proved reluctant to help migrants and others fleeing war-torn Libya. The arrival of thousands of Tunisian migrants in Italy beginning in January led leading EU governments to question free movement inside the EU, one of its fundamental pillars.

Move beyond the fine words and human rights in Europe are in trouble. A new (or rather a resurgent old) idea is on the march: that the rights of "problematic" minorities must be set aside for the greater good, and elected politicians who pursue such policies are acting with democratic legitimacy.

At first glance, the idea of a human rights crisis in Europe might seem far-fetched. But scratch beneath the surface and the trends are truly worrying. Four developments stand out: the rollback of civil liberties in state responses to terrorist attacks; the debate around the place of minorities and migrants in Europe, a debate too often laced with xenophobia; the rise of populist extremist parties and their baleful influence on public policy; and the diminishing effectiveness of traditional human rights institutions and tools. Unless governments wake up to the scale of the threat, the next generation of Europeans may see human rights as an optional extra instead of a core value.

Counterterrorism and the Attack on Rights

Terrorist violence in Europe is nothing new. Nor is human rights abuse as part of the effort to counter it. But the 9/11 attacks, and the subsequent attacks in Madrid and London, triggered policy responses in Europe that caused lasting damage to the human rights cause.

In the past decade, European governments too often have shown a willingness to chip away at the absolute global prohibition of torture, exposing terrorism suspects to violent abuse and illegal detention overseas, using the fruits of that torture at home, and denying terrorism suspects the rights accorded to others accused of crimes. Even now, we do not know the full extent of European complicity in US abuses (rendition, "black sites," and torture) under the Bush administration. (Some governments, like Norway, have resisted the temptation, responding to terrorist violence using the rule of law).

While many of these laws and policies were deeply problematic, and in some cases remain unchanged today (especially where courts or national parliaments were unable or unwilling to curb them), the rhetoric around them arguably represents an even worse legacy.

Many EU governments sought to construct a new paradigm in which human rights had to take second place to security or be set aside entirely. As then-British Prime Minister Tony Blair claimed after the July 2005 suicide attacks in London, "the rules of the game are changing." While public concern about terrorism has been largely supplanted by worries about jobs and social services (even though the threat remains), these poisonous ideas have taken root.

European politicians mounted a three-pronged attack on universal human rights in the context of combating terrorism. The first was that terrorism suspects deserve fewer rights than others. The second was that Europe could have security or human rights, but not both. The third was that human rights are a zero sum game, so that rights for the majority can only be secured by sacrificing the rights of the minority suspected of terrorism.

Driven by fear, many in Europe accepted these arguments. Offered a chance to trade away those rights to assuage their fear, people willingly did so, especially when the rights at risk were not, or did not seem to be, theirs.

The Place of Migrants and Minorities

Intolerance towards migrants and minorities in Europe is widespread. Polling data from 2010 shows that a majority in eight EU states shared the view that there are too many immigrants, with as many as half concluding the same of Muslims.

Fears about loss of culture, terrorism, crime, and competition for economic resources all help explain rising intolerance in Europe. Europe's current economic and financial crisis and resulting austerity is likely to exacerbate the intolerance.

Europe's Muslims and Roma experience persistent hostility and discrimination across the region, as an EU Fundamental Rights Agency survey from 2009 showed. Undocumented African migrants face significant problems, including discrimination and violence. While individual attacks are common in the region, in some cases this has spilled over into mob violence, including in Italy (against African migrants and Roma), in Greece (against migrants), and in Eastern Europe (against Roma).

European governments have responded in ways that are deeply corrosive of respect for universal rights. Rather than emphasizing that Europe's history has been shaped by migration, pointing to the many contributions made by minorities and migrants and forcefully condemning racism and intolerance, they have played on these fears.

Cultural and religious practices can of course violate human rights, and those who engage in discriminatory or abusive conduct must be held to account.

But what is happening in Europe goes far beyond concern with the conduct of specific individuals.

The response has included blaming marginalized communities for the conduct of a handful of people (as with Roma in Italy); seeking to close Europe's borders at the EU and national levels; restrictive and abusive asylum procedures and abusive migrant detention conditions (notably in Greece), with unaccompanied migrant children at particular risk; and in the name of integration, telling migrants (even second or third generation) that they must embrace majority culture, and if they do not, face sanction, or leave (in Germany, the Netherlands, Denmark and elsewhere).

Muslims in Europe have borne the brunt. Fears of so-called home-grown terrorism after the Madrid and London bombings, a string of alleged terrorism plots, and concerns over loss of culture prompted by the more visible presence of observant Muslims have put the continent's diverse Muslim communities under scrutiny, their loyalty implicitly challenged.

Fear of Muslims has impacted wider policy debates about "integration," a byword for a whole basket of anxieties and concerns about the place in society of migrants, especially Muslim migrants, and has led to calls for action.

At heart the anxiety about the place of Muslim migrants in Europe, as a recent report by the think tank Chatham House pointed out, is cultural. The headscarf and face-covering *niqab*, and to some degree minarets and mosques, have played such an important role in these debates because they are visual reminders that Muslims live in Europe and are here to stay.

Fear of the place of Muslims in Europe did not begin with al Qaeda's attacks on September 11, 2001. What changed that day was the characterization of Bangladeshi, Pakistani, Moroccan, and Turkish migrants in Europe. While many European officials sought to draw a clear distinction between the acts of a small group and Muslim communities as a whole, policy responses and debates about how to counter the home-grown threat frequently created the impression that Muslim communities were suspect.

The impact on human rights in Europe is real. On a practical level, forced integration and a concept of integration that requires no accommodation by the wider society is doomed to fail. When policymakers play into public fears about loss of culture and pursue policies that increase rather than lessen xenophobia, they put the rights of European minority communities at risk. Perhaps worse, they reinforce the dangerous zero-sum conception of rights—minorities must be forced to accept majority culture (or "Christian values" as the German chancellor suggested in 2010) and if they refuse to do so their rights must be set aside for the greater good.

Among Roma, Europe's largest minority, the picture on human rights is bleak. At the EU level there is recognition that the persistent discrimination and marginalization experienced by Roma requires positive intervention and support, and officials have devised a strategy to that end. But Roma continue to be stigmatized at national levels across the EU. And like migrant communities, Roma are likely to be disproportionately affected by austerity measures.

The experience of Roma migrants from Eastern to Western Europe and the problematic policy responses to them have some parallels with those faced by Muslims, but with fears of a purported epidemic of crime taking the place of fears of terrorism, and with economic rather than cultural concerns predominating. Forced evictions and expulsions of Eastern European Roma, who are EU citizens, by France and Italy exemplify the impact of these fears. Forced evictions remain a common feature of Roma policy across the EU.

Further east, in Hungary, Romania, Bulgaria, the Czech Republic, and Slovakia, the situation is even more alarming, with violent attacks and anti-Roma rhetoric and little progress towards ending housing and school segregation despite hundreds of millions of euros of EU funding and rulings of the European Court of Human Rights (ECtHR, a Council of Europe court that binds EU states).

This is bad news for Roma. But it is also bad news for human rights in general. Once again, policymakers in Europe prefer to yield to, and in some cases exacerbate, public concerns at the expense of an unpopular minority rather than saying loud and clear that Europe's values demand rights for all.

Populist Extremism

The failure of leadership and negative rhetoric by European governments is connected to a third worrying trend: the rise of populist extremist parties.

The terrorist act in July 2011 by Anders Breivik that left 77 Norwegians dead was a stark reminder that extremism and political violence are not confined to those acting in the name of Islam. Breivik's twisted manifesto cited with approval populist extremist parties across Europe, though the decision to engage in terrorism was his alone.

The growing success of these parties at ballot boxes across the continent is having a profound impact on mainstream politics. Where populist extremist parties form part of ruling coalitions (as in Italy and Switzerland), or formally support minority governments (as in the Netherlands), the impact on mainstream politics is immediately evident. More generally, mainstream parties have responded to the growing electoral share of populist extremist parties in ways that move away from human rights-respecting policies.

In Western Europe, extremist parties have put the place of Muslims and their alleged threat to European culture at the forefront. Some, like Italy's Northern League, also focus on migrant communities more generally.

The focus on Muslims and fears of terrorist attacks allows these parties to more easily resist accusations of racism and xenophobia (some even distinguishing "good" minority communities from Muslim minority communities) and to present the views held by conservative Muslims on women's rights and homosexuality as illustrative of the threat even though conservative Christians with similar views have not faced the same vilification.

Populist extremist parties in the eastern part of the EU are more focused on Roma than Muslims. Examples include Jobbik, the third largest party in Hungary's parliament, which has links to a paramilitary group implicated in

47

attacks on Roma, and the Slovak National Party, part of the ruling coalition, whose leader recently called for the creation of a separate Roma state.

At a time of growing voter anger over austerity measures and mass unemployment, these messages risk attracting greater support.

Many in Europe continue to defend the rights of migrants and minorities and the importance of universality. But rather than standing up against populist extremism, mainstream parties have responded with co-option through coalition politics, adopting watered-down versions of the same policies or rhetoric, or in the case of some centre-left parties, with paralysis and silence.

In some cases, it is argued that the electoral success of the parties mean that it would be undemocratic for mainstream parties not to take account of their views.

Far from neutralizing the political challenge posed by populist extremist parties, these strategies have served instead to legitimize them and make them respectable, sending a message to voters that xenophobic, anti-Muslim, or anti-Roma sentiment is acceptable rather than a cause for shame.

The growth of populist extremist parties poses a real challenge for human rights in Europe. It engenders divisive politics. It reinforces the idea that the rights of the majority can only be upheld and respected if those of the minority are set aside, moving us further away from universality. And it legitimizes abusive policies on democratic grounds.

Declining Leverage

There is always a risk in a democracy that without responsible leadership the majority will support measures that harm the interests of the minority. This dilemma helps explain why human rights protections, which are designed in part to protect against "tyranny of the majority," are more essential than ever. It is particularly alarming then that Europe's human rights tools and institutions are proving ineffective in tackling these negative trends.

One often valuable tool—naming and shaming—only works when the government being identified is embarrassed by the disclosure that it is not playing by the rules. But the state of politics in many EU states today means governments are no longer embarrassed to pursue abusive policies, arguing that doing otherwise would risk losing ground to populist extremist parties.

Criticisms of abusive policies and rhetoric from human rights NGOs, from the Council of Europe, from the United Nations, from religious leaders, and even in some cases from EU institutions, are brushed aside. Examples include France's forced evictions and expulsions of Roma, Spain's incommunicado detention of terrorism suspects, Italy's interdiction and pushbacks of migrants to Libya under Gaddafi, and Greece's abusive detention of migrants. The perceived domestic political benefits of engaging in these kinds of policies frequently outweigh the inconvenience caused by international or regional condemnation.

Two institutions remain hard to ignore: the ECtHR and the EU's European Commission.

The ECtHR still has real clout, although EU governments (notably Italy on terrorism expulsions) have begun to ignore some of its interim rulings and the court faces more general political attacks (particularly in the UK) for "straying" into domestic issues.

The European Commission has long had the power to hold EU states to account for breaking EU law. And after the Lisbon treaty, that includes human rights, with a dedicated fundamental rights commissioner.

France's expulsion of Roma in the summer of 2010 showed the commission's potential. Having ignored UN, Council of Europe, and European Parliament criticism of its policy, Paris reacted with fury when the commission took it to task.

Sadly, the commission eventually backed down, accepting in August 2011 legislative changes that did not address the fundamental discrimination motivating the expulsions. Its approach to Hungary's media law and to Greece's broken asylum system demonstrated a similar half-heartedness. In both cases, commission enforcement action was initiated but later discontinued or put on hold without adequately addressing the triggering problems.

Human rights are supposed to be integral to the European project. If the commission does not find more courage to hold member states to account when they break the rules, Europe's downward slide on rights looks set to continue.

Conclusion

Europe's declining respect for human rights has not gone unnoticed. Governments around the world have seized on abusive counterterrorism measures, attacks on migrants, Roma, and other minorities, and hostility towards Muslims both as justification for their own abusive policies and to undercut criticism by the EU. The European Parliament noted in 2009 the damage to the credibility of EU external human rights policy as a result.

Above all, Europe's human rights crisis matters for its own sake. If these dangerous ideas—that some deserve fewer rights than others, and that the democratic will of the majority can choose to set aside rights for minorities—are left unchecked, the ideals of those who tore down the Berlin Wall will be betrayed, and the loss incalculable.

Benjamin Ward is deputy director of the Europe and Central Asia Division at Human Rights Watch.

FROM PATERNALISM TO DIGNITY:
RESPECTING THE RIGHTS OF PERSONS WITH DISABILITIES

By Shantha Rau Barriga

Good intentions do not always make for good policy.

That is particularly true for people with disabilities, who are often stripped of the most fundamental of human rights—the right to make choices about their own lives—under the guise of "protecting" them from the challenges of decision-making and living independently."It happens to all persons with disabilities," Jennifer, a woman with a physical disability in northern Uganda, told Human Rights Watch. "It is as if we weren't human."[1]

In Croatia, for example, Human Rights Watch found that more than 70 percent of persons with intellectual or mental disabilities living in nine institutions that we visited were there without their consent or the opportunity to challenge the decision to keep them there. Living out grim and regimented days, they cannot even take a shower in private and are deprived of the ability to make even basic decisions, including what to eat and what time to sleep. Many residents have been there for most of their lives. As one young woman, Marija, told us, "Once you enter, you never leave."

Meanwhile in Peru the government excluded more than 23,000 people with intellectual and mental disabilities from the voter registry before the April 2011 national election. The decision was based on assumptions that people with such disabilities cannot make decisions on their own, and that the government was "protecting" individuals with disabilities from being penalized for not voting.[2] Pressured by local disability rights advocates and the Ombudsman's Office, the government invited people with disabilities to register. But with limited time and poor communication regarding the about-turn in policy, fewer than 60 people with disabilities were added back to the roster before the election.

As these examples show, restrictions on legal capacity are based on law, policy, accepted state practices, or arbitrary decision-making by state officials. Government laws and policies restricting or removing legal capacity of persons with disabilities reflect an understanding of disability as a medical issue. As Human Rights Watch's country-specific research has shown over the last two years, deprivation of legal capacity profoundly impacts people with disabilities, for example, when it comes to the right to health, political participation, access to justice, and freedom from arbitrary detention. Indeed in many countries, national laws recognize persons with disabilities as unequal citizens, sometimes allowing them fewer rights than children.

The Convention on the Rights of Persons with Disabilities (CRPD)—the most recent comprehensive human rights treaty—reaffirms that persons with disabilities have rights, and challenges the inequality and discrimination inherent in laws that infantilize individuals with disabilities.[3] Disability is described as long-term physical, mental, intellectual, or sensory impairments that—because of physical, communication, and attitudinal barriers—limit inclusion and full participation in society.[4] Respect for inherent dignity, independence, individual autonomy including the freedom to make one's own choices, and non-discrimination are among the CRPD's core principles.[5]

The convention compels us to start with the premise that people with disabilities have the same rights and equal recognition under the law as all others. The CRPD also acknowledges that persons with disabilities may, in certain situations, need support exercising their rights.

However, the convention does not spell out *how* the right to legal capacity and supported decision-making should be implemented. As a result, disability advocates, legal experts, and governments find themselves trying to interpret the scope of these provisions, while providing rights-affirming alternatives to old patterns of guardianship and substituted decision-making.

Disabled peoples' organizations (DPOs) and persons with disabilities, who were key actors in advocating for and drafting the treaty, must be engaged and take the lead in this process. Indeed, the CRPD itself requires that states involve DPOs and experts with disabilities in implementing and monitoring the treaty.

The Impact of Legal Capacity Restrictions

Losing one's legal capacity can be devastating. For example, Milica, a woman with an intellectual disability in Croatia, was stripped of her legal capacity by a court decision and forced to live in an institution for approximately 20 years.[6] She even had to ask her sister for permission before marrying her husband.[7]

In Peru, Roberto, a 37-year-old man with a mild intellectual disability, went to a regular school and now has a job, yet was denied the chance to open a bank account because of an arbitrary decision of bank officials. His national identity card is labeled "mentally disabled" on the back. His father told us, "The bank staff looked at him strangely. He understood. He felt bad, I felt bad.... Roberto doesn't need to wear a sign on his chest [that he has a disability]."[8]

In the United States, some immigrants with mental disabilities are unjustifiably detained for years on end, sometimes with no legal limits.[9] Why? Because they do not get the support they need, such as legal representation, to make claims against their deportation.

Despite the protections outlined in the CRPD, most countries still maintain a system of guardianship for those deprived of legal capacity. Guardians are usually appointed by a court and make decisions on behalf of the individual. With such power comes plenty of opportunity for abuse, emotionally, financially, sometimes even physically. What we once considered well-intended protection for persons with disabilities often resulted in abuses in access to justice.

To combat these abuses inherent in the guardianship system, governments must adapt their laws to ensure that an individual's rights, will, and preferences are respected. So far no government has completed the complex transition from substituted decision-making to a system of autonomous decision-making with adequate support mechanisms, as the CRPD requires. Some countries have set out on the right track, and others should benefit from these experiences.

Living in the Community

Persons with disabilities are at particular risk of arbitrary deprivation of liberty. This is because their compulsory placement and confinement in an institution may not be considered as "detention" under domestic law, especially when—as in a number of countries—it is done under the decision of a guardian.

"There, I was free," Marija, a young woman with mild intellectual and mental disabilities told Human Rights Watch about her experience living in a home in the community.[10] She now lives in an institution.

The CRPD recognizes the right to live in the community on an equal basis as others, including the choice of residence and development of a supportive and independent living arrangement.[11] There are a number of examples of how it can be done: Senada, who lived in an institution in Croatia for more than seven years, has lived in the community since 2006. Although she initially needed support from staff in her community living program, she now lives alone, has her own key, buys her own food, and cooks. She has a job and decides how she spends the money she earns.[12] In other words, she lives just like others.

Even long-term residents of institutions have shown they can successfully transition into community life. For example, Milica and her husband, whom she met in the institution, are able to cook, go to the market together, and take care of their daily living needs.[13] But because Milica has difficulty with numbers, she receives assistance with financial matters such as paying her bills and buying groceries.[14] Based on interviews with former residents of Croatian institutions, it is clear they took particular pride in their ability to live in the community, even if they did need support to make that possible. For them, independent living has led to a better, more productive life and given them a purpose and reason to live.

Political Participation

Disenfranchisement of people with disabilities, as seen in Peru, is not uncommon. However, Peru is also an example of where local disability groups and the Ombudsman's Office used the CRPD to advocate for change. In October 2011 the government reversed its policy and pledged to take prompt action to reinstate voting rights to the more than 20,000 persons with disabilities who were unable to vote in the presidential elections.[15] However, the victory was not complete as Peru's civil code still limits the rights of some people with disabilities to participate in the political process.

The practice of excluding those perceived as lacking the capacity to vote has a long history, and currently most democratic countries have capacity-related qualifications for voting.[16] In Germany, for example, the electoral law prevents some citizens from voting based on disability, including if someone is "not eligible to vote owing to a judicial decision, ... a custodian has been appointed ... and he or she is accommodated in a psychiatric hospital..."[17] The constitutions of Thailand, Kenya, India, and Ghana limit the right to vote for people with "unsound mind." In Hungary the new constitution adopted in June 2011 states that no one should be discriminated against based on disability, but also permits a judge to remove the right to vote from those with "limited mental ability." Similarly, the Council of Europe's advisory body on constitutional matters, known as the Venice Commission, has been considering amendments to protect the right to political participation of persons with disabilities, yet to date has deemed acceptable laws and practices that enable judges to restrict their right to vote.

The CRPD, however, requires governments to "ensure that persons with disabilities can effectively and fully participate in political and public life on an equal basis with others, directly or through freely chosen representatives, including the right and opportunity for persons with disabilities to vote and be elected."[18] The convention allows for no exceptions. The CRPD's treaty body has recently said that disability-based discrimination should be prohibited in all laws, "particularly those governing elections" and that "urgent adoption of legislative measures to ensure that the right of persons with disabilities, including persons who are currently under guardianship or trusteeship, can exercise their right to vote and to participate in public life on an equal basis with others."[19]

There is not, and cannot be, a clear and objective measure of knowledge related to participating in an electoral process. Already in any election, people vote for a range of reasons, including preference for a candidate's agenda or their image. Some publicly state their intention to vote for candidates randomly or to write in fictional candidates. En masse exclusion of persons categorized as "disabled" clearly violates the right of political participation. Especially when read together with its provisions on non-discrimination and legal capacity, the CRPD makes clear that there should be no case-by-case restrictions on this right on the grounds of disability. Governments can and should do much more to honor the right of citizens with disabilities to participate in the political process and provide them the necessary support to exercise this basic right.

Informed Consent

Free and informed consent is one of the pillars of the right to health and to legal capacity. For people with disabilities, this principle is often violated and undermined by paternalistic attitudes and actions. For example, Human Rights Watch found that women and girls with disabilities in Argentina are infantilized in the reproductive health system, and stripped of their capacity to make decisions about available services. One woman told Human Rights Watch that some doctors thought her incapable of remembering to take her daily contraceptive pill because she is blind.

The coerced sterilization of women and girls with disabilities is another issue of serious concern. In Nepal, women and girls with intellectual disabilities were sterilized without their free and informed consent. In these cases, the decision to perform the sterilization was made by the parents in consultation with a doctor.[20] Dr. Lalitha Joshi, mother of a young man with Down's Syndrome in Nepal, told Human Rights Watch: "If parents and society really care for children with disabilities, there's no need to sterilize them. We can train them to look after themselves."[21]

It is particularly common in institutions and other closed settings to deny people with mental or intellectual disabilities the right to consent to decisions that impact their lives. In visits to two psychiatric institutions in Peru, for example, staff told Human Rights Watch that if residents refuse to take their medications, they simply disguise the medications in meals or inject them with the drugs.[22] In some cases, as noted by the United Nations special rapporteur on torture and other cruel, inhuman or degrading treatment or punishment, forced medical treatment can amount to torture and ill-treatment without the person's free and informed consent.[23]

The Way Forward

Legal capacity is a most fundamental right: it is what makes a human being a subject in the legal system, rather than a mere object of the law. It is no coincidence that the CRPD calls on governments and communities not only to guarantee the rights of people with disabilities, but also to guarantee their human dignity.

In transitioning to community-based services and independent living programs, all relevant stakeholders—including governments, development agencies, society, and legal and health professionals—should share the experiences, models, and lessons they have learned. The continued leadership of individuals with disabilities is critical to this effort, as is the activism of local, regional, and international advocacy organizations. After all, the call to protect the rights and dignity of people with disabilities is never more powerful than when it comes from the very people who experience these injustices themselves.

Shantha Rau Barriga is researcher and advocate in the Health and Human Rights Division at Human Rights Watch.

[1] Human Rights Watch, "As if We Weren't Human": Discrimination and Violence against Women with Disabilities in Northern Uganda, August 2010, p.8, http://www.hrw.org/reports/2010/08/24/if-we-weren-t-human

[2] Human Rights Watch interview with Malena Pineda Angeles, chief, Program for the Defense and Promotion of the Rights of Persons with Disabilities, July 26, 2011, Lima, Peru. Jorge Yrivarren Lazo, "DERECHOS PARA TODOS, Los derechos de las personas con discapacidad," El Comercio, October 18, 2011 http://elcomercio.pe/impresa/notas/derechos-personas-discapaci-dad/20111018/1319463

[3] Convention on the Rights of Persons with Disabilities (CRPD), adopted December 13, 2006, G.A. Res. 61/106, Annex I, U.N. GAOR, 61st Sess., Supp. (No. 49) at 65, U.N. Doc. A/61/49 (2006), entered into force May 3, 2008.

[4] Ibid, art. 2.

[5] Ibid, art. 3.

[6] Human Rights Watch "Once You Enter, You Never Leave": Deinstitutionalization of Persons with Intellectual or Mental Disabilities in Croatia, ISBN: 1-56432-686-1, September 23, 2010, http://www.hrw.org/reports/2010/09/23/once-you-enter-you-never-leave-0

[7] Ibid.

[8] Human Rights Watch interview with Marcelino Velazco, father of three young men with intellectual disabilities, Lima, Peru, October 22, 2011.

[9] Human Rights Watch, Deportation by Default: Mental Disability, Unfair Hearings, and Indefinite Detention in the US Immigration System, ISBN: 1-56432-665-9, July 25, 2010, http://www.hrw.org/reports/2010/07/26/deportation-default-0

[10] Human Rights Watch, "Once You Enter, You Never Leave," p.1.

[11] CRPD, art. 19.

[12] Human Rights Watch, "Once You Enter, You Never Leave," p.49.

[13] Ibid.

[14] Ibid.

[15] RENIEC (Registro Nacional de Identificación y Estado Civil), Resolución Jefatural Nº 508-2011-JNAC/RENIEC)October 10, 2011), http://www.reniec.gob.pe/portal/TransparenciaAdm?id=005&anno=&valorInicial=16&valorMenu=13 (accessed November 16, 2011).

[16] Marta Mendiondo, Pamela Teaster and Susan Lawrence, "Public Guardianship: In the Best Interests of Incapacitated People?," August 10, 2011, ISBN: 0313378274.

[17] Federal Electoral Law (Bundewahlgesetz, BGW), s. 1. art. 13.

[18] CRPD, art. 29a.

[19] Concluding observations of the UN Committee on the Rights of Persons with Disabilities regarding Tunisia; Fifth session, April 11-15, 2011, paras. 13 and 35.

[20] Human Rights Watch, Futures Stolen: Barriers to Education for Children with Disabilities in Nepal, August 2011, http://www.hrw.org/reports/2011/08/24/futures-stolen.

[21] Human Rights Watch interview with Dr. Lalitha Joshi, gynecologist and president of the Down's Syndrome Association, Kathmandu, Nepal, March 30, 2011.

[22] Human Rights Watch interview with staff members at Hospital Hermilio Valdizan, Lima, Peru, October 25, 2011. Human Rights Watch interview with a nurse at Hospital Victor Larco Herrera, Lima, Peru, October 26, 2011.

[23] Report of the special rapporteur on torture and other cruel, inhuman and degrading treatment, Manfred Nowak. A/63/175, July 28, 2008.

A LANDMARK VICTORY FOR DOMESTIC WORKERS:
NEW CONVENTION ESTABLISHES FIRST GLOBAL LABOR STANDARDS FOR MILLIONS OF WOMEN AND GIRLS

By Nisha Varia and Jo Becker

If someone had told me 45 years ago that we would be here today, I would not have believed it. We do not have to be slaves anymore.

—MYRTLE WITBOOI, CHAIR OF THE INTERNATIONAL DOMESTIC WORKERS NETWORK AND FORMER DOMESTIC WORKER FROM SOUTH AFRICA, GENEVA, JUNE 10, 2011

On June 16, 2011, with the world's attention consumed by street protests in the Middle East and a stubbornly bleak global economy, a quiet revolution took place. Overcoming initial skepticism and resistance, members of the International Labour Organization (ILO)—governments, trade unions, and employers' associations—voted overwhelmingly in favor of a new ground-breaking treaty that, for the first time, established global labor standards for the estimated 50 to 100 million domestic workers worldwide who clean, cook, and care for children and the elderly in private households.

ILO Convention 189 Concerning Decent Work for Domestic Workers did not topple any dictators, but it does radically change how domestic workers—the vast majority of whom are women and girls—and their work inside the home are valued, recognized, and protected. Its desperately needed and long over-due protections shake deeply entrenched gender discrimination in social and legal norms, and, in some countries, the lingering legacies of slavery.

Many countries exclude domestic workers from labor laws partially or com-pletely, denying them basic labor protections that most other categories of workers can take for granted, such as a minimum wage or limits to hours of work. Such exclusion—together with discrimination and a profound devalua-tion of work associated with traditional, unpaid female roles has—led to a wide and disturbing range of abuses against domestic workers around the world, many of whom are migrants and an estimated 30 percent of whom are children under the age of 18.

Over the past 10 years, Human Rights Watch's research in countries as diverse as Indonesia, Saudi Arabia, the United States, Morocco, Guinea, and El Salvador has documented pervasive abuses and labor exploitation, including excessively long working hours without rest; unpaid wages for months or years; forced confinement in the workplace; food deprivation; verbal, physical, and sexual abuse; and forced labor including debt bondage and trafficking. Domestic workers who suffer such abuses typically have little access to redress.

Governments overwhelmingly voted in favor of the ILO convention, which guarantees domestic workers labor protections equivalent to those of other workers, including for working hours, minimum wage coverage, overtime compensation, daily and weekly rest periods, social security, and maternity leave. The new standards oblige governments to address the minimum age for children in domestic work and their right to attend school, protect domestic workers from violence and abuse, regulate recruitment agencies and fees, and set out measures for effective monitoring and enforcement.

While adoption of the convention was a major victory worthy of celebration, the toughest work lies ahead: ensuring that the convention is ratified, incorporated into domestic laws worldwide, and enforced. This essay describes the situation that domestic workers currently face, analyzes how a constellation of forces came together in 2011 to get the ILO convention adopted, and outlines steps that need to be taken now to ensure that this positive development leads to tangible improvements in the lives and working conditions of domestic workers.

Abuses against Domestic Workers

> *I woke up at 5 a.m., cleaned the house and made breakfast for the children and worked all day. I went to sleep at 3 a.m. I never got a chance to rest…. The wife of the employer shouted and beat me every day…. The employer had my passport. The door was locked. I was not allowed to go out or even talk to the neighbors. I never received my salary.*
>
> —CHAIN CHANNI, CAMBODIAN DOMESTIC WORKER, KUALA LUMPUR, MALAYSIA, APRIL 12, 2011

Domestic workers play a critical economic role globally, helping households manage responsibilities of child care, cooking, and cleaning. They also free up their employers to participate in the workforce themselves and provide care for the industrialized world's increasingly aging population. Migrant domestic workers send home billions of dollars in remittances to developing countries each year, but despite their economic contributions, sending governments have largely ignored protection concerns.

Domestic workers, who often make extraordinary personal sacrifices to support their families, have routinely been denied basic protections guaranteed others workers and are among the most exploited workers in the world. Gaps in legal protections, isolation in private homes, and social norms that have sanctioned exploitation of a "servant" class have given rise to abuses ranging from endemic labor exploitation in which workers toil around the clock for little or no pay, to trafficking into domestic servitude and slavery.

In a review of 72 countries' labor laws, the ILO found that 40 percent did not guarantee domestic workers a weekly rest day, and half did not limit hours of work. Many national child labor laws currently exclude domestic workers, meaning employers can employ young children and make them labor for long hours, often at the cost of their education and health. A Human Rights Watch study in Indonesia found that only 1 in 45 child domestic workers interviewed was attending school.

Many domestic workers are international migrants who confront additional risks posed by language barriers, precarious immigration status, excessive recruitment fees, and employers' confiscation of passports. Human Rights Watch investigations across Asia and the Middle East have documented the failure of many governments to monitor recruitment agencies that impose heavy debt burdens or to ensure that migrant domestic workers have access to courts, information about their rights, and support services when they face abuse.

Trade unions have begun organizing domestic workers in recent decades in places such as South Africa, Hong Kong, and Brazil, but for the most part the organized labor movement has been slow to take up domestic workers' concerns and the particular risks faced by children and migrants. The process of negotiating global labor standards on domestic work brought together a diverse alliance of domestic worker organizations, NGOs, and trade unions working to reverse this dynamic.

Forging Global Labor Standards

> *The lack of protection for domestic workers represents a significant gap in the coverage of international labor standards.... Domestic workers around the world are looking to the ILC [International Labour Conference] to adopt a convention that would help to overcome past injustices and give domestic workers a better future.*
> —MARIA LUISA ESCOREL, MINISTER COUNSELOR, PERMANENT MISSION OF BRAZIL, GENEVA, JUNE 2011

The ILO convention adopted in June 2011 was unthinkable just a few years ago. It represents the culmination of years of efforts by domestic workers, advocates, and officials to shine a spotlight on a long-ignored but significant sector of the workforce. These efforts properly focused on the ILO, with its unique tripartite structure in which workers' groups, employers' groups, and governments (183 countries are members) negotiate international standards, with all three component groups having a vote.

The push for new global labor standards began in earnest in March 2008 when domestic worker advocacy groups, migrants' groups, and global trade unions successfully pressed to get domestic work formally on the ILO agenda. This was followed by a series of intensive consultations with ILO members and opportunities for them to comment on draft instruments between 2008 and 2010, and two rounds of on-the-floor negotiations at the International Labour Conference in Geneva in June 2010 and June 2011.

Many governments initially expressed hesitation or direct opposition to a legally binding convention on domestic work, citing the impracticality of monitoring work in private households and their reluctance to add to a growing body of international labor standards, many of which had poor rates of ratification. However, the ILO survey of laws and practices around the world, opening statements at the negotiations by the workers' group and key governments, and lobbying by domestic workers' organizations and NGOs made a strong case that the pervasive exploitation and abuse in this sector could no longer be neglected.

The workers' position was formally represented by the International Trade Union Confederation (ITUC), the global umbrella for national trade union federations, and supported by the ILO unit assisting workers (ACTRAV). The newly formed International Domestic Workers Network (IDWN), supported by the main global trade union for food workers (IUF), ensured domestic workers' voices were represented in the negotiations. They brought domestic workers from around the world to participate in and observe the negotiations, and several of them were selected for their country's official worker delegations, including those from Mexico, Brazil, South Africa, Jamaica, the US, and the United Kingdom. Anti-Slavery International facilitated a delegation of child domestic workers to share their experiences and recommendations to the negotiating committee.

The employers' position was formally represented by the International Organization of Employers (IOE), which had little previous experience with the issue.

From the outset of the negotiations, the employers pushed strongly for a non-binding recommendation in lieu of a legally binding convention, and were particularly concerned by additional regulation of private employment agencies that they feared was unrealistic and impractical. However, a change in leadership between the second and third years of negotiations, engagement with NGOs to learn more about abusive practices by recruitment agencies in some parts of the world, and a clear signal of overwhelming support for a binding convention led the employers to back down from their opposition. The employers' representative spoke strongly on behalf of the new standards during the final vote, and more than half of the employers cast their votes in favor of adopting the convention.

Some of the most contentious debates during the negotiations included regulation of employment agencies, elements of written contracts for domestic workers, provisions on social security and a healthy working environment, and how to account for working hours when domestic workers are not actively working but must be available to be "on-call." Surprisingly, provisions on monitoring and inspections of private homes garnered little controversy during the final debate.

From the outset of negotiations, key governments provided decisive support, advocating strongly for binding standards that would extend equal labor protections to domestic workers. Delegates from Australia, Brazil, South Africa (speaking on behalf of the Africa group), the US, Argentina, and Uruguay spoke up repeatedly to introduce and defend strong provisions and to point to effective country-level examples of legislation and implementation.

Although European Union countries, with the exception of the UK and the Czech Republic, cast their final votes in favor of the convention, the EU played a disappointing role during the negotiations, often attempting to weaken suggested provisions. In part, this emanated from the EU's desire to avoid highly politicized debates on migrants' rights in their home countries and, in general, to work around specific provisions in EU directives and reflect existing national legislation. ILO members made a number of concessions in order to accommodate EU concerns, hoping to win their support and avoid the credibility problems faced by the United Nations Migrant Worker

Convention, which has been primarily ratified by migrant-sending countries and ignored by migrant-receiving countries.

As negotiations progressed, support for the convention grew. Some states with initially hostile attitudes changed their positions as they heard evidence of the abuses against domestic workers and concrete examples of how legislation in a diverse array of countries could improve domestic workers' rights. Members of the Gulf Cooperation Council (Bahrain, Kuwait, Oman, Qatar, the United Arab Emirates (UAE), and Saudi Arabia), along with Bangladesh, Indonesia, and India, reversed early opposition to a legally binding convention and expressed support in the final vote.

On June 16, 2011, the newly negotiated standards won overwhelming support, with 396 delegates (representing governments, workers, and employers' associations) voting for the convention, 16 voting against, and 63 abstaining. Swaziland was the only government to vote against the convention.

Translating Standards into Change on the Ground

While we celebrate this historic moment, we also know that there are many challenges to face in our struggle to ensure that these rights, now enshrined in Convention form, are upheld, protected, and defended.
—MIGRANT FORUM IN ASIA, STATEMENT, MANILA, JUNE 16, 2011

Adopting a new convention is only the first step in a long, difficult campaign for widespread ratification and implementation. However, the process of negotiating the convention has already played a critical role in raising awareness about a labor sector once largely hidden from public view. This has already begun to shift attitudes away from perceiving household work as informal labor, to recognizing it as work deserving of comprehensive protections. The negotiations also served as a focal point to mobilize a diverse array of actors committed to enshrining these standards in national laws and practices on the ground.

Two ratifications are required for the convention to come into force, and several countries have already expressed their intention to ratify, including Belgium, Brazil, Namibia, Norway, Peru, the Philippines, and Uruguay. National consultations on the convention are taking place in others. Whether governments are close to ratifying the convention or not, they will feel pressure to respect the standards it sets forth. For example, several countries are currently drafting or revising legislation on domestic work, such as Kuwait, the UAE, Lebanon, Indonesia, and the Philippines, and they will consult the standards as they finalize their laws. Singapore and Malaysia, two of the nine countries that did not vote in the convention's favor, will find it in their interest to introduce reforms anyway to remain an attractive destination for migrant domestic workers who can increasingly opt for better working conditions and pay elsewhere.

Discrimination and exploitative practices are deeply entrenched and recognition and respect for domestic workers' rights will not improve overnight. To make the new standards count, domestic workers' groups, migrants' groups, trade unions, the ILO, NGOs, and other advocates must strengthen efforts at the national level to replicate their success in Geneva at the international level. They must also raise public awareness among key constituencies such as national labor officials, employers, trade unions, and media. They will then need to mobilize and build momentum around national consultations, ILO ratification, and related legislative reforms.

Because the strength and diversity of the domestic workers' movement varies greatly by country and region, a third priority is to provide international support to national and regional groups as needed. This may entail working to ensure freedom of association for domestic workers, providing financial and organizational support to fledgling groups, or building alliances among domestic workers, labor, migrants, women's rights, and children's rights organizations.

Finally, dissemination of best practices and lessons learned, particularly on experiences with implementing domestic worker protections and instituting monitoring mechanisms, will be crucial for ensuring that strong global standards turn into concrete improvements in local practices.

As Myrtle Witbooi, the IDWN chair quoted earlier, said when celebrating adoption of the ILO convention:

> *The fight is not over. We need to go back home. We need to campaign. We need to be sure that what we vote for is implemented. We must not rest until our governments ratify the convention. We cannot be free until we free all the domestic workers.*

Nisha Varia is senior researcher in the Women's Rights Division at Human Rights Watch; Jo Becker is advocacy director of the Children's Rights Division.

UPRISING
PHOTOGRAPHS FROM THE ARAB SPRING

On December 17, 2010, a 26-year-old Tunisian man set himself ablaze after abusive police confiscated his unlicensed vegetable cart, his only source of income. This desperate act of protest inspired a movement that swept the country and ignited calls for reform throughout the region. Thousands of Tunisians took to the streets to denounce their tyrannical government and, within weeks successfully ousted President Zine el-Abidine Ben Ali from power. On January 25, 2011, Egyptians came together by the thousands to launch a massive pro-democratic movement that within 18 days ended President Hosni Mubarak's 30-year reign. Emboldened anti-government protests quickly erupted in Jordan, Yemen, Algeria, Bahrain, Iran, Iraq, Syria, Oman, and Libya.

EGYPT A crowd celebrates Mubarak's resignation in Tahrir Square, Cairo, on February 11, 2011.

© 2011 Yuri Kozyrev/NOOR for TIME Magazine

EGYPT Laila Said with Wael Ghonim. Laila is the mother of 28-year-old Khaled Said, whose torture and murder by Egyptian police on June 6, 2010, helped to spark the discontent that eventually led to the Tahrir Square protests and President Hosni Mubarak's downfall. Laila, who spoke out about the murder of her son, became known as the "Mother of Egypt," and as an emblem of the consequences of endemic police torture and impunity. Wael is a Google regional marketing executive who administered the "We are all Khaled Said" Facebook page after the young man's killing.

© 2011 Platon for Human Rights Watch

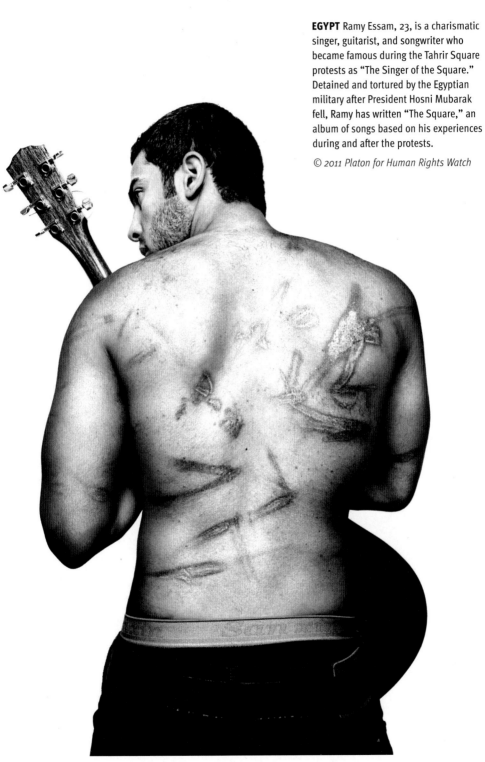

EGYPT Ramy Essam, 23, is a charismatic singer, guitarist, and songwriter who became famous during the Tahrir Square protests as "The Singer of the Square." Detained and tortured by the Egyptian military after President Hosni Mubarak fell, Ramy has written "The Square," an album of songs based on his experiences during and after the protests.

© 2011 Platon for Human Rights Watch

YEMEN A poster of Yemen's President Ali Abdullah Saleh on a roof of a house in the old city of Sanaa. After more than three decades of autocratic rule, Saleh bowed to unrelenting street protests and signed an agreement on November 23, 2011, to relinquish power over three months.

© 2011 Yuri Kozyrev/NOOR for TIME Magazine

TUNISIA A protester rests during a day marked by clashes with the police in Tunis on January 21, 2011. The slogan behind him reads: "Death to dictatorship."

© 2011 Alex Majoli/Magnum

BAHRAIN The funeral procession of anti-government protester Abdul Ridha BuHameed in Malkiya on February 22, 2011. BuHameed was shot in the head when Bahraini military and security forces attacked peaceful anti-government demonstrators marching toward the Pearl Roundabout, in the capital, Manama.

© *2011 Yuri Kozyrev/NOOR for TIME Magazine*

SYRIA A cell phone image of Ismail Bakir who was reportedly tortured and killed by Syrian security forces while trying to cross the border with Turkey.

© 2011 Stanley Greene/NOOR

LIBYA A Libyan reacts while touring Libyan leader Muammar Gaddafi's massive Bab al-Aziziya compound in central Tripoli, which opposition fighters overran in August 2011.

© *2011 Yuri Kozyrev/NOOR for TIME Magazine*

MALI

A Poisonous Mix

Child Labor, Mercury, and Artisanal Gold Mining in Mali

HUMAN
RIGHTS
WATCH

WORLD REPORT

2012

AFRICA

ANGOLA

In 2011 President Jose Eduardo dos Santos, in power for 32 years, faced an unprecedented wave of criticism. Inspired by the pro-democracy Arab Spring movements, Angola witnessed an incipient movement of anti-government protests. In response, authorities used excessive force to crack down on the protests, most of which were organized via the internet, and curtailed media coverage of the demonstrations.

More broadly, Angola's government continued restrictions on the rights to freedom of expression, association, and assembly, despite strong guarantees protecting these rights in the 2010 constitution.

Freedom of Media

Media face a wide array of restrictions that impair free expression and encourage self-censorship. The ruling party limits access to information and, by controlling the state-owned as well as some private media, severely restricts media criticisms of the government. Educated urban classes often use the internet and social media as channels to criticize the government due to constraints on traditional media. At this writing the necessary by-laws and other complementary laws to the 2006 press law that would lift administrative restrictions on private radio broadcasting had yet to be tabled before parliament.

On March 31 parliament passed an information technology crime bill that undermined freedom of expression and information. After domestic and international criticism, parliament eventually withdrew the bill, but government officials announced that some of its provisions would be integrated into a new criminal code that parliament has yet to pass.

Defamation remains a criminal offense in Angola, and offenses, such as "abuse of press freedom," defined by the 2006 press law, are vague and open to use against journalists and media outlets.

On March 3 a judge of the provincial court of Namibe sentenced Armando Chicoca, a journalist for Voice of America and the private weekly newspaper

Folha 8, to one year in prison for defamation. On April 6 he was released on bail while awaiting appeal. On October 10 a court gave William Tonet, director of *Folha 8*, a one-year suspended sentence for defaming four senior government officials. He was also ordered to pay US$100,000 in damages, an unusually high sum. Tonet's appeal was pending at this writing.

In September the police arrested and briefly detained several journalists, who intended to cover anti-government rallies; individuals apparently acting under police instructions physically attacked and injured several journalists. Their equipment was confiscated or destroyed.

Right to Peaceful Assembly

The 2010 constitution guarantees freedom of assembly and peaceful demonstration, and Angolan laws explicitly allow public demonstrations without government authorization. However, since 2009 the government has banned or obstructed a number of anti-government demonstrations, and the police have prevented the majority of peaceful demonstrations from taking place.

Since early 2011 a non-partisan youth movement, inspired by the pro-democracy Arab Spring movements, has organized a number of demonstrations in Luanda, the capital, calling for freedom of expression, social justice, and the president's resignation. The authorities responded in high-handed fashion, intimidating protesters and organizers and spreading fear among the population by alleging an imminent risk of civil war. On September 15 the Luanda provincial government banned all demonstrations in Luanda's city center, effectively undermining the right to peaceful assembly. The banning order was withdrawn after opposition parties appealed at the Constitutional Court.

On March 7, police briefly detained 17 rap musicians who intended to join an anti-government rally organized anonymously via the internet at Luanda's Independence Square; three journalists of the private weekly newspaper *Novo Jornal,* who intended to cover the events, were also arrested. Representatives of three opposition parties who planned to join the protests withdrew following anonymous death threats. In order to discourage people from participating, the ruling Popular Movement for the Liberation of Angola (MPLA) party organized a campaign to discredit anti-government protests as an attempt to throw the country back to civil war, and on March 5 the ruling party organized a nation-wide peace march.

On April 2 several hundred people from the same youth movement demonstrated peacefully at the Independence Square in Luanda. The protests took place without any incident. However, protesters said they received anonymous death threats and were subject to other forms of intimidation ahead of the protests. On May 25 police dispersed a demonstration organized by the youth movement, and briefly detained 12 protesters.

On September 3 police violently dispersed an anti-government rally of several hundred youth, and arrested at least 24 people. During the rally, groups of unidentified men acting under police coverage attacked and injured demonstrators. Several journalists and demonstrators were injured. On September 12 a police court convicted 18 demonstrators to prison sentences of 45 to 90 days for alleged disobedience, damage, and the injuring of four police agents. The detainees were denied due process, as well as access to lawyers and family members ahead of the hearings, and defense witnesses said they were intimidated and threatened by supposed state security agents.

Twenty-seven people were arrested at a September 8 protest that called for the release of the detainees. The police also briefly detained two journalists from the state news agency Angop and the private weekly newspaper *Continente*, who were covering the protests. On September 19 a police court acquitted for lack of evidence all 27 detainees of charges of disobedience, incitement to violence, and damage. On October 14 the Supreme Court ordered the release of the demonstrators convicted on September 12, admitting lack of evidence.

Police have also used excessive force to disperse spontaneous demonstrations in Cabinda, Bié, and Benguela. On September 8, policemen killed two alleged demonstrators in Kuito, Bié, as motorcycle taxi drivers protested against police violence. On September 26, police briefly arrested a dozen protesters for alleged illegal land expropriation in Benguela.

Cabinda

An intermittent conflict with a separatist movement has persisted in the enclave of Cabinda since 1975, despite a 2006 peace agreement. In March the government officially resumed military counter-insurgency operations in the enclave. The authorities continued using the conflict to justify restrictions on freedom of expression, assembly, and association.

In December 2010 all political dissidents who had been convicted and imprisoned following the armed attack on the Togolese soccer (football) team during the Africa Cup of Nations in Cabinda on January 8, 2010, were released, following a parliamentary review of the abusive 1978 state security crime law under which they were sentenced.

However, on February 13 the government banned anti-government protests in Cabinda, and on March 7 and April 10 the police briefly detained a number of alleged protesters. They were released without charge. On July 26, police arrested nine activists who intended to present a letter to a visiting delegation of European Union ambassadors. Although a judge acquitted them on August 3, ruling that the police maltreated them upon arrest, the police sued a Voice of America journalist who covered the event for defamation, as well as two of his interviewees who commented on police violence and arrests. At this writing there had been no progress in the case.

Mass Expulsions of Irregular Migrants

On July 7 a law seeking to prevent and punish perpetrators of domestic violence entered into force. The law defines sexual violence more broadly than in previous legislation. While this is a positive step, the government failed to investigate and punish those who perpetrated sexual violence against female immigrants during the most recent wave of mass expulsions of irregular migrants that started in October 2010.

In March the United Nations special rapporteur on torture and the UN special rapporteur on violence against women questioned Angola's government on new allegations of serious human rights abuses, including widespread sexual violence against irregular, mostly Congolese migrants during the recent wave of mass expulsions in the Cabinda, Zaire, and Lunda Norte provinces. As in previous years, the government denied the allegations, claiming that it was cleared by a commission set up to investigate such allegations.

Following the visit of Margot Wallström, UN special representative on sexual violence in conflict, to Angola in March, the Angolan government said it could verify only one isolated case of rape that was being addressed through the courts. The authorities have not published any report of their own investigation, as promised to the UN, nor have they disclosed any detail on the alleged court case.

However, accounts gathered by Human Rights Watch in Kamako and Muanda in May and June suggest the urgent need for a credible, independent, and thorough investigation on both sides of the border of Angola and the Democratic Republic of Congo. Human Rights Watch research found that members of the security service—including border police, rapid intervention police, and immigration officials—continue to routinely commit violence against female Congolese migrants in a number of transit prison facilities where migrants are detained before deportation. Corroborated abuses targeting women include rape, sexual coercion, beatings, deprivation of food and water, and—in some cases—sexual abuse in the presence of children and other female inmates.

Key International Actors

Angola remains one of Africa's largest oil producers and China's second most important source of oil and most important commercial partner in Africa. This oil wealth, and Angola's regional military power, has greatly limited leverage of other governments and regional and international organizations pushing for good governance and human rights.

In August Angola took over the Southern Africa Development Community (SADC) chair. Yet, the government refuses to grant entry visas to regional NGO activists planning to attend parallel events during the August SADC heads of state summit.

BURUNDI

Violence increased in Burundi in 2011 as the country's political situation failed to stabilize. Reciprocal killings by members of the ruling National Council for the Defense of Democracy-Forces for the Defense of Democracy (CNDD-FDD) and the former rebel group the National Liberation Forces (FNL) increased, particularly in Bujumbura, the capital, and in Bujumbura Rural Province. Impunity for these crimes remains one of the most serious obstacles to peace. The single largest incident of killings took place in September in Gatumba, near the Congolese border.

The political space in 2011 continued to narrow, with the CNDD-FDD still in a position of near-monopoly following the main opposition parties' boycott of the 2010 elections. The government continued to harass and intimidate journalists, lawyers, and civil society actors who exposed abuses, often labeling them opposition supporters.

The creation of a National Independent Human Rights Commission (CNIDH), whose members were sworn in in June, was a positive step, but the CNIDH's activities in 2011 were poorly funded.

Political Space

The CNDD-FDD continued to dominate political space, sending contradictory messages to the opposition. On the one hand, President Pierre Nkurunziza, during his Independence Day speech on July 1, appealed to exiled opposition leaders to return to Burundi peacefully and help contribute to the construction of the country. On the other, the government and the opposition were unable to agree on the preconditions for dialogue, despite international appeals to do so. The situation was exacerbated by the disarray of the opposition and the lack of official recognition of the opposition coalition, ADC-Ikibiri.

Escalation of Political Violence

After exiting the political process in 2010, some FNL members again took up arms and began launching attacks inside Burundi and from neighboring

Democratic Republic of Congo. A number of other unknown armed groups have also emerged. In response, the CNDD-FDD increased attacks on FNL members and former members, notably through its *imbonerakure* youth wing and the National Intelligence Services (SNR).

Killings targeted prominent members of the FNL as well as the rank and file. Demobilized FNL commander Audace Vianney Habonarugira was shot dead in July 2011. He had first been shot and seriously injured by a policeman in March 2011, and he was repeatedly threatened and sought after by state security agents in the months before his death. Dédithe Niyirera, FNL representative in Kayanza province, was killed in Kayanza in late August after receiving numerous death threats. Médard Ndayishimiye, a local FNL leader in Mwaro province who was also threatened, was found dead in Rutana province in October after being abducted in Gitega town where he had fled for his safety. Demobilized FNL combatants were also pressured to join the SNR and the *imbonerakure* or face death, in an effort to recruit members who can more easily identify current and former FNL members. Many FNL members and former members went into hiding after receiving threats.

In response to these attacks, armed groups, some of whom were believed to be associated with the FNL, increased attacks on CNDD-FDD members and local officials. Among the victims were Pascal Ngendakumana and Albert Ntiranyibagira, two low-ranking CNDD-FDD members, killed on April 6 by individuals believed to be associated with the FNL.

On September 18, gunmen killed around 40 people in an attack on a bar in Gatumba, Bujumbura Rural province. It was the largest massacre in the country in several years. The majority of victims were not known to be affiliated with a particular political party. Nine days later the intelligence services blamed FNL leaders for the attack. However, the findings of the commission of inquiry have not yet been published.

Impunity

Following the Gatumba killings, President Nkurunziza announced that the government would find the perpetrators within one month. A special commission was established to conduct an investigation and submitted its report to the prosecutor general in October. By the end of October, 20 people were in pre-trial detention in connection with the Gatumba attack. Other commissions have been established since late 2010 to investigate extrajudicial killings and other abuses before, during, and since the 2010 elections. At this writing none of these commissions had published their findings.

Almost all political killings by individuals affiliated with the CNDD-FDD or the security forces were conducted with impunity. In some cases, the police or the prosecutor opened investigations, but these rarely led to arrests. When crimes were believed to have been perpetrated by opposition groups, the typical government response was to arbitrarily target FNL or ex-FNL members, even when there was no credible evidence that the individuals punished were responsible for these crimes.

Hearings into the killing of Ernest Manirumva, vice-president of the anti-corruption organization OLUCOME, have stalled since 2010. Eleven suspects remain in preventive detention since 2009 while high-level security force suspects have still not been questioned.

Journalists, Civil Society Activists, and Lawyers

Jean Claude Kavumbagu, a journalist charged with treason following his 2010 article questioning the army's ability to respond to attacks from al-Shabaab, was released on May 13, 2011. He was found guilty of "publishing an article likely to discredit the state or economy" and sentenced to eight months, but was released shortly after the trial since he had spent 10 months in pre-trial detention.

Bob Rugurika, chief editor of African Public Radio (RPA), was summoned multiple times to the public prosecutor's office and questioned about RPA's radio broadcasts. He was accused of disseminating information that "incites the population to civil disobedience" and "incites ethnic hatred" after broadcasting programs that called for dialogue with the opposition. Rugurika also faced questions about programs that touched on the composition of a committee set up by the government to prepare a Truth and Reconciliation Commission.

Patrick Mitabaro, editor-in-chief of Radio Isanganiro, was also summoned after his station aired an interview with former spokesperson of the FRODEBU party, Pancrace Cimpaye. He was accused, among other things, of disseminating information that could affect state security. Neither journalist was charged.

The National Security Council issued a one month media blackout on the Gatumba killings, prohibiting journalists from reporting, commenting on, or analyzing the incident and any other case under investigation. Five radio stations and one newspaper briefly defied the order.

Civil society leaders were likewise harassed by the authorities and accused of siding with the opposition. Pierre-Claver Mbonimpa, president of the human rights organization APRODH, and Gabriel Rufyiri, president of OLUCOME, were repeatedly summoned for questioning by the public prosecutor's office, but were not charged with any offense. In late August President Nkurunziza publicly warned that civil society organizations should be "on guard" in a response to their criticism of state pressure on journalists, lawyers, and civil society activists.

In April the government refused to allow civil society leaders to march in support of justice for Manirumva. When the organizations attempted to march without permission, two members were arrested and detained for several hours before being released.

State authorities also targeted lawyers. On July 15 lawyer Suzanne Bukuru was arrested on espionage charges after facilitating an interview between her clients and journalists. Isidore Rufyikiri, president of the Burundi Bar Association, was arrested on July 27 on charges of "insulting magistrates" after organizing a rally in defence of Bukuru. Bukuru was released on August 1 and the charges were dropped. Rufyikiri was released on August 4 after paying a fine.

François Nyamoya, lawyer and spokesman for the opposition party Movement for Solidarity and Democracy (MSD), was arrested on July 29 on charges of witness tampering in a 2004 murder trial. At this writing he remained in detention. Nyamoya, who is also the lawyer for journalist Rugurika of RPA, had previously been arrested in 2010 on charges of "threatening state security."

National Independent Human Rights Commission

CNIDH began working in June and issued its first public statement on an alleged extrajudicial execution by the police. However, the commission's activities in 2011 were poorly funded. Following pressure from the Burundian government and other African governments, the United Nations Human Rights Council (HRC) hastened the termination of the mandate of the UN independent expert on the situation of human rights in Burundi, on the basis that a national human rights commission had been created.

Transitional Justice

After years of delay, measures were put in place relatively quickly to prepare the establishment of a Truth and Reconciliation Commission (TRC) to cover grave crimes in Burundi since 1962. The government appointed a technical committee in July to create a framework for a TRC, and in October the committee submitted its report to the president. At this writing the report had not been officially published. The government has not made a commitment to establish a special tribunal to investigate past war crimes.

Key International Actors

On January 1 the UN Security Council adopted a resolution scaling down the UN Office in Burundi (BNUB). Staffing reduction affected BNUB's human rights monitoring capacity.

In June the UN independent expert on the situation of human rights in Burundi presented his first report since September 2008. Burundi officials and the African Group at the HRC had repeatedly blocked previous publication attempts. The expert called for measures to end impunity and promote greater respect for freedom of expression.

International diplomats in Bujumbura continued to follow high-profile court proceedings including that of Kavumbagu. In May European diplomats in Burundi, in a joint statement, expressed concern over reports of extrajudicial executions and torture in 2010 and 2011. The UN secretary-general and several governments, including those of the United States and Belgium, condemned the Gatumba attack and called for an investigation. The United Kingdom's Department for International Development (DFID) announced that it would close its aid programme in Burundi in 2012, citing internal reprioritization. Other international donors expressed concerns over state corruption.

CÔTE D'IVOIRE

At least 3,000 people were killed and more than 150 women and girls raped during the six months of political violence and armed conflict which followed the November 28, 2010 presidential run-off election between opposition leader Alassane Ouattara and incumbent President Laurent Gbagbo. Despite internationally recognized results proclaiming Ouattara the winner, Gbagbo refused to step down. Large-scale violence ended in May, after the April capture of Gbagbo and Abidjan, the commercial capital, by pro-Ouattara troops.

After consolidating power President Ouattara made repeated commitments to investigate and ensure impartial justice for the massive human rights and international humanitarian law violations that characterized the period. However, one-sided domestic justice efforts, which excluded charges against any member of his camp, threatened further communal divisions and undermined the return to the rule of law.

International actors that had rightfully taken a hardline stance against the Gbagbo camp's abuses during the conflict—including the United Nations, the European Union, France, and the United States—appeared less willing to publicly pressure Ouattara's government on the same issues and on the importance of impartial accountability.

Post-Election Violence

From December 2010 to late February 2011 the post-election violence was primarily perpetrated by security forces and allied militia loyal to Gbagbo, which sought to maintain power by systematically targeting real or perceived Ouattara supporters. Pro-Gbagbo forces "disappeared" neighborhood political leaders from Ouattara's coalition, gang-raped women and girls who had helped mobilize voters, and violently suppressed any demonstration against Gbagbo's refusal to step down. State-controlled media routinely incited hatred and violence against northern Ivorians and West African immigrants. As a direct consequence, pro-Gbagbo militias established roadblocks around Abidjan and killed scores from these typically pro-Ouattara groups during moments of tension.

In early March forces loyal to Ouattara—composed primarily of soldiers who fought with his prime minister, Guillaume Soro, during the 2002 to 2003 conflict and its aftermath—launched a military offensive to remove Gbagbo from power. Once the crisis escalated to armed conflict, it was marked by war crimes and likely crimes against humanity by both sides.

The west of the country, which has long been its most volatile region, was the scene of massacres committed by both sides in late March. In Bloléquin and Bédi-Goazon, pro-Gbagbo militiamen and Liberian mercenaries killed at least 130 men, women, and children from groups that largely supported, or were perceived to support, Ouattara. In Duékoué, the Republican Forces and allied militias killed several hundred men from pro-Gbagbo ethnic groups after taking control of the town on March 29. Throughout the west, pro-Ouattara forces killed, raped, and burned villages. At the conflict's peak more than 180,000 Ivorians fled to Liberia; at this writing most refugees remained there, often without a home to return to, and afraid of abuse should they return to villages that still exist. Several hundred thousand more remain internally displaced for similar reasons.

After taking over the west, the Republican Forces advanced to Abidjan in several days as most Gbagbo fighters laid down their weapons and fled. However, intense fighting engulfed Abidjan in early April, before Gbagbo's April 11 capture. In subsequent days pro-Gbagbo militiamen rampaged in areas they still controlled, killing hundreds of perceived Ouattara supporters. The Republican Forces engaged in widespread summary executions, torture, arbitrary detention, and looting as they consolidated control of the commercial capital.

National-Level Justice and Accountability

The capture of Gbagbo and his wife Simone began a wave of arrests against the former regime's military and political leaders. At this writing military and civilian prosecutors had brought charges against at least 118 of these officials including Gbagbo, Simone, Charles Blé Goudé, Gen. Guiai Bi Poin, and Gen. Bruno Dogbo Blé. The civilian prosecutor primarily limited the charges to economic crimes and crimes against the state—including charges against Gbagbo—whereas the military prosecutor included charges for murder, rape,

COTE D'IVOIRE

"They Killed Them Like It Was Nothing"

The Need for Justice for Côte d'Ivoire's Post-Election Crimes

HUMAN
RIGHTS
WATCH

and other violent crimes. In stark contrast, at this writing not a single member of the pro-Ouattara forces had been charged for crimes committed during the post-election crisis.

Almost immediately after the conflict ended Ouattara called for a Dialogue, Truth, and Reconciliation Commission (DTRC) and then named former Prime Minister Charles Konan Banny as the commission's president. The commission formally began working on September 28. The DTRC's potential efficacy was undermined by inadequate consultation with Ivorian civil society, lack of independence from the presidency, an unclear relationship with prosecution efforts, and ill-defined powers.

The president also established a national commission of inquiry to provide conclusions on how and why massive human rights violations occurred. The commission, which began its work on September 13 and had a six-month mandate that could be extended for another six months, was tasked most importantly with identifying individuals who should be subject to criminal prosecution. However, the nomination of a commissioner perceived to be close to the president, as well as the process that created the commission, raised concerns about its independence from the presidency and commitment to faithfully and impartially investigate abuses perpetrated by both sides.

International Criminal Court

In December 2010 and again in May 2011 Ouattara confirmed the authority of the International Criminal Court (ICC) to investigate crimes under its jurisdiction. Although not a state party to the Rome Statue, the Ivorian government under Gbagbo had accepted the ICC's jurisdiction in April 2003. However, in Ouattara's May request reconfirming the court's jurisdiction, he asked it to limit its investigation to crimes committed after November 28, 2010. Ouattara did publicly express his expectation that the ICC would examine both sides' crimes, and that the government would cooperate in handing over any individuals requested.

On June 23 the ICC prosecutor asked the pre-trial chamber for authorization to open an investigation, limiting his inquiry into post-election crimes. This request for a temporal restriction drew criticism from many, including a coalition of Ivorian civil society organizations that stressed the importance of investigations going back to 2002, given the gravity, scale, and complete impunity for these crimes.

On October 3 the pre-trial chamber authorized the prosecutor's investigation into the post-election crimes and requested that he provide further information on crimes committed between 2002 and 2010 to determine possible expansion of the investigation.

Ongoing Insecurity and Reestablishing the Rule of Law

Widespread recruitment of ethnic-based militia by both sides, as well as long-standing weaknesses within the Ivorian judiciary, contributed to ongoing levels of criminal and political violence countrywide, illuminating the urgent need for a credible disarmament program. Several cross-border attacks on Ivorian villages by former Gbagbo militiamen, who have taken refuge in Liberia raised concerns about continued instability in the long-volatile west.

At this writing most gendarmes and police—particularly outside Abidjan—were still unarmed, leaving security functions largely in the hands of soldiers and youth volunteers loyal to Ouattara. The result is an extra-judicial system similar to that which plagued the north when controlled by Soro's forces after 2002: arbitrary detention, disputes "resolved" by soldiers, and extortion. By September the Ouattara government had notably removed most roadblocks along the main roads, and threatened to dismiss soldiers found extorting the population. These steps helped combat the rampant checkpoint extortion that has impacted northern and southern Côte d'Ivoire since 2002.

Legislative elections were scheduled for December 11. If free and fair, they offer an important step in the return to rule of law, instead of rule by presidential decree.

Key International Actors

Gbagbo's refusal to recognize defeat elicited widespread condemnation by the international community, notably the UN, Economic Community of West African States (ECOWAS), EU, France, and the US. Concerted diplomatic pressure on Gbagbo to step down was exerted through repeated demarches, threat of military intervention by ECOWAS, and economic strangulation. The Central Bank of West African States cut off funds, and the EU and US imposed targeted sanctions against leading members of the regime and key Ivorian entities supporting the regime financially.

The UN, which had for years failed to adequately confront Gbagbo on his human rights record and the repeated delays in organizing elections, took a committed stand on enforcing the election result. The UN's endorsement of Ouattara's victory led to repeated threats and attacks by Gbagbo's forces against peacekeepers and civilian UN staff, and at times a closing of humanitarian space.

Citing Gbagbo's use of heavy weapons in indiscriminate attacks that killed civilians, the UN Security Council authorized the UN Operations in Côte d'Ivoire (UNOCI) to use "all necessary means" to protect civilians, including through "prevent[ing] the use of heavy weapons against [civilians]." UNOCI and French forces deployed since 2004 quickly began targeting heavy weapons, culminating in an attack on Gbagbo's residence that led to his arrest. Throughout the conflict, UNOCI played a key, if inconsistent, role in civilian protection, including reinforcing its presence in the west ahead of legislative elections.

The UN Human Rights Council established a commission of inquiry in late March to investigate post-election crimes. In mid-June it presented the Council with its report that found both sides responsible for war crimes and likely crimes against humanity. The Council then established an independent expert on the situation of human rights in Côte d'Ivoire. The commission of inquiry's report included an annex containing names of individuals deemed to merit criminal investigation for their role in crimes. While this annex has been provided to the Office of the High Commissioner for Human Rights, it had not been made available to relevant Ivorian authorities at this writing, thereby failing to contribute to accountability. The UN Security Council has also not published the findings of the 2004 commission of inquiry that investigated serious violations of human rights and international humanitarian law during the 2002 to 2003 armed conflict. The report was delivered to the UN secretary-general in November 2004.

DEMOCRATIC REPUBLIC OF CONGO

The human rights situation in the Democratic Republic of Congo (DRC) remained grave. All sides in the country's ongoing armed conflicts continued to attack civilians and commit other serious human rights abuses. Military operations against foreign and domestic armed groups in the east and north were on a smaller scale than in previous years. Efforts to integrate armed groups into the national army were hampered by former rebel leaders, such as Bosco Ntaganda, who flouted orders from the army's central command and pursued their own interests. Ntaganda is facing an International Criminal Court (ICC) arrest warrant but remains in charge of military operations in eastern Congo.

Preparations for elections preoccupied Congolese authorities and international partners for much of the year. The months before the elections were marked by threats and physical attacks against opposition members, media, and human rights defenders. The United Nations peacekeeping mission in Congo (MONUS-CO) continued to implement its civilian protection mandate and supported logistics for the elections, but was hampered by a serious shortage of helicopters, which impeded its mobility and effectiveness.

Presidential and Legislative Elections

Much attention was focused on preparing for elections set for late 2011 as President Joseph Kabila sought a second term. In January Kabila's government pushed a hasty constitutional change altering the voting system for presidential elections from a two-round to a single-round poll. A month later a close Kabila ally, Pastor Daniel Mulunda Ngoy, was sworn in as head of the National Independent Electoral Commission (CENI). Opposition groups protested the changes, which they said were designed to benefit Kabila.

Politically motivated human rights violations increased as elections approached. UN investigators reported 188 cases before the official campaign began in October. Violence perpetrated by police and other state security services included restrictions on political activities, unnecessary force against demonstrators, and arbitrary arrests primarily directed toward opposition parties, their supporters, and journalists. For example, on October 6 the police violently crushed a demonstration by the Union pour la Democratie et le Progres Social (UDPS) opposition party in Kinshasa, using teargas and firing live rounds in the air. One person was killed and at least 10 others were wounded. Some candidates and their supporters also used inflammatory language and hate speech, inciting youth groups and others to use violence against their opponents.

Attacks on Civilians

The east and the north of the country remained volatile and were marked by frequent attacks on civilians, particularly sexual violence against women and girls. Nearly 1.7 million people are displaced, including the newly displaced, and a further 476,000 are refugees in neighboring countries.

In the east, the army continued military operations against the Democratic Forces for the Liberation of Rwanda (FDLR), a predominately Rwandan Hutu rebel group, and the Allied Democratic Forces (ADF), a Ugandan rebel group, though on a reduced scale from previous years. The government opened secret negotiations with the FDLR to encourage the group to disarm and resettle in another part of Congo, but the talks failed.

As in the past, government soldiers frequently killed and raped civilians and pressed them into forced labor or looted their belongings. In one case, on the night of January 1 soldiers raped at least 67 women and girls and arbitrarily detained and tortured dozens of other civilians in Fizi, South Kivu. Also in January soldiers raped at least 47 women and girls in Bushani, North Kivu, and looted and burned some 100 homes.

Government soldiers also attacked civilians while fighting in the north against the Lord's Resistance Army (LRA), a Ugandan rebel group with a long record of atrocities. The worst attacks were against the Mbororo nomadic cattle herders who frequently traverse the border between Congo and the Central African Republic (CAR). At least 35 Mbororo women and girls were raped. Some women were taken to army camps where they were held and repeatedly raped. Soldiers also beat and arbitrarily detained Mbororo men and pillaged their cattle. The army claimed the Mbororo were aligned with the LRA, but provided no evidence to support the claim.

Armed groups also attacked civilians. In the east, the FDLR and Congolese armed groups occupied areas vacated by government soldiers when they were temporarily recalled for training, attacking civilians who resided there. For example, in May FDLR combatants attacked numerous villages in Masisi territory, killing six civilians, raping two women, and abducting at least 48 people whose whereabouts remain unknown. In Bwale, South Kivu, in January and February at least 65 women and girls were raped by FDLR combatants during four attacks.

In the north the LRA carried out at least 250 attacks against civilians and continued to abduct children and adults, although deadly attacks were less frequent than in previous years. In LRA-affected areas in Congo, CAR, and South Sudan, 2,400 people were killed and 3,400 were abducted by the LRA since September 2008. The Ugandan army, in coalition with armed forces from neighboring countries, continued its military operations against the LRA. No progress was made in apprehending three of the LRA's top leaders sought by the ICC for war crimes committed in northern Uganda, and relations between the coalition partners began to deteriorate. Congolese army and MONUSCO efforts to protect civilians in LRA-affected areas remained inadequate, though some efforts were made to avert attacks around the 2010 Christmas period, a time of previous LRA violence.

Abuses by Bosco Ntaganda

The Congolese army's attempts to restructure and integrate former armed groups into its ranks continued to be fraught with problems. The creation of new regiments mixing government soldiers with former rebels caused confusion and weakened command and control. It further permitted former rebel leader Bosco Ntaganda to increase his power base by expanding his parallel command over parts of the army and local administration.

Ntaganda continued his brutal campaign against perceived opponents, both military and civilian, by ordering assassinations, arbitrary arrests, and other forms of intimidation. Troops under his command were implicated in attacks on civilians. He continued to recruit children and thwarted efforts to demobilize them. He blocked judicial investigations into abuses committed by his loyalists, violated a government export ban on minerals from eastern Congo, and used his influence in the military to confiscate land and expand his business interests.

Despite the flagrant abuses, the government did not enforce the ICC arrest warrant against Ntaganda. Officials said they feared his arrest could disrupt the integration of former rebel groups into the army and harm diplomatic relations with Congo's neighbor, Rwanda, which supports Ntaganda. Failure to arrest Ntaganda further harmed peace and stabilization efforts.

Journalists and Human Rights Defenders

Congolese human rights defenders and journalists continued to be targeted in 2011. On June 21 Witness-Patchelly Kambale Musonia—a journalist and talk show host at Radio Paysanne, a community radio station in Kirumba, North Kivu—was shot dead by unidentified armed men following a broadcast about the trafficking of weapons. On March 24, government soldiers in Baraka, South Kivu, threatened a human rights defender from Federation des Femmes pour la Paix for her activities in defense of rape victims.

Threats increased as elections approached. On September 6, unidentified armed men threw tear gas, gasoline, and incendiary grenades into the studio of Radio Lisanga Télévision (RTLV), a private television station favorable to opposition candidate Etienne Tshisekedi. In June armed men attacked and injured an RTLV presenter. In Fungurume, Katanga province, Dédé Ilunga, a journalist with Radio Océan, was arbitrarily arrested and detained by police for 17 days in September following a broadcast criticizing President Kabila's development program. He was released without charge.

Journalists covering demonstrations and political rallies were also repeatedly targeted. In August security guards at a ruling party congress at a Kinshasa stadium attacked cameraman Serge Kembila of Radio Télévision Groupe l'Avenir (RTGA) for filming empty seats and confiscated his footage.

Congolese authorities have largely failed to investigate and prosecute those responsible for the attacks. In one exception, a military court in Kinshasa found five senior police officers guilty of murdering Floribert Chebeya Bahizire, the executive director of Voice of the Voiceless, and his driver, Fidèle Bazana, in June 2010. At this writing three of the five remained at large. Congolese human rights groups criticized the trial for failing to take into account the role of the national police chief in the murder.

Justice and Accountability

There was mixed progress in the government's efforts to hold perpetrators of serious violations to account.

Congo's judicial officials had some notable successes in prosecuting sexual violence and other crimes. Following the January mass rape in Fizi, South Kivu, a military court found 10 soldiers and their commanding officer guilty of crimes against humanity. In March another military court sentenced 11 soldiers, including three officers, for crimes against humanity committed in Katasomwa in September 2009. On March 25 the High Military Court in Kinshasa began the trial of Gen. Jérôme Kakwavu, on war crimes charges for rape and torture. Kakwavu is the first general in Congo's history to be arrested on rape charges.

No progress was made in apprehending the perpetrators of a mass rape of 387 women, men, and children, committed by a coalition of armed groups in Walikale territory, North Kivu, in July and August 2010. One of those facing an arrest warrant for the crime against humanity of rape, Ntabo Ntaberi Sheka, ran as a candidate for the National Assembly. Efforts to combat impunity also suffered a serious blow with the promotion and growing power of Ntaganda, living openly in Goma, and the escape from prison of Gedeon Kyungu Mutanda and many of his co-perpetrators, who had been found guilty of crimes against humanity in 2009. Authorities had ignored many earlier requests from civil society to incarcerate Mutanda at a maximum security prison.

The Congolese government took action in response to the 2010 human rights "mapping report" published by the UN Office of the High Commissioner for Human Rights (OHCHR), which documented 617 incidents of serious violations of international humanitarian law between 1993 and 2003. In August the government presented a draft law to parliament to establish a specialized mixed court with national and international judicial staff to try those responsible for the most serious crimes. Congolese civil society groups strongly supported the draft legislation, but the Senate rejected it and asked the government to harmonize its proposal with other draft laws to combat serious human rights violations.

International trials against those responsible for crimes continued. In Germany two FDLR leaders stood trial for war crimes and crimes against humanity. At the ICC three former Congolese armed group leaders were tried for similar crimes and judges deliberated whether the case of a Rwandan FDLR leader would move forward to trial.

Key International Actors

International actors focused their attention on the elections. The UN Security Council renewed MONUSCO's mandate with a continued focus on protecting civilians, though UN member states failed to provide it with the logistical capabilities it required.

OHCHR took few steps to follow-up on its "mapping report." Few diplomats and UN officials raised public concerns about the government's failure to arrest Ntaganda, though some said they raised it privately.

United States President Barack Obama announced in October that the US would send 100 military advisors to central Africa to help regional forces apprehend LRA leaders and end the group's violence. The US also said it would withhold US$1.3 million in foreign military financing until the Congolese government takes concrete steps to end its use of child soldiers.

EQUATORIAL GUINEA

Equatorial Guinea remains mired in corruption, poverty, and repression under President Teodoro Obiang Nguema Mbasogo, who has been in power since 1979. Vast oil revenues fund lavish lifestyles for the small elite surrounding the president, while most of the population lives in poverty. The government regularly engages in torture and arbitrary detention. Journalists, civil society groups, and members of the political opposition face heavy government repression.

President Obiang, who became Africa's longest-serving ruler with the fall of Muammar Gaddafi, continued seeking to enhance his international standing. In 2011 he assumed the one-year rotating presidency of the African Union but failed to persuade the United Nations Educational, Scientific and Cultural Organization (UNESCO) to award a long-stalled prize in his name.

Despite some positive steps, including the release of 22 political prisoners, overall human rights conditions remained poor and, in some respects, worsened as freedoms were clamped down on ahead of the AU summit President Obiang hosted in June. Constitutional changes proposed in March were not open to debate and seemed designed to transfer power from the president to his eldest son. Obiang and his family remained ensnared in multiple foreign corruption investigations, which gathered momentum during the year.

Economic and Social Rights

Fulfillment of key socio-economic rights, such as the right to education and basic healthcare, remained poor, despite significant oil revenues and the country's small population, which make Equatorial Guinea's per capita gross domestic product—at approximately US$30,000 according to UN figures—among the highest in the world, and the highest in Africa.

Although the country saw notable progress in reducing rates of maternal and child mortality, these rates still remained high. For example, 2010 UN and World Bank statistics indicate that nearly one in every eight child dies before his or her fifth birthday. A reduction of the high incidence of malaria resulted from a prevention campaign largely funded by Western oil companies.

The quality of education remained poor in Equatorial Guinea. According to UNESCO figures, nearly one-quarter of primary students repeat a grade. The government acknowledged problems in its education system in October when a workshop on girls' education identified barriers to learning, including inadequate facilities, a high student-to-teacher ratio, low teacher quality, and poor nutrition. Although the country ratified the African Charter on Human and People's Rights on the Rights of Women in Africa—the Maputo Protocol—in June, there is no indication that it will be implemented vigorously.

The government increased social spending levels but prioritized public investments in projects that have little benefit for the poor, such as a lavish $830 million resort complex built for the AU summit.

Ongoing legal challenges in France, Spain, and the United States, as well as a complaint before the African Commission on Human and Peoples' Rights, allege misuse of Equatorial Guinea's oil funds. In connection with their investigation, in September French police seized 11 luxury cars belonging to President Obiang's eldest son and minister of agriculture and forestry—known by the nickname Teodorín—from outside his Paris residence. Also in September a French court ruled against President Obiang's claims of defamation against the French NGO CCFD-Terre Solidaire for its 2009 report on the ill-gotten gains of the president and other public officials. In October US authorities filed legal claims against Teodorín's US assets—including a Malibu mansion, luxury vehicle, and valuable collectables—alleging they were illegally purchased with the proceeds of corruption.

Freedom of Expression and Association

Equatorial Guinea is notorious for its lack of press freedom. Freedom of expression was curtailed even further in 2011. Journalists from state-owned media outlets are not permitted to criticize the government. The few private media outlets that exist are generally owned by persons close to President Obiang; self-censorship is common. Foreign news is available to those with access to satellite broadcasts and the internet, which is a small minority of the population; others have access only to limited foreign radio programming.

In February the government ordered the staff of state radio and TV not to cover the pro-democracy Arab Spring movements. In March the host of a French-language state radio program was removed after he referred briefly to Libya on air. In an official statement denying claims of censorship, the government said he was sacked for "his lack of rigor and professionalism."

The government is also intolerant of critical views from abroad. It denies visas and uses surveillance, harassment, and detention to hamper independent foreign journalists. In March 2011 the government informed Reporters Without Borders that it would not grant a visa to carry out a fact-finding visit "as long as the offensive references to our President continue to appear on your website." Some foreign journalists reported being detained and forced to delete photographs before and during the AU summit. In one incident, security agents detained and interrogated journalists from the German television network ZDF and deleted some of their footage, including images of poverty.

In February novelist, blogger, and editor Juan Tomás Ávila Laurel began a hunger strike calling for democratic reforms. He soon left for Spain, claiming that he was harassed.

In March the government banned demonstrations and blocked an opposition party from staging a rally. Activists from another opposition party were prevented from staging a Labor Day protest in May.

Human Rights Defenders

The government imposes restrictive conditions on the registration and operation of NGOs, and the country has no legally registered independent human rights groups. As reported by EG Justice, a US-based NGO, a local organization was told its registration application would not be approved until it removed the reference to human rights.

The few local activists who seek to address human rights related issues are vulnerable to intimidation, harassment, and reprisals. In July authorities demanded that a local organization—Centro de Estudios e Iniciativas para el Desarrollo (CEID)—halt a series of civil society training seminars it had been conducting. The head of CEID, Alfredo Okenve Ndo, had previously been removed from two posts at the National University after critiquing the government's transparency record at a May 2010 event in Washington, DC.

After more than a year of unsuccessfully seeking permission to hold an event in Malabo to discuss follow-up to the government's commitments under its UN Universal Periodic Review, CEID and other local organizations moved the meeting to Madrid.

Political Parties and Opposition

The ruling Democratic Party of Equatorial Guinea (PDGE) maintains a monopoly over political life and the government continued its harsh repression of political rights and civil liberties during the year.

In March, in the wake of the Arab Spring events, President Obiang announced that he would introduce constitutional reforms. Far from signaling a democratic opening, however, the process was conducted in a heavy-handed manner. In October the president set a November 13 date for a national referendum to approve the changes, which had not been open to debate and were not shared with political parties until the day before the campaign opened. Instead, various government bodies rubber-stamped proposals that increase the near-absolute powers of the presidency. Although the changes create some new institutions, including an audit body, these are controlled by the president. The proposals also provide for the creation of a vice-presidential post filled at his discretion. Observers consider the creation of a vice-presidency a further move to position his son, Teodorín, to replace him. Teodorín was named to head the national election campaign to promote the referendum. A year earlier he was made the vice-president of the ruling party.

Most political parties are aligned with PDGE; members of the only two political parties that maintain independence—the Convergence for Social Democracy (CPDS) and the People's Union (UP)—are pressured through various means, including arbitrary arrest and harassment. For example, in November police arrested and held for three days a prominent CPDS figure and civil society activist, Marcial Abaga Barril, on a dubious pretext.

The opposition is also hampered by the ruling party's virtual monopoly on power, funding, and access to national media. Both beleaguered parties were further weakened during the year by internal splits. At least one CPDS leader left the party for a government post.

Torture, Arbitrary Detention, and Unfair Trials

There is no independent judiciary in Equatorial Guinea. The government commonly conducts arbitrary arrests and denies detainees due process, for example by holding them indefinitely without telling them the charges against them. Basic fair trial standards are disregarded. Torture remains a serious problem despite a national law prohibiting it. The International Committee of the Red Cross, which resumed prison visits in the country in 2009 after a one-year suspension, opened an office in Equatorial Guinea in 2011.

Political activists and others were detained in the lead-up to the AU summit. In May security forces detained more than 100 young people and some political opponents in Bata. Migrants were also rounded up between April and June. According to Amnesty International, many of them were reportedly ill-treated. The organization also received reports of road blocks and arbitrary searches by security forces.

In June President Obiang released 22 political prisoners on his 69th birthday. The release was consistent with past patterns of amnesties on special occasions. Those remaining in custody included relatives and associates of escaped prisoners—one a former military officer—who have been held without charge for over a year in apparent retribution for the October 2010 escape. Among those being held was a child under the age of two and his mother.

Key International Actors

As AU chair, President Obiang gained a prominent platform during the year. He traveled widely in that capacity, including to the G-20 summit of world leaders in France, and also sought new or improved bilateral ties. Equatorial Guinea is slated to co-host the African Cup of Nations soccer (football) tournament in early 2012.

UNESCO resisted President Obiang's efforts to reinstate a long-stalled prize in his name. He secured an AU resolution that forced the issue back onto UNESCO's agenda but UNESCO diplomats deferred any decision until May 2012.

The US is Equatorial Guinea's main trading partner and US companies dominate the country's oil sector. Although some US diplomats have defended President Obiang in press interviews and leaked cables, the US government took steps to hold Equatorial Guinea to global standards, notably maintaining a strong stance at UNESCO against the Obiang prize.

Spain, the former colonial power, generally has declined to apply pressure on Equatorial Guinea regarding human rights issues. However, the Spanish government opposed the UNESCO prize, as did the European Union.

Germany opened an embassy in the country during the year. Following the deportation of German journalists in June, the German Foreign Ministry summoned the Equatorial Guinean ambassador in Berlin.

ERITREA

Eritrea marked 20 years of independence in 2011, but its citizens remain victimized by one of the world's most repressive governments. They suffer arbitrary and indefinite detention; torture; inhumane conditions of confinement; restrictions on freedom of speech, movement, and belief; and indefinite conscription and forced labor in national service.

Arbitrary Detention

Since September 2001 or even before, Eritreans from all walks of life—government officials, leaders of government-controlled labor unions, businesspeople, journalists, and national service evaders or escapees—have been jailed for explicit or inferred opposition to President Isaias Afwerki and his policies. The number of Eritreans jailed for such opposition is difficult to confirm, but ranges from 5,000 to 10,000, excluding national service evaders and deserters, who may number tens of thousands more. Twenty prominent critics and journalists have been held in incommunicado isolation for a decade; nine are feared dead.

Prisoners are often held indefinitely without access to family members, prison monitors, or lawyers. There are no public trials and no appeals. Persons inquiring about a relative's whereabouts risk being jailed themselves.

Families are punished for the acts of one of its members, especially for draft evasion or desertion. The family is given no opportunity to defend itself. Families are fined Nakfa 50,000 (US$3,333) for evasion or desertion. Those who do not or cannot pay are jailed and may have property confiscated.

Forced Labor and Other Abuses in "National Service"

Since 2002 Eritrea has misused its national service system to keep a generation of Eritreans in bondage. Service is indefinitely prolonged, extending for much of a citizen's working life. Pay is barely sufficient for survival. Recruits are used as cheap labor for civil service jobs, development projects, and the ruling party's commercial and agricultural enterprises. Female recruits have reported sexual abuse by higher-ranking officers.

Thousands of Eritreans, mostly of younger generations, flee the country because of the harsh conditions in national service. The United Nations High Commissioner for Refugees (UNHCR) reported in early 2011 that 220,000 Eritreans, about 5 percent of the population, have fled. During a visit to a refugee camp in Ethiopia in mid-2011, an assistant high commissioner said she was shocked to see such a "sea of young faces." The new refugees included a significant number of unaccompanied children, some as young as six-years-old.

Among the most prominent defectors in 2011 were 13 members of a 25-member soccer (football) team who refused to return after a regional tournament in Tanzania. Such defections are not new. In 2009, 12 soccer players absconded in Kenya. Earlier in 2011, fearful of further defections, the government refused to allow a soccer team that won a first-round game in Eritrea to play a return match in Kenya.

A UN Monitoring Group on Somalia and Eritrea found strong evidence that high-level Eritrean officials facilitate escapes to earn hard currency: "People smuggling is so pervasive that it could not be possible without the complicity of Government and party officials, especially military officers...." Military officers charge about $3,000 per person for a border crossing and up to $20,000 for smuggling escapees through Sudan and Egypt. According to the UN group, receipts are funneled through Eritrean embassy staff into a Swiss bank account.

Torture and Cruel, Inhuman, and Degrading Treatment

Escaping Eritreans, including prison guards, report that torture and other forms of cruel, inhuman, and degrading treatment in detention are systematic and routine. Aside from severe beatings, punishments include mock drowning, hanging by the arms from trees, being tied up in the sun in contorted positions for hours or days, and being doubled up inside a tire. One investigative technique is to tighten handcuffs so that circulation to the hands is cut off and pain from the swelling hands becomes unbearable.

Many prisoners are held in unlit underground bunkers and in shipping containers with broiling daytime and freezing nighttime temperatures. Prisoners are held in isolation or are packed tightly in severely crowded cells. Food rations generally consist of lentils and a bread roll once a day and tea twice a day. Deaths in prison from torture, disease, inadequate food, and other harsh conditions are frequent.

Freedom of Expression and Association

The government destroyed Eritrea's private press in September 2001 and arrested its journalists. Since then propaganda outlets run by the Ministry of Information—television, radio, and newspapers—serve as the only domestic sources of news. Information inconsistent with President Isaias's preconceptions is suppressed. It took a month for government media to mention the Tunisian, Libyan, and Egyptian revolutions. When they did, it was to assert that Egyptian President Hosni Mubarak's government deserved to fall for not adopting Isaias's policy of self-reliance.

According to Reporters Without Borders, four additional journalists were detained in 2011 and remain in custody: Neibel Edris, Ahmed Usman, Mohammed Osman, and Tesfalidet Mebratu.

Internet access is available but difficult. Penetration is under 4 percent, primarily through cyber cafés in Asmara. Users are closely monitored. Some users were reportedly arrested in early 2011.

No political or civic organizations are permitted except those controlled by Isaias's People's Front for Democracy and Justice (PFDJ). Nongovernmental public gatherings of over seven persons are prohibited. Critical questions at government-convened meetings constitute grounds for arrest.

Freedom of Religion

In 2002 the Eritrean government banned religious activities, except those organized by four registered religious organizations: Sunni Islam, the Eritrean Orthodox Church, the Roman Catholic Church, and the Evangelical (Lutheran) Church of Eritrea. It deposed the Orthodox patriarch in 2005, has held him in house arrest since 2007, and chose his successor. The government also appointed the current Sunni *mufti*.

Adherents of "unrecognized" religions are seized in raids on churches and homes and imprisoned and tortured until they renounce their faiths. Jehovah's Witnesses are especially victimized. As of April 2011, the Jehovah's Witness media website lists 51 Witnesses incarcerated as conscientious objectors, for participation in religious meetings, or for unknown reasons; three conscientious objectors have been imprisoned for 17 years.

Usually reliable sources who monitor religious persecutions reported continuing persecution of religious practitioners in 2011. Thirty members of an evangelical Christian church were arrested in Asmara in January. In May and June authorities reportedly arrested over 90 members of unrecognized Christian churches, including 26 college students. Two women and one man in their twenties, arrested in 2009 for participating in prayer meetings while serving in national service, reportedly died in captivity at military camps in 2011. A 62-year-old Jehovah's Witness arrested in 2008 died in July, a week after he was placed in solitary confinement in a metal shipping container.

United Nations Sanctions and Horn of Africa Relations

The UN Security Council imposed sanctions on Eritrea in 2009 for providing political, financial, and logistical support to insurrectionary groups in Somalia and for occupying Djibouti territory it had invaded in 2008. In 2011 the council's Monitoring Group on Somalia and Eritrea reported that Eritrea was still funneling funds through its embassies to al-Shabaab and other groups fighting the UN-recognized Somali government. Although Eritrea had withdrawn from Djibouti territory by 2011, it continues to hold 19 Djiboutian prisoners of war to whom it has not permitted third-party access.

The Monitoring Group also concluded that Eritrea had sponsored an unsuccessful attempt to bomb an African Union Heads of State Summit in Addis Ababa, the Ethiopian capital, in January 2011. Eritrea and Ethiopia have been bitter enemies since Eritrea began a border war in 1998. The bitterness continues partly because of animosity between the leaders of the two countries, and partly because Ethiopia refuses to vacate land that a neutral boundary commission, whose decision both countries agreed would be binding, held belongs to Eritrea.

Key International Actors

Eritrea received modest amounts of foreign aid from China (in the form of soft loans), the United Arab Emirates, Iran, Libya, and Qatar in recent years; no loans or grants were announced in 2011. The European Union provides some development and emergency assistance, but the bulk of this remains undisbursed because of concerns about transparency and accountability.

The Isaias government lost a key political and financial supporter with the death of Libyan leader Muammar Gaddafi. The emir of Qatar and president of Sudan remain important supporters. Qatar is financing a four-star resort on Dahlak Kebre island, not far from a notorious underground prison. In October 2011 Sudan refouled over 300 Eritreans without screening them for refugee status, ignoring an agreement with the UNHCR calling for such screening.

Eritrea in 2011 began to re-engage with other African countries, announcing that it would rejoin the regional organization, the Intergovernmental Authority for Growth and Development.

Eritreans who fled the country in 2011 report a lack of food and soaring prices for what food remains available because of a serious regional drought, but Eritrea insists it needs no food assistance. It has not allowed access by humanitarian organizations to assess needs. In 2009 Isaias privately told the UN Children's Fund that Eritrea was suffering from famine even as he publicly denied food shortages. It continues to receive UN funding for health, sanitation, and safe-water projects, but it ended its relationship with the World Bank in 2011.

Isaias told Eritreans in May 2011 that international NGOs harbor "a pathological compulsion for espionage."

ETHIOPIA

Ethiopian authorities continued to severely restrict basic rights of freedom of expression, association, and assembly. Hundreds of Ethiopians in 2011 were arbitrarily arrested and detained and remain at risk of torture and ill-treatment.

Attacks on political opposition and dissent persisted throughout 2011, with mass arrests of ethnic Oromo, including members of the Oromo political opposition in March, and a wider crackdown with arrests of journalists and opposition politicians from June to September 2011.

The restrictive Anti-Terrorism Proclamation (adopted in 2009) has been used to justify arrests of both journalists and members of the political opposition. In June 2011 the Ethiopian House of Federations officially proscribed two armed groups—the Ogaden National Liberation Front (ONLF) and the Oromo Liberation Front (OLF) and one opposition party, Ginbot 7—labeling them terrorist organizations.

Political Repression, Pre-Trial Detention, and Torture

In March 2011, authorities arrested more than 200 members and supporters of registered Oromo opposition parties—the Oromo Federal Democratic Movement (OFDM) and the Oromo People's Congress (OPC)—during mass roundups. Those arbitrarily arrested and detained included former members of parliament, long-serving party officials, and candidates in the 2010 regional and parliamentary elections. They were publicly accused of being involved with the banned OLF; at least 89 have been charged with a variety of offenses, some relating to terrorism.

On August 27 Bekele Gerba, deputy chairman of OFDM; Olbana Lelisa, a spokesman for OPC; and seven other opposition party members were arrested on charges of involvement with the OLF. They were held in pre-trial detention at the Federal Police Crime Investigation Department, also known as Maekelawi, where torture is reportedly common. At least 20 other ethnic Oromo were arrested in this same sweep.

On September 8 popular actor Debebe Eshetu was arrested and accused of belonging to the banned opposition party Ginbot 7. The following week, on September 14, Andualem Aragie, vice-chairman of the opposition party Unity for Democracy and Justice (UDJ), two other active members of UDJ, and the general secretary of another opposition party, the Ethiopian National Democratic Party (ENDF), were arrested in Addis Ababa, the capital, on similar accusations.

Human Rights Watch continues to receive credible reports of arbitrary detention and serious abuses of civilians alleged to be members or supporters of ONLF. These civilians were being held in detention facilities in Ethiopia's Somali region.

Long-term pre-trial detention without charge, often without access to counsel, is common, notably under the Anti-Terror law, which allows police to request additional investigation periods of 28 days each from a court before filing charges, for up to four months. Human Rights Watch is aware of at least 29 opposition party members, journalists, and an actor who at this writing were currently held in remand detention under the Anti-Terror law.

No independent domestic or international organization has access to all of Ethiopia's detention facilities; it is impossible to determine the number of political prisoners and others arbitrarily detained or their condition.

Freedom of Expression and Association

What little remains of the private independent media and foreign media faced further attacks and restrictions during 2011. Self-censorship is rampant. Journalists working for the few remaining "independent" domestic newspapers have faced regular harassment and threats. Several journalists were arbitrarily arrested and detained in 2011.

On June 19 and 21 respectively Woubshet Taye of *Awramba Times* and Reeyot Alemu of *Feteh*, journalists for two newspapers often critical of the government, were arrested, along with seven other individuals, including two ENDP members, and accused of conspiring to commit terrorist acts. After almost three months of detention, without access to their lawyers, the two were charged on September 6 of several counts of terrorism. Charges were also leveled against

Elias Kifle, editor of the online *Ethiopian Review,* in absentia. One ENDP member, Zerihun Gebre-Egzabiher, was also charged.

On September 14, 2011, veteran journalist Eskinder Nega was arrested on charges of involvement with Ginbot 7. Eskinder, like Elias Kifle, was among the 121 opposition party members, journalists, and human rights activists arrested following the 2005 elections, and accused of treason and other related crimes, and among the 76 who were later convicted. He has faced ongoing harassment since his release and has been repeatedly denied a license to practice journalism.

Journalists working for foreign media have not been spared from these attacks. In September 2011 the Ethiopian correspondent of the Kenyan *Daily Nation,* Argaw Ashine, was forced to flee the country after he was named in an unedited WikiLeaks United States diplomatic cable regarding planned attacks, by the governmental Communication Affairs Office (GCAO), on journalists from the *Addis Neger* newspaper. The GCAO and Federal Police summoned Argaw for questioning regarding his sources within the GCAO. *Addis Neger* editors and journalists were forced to close their newspaper and flee the country in November 2009 after threats of arrest under the Anti-Terror law.

Independent reporting on the conflict-affected areas of the Somali region remains severely restricted. On July 1, 2011, two Swedish journalists who had entered Ethiopia in order to report on the situation were arrested. They were held without charge for two months in Jijiga and Addis Ababa before being charged on September 6 with terrorism. Their trial continued at this writing.

Restrictions on Human Rights Reporting

The restrictive Charities and Societies Proclamation, adopted in 2009, which prohibits organizations receiving more than 10 percent of their funding from abroad from carrying out human rights and governance work, continues to severely hamper basic rights monitoring and reporting activities. Two former leading rights organizations, the Ethiopian Women's Lawyers Association (EWLA) and the Human Rights Council (HRCO, formerly EHRCO), have had to slash their budgets, staff, and operations. Their bank accounts, which the government arbitrarily froze in December 2009, remain frozen.

The government-affiliated Ethiopian Human Rights Commission lacks independence and is not yet compliant with the Paris Principles, which the United Nations General Assembly adopted in 1993 and which promote the independence of national human rights institutions.

On August 27, 2011, an Amnesty International delegation to Ethiopia was ordered to leave the country following a series of meetings with members of the political opposition; two of these members were arrested after their meeting with Amnesty International.

Discrimination in Government Services

In October 2010 Human Rights Watch published *Development without Freedom: How Aid Underwrites Repression in Ethiopia*, a report that documented discrimination in the administration of foreign donor-funded government services, including agricultural assistance, food-for-work programs, educational training opportunities, and civil-service reform programs. The report also showed how donor-funded facilities, such as schools and teacher training colleges, underwrite the indoctrination of civil servants and school children in political propaganda. Human Rights Watch's research suggested that donors in the Development Assistance Group (DAG), including the US, Canada, the United Kingdom, and the European Union, were aware of such allegations, but were taking insufficient steps to investigate the misuse of their aid money.

DAG denied that aid was politicized, citing as evidence a UK Department for International Development-led report, "The Aid Management and Utilization Study," which concluded that existing monitoring mechanisms would not detect politicization if it were occurring. That report also promised a second phase, a field investigation, which it said was crucial to establishing whether or not politicization was occurring on a broad scale. In April 2011 DAG told Human Rights Watch that this second phase, the field investigation, had been cancelled. A 2009 US diplomatic cable released by WikiLeaks said that the US embassy in Ethiopia was "keenly aware that foreign assistance ... is vulnerable to politicization," but that monitoring the problem, "risks putting the assistance programs themselves in jeopardy from a ruling party that has become confident that its vast patronage system is largely invulnerable."

Key International Actors

International donor assistance continues to pour into Ethiopia, one of the world's largest recipients of aid, but this has not resulted in greater international influence in ensuring government compliance with its human rights obligations. Conversely, donors appear to be reluctant to criticize the Ethiopian government's human rights record so as not to endanger the continuity of their assistance programs.

Nonetheless, government spending remains hugely reliant (between 30 and 40 percent) on foreign assistance, and donors retain significant leverage that they could use to greater effect to insist on basic measures, such as the repeal or amendment of the Charities and Societies Proclamation and the Anti-Terrorism Proclamation, admission of UN special rapporteurs on human rights, the release of political prisoners, and better monitoring of foreign-funded programs to make sure they are not being used to bolster the ruling party.

GUINEA

President Alpha Condé, who was elected in largely free and fair elections in December 2010, made limited progress in addressing the serious governance and human rights problems he inherited. The elections ended a period of profound political instability that began in December 2008, when Captain Moussa Dadis Camara seized power in a coup after the death of Lansana Conté, Guinea's authoritarian president of 24 years.

Progress towards a full transition to democratic rule and greater respect for the rule of law was undermined by delays in organizing parliamentary elections, rising ethnic tension, the president's frequent use of the presidential decree, and inadequate gains in strengthening the chronically neglected judiciary.

Continued indiscipline by members of the security services and the July attempted assassination of President Condé, allegedly by disgruntled members of the army, illuminated the fragility of recent democratic gains. However, there were some efforts to professionalize and reduce the size of the 45,000-strong security sector, which has long been steeped in a culture of indiscipline and impunity.

There was inadequate progress for ensuring accountability for past atrocities, notably the 2007 and 2009 massacres of unarmed demonstrators by security forces. Preliminary moves towards establishing a reconciliation commission and independent human rights body were positive steps; however, inadequate consultation with civil society about the composition and mandate of these institutions threatened to undermine their efficacy. President Condé took a few concrete actions to improve the state of the judiciary and address endemic corruption.

International actors—including France, the United States, European Union, Economic Community of West African States (ECOWAS), and African Union—exerted pressure on President Condé to organize parliamentary elections, but they remained virtually silent on the need for justice for past crimes.

Truth and Reconciliation Commission and Independent Human Rights Institution

In June Condé issued a presidential decree creating a "Reflection Commission" to promote reconciliation, and in August appointed two leading religious figures as co-presidents. There was, however, inadequate consultation with civil society about the mandate, composition, or powers of the commission. While the president appeared to limit its mandate to promoting reconciliation, local human rights groups pushed for a commission that could meaningfully address impunity, including the inclusion of provisions to recommend individuals for prosecution.

Communal violence in the southeast that left some 25 dead in May, the appointment by the president of a disproportionate number of senior civil servants from his Malinke ethnic group, and rising tension between the Malinke and Peuhl communities demonstrated the urgent need for a truth and reconciliation mechanism with the capacity to make recommendations aimed at addressing the root causes of communal conflicts.

The new 2010 constitution mandated the establishment of Guinea's first-ever independent national human rights institution. In July the ad hoc parliamentary body passed a law establishing the National Human Rights Commission, to be comprised of 20 members from all over the nation. Civil society groups have raised concerns over inadequate consultation about the mandate and composition of the commission.

Parliamentary Elections and Governance

The president's insistence on redoing the electoral register and a leadership crisis within the national electoral body delayed parliamentary elections (not held since 2002) and generated considerable frustration within Guinean civil society and among the country's international partners. Progress on addressing corruption included eliminating discretionary funds within various ministries, passing a new mining code envisioned to improve management of Guinea's extensive natural resources, and establishing a hotline to report cases of graft and state corruption.

On several occasions the president appeared to use the security forces and judiciary for partisan ends. In April the government banned a gathering to welcome back to Guinea an opposition leader. Several opposition supporters were later tried and convicted for their participation in the gathering. In July all media outlets were banned from reporting on the attack against the president, and in September the government disallowed a ceremony by human rights groups and a march by the political opposition to commemorate the 2009 massacre. In the absence of a functioning parliament, the president frequently issued presidential decrees.

Judiciary and Detention Conditions

Decades of neglect and manipulation of the judiciary by successive regimes have led to striking deficiencies in the sector and have allowed perpetrators of all classes of abuses to enjoy impunity for crimes.

Allocations for the judiciary for several years, including 2011, have stood at less than 0.5 percent of the national budget. This led to severe shortages of judicial personnel and insufficient infrastructure and resources that, when coupled with unprofessional conduct and poor record-keeping, contributed to widespread detention-related abuses, notably prolonged pre-trial detention and poor prison conditions. Prison and detention centers are severely overcrowded and inmates and detainees lack adequate nutrition, sanitation, and medical care. The largest detention facility—designed for 300 detainees—accommodates over 1,000. Between 80 and 90 percent of prisoners in Guinea are held in prolonged pre-trial detention.

Concrete progress in this sector included the removal of several judges and other judicial personnel who were implicated in corrupt practices, the July swearing-in of 38 new judges into the Conakry Court of Appeals, and the May liberation of numerous detainees who had been held in extended pre-trial detention for minor offenses.

Accountability for the September 28, 2009 Massacre and Other Crimes

There was insufficient progress in holding to account members of the security forces implicated in the September 28, 2009 massacre of some 150 people and the rape of over 100 women during the military regime of Dadis Camara. A 2009 report by the United Nations-led International Commission of Inquiry concluded that the abuses committed by security forces very likely constituted crimes against humanity. In 2010 the then-government committed to bringing the perpetrators to justice, and appointed three investigating judges to the case.

At this writing there was little public evidence of the investigation's progress, and no evidence of government efforts to locate the over 100 bodies believed to have been disposed of secretly by the security forces. The government's refusal for much of the year to provide security to the investigating judges and President Condé's appointment of two men implicated in the massacre to high-level positions within his administration brought into question his commitment to ensure justice for the crimes.

The International Criminal Court (ICC), which in October 2009 confirmed that the situation in Guinea was under preliminary examination, visited the country in March, April, and October to assess progress made in national investigations. The ICC has expressed its willingness to take on the case should the Guinean government fail to do so. Meanwhile, there have been no attempts by the authorities to investigate, much less hold accountable, members of the security forces responsible for the 2007 killing of some 130 demonstrators.

Conduct of the Security Forces

The July 19 attack on the residence of President Condé, allegedly by disgruntled members of the military, resulted in the arrest of at least 38 individuals, including 25 soldiers. The arrest and detention of some of the military personnel was accompanied by physical abuse and, in a few cases, torture. The attempt illuminated the continuing divisions along ethnic and regional lines within the military and the fragility of the political process.

Allegations of excessive use of lethal force in responding to protestors diminished in 2011, although security forces killed at least five protestors during opposition marches in April and September. During the violence, the security forces also engaged in theft, robbery, sexual violence, and assault. Throughout the year soldiers were credibly implicated in numerous acts of criminality. There were no attempts to investigate, discipline, or prosecute those implicated. The emergence of a militia recruited from the president's ethnic group was cause for alarm.

Efforts by the military hierarchy to professionalize the army resulted in a reduced presence of soldiers on the streets, and some responsibilities that had long been held by the army were relinquished to police and gendarmes.

Meanwhile police were repeatedly implicated in extortion and soliciting bribes. Crime victims are frequently required to pay for investigations, while authorities commonly fail to conduct adequate investigations and, in some cases, free alleged criminals. Police leadership made no effort to address these problems.

Key International Actors

Guinea's key international partners—notably the EU, ECOWAS, the UN Office in West Africa, France, and the US—remained primarily focused on ensuring progress in the long-delayed parliamentary elections. However, Guinea's partners remained largely silent on the need for those responsible for the September 28, 2009 violence to be held accountable for their crimes. They did successfully exert pressure on the government to overturn a ban on media reporting about the assassination attempt against Condé.

The Office of the UN High Commissioner for Human Rights and the EU took the lead in strengthening Guinea's judicial system. However, much of the EU's support was conditioned on the conduct of transparent legislative elections. During a March visit the UN High Commissioner for Human Rights Navi Pillay urged the government to step up its efforts to address impunity. The UN Office on West Africa led the other international partners in advising the government how to reform the security sector.

KENYA

Human rights developments in Kenya were dominated by the implementation of a new constitution and related judicial and police reforms, and the International Criminal Court (ICC) cases against six Kenyans whom the ICC prosecutor accused of crimes against humanity. The alleged crimes were committed during Kenya's post-election violence in 2007 and 2008. Kenyan politicians resisted the ICC process, claiming the judicial and police reforms underway gave sufficient cause to return the cases to Kenya. But there was little progress on the ground in terms of accountability for post-election violence or human rights violations by security forces.

The New Constitution and the Reform Process

The new 2010 constitution propelled a series of reforms, including in the judiciary and the police. It transferred many powers of the attorney general—a political appointee—to the newly autonomous Directorate of Public Prosecutions; this was a critical shift, given that outgoing Attorney General Amos Wako's record was marked by refusing to prosecute, or arbitrarily terminating, cases against political heavyweights, including for political violence and large-scale corruption.

The constitution provided for new appointments for chief justice, deputy chief justice, director of public prosecutions, and attorney general. In an initial false start in January, President Mwai Kibaki unilaterally announced appointments for the first three positions. Civil society groups filed a lawsuit against Kibaki, charging that the move violated the constitutionally mandated consultative process for appointments, and a court ruled in their favor. Parliament also rejected the appointments as unconstitutional. Under pressure, Kibaki withdrew the appointments. In May the Judicial Services Commission conducted a transparent interview process, leading to the naming of Dr. Willy Mutunga and Nancy Baraza, well-respected reformers, as chief justice and deputy chief justice. However, the procedure for selecting the director of public prosecutions was not transparent. Further reforms included the naming of judges to a new Supreme Court.

KENYA

"Turning Pebbles"

Evading Accountability for Post-Election Violence in Kenya

HUMAN RIGHTS WATCH

Police reform proceeded slowly. In August and September parliament passed two police reform bills that bring the Kenya Police and the previously separate (and often politicized) Administration Police under one command structure, and establish a civilian National Police Service commission, which will play a role in police recruitment, training, and disciplinary proceedings. In November, parliament passed an Independent Policing Oversight Authority bill, which could be critical in assuring accountability. Police attempted to initiate a purely internal vetting process in June, but the process was suspended over criticism of the lack of civilian oversight.

The ICC Kenya Cases

In December 2010 ICC Prosecutor Luis Moreno Ocampo requested summonses for six Kenyans suspected of organizing and funding crimes against humanity during Kenya's post-election violence in 2007 and 2008. Although the government has regularly pledged cooperation with the ICC, the naming of suspects—Francis Muthaura, Uhuru Kenyatta, and Hussein Ali in one case, and William Ruto, Henry Kosgey, and Joshua arap Sang in another—provoked attempts by the government and parliament to avoid ICC jurisdiction.

In December 2010 parliament called on the government to withdraw from the Rome Statute. The government did not heed parliament's call, but launched an unsuccessful campaign to convince the United Nations Security Council that the Kenya cases should be deferred, claiming they posed a threat to international peace and security.

Kenya then filed an "admissibility challenge," claiming the ICC could not exercise its jurisdiction as a court of last resort because Kenya was already investigating the election violence. The ICC rejected the challenge, finding no evidence that Kenya was investigating the same suspects for the same crimes.

In September the court initiated "confirmation of charges" hearings to determine whether the cases should continue to trial. The hearings were marked by attempts by opponents of accountability to intimidate persons perceived to support the ICC. In September relatives of one ICC witness were physically assaulted and forced to relocate.

Accountability and Impunity in Kenya's National Justice System

Efforts to convince the ICC of progress toward bringing election violence suspects to book in Kenya were not matched by concrete actions. President Kibaki announced in December 2010 that the government would establish a local tribunal, but took no steps toward doing so. A few election violence cases proceeded through the justice system, with one new murder conviction in 2011, but cases that resulted in convictions did not target planners of the violence. At this writing no security officers had been convicted for hundreds of killings and scores of rapes attributed to them during the election violence. At least 19 victims of police shootings have won civil suits, but the government has not paid the court-ordered compensation.

The government continued to deny responsibility for extrajudicial executions, enforced disappearances, and torture during a 2008 security operation in Mt. Elgon region. NGOs filed cases against the government at the East African Court of Justice, the UN Working Group on Enforced or Involuntary Disappearances, and the African Commission on Human and People's Rights. Local organizations documented over 300 cases of persons "disappeared" between 2006 and 2008, some by the Sabaot Land Defence Forces, a militia, but most by the army. The government took no new steps to investigate the "disappearances," with the exception of one inquest, or to exhume mass graves.

Extrajudicial killings attributed to the police remained unpunished. No one was arrested for the killings of police whistleblower Bernard Kiriinya in 2008; human rights activists Oscar Kamau King'ara and John Paul Oulu in 2009; or Kenneth Irungu, a teacher killed in March after inquiring into the abduction and murder of two of his cousins by suspected police. Police caught on camera shooting unarmed civilians on Nairobi's Langata Road in January 2011 were suspended but later reinstated. In one exception to the impunity trend, in May a Kilifi magistrate filed murder charges against four police suspected of killing unarmed civilians in 2007; the case was proceeding at this writing.

The Truth, Justice and Reconciliation Commission began public hearings in April on human rights violations committed in Kenya from 1963 to 2008. The hearings afforded victims an important opportunity to testify about abuses by state agents in an official forum, but the commission's insufficient funds, short operational time frame, and organizational shortcomings limited its impact.

A witness protection agency was formally launched in mid-2011, but has been unable to operate due to inadequate funding.

Human Rights Defenders

In September 2010, Ugandan police arrested Al-Amin Kimathi, director of the Nairobi-based Muslim Human Rights Forum, when he visited Uganda to observe proceedings against Kenyans accused of the July 2010 Kampala bombings who had been rendered to Uganda without due process. Kimathi, charged with terrorism, murder, and attempted murder, was held in pre-trial detention in Uganda for a year before the charges were dropped in September 2011. In May Kenya deported Clara Gutteridge, a British fellow with the Open Society Justice Initiative who was researching abuses by East African governments in the context of counterterrorism operations, including Kimathi's case. Kenya claimed Gutteridge's activities were "a threat to national security."

Somalia and Refugee Rights

In March Kenya intervened in Somalia's civil war, supporting pro-Transitional Federal Government militias that committed human rights violations. In October, following the abduction of four foreigners from Kenya by Somali militants or pirates, Kenyan troops invaded areas of Somalia controlled by the militia group al-Shabaab.

Police arrested and unlawfully returned some Somali asylum seekers crossing into Kenya. Most reached Kenya's refugee camps via dangerous back roads to avoid police arrest and extortion, exposing themselves to bandits who rob and rape. The Liboi screening center near the border remained closed.

Kenya delayed opening two new camps—Ifo Extension and Kambios—claiming they would attract more Somalis. Instead, it proposed building new camps in Somalia, a dangerous proposition given the ongoing fighting. By August when the two camps finally opened, over 400,000 refugees lived in three camps built for 90,000. Movement to the new camps encountered delays due to local community opposition. Reports of rape in the camps increased dramatically and almost always went unpunished. People with disabilities, especially mental disabilities, had limited access to medical and social services.

Women's, Children's, and LGBT Rights

The Kenyan government undertook to improve access to pain treatment and palliative care. Access to such care has been poor, particularly for hundreds of thousands of children suffering pain from cancer, HIV/AIDS, or other diseases. Eleven government hospitals are in the process of creating palliative care units, and at least three were functional by September. In August the government launched the first National Cancer Control Strategy, which recognizes the importance of pain treatment and palliative care.

Kenya's maternal mortality ratio remains high, at 488 deaths per 100,000 live births. About 3,000 fistula injuries occur annually. The department of reproductive health is developing a fistula policy, but the government has failed to effectively address recurrent health system problems, including inadequate emergency obstetric care facilities and lack of accountability, which contribute to fistula and maternal deaths.

In December 2010 the Kenyan High Court ruled in favor of Richard Muasya, an intersex individual, for the inhuman and degrading treatment Muasya suffered at Kamiti Maximum Prison. Muasya and other intersex individuals are appealing the court's decision not to recognize intersex persons in Kenyan law. Kenyan law continues to criminalize homosexual conduct, despite mounting evidence that the law inhibits effective HIV/AIDS prevention and treatment programs.

Key International Actors

The African Union supported Kenya's drive to defer ICC cases against post-election violence suspects, increasing concerns over the body's commitment to accountability. The UN Security Council, however, did not grant the deferral request.

The United States supported counterterrorism initiatives in Kenya and East Africa. FBI agents were involved in the interrogations of Kimathi and other Kenyans held in Uganda, despite their knowledge of due process violations against the suspects.

The UN and most donor states appropriately rejected Kenya's suggestion that camps be built in south-central Somalia to house Somalis fleeing conflict, human rights abuses, and famine.

MALAWI

The human rights situation in Malawi deteriorated significantly in 2011, with President Bingu wa Mutharika's government acting in an increasingly repressive manner. Fuel and foreign currency shortages and increasing food prices have taken a toll on the country, reversing the economic gains made during Mutharika's first term in office.

The government's failure to adequately address the country's economic problems and the clampdown on its critics triggered a protest by civil society activists. The government reacted to these street protests with increasing heavy-handedness.

Freedom of Expression and Assembly

In the past year Mutharika signed repressive new legislation, including Section 46 of the penal code, which allows the minister of information to ban publications deemed "contrary to the public interest." The president also signed the Injunctions Law, which prevents Malawians from filing civil suits against government officials. These new laws, which were severely criticized by civil society activists, limit the ability of the media to operate freely and deny Malawians the protection of the law.

Authorities also intimidated and harassed university lecturers and students who have been at the forefront of criticizing the government's poor human rights and governance records. In September plainclothes police interrogated staff of the Polytechnic University of Malawi about the existence of a political group, Youth for Freedom and Democracy (YFD). A week later Robert Chasowa—vice-president of YFD, university student, and outspoken government critic—was found dead at the Polytechnic campus with a deep cut to his head. Although police ruled his death a suicide, civil society activists accused the government of involvement in Chasowa's death.

In February the inspector general of police, Peter Mukhito, interrogated University of Malawi lecturer Blessing Chisinga after he delivered a lecture on the causes of mass protests in Malawi. In reaction, university lecturers boycotted classes, demanding an apology from Mukhito and calling on the authorities to respect academic freedom. The Chancellor College section of the University of Malawi's academic staff union supported the boycott and Jessie Kabwila Kapusula, the union's acting president, received anonymous death threats. Kapasula and three colleagues were later dismissed by the university for supporting the boycott.

The government has also shown increasing intolerance towards peaceful demonstrations. On October 11, police arrested five civil society activists—Habiba Osman, Billy Mayaya, Brian Nyasulu, Ben Chiza Mkandawire, and Comfort Chiseko—on charges of "holding an illegal demonstration." They were taking part in a small demonstration outside parliament, calling on Mutharika to hold a referendum, for his resignation, and an early election. The activists were released on bail five days later.

The most brutal crackdown on a peaceful demonstration took place on July 20 when police fired live ammunition and tear gas at unarmed demonstrators and bystanders Lilongwe, the capital, Blantyre, and Mzuzu, killing 19 and leaving scores more wounded. The police also arrested around 500 demonstrators. The demonstrators were protesting deteriorating economic conditions and increasing repression by the authorities. On August 10 Mutharika said he would establish an independent commission of inquiry into the July killings. However, at this writing the government had not set up the commission and there had been little progress in investigating and bringing to account those responsible for the killings.

Further civil society vigils and demonstrations were planned for August 17 and 18 to commemorate those killed in July and to raise concerns about the economy and human rights situation. These nationwide protests were indefinitely postponed by the organizers after the High Court issued an injunction banning them. Persons believed to be affiliated with the ruling Democratic Progressive Party (DPP) had applied for the injunction.

Human Rights Defenders and Journalists

There is a climate of fear in the country as journalists and civil society activists who attempt to report on the human rights situation have come under increasing attack from security forces and supporters of the DPP. Several human rights activists have received death threats and been forced to go into hiding. In September unknown assailants threw petrol bombs at the homes and offices of several government critics, including activists Mcdonald Sembereka and Rafiq Hajat and opposition politician Salim Bagus. Human rights activists alleged that the government and DPP supporters orchestrated the attacks. At this writing the police had neither conducted any investigations nor arrested those responsible for the attacks.

Freedom of Press

Police and DPP supporters have also been implicated in the intimidation, arbitrary arrest, and beating of journalists attempting to report on political events in the country.

On October 11, police summoned deputy editor Innocent Chitosi and reporter Archibald Kasakura, both of *Malawi News,* as well as George Kasakula of *Weekend Nation,* after the two papers published stories about the death of student activist Chasowa. On September 12, police arrested journalist Ernest Mhwayo for allegedly taking pictures of President Mutharika's farm without permission.

Police conducted a violent crackdown on journalists attempting to cover the July protests. According to the Media Institute of Southern Africa, police beat 14 journalists, arrested three, and harassed 10 more, as they attempted to cover the protests in Lilongwe and Blantyre. Authorities also prevented independent radio stations from reporting on the protests. On July 20 the Malawi Communications Regulatory Authorities, the state broadcasting regulator, directed three independent radio stations, Capital FM, Joy Radio, and Zodiak Broadcasting Station (ZBS), to stop live coverage of the demonstrations because this was viewed as perpetuating violence. Although all the stations complied with the directive, they were taken off air for several hours on the following day, a move that denied Malawians vital information about how best to negotiate a dangerous situation.

Key International Actors

The deteriorating human rights situation in the country has led to increasing concern from the international community and donors. In October the Malawian government faced widespread international criticism and condemnation by local and international civil society groups when it invited and hosted Sudanese President Omar al-Bashir at the Common Market for Eastern and Southern Africa (COMESA) summit in Lilongwe. Despite being a state party to the International Criminal Court, Malawi did not arrest al-Bashir—who is wanted by the court on charges of genocide, crimes against humanity, and war crimes— upon his arrival in the country.

In August the United Nations pushed for dialogue between the Malawian government and civil society activists to address the political and economic crisis in the country. However, dialogue broke down after human rights activists alleged that the government orchestrated attacks against them, accusations that the government rejected.

In July the United Kingdom, Malawi's biggest bilateral donor, withheld US$30 million of direct aid in reaction to the expulsion of the UK high commissioner, Fergus Cochrane Dyet, and concerns over the deteriorating human rights situation. President Mutharika's brother, Justice Minister Peter Mutharika, visited the UK in October in an attempt to repair relations between the two governments. On July 26 the United States government said it would suspend a $350 million aid package in reaction to the July killings of 19 protesters and bystanders.

NIGERIA

Deeply entrenched human rights problems, as well as the growing threat posed by a militant Islamist group, underscored the pressing need for President Goodluck Jonathan to strengthen and reform the institutions that ensure security and the rule of law. National elections in April were heralded by many as Nigeria's fairest. Still, campaign violence, allegations of vote rigging, and inflation of results—particularly in the rural areas of southeastern Nigeria, President Jonathan's stronghold—marred the elections.

Episodes of intercommunal violence continued to claim hundreds of lives, including ongoing violence in Plateau State, and post-presidential election riots and sectarian killings in northern Nigeria that left more than 800 dead. Meanwhile abuses by government security forces and the ruling elite's mismanagement and embezzlement of the country's vast oil wealth continued largely unabated. Endemic corruption, poverty, poor governance, and unchecked police abuses have created an environment where militant groups thrive and find ready recruits in the vast cadre of Nigeria's unemployed youth.

A series of bombings and numerous targeted killings by the Boko Haram militant Islamist group in northern Nigeria had at this writing left more than 425 people dead in 2011, raising concern about the government's use of heavy-handed tactics in responding to the problem. Suspected members of the group carried out dozens of attacks in the northern city of Maiduguri, gunning down police officers, politicians, traditional leaders, and opposing clerics. The group also claimed responsibility for the November bombings in the town of Damaturu, Yobe State, that left at least 100 people dead, and a suicide bomb attack in August on the United Nations building in Abuja that killed 24 people and injured more than 100 others.

The administration took some steps to improve government transparency. In May the National Assembly passed, and President Jonathan signed into law, the Freedom of Information Act, which guarantees the public the right to access public records. Free speech and the independent press remained robust. Nigeria's judiciary continued to exercise a degree of independence but was dogged by public allegations of corruption. Meanwhile, many of the corruption cases against senior political figures remained stalled in the courts. Foreign partners took some important steps to confront endemic corruption in Nigeria, but appeared reluctant to exert meaningful pressure on the government over its human rights record.

Intercommunal and Political Violence

Intercommunal, political, and sectarian violence has claimed more than 16,000 lives since the end of military rule in 1999. Protests by opposition supporters in 12 northern states following the April 16 presidential election degenerated into three days of violent riots and sectarian killings between Christians and Muslims that left hundreds dead, including at least 680 in Kaduna State.

Episodes of intercommunal violence continued in Plateau State, in central Nigeria. At this writing more than 350 people had died in 45 separate incidents in 2011. Victims, including children, were hacked to death, shot, burned alive, and dragged off buses and killed, in many cases simply based on their ethnic or religious identity. Intercommunal clashes in 2011 in Bauchi, Benue, Nassarawa, Niger, and Taraba states left more than 120 dead and hundreds more displaced.

State and local government policies that discriminate against "non-indigenes"—people who cannot trace their ancestry to what are said to be the original inhabitants of an area—continue to exacerbate intercommunal tensions and perpetuate ethnic-based divisions. Federal and state authorities failed to break the cycle of violence by holding the perpetrators of these crimes accountable.

Conduct of Security Forces

As in previous years, the undisciplined Nigeria Police Force was implicated in frequent human rights violations, including extrajudicial killings, torture, arbitrary arrests, and extortion-related abuses. The police routinely solicit bribes from victims to investigate crimes and from suspects to drop investigations. Embezzlement of police funds is rife among senior police officials who also often demand monetary "returns" from money extorted from the public by their subordinates. Meanwhile, soldiers were implicated in several attacks on vil-

NIGERIA

Corruption on Trial?

The Record of Nigeria's Economic and
Financial Crimes Commission

HUMAN
RIGHTS
WATCH

lages in Plateau State in August and September, and in extrajudicial killings in response to Boko Haram attacks in Maiduguri.

In July the attorney general's office filed criminal charges against five police officers, including three assistant commissioners of police, for the 2009 extra-judicial killing of the Boko Haram leader Mohammed Yusuf and his followers. But the authorities have still not prosecuted members of the police and military for the unlawful killing of more than 130 people during the November 2008 sec-tarian violence in Plateau State, the soldiers who massacred more than 200 people in Benue State in 2001, or the members of the military involved in the complete destruction of the town of Odi, Bayelsa State, in 1999.

Government Corruption

Nigeria made only limited progress with its anti-corruption campaign in 2011. The Economic and Financial Crimes Commission (EFCC) at this writing had arraigned 35 nationally prominent political figures on corruption charges since 2003, including in 2011 a former federal minister, four former state governors, and a former speaker and deputy speaker of the House of Representatives.

But executive interference with the EFCC, a weak and overburdened judiciary, and the agency's own failings have undermined the effectiveness of its work. At this writing the commission had only secured four convictions of senior politi-cal figures, and they faced relatively little or no prison time. The EFCC has failed to prosecute other senior politicians widely implicated in corruption, and the political elite continues to squander and siphon off the country's tremendous oil wealth, leaving poverty, malnutrition, and mortality rates among the world's highest.

Violence and Poverty in the Oil-Producing Niger Delta

The 2009 amnesty—which saw a few thousand people, including top militant commanders, surrendering weapons in exchange for cash payments—has reduced attacks on oil facilities, but kidnappings, mostly of family members of wealthy Nigerians, continued in the Niger Delta and southeastern Nigeria. The government made little effort to address the environmental damage from oil pollution, state and local government corruption, and political sponsorship of armed groups, which drive and underlie violence and poverty in the oil-rich region.

Decades of oils spills—from multinational oil company operations, sabotage of pipelines, and bunkering (theft) of crude oil—and widespread gas flaring have left the Niger Delta heavily polluted. A UN report in August found that oil pollution in the Ogoniland region of Rivers State may require the world's largest clean up ever, at an initial cost of US$1 billion, and take up to 30 years. The UN team found that oil contamination had migrated into the groundwater in at least eight spill sites that Shell—the largest oil company in Nigeria—had claimed they had remediated.

Human Rights Concerns in the Context of Sharia

State governments in 12 northern states apply Sharia law as part of their criminal justice systems, which include sentences—such as the death penalty, amputations, and floggings—that amount to cruel, inhuman, and degrading punishment. In September a court in Zamfara State sentenced two men to amputation of their right hands. At this writing the case was under appeal. Serious due process concerns also exist in these proceedings, and evidentiary standards in the Sharia codes applied in these states discriminate against women, particularly in adultery cases.

Sexual Orientation and Gender Identity

Nigeria's federal criminal code punishes consensual homosexual conduct with up to 14 years in prison. In states applying Sharia, consensual homosexual conduct among men is punishable by death (stoning), and by flogging and six months in prison in the case of women. Federal legislation that would criminalize anyone who enters into or assists a "same gender" marriage was introduced in the Senate in July. Similar legislation has been introduced in the National Assembly at least twice before and stalled amid opposition from domestic and international human rights activists.

Health and Human Rights

Widespread lead poisoning from artisan gold mining in Zamfara State has killed at least 500 children since 2010. At this writing 1,500 children were being treated for lead poisoning, but hundreds of other affected children had not received any medical care. The government has also failed to adequately clean up the environment and regulate ongoing mining practices.

Freedom of Expression and Media

Civil society and the independent press openly criticize the government and its policies, allowing for robust public debate. Yet journalists are still subject to arrest and intimidation when reporting on issues implicating Nigeria's political and economic elite. The police arrested six journalists from the *Nation* newspaper in October after they published a purported letter from former President Olusegun Obasanjo. In October Zakariyya Isa, a journalist with the state National Television Authority, was gunned down in Maiduguri. Boko Haram claimed responsibility for the killing.

Key International Actors

Because of Nigeria's role as a regional power, Africa's leading oil exporter, and a major contributor of troops to UN peacekeeping missions, foreign governments—including the United States and the United Kingdom—have generally been reluctant to publicly criticize Nigeria over its poor human rights record.

US government officials did speak out forcefully against the country's endemic government corruption, but they were less willing to condemn the serious abuses committed by Nigeria's security forces. The UK government continued to play a leading role in international efforts to combat money laundering by corrupt Nigerian officials, demonstrated by the April extradition from Dubai of powerful former Delta State governor James Ibori. However, the UK increased funding to £180 million ($280 million) in aid to Nigeria in 2011, including security sector assistance, without demanding accountability for government officials or members of the security forces implicated in corruption or serious human rights abuses.

During the UN secretary-general's visit to Nigeria in May he expressed concern about intercommunal violence, but failed to put meaningful pressure on the Nigerian government to allow a mission to Plateau State by his special adviser on the prevention of genocide, after the government failed to approve the visit.

RWANDA

Progress continued in Rwanda in 2011 in the fields of development, delivery of public services, health, and the economy. Draft revisions of the laws on genocide ideology and media contained some positive amendments, but leave open the possibility for inappropriate prosecutions for "genocide ideology." Moreover, freedom of expression and political space are still severely restricted. Members of opposition parties, journalists, and other perceived critics of the government were arrested, detained, and tried, some solely for expressing their views. Charges such as endangering state security and inciting public disobedience were increasingly used to prosecute government critics.

Community-based *gacaca* courts had almost completed their work by the end of the year, after trying more than 1.2 million cases related to the 1994 genocide since 2005. A number of applications for review of *gacaca* decisions remained pending.

The International Criminal Tribunal for Rwanda (ICTR) ruled that the case of Jean-Bosco Uwinkindi should be transferred to Rwanda's national courts.

Government Opponents and Other Critics

Bernard Ntaganda, leader of the PS-Imberakuri opposition party, was tried and sentenced to four years imprisonment in February 2011. He was found guilty of endangering national security, divisionism, and attempting to organize demonstrations without authorization.

The trial of Victoire Ingabire, leader of the FDU-Inkingi opposition party, began in earnest in September after multiple adjournments. Ingabire faces six charges: creating an armed group, complicity in terrorist acts, complicity in endangering the state through terrorism and armed violence, inciting the public to rise up against the state, genocide ideology, and divisionism. She was being tried alongside four current or former members of the Democratic Forces for the Liberation of Rwanda (FDLR), an armed group operating in the Democratic Republic of Congo, composed partly of individuals who participated in the

Rwandan genocide. All four have incriminated Ingabire. The trial was ongoing at this writing.

Other FDU-Inkingi and PS-Imberakuri members were harassed and intimidated. FDU-Inkingi representatives Anastase Hagabimana and Norbert Manirafasha were arrested on April 20 in connection with a draft statement by their party criticizing the increase in the cost of living in Rwanda. Manirafasha was released on May 3 without charges. Hagabimana was held in pre-trial detention until August 26, when he was provisionally released. He was tried on charges of endangering state security. At this writing the judgment was expected in November.

There was no progress in the case of the July 2010 murder of André Kagwa Rwisereka, vice-president of the opposition Democratic Green Party of Rwanda. No one has been charged with his murder.

Four former senior government and army officials turned outspoken critics, now in exile—Faustin Kayumba Nyamwasa, Patrick Karegeya, Gerald Gahima, and Théogène Rudasingwa—were tried in absentia by a military court in January. The trial focused on the defendants' public criticisms of the government and President Paul Kagame. They were found guilty of endangering state security, destabilizing public order, divisionism, defamation, and forming a criminal enterprise. Karegeya and Gahima were each sentenced to 20 years imprisonment and Nyamwasa and Rudasingwa to 24 years, with an additional charge of army desertion. The trial of six people accused of involvement in a failed assassination attempt on Nyamwasa in 2010 opened in South Africa in June and hearings continued through October. At this writing the trial had not yet concluded.

Nyamwasa's brother, Lt.-Col. Rugigana Ngabo, held incommunicado since his arrest in August 2010, appeared before a military court in January, charged with endangering state security. Details of his alleged offenses were not disclosed in the initial hearings. At the military prosecutor's request, subsequent hearings were held behind closed doors.

Less prominent individuals were also punished for criticizing state policies. Abbé Emile Nsengiyumva, a priest in eastern Rwanda, was arrested following a

Christmas sermon in December 2010 in which he had opposed a state policy to destroy thatched houses and proposals for family planning restrictions. He was accused of endangering state security and inciting civil disobedience. In July he was sentenced to 18 months imprisonment.

The law on genocide ideology, which has been used to target critics, went through a process of revision. If adopted, some draft amendments would help limit the scope for misuse of the law by defining the offense more precisely and requiring that intent behind the crime be proven. However, vague offenses such as approving of the genocide by "mocking" a person or group on the basis of shared characteristics are included in the draft and are ripe for abuse. The new draft law proposes a reduction in penalties.

Independent Media

The government made draft amendments to media laws, which, if adopted, would lift some of the burdensome restrictions on journalists and introduce self-regulation by media. However, after years of intimidation and a further crackdown on independent media in 2010, there are almost no independent Rwandan journalists operating in Rwanda. Several leading independent journalists remain in exile.

In February Agnès Nkusi Uwimana and Saidati Mukakibibi, of the newspaper *Umurabyo*, were tried and sentenced to 17 years and 7 years, respectively, for publishing articles critical of the government and President Kagame. The court ruled that the two women had incited the public to rise up against the state and found them both guilty of endangering public order. Uwimana, the newspaper's editor, was also found guilty of minimizing the genocide, divisionism, and defamation.

In September the Supreme Court heard the appeal of Didace Nduguyangu and Antoine Karemera, convicted of the murder of *Umuvugizi* journalist Jean-Léonard Rugambage in 2010. The case rested on the theory that they had killed Rugambage to avenge the death of a relative, whom Rugambage had allegedly killed during the genocide. Both men were sentenced to life imprisonment in 2010. On appeal, Nduguyangu's sentence was reduced to 10 years and

RWANDA

Justice Compromised

The Legacy of Rwanda's Community-Based *Gacaca* Courts

HUMAN
RIGHTS
WATCH

Karemera was acquitted. Judicial authorities are not known to have pursued leads suggesting that Rugambage may have been killed because of his investigative work as a journalist.

Human Rights Defenders

The government's intolerance of criticism and hostility toward human rights organizations means there is little scope for Rwandan organizations to report on human rights violations by the state. Threats and intimidation of human rights defenders by individuals close to the government, combined with a degree of self-censorship, have ensured that few Rwandan civil society groups publicly criticize the government's human rights record.

In August Joseph Sanane and Epimack Kwokwo, the president and acting executive secretary of the Regional Human Rights League in the Great Lakes Region (LDGL)—one of the few remaining active human rights organizations in Rwanda—were prevented from travelling to Burundi and were detained by the police. They were questioned about the LDGL's internal administration and finances, and accused of helping its former secretary general leave the country. Kwokwo was released the same day; Sanane was detained overnight. Neither was charged with any criminal offense.

Senior government officials and pro-government media continued to discredit international human rights organizations in public speeches, articles, and interviews. Pro-government media and websites also launched personal attacks against human rights defenders, academics, and other individuals for painting a negative picture of the human rights situation in Rwanda.

Justice for the Genocide

Community-based *gacaca* courts, which have tried more than 1.2 million genocide-related cases since 2005, had almost completed their work by the end of 2011. They leave behind a mixed legacy, with a number of positive achievements—including the swift work of the courts, the extensive participation of the local population, and the revelation of information about events during 1994— alongside violations of the right to a fair trial, intimidation of witnesses, corruption of judges and other parties, and political interference. As *gacaca* prepares to close, the government is considering how to handle applications for reviewing *gacaca* courts' decisions.

In June the referral chamber of the ICTR ruled that the case of Jean-Bosco Uwinkindi should be transferred to Rwanda's national jurisdictions. In the past the ICTR and jurisdictions in other countries had declined to transfer genocide cases to Rwanda due to fair trial concerns. Uwinkindi's appeal against the decision was pending at this writing. In October the European Court of Human Rights held that the extradition of Sylvère Ahorugeze from Sweden to Rwanda would not expose him to a real risk of a flagrant denial of justice, and so would not violate the European Convention on Human Rights. Ahorugeze was arrested in Sweden in 2008 following an extradition request by Rwanda.

Trials Linked to 2010 Grenade Attacks

Twenty-nine people were tried in connection with a series of grenade attacks in Rwanda in 2010 and previous years. Most of the defendants plead guilty. Several stated in court that they had been illegally detained in military detention for several months and tortured. The trial, which began in February, was ongoing at this writing.

In a separate case, university professor Lambert Havugintwari was arrested in Huye on February 9 and held illegally in military custody in an undisclosed location for several weeks. He and his co-accused, Alexandre Munyentwali, were accused of bringing grenades into the country and charged with endangering state security and forming a criminal gang. They were tried in November and were awaiting the court's verdict at this writing.

Cases Related to the Democratic Republic of Congo

There was no progress on the case of Laurent Nkunda, former leader of the Congolese armed group National Congress for the Defense of the People (CNDP), who remained illegally detained under house arrest in Kigali, the capital, since January 2009, with no access to lawyers and occasional access to relatives. Continued attempts to get his case heard in Rwandan courts remained blocked.

Rwandan authorities are not known to have taken any action in response to allegations of grave crimes committed by the Rwandan army in Congo in 1996 and 1997, contained in the 2010 mapping report of the United Nations Office of the High Commissioner for Human Rights.

Refugee Protection

Rwanda placed considerable pressure on states hosting Rwandan refugees and on the office of the UN High Commissioner for Refugees (UNHCR) to invoke the 1951 UN Refugee Convention's "cessation clause" by December 31, 2011, under which host countries can declare that a given group of refugees no longer needs protection and should return home. The Zambian government and UNHCR announced steps to prepare cessation on September 5. In a joint communique with the Rwandan government on October 7, UNHCR recommended that states invoke cessation by December 31, 2011, effective from June 30, 2012. International NGOs voiced concern about human rights violations in Rwanda, as well as fears that countries hosting large numbers of Rwandan refugees may not have adequate procedures to process claims for exemption under the clause.

Key International Actors

Most foreign governments continued to broadly support the Rwandan government and to applaud its development successes. However, some governments expressed increasing concern about restrictions on free speech and political space following the 2010 elections. A warning by the London Metropolitan Police about security threats against two Rwandans living in the United Kingdom in May affected Western perceptions of the government's human rights record, particularly in the UK, one of Rwanda's most important partners. However, these developments did not fundamentally alter the foreign and development policies of most Western governments.

Following the resumption of diplomatic relations between Rwanda and France and French President Nicolas Sarkozy's visit to Kigali in 2010, President Kagame visited Paris for the first time in September 2011.

SOMALIA

The year was marked by ongoing fighting in Somalia and abuses by the warring parties, including indiscriminate attacks harming civilians. While the armed Islamist al-Shabaab group continued to control more territory than any other group in South and Central Somalia, the Transitional Federal Government of Somalia (TFG)—with the support of the African Union Mission in Somalia (AMISOM) and militias aligned to the TFG, notably Ahlu Sunna Wal Jama'a (ASWJ) and Raskamboni—gained control over new areas in Mogadishu, the capital, and small areas along the border with Kenya and Ethiopia. On August 6 al-Shabaab withdrew from Mogadishu, citing tactical reasons, but has continued to attack the capital, including with suicide bombings.

Al-Shabaab continued to administer arbitrary justice in the areas It controls, including beheadings, beatings, and torture. TFG forces and TFG-aligned militias also committed serious abuses against civilians, and the TFG has largely failed to protect the basic human rights of the population in areas under its control. The war contributed directly to the worsening humanitarian emergency and famine that struck Somalia in mid-2011. Abuses by al-Shabaab and to a lesser extent the TFG restricted humanitarian aid from reaching intended beneficiaries in the country.

Violations of the Laws of War

Indiscriminate attacks were committed by all parties to the conflict during a series of military offensives led by the TFG, with the support of AMISOM and ASWJ, in late 2010 and between February and May 2011. Al-Shabaab regularly fired mortars indiscriminately from densely populated areas towards TFG/AMISOM positions, often unlawfully placing civilians at risk. TFG and AMISOM forces frequently responded with indiscriminate counter-attacks, notably in and around Bakara market. According to the World Health Organisation (WHO), between January and late September three hospitals in Mogadishu treated 8,430 casualties for weapon-related injuries. Hospital records show that a significant proportion of civilian casualties were women and children.

SOMALIA

"You Don't Know Who to Blame"

War Crimes in Somalia

HUMAN
RIGHTS
WATCH

Indiscriminate fire on civilian areas has also occurred during offensives by TFG-affiliated militias in the border areas of Dhobley and Baardhere during clashes with al-Shabaab. An outburst of renewed fighting between Raskamboni and other TFG-affiliated militias against al-Shabaab in Dhobley in early October resulted in at least 11 civilian deaths, reportedly due to crossfire.

There have been no attempts to hold to account those responsible for indiscriminate attacks.

On October 4 a suicide bombing in Mogadishu, claimed by al-Shabaab, occurred outside a compound housing several government ministries, including the Ministry of Education. At least 100 civilians were killed, including students and parents awaiting exam results at the ministry.

Abuses in TFG-Controlled Areas

Many civilians were killed and wounded during fighting between TFG forces and insurgents and during TFG "law enforcement" operations. In an incident in late January TFG forces reportedly fired on civilians in Mogadishu, killing between 12 and 20 people and wounding at least 30.

TFG forces and aligned militias have committed a range of abuses against internally displaced persons (IDPs) in Mogadishu, including looting food aid in IDP camps, carrying out arbitrary arrests and detentions, and raping. Despite the TFG's public claims that it would consider a moratorium on the death penalty, the military court has tried and sentenced at least 17 TFG soldiers and one civilian to death since August, when TFG President Sheikh Sharif Sheikh Ahmed declared a state of emergency in areas of Mogadishu. On August 22 two TFG soldiers were executed.

In areas under the control of TFG-affiliated militias, civilians have been arbitrarily arrested and detained. In March in Bula Hawo ASWJ arbitrarily arrested hundreds of civilians, including women and children, after a bomb attack. Those fleeing to Kenya via Dhobley reported being arrested and accused of being al-Shabaab sympathizers by men in uniform they believed to be associated with the TFG. Individuals alleged or perceived to support al-Shabaab were also unlawfully killed. At least three civilians were summarily executed by ASWJ following their takeover of Bula Hawo in March; one was reportedly a 17-year-old boy. In May media quoted an ASWJ spokesperson as saying the group would execute those found spying for al-Shabaab.

Indiscriminate shooting by AMISOM has also resulted in civilian deaths; some incidents have led to internal investigations. On September 2, AMISOM forces in Mogadishu shot dead a Malaysian journalist and injured his colleague. An internal investigation found three Burundian soldiers responsible for the killing. The three have been returned to Burundi, reportedly to face trial.

Abuses in Opposition Controlled Areas

Al-Shabaab remained in control of most of southern Somalia where every area of people's lives is regulated by an extreme form of Islamic law. Women and girls in particular have suffered from these harsh laws. Freedoms previously enjoyed by women in Somali culture have been severely curtailed to prevent them from mixing with men. This has also limited women's ability to engage in small-scale commercial enterprises. Harsh punishments—notably floggings, summary executions, and public beheadings—are common. Such punishments generally take place after summary proceedings without due process. On August 23 al-Shabaab publicly executed three men accused of spying for the TFG in the Daynile district of Mogadishu.

Children Associated with Armed Forces and Groups

Schools have featured heavily in al-Shabaab's combat operations. The group has fired on AMISOM and TFG forces from schools, deliberately exposing students and teachers to retaliatory fire and, in some cases, directly attacking students and school buildings and interfering with teaching. As a result of ongoing attacks, teachers have fled and—where schools have not shut down entirely—children, deprived of any meaningful education and afraid for their safety, have dropped out in large numbers. Forced recruitment of adults and children by al-Shabaab is widespread and ongoing. Al-Shabaab routinely uses children in its ranks. Children continue to also be found within the TFG armed forces and TFG-affiliated militias; the TFG has at this writing failed to ensure that all its recruits, including those formerly associated with aligned militias, undergo effective age vetting to prevent the recruitment of children.

Restrictions on Humanitarian Assistance

On July 20 the regions of South Bakool and Lower Shabelle were declared to be in a state of famine and by August the United Nations had declared six areas, primarily in southern Somalia, to be in a state of famine. As of August 2011 more than half of the Somali population—an estimated 4 million people—was in need of food aid.

Al-Shabaab restrictions on humanitarian assistance persisted despite the unfolding humanitarian disaster. It continued to prohibit over a dozen humanitarian organizations from working in areas under its control, with continued attacks on humanitarian workers.

Al-Shabaab has also imposed taxation, both monetary and on livestock, on the population under its control, causing significant hardship. It also severely restricted the movement of those in need of assistance, preventing people, particularly boys and young men, from fleeing to Kenya for assistance. In late September al-Shabaab prevented IDPs from reaching Mogadishu, stopping them in the Afgooye corridor on the outskirts of the city and transporting them back to their places of origin. It also returned IDPs from Baidoa to rural areas.

The diversion of humanitarian aid within Mogadishu and the perpetration of violence during food distribution by TFG forces and allied militias have further limited IDPs' access to greatly needed assistance. On August 5 at least three civilians were killed in a Badbado camp after militias reportedly allied to the TFG opened fire on a food distribution site. Newly appointed Prime Minister Abdiweli Mohamed Ali created a committee to investigate the incident. In addition, United States sanctions on terrorist groups have restricted US aid going into southern and central Somalia and support for certain humanitarian organizations.

Key International Actors

Western governments, the UN, the AU, and neighboring countries, with the exception of Eritrea, are united in supporting the TFG as the legitimate government of Somalia. Support for the TFG was forthcoming despite concerns about political infighting and lack of progress on the basic priorities of the Djibouti agreement, such as the drafting of the constitution, the reformation of the parliament and addressing issues of corruption.

Eritrea uses Somalia as a convenient theater in its proxy war against Ethiopia. In July the UN Monitoring Group on Somalia and Eritrea reported Eritrea's continued support for al-Shabaab.

Kenya closed its border with Somalia in January 2007; it has forcibly returned Somalis, including asylum seekers, to their country and has repeatedly called for Somalis to receive assistance only within Somalia, and yet at this writing Kenya continues to accommodate the arrival of around 1,000 new Somali refugees daily in the sprawling refugee camps around the northern town of Dadaab.

Kenya and Ethiopia have trained and offered military support to TFG-affiliated militia groups, notably Raskamboni and ASWJ. Reports suggest that both Ethiopian and Kenyan forces have also entered Somalia for security operations near the border. On October 16, Kenyan military forces entered Somalia and declared war on al-Shabaab, following a series of kidnappings of foreigners in Kenya.

The US military has carried out targeted strikes using aerial drones on alleged al-Shabaab targets.

The UN Security Council has authorized an AU force of 12,000 peacekeepers for Somalia, but thus far only 9,000 Ugandan and Burundian troops have been deployed, despite calls by the AU for an increase in the number of troops.

The UN independent expert on Somalia and some other key international actors have recognized that accountability for past abuses in Somalia is crucial to establishing a meaningful and inclusive peace process, but they have not prioritized this issue. Such accountability efforts should include documenting abuses since the end of the Siad Barre regime in 1988 and, ultimately, a UN commission of inquiry into war crimes committed since then.

SOUTH AFRICA

South Africa continues to grapple with corruption, growing social and economic inequalities, and the weakening of state institutions by partisan appointments and one-party dominance. Attacks on freedom of expression, particularly attempts by the ruling African National Congress (ANC) to tamper with media independence, raised serious concerns about the government's commitment to the protection of basic civil and political rights. In April 2011, images of the brutal, public murder by the police of Andries Tatane during a peaceful protest in Ficksburg to demand better service delivery elicited public ire regarding police brutality. Despite these concerns, institutions of democracy, among them the South African Human Rights Commission and the Public Protector, remain highly active.

The Foreign Policy White Paper, published in late May, failed to clarify the thrust of South Africa's international agenda, dashing hopes that a country with strong constitutional protections of rights at home is ready to assume a leadership position on the realization of rights worldwide.

Freedom of Expression

Following year-long deliberations, the Ad-Hoc Committee on the Protection of Information Bill tabled a new draft for parliamentary approval in September 2011. The bill is designed to regulate classification procedures of state information and proposes prison sentences of 15 to 20 years for publishing information deemed to threaten national security. Public engagement on the bill has been vociferous, with civil society arguing that, if promulgated, the bill would silence the media and whistleblowers and condone overreaching state secrecy. Despite improvements to the bill—such as the establishment of an independent Classification Review Panel and limitations on institutions that can classify information—it remains flawed. The absence of a public interest defense, permitting the publication of information that serves the public, is its most notable weakness. Public pressure—coordinated through the Right2Know Campaign, a civil society network of organizations opposed to the Protection of Information Bill—forced the ANC's bill on September 20 to allow for further consultation.

Concerns regarding the ANC's attempts to curtail freedom of media persist. The party periodically invokes the spectre of a media appeals tribunal, which would see statutory regulation of the media. Also of concern is ANC's growing hold over the country's public broadcaster, the South African Broadcasting Corporation.

Vulnerable Workers

Despite legislation protecting the rights of workers and being highly organized, workers in various sectors of the economy continue to face severe challenges; farmworkers are particularly vulnerable. The failure of the government to enforce labor and tenure laws renders them defenseless against powerful employers. Human Rights Watch's research in the Western Cape, the second-richest province with the largest number of farmworkers in South Africa, uncovered a number of exploitative conditions under which farmworkers interviewed work and live. These range from occupational health and safety hazards, including exposure to harmful pesticides; evictions without access to short-term shelter and poor housing conditions on farms; difficulties in forming or joining unions; and unfair labor conditions, such as pay below minimum wage. In response to a report that was the outcome of the Human Rights Watch research, and the efforts of other civil society organizations, several South African government officials committed to addressing abuses and enforcing labor laws, in spite of negative reactions from farm owners.

Women's Rights

South Africa's maternal mortality ratio has more than quadrupled in the last decade, increasing from 150 to 625 deaths per 100,000 live births between 1998 and 2007, with HIV playing a role in many of the deaths. The United Nations estimates that 4,500 women die each year in South Africa due to pre-ventable and treatable pregnancy-related causes. This is despite South Africa's wealth, reasonably good health infrastructure, and strong legal and policy framework, which includes a constitutional guarantee of the right to health.

Generally poor health outcomes—especially maternal and child mortality—are a result of various factors, including fragmentation; inequalities between the

SOUTH AFRICA

Ripe with Abuse

Human Rights Conditions in South Africa's
Fruit and Wine Industries

HUMAN
RIGHTS
WATCH

public and private health sectors regarding the availability of financial and human resources; the accessibility and delivery of health services; and a high disease burden, particularly HIV/AIDS. The government's failure to provide effective oversight for the implementation of existing reproductive and sexual health-related laws and policies contributes to South Africa's high and increasing maternal death rate, as does a lack of accountability for recurrent problems in the health system, including abuses committed by health personnel.

The country's women and girls continue to live with insecurity despite efforts to curb violence against women, specifically sexual violence, which has been on the rise. Several studies indicate that the failure of the criminal justice system to investigate and punish sexual violence has created a culture of impunity for rape. The rulings of magistrates and judges sometimes trivialize the gravity of rape. Judge Mogoeng Mogoeng's nomination and subsequent appointment as chief justice by President Jacob Zuma could erode the gains that have been made in addressing violence against women. Many civil society groups have accused Mogoeng of undermining the rights of women and girls by issuing lenient sentences in cases of rape and domestic violence, and invoking in his rulings myths about rape that often blame the victims and excuse perpetrators.

Sexual Orientation and Gender Identity

During the 17th UN Human Rights Council session, South Africa successfully pushed through the adoption of the first-ever UN resolution on sexual orientation and gender identity. This action affirmed South Africa's endorsement of the rights of lesbian, gay, bisexual, and transgender (LGBT) people worldwide, but does not address the concerns of the LGBT community at home. A 2011 Human Rights Watch report found that, despite the country's progressive legislation, discrimination on the grounds of sexual orientation and gender identity is widespread in the society and evident in the behavior of government officials, including the police and teachers. Black lesbians and transgender men are especially vulnerable and live under constant threat of verbal, physical, and sexual violence from acquaintances and strangers. Civil society pressure following recent cases of rape, torture, and murder of black lesbians and transgender people has prompted the Department of Justice and Constitutional

SOUTH AFRICA

"Stop Making Excuses"

Accountability for Maternal Health Care in South Africa

HUMAN
RIGHTS
WATCH

SOUTH AFRICA

"We'll Show You You're a Woman"

Violence and Discrimination against Black Lesbians and
Transgender Men in South Africa

HUMAN
RIGHTS
WATCH

Development to form a multi-sectoral task team to formulate legal and judicial responses to violence against members of the LGBT community.

Refugee Rights

In 2011 South Africa prevented Zimbabwean asylum seekers from entering the country, and forcibly returned registered Zimbabwean asylum seekers because they did not possess "travel documents," an unlawful requirement under international law. On June 1 South Africa closed its largest refugee reception office in Johannesburg. Local groups and Human Rights Watch raised concerns this would further exacerbate registration problems faced by refugees and asylum seekers, lead to increased unlawful deportation, and further increase the backlogs in a system already struggling to process over 250,000 cases.

Some South African officials indicated that the country was considering moving refugee reception offices to its borders with Mozambique and Zimbabwe and detaining all asylum seekers while their cases were being considered. Local civil society voiced concerns this would bring chaos and possibly a humanitarian crisis to the South Africa-Zimbabwe border area in particular and lead to a sharp deterioration of already poor decision-making, which would likely lead to increased refoulement of genuine refugees.

International Role

South Africa's role as a non-permanent member of the UN Security Council has been mixed. In Cote d'Ivoire, for example, as forces loyal to former President Laurent Gbagbo were killing Ivorians known or suspected of supporting rival and current President Alassane Ouattara, South Africa chose to focus on the validity of the contested November 2010 elections, which it claimed were inconclusive. That foot-dragging stalled international and regional efforts to resolve the electoral crisis and protect civilians under siege.

In the case of Libya, South Africa surprised its critics by voting in favor of UN Security Council Resolutions 1970 and 1973; the latter permitted military action against to protect civilians Muammar Gaddafi's regime. Zuma was harshly criticized by his African Union peers, as well as some within his administration and the ANC, for this vote. Zuma later backtracked, claiming that South Africa was misled into supporting a NATO-led, Western regime-change agenda. Afterward the Zuma administration failed to criticize the abusive actions of the Libyan regime, as the human rights situation in the country deteriorated. Since then the government of South Africa has used the Libya situation to explain its failure to support UN Security Council action on country situations such as Syria.

In an unprecedented development President Zuma's more assertive leadership as Southern African Development Community (SADC) mediator on Zimbabwe saw SADC taking a tougher stance against President Robert Mugabe's continued repressive rule. At a SADC meeting in Livingstone, Zambia, in March SADC leaders challenged Mugabe on his failure to institute agreed reforms under the Global Political Agreement. Later Mugabe launched a scathing attack against Zuma and his mediation panel for interfering in Zimbabwe's affairs.

SOUTH SUDAN

Following an overwhelming vote for secession from Sudan in the January 2011 referendum, South Sudan declared independence on July 9. The new nation faces major human rights challenges. However, officials have expressed the new government's intention to ratify major human rights treaties.

An influx of refugees and returnees from the North has presented severe humanitarian challenges to South Sudan. Between January and August political, inter-communal, and resource-driven clashes killed over 2,600 people, according to the United Nations. The government failed to fulfill its responsibility to protect civilians from this violence, as security forces fighting against armed militias committed serious abuses against civilians. Across the country, lack of capacity and inadequate training of police, prosecutors, and judges have resulted in numerous human rights violations in law enforcement and in the administration of justice.

Political and Legislative Developments

The January referendum was held under the terms of Sudan's 2005 Comprehensive Peace Agreement, which ended over two decades of civil war. Southern Sudanese cast ballots either for the continued unity of Sudan or for secession from the North. Over 98 percent of votes were cast in favor of separation.

In late January the president of the new nation, Salva Kiir, established a constitutional review committee to draft a transitional constitution. Opposition political parties complained of the committee's work being dominated by the ruling Sudan People's Liberation Movement (SPLM), and several withdrew in protest.

The Transitional Constitution entered into force on July 9 for a period of four years, to be followed by national elections and the adoption of a permanent constitution. It expanded presidential powers and created a new and enlarged bicameral legislative body, which incorporated South Sudanese who left legislative positions in Sudan's former Government of National Unity. It also provided for the transformation of the Sudan People's Liberation Army (SPLA) into the South Sudan Armed Forces.

Tensions along the North-South Border

Tensions between Sudan and South Sudan rose steadily throughout 2011. Negotiations between the southern ruling SPLM and the Sudan's ruling National Congress Party (NCP) regarding post-secession issues—such as oil revenue sharing, border management, and the status of the contested area of Abyei— stalled on several occasions. Many issues remain unresolved.

Conflict in border areas has had a significant impact on South Sudan. In May Sudan's violent occupation of Abyei displaced an estimated 110,000 people, mostly to Warrap state in South Sudan. Fighting between the Sudan Armed Forces (SAF) and elements of the SPLA in Southern Kordofan drove some 20,000 people to South Sudan's Unity state. Approximately 4,000 more people arrived in Upper Nile state following the September clashes between Sudanese government forces and the SPLM-North in Southern Kordofan. Humanitarian agencies are struggling to meet the health, nutrition, and security needs of these displaced people and refugees.

South Sudanese continue to return from the North, with over 340,000 arriving between October 2010 and October 2011, according to the UN. Many moved in the months prior to the referendum. Returnees cited a rise in anti-southerner sentiments and uncertainty of citizenship status in the North as reasons for their decision to return. Less than two weeks after the secession of the South, Sudan amended its nationality law, raising concerns that people of South Sudanese origin residing in Sudan will be discriminatorily stripped of citizenship, and as a consequence might be made stateless.

Clashes between SPLA and Armed Militia Groups

Armed insurgencies by rebel militia groups against the South Sudan government, originally triggered by disapproval of the outcome of the April 2010 general elections, continued in 2011. Hundreds of civilians, including women and children, were killed, and tens of thousands of people were displaced, primarily in Upper Nile, Unity, and Jonglei states.

Both opposition militias and government soldiers have failed to take adequate precautions to protect civilians. Human Rights Watch documented grave human rights abuses and violations of humanitarian law by SPLA soldiers in the course of fighting in Upper Nile, including unlawful killings of civilians and the destruction of homes and civilian property. According to UN reports, SPLA soldiers in May opened fire indiscriminately on civilians during a confrontation with a militia group in Jonglei.

President Kiir has offered a general amnesty for armed militias in exchange for the promise to lay down arms and integrate their forces into the national military. Several militia leaders have entered into ceasefire agreements with the government, but others continue to clash with government forces.

Inter-Communal Violence

Cyclical fighting between ethnic communities caused by cattle-raiding, competition over land resources, and kidnapping of women and children continued to put civilians at risk of injury and death. The most intense clashes occurred between the Lou Nuer and Murle communities in Jonglei state, where over 1,000 people were killed between April and August.

The government has taken some steps to promote reconciliation between neighboring communities. However, both the government and the UN peacekeepers have been unable to protect civilians and prevent these often predictable outbreaks of violence. Land mines and ongoing insecurity have hampered humanitarian access. The government has also failed to conduct public investigations into abuses against civilians and ensure accountability.

Attacks by the Lord's Resistance Army

Attacks and abductions by the Lord's Resistance Army, a Ugandan rebel group, continued to pose a threat to civilians. The UN reported over 25 separate attacks in 2011, mostly in western areas of the country bordering the

Democratic Republic of Congo and Central African Republic. The displacement of populations in response to this violence has threatened food security, according to local officials. The SPLA and Ugandan People Defence Force (UPDF) continued efforts to improve safety, relying frequently on a local defense group known as the Arrow Boys.

Law Enforcement and the Administration of Justice

Human Rights Watch has documented numerous violations by security forces. These include unlawful killings, beatings, and looting, particularly when conducting forcible community disarmament operations, as well as unlawful arrests and detentions. Security forces have also used arrests and intimidation to suppress opponents of the ruling party and independent journalists.

UN and humanitarian aid groups have reported that police, soldiers, and local authorities have harassed staff, hijacked vehicles, and stolen aid supplies. In August police officers in Juba severely assaulted the UN human rights chief in South Sudan, forcing him to seek medical treatment. President Kiir has warned security forces against such abuses.

There are serious human rights violations in the administration of justice such as prolonged periods of pre-trial detention and poor conditions of detention. Children are often detained with adults, while persons with mental disabilities languish in prison without any legal basis for their detention and do not receive treatment. Lack of legal aid also renders defendants vulnerable to due process violations.

Economic and Social Rights

Millions of South Sudanese suffer from lack of access to education, health care, food, and water. The government estimates that 47 percent are under-nourished. Less than half of primary school age children are in schools and only 16 percent of women are literate. The maternal mortality rate of 2,054 per 100,000 live births is the highest in the world.

Women's and Girls' Rights

Women and girls are routinely deprived of the right to choose a spouse or to own and inherit property. They are subjected to degrading practices such as forced and early marriage, wife-inheritance, the use of girls to pay debts, and various forms of domestic violence. Domestic disputes are resolved by traditional courts that often apply discriminatory customs.

Key International Actors

There was a high level of international engagement in support of the January referendum. Some 600 international observers—including delegations from the African Union (AU), the Arab League, the European Union, and the Intergovernmental Authority on Development—monitored the polling process, which was found to comply with international standards

Sudan officially recognized the Republic of South Sudan on July 8, and many other countries immediately followed suit. Approximately 30 heads of state as well as UN Secretary-General Ban Ki-moon attended independence ceremonies in Juba. South Sudan became a UN member on July 14 and joined the AU on July 27.

When the mandate of the UN Mission in Sudan (UNMIS) expired with the independence of South Sudan, the Security Council unanimously approved a successor mission, the UN Mission in South Sudan (UNMISS), to include 7,000 military personnel. It has the mandate to "consolidate peace and security," to help establish conditions for development, and to strengthen the capacity of South Sudan to govern effectively and democratically.

The AU's High-Level Implementation Panel continued to play a key role in facilitating negotiations between the SPLM and the NCP, including a June agreement for the demilitarization of Abyei and monitoring by Ethiopian troops. This led the Security Council to establish the UN Interim Security Force for Abyei (UNISFA), to comprise a maximum of 4,200 troops.

At its 18th session, the UN Human Rights Council did not appoint an independent expert as it did for Sudan, but instead called for the identification of areas for technical assistance and capacity-building to promote respect for human rights in South Sudan and requested that the high commissioner for human rights present a report on the human rights situation in the country at its September 2012 session.

SUDAN (NORTH)

South Sudan seceded from Sudan on July 9 under the terms of the 2005 Comprehensive Peace Agreement (CPA) that ended Sudan's 22-year civil war. The split was peaceful but Sudan saw increasing popular unrest and widening armed opposition in the months that followed. In Khartoum, the capital, government authorities pursued familiar repressive tactics including harassing, arresting, detaining, and torturing perceived opponents of the government; censoring media; and banning political parties.

Volatile areas north of the South Sudan border descended into conflict while a peace agreement signed by the government and one rebel group did not end simmering conflict or improve the human rights situation in the western province of Darfur. At this writing Sudan's proposed new constitution had not been adopted amid calls by President Omar al-Bashir to impose a strict version of Islamic law without exception for religious and ethnic minorities.

New Conflict Near South Sudan Border

The ruling National Congress Party (NCP) and the South's ruling Sudan People's Liberation Movement (SPLM) remained deadlocked on the disputed territory of Abyei. In May Sudan conducted a military offensive to take over Abyei in which government forces and allied militia burned and looted homes and other property, causing more than 100,000 civilians to flee. In June the parties agreed to demilitarize the area and deploy an Ethiopian peacekeeping force under the auspices of the United Nations.

In June fighting started in Southern Kordofan between Sudan government forces and elements of the South's Sudan People's Liberation Army (SPLA) after weeks of growing tension over security arrangements and a state election in which Ahmed Haroun—whom the International Criminal Court (ICC) wants for war crimes and crimes against humanity in Darfur—narrowly won the governorship in May.

In Kadugli, the capital of Southern Kordofan, government soldiers and militia shot civilians and arrested suspected SPLM supporters during house-to-house searches and checkpoint stops, and looted and burned churches and homes. A report released in August by the Office of the United Nations High Commissioner for Human Rights documented patterns of unlawful killings and widespread attacks on civilian properties that could amount to war crimes and crimes against humanity.

Sudan bombed indiscriminately across the Nuba Mountains, forcing the population to seek shelter in caves and mountains where they lacked food, shelter, and hygiene. The government refused to allow aid groups to affected areas, effectively blockading much of the Nuba Mountains.

In early September conflict spread to the Blue Nile state, with fighting between government forces and an armed opposition linked to SPLM-North, the successor to the SPLM in Sudan. Tens of thousands of civilians fled across the border to Ethiopia to escape the conflict. The Sudanese government bombed areas held by opposition forces, and again blocked aid groups from accessing the area.

Ongoing Conflict in Darfur

In December 2010 and early 2011 a surge in government-led attacks on populated areas in North and South Darfur killed and injured scores of civilians, destroyed property, and displaced more than 70,000 people, largely from ethnic Zaghawa and Fur communities with perceived links to rebel groups. The fighting followed a break between the government and Minni Minawi, the only major Sudan Liberation Army (SLA) rebel leader to have signed the 2006 Darfur Peace Agreement.

Much of Darfur remained off limits to the African Union/UN Mission in Darfur and aid groups, curtailing the peacekeepers' ability to protect civilians or monitor the human rights situation. The vast majority of Darfur's displaced population, estimated at 2.5 million people, remained in camps in Darfur and Chad. On several occasions, security forces carried out violent search-and-cordon operations, arresting dozens of camp residents. Government forces were also responsible for sexual violence against displaced women and girls.

SUDAN

Darfur in the Shadows

The Sudanese Government's Ongoing Attacks
on Civilians and Human Rights

HUMAN
RIGHTS
WATCH

A peace agreement signed in July by the Sudanese government and one rebel group, the Liberation and Justice Movement, did not stop sporadic fighting or address ongoing human rights abuses and impunity. The government, with support from AU/UN peacekeepers, pursued controversial plans for a "domestic political process" to end the Darfur conflict.

Although President al-Bashir announced in March that he would lift the state of emergency in Darfur, he had not done so at this writing. Authorities relied on emergency and national security laws to detain perceived opponents for long periods without judicial review, often subjecting them to ill-treatment or torture while in detention. Those detained in 2011 included Sudanese employees of the AU/UN peacekeeping mission and of an international aid group. Four displaced leaders, held under emergency laws in North Darfur since 2009, remained in prison.

Crackdown on Protesters

In January in response to demonstrations inspired by the popular uprisings in Egypt and Tunisia, security forces arrested more than 100 protesters in Khartoum and Omdurman alone. The National Intelligence and Security Service (NISS) detained dozens of protesters for several weeks, subjecting them to beatings, sleep deprivation, electric shock, and other forms of physical and mental abuse, including death threats and threats of rape.

Throughout the year security forces used violence to disperse peaceful protests across the country, often at universities where students gathered to protest a range of government policies and price hikes, and detained many. Security officials were also implicated in sexual violence and harassment of female activists, including the brutal rape in mid-February of Safiya Ishaq, a youth activist who was forced to flee the country after speaking out about her ordeal.

Arrest and Detention of Perceived Opponents

The NISS also targeted opposition party members, activists, and other perceived opponents. In January officials arrested and detained opposition figure

Hassan al-Turabi and members of his Popular Congress Party for four months after he warned of an uprising if the government refused to make reforms.

In June, when fighting broke out in Southern Kordofan, security forces rounded up ethnic Nuba suspected to be SPLM members or supporters. Among those arrested by NISS was Dr. Bushra Gammar Hussein Rahma, a prominent Nuba human rights activist, who remained in detention without charge at this writing.

In September, when fighting spread to Blue Nile, security forces, including NISS, arrested more than 100 suspected party members of SPLM-North, including the well-known Sudanese writer, artist, activist, and former state adviser on cultural affairs, Abdelmoniem Rahma. Some were released following renunciations of their political affiliation to the party. In September the government also banned 17 political parties including SPLM-North citing their southern links.

Media Restrictions

Sudanese authorities continued to stifle the media by arresting, detaining, and prosecuting journalists reporting on sensitive topics, and by confiscating publications.

Between October 30 and November 2, 2010, NISS arrested a group of Darfuri journalists and activists affiliated with Radio Dabanga, a news service reporting on Darfur, and subjected them to beatings and other ill-treatment and torture while in detention for weeks and months. Seven faced criminal charges, including espionage, punishable by death.

In May security officials detained and interrogated two Sudanese journalists because they tried to report on elections in Southern Kordofan. In June and September security officials arrested Al Jazeera journalists attempting to cover events in Southern Kordofan and Blue Nile.

Two prominent journalists were charged with defamation for their coverage of the February rape of Safiya Ishag by security officials. Other journalists have also been harassed or threatened with defamation charges for reporting on the case.

NISS officials confiscated editions of major newspapers for their coverage of conflicts or because of articles critical of the ruling party. Authorities also suspended a dozen newspapers, including opposition paper *Ajras al Hurriya,* citing their links to South Sudan.

Justice and Accountability

In 2005 the UN Security Council referred the situation in Darfur to the ICC, which has issued arrest warrants for three individuals, including President al-Bashir, on charges of war crimes, crimes against humanity, and genocide. Sudan continued to refuse cooperation with the ICC in its cases for crimes in Darfur or to meaningfully prosecute the crimes in its own courts. Despite the appointment of several special prosecutors for Darfur, Sudan has done little to promote accountability and made none of the justice reforms recommended by the AU's High-level Panel on Darfur, headed by former South Africa President Thabo Mbeki, in its 2009 report.

Key International Actors

World leaders congratulated Sudan for allowing the South's secession, but were largely mute in response to the human rights and laws of war violations in Southern Kordofan and Blue Nile. Neither the UN nor the AU condemned the serious violations, despite calls by the Office of the UN High Commissioner for Human Rights for an investigation into possible war crimes and crimes against humanity, or took other action to protect civilians from the conflicts.

Three ICC member states—Djibouti, Chad, and Malawi—welcomed al-Bashir to their territories, flouting their obligation to arrest him. China also welcomed him.

The European Union, United States, United Kingdom, Germany, and France criticized the visits and urged Sudan and other states to cooperate with the court, including in the surrender of ICC suspects. Malaysia cancelled an anticipated visit by al-Bashir after public outcry.

The Mbeki-led AU Panel mediated between Sudan and South Sudan on critical outstanding issues, such as oil revenue sharing, border management, and the status of the contested area of Abyei. Ethiopian Prime Minister Meles Zenawi and UN and US special envoys played key roles. In June the UN authorized 4,200 Ethiopian peacekeepers for Abyei. The US also played a major role mediating a new peace agreement for Darfur, signed by the government and one rebel group at Doha.

However, key international actors did not take a unified approach to addressing the protection of civilians and ending human rights violations, particularly in Southern Kordofan and Blue Nile. The mandate of the UN peacekeeping mission in Sudan (UNMIS) expired in July, effectively ending international monitoring in Sudan, except in Darfur, where the AU/UN mission continued to face significant restrictions.

In September the UN's Human Rights Council renewed the mandate of the UN expert on Sudan for another year, but the resolution fell short of reflecting the gravity of the situation on the ground and of calling for an international investigation or any other meaningful response to the human rights and humanitarian crisis in Sudan's border regions of Abyei, South Kordofan, and Blue Nile.

SWAZILAND

The Kingdom of Swaziland, ruled by King Mswati III since 1986, is in the midst of a serious crisis of governance. Years of extravagant expenditure by the royal family, fiscal indiscipline, and government corruption have left the country on the brink of economic disaster.

Under Swazi law and custom, all powers are vested in the king. Although Swaziland has a prime minister who is supposed to exercise executive authority, in reality, King Mswati holds supreme executive powers and control over the judiciary and legislature. The king appoints 20 members of the 65-member house of assembly and approves all legislation that parliament passes. Political parties have been banned in the country since 1973.

Swaziland has one of the highest HIV prevalence rates in the world at 26 percent, but has failed to secure sufficient treatment for its population, including anti-retroviral drugs. With 80 percent of the population subsisting on less than US$2 per day, a 40 percent unemployment rate, and thousands of civil servants facing wage cuts, Swazi authorities have faced increasing pressure from civil society activists and trade unionists to implement economic reforms and open up the space for civil and political activism. Dozens of students, trade unionists, and civil society activists have been arrested during protests against the government's poor governance and human rights record.

Freedom of Association and Assembly

The government has intensified restrictions on freedom of association and assembly in the past few years. The Swazi constitution guarantees these rights, but the provisions protecting these rights have been undermined by clauses that permit restrictions by the state. Authorities have also restricted political participation and banned political parties.

Permission to hold political gatherings is often denied, and police routinely disperse and arrest peaceful demonstrators. On September 7, police beat and injured several students in Mbabane as they attempted to deliver a petition to the minister of labour and social security. Police detained two students, later releasing them without charge.

On September 5, local civil society groups, trade unionists, workers, and students embarked on a week of action calling for, among other things, multi-party democracy, the release of political prisoners, and a freeze on wage cuts for civil servants. The week of action was supported by various trade union groups around the world, including the Congress of South African Trade Unions (COSATU), which sent representatives to Swaziland. The demonstrations turned violent. On September 7, police attempted to prevent the deputy president of COSATU, Zingiswa Losi, from addressing a rally and fired live ammunition, rubber bullets, and tear gas at crowds, resulting in several injuries in the town of Siteki. Losi and the deputy head of COSATU's international department, Zanele Matebula, were later deported.

On September 9, police attempted to prevent leaders from the political movement Peoples' United Democratic Movement (PUDEMO) from speaking at a rally in Manzini, beating PUDEMO and trade union leaders.

On April 12, authorities responded to civil society plans for a mass demonstration against poor economic and human rights conditions by arresting about 150 civil society and trade union leaders. Police and security forces detained and beat several activists and placed many others under house arrest.

Human Rights Defenders

Police harassment and surveillance of civil society organizations increased in 2011. Political activists were arrested, detained, and tried under security legislation. They have also faced common law charges such as treason.

Civil society activists and government critics have reported increased incidents of harassment, searches, and seizures of office materials, as well as monitoring of electronic communications, telephones calls, and meetings by the authorities. Police and other security officials routinely use excessive force against political activists. Local activists reported that police often use torture and other ill-treatment against activists with impunity. No independent complaints investigation body exists for victims of police abuses.

Freedom of Expression and Media

Journalists and the media face continued threats and attacks by the authorities. Self-censorship in media is widespread. Publishing criticism of the ruling party is banned. On July 12, police stormed the offices of the *Times* newspapers and served the editor with a court order to stop publishing any articles related to the chief justice. A high court later rescinded the order after finding no basis for it.

The government has passed draconian security legislation such as the Sedition and Subversive Activities Act, which severely curtails the enjoyment of freedom of expression, among other rights, and allows for extensive imprisonment without the option of a fine if one is found guilty. The act has been used to harass activists and conduct searches of their homes and offices.

Rule of Law

Serious deficiencies in Swaziland's judicial system persist. In an ominous precedent for the independence of the judiciary, Chief Justice Michael Ramodibedi in August suspended Justice Thomas Masuku for insubordination and for insulting the king, among other charges, in reaction to a January judgment by Justice Masuku in which he said King Mswati was speaking with a "forked tongue." On August 11 Justice Masuku appeared before the Judicial Services Commission (JSC), whose six members are appointed by the king. On September 27 the king relieved Judge Masuku of his duties for "serious misbehavior." Justice Masuku had in the past made several rulings in favor of human rights.

Control over the daily allocation of cases for hearings, including urgent ones, has been placed solely in the hands of the chief justice, creating what is perceived by lawyers as an unacceptable bias in the administration of justice. In August the Law Society of Swaziland instituted a boycott of the courts to protest these developments and the failure of the authorities to hear its complaints regarding the running of the courts, including the chief justice's allocation of cases. On September 21, Law Society members delivered a petition to the minister of justice calling for action to address the decisions of the chief justice and the general administration of justice in the court system.

Victims of human rights abuses and those seeking to advance the protection of human rights through the courts have little or no access to effective legal remedies. In June the chief justice published a directive protecting the king from civil law suits in the high court or any other courts, a clear violation of a citizen's right to be protected by the law and to be heard before an independent judiciary.

Key International Actors

In August the International Monetary Fund expressed serious concerns about Swaziland's deepening fiscal crisis and called on the government to implement significant fiscal reforms.

On August 3 South Africa agreed to a $355 million loan to help ease Swazi economic woes. However, in a move widely lauded by civil society groups in Swaziland and South Africa, the South African government insisted on political and economic reforms as conditions for the loan. The Swazi authorities declined the conditions, leading to delays in the loan's disbursement.

UGANDA

During demonstrations in April, following February's presidential elections, the unnecessary use of lethal force by Ugandan security forces resulted in the deaths of nine people. Opposition politicians and hundreds of supporters were arrested and charged with unlawful assembly and incitement to violence, and state agents beat and harassed journalists covering the unrest.

Several bills with negative implications for human rights, including the Anti-Homosexuality Bill, which proposes the death penalty for some consensual same-sex activity, failed to advance but remain in parliament.

Freedom of Assembly and Expression

Security forces' unjustified use of lethal force remains a significant problem. In April military and police shot and killed nine people—six in Kampala, the capital, two in Gulu, and one in Masaka—during demonstrations. None of the dead carried weapons or posed a serious threat. At least two were shot in the back as they fled and two, including a child, were inside buildings.

The protests began in April when Activists for Change, a non-profit group, called on the public to "foster peaceful change in the management of public affairs." The first action was a "Walk to Work" to protest rising fuel and food prices. The government argued that these walks constituted an unlawful assembly.

The government responded by unleashing security forces on the protesters. In some instances protestors were aggressive, throwing stones and setting debris alight. State forces failed to distinguish between individuals actively participating in violence and those uninvolved, firing randomly into crowded areas and throwing tear gas at people or into houses. Passersby were forced at gunpoint or on threat of violence to clear burning debris. Security forces beat or shot at over 30 journalists, confiscated audio recorders and cameras, and deleted images of the violence. Several opposition politicians, including two former presidential candidates, were violently arrested and charged with unlawful assembly and inciting violence. All charges were eventually dropped.

In mid-October at least 27 members of Activists for Change were arrested and charged with incitement to violence, concealment of treason, or treason as the group planned more protests to highlight corruption and inflation. Opposition leader Kizza Besigye was arrested several times throughout the year while walking to work and held in "preventative detention" at his home.

The government has not conducted effective criminal investigations into the April killings and other state abuses, although there was one arrest for the killing of a child in Masaka. In some instances, the government paid families money following cursory inquiries. The government has a history of not holding state actors to account for the unnecessary use of lethal force. In protests in September 2009 at least 40 persons were killed, but there has been no meaningful attempt to investigate and prosecute those responsible.

Torture, Extrajudicial Killings, and Arbitrary Detention

The Rapid Response Unit (RRU), a section of the police created to combat armed crimes, continues to arrest and in some instances torture criminal suspects. RRU frequently illegally detains people without charge beyond the constitutionally mandated 48 hours in its headquarters in Kireka, Kampala, and other locations. RRU officers routinely use unlawful force during arrests, including beating suspects, using torture during interrogations to extract confessions, and the alleged extrajudicial killings of at least six individuals in 2010 alone.

No one has been charged for the May 2010 killing of Henry Bakasamba while he was in RRU custody, or for four suspects who were gunned down by RRU operatives on the Kyengera-Natete road in January 2010. In a positive step, three RRU officers were arrested for the August 2010 killing of detainee Frank Ssekanjako, though the trial has not taken place. This case could be the first time that RRU officers are held criminally accountable for murder. In past incidents, alleged perpetrators have been arrested only to be granted bail and never brought to trial.

Due Process Violations

Uganda's military court system violates international standards on fair trials and due process by its infrequent sessions, painfully slow processes, lack of adequate defense preparation, and lack of legal expertise among the army officers who act as judges. Suspects have waited in some cases up to nine years for trial resolutions. Some await trial for periods exceeding the maximum sentence for their charges. The military court has in the past admitted into evidence confessions extracted by torture. Suspects on remand often feel they must plead guilty to conclude their case. In contravention of international legal standards and Ugandan constitutional law, military courts have routinely prosecuted civilians, particularly for gun possession, although there were indications during 2011 that this practice would end.

The slow pace of the civilian justice system also violates human rights law. Fifty-five percent of the Ugandan prison population is held on remand, though international law requires pre-trial detention be an exception and as short as possible. While the donor-driven Justice Law and Order Sector program has made progress in reducing the case backlog, detainees are still in custody for several years, pending trial. Most detainees, including those accused of serious crimes and face long remand times, lack legal representation or the practical ability to apply for bail without counsel.

Health Care and Forced Labor in Prisons

Uganda's prisons are at 225 percent of capacity. Thousands of convicted and remanded prisoners are forced to work long hours on prison farms, private land, or prison staff's fields, and are brutally beaten if slow. The funds raised from prison labor are never fully accounted for, fueling corruption. A lack of basic necessities, as well as the use of abusive corporal punishment, remained widely reported, in contradiction of international standards.

A 2008 survey found HIV and tuberculosis rates for prisoners approximately double those in the general population. Meanwhile, only 63 of Uganda's 223 prisons have health workers, and only one prison hospital provides comprehen-

UGANDA

"Even Dead Bodies Must Work"

Health, Hard Labor, and Abuse in Ugandan Prisons

HUMAN
RIGHTS
WATCH

sive HIV and tuberculosis treatment. Medically unqualified officers routinely assess the health needs of prisoners and deny access to care.

The International Crimes Division

The new International Crimes Division of the High Court (ICD), created following failed peace talks with the insurgent Lord's Resistance Army (LRA) in 2008, brought Uganda's first domestic war crimes prosecution. In July LRA combatant Thomas Kwoyelo faced 12 counts of grave breaches of the Geneva Conventions and 53 counts of penal code violations, including murder, kidnapping, and aggravated robbery. His lawyers challenged the state's failure to grant amnesty, which was granted to over 12,000 LRA combatants since 2000. In September the constitutional court ruled that the amnesty act was constitutional, and thus Kwoyelo should be granted amnesty, and his prosecution cease. At this writing the government appeal was pending.

Defendants arrested for the July 2010 bombings also face trial before the ICD. Al-Shabaab, the militant group fighting to overthrow the government of Somalia, claimed responsibility as retaliation for the Ugandan army's role in the African Union mission in Somalia. Ugandan police arrested scores of Muslims and detained many for months without charge, torturing some to elicit confessions. Kenyan police handed over suspects without respect for national extradition requirements. Twelve Muslim men from Uganda, Somalia, Tanzania, and Kenya were on trial at this writing; two others pled guilty to conspiracy and terrorism and were sentenced.

Bills Violating Human Rights Law

Due to a motion to maintain the legislative agenda of the previous parliament, several repressive bills remain. The Anti-Homosexuality Bill, which proposes the death penalty for some consensual same-sex activities, and the HIV/AIDS Prevention and Control Act, which criminalizes intentional or attempted transmission of HIV, could still come up for debate and vote. The Public Order Management Bill, which grants police overly broad discretionary powers in the management of all public meetings, was also presented in parliament.

Human Rights Defenders

Prominent Kenyan Muslim rights defender Al-Amin Kimathi, who had been charged with terrorism in Uganda for the July 2010 bombings, was released in September after a year in prison without trial. Six other human rights activists (one from the United Kingdom, five from Kenya) on two occasions were denied entry to Uganda while trying to observe legal proceedings or meet with authorities to raise due process concerns.

A leading lesbian, gay, bisexual, and transgender (LGBT) activist who advocated against the Anti-Homosexuality Bill, David Kato of Sexual Minorities Uganda, was murdered in January, allegedly by an acquaintance who confessed. The defendant pled guilty and was sentenced to 30 years in prison.

Key International Actors

The rights of the LGBT community, corruption, and governance mismanagement dominated international attention, although after the brutal responses to the protests, the United States spoke out in support of Ugandans' rights to free expression and assembly.

Donor countries criticized President Yoweri Museveni's massive off-budget expenditures to support elections, pay-outs to parliamentarians, and the procurement of several fighter jets worth over US$740 million. As inflation rose, the International Monetary Fund delayed approval of Uganda's economic framework because government spending was found to be out of compliance with agreed-upon principles of macroeconomic stability.

The UK and Ireland suspended a €2 million (US$2.7 million) police training program focusing on public order management after the April protests, but support from both countries remains strong, with the UK providing £390 million ($614.5 million) over the next three years despite concerns about corruption.

The US reliance on the Ugandan army has to some extent shielded Uganda from meaningful criticism of its poor domestic human rights record. The Ugandan army continued to receive logistical support and training from the US for counterterrorism, for the African Union mission in Somalia, and for operations against the LRA. In October US President Barack Obama announced the deployment of 100 US military advisors to provide assistance in ending the LRA conflict.

ZIMBABWE

Zimbabwe's inclusive government has made significant progress in improving the country's economic situation and reversing the decline of the past decade. For example, Zimbabwe has seen a marked improvement in its health system. However, despite a decline in HIV prevalence over the past decade and adoption of new guidelines on treatment in 2011, the number of HIV-positive Zimbabweans requiring but not receiving treatment remained high. Huge challenges also remain on the political front, with elections a key point of contention within the Government of National Unity (GNU).

The two main parties to the GNU, the Zimbabwe African National Union-Patriotic Front (ZANU-PF) and the Movement for Democratic Change (MDC), differ sharply over when elections should be held and the role of the security forces, often seen as staunch allies of President Robert Mugabe and ZANU-PF. ZANU-PF insists that the environment in the country is conducive to the holding of free, fair, and credible elections while the MDC contends that elections should not take place in the absence of human rights and electoral reforms. Questions also remain over the independence of key institutions that are vital to the proper implementation of free and fair elections, such as the electoral commission and the judiciary.

Mugabe's announcement in December 2010 that elections would be held in 2011 triggered an increase in violence and abuses across the country. The beginning of the year saw ZANU-PF and elements within the security forces resort to old campaign tactics of violence, intimidation, and harassment. State security agents, police, and ZANU-PF supporters have been implicated in beatings, arbitrary arrests, and harassment of members of the MDC, cabinet ministers, human rights activists, and journalists, deepening the pervasive climate of fear in the country. In reaction to the abuses, Prime Minister Morgan Tsvangirai threatened to withdraw the MDC from the inclusive government in March.

Political Violence

After a period of relative calm, 2011 saw an increase in politically motivated violence across the country. Tensions flared between the ZANU-PF and the MDC as a result of the anticipated elections. The main perpetrators of the violence have been ZANU-PF supporters and youth who have attacked scores of people, mainly MDC supporters and members, in the high-density neighborhoods of Harare, the capital, as well as outside of Harare. Over several days of violence in early February, scores of MDC supporters were injured and some were hospitalized as a result of attacks by alleged ZANU-PF youth in Mbare.

Police and prosecutors have been highly partisan and biased in their investigations and prosecution of acts of violence between supporters of the two parties. Groups allied to ZANU-PF continue to beat and intimidate citizens in the high-density suburbs of Harare with impunity, while MDC activists accused of violence are disproportionately arrested. In March police raided the MDC party headquarters and arrested three MDC officials and seven MDC youth on assault charges. Three days later they were all released. Several MDC parliamentarians and officials are facing various criminal charges, including inciting and participating in violence. In contrast, there have been few arrests or charges laid against ZANU-PF supporters implicated in violence.

Human Rights Defenders

The Zimbabwean authorities continue to use repression and intimidation to silence human rights advocates and to prevent them from exposing abuses and promoting respect for human rights. Harassment and arbitrary arrests of human rights defenders have intensified since January 2011. For example, on February 8, police arrested two employees of the Zimbabwe Human Rights NGO Forum as they tried to conduct a survey on transitional justice. In the same period police also raided the offices of a number of human rights NGOs and questioned the employees.

On May 23, police in Matabeleland North arrested two activists from the human rights organization ZimRights for convening a workshop on torture and its effects. Lawyers were denied access to the activists for three days before they were released.

ZIMBABWE

Perpetual Fear

Impunity and Cycles of Violence in Zimbabwe

HUMAN
RIGHTS
WATCH

Freedom of Association and Assembly

Minimal changes to repressive laws such as the Public Order and Security Act (POSA) and the Access to Information and Protection of Privacy Act (AIPPA) have failed to open up space for the political opposition and civil society. ZANU-PF continues to selectively apply these laws and others, such as the Criminal Law (Codification and Reform) Act, to justify arrests that violate basic rights and systematically deny civil society activists the right to peacefully assemble and associate. The police use provisions of POSA to strictly monitor and prevent public meetings or disrupt peaceful demonstrations.

On September 21, police arrested 12 activists from the organization Women of Zimbabwe Arise (WOZA) during a peaceful march commemorating the international day of peace. Ten of the activists were released without charge but two leaders of the organization, Jenni Williams and Magodonga Mahlangu, spent 13 days in custody.

On February 19, police arrested 45 activists who were meeting in Harare to discuss events in the Middle East. Six of the activists spent three weeks in custody before they were released on bail, initially charged with treason and attempting to overthrow the government by unconstitutional means. On September 14 the trial of the activists began in Harare, but the charges were revised to allegedly conspiring to commit public violence and participating in a gathering with intent to promote public violence.

The Office of the Attorney General has often been accused of a strong partisan bias toward ZANU-PF and of using criminal laws to prevent peaceful political activism. Prosecutors routinely invoke section 121 of the Criminal Procedure and Evidence Act to deny bail to political and civil society activists despite judicial rulings granting them bail, thus nullifying judicial checks on the excesses of the executive.

Freedom of Expression

There continue to be serious limits on the rights to freedom of expression and information in Zimbabwe, particularly in the form of threats of closure of independent media organizations, as well as the intimidation, arbitrary arrest, and criminal prosecution of journalists. The government's actions seem primarily designed to inhibit criticism of government officials and institutions, and to muzzle reporting and commentary on the political situation in the country.

While the government has allowed independent local daily papers to resume operations, it has not fully reformed media-related laws as promised. It has also not reviewed criminal defamation laws that impose severe penalties, including prison terms, on journalists. Media laws such as AIPPA give the Zimbabwe authorities discretionary control over which individuals may practice journalism and operate a media outlet, as well as broad powers to prosecute persons critical of the government. Laws such as AIPPA and POSA continue to be selectively used to restrict the media. Journalists and media practitioners routinely face arrest for allegedly violating the state's repressive media laws. Journalists and media outlets have also been subjected to threats and harassment from the authorities and security forces, creating major obstacles to reporting on Zimbabwe's political system and continuing abuses by ZANU-PF.

Human Rights Violations in Marange Diamond Fields

While violence has decreased in the Marange diamond fields over the past year, Human Rights Watch research in June found that Zimbabwe police and private security guards employed by mining companies in the Marange diamond fields were implicated in abuses against local unlicensed miners. Private security guards working with the police routinely beat and set dogs to attack and maul local miners who stray into areas of the fields controlled by the companies. During patrols, police also fired live ammunition at miners as they fled the fields.

These findings contradict claims by the Zimbabwe government and some members of the international diamond monitoring body, the Kimberley Process, that areas controlled by private mining companies are relatively free of abuses and that diamonds from these companies should be certified and allowed on to international markets. The violence followed claims in June by the government and the chairman of the Kimberley Process, Mathieu Yamba, that conditions in the Marange fields are sufficient for it to be allowed to resume exports of diamonds.

Key International Actors

Leaders of the Southern African Development Community (SADC) grew increasingly frustrated with the slow pace of political and human rights reforms in Zimbabwe, in particular ZANU-PF's reluctance to implement key parts of the Global Political Agreement (GPA), which paved the way for the formation of the GNU. Throughout the year SADC and South African President Jacob Zuma, appointed by SADC to facilitate reforms, exerted concerted pressure on the GNU to increase the pace of reforms and to adhere to a SADC-drafted electoral road map that would lead to free, fair, and credible elections.

At an extraordinary meeting held in Zambia in March, President Zuma reported back to SADC leaders on the situation in Zimbabwe. The report highlighted concerns about widespread human rights violations, including violent attacks on MDC supporters and arbitrary arrests. SADC issued a strong communiqué in support, demanding an end to political violence and arbitrary arrests and calling for an expanded facilitation team to engage with the GNU. ZANU-PF's response to the communiqué was highly critical of Zuma's facilitation, publicly accusing SADC of interfering in the country's sovereignty and its right to hold elections at a time of its choosing. Subsequent communiqués issued by SADC at an extraordinary meeting in June and at its annual summit in August called for greater progress in the implementation of the GPA and the creation of a conducive environment to hold free and fair elections "under conditions of a level playing field."

SADC and Zuma's more robust engagement has led to progress in implementing certain parts of the GPA, including the formation of the electoral road map, finalizing the constitution making process, appointing a new election commission, and the introduction of the Zimbabwe Human Rights Commission Bill and the Electoral Amendment Bill. Zuma and his facilitation team's insistence that the environment in the country was not conducive to the holding of free and fair elections forced Mugabe and ZANU-PF to relent on holding the elections in 2011. Meanwhile SADC has been unable to make any gains on important issues such as security sector reform, accountability for past abuses, and ending politically motivated violence and other human rights abuses.

The United Nations Human Rights Council's first Universal Periodic Review of Zimbabwe took place in October 2011. Zimbabwe rebuffed at the outset all recommendations pertaining to investigating allegations of violations, combating impunity, and bolstering protection in the Marange region, and related to freedoms of assembly and expression, including repealing or amending the POSA.

Due to the absence of meaningful human rights improvements, the European Union and United States have maintained targeted sanctions on Mugabe and others within his government.

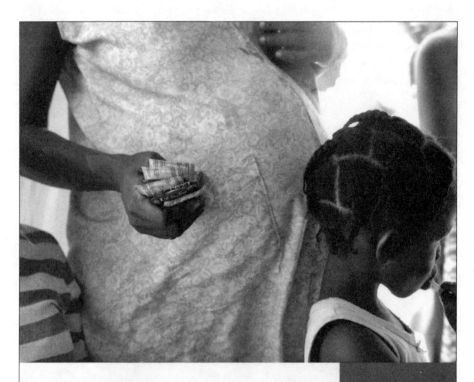

HAITI

"Nobody Remembers Us"

Failure to Protect Women's and Girls' Right
to Health and Security in Post Earthquake Haiti

HUMAN
RIGHTS
WATCH

WORLD REPORT

2012

AMERICAS

ARGENTINA

Argentina continues to make significant progress prosecuting military and police personnel for enforced disappearances, killings, and torture during the country's "dirty war" between 1976 and 1983, although trials have been subject to delays.

Argentina adopted comprehensive legislation to regulate broadcast and print media in 2009, and was still in 2011 considering bills to promote access to information. The impact of this legislation on freedom of expression will depend on how it is implemented by a new regulatory body established in the law.

Significant ongoing human rights concerns include deplorable prison conditions, torture, and arbitrary restrictions on women's reproductive rights.

Confronting Past Abuses

Several important human rights cases from Argentina's last military dictatorship (1976-1983) were reopened in 2003 after Congress annulled the 1986 "Full Stop" law, which had stopped prosecution of such cases, and the 1987 "Due Obedience" law, which granted immunity in such cases to all members of the military except those in positions of command. Starting in 2005, federal judges struck down pardons that then-President Carlos Menem issued between 1989 and 1990 to former officials convicted of or facing trial for human rights violations.

As of October 2011, according to the Center for Legal and Social Studies (CELS), 379 cases involving killings, "disappearances," and torture (in which CELS participated) were under judicial investigation or being tried in court. Of 1,774 alleged perpetrators, 749 were facing charges for these crimes, and 210 had been convicted.

Trials have been subject to delays at the appellate level, with appeals normally taking more than two years to be heard after the sentence of the trial court. At this writing the Supreme Court had confirmed final sentences in only four of the cases reactivated after the annulment of the amnesty laws.

In March 2011 the First Federal Oral Court sentenced an army general to life imprisonment and three agents to prison terms between 20 and 25 years for the murder, torture, and illegal arrest of detainees held in the 1970s in a secret detention center in Buenos Aires, the capital, known as Automotores Orletti. It was the first conviction in Argentina of participants in Plan Condor, a scheme by which the military rulers of the region coordinated the abduction, interrogation, and "disappearance" of political opponents. More than 30 Uruguayans abducted in Argentina in 1976 were held at Automotores Orletti, before some were transferred back to Uruguay. Others "disappeared."

Security of witnesses in human rights trials continues to be a concern. Jorge Julio López, 79, a former torture victim who disappeared from his home in September 2006, the day before he was due to attend one of the final days of a trial, remains missing.

Freedom of Expression and Access to Information

A bill to regulate the broadcast media, which Congress approved in October 2009, aims to promote diversity of views by limiting the ability of corporations to own large portions of the radio frequency spectrum. The law contains vague definitions of what "faults" could lead to sanctions—including the revocation of broadcasting licenses—and establishes a new regulatory body to interpret and implement its provisions. The law has faced numerous legal challenges. In October 2010 the Supreme Court upheld an injunction suspending application of an article of the law that would oblige companies to sell within a year outlets that exceed the new legal limits.

The Supreme Court has defended the right of print media not to be discriminated against in the allocation of official advertising. In March 2011 it unanimously upheld an administrative court ruling in favor of Perfil publications, which had filed a petition for an injunction against the government for refusing to allocate advertising to *Noticias* and *Fortuna* magazines, and to the *Perfil* newspaper, because of their editorial positions. The Supreme Court had published a similar ruling in 2007 against the provincial government of Neuquén in a complaint filed by the *Rio Negro* newspaper.

In September 2011 a judge subpoenaed Argentina's leading newspapers to provide the contact information of journalists and editors who have covered the Argentine economy since 2006, so that he could question them about their sources. Official statistics on the inflation rate have been widely questioned in recent years and many newspapers rely for inflation estimates on private consultancies, one of which the Commerce Secretary had accused of willfully falsifying the figures, a criminal offense in Argentina. The subpoenas threatened the press's freedom to freely publish information of public interest.

A proposed law to ensure public access to information held by state bodies has been stalled in the Chamber of Deputies since it received Senate approval in September 2010.

Conditions in Detention Facilities

Overcrowding, inadequate physical conditions, abuses by guards, and inmate violence continue to be serious problems in detention facilities. Following a visit to the province of Buenos Aires in June 2010, the Organization of American States' special rapporteur on the rights of persons deprived of their liberty reported that, according to official figures, 4,040 inmates (out of a provincial prison population of 30,132) were being held in police lockups not designed or equipped to hold detainees for long periods. The special rapporteur expressed concern about the abusive use of pre-trial detention, torture and ill-treatment by police guards, poor sanitary conditions, and deficient medical attention in these facilities.

According to CELS, the situation in February 2011 had scarcely improved. Despite a slight decline in the number held in preventive detention and in police lockups, conditions remained deplorable, and overcrowding and violence in the prison system had increased. According to CELS, there were 124 prison deaths due to abusive conditions in 2010.

Torture

Torture and ill-treatment are common problems. Government authorities and the legislature have taken some steps to curb abuse of detainees. In December 2010 the Public Defender's Office set up a National Register of Torture and Ill-treatment, a torture data bank aimed at registering, documenting, and following up on denunciations of torture, "other forms of institutional violence," and inhumane conditions of detention. Legislation creating a national system of torture prevention, drafted by a wide range of civil society groups, was approved unanimously in the Chamber of Deputies in September 2011. It awaits a final vote in the Senate to become law. Argentina is a party to the Optional Protocol to the Convention against Torture, which it ratified in September 2004.

Transnational Justice

At this writing no one had been convicted for the 1994 bombing of the Jewish Argentine Mutual Association in Buenos Aires in which 85 died and over 300 were injured. Criminal investigations and prosecutions have been hindered by judicial corruption and political cover-ups in Argentina, and by the failure of Iran, which is suspected of ordering the attack, to cooperate with the Argentine justice system. An Argentine federal court issued an international warrant for the arrest of former Iranian President Ali Akbar Hashemi-Rafsanjani and six Iranian officials in 2006, but demands for their extradition fell on deaf ears. President Fernández de Kirchner has repeatedly called for justice in annual speeches at the United Nations since taking office in 2007, as did her husband, former President Néstor Kirchner, who died in 2010. In September 2011 she told the UN that she would accept an Iranian government proposal to open a dialogue about the case, but only if it brought concrete results.

Reproductive Rights

Abortion is illegal, with limited exceptions, and women and girls face numerous obstacles to reproductive health products and services such as contraception, voluntary sterilization procedures, and abortion after rape. The most common barriers are long delays in obtaining services, unnecessary referrals to other clinics, demands for spousal permission (contrary to law), financial barriers, and, in some cases, arbitrary denials. In addition, government oversight of reproductive health care and accountability practices are woefully deficient. As a result of these barriers, women and girls may face unwanted or unhealthy pregnancies. Approximately half-a-million illegal abortions occur every year, and unsafe abortions have been a leading cause of maternal mortality for decades. Several proposals to decriminalize abortion were pending before the Chamber of Deputies at this writing.

Key International Actors

In December 2010 the Inter-American Commission on Human Rights took the case of Jorge Fontevecchia and Héctor D'Amico, founder and director respectively of the magazine *Noticias*, to the Inter-American Court of Human Rights. In 2001 the Supreme Court ordered the two journalists and Perfil Publications (the owner of *Noticias*) to pay damages of US$60,000 to former President Carlos Menem for articles published in 1995 about his extramarital affair with a former schoolteacher, on the grounds that the articles violated his right to privacy. It was the first time the court has been asked to deliver a judgment on a privacy claim for damages involving a question of public interest.

Argentina has continued to positively engage on human rights issues at the UN Human Rights Council and in other international settings. At the Council Argentina has consistently voted in a principled way to ensure scrutiny of human rights violators. In 2011, for example, it co-sponsored special sessions on Libya and the Côte d'Ivoire, and voted in favor of all resolutions addressing country situations that were put to a vote.

BOLIVIA

Bolivian courts made some progress in clarifying responsibilities for human rights abuses in 2011, including convicting seven high-ranking military officers and politicians for deaths in the 2003 street protests. However, lack of account-ability remains a serious problem. The fate of scores who "disappeared" before democracy was re-established in 1982 has still not been clarified, and trials of those responsible for killings during marches and demonstrations in recent years have been subject to long delays. The insistence of military courts on try-ing military accused of abuses continues to be an obstacle.

Laws passed in 2010 and 2011 posed risks to the media's ability to freely criti-cize the government. However, in 2011 President Evo Morales took some steps to address objections from media groups by amending some disputed laws.

Accountability for Past Human Rights Abuses

In August 2011 a Supreme Court panel sentenced five generals to 10 to 15 years imprisonment for killing at least 60 people during anti-government protests in September and October 2003, when the army used lethal force to quell violent demonstrations in the highland city of El Alto (an event known as Black October). Two members of former President Gonzalo Sánchez de Losada's cabi-net received three-year suspended sentences. Sánchez de Losada and other accused senior government members left the country immediately after the events.

The trial, which began in May 2009, followed an impeachment procedure known as a "trial of responsibilities." The law, which dates from 2003 and was rewritten in 2010, requires that trials of heads of state and ministers must first be authorized by the vote of two-thirds of Congress, after which the Supreme Court's criminal bench must approve the charges. The full Supreme Court then conducts the trial without the criminal bench. All members of the six-person panel that heard the case were appointed by pre-established and lawful proce-dures, without credible evidence of government interference.

Trial Delays in Political Violence Cases

Trials of opposition leaders, local government officials, and others accused of killings during violent clashes between supporters and opponents of President Morales have been subject to long delays. In September 2011 a La Paz court was still hearing evidence against 26 defendants in connection with a massacre in Porvenir, Pando department, on September 11, 2008, in which at least nine pro-Morales demonstrators were killed. The former prefect of Pando department, Leopoldo Fernández, who was indicted in October 2009 on charges of homicide, terrorism, and conspiracy, had been held for three years in a maximum security prison in La Paz, the capital.

A trial of former members of the regional government of Chuquisaca and former Sucre city officials in connection with a incident in May 2008, in which Morales supporters were taken hostage and made to strip to the waist, kneel, and beg forgiveness in the city square, did not start until March 2011. The trial has since been repeatedly postponed.

Military Jurisdiction

The determination of Bolivia's military courts to assert jurisdiction over human rights abuses has been an obstacle to accountability for many years. The military has often refused to allow members of the armed forces to testify before civilian courts, instead insisting on trying the cases in military court, which invariably ends in acquittals.

In a case involving a 26-year-old conscript, Gróver Poma, who died in February 2011 following a hand-to-hand combat training exercise—allegedly after instructors beat him on the head and chest—the Supreme Military Tribunal insisted that a military court try three implicated officers. A military investigation claimed Poma's death had been accidental, while the human rights ombudsman concluded that he had been brutally beaten. The military disregarded the ombudsman's requests to hand the case to a civilian court. It also disregarded a Senate resolution ordering it to do so, appealing the resolution before the Constitutional Court. Meanwhile, an investigation by a civilian prosecutor continued. At this writing the military still insisted on retaining jurisdiction. In

September 2011 the civilian prosecutor began criminal proceedings against four junior officers who allegedly participated in the beating, but at this writing the military had still insisted on retaining jurisdiction.

In October 2010 the armed forces did agree to order four officers to appear before a civilian judge in a case involving the water torture of a recruit during a training exercise, after President Morales ordered that a civilian court try those responsible. In April 2011 the judge dropped charges against four suspects after accepting a defense argument that torture could only be committed against someone in detention, and ordered their release. However, in July an appeals court overruled this decision, and the case continued at this writing.

Excessive Use of Force

In September 2011, police in riot gear used tear gas and batons to disperse demonstrators marching against a proposed highway project through the Isiboro-Sécure National Park, a protected indigenous territory in the Bolivian tropics. More than one hundred protesters were injured, according to the Bolivia office of the Office of the United Nations High Commissioner on Human Rights. The previous day, after skirmishes in which some police were reportedly wounded by arrows, the marchers had detained Foreign Minister David Choquehuanca, who had come to negotiate with them on the government's behalf, and forced him to march with them before releasing him. By the time the police acted the foreign minister had been released and the skirmishes had ended. On September 28 President Morales publicly apologized for the crack-down, saying there had been no presidential order to disperse the protesters.

Freedom of Media

Bolivia enjoys vibrant public debate, with a variety of critical and pro-govern-ment media outlets. However, in what remains a politically polarized atmos-phere, President Morales sometimes aggressively criticizes the press, accusing journalists of distorting facts and seeking to discredit him.

Under a law against racism and other forms of discrimination passed in October 2010, media that "authorize or publish racist or discriminatory ideas" can be fined and have their broadcasting licenses suspended. Journalists "spreading ideas based on racial superiority or hatred" could face up to five years in prison. Media outlets protested these provisions, claiming they were so broad they could be used against media and journalists critical of the government.

Regulations governing the application of the law, which Morales signed into law in January 2011, addressed these criticisms in part by defining punishable offenses more precisely. The regulations stipulate that outlets could not be suspended for longer than 360 days at a time. Media would not be liable under the law if they report on expressions of racism, or if they broadcast racist expressions by third parties in live transmissions provided they caution or cut off the speaker.

A law governing the October 16, 2011 elections to the Supreme Court and Constitutional Court, promulgated in June 2010, would have banned any media comment on the candidates in the final three months before the elections, allowing only the Supreme Court to give information about them. Following criticism by opposition and media groups, the Supreme Court presented an amendment at Morales's invitation, which Congress approved. It allowed candidates to participate in debates and give press interviews, while the press was permitted to praise and criticize candidates as well as publish information different from that issued by the Supreme Court. Paradoxically, however, media were still banned from showing opinion programs on the candidates or giving them space to publicize their candidacy.

A draft law on telecommunications tabled in Congress in May 2011 has a clause obliging all radio and TV outlets as well as cable networks to broadcast presidential messages to the nation at their own expense. The absence of any limitations in this provision raises concerns that it may be abused in situations where there is no public interest to justify state intervention in broadcasting content.

Human Rights Defenders

In April 2011 a public prosecutor brought charges against lawyers Jorge Quiroz and Claudia Lecoña, who were representing the parents of two students killed after police broke up a protest in May 2010 in Caranavi, a department of La Paz. They were accused of *desacato* ("lack of respect") toward Marcos Farfán, deputy minister for the interior and police, for saying that he had committed a "cowardly act" by accusing them of procuring women for sex. Even though many Latin American nations have abolished *desacato* provisions, Bolivia still retains them: insulting a government minister can incur a three-year prison sentence.

In 2010 government officials had accused Quiroz of a string of offenses, including drug-trafficking, immigration irregularities, trafficking prostitutes, and acting as an "infiltrator" for the United States embassy in the Caranavi protests. However, no proof was provided or charges leveled, raising concerns that the government was targeting Quiroz because of his accusations that government officials and police were responsible for the deaths of the Caranavi students.

Key International Actors

The US government has failed to reply to a request by the government of Bolivia, first made in November 2008, to extradite former President Gonzalo Sánchez de Lozada and two of his ministers so they can stand trial in Bolivia for the Black October events. In September 2011 UN High Commissioner for Human Rights Navi Pillay welcomed the sentences handed down by the Supreme Court as "an important step in the fight against impunity."

BRAZIL

Brazil is among the most influential democracies in regional and global affairs, yet it continues to confront very serious human rights challenges at home. Faced with high levels of violent crime, some Brazilian police units engage in abusive practices with impunity, instead of pursuing sound policing practices. Justice officials who seek to hold police officers accountable for unlawful practices face threats of violence. In August 2011 Judge Patricia Acioli was gunned down outside her home in the state of Rio de Janeiro, apparently in retaliation for ordering the detention of police officers suspected of murder.

Detention centers in various states are severely overcrowded, lengthy pre-trial detention is the norm, and torture continues to be a serious problem. Forced labor persists in some states despite federal efforts to eradicate it.

Public Security and Police Conduct

Widespread violence perpetrated by criminal gangs and abusive police plague many Brazilian cities. Violence especially impacts low-income communities. In Rio de Janeiro, for example, drug gangs that routinely engage in violent crime and extortion control hundreds of shantytowns. In November 2010, drug gangs unleashed a wave of attacks in the streets of Rio, setting vehicles ablaze and staging mass robberies, leading to massive deployment of police and armed forces to the Complexo do Alemão community.

Police abuse, including extrajudicial execution, is also a chronic problem. According to official data, police were responsible for 372 killings in the state of Rio de Janeiro and 252 killings in the state of São Paulo in the first six months of 2011. Police often claim these are "resistance" killings that occur in confrontations with criminals. While many police killings undoubtedly result from legitimate use of force by police officers, many others do not, a fact documented by Human Rights Watch and other groups and recognized by Brazilian criminal justice officials.

Reform efforts have fallen short because state criminal justice systems rely almost entirely on police investigators to resolve these cases, leaving the police largely to regulate themselves. In 2010 São Paulo's attorney general took an important step to address the problem of police violence by establishing that all cases involving alleged police abuse be investigated by a special unit of prosecutors.

The state of Rio de Janeiro launched the System of Goals and Results Tracking in 2009, whereby police are awarded financial compensation for meeting crime reduction targets. These targets were redesigned in January 2011 to include police homicides. In addition, almost 20 Pacifying Police Units (UPP) have been installed in Rio since 2008, in order to establish a more effective police presence at the community level. However, the state has not yet taken adequate steps to ensure that police who commit abuses are held accountable.

Many Rio communities formerly controlled by drug dealers are now in the hands of militias composed of police, jail guards, firefighters, and others who coerce residents to pay for illegal utility hookups, transportation, and security. These militias have been implicated in execution-style killings, far-reaching extortion schemes, and the kidnapping and torture of a group of journalists investigating their activities. In October 2011 Rio Congressman Marcelo Freixo announced his decision to leave Brazil temporarily due to escalating death threats. He presided over a parliamentary commission of inquiry that investigated militia activity in Rio in 2008 and has been outspoken in denouncing links between certain militia groups and local elected officials.

Judges and magistrates who take on cases of violence by illegal militia face threats of violence. In August 2011 Judge Patricia Lourival Acioli was gunned down outside her home in the city of São Gonçalo, apparently in retaliation for ordering the detention of police officers suspected of murder. She had received four death threats prior to her murder. The head of Rio's military police subsequently resigned and several São Gonçalo police officers were indicted. Nevertheless, the Brazilian Association of Judges has reported that the number of judicial workers requesting government protection increased 400 percent since Acioli's killing.

Detention Conditions, Torture, and Ill-Treatment of Detainees

Many Brazilian prisons and jails are violent and severely overcrowded. According to the Ministry of Justice's Penitentiary Information Integrated System (INFOPEN), Brazil's incarceration rate tripled over the last 15 years and the prison population now exceeds half a million people. Delays within the justice system contribute to the overcrowding: almost half of all inmates are in pre-trial detention. On July 4, 2011, Congress passed a law prohibiting pre-trial detention for crimes punishable by less than four years in jail.

Torture is a chronic problem throughout Brazil's detention centers and police stations. A 2010 report by the Pastoral Prison Commission documented cases of torture in 20 out of 26 Brazilian states. HIV and tuberculosis prevalence rates in Brazilian prisons are far higher than rates in the general population; inhumane conditions facilitate the spread of disease, and prisoners' access to medical care remains inadequate. In early September 2011, hundreds of detainees in Maranhão state rioted against prolonged pre-trial detention, unsanitary facilities, limited access to drinking water, and sexual abuse by prison wards. Rival factions killed at least 18 prisoners.

On September 30, 2011, President Dilma Roussef proposed legislation to create a national mechanism—the National System to Prevent and Combat Torture—to monitor detention centers throughout the country and investigate allegations of torture and ill-treatment.

Women's Health and Reproductive Rights

Although Brazil has significantly lowered its maternal mortality rate over the last two decades, national statistics mask severe disparities based on race, economic status, region, and urban or rural settings. In August 2011 the United Nations Committee on the Elimination of All Forms of Discrimination Against Women held that in the case of Alyne da Silva Pimental, who died after being denied timely care at a public health facility, Brazil failed to fulfill its obligation to guarantee timely, nondiscriminatory, and appropriate maternal health services.

The Brazilian Criminal Code criminalizes abortion except in cases of rape or when necessary to save a woman's life. Women and girls who undertake the procedure voluntarily may be sentenced to up to three years in jail, and their doctors to up to ten years. Raids on family planning clinics and aggressive prosecution of abortion further limit women's and girls' access to reproductive health services. There are currently more than 40 draft laws before the House of Representatives proposing to further restrict access to contraception or punish abortion more harshly. The Health Ministry estimates that more than one million illegal abortions are performed every year and hundreds of women and girls annually seek hospital attention due to complications arising from illicit abortions.

Sexual Orientation and Gender Identity

In May 2011 the Supreme Court unanimously decided to legalize same-sex civil unions in light of the constitutional guarantee of non-discrimination. Same-sex spouses now have the same legal rights as their heterosexual counterparts: broader health insurance coverage, hospital visits, pension plans, and inheritance rights. The following month a trial court in the state of São Paulo recognized the first same-sex civil marriage in Brazil. The Superior Justice Court followed suit in October, setting an important precedent by interpreting the Brazilian Civil Code as allowing same-sex marriages.

Forced Labor

The federal government has taken important steps to eradicate forced labor since 1995, including creating mobile investigation units to examine conditions in rural areas and publishing a "black list" of employers found to have used forced labor. Official data suggests that more than 39,000 workers have been freed since 1995. However, the Pastoral Land Commission reported that more than 4,000 workers were subject to forced labor in 2010. Criminal accountability for offending employers remains relatively rare.

Rural Violence

Indigenous leaders and rural activists continue to face threats and violence. According to the Pastoral Land Commission, 34 people were killed and 55 were victims of attempted murder throughout the country in 2010. Over 1,900 rural activists have received death threats over the past decade; of these 42 have been killed. The south of Pará state has long been a focal point of rural violence, but frontier areas where illegal loggers and ranchers operate in Maranhão, Mato Grosso, and Rondônia states are becoming dangerous for environmentalists and government officials alike.

Confronting Past Abuses

Brazil has granted over US$1 billion in financial compensation to more than 12,000 victims of abuses committed by state agents during the military dictatorship from 1964 to 1985. On October 26, 2011, Congress approved a law creating a truth commission charged with "examining and clarifying" human rights abuses committed between 1946 and 1988.

However, there has been little progress in prosecuting those responsible for atrocities. A 1979 amnesty law has thus far been interpreted to bar prosecutions of state agents, an interpretation that the Supreme Court reaffirmed in April 2010.

Freedom of Expression and Access to Information

In July 2009 the Federal District Court of Justice issued an injunction prohibiting the newspaper O Estado de São Paulo from publishing stories containing information on the "Operação Faktor" police investigation involving Fernando Sarney, son of Senate President José Sarney. Despite strenuous criticism from national and international press freedom organizations, the Supreme Court upheld the ruling in December 2009.

On June 15, 2011, the Supreme Court unanimously held that peaceful demonstrations calling for marijuana to be legalized are protected under the constitutional guarantees of freedom of expression and assembly. Certain state judges have prohibited such demonstrations on the grounds that they encouraged or glorified drug use.

In September 2011 the host of a radio show on Radio Frontera, Vanderlei Canuto Leandro, was shot by unidentified assailants in the city of Tabatinga, Amazonas state, purportedly in retaliation of his investigations of corruption by local government officials. It was the fifth such killing of a journalist in Brazil in 2011, according to the Inter-American system's special rapporteur for freedom of expression.

Key International Actors

The Inter-American system has played an important role in addressing key human rights issues. In November 2010 the Inter-American Court of Human Rights ruled that Brazil's amnesty law cannot prevent the investigation and prosecution of serious human rights violations and crimes against humanity committed by state agents during the military regime. In resolutions in February and September 2011 the court also instructed the state of Espírito Santo to take steps to address alleged abuses against juveniles detained at the Unidade de Internação Socioeducativa (UNIS) detention center.

In April 2011 the Inter-American Commission on Human Rights issued precautionary measures for Brazil due to an alleged failure to consult with indigenous groups prior to beginning the construction of the Belo Monte hydroelectric dam, slated to be the world's third largest. The Rousseff administration publicly rejected the commission's findings and characterized them as "premature and unjustified." On July 29, 2011, the commission modified its precautionary measures on the basis of information provided by the Brazilian government. A federal judge in the state of Pará enjoined work at the Xingu River basin in September 2011 in order to protect local fish stocks deemed essential to the livelihood of indigenous communities. The consortium building the dam appealed the decision in November.

In May 2011 the UN special rapporteur on contemporary forms of slavery encouraged Brazil to strengthen efforts to close loopholes perpetuating the practice of slavery, including forced labor in the country's rural areas.

Brazil has emerged as an important and influential voice in debates over international responses to human rights issues at the UN. At the UN Human Rights Council during the July 2010 to June 2011 period, Brazil consistently voted in support of resolutions addressing country situations, including on Sudan, North Korea, Iran, Belarus, and Syria. However, at the UN Security Council in October 2011 it refused to support a resolution condemning state-sponsored violence in Syria.

CHILE

Sebastián Piñera's government has reformed Chile's counterterrorism law and military justice system, eliminating important elements that were incompatible with international standards of due process. Nonetheless, while military courts no longer exercise jurisdiction over civilians, they continue to try police accused of human rights abuses. And while the Piñera administration has not pressed "terrorism" charges against indigenous protesters, some prosecutors have continued to charge them under the counterterrorism law for actions that should be considered common crimes.

The government took some important steps in 2011 to remedy overcrowding and inhumane conditions in Chilean prisons, but they remain a serious problem.

Most recorded cases of extrajudicial executions and enforced disappearances committed during military rule (1973-1990) have been heard in court or are now under judicial investigation. Judges continue to convict former military personnel for these crimes. However, given the seriousness of the crimes, final sentences are often unacceptably lenient.

Police Abuses

Cases of excessive use of force by police when dealing with detainees during demonstrations and Mapuche land occupations continue to be reported. In August 2011 a carabinero (uniformed policeman) shot and killed a 16-year-old student, Manuel Gutiérrez Reynoso, who had been watching a demonstration from a Santiago footbridge during a national strike. A police general—who had brushed aside accusations that the police were responsible for the incident—was fired, together with the alleged culprit and several other junior officers. A military prosecutor was investigating the case at the end of September.

Since 2002, police have been responsible for the deaths of at least three Mapuches (Chile's largest indigenous group). A military court trial of a police sergeant who, in August 2009, shot dead Jaime Mendoza Collío, a 24-year-old Mapuche who had been participating in a land occupation near Ercilla, continued in 2011. Police claimed the officer acted in self- defense, but forensic reports indicated the bullet hit Mendoza's back and that he had not fired a weapon.

Military Jurisdiction

Following the recommendations of the Inter-American Court of Human Rights in its 2005 ruling against Chile in the Palamara case, legislation introduced by Piñera's administration— and approved by Congress in September 2010—finally ended the jurisdiction of military courts over civilians. However, the reforms did not address jurisdiction over abuses against civilians by police, which is still exercised by military courts that are not fully independent.

Counterterrorism Laws

The inappropriate use of counterterrorism legislation to deal with common crimes against property, such as arson committed by indigenous Mapuche activists, remains an important due process issue. In September 2010, following concern expressed by the United Nations and regional human rights bodies and a hunger strike by Mapuche prisoners, the government amended the counterterrorism law. Some due process guarantees were strengthened, such as allowing witnesses whose identity can be concealed by prosecutors to be cross-examined by defense attorneys. However, the inclusion in the law of crimes against property without violence to persons was left unchanged, and public prosecutors continued to apply the law to such cases.

In February 2011 a court in Cañete, in the Araucanía region, sentenced a Mapuche leader to 25 years in prison and three others to 20 years for "the attempted murder" of a senior prosecutor and the "robbery with intimidation" of a landowner. The charges were initially brought under the counterterrorism law, but the court dismissed terrorism charges against all the defendants, and acquitted 17 other defendants. Defense lawyers appealed the convictions, alleging the court had allowed counterterrorism procedures such as the use of anonymous witnesses during the trial even though it had thrown out counterterrorism charges. In June the Supreme Court downgraded the murder charge to one of "wounding" and reduced the 25 and 20 year sentences to 14 and 8 years respectively.

In May 2011 the National Institute of Human Rights, an official body created in 2009 to promote and defend human rights, issued a statement criticizing use of counterterrorism law against Mapuches.

Prison Conditions

Conditions in many prisons are deplorable. Sanitation, ventilation, and nutrition are poor and potable water insufficient. Despite conditions conducive to ill-health and the spread of infectious disease, access to medical care remains inadequate. In December 2010, 81 prisoners died and 14 were seriously injured in a fire at Santiago's San Miguel prison that started after a fight between inmates in which a flame thrower made from gas cylinder was used. The prison, which has room for 1,100 inmates, held 1,900 prisoners at the time; only four prison guards were reportedly on duty inside the building.

In his annual address in March 2011 Chief Justice Milton Juica stated that the prison system was in "absolute collapse" and constituted a "grave lack of respect for the rights and guarantees of those who are deprived of their liberty." Government officials acknowledged that prisons were 60 percent over capacity, reaching 200 percent in the worst affected ones. According to a report issued in March 2010 by a government-appointed prison review commission, the problems stem from delays in building new facilities, the introduction of faster criminal procedures and harsher sentencing policies, and the failure to effectively implement alternatives to prison.

Responding to the crisis, the Ministry of Justice has introduced legislation to allow the release of low-risk prisoners, and to strengthen alternatives to custodial sentences. In August 2011 the Senate approved two bills to this effect: the first allows the release of individuals imprisoned for non-payment of fines, and would prevent their future incarceration by replacing prison sentences for this offense with community service; the second allows the release of convicted prisoners already on day release and women who had served two-thirds of their sentence, unless serious crimes were involved. At this writing approval of the legislation depended on a vote in the Chamber of Deputies.

Confronting Past Abuses

More than three-quarters of the 3,186 documented killings and "disappearances" under military rule have been heard by courts or are now under court jurisdiction, according to Diego Portales University's Human Rights Observatory, an NGO that monitors progress in human rights trials. By the end of May 2011, 1,446 judicial investigations into human rights abuses under military rule had been completed or were underway, and 245 former security service agents had been convicted and sentenced in the final instance. However, only 66 were actually serving prison sentences at the end of May.

In many cases, the Supreme Court has used its discretionary powers to reduce sentences against human rights violators in recognition of the time elapsed since the criminal act. Often the sentence finally imposed is low enough to exempt those convicted from going to prison. This practice raises concerns about Chile's fulfillment of its obligation to hold accountable perpetrators of crimes against humanity by imposing appropriate punishment or sanctions.

Reproductive Rights

Chile is one of only three countries in Latin America (El Salvador and Nicaragua are the other two) with an absolute prohibition on abortion, even in cases of medical necessity. The prohibition has existed in Chile's Constitution since 1989. Women prevented from receiving therapeutic abortions sometimes turn to unsafe and clandestine procedures that can threaten their life and safety. Such an absolute prohibition violates a woman's fundamental right to the highest attainable standard of health, life, nondiscrimination, physical integrity, and freedom from cruel, inhuman, or degrading treatment. Legislation pending before Congress would provide avenues for legal therapeutic abortions in certain cases.

Sexual Orientation and Gender Identity

In August 2011 Piñera tabled a bill in the Senate seeking to legalize informal unions, whether of heterosexual or gay couples, a reform he had promised during the 2009 electoral campaign. Some 2 million Chileans currently live in informal unions without the legal rights that married couples enjoy.

Following the presentation of a writ asking for protection of their constitutional rights by two gay couples, the Santiago Appeals Court asked the Constitutional Tribunal to rule on the constitutionality of a civil code article affirming that marriage is a contract between a man and a woman. In November the court ruled that the regulation of marriage was a legal and not a constitutional matter, and was therefore subject to a vote in the legislature.

In November the Senate voted to include discrimination based on gender or sexual orientation in an anti-discrimination bill currently under debate in the legislature.

Key International Actors

In August 2011 the Inter-American Commission on Human Rights took the case of seven Mapuche leaders and a pro-Mapuche activist who were tried in 2003 under Chile's counterterrorism law to the Inter-American Court of Human Rights, alleging their prosecution under the law was discriminatory.

COLOMBIA

Colombia's internal armed conflict continued to result in serious abuses by irregular armed groups in 2011, including guerrillas and successor groups to paramilitaries. Violence has displaced millions of Colombians internally, and continues to displace tens of thousands every year. Armed actors frequently threaten or attack human rights defenders, journalists, community leaders, teachers, trade unionists, indigenous and Afro-Colombian leaders, displaced persons' leaders, and paramilitaries' victims seeking land restitution or justice.

During its first year in office, President Juan Manuel Santos' administration showed a greater concern for human rights than the government of former President Álvaro Uribe, which was racked by scandals over extrajudicial killings by the army, a highly questioned paramilitary demobilization process, and abuses by the national intelligence service. In 2011 President Santos won the passage of the Victims and Land Restitution Law, which aims to return millions of acres of land to displaced persons and provide financial compensation to victims of human rights abuses and of violations of international humanitarian law.

However, paramilitary successor groups continue to grow, maintain extensive ties with public security force members and local officials, and commit widespread atrocities. There has also been ongoing violence against rights defenders, community leaders, and trade unionists. Candidates campaigning for the nationwide and local elections in October 2011 were also frequently killed amid reports of alleged links between candidates and armed groups. According to the Colombian NGO Mision de Observacion Electoral, 40 candidates were killed in 2011, representing a 48 percent increase in such crimes reported during the 2007 local elections. Moreover, new constitutional reform proposals promoted by the Santos administration could facilitate impunity for human rights abuses by giving a greater role to military courts in prosecuting military abuses, and by opening the possibility for amnesties for serious violations by all actors.

Guerrilla Abuses

The Revolutionary Armed Forces of Colombia (FARC) and the National Liberation Army (ELN) continue to commit serious abuses against civilians. The FARC especially is often involved in killings, threats, forced displacement, and recruiting and using child soldiers. On May 22, 2011, presumed FARC members attacked a boat traveling down the Atrato River in Choco department, killing three civilians and injuring another two.

The FARC and ELN frequently use antipersonnel landmines and other indiscriminate weapons. The government reported 16 civilians killed and 104 injured by landmines and unexploded munitions between January and August 2011. On July 9, 2011, the FARC set off a car bomb and fired homemade explosives in the town of Toribio in Cauca department, killing three civilians, injuring 122, and destroying dozens of homes.

Guerrilla groups are believed to be responsible for some of the threats and attacks against candidates in the local October 2011 elections. On May 30, 2011, the FARC reportedly killed two mayoral candidates in the municipality of Campamento in Antioquia department.

In November 2011 the Colombian military killed top FARC leader Guillermo León Sáenz, alias "Alfonso Cano," during a military operation in Cauca department.

Paramilitaries and Their Successors

Since 2003 more than 30,000 individuals have participated in a paramilitary demobilization process, although there is substantial evidence that many of the participants were not paramilitaries, and that a portion of the groups remain active.

Implementation of the Justice and Peace Law, which offers dramatically reduced sentences to demobilized paramilitaries who confess their atrocities, has been slow and uneven. At this writing, more than six years after the law was approved, special prosecutors had only obtained three convictions and recovered a small fraction of paramilitaries' illegally acquired assets. Paramilitary leaders' confessions in the Justice and Peace process suffered a setback when former President Uribe extradited most paramilitary leaders to the United States between May 2008 and August 2009 to face drug trafficking crimes.

Successor groups to the paramilitaries, led largely by members of demobilized paramilitary organizations, have grown to have approximately 5,700 members, according to official numbers as of October 2011. Toleration of the groups by public security force members is a main factor for their continued power. At least 180 police officers were jailed in 2011 because of alleged ties to successor groups.

Like the paramilitary organizations that demobilized, the groups engage in drug trafficking; actively recruit members, including children; and commit widespread abuses against civilians, including massacres, killings, rapes and other forms of sexual violence, threats, and forced displacement. They have repeatedly targeted human rights defenders, Afro-Colombian and indigenous leaders, trade unionists, and victims' groups seeking justice and recovery of land. Successor groups appear to be responsible for the 34 percent increase in cases of massacres registered in 2010 and the continued rise in cases reported during the first half of 2011. (The government defines a massacre as the killing of four or more people at the same time.) In January 2011 Colombia's national police chief publicly stated that such groups are the largest source of violence in Colombia.

Paramilitary Accomplices

Colombia's Supreme Court has in recent years made considerable progress investigating Colombian Congress members accused of collaborating with paramilitaries. In the "parapolitics" scandal, more than 120 former Congress members have been investigated, and approximately 40 convicted. In February 2011 former Senator Mario Uribe—former president of the Colombian Congress and second cousin of former President Uribe—was convicted for ties with paramilitaries. While demobilized paramilitaries have also made statements about extensive collaboration with local politicians, senior military officers, and businesspersons, the Attorney General's Office's investigations into such persons have advanced slowly.

There are concerns of ongoing infiltration of the political system by paramilitaries and their successor groups. As of September 2011 the Supreme Court had opened investigations against 10 current members of Congress for allegedly having had ties to paramilitaries. Colombia's Ombudsman's Office reported that 119 municipalities faced a high risk of electoral violence or interference by paramilitary successor groups during the October 2011 local elections.

In 2011 two former paramilitaries publicly claimed that former President Uribe had been directly involved with a paramilitary group while governor of Antioquia department in the 1990s. Uribe has denied the allegations.

Military Abuses and Impunity

Over the past decade the Colombian Army has committed an alarming number of extrajudicial killings of civilians. In many cases—commonly referred to as "false positives"—army personnel murdered civilians and reported them as combatants killed in action, apparently in response to pressure to boost body counts. The executions occurred throughout Colombia and involved multiple army brigades.

The government does not keep statistics for cases of "false positives" as a separate category of crimes, but the Office of the United Nations High Commissioner for Human Rights (OHCHR) in Colombia estimates that more than 3,000 people may have been victims of extrajudicial killings by state agents, and that the majority of cases were committed by the army between 2004 and 2008. There has been a dramatic reduction in cases since 2008; however, some alleged cases of extrajudicial killings attributed to state agents were reported in 2010 and 2011.

Investigations into such cases have advanced slowly: as of September 2011 the Human Rights Unit of the Attorney General's Office was investigating 1,622 cases of alleged extrajudicial killings committed by state agents involving 2,788 victims, and had obtained convictions for 77 cases. In July 2011 a judge convicted former army Col. Luis Fernando Borja Giraldo, the highest-ranking military officer to be sentenced for "false positives" at this writing.

Accountability achieved to date is due to the fact that civilian prosecutors are investigating most cases. However, as of July 2011, more than 400 cases involving alleged extrajudicial killings remained in the military justice system, where there is little chance that justice will be obtained.

At this writing the government had backed two constitutional reform proposals that threaten to facilitate impunity for military abuses: a "justice reform" bill that would increase the likelihood that military abuse cases are handled by military courts, and a "transitional justice" bill that would allow Congress, at the president's behest, to authorize the Attorney General's Office to drop prosecutions for human rights violations, including those committed by members of the military.

Abuses by National Intelligence Service

In October 2011 President Santos dissolved the National Intelligence Service (DAS), the Colombian intelligence service that answers directly to the president's office, and announced the creation of a new intelligence agency. In recent years media and judicial investigations revealed that the DAS, during the Uribe presidency, had illegally spied on the Supreme Court, as well as trade unionists, human rights defenders, journalists, and opposition politicians. The DAS has also been implicated in other criminal activity, including death threats, smear campaigns against government critics, and collaboration with paramilitaries. In September 2011 Jorge Noguera Cotes, who directed the DAS from 2002 to 2005, was convicted of having put the intelligence agency at the service of paramilitary groups, including in the 2004 killing of a university professor.

Violence against Trade Unionists

While the number of trade unionists killed every year is less today than a decade ago, it remains higher than any other country in the world: 51 trade unionists were murdered in 2008, 47 in 2009, 51 in 2010, and 26 from January to November 15, 2011, according to the National Labor School (ENS), Colombia's leading NGO monitoring labor rights. Threats against trade unionists—primarily attributed to paramilitary successor groups—have increased since 2007.

Impunity for anti-union violence is widespread: Colombia has obtained convictions for less than 10 percent of the more than 2,900 trade unionist killings reported by the ENS since 1986. As of June 2011 the Attorney General's Office's sub-unit of prosecutors dedicated to anti-union violence had opened investigations into 787 cases of trade unionist killings and reached a conviction for more than 185 such killings.

The sub-unit has made virtually no progress in obtaining convictions for recent killings. Of the more than 195 trade unionist killings that have occurred since the sub-unit started operating in 2007, the special office had obtained convictions in only six cases as of May 2011. It had not obtained a single conviction for the more than 60 homicide attempts, 1,500 threats, and 420 forced displacements reported by the ENS during this period.

Internal Displacement

Tens of thousands of Colombians continue to be forcibly displaced every year. The state agency Social Action has registered 3.7 million displaced persons between 1997 and May 2011, compared to 5.3 million that the respected Colombian NGO CODHES reports between 1985 and June 2011. Social Action registered more than 100,000 newly displaced people in 2010, while CODHES reports nearly 300,000 newly displaced during that year. The Permanent Human Rights Unit of the Personería of Medellín documented an 81 percent increase in reported cases of intra-urban displacement during the first half of 2011 in Medellín, where paramilitary successor groups are active. Massive displacements (affecting more than 10 households or 50 people) also increased in 2011, with Social Action reporting 80 cases between January and early November 2011, as compared to 59 in all of 2010.

The government's land restitution efforts have coincided with a rise in attacks and threats against leaders of displaced communities campaigning for land recovery. Nine leaders of displaced persons involved in such activity were murdered during the first half of 2011, according to CODHES.

Sexual Violence

Impunity remains a problem in cases of sexual violence, particularly conflict-related violence. In a 2008 decision the Constitutional Court recognized that sexual violence against women is "a habitual, extended, systematic and invisible practice in the context of the Colombian armed conflict … [perpetrated] by all illegal armed groups, and in some isolated cases, by individual agents of the public security forces." It instructed the Attorney General's Office to further investigate specific cases. Progress in these cases has been slow.

Legal Capacity of People with Disabilities

Colombia ratified the Convention on the Rights of Persons with Disabilities in May 2011. To comply with the standards established in the convention, it will need to adjust domestic legislation and policies to ensure that people with disabilities are not stripped of their legal capacity, resulting in restrictions on the right to vote, property rights, and the right to free and informed consent.

Human Rights Defenders

Human rights defenders are routinely threatened and attacked. In June 2011 a death threat signed by a paramilitary successor group called the "Rastrojos" targeted numerous rights organizations and individual defenders, including several prominent advocates for the rights of women and internally displaced persons.

The Ministry of Interior runs a protection program that covers more than 8,000 members of vulnerable groups, including human rights defenders and trade unionists.

Key International Actors

The US remains the most influential foreign actor in Colombia. In 2011 it provided approximately US$562 million in aid, about 61 percent of which was military and police aid. Thirty percent of US military aid is subject to human rights conditions, which the US Department of State has not enforced. In September 2011 the State Department certified that Colombia was meeting human rights conditions.

In October 2011 US President Barack Obama signed into the law the US-Colombia Free Trade Agreement, a treaty the US Congress had delayed ratifying for nearly five years, in part due to violence against trade unionists and impunity for that violence. In April 2011 Colombia and the US signed an "Action Plan" outlining key steps that Colombia had to take to protect workers' rights as a precondition for ratification; however, the commitments failed to address the paramilitary successor groups believed to be responsible for a large portion of anti-union violence.

The United Kingdom reportedly reduced military assistance to Colombia in 2009, apparently due to scandals over illegal surveillance and extrajudicial executions. The European Union provides social and economic assistance to Colombia.

The Organization of American States' Mission to Support the Peace Process in Colombia, charged with verifying paramilitary demobilizations, issued a report in 2011 expressing alarm over the activities of paramilitary successor groups and noting that, "massacres have continued, wiping out entire families."

The Office of the Prosecutor of the International Criminal Court continued to monitor local investigations into human rights crimes. OHCHR is active in Colombia, and in November 2010 its mandate in the country was extended for three years. The International Committee of the Red Cross is also active in Colombia, and its work includes providing assistance to internally displaced persons.

In October 2010 Colombia was elected as a non-permanent member of the UN Security Council for 2011-2012.

CUBA

Cuba remains the only country in Latin America that represses virtually all forms of political dissent. In 2011 Raúl Castro's government continued to enforce political conformity using short-term detentions, beatings, public acts of repudiation, forced exile, and travel restrictions.

In 2011 the Cuban government freed the remaining 12 political prisoners from the "group of 75" dissidents—human rights defenders, journalists, and labor leaders who were sentenced in 2003 in summary trials for exercising their basic rights—having forced most into exile in exchange for their freedom. Also in 2011 the government sentenced at least seven more dissidents to prison for exercising their fundamental rights, and human rights groups on the island said dozens more remain in prison.

The government increasingly relied on arbitrary arrests and short-term detentions to restrict the basic rights of its critics, including the right to assemble and move about freely. Cuba's government also pressured dissidents to choose between exile and continued repression or even imprisonment, leading scores to leave the country with their families during 2011.

Political Prisoners

Cubans who criticize the government are subject to criminal charges. They are exempt from due process guarantees, such as the right to a defense or fair and public hearings by a competent, independent, and impartial tribunal. In practice, courts are "subordinated" to the executive and legislative branches, denying meaningful judicial protection.

Dozens of political prisoners remain in Cuban prisons, according to respected human rights groups on the island. In June 2011 the Cuban Council of Human Rights Rapporteurs issued a list of 43 prisoners whom it said were still incarcerated for political reasons. In May 2011, four dissidents from Havana—Luis Enrique Labrador, David Piloto, Walfrido Rodríguez, and Yordani Martínez—were prosecuted on charges of contempt and public disorder for demonstrating in Havana's Revolutionary Square and throwing leaflets with slogans such as

"Down with the Castros." They were sentenced to three to five years in prison. The council estimates that there are many more political prisoners whose cases they cannot document because the government does not let independent national or international human rights groups access its prisons.

Arbitrary Detentions and Short-Term Imprisonment

In addition to criminal prosecution, Raul Castro's government has increasingly relied on arbitrary detention to harass and intimidate individuals who exercise their fundamental rights. The Cuban Commission for Human Rights and National Reconciliation documented 2,074 arbitrary detentions by security forces in 2010, and 2,224 between January and August 2011. The detentions are often used preemptively to prevent individuals from participating in meetings or events viewed as critical of the government.

Security officers hardly ever present arrest orders to justify detentions, and threaten detainees with criminal prosecution if they continue to participate in "counterrevolutionary" activities. Victims of such arbitrary arrests said they were held incommunicado for several hours to several days, often at police sta- tions. Some received an official warning (*acta de advertencia*), which prosecu- tors may later use in criminal trials to show a pattern of delinquent behavior. Dissidents said these warnings aimed to dissuade them from participating in future activities considered critical of the government.

For example, on July 24, 2011, state security agents arbitrarily detained 28 human rights activists for 4 to 30 hours in Palma Soriano, Santiago de Cuba province, when they tried to participate in a religious service to pray for the release of political prisoners.

Forced Exile

The death of political prisoner Orlando Zapata Tamayo in February 2010 follow- ing his 85-day hunger strike, and the subsequent hunger strike by dissident Guillermo Fariñas, pressured the Cuban government to release the remaining political prisoners from the "group of 75," who were detained during a 2003 crackdown on dissent. Yet while the final 12 prisoners from the group were released in March 2011, most were forced to choose between ongoing prison and forced exile.

Since that time dozens of other prominent dissidents, journalists, and human rights defenders have been forced to choose between exile and ongoing harassment or even imprisonment. For example, Néstor Rodríguez Lobaina, an outspoken human rights activist, former political prisoner, and president of a dissident youth group in Guantánamo, was arrested in December 2010. Held for months while awaiting trial, he said authorities told him that unless he agreed to go into exile, he would be sentenced to five years of prison. He accepted forced exile to Spain in April 2011.

Freedom of Expression

The government maintains a media monopoly on the island, ensuring there is virtually no freedom of expression. The government controls all media outlets in Cuba, and access to outside information is highly restricted. Limited internet access means only a tiny fraction of Cubans can read independently published articles and blogs.

Although a few independent journalists and bloggers manage to write articles for foreign websites or independent blogs, they must publish work through back channels, such as writing from home computers, saving information on memory sticks, and uploading articles and posts through illegal internet connections; others dictate articles to contacts abroad.

Independent journalists and bloggers are subjected to short-term arrests and harassment by police and state security agents, as well as threats of imprisonment if they continue to work. For example, independent journalists Magaly Norvis Otero Suárez and Roberto de Jesús Guerra Pérez were detained and beaten in Havana on February 23, 2011, as they walked to an event with two members of the Women in White—a respected human rights group comprised of wives, mothers, and daughters of political prisoners—to honor the one year anniversary of Orlando Zapata Tamayo's death. They later said they were transported to a police station, where they were assaulted and held incommunicado for roughly 14 hours.

Bloggers and independent journalists have also been the victims of public smear campaigns, such as a March 2011 episode of a government-produced news program—broadcast widely on public television—which referred to independent bloggers as "cyber-mercenaries" and "puppets of the empire."

The Cuban government uses the granting of press credentials and visas, which foreign journalists need to report from the island, to control coverage of Cuba and punish media outlets considered overly critical of the regime. In September, for example, the government refused to renew the press credentials of a journalist from Spain's *El Pais* newspaper, arguing he presented a biased and negative image of Cuba.

Human Rights Defenders

Refusing to recognize human rights monitoring as a legitimate activity, Cuba's government denies legal status to local human rights groups and uses harassment, beatings, and imprisonment to punish human rights defenders who try to document abuses. For example, Enyor Díaz Allen, Juan Luis Bravo Rodríguez, and Óscar Savón Pantoja—members of a human rights group in Guantanamó— were trying to enter a hospital on March 10 to visit a dissident on a hunger strike when security forces detained and transferred them without explanation to a police station and held them for three days in solitary confinement, Díaz Allen said.

Travel Restrictions and Family Separation

The Cuban government forbids the country's citizens from leaving or returning to Cuba without first obtaining official permission, which is often denied. For example, well-known blogger Yoani Sanchez, who has criticized the government, has been denied the right to leave the island to accept awards and participate in conferences at least 16 times in the past four years. The government uses widespread fear of forced family separation to punish defectors and silence critics, and frequently bars citizens engaged in authorized travel from taking their children with them overseas, essentially holding the latter hostage to guarantee their parents' return.

The government restricts the movement of citizens within Cuba by enforcing a 1997 law known as Decree 217. Designed to limit migration to Havana, the decree requires that Cubans obtain government permission before moving to the capital. It is often used to prevent dissidents from traveling to Havana to attend meetings, and to harass dissidents from other parts of Cuba who live in the capital.

Prison Conditions

Prisons are overcrowded, unhygienic, and unhealthy, leading to extensive malnutrition and illness. Prisoners who criticize the government, refuse to undergo ideological "reeducation," or engage in hunger strikes and other protests are often subjected to extended solitary confinement, beatings, and visit restrictions, and denied medical care. Prisoners have no effective complaint mechanism to seek redress, giving prison authorities total impunity.

Key International Actors

The United States's economic embargo on Cuba, in place for more than half a century, continues to impose indiscriminate hardship on Cubans, and has failed to improve human rights in the country. At the United Nations General Assembly in October, 186 of the 192 member countries voted for a resolution condemning the US embargo; only the US and Israel voted against it.

In January 2011 US President Barack Obama used his executive powers to ease "people-to-people" travel restrictions, allowing religious, educational, and cultural groups from the US to travel to Cuba, and permitting Americans to send remittances to assist Cuban citizens. In 2009 Obama eliminated limits on travel and remittances by Cuban Americans to Cuba, which had been instituted during George W. Bush's administration.

In March US citizen Alan Gross—a subcontractor for the US Agency for International Development—was sentenced to 15 years in jail for distributing telecommunications equipment for religious groups in Cuba. Gross was detained in December 2009 and accused by state prosecutors of engaging in a "subversive project aiming at bringing down the revolution." Cuba's highest court upheld his sentence in August. He remains in prison.

The European Union continues to retain its "Common Position" on Cuba, adopted in 1996, which conditions full economic cooperation with Cuba on its transition to a pluralist democracy and respect for human rights.

At this writing Cuba's government had yet to ratify the core international human rights treaties—the International Covenant on Civil and Political Rights and the International Covenant on Economic, Social and Cultural Rights—which it signed in February 2008. Cuba is currently serving a three-year term on the UN Human Rights Council, having been re-elected in May 2009.

ECUADOR

In a referendum held in May 2011, President Rafael Correa obtained a popular mandate for constitutional reforms that could significantly increase government powers to constrain media and influence the appointment and dismissal of judges.

Those involved in protests in which there are outbreaks of violence may be prosecuted on inflated and inappropriate terrorism charges. Criminal defamation laws that restrict freedom of expression remain in force and Correa has used them repeatedly against his critics. Some articles of a draft communications law in the legislature since 2009 could open the door to media censorship.

Misuse of Anti-Terror Laws in Dealing with Social Protests

Prosecutors have applied a "terrorism and sabotage" provision of the criminal code in cases involving protests against mining and oil projects and in other incidents that have ended in confrontations with police. Involvement in acts of violence or obstructing roads during such protests should be ordinary criminal offenses. Yet Ecuador's criminal code includes, under the category of sabotage and terrorism, "crimes against the common security of people or human groups of whatever kind or against their property," by individuals or associations "whether armed or not." Such crimes carry a possible prison sentence of four to eight years. In July 2011 the Center for Economic and Social Rights, an Ecuadorian human rights group, reported that 189 indigenous people were facing terrorism and sabotage charges. Most of them were in hiding and only eight had been convicted.

Accountability

Impunity for police abuses is widespread and those responsible for murders often attributed to a "settling of accounts" between criminal gangs are rarely brought to justice. In June 2010 a truth commission created by the Correa administration published a report documenting 68 extrajudicial executions and

17 enforced disappearances between 1984 and 2008, and named 458 alleged perpetrators of abuses. According to the commission, few of those responsible for the abuses had been held accountable, due to statutes of limitations, jurisdictional disputes, and procedural delays. In October 2010 the attorney general appointed a team of prosecutors to reopen investigations into cases reported by the commission. As of September 2011 the prosecutors were reported to have renewed investigations into several key cases, but no suspects had been charged.

Freedom of Expression

Ecuador's Criminal Code still has provisions criminalizing *desacato* ("lack of respect"), under which anyone who offends a government official may receive a prison sentence up to three months and up to two years for offending the president. In September 2011 the Constitutional Court agreed to consider a challenge to the constitutionality of these provisions submitted by Fundamedios, an Ecuadorian press freedom advocacy group. A new criminal code presented by the government to the National Assembly in October does not include the crime of *desacato*, but if approved would still mandate prison sentences of up to three years for those who defame public authorities.

Under the existing code, journalists face prison sentences and crippling damages for this offense. According to Fundamedios, by October 2011 five journalists had been sentenced to prison terms for defamation since 2008, and 18 journalists, media directors, and owners of media outlets faced similar charges.

President Correa frequently rebukes journalists and media that criticize him and has personally taken journalists to court for allegedly defaming him. In July 2011 a judge in Guayas province sentenced Emilio Palacio, who headed the opinion section of the Guayaquil newspaper *El Universo*, and three members of the newspaper's board of directors, to three years in prison and ordered them to pay US$40 million in damages to the president for an article the judge considered defamatory. In an opinion piece Palacios had referred to Correa as a "dictator" and accused him of ordering his forces to fire on a hospital, which was "full of civilians and innocent people," during the September 2010 police revolt.

In September 2011 a three-person appeals court confirmed the prison sentence and the fine by majority vote. Correa said in a press conference that he would consider a pardon if the newspaper confessed that it had lied, apologized to the Ecuadorian people, and promised to be more "serious, professional and ethical" in the future.

In order to rebut media criticism the government has also used a provision of the broadcasting legislation that obliges private broadcasters to interrupt scheduled programs to transmit government messages known as *cadenas*. According to an independent media observation group, between January 2007 and May 2011, there were 1,025 *cadenas* totaling 151 hours of broadcasting time, many of which included attacks on government critics.

Legislation to regulate broadcasting and print media has been under congressional debate since 2009. In the May 2011 referendum voters supported, by a small majority, a proposal to create an official council to regulate the content of television, radio, and print media. Proposals by six ruling party legislators under discussion in the National Assembly in July 2011 would grant broad powers to this council, allowing it to punish media that disseminate "information of public relevance that harms human rights, reputation, people's good name, and the public security of the state," terms so vague that they could easily lead to sanctions against critical outlets.

Judicial Independence

Corruption, inefficiency, and political influence have plagued the Ecuadorian judiciary for many years. Correa's efforts to reform the system could lead to a significant increase in the government's influence over the appointment and dismissal of judges. Voters in the May 2011 referendum approved a proposal to dissolve the Judicial Council, a body composed of independent jurists responsible for the selection, promotion, and dismissal of judges, whose efficiency had been widely questioned. It was to be replaced for 18 months by a tripartite transitional council to be appointed by the president, the legislature (in which Correa has majority support), and the "Transparency and Social Control Function," the citizens' branch established in the 2008 Constitution. This transitional council dismissed scores of judges in August and September 2011.

Also approved in the referendum was a constitutional reform giving the executive branch and its appointees a direct role in a new judicial council that would eventually replace the one dissolved. One of the new council's five members would be chosen by the executive; its other members would include the attorney general and the public defender.

In September 2011, at the request of the transitional council, Correa declared a "state of emergency in the judicial branch," to resolve the "critical situation" of the justice system. The decree declared a "national mobilization, especially of all the personnel of the judicial branch." Lack of clarity about the meaning of "mobilization" could threaten judges' independence by suggesting they must get behind government goals or risk dismissal.

Human Rights Defenders

The Correa administration has proposed to tighten regulations regarding the operation of both domestic and international NGOs in the country, including those working on human rights and the environment. In a draft decree announced in December 2010, domestic NGOs, including those working on human rights, would have to re-register and submit to continuous government monitoring. The decree would give the government broad powers to dissolve groups for "political activism," and "compromising national security or the interests of the state," ill-defined terms that could seriously compromise NGOs' legitimate activities. At this writing the proposed decree had not been adopted.

Another presidential decree adopted in July 2011, regulating international NGOs with offices in Ecuador, allows the government to monitor all their activities and rescind their authorizations if they engage in activities different from those described in their application, or "attack public security and peace." In August the government announced it planned to halt the operations of 16 foreign NGOs because they had failed to provide information about their activities.

In a radio broadcast in June Correa accused Fundamedios and another NGO, Participación Ciudadana (Citizen Participation), of trying to destabilize his government, and questioned their alleged receipt of funds from foreign donors. In response to a statement by Fundamedios pointing out that its receipt of foreign funding complied with the law, the communications secretary accused NGOs of implementing "political strategies and military tactics aimed at creating confusion or promoting currents of public opinion favorable to the interests of some of their funders."

Key International Actors

In August 2011 the Inter-American Commission on Human Rights filed a case accusing Ecuador of violating the right to due process of 27 Supreme Court justices who were arbitrarily dismissed by Congress during a constitutional crisis in 2004.

In October 2011 the Inter-American Commission on Human Rights held a thematic hearing on freedom of expression in Ecuador. Addressing the ongoing use of criminal libel laws to prosecute people for criticizing public authorities over matters of public interest, the commission noted that the protection of reputation in such cases must be guaranteed only through civil sanctions. The commission also expressed its "deepest concern" at a government broadcast (which all television and radio stations had to air) seeking to discredit Fundamedios, whose representatives had testified at the hearing.

GUATEMALA

Guatemala's weak and corrupt law enforcement institutions have proved incapable of containing the powerful organized crime groups and criminal gangs that contribute to one of the highest violent crime rates in the Americas. Illegal armed groups are believed to be responsible for ongoing threats and targeted attacks against civil society actors and justice officials.

Although impunity remains the norm for human rights violations, there were significant advances for accountability in 2011, including convictions of four former officers for a notorious massacre in 1982 and the first arrest of a top-ranking official for human rights violations.

Public Security, Police Conduct, and the Criminal Justice System

Illegal armed groups and criminal gangs significantly contribute to violence and intimidation, which they use to further political objectives and illicit economic interests, including drug-trafficking.

Powerful and well-organized youth gangs, including the Mara Salvatrucha and Barrio 18, have also contributed to escalating violence. The gangs use lethal violence against those who defy their control, including gang rivals, former gang members, individuals who collaborate with police, and those who refuse to pay extortion money. They are believed responsible for the widespread killing of bus drivers targeted for extortion. According to local media, 183 bus drivers or their assistants were murdered in 2010, and 105 in the first eight months of 2011.

Mexican drug cartels, in particular the Zetas, have added to violence and lawlessness in Guatemala. In December 2010 President Alvaro Colom declared a state of siege and martial law in Alta Verapaz, a department near Guatemala's northern border with Mexico, claiming the Zetas's criminal activities had made the region ungovernable. The state of siege, which was renewed for a further month in January, enabled the security forces to prohibit meetings and carry out arrests and searches without warrants. However, violence by the Zetas continued. In May 2011 the group claimed responsibility for a massacre at a ranch in neighboring Petén department, in which 27 peasants were murdered in cold blood and all but two were beheaded.

Guatemala's justice system has proved largely incapable of curbing violence and containing criminal gangs and mafias. According to official figures, there was 95 percent impunity for homicides in 2010. Deficient and corrupt prosecutorial and judicial systems and police, as well as the absence of an effective witness protection system, all contribute to Guatemala's alarmingly low prosecution rate. In addition, members of the judicial system are routinely subject to attacks and intimidation. Despite these enormous obstacles, there were a number of successful prosecutions in 2011, due partly to the work of Attorney General Claudia Paz y Paz, and the key role played by the United Nations's International Commission against Impunity in Guatemala (CICIG).

Police have used repressive measures to curb gang activity, including arbitrary detentions and extrajudicial killings. As part of an investigation into police involvement in extrajudicial executions in 2010 and 2011, CICIG assisted in the prosecution of two former members of the National Police's criminal investigation division, who were sentenced in June 2011 to 25 years in prison for the enforced disappearance of an alleged extortionist in October 2009.

Accountability for Past Abuses

Guatemala continues to suffer the effects of its 36-year civil war. A UN-sponsored Commission on Historical Clarification (CEH) estimated that as many as 200,000 people were killed during the conflict. The CEH attributed 93 percent of the human rights abuses it documented to state security forces and concluded the military had carried out "acts of genocide."

Very few of those responsible for the abuses have been prosecuted. However, 2011 saw the first arrest of a top-ranking official for human rights violations. In June Gen. Héctor Mario López Fuentes, former defense minister in the de facto government of Gen. Oscar Humberto Mejía Victores, was detained for his alleged role in massacres committed in 1982 to 1983. A judge also issued a warrant for the arrest of Mejía Victores, who seized power in a coup in 1983, but as of October 2011 he was in the hospital after having suffered a stroke, according to his lawyer.

In August 2011 a court sentenced four other former army officers to a total of 6,050 years in prison for participating in a brutal massacre in 1982 in Dos Erres, in which more than 250 people, including children, were murdered. Of 626 documented massacres, the Dos Erres case was only the fourth to have led to a conviction.

Guatemala's first conviction for the crime of enforced disappearance occurred in August 2009, when an ex-paramilitary leader was sentenced to 150 years in prison for his role in "disappearing" individuals between 1982 and 1984. The verdict was made possible by a landmark ruling by the country's Constitutional Court in July 2009, which established that enforced disappearance is a continuing crime that is not subject to a statute of limitations, as long as the whereabouts or fate of the victims are still unknown.

The discovery in July 2005 of approximately 80 million documents of the disbanded National Police, including files on Guatemalans killed or "disappeared" during the conflict, could play a key role in prosecutions for past human rights violations. Documents from the archive led to the arrest in March 2009 of two former National Police agents for their participation in the "disappearance" in 1984 of student leader and activist Edgar Fernando García. In October 2011 a court sentenced both men to 40 years in prison for the crime. Jorge Alberto Gómez—the former head of a unit that coordinated police and army counterinsurgency operations, who was arrested in April 2011—and ex-Col. Héctor Bol de la Cruz—the National Police's former director, who was arrested in June—are currently facing trial for their alleged responsibility for García's "disappearance."

In September 2008 Congress passed the Law of Access to Public Information, which prohibits "information related to investigations of violations of fundamental human rights or crimes against humanity" from being classified as confidential or reserved under any circumstances. In March 2009 President Colom created the Military Archive Declassification Commission, tasked with sorting and declassifying military documents from 1954 to 1966. In June 2011 the government made 12,287 declassified documents publicly available. According to a commission member, 55 were kept secret on national security grounds, but could be consulted by a court if required.

Labor Rights and Child Labor

Freedom of association and the right to organize and bargain collectively are endangered by a high level of anti-union violence, including attacks on trade union offices and threats, harassment, and killings of trade unionists. The International Trade Union Confederation reported the killing of 16 trade unionists in 2009 and 10 in 2010. In May 2011 two unidentified men on a motorcycle shot and killed Idar Joel Hernández, finance secretary of the Izabal Banana Workers' Union (SITRABI). In April Oscar González—another SITRABI official who worked at a Del Monte subsidiary in Morales, Izabal—was shot to death.

Guatemala has one of the highest rates of child labor in the Americas. The International Labour Organization reported in 2008 that 16.1 percent of children aged five to fourteen are obliged to work, many in unsafe conditions. Some of these children are employed in the construction, mining, and sex industries.

Gender-Based Violence

Violence against women is a chronic problem in Guatemala and most perpetrators are never brought to trial. According to the UN special rapporteur on extrajudicial, summary or arbitrary executions, investigations into crimes against women are often inadequate and obstructed by investigating police operating with a gender bias.

Palliative Care

Available palliative care is very limited in Guatemala, even though more than 10,000 people die of cancer or HIV/AIDS each year, many in severe pain. The government has not made oral morphine available in most of the country and has failed to ensure health care workers are adequately trained in modern pain treatment methods. Guatemala has some of the most restrictive regulatory policies in the region, discouraging doctors from prescribing pain medication and preventing patients in severe pain from accessing treatment. As a result, thousands of Guatemalans unnecessarily suffer from severe pain and other distressing symptoms every year.

Human Rights Defenders

Attacks and threats against human rights defenders are common, significantly hampering human rights work throughout the country. There is a routine failure to prosecute those responsible. In a rare exception, in July 2011 a court handed down a three-year prison sentence to a man found guilty of repeatedly threatening Norma Cruz Córdoba, director of the Fundación Sobrevivientes, a group that supports women who are victims of violence, and her coworker Gloria Ayala Pinto. The sentence was commuted to a fine.

In August 2011 four forensic experts from the Guatemalan Forensic Anthropology Foundation (FAFG) received death threats after giving evidence in the Dos Erres case. Four days earlier someone had slashed the tire of a pickup truck belonging to FAFG's director while he was waited in traffic in Guatemala City. As of October the Attorney General's Office had not identified those responsible for these threats.

Key International Actors

The CICIG, established in 2007, plays a key role in assisting the Guatemalan justice system in prosecuting violent crime. The commission's unique mandate allows it to work with the Attorney General's Office, the police, and other government agencies to investigate, prosecute, and dismantle the criminal organizations operating in Guatemala. The CICIG can participate in criminal proceedings as a complementary prosecutor, provide technical assistance, and promote legislative reforms. As of September 2011 it had initiated 62 investigations, and was directly participating in 20. The Office of the UN High Commissioner for Human Rights has maintained an office in Guatemala since 2005 that provides observation and technical assistance on human rights practices.

In January 2011 Jorge Sosa Orantes, a former army officer who faces charges in Guatemala as the commander responsible for the Dos Erres massacre, was detained in Calgary, Canada, after fleeing from the United States where he was accused of lying in an immigration application. Both Guatemala and Spain sought Sosa's extradition on war crimes charges. In September a Calgary judge ordered that he be extradited to the US to be tried for immigration fraud.

Haiti

Still reeling from the devastating January 12, 2010 earthquake and subsequent deadly cholera epidemic, Haiti inaugurated Michel Joseph Martelly as president on May 14, 2011, after a contested electoral process. The government stalled for over four months as parliament failed to ratify two consecutive nominees for prime minister, before confirming Martelly's third pick, Garry Conille, on October 4, 2011.

Weakened by the electoral and political crises, reconstruction efforts made little progress in rebuilding government or private structures. Despite this, the number of people living in informal settlements created after the earthquake dropped from some 1.3 million people in late 2010 to approximately 550,000 by September 2011.

The continuing humanitarian crisis created by the earthquake and cholera epidemic hindered Haiti from addressing many of the chronic human rights problems exacerbated by the quake, including violence against women and girls, inhuman prison conditions, and impunity for past human rights abuses. Moreover, increasing pressure to close camps on both private and public land has led to a growing number of evictions.

The Justice System

Haiti has been plagued by high levels of violent crime for years, but the United Nations secretary-general noted that trends since the earthquake demonstrate an increase in all major categories of crimes, including murder, rape, and kidnapping. Violent demonstrations and civil unrest related to the extended and contested electoral process contributed to this rise.

The weak capacity of the Haitian National Police (HNP) has contributed to overall insecurity in Haiti. The reform and strengthening of police remains a priority of the government and of the UN Stabilization Mission in Haiti (MINUSTAH). There has been progress in adding to HNP ranks, but obstacles such as the continued employment of compromised officers threaten Haiti's stability.

Police abuses and deaths in detention in select commissariats threaten to taint HNP's improving reputation of professionalism. In 2011 MINUSTAH and the Office of the UN High Commissioner for Human Rights (OHCHR) investigated several alleged cases of extrajudicial killings, arbitrary arrests, and ill-treatment of detainees and urged the police and judiciary to make systematic responses to cases of abuse. A trial in the case of alleged police killings in Les Cayes prison on January 19, 2010, began in mid-October. The outcome of the trial was unknown at this writing.

Haiti's justice system, long-troubled by politicization, corruption, resource shortages, and lack of transparency, worked slowly to recover in 2011. Some tribunal buildings were constructed and some magistrates received training in the country, while others did so in France. President Martelly appointed a chief judge and one other judge approved by the Senate to the Supreme Court of Haiti in October, but a political stalemate between President Martelly and the Senate prevented the remaining four vacant positions from being filled.

Detention Conditions

Haiti's chronically and severely overcrowded prison system suffered damage in the earthquake, leading to even more limited cell space as well as dire prison conditions. Reconstruction projects increased cell space by 28 percent this year. The percentage of pre-trial and illegal detainees is still very high, but international actors worked with prison and judicial officers to review cases of potential illegally detained inmates, leading to the release of several hundred people.

The negative health impact of substandard prison conditions became life-threatening with the arrival of cholera. In the first month of the epidemic, the HNP announced that 19 prisoners nationwide had died from the disease. In January a recent deportee from the United States died of cholera-like symptoms after less than two weeks in detention, leading the Inter-American Commission for Human Rights to grant a petition for precautionary measures calling for the suspension of further deportations from the US.

Women's and Girls' Rights

High rates of sexual violence existed before the earthquake, but the precarious safety and economic situation after the earthquake has left some women and girls even more vulnerable to such abuse. Many women lost their homes and livelihoods in the quake and now live in informal settlements or rely on host families for shelter. The UN and HNP have increased their security presence in some camps, and the UN Population Fund and humanitarian organizations have worked to increase lighting in many camps. Yet Human Rights Watch found that some victims have difficulty accessing post-rape medical services in sufficient time to prevent unwanted pregnancy.

Some women and girls in post-earthquake Haiti lack access to family planning and prenatal and obstetric care. Pregnancy rates in camps for displaced people are three times higher than urban rates of pregnancy were before the earthquake. Human Rights Watch found that many women and girls in camps do not know where to get birth control or prenatal care even though these services exist. Many have given birth in tents or some on the street en route to the hospital because of transportation difficulties.

Human Rights Watch also found that women's lack of access to economic security leads some women to trade sex for food or other necessities without using contraception, compounding the impact of their lack of access to reproductive health services and increasing chances for unintended pregnancy and disease. In particular, pregnant women and lactating mothers face increased hardships, as do women with disabilities and elderly women, due to constrained mobility and greater need for health services, food, and water.

Women also have difficulty participating in decision-making about recovery and reconstruction.

Children's Rights

Prior to the earthquake, only about half of Haiti's primary school-age children attended school. The UN Children's Fund estimates that the quake damaged or destroyed almost 4,000 schools and that 2.5 million children experienced prolonged interruption in their education. Schools resumed several months after the earthquake; however, many experienced a sharp drop in enrollment. President Martelly introduced a plan for free universal education early in his administration, and classes began October 3, 2011, with the first phase of his plan in place.

The use of child domestic workers in Haiti, known as *restavèks*, continues. *Restavèks* are children, 80 percent of whom are girls, from low-income households sent to live with other families in the hope they will be cared for in exchange for performing light chores. These children are often unpaid, denied education, and physically and sexually abused. UN and civil society organizations warn that a number of unaccompanied minors remaining in camps are vulnerable to this form of forced labor or to trafficking.

Accountability for Past Abuses

Former President-for-Life Jean-Claude Duvalier returned to Haiti on January 16, 2011, after nearly 25 years in exile. He was quickly charged with financial and human rights crimes allegedly committed during his 15-year tenure.

From 1971 to 1986 Duvalier commanded a network of security forces that committed serious human rights violations, including arbitrary detentions, torture, enforced disappearances, rape, and summary executions. Thousands of Haitians were victims of extrajudicial killings or otherwise died from torture or inhuman detention conditions. Many more were forced to flee the country, building the modern Haitian diaspora.

Duvalier's prosecution faces many obstacles, including the fragility of Haiti's justice system and the absence of a safe environment for his continued investigation and prosecution. Lack of political will from the international community to support the prosecution leaves the government without the adequate resources or technical assistance needed for a robust judicial process. Victims

and their families feel intimidated by Duvalier's lawyers and supporters, who have interrupted victims' audiences before the investigative judge, yelled at victims in public markets, and otherwise created an environment that discourages witnesses and victims from coming forward. In September Duvalier's lawyers disrupted an Amnesty International press conference supporting the prosecution.

Key International Actors

MINUSTAH has been present in Haiti since 2004, playing a prominent role in increasing stability. A contingent of the peacekeeping mission stationed in central Haiti is alleged to be the source of the cholera epidemic, leading to demonstrations against the force during the year. A UN independent investigation found that the cholera epidemic was caused by a confluence of circumstances, while numerous scientific analyses claim evidence that MINUSTAH soldiers most likely introduced the strain.

In September media outlets released a video of Uruguayan soldiers harassing an 18-year-old Haitian young man in a sexually explicit manner. The boy alleges he was raped, and members of the Uruguayan contingent were sent home to face a criminal investigation. The incident fueled anti-MINUSTAH sentiments ahead of the renewal of its mandate in October. The Security Council nevertheless extended the mission's mandate through October 15, 2012, with a reduction in the number of troops to pre-quake levels.

The Interim Haiti Recovery Commission (IHRC), provided for in the state of emergency law that parliament passed in April 2010, continued to operate through most of 2011. An extension of the IHRC did not pass parliament before the end of its mandate, making its future uncertain at this writing. The commission's mandate is to oversee billions of dollars in reconstruction aid and to conduct strategic planning and coordination among multi-lateral and bilateral donors, NGOs, and the private sector. Former US President Bill Clinton remains a co-chair of the IHRC and UN special envoy for Haiti.

Honduras

Honduras failed in 2011 to hold accountable those responsible for human rights violations under the de facto government that took power after the 2009 military coup. Impunity remained a serious problem, despite the government's establishment of a truth commission in May 2010 to examine events surrounding the coup, and efforts by the human rights unit in the Attorney General's Office to investigate abuses.

Violence and threats against journalists, human rights defenders, political activists, and transgender people continued. Those responsible for these abuses are rarely held to account.

Lack of Accountability for Post-Coup Abuses

Following the 2009 military coup, the de facto government suspended key civil liberties, including freedom of the press and assembly. In the ensuing days the military occupied opposition media outlets, temporarily shutting down their transmissions. Police and military personnel responded to generally peaceful demonstrations with excessive force. This pattern of the disproportionate use of force led to several deaths, scores of injuries, and thousands of arbitrary detentions.

In July 2011 a truth commission, established by President Porfirio Lobo's administration to investigate events before and after the coup, delivered its report. The commissioners documented the cases of 20 people, 12 of whom they concluded had been killed due to excessive police or army force, and eight of whom had died in selective killings by government agents. The commission also reported that police and army officials were responsible for "systematic obstruction" of investigations into these abuses, including altering crime scenes and official documents, criminal negligence, and helping suspects escape.

According to information provided in October 2011 by the Human Rights Unit of the Attorney General's Office, no one had been held criminally responsible for any of the serious abuses attributed to the security forces that occurred after the coup in the context of protests in support of Manuel Zelaya, the former president. Human rights prosecutors continue to face obstacles conducting investigations, including limited collaboration by security forces, lack of sufficient resources, and lack of implementation of a witness protection program.

Attacks on Journalists

Between President Lobo's January 2010 inauguration and November 2011, at least 12 journalists died—including three in 2011—at the hands of unidentified attackers. Many victims had opposed the coup or reported on corruption or human rights abuses. Other journalists have received death threats.

In July 2011 Nery Jeremias Orellana, a 26-year-old radio journalist, was riding to work on his motorbike in Candelaria, Lempira department, when unidentified assailants shot him in the head. He died in the hospital a few hours later. Orellana managed Radio Joconguera de Candelaria, which reported on human rights abuses in the area and had frequently aired the views of coup opponents. He had reportedly received death threats.

The individuals responsible for most of these crimes have not been identified or charged. In March 2011 the minister for human rights told the United Nations Human Rights Council that four cases were in court and six were still under investigation. Several government officials, including the minister of security and the minister of justice and human rights, have rejected suggestions that the killings were related to the victims' professional activities.

Rural Violence

More than 30 people were killed between January and August 2011 in the Bajo Aguan valley, a fertile palm oil-producing zone in northern Honduras. A long-simmering land conflict erupted in May when peasants occupied land being cultivated by large privately owned agricultural enterprises. Many victims were members of peasant associations who were allegedly gunned down by security guards working for the enterprises. In addition, four security guards were shot and killed in August 2011, when individuals armed with assault rifles and other arms reportedly tried to take over a ranch. In the absence of criminal investiga-

HONDURAS

After the Coup

Ongoing Violence, Intimidation, and Impunity in Honduras

HUMAN
RIGHTS
WATCH

tions, the circumstances of each incident remained unclear. By September no one had been charged for the killings in the Bajo Aguán region.

Excessive Use of Force against Demonstrators

There were credible reports in March 2011 that members of the national police fired tear gas canisters indiscriminately and beat people with batons during demonstrations by teachers' unions protesting proposed changes in the public education system. Ilse Velázquez Rodríguez, a teacher and member of a human rights organization, passed out after a tear gas bomb allegedly struck her forehead and was killed a few minutes later when a car ran her over.

Violence against Transgender Persons

Bias-motivated attacks on transgender people are a serious problem in Honduras. Six transgender women were murdered between November 2010 and January 2011 on the streets or in their homes in Tegucigalpa, the capital, and in the cities of Comayagüela and San Pedro Sula. The attacks ranged from gunshots to setting the victims on fire. Some victims appeared to have been tortured before being killed. Four additional murders of transgender women have been documented by local rights advocates between January and November 2011.

The alleged involvement of members of the Honduran police in some of these violent abuses is of particular concern. They are rarely followed by rigorous investigations, let alone criminal convictions. In January 2011 the minister of justice and human rights condemned "hate crimes" against members of the lesbian, gay, bisexual, and transgender (LGBT) community. In February the government established a special unit in the Attorney General's Office to investigate killings of transgender women among other vulnerable groups, and in November a similar unit was established in San Pedro Sula.

Honduras lacks anti-discrimination legislation, and current criminal laws expose LGBT community members to arbitrary arrest for vaguely defined conduct such as "offenses against decency."

Judicial Independence

Until recently the Supreme Court enjoyed absolute powers over personnel matters. In May 2010 it abused these powers by firing four judges who had publicly
opposed the coup on grounds that they had participated in politics, while taking no action against judges who had publicly supported the ouster of former
President Zelaya. In August 2011 the Council of the Judicial Career upheld the
dismissal of three of the judges, ordering monetary compensation for only one
of them, and reinstated the fourth judge.

In February 2011 the Honduran Congress approved constitutional reforms creating a new body, the Council of the Judiciary and Judicial Career, an elected body
responsible for appointing and dismissing judges. In November 2011, after long
delays due to political disagreements, Congress approved key articles of a law
regulating the council's membership and powers. Legislators agreed not to
include a representative of the executive branch on the council, whose five
members would be elected by Congress after public hearings.

Human Rights Defenders

Government officials have sometimes fueled hostility among some sectors of
the public towards human rights advocates who defend the rights of victims of
police abuses. In May 2011 the head of the Human Rights Unit of the Attorney
General's Office, Sandra Ponce, received intimidating text messages after the
deputy minister of security publicly criticized her for opening an investigation
into the deaths of seven alleged youth gang members in Ciudad Planeta, near
San Pedro Sula.

Leo Valladares, one of Honduras's most distinguished human rights advocates
and a former president of the Inter-American Commission of Human Rights, told
Human Rights Watch that he had received intimidating phone calls, and noticed
people monitoring his home and following him after he questioned the increasing power of the Honduran military since the 2009 coup.

Key International Actors

In June 2011 the Organization of American States General Assembly voted to readmit Honduras, having suspended its membership immediately after the 2009 coup. A few days earlier Zelaya returned to Honduras from exile after a Honduran appeals court dropped corruption charges against him.

In June 2011 the Center for Constitutional Rights filed a complaint under the United States Alien Tort Statute against former de facto president Roberto Micheletti on behalf of the parents of Isis Obed Murillo, a teenager who was shot and killed by members of the Honduran military in July 2009 during a demonstration against the coup. At this writing the civil action was pending before a US District Court in the Southern District of Texas.

The Inter-American Commission on Human Rights has played a critical role in Honduras since the coup, producing comprehensive reports documenting abuses, including killings, threats, and attacks on journalists.

Since August 2010 the Office of the UN High Commissioner for Human Rights has maintained a human rights advisor in Honduras, who provides advice to the government on strategies to protect and promote human rights, and advice and support to civil society groups defending human rights.

President Lobo continued in 2011 to support the creation of a UN-backed international commission against impunity in Honduras, in the context of international efforts to assist governments combating organized crime, drug-trafficking, and corruption in Central America.

Mexico

Mexico has experienced a dramatic surge in homicides in recent years, driven in large part by the violent struggle between and within powerful criminal organizations to control the drug trade and other lucrative illicit businesses such as human trafficking. Efforts by the administration of President Felipe Calderón to combat organized crime have resulted in a significant increase in killings, torture, and other abuses by security forces, which only make the climate of lawlessness and fear worse in many parts of the country.

Journalists, human rights defenders, and migrants are targeted for attack by criminal groups and members of security forces, yet Mexico has failed to provide these vulnerable groups with protection or to adequately investigate the crimes against them.

Efforts to implement comprehensive reform of the criminal justice system, which would address endemic problems such as torture to extract confessions, continued to progress slowly in 2011, leaving in place a system rife with abuses.

Impunity for Military Abuses

President Calderón has relied heavily on the military to fight drug-related violence and organized crime. While engaging in law enforcement activities, the armed forces have committed serious human rights violations, including killings, torture, and enforced disappearances. Mexico's National Human Rights Commission has issued detailed reports of nearly 90 cases since 2007 in which it found that members of the army had committed serious human rights abuses, and it has received complaints of nearly 5,800 additional human rights violations from 2007 to October 2011.

In September 2011 Gustavo Acosta, 31, and his family awoke to the sound of shooting outside their house in Apodaca, Nuevo León. Several armed members of the navy banged on their front door and, when Acosta opened it, they demanded to know why the family had been shooting at them. When Acosta responded that they were unarmed, one of the navy officers shot him dead, according to his father and brother, who witnessed the shooting. At this writing no members of the navy had been charged in the crime.

One of the main reasons military abuses persist is because soldiers who commit human rights violations against civilians are almost never brought to justice. Such cases continue to be investigated and prosecuted under military jurisdiction, despite rulings by Mexico's Supreme Court and the Inter-American Court of Human Rights that civilian prosecutors and courts should handle military abuses. The Military Prosecutor's Office opened 3,671 investigations into human rights violations committed by the army against civilians from 2007 to June 2011. Only 15 soldiers were convicted during that period. An additional 14 army members were sentenced in a case in November 2011.

Criminal Justice System

The criminal justice system routinely fails to provide justice to victims of violent crimes and human rights violations. The causes of this failure are varied and include corruption, inadequate training and resources, and abusive policing practices without accountability.

Torture remains a serious problem and is most often applied in the period between when victims are arbitrarily detained and when they are handed to prosecutors, a period in which they are routinely held incommunicado. Common tactics include beatings, asphyxiation with plastic bags, waterboarding, electric shocks, and death threats.

One perpetuating factor is the acceptance by some judges of confessions obtained through torture and other ill-treatment, as well as the complicity of public defenders entrusted with safeguarding detainees' rights. Another is the failure to investigate and prosecute most cases of torture, including the failure of authorities to insist that legally mandated medical tests, designed to assess the physical and psychological condition of a potential victim of torture, are adequately carried out.

In June 2008 Mexico passed a constitutional reform that creates the basis for an adversarial criminal justice system with oral trials, and contains measures that are critical for promoting greater respect for fundamental rights, such as

Mexico

Neither Rights Nor Security

Killings, Torture, and Disappearances in Mexico's
"War on Drugs"

HUMAN
RIGHTS
WATCH

including presumption of innocence in the Constitution. The government has until 2016 to implement the reform. At this writing only a handful of states have undertaken substantive changes.

In addition to its positive aspects, the reform also introduced the provision of *arraigo*, which allows prosecutors, with judicial authorization, to detain individuals suspected of participating in organized crime for up to 80 days before they are charged with a crime, a power that is inconsistent with Mexico's due process obligations under international law.

Freedom of Expression

Journalists, particularly those who have reported on drug trafficking or have been critical of security forces and authorities, have faced serious harassment and attacks. From 2000 to September 2011, 74 journalists were killed, including at least eight killed in 2011. While many attacks on the press in 2011 were attributed to organized crime, evidence points to the possible involvement of state officials in some instances.

Participants in social media networks have increasingly been the targets of violence and intimidation. In September 2011 three mutilated bodies were left in public places with notes warning against the use of social media networks, such as Twitter, to report on violence by organized crime groups.

Authorities have routinely failed to adequately investigate and prosecute crimes against members of the press or to protect journalists who face serious risk, fostering a climate of impunity and self-censorship. While Mexico broadened the mandate and autonomy of its special prosecutor for crimes against the press in 2010, the special prosecutor's office has since failed to improve on its poor record of prosecuting cases. Similarly, while the Calderón administration created a protection mechanism for journalists in December 2010, it lacks clear functions and operating guidelines, and has until now failed to offer effective protection to journalists under threat.

Domestic Violence, Reproductive Rights, and Same-Sex Marriage

Mexican laws do not adequately protect women and girls against domestic violence and sexual abuse. Some provisions, including those that make the severity of punishments for some sexual offenses contingent on the "chastity" of the victim, contradict international standards. Women who have suffered human rights violations generally do not report them to authorities, while those who do report them are generally met with suspicion, apathy, and disrespect. Such underreporting undercuts pressure for necessary legal reforms and leads to impunity for violence against women and girls.

In August 2008 the Supreme Court affirmed the constitutionality of a Mexico City law that legalized abortion in the first 12 weeks of pregnancy. Since that time more than 15 of Mexico's 32 states have adopted reforms that recognize the right to life from the moment of conception. In September 2011 the Supreme Court upheld the state reforms as constitutional by a single vote. In May 2010 the Supreme Court ruled that all states must provide emergency contraception and access to abortion for rape victims. However, only five states have reformed their procedural codes accordingly and efforts to inform women and girls of their rights have been very limited.

In August 2010 the Supreme Court recognized the right of same-sex couples in Mexico City to adopt children and to marry, and ruled that all states in Mexico must recognize same-sex marriages that take place in Mexico City.

Labor Rights

Legitimate labor-organizing activity continues to be obstructed by agreements negotiated between management and pro-management unions. These agreements often fail to provide worker benefits beyond the minimums mandated by Mexican legislation. Workers who seek to form independent unions risk losing their jobs, as loopholes in labor laws and poor enforcement generally fail to protect them from retaliatory dismissals.

Migrants

Hundreds of thousands of migrants pass through Mexico each year and many are subjected to grave abuses en route, including physical and sexual assault, extortion, and theft. Approximately 18,000 migrants are kidnapped annually, often with the aim of extorting payments from their relatives in the United States. Authorities have not taken adequate steps to protect migrants, or to investigate and prosecute those who abuse them. Migration officials rarely inform migrants of their rights, such as the right to seek asylum, and the authorities themselves are often the perpetrators of abuses.

Human Rights Defenders

Human rights defenders continue to suffer harassment and attacks, sometimes directly at the hands of state officials. Meanwhile authorities consistently fail to provide defenders with adequate protection or investigate the crimes against them.

In February 2011 the homes of human rights defenders María Luisa García Andrade and Sara Salazar—both of whom worked with the organization Return our Daughters in Ciudad Juárez—were set ablaze in separate incidents. They followed a series of attacks and threats against these and other defenders, including the disappearance of two of Salazar's children and her daughter-in-law, who were later found dead. The Inter-American Commission on Human Rights had granted García and Salazar protection measures in June 2008, but federal and state authorities failed to take adequate steps to protect them. They later fled Ciudad Juárez with their families.

In July 2011 President Calderón signed an agreement pledging to create a mechanism to protect human rights defenders. However, at this writing it was unclear what progress, if any, had been made towards creating that mechanism.

Key International Actors

The US has allocated US$1.6 billion in aid to Mexico through the Merida Initiative, a multi-year aid package agreed upon in 2007 to help Mexico combat organized crime. Fifteen percent of select portions of the assistance can be disbursed only after the US secretary of state reports to the US Congress that the Mexican government is meeting four human rights requirements: ensuring that civilian prosecutors and judicial authorities investigate and prosecute federal police and military officials who violate basic rights, consulting regularly with Mexican civil society organizations on Merida Initiative implementation, enforcing the prohibition on use of testimony obtained through torture or other ill-treatment, and improving transparency and accountability of police forces.

However, the impact of these requirements has been undermined by the fact that the US has repeatedly allocated the conditioned funds despite evidence that Mexico has not met the requirements, most recently in September 2010. While the US State Department announced in September 2010 that it would withhold an additional $26 million in Merida aid for 2010, it pegged the funds to a different set of conditions, and then released the funds in 2011. In January 2011 US Secretary of State Hillary Clinton said that Mexico needed to "make sure that any human rights violations committed by the military against civilians are tried in civilian courts."

In November 2009 the Inter-American Court ruled that Mexico was responsible for the 1974 enforced disappearance of Rosendo Radilla Pacheco, and had failed to adequately investigate the crime. The binding decision ordered Mexico to modify its Code of Military Justice to ensure that "under no circumstances can military jurisdiction be applied" in cases where the military violates the human rights of civilians.

In August 2010 the court found that members of the army had in 2002 raped and tortured Valentina Rosendo Cantú and Inés Fernández Ortega, indigenous women from Guerrero, and again ordered Mexico to modify its military code. The ruling was repeated in December 2010, when the court found Rodolfo Montiel and Teodoro Cabrera—peasant leaders from Guerrero state involved in environmental activism—had been arbitrarily detained and tortured by the military. Despite these four binding rulings, Mexico continues to judge soldiers who commit abuses in military jurisdiction.

The United Nations Working Group on Enforced or Involuntary Disappearances conducted a fact-finding mission to Mexico in March 2011. In its preliminary observations, it concluded that "enforced disappearances happened in the past and continue to happen in the present [in Mexico]," and that "the increased numbers of newly admitted cases in 2010 and the high number of new allegations received during the visit could indicate a deterioration regarding enforced disappearances in Mexico." Among its recommendations, the group suggested Mexico create a national database of the disappeared, and end the practice of requiring victims' families to gather evidence of the disappearance of relatives and possible participation of state officials before opening investigations.

PERU

In the June 2011 elections, Ollanta Humala, a former army colonel, won a narrow victory over Keiko Fujimori, daughter of former President Alberto Fujimori. Fujimori is serving a 25-year prison sentence for human rights violations during his first presidency.

Progress in holding others responsible for abuses during Peru's internal armed conflict remained slow. Top officials in the government of President Alan García, whose term ended in July 2011, often criticized judicial investigations. In 2010 García signed a decree amounting to a blanket amnesty that would leave most of the crimes unpunished. The measure was eventually withdrawn after national and international protests. Still, the military's refusal to provide information continues to obstruct judicial investigations, and most perpetrators have evaded justice.

In recent years there have been a rising number of social conflicts involving communities protesting actions by the government or mining and other private companies. These have in several cases resulted in violent clashes between protesters and police, and fatalities on both sides.

Confronting Past Abuses

Peru's Truth and Reconciliation Commission estimated that almost 70,000 people died or were subject to enforced disappearances during the country's internal armed conflict between 1980 and 2000. Many were victims of atrocities committed by the Shining Path and other insurgent groups, as well as human rights violations by state agents.

Efforts to prosecute those responsible for these abuses have had mixed results. In August 2011 the Constitutional Tribunal rejected former President Fujimori's appeal requesting annulment of the verdict of a Supreme Court panel that had unanimously confirmed his 25-year prison sentence for killings and "disappearances" in 1991 and 1992. In July 2011, amid rumors that Fujimori might have cancer, politicians linked to President García's party and presidential candidate

Keiko Fujimori advocated that he receive a "humanitarian pardon," but he continued to serve his sentence at this writing.

Progress in other cases has been slow. According to the Institute for Legal Defense (IDL), a rights organization that monitors trials, by December 2010 the National Criminal Court—which was given jurisdiction in many human rights cases in 2004—had handed down only 20 sentences, of which 85 percent were acquittals. The only sentence of note by another court was the conviction of 19 former military personnel for kidnapping and killing 35 victims in three different incidents during Fujimori's government.

A major obstacle has been the military's failure to cooperate by identifying officers present at army bases during the conflict. The low conviction rate also reflects the National Criminal Court's insistence there be direct and documentary proof of the responsibility of superior officers, and its unwillingness to credit the testimony of victims' relatives.

Senior officials of García's administration, including the minister of defense and the vice-president, frequently criticized human rights trials. In August 2010 García signed a decree that would have halted prosecutions in many cases by applying a statute of limitations. He later withdrew it after intense domestic and international criticism. Officials of the current government have also opposed human rights trials, including the current minister of defense, retired Gen. Daniel Mora, who said in a September 2011 radio interview: "I think that we should arrive at a full-stop solution and reconciliation of the country."

Unjustified Use of Lethal Force

In June 2011 the human rights ombudsman reported more than 200 ongoing social conflicts, many related to new mining ventures. Several have resulted in violent clashes between protesters and police, in which the latter appear to have used unlawful force. In April 2011, for example, three civilians were killed and more than 31 injured in Islay province when police reportedly opened live fire to clear a roadblock during protests against a proposed copper mining project. In May 2011 a civilian judge opened trial proceedings against two police generals and three other police officers for killing protesters during violent clashes in June 2009 in Utcubamba and Bagua provinces, in which 23 police and 10 civilians were killed. The trial was underway at this writing.

Torture

Beatings by police and military personnel, prison guards, and members of municipal security patrols is a serious problem in Peru, according to the National Human Rights ombudsman. In April 2011, police in San Borja, Lima, detained 26-year-old Gerson Falla, reportedly after he sought refuge in a bakery thinking he was going to be robbed. Police arrested him and allegedly beat him brutally. Falla died 48 hours later. A police video featured on television showed officers twisting his arm behind his bruised back and dragging him across the floor.

Military Justice

Military courts that lack independence and impartiality continue to conduct trials of police and military officials accused of human rights abuse. Decrees 1094, 1095, and 1096—issued by President García in September 2010—gave military officers on active service powers to investigate and judge abuses committed by police and military personnel engaged in policing duties. This violates international principles on fair trial and earlier rulings of Peru's Supreme Court and Constitutional Tribunal.

Reproductive Rights

Women and girls in Peru have the right to seek therapeutic abortions in specific cases of medical necessity. The United Nations Human Rights Committee in the 2005 case *K.L. v. Peru* concluded that Peru needed to provide clear national protocols for when abortions may be performed legally. Human Rights Watch found that the absence of such protocols endangers the lives and health of women and girls, because it is nearly impossible to have an abortion in a public facility without clear guidelines on the legality of procedures. Women prevented from receiving therapeutic abortions sometimes turn to unsafe and clandestine procedures that can threaten their lives and safety, and violate a women's fundamental right to the highest attainable standard of health, life, non-discrimination, physical integrity, and freedom from cruel, inhuman or degrading treatment. The Ministry of Health is currently reviewing national protocols.

Disenfranchisement of People with Disabilities

People with disabilities face systematic barriers to political participation. Prior to presidential elections in April and June 2011, el Registro Nacional de Identificación y Estado Civil (RENIEC), the government agency responsible for the electoral rolls, excluded more than 23,000 persons with intellectual and mental disabilities from the voter registry.

After pressure from the disability community, people with disabilities were invited to re-register. But with limited time and poor communication about this decision, less than 60 people were added back to the registry before the election. In September 2011 RENIEC acknowledged this disenfranchisement of certain people with disabilities and pledged to rectify the situation.

People living in institutions and those under guardianship also face restrictions in the right to vote. Other barriers to political participation include lack of Braille ballots, ramps at polling sites, and easy-to-understand information about candidates and the political process.

Freedom of Media

Journalists in Peru's provinces face intimidation and threats. Individuals supporting or working for municipal authorities have assaulted and even murdered journalists who publicize abuses by local government officials. In 2010, in a measure intended to ensure these cases are brought to justice, the judiciary's executive branch placed violent crimes against journalists under the jurisdiction of the Lima-based National Criminal Court. The court specializes in serious crimes like human rights violations and terrorism.

In July 2011 a parliamentary commission approved a bill to end the imprisonment of journalists convicted of criminal defamation. If passed in the plenary, the bill will replace prison sentences of up to three years, as stipulated in the current law, with community service and fines. When the bill was approved, several journalists faced prison for criticizing public officials. They included Francisco Andrade Chávez, a journalist for America TV in Chepén province, who was sentenced in July 2011 to two years in prison, a fine, and civil damages, for defaming a municipal official. As of October 2011 President Humala had not yet signed or endorsed the bill.

Radio La Voz de Bagua faced legal reprisals in 2011 for its coverage of the civil unrest in Bagua. In June 2009 the government revoked its broadcasting license after government officials and ruling party leaders accused the station of inciting violence. The license was provisionally restored in October 2010, and a Ministry of Communications and Transport investigation into the station's allegedly unauthorized use of broadcasting frequencies was closed. However, in February 2011 a local prosecutor accused the station's owner of "aggravated theft of the radio spectrum" in relation to the same events. The accusation was dismissed on appeal, but reinstated in June 2011 by an Utcubamba appeals court. The station's owner could face four years in prison if convicted.

Human Rights Defenders

In September 2011, in a speech in Congress, the minister of defense accused two of Peru's best known human rights organizations, the National Coordinator for Human Rights and the Institute for Legal Defense, of seeking "to destroy the armed forces." Both organizations have advocated for years for accountability for human rights violations during the armed conflict. They were the target of similar comments by the vice-president and defense minister during García's presidency.

Key International Actors

In July 2011 the United States extradited former army major Telmo Hurtado to stand trial in Peru for the 1985 massacre of 69 civilians at Accomarca, Ayacucho department. In March 2008 a US federal court in Miami ordered Hurtado to pay US$37 million in damages to two relatives of victims of the massacre in a suit filed under the Alien Tort Statute. Hurtado was among 29 former military facing trial by the National Criminal Court in Lima at this writing.

VENEZUELA

The weakening of Venezuela's democratic system of checks and balances under President Hugo Chávez has contributed to a precarious human rights situation. Without judicial checks on its actions, the government has systematically undermined the right to free expression, workers' freedom of association, and the ability of human rights groups to protect rights.

Weeks before the new National Assembly—with a substantial opposition composition—took office in January 2011, Chávez's supporters in the legislature adopted several laws that increased the government's ability to undercut rights.

Police abuses and impunity remain a grave problem. Prison conditions are deplorable, and fatality rates high due to inmate violence.

Judicial Independence

In 2004 Chávez and his legislative allies conducted a political takeover of the Supreme Court, filling it with government supporters and creating new measures that make it possible to purge justices from the court. In December 2010 the outgoing legislators from Chávez's political party modified the timeline so they could make appointments before leaving office: they appointed 9 permanent justices and 32 stand-ins, including several allies. Since 2004, the court has largely abdicated its role as a check on executive power, failing to protect fundamental rights enshrined in the constitution.

In 2011 Supreme Court President Luisa Estella Morales declared that laws in Venezuela "respond to an ideological purpose," while Justice Fernando Torre Alba stated that courts "must severely ... sanction behaviors or cases that undermine the construction of [Bolivarian] socialism."

Individual judges may face reprisals if they rule against government interests. In December 2009 Judge María Lourdes Afiuni was detained on the day she authorized the conditional release of Eligio Cedeño, a banker accused of corruption. Afiuni was following a recommendation by the United Nations Working

Group on Arbitrary Detentions, given that Cedeño had been in pre-trial detention for almost three years, although Venezuelan law prescribes a two-year limit. The day after her arrest, Chávez publicly branded Afiuni a "bandit" who should receive the maximum 30 years in prison. Accused of corruption, abuse of authority, and "favoring evasion of justice," her case is pending before a judge who has stated publicly: "I would never betray my Commander because I take the Revolution in my blood..."

Judge Afiuni was held in pre-trial detention in deplorable conditions in a violent prison for over a year, and remains under house arrest. Three UN human rights special rapporteurs and the Inter-American Commission on Human Rights have denounced her arrest and called for her release.

Legislating by Decree

In December 2010 the outgoing National Assembly passed an enabling law that granted Chávez broad powers to legislate by decree on a wide range of issues for 18 months. The law's vague provisions could directly impact the exercise of rights by, for example, allowing the president to determine which penalties can be imposed when someone commits a crime. As of November 2011 Chávez had adopted over 20 legislative decrees, including one reinstating crimes previously derogated by the legislature. The Supreme Court upheld the constitutionality of this decree, which criminalized several banking practices, arguing that economic crimes are "crimes against humanity" and could not be decriminalized.

Freedom of Media

Venezuela enjoys a vibrant public debate in which anti-government and pro-government media criticize and defend the president. However, the government has discriminated against media that air political opponents' views, strengthened the state's ability to limit free speech and created powerful incentives for government critics to self-censor.

Laws contributing to a climate of self-censorship include the 2005 amendments to the criminal code extending the scope of desacato laws that criminalize disrespect of high government officials, and a broadcasting statute allowing arbitrary suspension of channels for the vaguely defined offense of "incitement." In December 2010 the National Assembly extended the scope of this statute to include the internet. It also amended the telecommunications law, granting the government power to suspend or revoke concessions to private outlets if it is "convenient for the interests of the nation" or demanded by public order and security.

The government has abused its control of broadcasting frequencies to punish radio and television stations with overtly critical programming. In 2009 the government broadcasting authority CONATEL closed 32 radio stations and reported that over 200 others were under review, without providing a list of the stations being investigated. Several stations have since limited their critical programming. In November 2011 CONATEL suspended several radio stations while it investigated them, but no additional stations had been closed at this writing.

RCTV, Venezuela's most popular critical television station, was pulled from public airwaves in 2007. RCTV International, the cable channel that replaced it, was removed from cable broadcasting in 2010 after CONATEL ordered that cable providers suspend transmitting channels that it had not certified as "international" channels. RCTV's lawyers say CONATEL has rejected RCTV's requests to obtain this certification, and the channel remains unable to transmit in Venezuela.

CONATEL has opened seven administrative investigations against Globovisión—the only TV channel available without cable critical of the government—that could lead to the station's suspension or revocation of its license. In October 2011 CONATEL fined Globovisión US$2.1 million for allegedly violating the broadcasting statute when it aired images of a June prison riot. The other six cases have yet to be resolved; some have been pending for over a year.

In 2010 the government adopted vague norms that expand its power to limit access to almost any information it holds, including creating a Center for Situational Studies of the Nation with broad powers to limit public dissemination of "information, facts or circumstance[s]" it deems confidential.

Prosecuting Government Critics

Several prominent critics of Chávez's government have been targeted for criminal prosecution in recent years. The courts' lack of independence reduced the chances of them receiving a fair trial.

In July 2011 Oswaldo Álvarez Paz, a former governor of Zulia state and member of an opposition political party, was sentenced to two years in prison for criticizing the Chávez administration on TV. Álvarez Paz was convicted of disseminating false information for saying that Chávez was not a democrat and that "Venezuela has turned into a center of operations that facilitates the business of drug-trafficking." Álvarez Paz is serving his sentence on conditional liberty but cannot leave the country without judicial authorization.

Guillermo Zuloaga, president of Globovisión, remains under criminal investigation for allegedly disseminating false information and for offending the president. At a public meeting in March 2010, Zuloaga accused Chávez of ordering the shooting of demonstrators during the 2002 coup. In a June televised speech, Chávez expressed outrage that Zuloaga was still free. A week later police arrived at Zuloaga's house to arrest him and his son for alleged irregularities in their car sales business, an investigation their lawyers said had been stalled for months. The two men, who were not at home, subsequently fled the country.

In March 2011 Rubén González, secretary general of the Ferrominera Orinoco Union, was sentenced to over seven years in prison for organizing and participating in a strike with 2,000 workers in Guyana to protest a government-owned company's failure to comply with a collective bargaining agreement. González was convicted for incitement to commit crimes, restricting freedom to work, and violating the prohibition to enter security zones. Not only was the prosecution of González criticized by the International Labour Organization and Venezuelan unions, but it was also denounced by pro-government labor leaders in Venezuela. Upon appeal, the Supreme Court ordered another judge to re-try González. The case against González, who was released on conditional liberty, remained pending at this writing.

Human Rights Defenders

Chávez's government has aggressively sought to discredit human rights defenders. In June Justice Minister Tarek El Aissami accused Humberto Prado of the Venezuelan Observatory of Prisons of "destabilizing the prison system" and having been "an accomplice in the massacre of inmates" in the past. After several official media outlets discredited Prado, he received multiple death threats and left Venezuela for two months.

In July 2010 the Supreme Court ruled that "obtaining financial resources, either directly or indirectly, from foreign states with the intent of using them against the Republic, [and] the interest of the people [could constitute] treason." That same month members of Chávez's political party filed a criminal complaint with the Attorney General's Office, alleging that several local human rights NGOs had committed treason by receiving funding from foreign donors. Over 30 NGOs are currently under investigation, according to local media.

In December 2010 the National Assembly adopted two laws that, if applied to human rights organizations, could severely undermine their ability to work independently. The "Law for the Defense of Political Sovereignty and National Self Determination" blocks NGOS that "defend political rights" or "monitor the performance of public bodies" from receiving international funding. It also imposes stiff fines on organizations that invite foreigners who express opinions that offend institutions or undermine national sovereignty. The "Organic Law on Social Control"—which regulates the work of organizations and individuals that have an impact on "general or collective interests"—states that individuals must follow the law's socialist principles and values: those who violate the law may face civil, administrative, or criminal sanctions.

Police Abuses

Violent crime is rampant in Venezuela, where extrajudicial killings by security agents remain a problem. The minister of the interior and justice has estimated that police commit one of every five crimes. According to the most recent official statistics, law enforcement agents allegedly killed 7,998 people between January 2000 and the first third of 2009.

Impunity for human rights violations remains the norm. In 2010, prosecutors charged individuals allegedly responsible for abuses in less than 3 percent of cases investigated.

In April 2008 Chávez's administration issued a decree that established a new national police force and enacted measures to promote non-abusive policing proposed by a commission comprised of government and NGO representatives. At this writing there had been no independent evaluation of the new police force's performance.

Prison Conditions

Venezuelan prisons are among the most violent in Latin America. Weak security, deteriorating infrastructure, overcrowding, insufficient and poorly trained guards, and corruption allow armed gangs to effectively control prisons. Hundreds of violent prison deaths occur every year. In June 2011, at least 25 people were killed and over 60 seriously injured, including prisoners and National Guard members, after clashes between inmates in the El Rodeo prisons.

Labor Rights

The National Electoral Council (CNE), a public authority, has the power to organize and certify all union elections, violating international standards that guarantee workers the right to elect their representatives in full freedom, according to conditions they determine. Established unions whose elections have not been CNE-certified may not participate in collective bargaining.

For several years the government has promised to reform the relevant labor and electoral laws to restrict state interference in union elections. Reforms that explicitly state that union elections held without CNE participation are legally valid were still pending before the National Assembly at this writing.

Key International Actors

Venezuela's government has increasingly rejected international monitoring of its human rights record. In September 2011 the Supreme Court president held that Venezuela will "respect all international agreements only if ... international bodies respect [Venezuelan] sovereignty and ... jurisdiction."

In September 2011 the Inter-American Court of Human Rights ruled that Venezuela must allow Leopoldo López, a prominent opposition leader, to run for public office. López, a former Caracas district mayor, has been barred from seeking elected office by the country's comptroller general since 2008 due to corruption allegations for which he has never been formally charged, prosecuted, or convicted. The court has also found that Venezuela is failing to adopt measures it ordered to protect individuals facing imminent risks to their lives or physical integrity.

In October 2011 many governments expressed concern regarding the human rights situation in Venezuela during the UN Human Rights Council's Universal Periodic Review of the country. Venezuela's government accepted most recommendations that states made, but rejected several key recommendations aimed at protecting free speech, strengthening judicial independence, complying with the Inter-American Court's binding rulings, and supporting the independent work of NGOs.

LAO PDR

Somsanga's Secrets

Arbitrary Detention, Physical Abuse, and Suicide
inside a Lao Drug Detention Center

HUMAN
RIGHTS
WATCH

WORLD REPORT

2012

ASIA

AFGHANISTAN

Armed conflict with the Taliban and other insurgents escalated in 2011, but Afghanistan's military allies made it clear they were intent on withdrawing troops as soon as possible, with a deadline for Afghan national security forces to take over from international forces by the end of 2014.

Rising civilian casualties, increased use of "night raids" by the International Security Assistance Force (ISAF), and abuses by insurgents and government-backed militias widened the impact of the war on ordinary Afghans. Stability was further undermined by a political crisis following parliamentary elections and panic caused by the near-collapse of the country's largest private bank.

The Afghan government continues to give free rein to well-known warlords and human rights abusers as well as corrupt politicians and businesspeople, further eroding public support. And it has done far too little to address longstanding torture and abuse in prisons and widespread violations of women's rights.

In 2011 support grew within the government and with its international partners for a negotiated peace agreement with the Taliban, given waning international willingness to continue combat operations. However, moves toward a peace agreement proved difficult with several false starts, the killing by the Taliban of a key government negotiator, pressure from Pakistan for a key role in the process, and lack of trust and differing priorities among the government and its international partners.

The possibility of an agreement raised fears (and, reportedly, re-arming) among non-Pashtun communities, who are concerned about an alliance between the government and the Taliban. It also renewed grave concerns that human rights, especially women's rights, would be bargained away in the negotiation process.

Flawed parliamentary elections in September 2010 led to fallout that, in 2011, threatened to seriously destabilize the country. Following the certification of election results by the Independent Election Commission (IEC), President Hamid Karzai took the unprecedented step of creating a special court to review the results. After street protests in Kabul and eight months during which parlia-

AFGHANISTAN

"Just Don't Call It a Militia"

Impunity, Militias, and the "Afghan Local Police"

HUMAN
RIGHTS
WATCH

ment was immobilized by uncertainty, the special court disqualified 62 members of parliament out of 249 seats. A compromise in September 2011 resulted in nine members of parliament being removed.

The Armed Conflict

The armed conflict escalated in 2011. The Afghan NGO Security Office (ANSO) reported that opposition attacks increased to 40 a day in the first six months of the year, up 119 percent since 2009 and 42 percent since 2010. ANSO also reported a 73 percent increase since 2010 in attacks against aid workers, which included a fatal mob attack—sparked by the burning of the Koran by an American pastor in Florida—against a United Nations office in the city of Mazar-e-Sharif. Insurgent attacks reached previously secure areas including Parwan and Bamiyan as the war spread to many new parts of the country.

Civilian casualties rose again, with the UN Assistance Mission in Afghanistan (UNAMA) recording 1,462 conflict-related civilian deaths in the first six months of the year, a 15 percent increase since 2010. Some 80 percent were attributed to anti-government forces, most commonly caused by improvised explosive devices (IEDs). Most IEDs that the ISAF encounters are victim-activated devices detonated by pressure plates, effectively antipersonnel landmines, which the 1997 Mine Ban Treaty—to which Afghanistan is a party—prohibits.

The death of 368 civilians in May was the highest monthly toll since UNAMA began tracking figures in 2007. The use of "night raids" by international forces—nighttime snatch operations against suspected insurgents widely despised by Afghans because of their infringement on family life—increased to a reported 300 per month. While pro-government forces succeeded in reducing the number of civilian deaths directly caused by their operations, more could still be done to protect civilian lives.

The NATO mission aimed to train a 134,000-strong police force and 171,600 soldiers by October 2011 to replace foreign forces. But the effort faces serious challenges, including attrition, insurgent infiltration, and illiteracy and substance abuse among recruits. In multiple incidents, trainees attacked and killed their international mentors. One in seven Afghan soldiers, a total of 24,000, deserted in the first six months of the year, twice as many as in 2010.There are concerns that the buildup of the armed forces is moving too fast for necessary training and vetting, and that the size of the force will be financially unsustainable.

In an effort to combat insurgency the Afghan government continues to arm and provide money, with little oversight, to militias in the north that have been implicated in killings, rape, and forcible collection of illegal taxes. As part of its exit strategy, the United States is backing "Afghan Local Police" (ALP), village-based defense forces trained and mentored primarily by US Special Forces, which have been created since 2010 in parts of the country with limited police and military presence. In its first year ALP units were implicated—with few consequences for perpetrators—in killings, abductions, illegal raids, and beatings, raising serious questions about government and international efforts to vet, train, and hold these forces accountable.

A campaign of assassinations of public figures by the Taliban in the north and the south seeks to destabilize the government. Prominent figures killed included the mayor of Kandahar, Ghulam Haidar Hameedi; a northern police commander, Gen. Daud Daud; and President Karzai's half-brother, Ahmad Wali Karzai, a key southern powerbroker. Shifting power structures have led to the appointment of individuals implicated in serious human rights abuses, including Matiullah Khan as Uruzgan police chief and Abdur Rezaq Razziq as Kandahar police chief. The Taliban and other insurgent groups continue to target schools, especially those for girls. The Taliban also use children, some as young as eight, as suicide bombers.

Detainee Transfers

Torture and abuse of detainees in Afghan jails in 2011 led the ISAF to temporarily suspend the transfer of prisoners in eight provinces. Abuses in these jails documented by the UN Assistance Mission in Afghanistan include beatings, application of electric shock, threats of sexual assault, stress positions, removal of toenails, twisting and wrenching of genitals, and hanging detainees by their wrists. Inadequate due process protections for detainees held within the parallel US-administered system and for those prosecuted under Afghan law following US detention also continue to be a serious concern.

Violence and Discrimination against Women and Girls

Attacks and threats against women continue, frequently focusing on women in public life, school girls, and the staff of girls' schools. The incarceration of women and girls for "moral crimes" such as running away from home—even when doing so is not prohibited by statutory law—also continues to be a major concern, with an estimated half of the approximately 700 women and girls in jail and prison facing such charges.

A government-proposed regulation in 2011 would have prevented NGOs from independently operating shelters for women and jeopardized the existence of Afghanistan's few existing shelters. Afghanistan at present has 14 shelters, each able to house an average of around 20 to 25 women and their children. This does not meet even a small fraction of the need in a country where an estimated 70 to 80 percent of marriages are forced and 87 percent of women face at least one form of physical, sexual, or psychological violence or forced marriage in their lifetimes. Although the regulation was significantly improved following strong domestic and international criticism, it exemplifies the hostility felt by many parts of Afghan society, including within the government, to women's autonomy and ability to protect themselves from abuse and forced marriage.

Weak Rule of Law and Endemic Corruption

Afghanistan's justice system remains weak and compromised, and a large proportion of the population relies instead on traditional justice mechanisms, and sometimes Taliban courts, for dispute resolution. Human rights abuses are endemic within the traditional justice system, with many practices persisting despite being outlawed. For example *Baad*, where a family gives a girl to another family as compensation for a wrong, continues even though it is banned by the 2009 Law on Elimination of Violence against Women.

Prison overcrowding is extreme and increasing at an alarming rate, with the number of prisoners increasing from 600 in 2001 to 19,000 in 2011. Following the escape of 476 prisoners from Sarposa Prison in Kandahar, the government ordered the transfer of responsibility for prisons from the Ministry of Justice to the Ministry of Interior, despite international concerns that doing so would increase the likelihood of abusive interrogation and lead to gaps in training, management, and oversight.

Key International Actors

For many international actors, particularly the US, a desire to bow out of what increasingly appears to be an unwinnable war has entirely overshadowed concerns about human rights. Activists' demands that negotiations with the Taliban not imperil human rights, especially women's rights, have been met by bland international assurances that any agreement would require the Taliban to commit to respecting the constitution. Such promises are of little use when many in Afghanistan, both government and insurgent supporters, interpret the constitution as elevating religious principles over international human rights obligations. The Taliban has in practice shown no willingness to respect international human rights laws and norms.

Internationally supported efforts to promote human rights, civil society, education, rule of law, governance, and access to health care are imperiled by declining international aid. Aid budgets are expected to decline precipitously in 2012. The looming date of 2014 for withdrawal of most international troops—which is advancing against a backdrop of rising civilian casualties particularly from insurgent attacks, increased use of "night raids," abuses by armed groups, and persistent human rights violations—begs the question of exactly what kind of Afghanistan the troops will be leaving behind.

BANGLADESH

The Awami League government failed to use its significant parliamentary mandate in 2011 to push through policies to ensure strong protections of human rights. Instead of prosecuting members of the Rapid Action Battalion (RAB), who engage in extrajudicial killings, the home minister chose to deny that such violations occur, even in cases where internal ministry investigations found evidence of wrongdoing. The practice of disguising extrajudicial killings as "crossfire" killings seeped from the RAB into other law enforcement institutions, particularly the police. New allegations of torture, arbitrary arrest, and enforced disappearances by police continue to emerge.

The government in 2011 tightened controls over civil society organizations by prosecuting labor union leaders and delaying foreign grants to NGOs. At this writing a bill proposing restrictions on media, which would prohibit the broadcast of certain religious and political speech, was under consideration.

Violence against women including rape, dowry-related assaults, acid attacks, and sexual harassment continue.

Torture, Extrajudicial Killings, and Other Abuses

Despite strong evidence that security forces were continuing to arbitrarily arrest people, often torturing and then killing them in custody, the home minister refused to acknowledge the need for accountability. Prime Minister Sheikh Hasina said her government had zero tolerance for extrajudicial killings, but failed to properly investigate allegations and prosecute the perpetrators.

On May 21, 2011, William Gomes, a representative of the Asian Human Rights Commission, was allegedly picked up by plainclothes RAB personnel and taken to a place his abductors described as "headquarters," where he was stripped naked, had his hands and legs cuffed, was forced into stress position, and was verbally abused and threatened with physical torture. He was interrogated about his work documenting human rights violations.

BANGLADESH

"Crossfire"

Continued Human Rights Abuses by Bangladesh's
Rapid Action Battalion

HUMAN
RIGHTS
WATCH

In at least two cases, the Home Ministry ignored its own findings that RAB was responsible for wrongful killings. According to Odhikar, a Dhaka-based human rights organization, at least 1,600 people have been victims of extrajudicial killings since 2004. Before the Awami League came to power, its leaders had accused RAB of widespread extrajudicial killings; they now claim that all deaths occur during armed exchanges with criminals.

The military and police continue to employ torture and cruel, inhuman, or degrading punishment against suspects, violating both domestic and international law. Many deaths in custody are never investigated. According to Odhikar, at least 12 people died in custody due to police torture in 2011.

Trials for Bangladesh Rifles Abuses

Military tribunal hearings against members of the Bangladesh Rifles (BDR) accused of participating in a February 2009 mutiny continued through 2011. Military courts convicted nearly 1,000 soldiers in mass trials that did not meet fair trial standards, among other things because the prosecution failed to produce individualized evidence against each detainee. In a single trial that concluded on June 27, 657 of 666 defendants were found guilty and sentenced to prison terms ranging from four months to seven years.

Several thousand other soldiers remain in custody awaiting trial in military courts, while another 847 have been charged under the Bangladesh Criminal Code. Some of those charged under the criminal code face the death penalty and many do not have lawyers.

The government did not investigate allegations of torture and possibly as many as 70 custodial deaths during investigations after the mutiny. Many suspects were denied access to legal counsel, particularly in the few months directly after the mutiny.

Civil Society

The government increased surveillance of Odhikar and in particular, Adilur Rahman Khan, Odhikar's secretary advocate; threatening and harassing staff; and delaying approvals of projects.

After Nobel Peace Laureate Mohmmad Yunus, founder of the Grameen Bank, was removed from his position at the bank because he had exceeded the mandatory retirement age, there were mysterious attacks on his supporters. In May Sagirur Rashid Chowdhury, an accounts officer at the bank, was picked up outside the office by plainclothes men. When he was released his body bore signs of severe beatings. He said his abductors had asked him to issue a public statement withdrawing support for Yunus. In September six women directors and one former director of the board of directors of the Grameen Bank, all bene-ficiaries of the microcredit system, suffered intimidation by police who came and searched their rooms.

The government continued legal action aimed at intimidating the Bangladesh Center for Worker Solidarity (BCWS), a trade union group. After revoking BCWS's registration one agency demanded that two union leaders, Kalpona Akhter and Babul Akhter, both facing criminal charges, resign as a precondition to renewed registration of the organization. BCWS has denied all allegations against it.

International Crimes Tribunal

To address fair trial concerns, the government in June 2011 amended the International Crimes (Tribunals) Act of 1973 to include some basic due process concerns, such as the right to the presumption of innocence and a fair and pub-lic hearing. But the law, established to prosecute those responsible for atroci-ties in the war of 1971, still fell short of international standards. The definitions of war crimes, crimes against humanity, and genocide did not conform to inter-national standards and the government failed to amend the law to ensure due process. Defense lawyers, witnesses, and investigators said they had been threatened.

The tribunal in 2011 began proceedings in its first case, that of Jamaat-e-Islami leader Delawar Hossein Sayedee, accused of involvement in war crimes in the 1971 war.

Women's and Girls' Rights

Violence against women and girls and their discriminatory treatment under personal status laws persists. New cases were reported in 2011 of beatings, isolation, and other public humiliation of girls, all imposed following religious leaders' issuance of fatwas on issues such as talking to a man, pre-marital relations, having a child outside wedlock, and adultery. Women's groups are particularly concerned that such abuses continue even though the High Court division of the Bangladesh Supreme Court ordered government authorities to take preventive measures and prosecute perpetrators.

The Bangladesh parliament in 2011 enacted a law against domestic violence and rules are currently being framed for its implementation. The government also introduced a national policy to advance women's rights.

Recruiters in the Middle East are increasingly turning to Bangladesh to hire women domestic workers as other labor-sending countries tighten their regulations or impose bans in response to widespread exploitation. The Bangladeshi government has failed to introduce minimum protection measures for these workers during training or recruitment or to ensure that embassies abroad are adequately equipped with labor attaches and shelters to respond to cases of abuse.

Protection of Indigenous People

Bangladeshi authorities did little to prevent intensifying violence and discrimination against indigenous groups residing in the Chittagong Hill Tracts. There were repeated clashes between ethnic and religious minority groups and "settlers" who belong to the majority Bengali community. These clashes were in part a result of government failure to implement its agreement with the indigenous communities to protect their rights.

Key International Actors

The United States and United Kingdom expressed concern in 2011 about continuing impunity for human rights violations by the RAB. Both countries have provided assistance and training for RAB, though the UK ended such programs in 2011. The US recommended creation of an independent unit to investigate allegations of torture, disappearances, and extrajudicial killings by the RAB.

Bangladesh and India signed trade and security agreements in 2011. Despite Indian government commitments to order its border forces to act with restraint against Bangladeshi nationals who cross into Indian territory, it failed to properly investigate and prosecute those responsible for abuses, including killings.

BURMA

Burma's human rights situation remained dire in 2011 despite some significant moves by the government which formed in late March following November 2010 elections. Freedoms of expression, association, and assembly remain severely curtailed. Although some media restrictions were relaxed, including increased access to the internet and broader scope for journalists to cover formerly prohibited subjects, official censorship constrains reporting on many important national issues. In May and October the government released an estimated 316 political prisoners in amnesties, though many more remain behind bars.

Ethnic conflict escalated in 2011 as longstanding ceasefires with ethnic armed groups broke down in northern Burma. The Burmese military continues to be responsible for abuses against civilians in conflict areas, including forced labor, extrajudicial killings, sexual violence, the use of "human shields," and indiscriminate attacks on civilians. Despite support from 16 countries for a proposed United Nations commission of inquiry into serious violations of international humanitarian law by all parties to Burma's internal armed conflicts, no country took leadership at the UN to make it a reality. Foreign government officials expressed their optimism about government reforms despite abundant evidence of continuing systematic repression.

Signs of Change, But Unclear If They Will Result in Lasting Change?

Burma's national parliament and 14 regional and state assemblies convened in late January 2011. The formal transfer of power from military rule to the new government took place on March 30. Former generals hold most senior ministerial portfolios, and serving generals are constitutionally guaranteed the posts of ministers of defense, home affairs, and border affairs security. Thein Sein, a former general and prime minister, was elected president. The speaker of the lower house is also a former general, and many former military officers hold important positions in the ruling military-backed Union Solidarity and Development Party.

President Thein Sein's inaugural speech in March was notably moderate and constructive in tone and he promised more reforms than had any leader during the preceding 23 years of military rule. The government's stated priorities include economic reform, improved education, ending corruption, and environment protection. In August senior government officials called on exiled political dissidents to return home without reprisal.

In the national parliament, members of parliament are permitted to raise issues with two weeks prior notice and upon official approval. Some previously sensitive issues have been discussed in the new parliament such as calls for a political prisoner amnesty, citizenship for the long repressed Rohingya Muslim minority, and education reform including the currently banned teaching of ethnic languages. In addition, the government worked on a bill that, if not watered down before being enacted, would liberalize citizens' ability to form unions and associations.

Reform bills have been tabled in the new parliament on forming trade unions, permitting peaceful assembly, and amending of the political party registration rules in ways that could open the way for participation by the long repressed opposition party, the National League for Democracy. These changes are encouraging on paper, but it remains to be seen how they will be implemented and the level of social participation.

Media freedoms have been relaxed in some cases, with propaganda slogans removed from magazines and newspapers; mention of Aung San Suu Kyi and display of her photo is now permitted after a long ban. Nevertheless, the censorship board continues to ban stories deemed politically sensitive, an estimated 20 media workers are in prison, including a 21-year-old videographer who received a 16-year sentence in September 2011 for taking video footage after a bomb blast in central Rangoon.

On September 5 the government formed a new National Human Rights Commission, composed of 15 former ambassadors, academics, and civil servants.

Since March Aung San Suu Kyi has been permitted much greater freedom to travel and meet her supporters in the National League for Democracy, even though the party is technically illegal under the electoral laws. Suu Kyi travelled to Naypyidaw in August to meet President Thein Sein; it was the first time she has visited the capital city, which formally opened in 2005.

In November the NLD announced the party would formally re-register as a political party, and expressed their intention to contest scheduled bi-elections in 2012, with Suu Kyi stating she would consider running as a candidate.

Ethnic Conflict and Displacement

Fighting between government forces and ethnic armed groups spread in Burma during 2011, as many longstanding ceasefire agreements unraveled. In Karen State, eastern Burma, a breakaway faction of the Democratic Karen Buddhist Army (DKBA) took up arms following the November 2010 elections. Intensified fighting along the border forced an estimated 20,000 refugees into Thailand. Most DKBA soldiers refused to complete their transformation into Burmese-army-controlled Border Guard Force units and ended their 16-year ceasefire.

In March the Burmese army attacked the Shan State Army-North, breaking a ceasefire reached in 1989, as the Shan army resisted pressure to demobilize and form a government-controlled people's militia. Fighting in northern Shan State displaced an estimated 30,000 civilians.

In June fighting broke out between Burma's second largest opposition armed group, the Kachin Independence Army (KIA), and the Burmese army in northern Burma near the Chinese border, ending a ceasefire signed in 1994. Local women's rights groups reported high levels of sexual violence with more than 35 women and girls raped in the first two months of the fighting alone. Over 30,000 civilians were internally displaced, fleeing Burmese army abuses such as forced labor, extrajudicial killings, and indiscriminate fire, with several thousand seeking refuge in China.

The Burmese military continues to violate international humanitarian law through the use of anti-personnel landmines, extrajudicial killings, forced labor, torture, beatings, and pillaging of property. Sexual violence against women and girls remains a serious problem and perpetrators are rarely brought to justice. The army continues to actively recruit and use child soldiers, even as

BURMA

Dead Men Walking

Convict Porters on the Front Lines in Eastern Burma

HUMAN
RIGHTS
WATCH

KHRG Karen Human Rights Group
Documenting the voices of villagers in rural Burma

the government cooperates with the International Labour Organization on demobilizing child soldiers.

In January Burmese army units in Karen State forced convicts to work as porters in ongoing operations in combat zones. This longstanding practice saw hundreds of prisoners drawn from prisons and labor camps transported to frontline units, and forced to carry military supplies and material to the frontline, often being used as "human shields" to deter attacks or clear anti-personnel landmines. Porters are often tortured, beaten, and subjected to ill-treatment during their forced service.

Ethnic armed groups have also been implicated in serious abuses, such as recruiting child soldiers, extrajudicial executions, and using antipersonnel landmines around civilian areas.

Approximately 500,000 people are internally displaced due to conflict in eastern Burma, with an additional 140,000 refugees in camps in Thailand. Thai authorities in 2011 increased calls for repatriation of the refugees, a proposal that Burmese officials welcomed, and European Union authorities gave greater priority in refugee aid allocations to preparations for repatriation despite serious security concerns about returning populations to active conflict zones. Bangladeshi authorities increased threats to close Rohingya refugee camps and drive the Rohingya minority back into Burma. Some 28,000 Rohingya refugees live in official camps in Bangladesh and another 200,000 live in makeshift settlements or mixed in with the local population in border areas.

Millions of Burmese migrant workers, refugees, and asylum seekers live in Thailand, India, Bangladesh, Malaysia, and Singapore.

Key International Actors

In 2011, 16 countries publicly supported calls for a UN-led commission of inquiry into violations of international human rights and humanitarian law in Burma, but none was prepared to lead efforts to make this a reality. Most countries adopted a "wait and see" approach to Burma, noting government pledges of reform and citing Aung San Suu Kyi's expression of cautious optimism that there might be an "opportunity for change."

In May Vijay Nambiar, the UN secretary-general's special envoy on Burma, visited Burma and expressed optimism over stated reform goals, but also noted that political prisoner releases fell short of international expectations. In his August report on the human rights situation, Secretary-General Ban Ki-moon encouraged the government to turn its reform agenda into reality, but cautioned that failure to release political prisoners, seek peace with ethnic groups, and lift all restrictions on Aung San Suu Kyi would erode international confidence in the process.

Tomas Ojea Quintana, the UN special rapporteur on Burma, visited Burma in August and later stated that despite positive signs of change there remain "serious and ongoing human rights concerns," including "continuing allegations of torture and ill-treatment during interrogation." In his September report to the General Assembly, Quintana said "many serious human rights issues encompassing the broad range of civil, political, economic, social and cultural rights remain and they need to be addressed."

The United States, EU, Australia, Canada, and Switzerland continue to impose restrictive trade and financial sanctions on Burma, arguing that recent government actions are insufficient to consider lifting the sanctions. In September and November Derek Mitchell, the newly appointed US special representative and policy coordinator on Burma, made official visits to the country. Mitchell expressed cautious optimism that reforms could evolve into far-reaching change, but urged the government to "take concrete actions in a timely fashion to demonstrate its sincerity and genuine commitment to reform and national reconciliation." US Senator John McCain visited refugee communities along the Thailand-Burma border and met government and opposition leaders inside Burma in May and June.

In December US Secretary of State Hillary Clinton visited Burma, the first visit by such a senior US official in 50 years—the result, President Barack Obama said, of encouraging "flickers of change" in Burma.

During the Association of Southeast Asian Nations (ASEAN) Summit in November, it was announced that Burma would become chair of the regional grouping in 2014 and host all of ASEAN's meetings that year.

Burma's neighbors—China, India, and Thailand—continue to invest in and trade extensively with Burma, especially in the extractive and hydro-electric energy industries. Burma continued to earn billions of US dollars in natural gas revenues, little of which is directed into social services such as health care and education.

China began construction on two energy pipelines from western Burma to Yunnan, including a planned rail link. The building of a series of massive hydro-electric dams on the Irrawaddy River in upper Burma sparked heated domestic debate over its effects on the environment and the ethnic minority population, some of whom have already been forcibly displaced by the project. In late September President Thein Sein suspended work on the Myitsone dam, the largest in a series of several planned dams. The move was received positively inside Burma, but criticized by the Chinese government.

There are negative impacts of certain other Chinese investments, including agri-business ventures in northern Burma, which have involved land seizures by Burmese authorities. India's construction of a major infrastructure project for the Kaladan River in western Burma continued in 2011, as did Indian investments in mining projects. Sales of natural gas to Thailand still account for the largest share of the Burmese government's foreign exchange earnings, which will increase markedly when the Chinese gas pipeline project is completed in 2013.

Russia, China, and North Korea continue to sell arms to Burma, despite frequently voiced US concerns that North Korean sales could breach UN Security Council resolutions on non-proliferation.

CAMBODIA

Twenty years after the signing of the Paris Agreements in 1991, Cambodia's human rights record remains poor. The government of the ruling Cambodian People's Party (CPP) continues to use the judiciary, penal code, and threats of arrest or legal action to restrict free speech, jail government critics, disperse peaceful protests by workers and farmers, and silence opposition party members. In 2011 it threatened one of the key accomplishments of the Paris Agreements—the spectacular growth of NGOs, community-based civic groups, informal associations, and grassroots networks—by proposing a law that would give it wide discretion to shut down associations and NGOs.

In 2011 the government failed to take meaningful steps to ensure that the judiciary was impartial and independent. The courts continued to operate as an arm of the CPP, symbolized by the chief justice of the Supreme Court, Dith Munthy, remaining a member of the party's highest decision-making body. Allegations that Prime Minister Hun Sen was pressuring Khmer Rouge tribunal officials to drop cases dealt a further blow to the judiciary.

Opposition party leader Sam Rainsy remains in exile rather than face long prison sentences as a result of politically motivated and manifestly unfair trials. Noting that criticism of policy decisions is "one of the basic functions of leaders of opposition parties," Surya Subedi, the United Nations special rapporteur on human rights in Cambodia, wrote that opposition leaders "should not be subjected to criminal proceedings for discharging their responsibilities in a peaceful manner."

Freedom of Expression, Assembly, and Association

The Cambodian government in 2011 pressed forward with a vaguely worded draft law on associations and NGOs that would require NGOs to register and would enable the government to order the closure of organizations on arbitrary grounds. Civil society groups fear that the law will be used to intimidate groups and associations into silence. National and international NGOs mounted a campaign opposing the draft law and the UN and key donors such as the United States and European Union made their concerns known publicly and privately.

NGO fears were deepened on August 2 when the Ministry of Interior (MOI) sent a letter to local NGO Sahmakum Teang Tnaut (STT) suspending its activities for five months without specifying the legal grounds for the action. On August 13 the MOI publicly accused STT of "incitement" of persons to oppose development projects. Authorities issued formal warning letters to two other groups, Bridges Across Borders Cambodia (BABC) and NGO Forum on Cambodia, and threatened a fourth group, the Housing Rights Task Force.

The government increasingly is using criminal defamation and incitement laws to intimidate critics. NGOs identified at least 12 persons imprisoned under such laws for peaceful expression of views since December 2010. They include Seng Kunnakar, UN World Food Program employee; Sam Chankea, provincial field coordinator of Cambodian Human Rights and Development Association (ADHOC); Leang Sokchouen, staff member from Licadho; and Hang Chakra, editor of the *Khmer Machas Srok* newspaper.

The government continues to use a 2009 law on demonstrations to deny protest requests or compel smaller protests to use remotely placed, so-called freedom parks for rallies. Many people have staged protests regardless, particularly over land. In March the government denied permission for a public rally organized by the Cambodian Women's Movement Organization and women workers in central Phnom Penh to celebrate the 100th anniversary of international women's day, even though the minister of women's affairs was scheduled to speak.

The government also continues to push for a trade union law that would significantly weaken union rights by amending registration, collective bargaining, and strike provisions. The draft provisions violate international labor rights standards. Authorities have prevented at least three public showings in Phnom Penh of a documentary about the 2004 assassination of labor leader Chea Vichea. There has been no progress in his case or that of two other union leaders killed in 2004.

Torture and Arbitrary Detention

Police and the military police routinely use torture to extract confessions that are used to obtain convictions. Cambodia's prisons continue to be overcrowded and lack sufficient food, water, sanitation, and healthcare. A survey by Licadho found that prisons are "bursting at the seams," with reported occupancy at 179 percent in April 2011. Campaigners have demanded reforms to limit widespread use of pre-trial detention and step up implementation of parole procedures and non-custodial sentences.

Reportedly, Cambodian authorities are arbitrarily detaining more than 2,000 people—including the homeless; street children, some as young as 13; and people with mental disabilities—in 11 government drug detention centers created to "treat" and "rehabilitate" drug users. Detainees in such centers are subjected to torture; violence, including electric shocks and whippings; forced labor; and military-style drills. Vietnam continued to strongly influence Cambodian drug treatment policies.

Women and girls—including transgender women—involved in sex work face beatings, rape, sexual harassment, extortion, arbitrary arrest, and detention by police and government-hired security guards. A 2008 law on trafficking and sexual exploitation that criminalizes trafficking also makes "solicitation" illegal, which has exposed sex workers to arbitrary detention and abuse. Homeless children, families, beggars, people with mental disabilities, and other indigent people gathered in police sweeps have been detained and mistreated in government social affairs centers.

Land Confiscation and Forced Evictions

Illegal land confiscation and forced evictions by government officials and security forces on behalf of powerful companies and individuals remains a pressing issue. Land rights activists face violence and arrest, with more than 60 people imprisoned or awaiting trial at this writing, for protesting forced evictions and land grabbing.

In August more than 100 protesters from the Prey Lang forest reserve were arrested in Phnom Penh, the capital, while distributing pamphlets advocating preservation of the forest. Ten people were injured in June in Kompong Speu when a prosecutor led over 100 soldiers and police to forcibly take control of disputed land awarded by courts to a Taiwanese company.

Since 2007 Phnom Penh municipal authorities, supported by military and police, have sought to evict the approximately 4,200 families living in the Boeung Kak Lake area.The land was transferred by the government in a 99-year lease to a joint venture between a Chinese company and Shukaku, a Cambodian company owned by Lao Meng Kim, a senator and senior CPP member. Intimidation and violence by security forces have forced many families to accept paltry compensation packages and resettle in remote sites on the city outskirts.

Khmer Rouge Tribunal

Prime Minister Hun Sen has continued to undermine the independence of the Extraordinary Chambers of the Courts of Cambodia (ECCC), demanding that the court not pursue cases 003 and 004 against five suspects submitted for indictment by the international co-prosecutor. In April You Bunleng and Siegfried Blunk, the co-investigating judges, closed their investigation into case 003 without having appeared to give the cases the rigorous scrutiny warranted. The international co-prosecutor Andrew Cayley challenged this decision in early May; a month later the co-prosecuting judges refused his request and threatened him with contempt of court on specious grounds of violating judicial confidentiality. The co-investigating judges also significantly narrowed their definition of "victim," thereby largely shutting down civil party applications to present evidence in those cases. In October Human Rights Watch called for the co-investigating judges to resign for failing to perform their judicial duties. One week later Blunk resigned, citing government interference in the court.

Refugees and Asylum Seekers

Asylum seekers, especially from Vietnam and China, remain at risk of forced repatriation in violation of the Refugee Convention. On February 15 the government ordered closed the refugee center in Phnom Penh sheltering Montagnard refugees from Vietnam. Despite international urging, the government did not amend its sub-decree on determining refugee status, which fails to incorporate the Refugee Convention's definition of refugee and otherwise to fulfill Cambodia's obligations as a party to that convention.

Cambodian authorities still do not grant asylum to Khmer Krom—ethnic Khmer from southern Vietnam—who fled Vietnam. Despite promises to treat them as Cambodian citizens, authorities have failed to grant many of them citizenship or residence rights.

Migrant Domestic Workers

Since 2008, 40,000 to 50,000 Cambodian women and girls have been recruited as migrant domestic workers in Malaysia. Recruitment agents often forge fraudulent identity documents for children, offer cash and food incentives as "loans" that leave migrants deeply indebted, confine recruits in training centers in Cambodia for months, and intimidate those who try to escape. Many recruitment centers have inadequate food, water, and access to medical care. In 2011 three women recruits died while confined in the centers; authorities failed to undertake thorough investigations into their deaths or hold anyone accountable.

A revised labor regulation in August fell far short of guaranteeing minimum rights protections for Cambodian migrants going abroad. Drafted with little consultation with migrants or civil society organizations, the regulation fails to tackle forced confinement, debt bondage, and child recruitment. Cambodian embassy officials in Kuala Lumpur and recruitment agencies frequently fail to protect workers fleeing abuses and in some cases have returned workers to abusive employers. In October Cambodia announced a ban on sending domestic workers to Malaysia.

Key International Actors

Cambodia's donors pledged US$2.8 billion in development aid for the 2009 to 2012 period. From 1998-2008, donors annually contributed approximately $600 million a year. Foreign assistance accounts for over 50 percent of Cambodia's

CAMBODIA/ MALAYSIA

"They Deceived Us at Every Step"

Abuse of Cambodian Domestic Workers Migrating to Malaysia

**HUMAN
RIGHTS
WATCH**

budget, yet donors have said little about Cambodia's worsening human rights environment.

A notable exception was a strong donor response to the draft NGO law, which at this writing had still not been enacted.

The World Bank suspended provision of new loans after the Cambodian government failed to address critical problems in a World Bank-supported land titling program. The bank had for many years raised concerns about high-level corruption but had rarely taken action.

Japan, Cambodia's largest donor, said little about human rights, the draft NGO law, or the Khmer Rouge tribunal debacle. China, another major investor and donor, continued to increase aid to Cambodia without conditions, undermining efforts by others to address human rights concerns.

CHINA

Against a backdrop of rapid socio-economic change and modernization, China continues to be an authoritarian one-party state that imposes sharp curbs on freedom of expression, association, and religion; openly rejects judicial independence and press freedom; and arbitrarily restricts and suppresses human rights defenders and organizations, often through extra-judicial measures.

The government also censors the internet; maintains highly repressive policies in ethnic minority areas such as Tibet, Xinjiang, and Inner Mongolia; systematically condones—with rare exceptions—abuses of power in the name of "social stability"; and rejects domestic and international scrutiny of its human rights record as attempts to destabilize and impose "Western values" on the country. The security apparatus—hostile to liberalization and legal reform—seems to have steadily increased its power since the 2008 Beijing Olympics. China's "social stability maintenance" expenses are now larger than its defense budget.

At the same time Chinese citizens are increasingly rights-conscious and challenging the authorities over livelihood issues, land seizures, forced evictions, abuses of power by corrupt cadres, discrimination, and economic inequalities. Official and scholarly statistics estimate that 250-500 protests occur per day; participants number from ten to tens of thousands. Internet users and reform-oriented media are aggressively pushing the boundaries of censorship, despite the risks of doing so, by advocating for the rule of law and transparency, exposing official wrong-doing, and calling for reforms.

Despite their precarious legal status and surveillance by the authorities, civil society groups continue to try to expand their work, and increasingly engage with international NGOs. A small but dedicated network of activists continues to exposes abuses as part of the *weiquan* ("rights defense")movement, despite systematic repression ranging from police monitoring to detention, arrest, enforced disappearance, and torture.

Human Rights Defenders

In February 2011, unnerved by the pro-democracy Arab Spring movements and a scheduled Chinese leadership transition in October 2012, the government launched the largest crackdown on human rights lawyers, activists, and critics in a decade. The authorities also strengthened internet and press censorship, put the activities of many dissidents and critics under surveillance, restricted their activities, and took the unprecedented step of rounding up over 30 of the most outspoken critics and "disappearing" them for weeks.

The April 3 arrest of contemporary artist and outspoken government critic Ai Weiwei, who was detained in an undisclosed location without access to a lawyer, prompted an international outcry and contributed to his release on bail on June 22. Tax authorities notified him on November 1 that he had to pay US$2.4 million in tax arrears and fines for the company registered in his wife's name. Most of the other activists were also ultimately released, but forced to adopt a much less vocal stance for fear of further reprisals. Several lawyers detained in 2011, including Liu Shihui, described being interrogated, tortured, threatened, and released only upon signing "confessions" and pledges not to use Twitter, or talk to media, human rights groups, or foreign diplomats about their detention.

The government continues to impose indefinite house arrest on its critics. Liu Xia, the wife of imprisoned Nobel Peace Laureate Liu Xiaobo, has been missing since December 2010 and is believed to be under house arrest to prevent her from campaigning on her husband's behalf. In February 2011 she said in a brief online exchange that she and her family were like "hostages" and that she felt "miserable." She is allowed to visit Liu Xiaobo once a month, subject to agreement from the prison authorities.

Chen Guangcheng, a blind legal activist who was released from prison in September 2010, remained under house arrest in 2011. Security personnel assaulted Chen and his wife in February after he released footage documenting his family's house arrest. Noted activist Hu Jia, who was released after completing a three-and-a-half-year prison sentence in June, is also under house arrest in Beijing, the capital, with his activist wife Zeng Jinyan and their daughter.

Grave concerns exist about the fate of lawyer Gao Zhisheng, who was "disappeared" by the authorities in September 2009 and briefly surfaced in March 2010 detailing severe and continuous torture against him, before going missing again that April.

On June 12, 2011, despite the steady deterioration in China's human rights environment, the Chinese government declared it had fulfilled "all tasks and targets" of its National Human Rights Action Plans (2009-2010).

Legal Reforms

While legal awareness among citizens continues to grow, the government's overt hostility towards genuine judicial independence undercuts legal reform and defeats efforts to limit the Chinese Communist Party's authority over all judicial institutions and mechanisms.

The police dominate the criminal justice system, which relies disproportionately on defendants' confessions. Weak courts and tight limits on the rights of the defense mean that forced confessions under torture remain prevalent and miscarriages of justice frequent. In August 2011, in an effort to reduce such cases and improve the administration of justice, the government published new rules to eliminate unlawfully obtained evidence and strengthened the procedural rights of the defense in its draft revisions to the Criminal Procedure Law. It is likely it will be adopted in March 2012.

However, the draft revisions also introduced an alarming provision that would effectively legalize enforced disappearances by allowing police to secretly detain suspects for up to six months at a location of their choice in "state security, terrorism and major corruption cases." The measure would put suspects at great risk of torture while giving the government justification for the "disappearance" of dissidents and activists in the future. Adoption of this measure—which is hotly criticized in Chinese media by human rights lawyers, activists, and part of the legal community—would significantly deviate from China's previous stance of gradual convergence with international norms on administering justice, such as the International Covenant on Civil and Political Rights, which China signed in 1997 but has yet to ratify.

China continued in 2011 to lead the world in executions. The exact number remains a state secret but is estimated to range from 5,000 to 8,000 a year.

Freedom of Expression

The government continued in 2011 to violate domestic and international legal guarantees of freedom of press and expression by restricting bloggers, journalists, and an estimated more than 500 million internet users. The government requires internet search firms and state media to censor issues deemed officially "sensitive," and blocks access to foreign websites including Facebook, Twitter, and YouTube. However, the rise of Chinese online social networks—in particularly Sina's Weibo, which has 200 million users—has created a new platform for citizens to express opinions and to challenge official limitations on freedom of speech despite intense scrutiny by China's censors.

On January 30 official concern about Egyptian anti-government protests prompted a ban on internet searches for "Egypt." On February 20 internet rumors about a Chinese "Jasmine Revolution" resulted in a ban on web searches for "jasmine." In August a cascade of internet criticism of the government's response to the July 23 Wenzhou train crash prompted the government to warn of new penalties, including suspension of microblog access, against bloggers who transmit "false or misleading information."

Ambiguous "inciting subversion" and "revealing state secrets" laws contributed to the imprisonment of at least 34 Chinese journalists. Those jailed include Qi Chonghuai, originally sentenced to a four-year prison term in August 2008 for "extortion and blackmail" after exposing government corruption in his home province of Shandong. His prison sentence was extended in June for eight years when the same court found him guilty of fresh charges of extortion and "embezzlement."

Censorship restrictions continue to pose a threat to journalists whose reporting oversteps official guidelines. In May *Southern Metropolis Daily* editor Song Zhibiao was demoted as a reprisal for criticism of the government's 2008 Sichuan earthquake recovery efforts. In June the government threatened to blacklist journalists guilty of "distorted" reporting of food safety scandals. In

July the *China Economic Times* disbanded its investigative unit, an apparent response to official pressure against its outspoken reporting on official malfeasance.

Physical violence against journalists who report on "sensitive" topics remained a problem in 2011. On June 1, plainclothes Beijing police assaulted and injured two *Beijing Times* reporters who refused to delete photos they had taken at the scene of a stabbing. The two officers were subsequently suspended. On September 19 Li Xiang, a reporter with Henan province's Luoyang Television, was stabbed to death in what has been widely speculated was retaliation for his exposé of a local food safety scandal. Police have arrested two suspects and insist that Li's murder was due to a robbery.

Police deliberately targeted foreign correspondents with physical violence at the site of a rumored anti-government protest in Beijing on February 27. A video journalist at the scene required medical treatment for severe bruising and possible internal injuries after men who appeared to be plain clothes security officers repeatedly punched and kicked him in the face. Uniformed police manhandled, detained, and delayed more than a dozen other foreign media at the scene.

Government and security bureaus prevented the biennial Beijing Queer Film Festival from screening in Beijing's Xicheng District. Parts of the festival were held surreptitiously in community venues.

Freedom of Religion

The Chinese government limits religious practices to officially-approved temples, monasteries, churches, and mosques despite a constitutional guarantee of freedom of religion. Religious institutions must submit data—including financial records, activities, and employee details—for periodic official audits. The government also reviews seminary applications and religious publications, and approves all religious personnel appointments. Protestant "house churches" and other unregistered spiritual organizations are considered illegal and their members subject to prosecution and fines. The Falun Gong and some other groups are deemed "evil cults" and members risk intimidation, harassment, and arrest.

In April the government pressured the landlord of the Beijing Shouwang Church, a "house church" with 1,000 congregants, to evict the church from its location in a Beijing restaurant. Over the course of at least five Sundays in April and May, the Shouwang congregation held its services in outdoor locations, attracting police attention and resulting in the temporary detention of more than 100 of its members.

The government continues to heavily restrict religious activities in the name of security in ethnic minority areas. See sections below on Tibet and Xinjiang.

Health

On August 2 the government announced the closure of 583 battery-recycling factories linked to widespread lead poisoning. However, it has failed to substantively recognize and address abuses including denial of treatment for child lead poisoning victims and harassment of parents seeking legal redress that Human Rights Watch uncovered in a June 2011 report of lead poisoning in Henan, Yunnan, Shaanxi, and Hunan.

People with HIV/AIDS continued to face discrimination. In September an HIV-positive female burn victim was denied treatment at three hospitals in Guangdong province due to stigma about her status. On September 8 an HIV-positive school teacher launched a wrongful dismissal suit against the Guizhou provincial government after it refused to hire him on April 3 due to his HIV status.

Disability Rights

The Chinese government is inadequately protecting the rights of people with disabilities, despite its ratification of the Convention on the Rights of Persons with Disabilities (CRPD), and its forthcoming review by the treaty's monitoring body.

CHINA

"My Children Have Been Poisoned"

A Public Health Crisis in Four Chinese Provinces

HUMAN
RIGHTS
WATCH

In September a group of part-time teachers with disabilities requested that China's Ministry of Education lift restrictions imposed by 20 cities and provinces on full-time employment of teachers with physical disabilities. On September 7, Henan officials freed 30 people with mental disabilities who had been abducted and trafficked into slave labor conditions in illegal brick kiln factories in the province. The discovery cast doubt on official efforts to end such abuses in the wake of a similar scandal in Shaanxi in 2007.

On August 10 the Chinese government invited public comment on its long-awaited draft mental health law. Domestic legal experts warn the draft contains potentially serious risks to the rights of persons with mental disabilities, including involuntary institutionalization, forced treatment and deprivation of legal capacity.

Migrant and Labor Rights

Lack of meaningful union representation remained an obstacle to systemic improvement in workers' wages and conditions in 2011.The government prohibits independent labor unions, so the official All-China Federation of Trade Unions (ACFTU) is the sole legal representative of China's workers. A persistent labor shortage linked to changing demographics—official statistics indicate that nationwide job vacancies outpaced available workers by five percent in the first three months of 2011—has led to occasional reports of rising wages and improved benefits for some workers.

In January a government survey of migrant workers indicated that the *hukou* (household registration) system continued to impose systemic discrimination on migrants. Survey respondents blamed the *hukou* system, which the government has repeatedly promised to abolish, for unfairly limiting their access to housing, medical services, and education. In August 2011 the Beijing city government ordered the closure of 24 illegal private schools that catered to migrant children. Most found alternate schools, although an estimated 10 to 20 percent had to be separated from their parents and sent to their *hukou*-linked rural hometowns due to their parents' inability to secure suitable and affordable schooling in Beijing.

Women's Rights

Women's reproductive rights remain severely curtailed in 2011 under China's family planning regulations. Administrative sanctions, fines, and forced abortions continue to be imposed, if somewhat erratically, on rural women, including when they become migrant laborers in urban or manufacturing areas, and are increasingly extended to ethnic minority areas such as Tibet and Xinjiang. These policies contribute to an increasing gender-imbalance (118.08 males for every 100 females according to the 2010 census), which in turn fuels trafficking and prostitution.

Sex workers, numbering four to ten million, remain a particularly vulnerable segment of the population due to the government's harsh policies and regular mobilization campaigns to crack down on prostitution.

Although the government acknowledges that domestic violence, employment discrimination, and discriminatory social attitudes remain acute and widespread problems, it continues to stunt the development of independent women's rights groups and discourages public interest litigation. A new interpretation of the country's Marriage Law by the Supreme People's Court in August 2011 might further exacerbate the gender wealth gap by stating that after divorce, marital property belongs solely to the person who took out a mortgage and registered as the homeowner, which in most cases is the husband.

Illegal Adoptions and Child Trafficking

On August 16 the Chinese government announced it would tighten rules to prevent illegal adoptions and child trafficking. Revised Registration Measures for the Adoption of Children by Chinese Citizens were expected to be introduced by the end of 2011 and would restrict the source of adoptions to orphanages, rather than hospitals or other institutions. The planned rule change follows revelations in May 2011 that members of a government family planning unit in Hunan had kidnapped and trafficked at least 15 babies to couples in the United States and Holland for US$3,000 each between 2002 and 2005. A subsequent police investigation determined there had been no illegal trafficking, despite testimony from parents who insist their children were abducted and subsequently trafficked overseas.

Sexual Orientation and Gender Identity

In 1997 the government decriminalized homosexual conduct and in 2001 ceased to classify homosexuality as a mental illness. However, police continue to occasionally raid popular gay venues in what activists describe as deliberate harassment. Same-sex relationships are not legally recognized, adoption rights are denied to people in same-sex relationships, and there are no anti-discrimination laws based on sexual orientation. On April 4, 2011, Shanghai police raided Q Bar, a popular gay venue, alleging it was staging "pornographic shows." Police detained more than 60 people, including customers and bar staff, and released them later that day. High-profile public support for overcoming social and official prejudice against lesbian, gay, bisexual, and transgender (LGBT) people is increasingly common. On July 5 a China Central Television talk show host criticized homophobic online comments posted by a famous Chinese actress and urged respect for the LGBT community.

Tibet

The situation in the Tibet Autonomous Region (TAR) and the neighboring Tibetan autonomous areas of Qinghai, Sichuan, Gansu, and Yunnan province, remained tense in 2011 following the massive crackdown on popular protests that swept the plateau in 2008. Chinese security forces maintain a heavy presence and the authorities continue to tightly restrict access and travel to Tibetan areas, particularly for journalists and foreign visitors. Tibetans suspected of being critical of political, religious, cultural, or economic state policies are targeted on charges of "separatism."

The government continues to build a "new socialist countryside" by relocating and rehousing up to 80 percent of the TAR population, including all pastoralists and nomads.

The Chinese government has given no indication it would accommodate the aspirations of Tibetan people for greater autonomy, even within the narrow confines of the country's autonomy law on ethnic minorities' areas. It has rejected holding negotiations with the new elected leader of the Tibetan community in exile, Lobsang Sangay, and warned that it would designate the next Dalai Lama itself.

In August Sichuan authorities imposed heavy prison sentences on three ethnic Tibetan monks from the Kirti monastery for assisting another monk who self-immolated in protest in March. Ten more Tibetan monks and one nun had self-immolated through mid-November, all expressing their desperation over the lack of religious freedom.

Xinjiang

The Urumqi riots of July 2009—the most deadly episode of ethnic unrest in recent Chinese history—continued to cast a shadow over developments in the Xinjiang Uighur Autonomous Region. The government has not accounted for hundreds of persons detained after the riots, nor investigated the serious allegations of torture and ill-treatment of detainees that have surfaced in testimonies of refugees and relatives living outside China. The few publicized trials of suspected rioters were marred by restrictions on legal representation, overt politicization of the judiciary, and failure to publish notification of the trials and to hold genuinely open trials as mandated by law.

Several violent incidents occurred in the region in 2011, though culpability remains unclear. On July 12 the government said it had killed 14 Uighur attackers who had overrun a police station in Hetian and were holding several hostages. On July 30 and 31 a series of knife and bomb attacks took place in Kashgar. In both cases the government blamed Islamist extremists. In mid-August it launched a two-month "strike hard" campaign aimed at "destroying a number of violent terrorist groups and ensuring the region's stability."

Under the guise of counterterrorism and anti-separatism efforts, the government also maintains a pervasive system of ethnic discrimination against Uighurs and other ethnic minorities, along with sharp curbs on religious and cultural expression and politically motivated arrests.

The first national Work Conference on Xinjiang, held in 2010, endorsed economic measures that may generate revenue but are likely to further marginalize ethnic minorities. By the end of 2011, 80 percent of traditional neighborhoods in the ancient Uighur city of Kashgar will have been razed. Many Uighur inhabitants have been forcibly evicted and relocated to make way for a new city likely to be dominated by the Han population.

Hong Kong

Hong Kong immigration authorities' refusal in 2011 to grant entry to several visitors critical of the Chinese government's human rights record raised concerns that the territory's autonomy was being eroded. Concerns about police powers also continue to grow following heavy restrictions imposed on students and media during the visit of a Chinese state leader in September 2011.

The status of migrant domestic workers in Hong Kong was strengthened in September when a court judged that rules excluding those workers from seeking the right of abode were unconstitutional. However, the Hong Kong government suggested it would appeal to Beijing for a review, further eroding the territory's judicial autonomy.

Key International Actors

Despite voting in favor of a Security Council resolution referring Libya to the International Criminal Court (ICC) in February, the Chinese government continued to ignore or undermine international human rights norms and institutions. In June, amidst outcry against the visit, China hosted Sudanese President Omar al-Bashir, who is wanted by the ICC on charges of war crimes, crimes against humanity, and genocide. In 2011 it significantly increased pressure on governments in Central and Southeast Asia to forcibly return Uighur refugees, leading to the refoulement of at least 20 people, and in October prevailed upon the South African government to deny a visa to the Dalai Lama, who wished to attend the birthday celebrations of Archbishop Desmond Tutu. That same month it exercised a rare veto together with Russia at the Security Council to help defeat a resolution condemning gross human rights abuses in Syria.

Although several dozen governments attended the 2010 Nobel Peace Prize ceremonies honoring activist Liu Xiaobo, relatively few engaged in effective advocacy on behalf of human rights in China during 2011. While the US emphasized human rights issues during Hu Jintao's January state visit to Washington, that emphasis—and the attention of other governments—declined precipitously once the Arab Spring began, making it easier for the Chinese government to silence dissent. Few audibly continued their calls for the release of Liu and others.

Perhaps demonstrating the influence of growing popular objections to abusive Chinese investment projects, the Burmese government made a surprise announcement in September that it would suspend the primarily Chinese-backed and highly controversial Myitsone Dam. In Zambia, Chinese-run mining firms announced a sudden wage increase following the election of the opposition Patriotic Front, which had campaigned in part on securing minimum wage guarantees.

INDIA

India, the world's most populous democracy, continues to have a vibrant media, an active civil society, a respected judiciary, and significant human rights problems.

Custodial killings, police abuses including torture, and failure to implement policies to protect vulnerable communities marred India's record in 2011 as in the past. Impunity for abuses committed by security forces also continued, particularly in Jammu and Kashmir, the northeast, and areas facing Maoist insurgency. New state controls over foreign funding of NGOs led to restrictions on legitimate efforts to protect human rights. However, killings by the Border Security Force at the Indo-Bangladesh border decreased dramatically.

Social unrest and protests deepened in resource-rich areas of central and eastern India, where rapid economic growth has been accompanied by rapidly growing inequality. Mining and infrastructure projects threaten widespread displacement of forest-dwelling tribal communities. The government has yet to enact comprehensive laws to protect, compensate, and resettle displaced people, although a new land acquisition law has been drafted.

Although at this writing deaths from terror attacks had decreased significantly from earlier years, there were serial bomb explosions in Mumbai on July 13, 2011. On September 7, 2011, a bomb explosion outside the Delhi High Court killed 15 people. The perpetrators remain unidentified. Progress was made in restraining the police from religious profiling of Muslims after bombings.

Despite repeated claims of progress by the government, there was no significant improvement in access to health care and education.

An anti-corruption movement erupted into public view in August and brought the government to a standstill, with widespread street protests and sit-ins demanding legal reform and prosecutions. Activists working with two prominent efforts to address poverty and accountability—India's rural employment guarantee scheme and right to information laws—came under increasing attack, facing threats, beatings, and even death.

Accountability

India has yet to repeal laws or change policies that allow de jure and de facto impunity for human rights violations, and has failed to prosecute even known perpetrators of serious abuses.

The Indian defense establishment resisted attempts to repeal or revise the Armed Forces Special Powers Act (AFSPA), a law that provides soldiers in "disturbed" areas widespread police powers. In September Home Minister P. Chidambaram said that there was an ongoing effort "to build a consensus within the government" to address the problems with AFSPA, but no action has been taken. Various government-appointed commissions have long called for repeal.

Jammu and Kashmir

Thousands of Kashmiris have allegedly been forcibly disappeared during two decades of conflict in the region, their whereabouts unknown. A police investigation in 2011 by the Jammu and Kashmir State Human Rights Commission (SHRC) found 2,730 bodies dumped into unmarked graves at 38 sites in north Kashmir. At least 574 were identified as the bodies of local Kashmiris. The government had previously said that the graves held unidentified militants, most of them Pakistanis whose bodies had been handed over to village authorities for burial. Many Kashmiris believe that some graves contain the bodies of victims of enforced disappearances.

The government of Jammu and Kashmir has promised an investigation, but the identification and prosecution of perpetrators will require the cooperation of army and federal paramilitary forces. These forces in the past, have resisted fair investigations and prosecutions, claiming immunity under the Armed Forces Special Powers Act (AFSPA) and section 197 of the Criminal Procedure Code.

Maoist Insurgency

Maoist insurgents, also known as Naxalites, operate in 10 states and claim to fight for the rights of the marginalized tribal, Dalit, and landless communities.

Governance has often been weak in regions where the Maoists have found popular support, with economic-development-related corruption and illegal mining severely limiting the revenue available for public services and infrastructure in many of the areas. With government oversight and regulation of the mining sector often wholly ineffective, irresponsible mine operators also pollute vital water supplies, destroy farmland, wreck roads and other public infrastructure, and create other serious health and environmental hazards.

Maoist forces continue to engage in killings and extortion, and target government schools and hospitals for attacks and bombings. At this writing the Naxalites had killed nearly 250 civilians as well as over 100 members of the security forces in 2011. Government officials assert that security forces killed more than 180 Naxalites between January and November 2011, though local activists allege that some of these were civilians.

Despite court rulings, the government has yet to properly implement a directive preventing security forces from using schools during counterinsurgency operations. Human rights activists seeking accountability for abuses such as arbitrary arrests, torture and other ill-treatment, and killings have come under threat from both Naxalite forces and security agencies.

In a welcome decision, the Indian Supreme Court ruled unconstitutional the use of Special Police Officers—inadequately trained militias—by the Chhattisgarh government in operations against the Maoists. SPOs have been implicated in many abuses.

Killings by Border Security Forces at Bangladesh Border

After a human rights report found that Border Security Force (BSF) personnel operating at the Bangladesh border had indiscriminately shot and killed over 900 Indians and Bangladeshis in the last 10 years, the government in March 2011 ordered restraint and issued BSF personnel rubber bullets. Killings dropped dramatically after the change in policy, but still continue. In their effort to contain illegal activities including the smuggling of cattle and narcotics, some BSF soldiers have continued to harass and beat border residents. No BSF soldier has been prosecuted for any of the killings or other abuses.

Right to Information Law

Citizens and activists have increasingly been using the Right to Information Act (RTI), passed in 2005, to expose official corruption and promote transparency and accountability. In a sad testament to the rampant corruption that exists in India, at least 12 RTI activists have been killed and several others assaulted over the past two years, according to the Asian Centre for Human Rights.

Bombings and Other Attacks

Three bomb explosions in Mumbai on July 13, 2011, killed 29 people and injured 130. On September 7, 2011, a bomb explosion outside the Delhi High Court claimed 15 lives and injured 50. Security and intelligence agencies did not conduct mass arrests of suspects based on little evidence, which in the past resulted in the torture of suspects for information and confessions. However, the failure of the authorities to identify alleged perpetrators led to widespread criticism of the agencies and calls for police reform and training.

Death Penalty

Capital punishment remains on the statute books. Although India has not carried out an execution since 2004, many death sentence appeals have been allowed to languish, some for decades. In 2011 the president rejected clemency petitions in five cases, including on behalf of three persons convicted for assassinating Rajiv Gandhi, the former prime minister.

Women's Rights

2011 census data revealed a further decline in India's female/male sex ratio, pointing to the failure of laws aimed at reducing sex-selective abortions. A series of "honor" killings and rapes rocked the country in 2011 but there has been no effective action to prevent and effectively prosecute such violence. The government has yet to improve health services for survivors of sexual assault but has taken steps to provide compensation for rape survivors. At this writing the government was revising its medico-legal protocols for evidence collection from rape survivors, excluding the degrading and inhuman "finger" test that classifies many rape survivors as "habituated to sexual intercourse," causing humiliation to victims and at times affecting the outcome of criminal trials. Despite considerable progress on maternal health, vast disparities remain and a spate of maternal deaths continues to be reported from Madhya Pradesh and Rajasthan states.

Palliative Care

Hundreds of thousands of persons with incurable diseases suffer unnecessarily from severe pain because the Indian government has failed to ensure access to safe, effective, and inexpensive pain drugs. In an important step forward, the Medical Council of India recognized palliative care as a medical specialty. But more than half of government-supported regional cancer centers still do not offer palliative care or pain management, even though more than 70 percent of their patients need it, resulting in severe but unnecessary suffering for tens of thousands.

International Role

As a member of the United Nations Security Council and the Human Rights Council (HRC), India in 2011 had an opportunity to align its foreign policy with the ideals it claims to stand for, but officials remained reluctant to voice concerns over even egregious human rights violations in countries such as Sri Lanka, Burma, Syria, and Sudan.

Despite concerns over the safety of its nationals in Libya, India did support UN Security Council resolution 1970 on Libya calling for protection of the Libyan people. India later abstained on resolution 1973, which authorized military force to protect civilians. During its rotating presidency at the Security Council, India was able to secure a consensus among sharply divided member states on Syria, leading to the first Council statement condemning the violence. India did not support the HRC resolution creating an international commission of inquiry on Syria in August, or the Syria text that called for a draft resolution that demanded an end to the violence and cooperation with the UN inquiry proposed by France and the United Kingdom at the Security Council in October.

While India claims it has privately pressed the Sri Lankan and Burmese governments on accountability for conflict-related abuses, it has not supported an independent international investigation into abuses in either country.

Key International Actors

Indian domestic human rights issues, terming such efforts interference in its internal affairs. The United States and European Union privately urge India to improve its human rights record, but say little in public. In July 2011, however, the European Parliament adopted a resolution concerning India's retention of the death penalty.

India's policy in the subcontinent continues to be heavily influenced by strategic and economic concerns about China's growing influence in countries like Burma, Nepal, Pakistan, and Sri Lanka.

INDONESIA

Over the past 13 years Indonesia has made great strides in becoming a stable, democratic country with a strong civil society and independent media. However, serious human rights concerns remain. While senior officials pay lip service to protecting human rights, they seem unwilling to take the steps necessary to ensure compliance by the security forces with international human rights and punishment for those responsible for abuses.

In 2011 religious violence surged, particularly against Christians and Ahmadiyah, a group that considers itself Muslim but that some Muslims consider heretical. Violence continued to rack Papua and West Papua provinces, with few effective police investigations to hold perpetrators accountable.

Freedom of Expression

While Indonesia today has a vibrant media, authorities continue to invoke harsh laws criminalizing those who raise controversial issues, chilling peaceful expression. Indonesia has imprisoned more than 100 activists from the Moluccas and Papua for peacefully voicing political views, holding demonstrations, and raising separatist flags.

The new Law on State Intelligence passed in October, contains vague and overbroad language that could facilitate abuse. For instance, anyone who even negligently leaks confidential information about intelligence activities is subject to imprisonment, raising fears the law could be used to prosecute journalists, political opposition members, or human rights activists who publish information in the public interest about government abuses.

Indonesia's criminal libel, slander, and "insult" laws prohibit deliberately "insulting" public officials and intentionally publicizing statements that harm another person's reputation. In July the Supreme Court overturned an acquittal of Prita Mulyasari, who complained of poor medical treatment over emails to friends, and convicted her on internet defamation charges. Despite acquitting Mulyasari in a related civil case, the Supreme Court sentenced her to a six-month suspended sentence.

Military Reform and Impunity

Impunity for members of Indonesia's security forces remains a serious concern, with no civilian jurisdiction over soldiers who commit serious human rights abuses. Military tribunals are held rarely, lack transparency, and the charges frequently fail to reflect the seriousness of the abuses committed.

In January a military tribunal in Jayapura, Papua, convicted three soldiers from Battalion 753 and sentenced them to between eight to twelve months imprisonment. Despite video evidence of six soldiers involved in brutally torturing two Papuans, the tribunal tried only three of the six soldiers, and on lesser military discipline charges rather than for torture. The soldiers have not been discharged.

In August the Jayapura military tribunal convicted three soldiers from the same battalion regarding an incident in which soldiers shot and killed Reverend Kinderman Gire on the suspicion he was a separatist. Again, the tribunal only convicted them of "disobeying orders," and sentenced them to six, seven, and fifteen months in prison respectively.

In June President Susilo Bambang Yudhoyono appointed his brother-in-law Lt.-Gen. Pramono Edhie Wibowo as the new army chief. Pramono commanded a Kopassus team that was deployed to East Timor in 1999. During that time, in the run up to a referendum on independence, pro-Indonesia militias or security forces killed more than 1,000 civilians.

The armed forces retain extensive business holdings despite a law requiring the government to shut down these businesses or take them over by October 2009.

Freedom of Religion

In 2011 incidents of religious violence got more deadly and more frequent, as Islamist militants mobilized mobs to attack religious minorities with impunity; short prison terms for a handful of offenders did nothing to dissuade mob violence. The government failed to overturn several decrees that discriminate between religions and foster intolerance. According to the Setara Institute, which monitors religious freedom, there were 216 cases of religious attacks in 2010 and 184 cases in the first nine months of 2011.

In February more than 1,500 Islamist militants attacked a house in Cikeusik, western Java, killing three and seriously wounding five Ahmadiyah men. The incident was caught on film. Public outrage generated around the case prompted the authorities to act quickly in investigating the attack. In July the Serang district court sentenced 12 men to between three and six months imprisonment for disturbing public order, incitement, and assault, but not for manslaughter. Police and prosecutors failed to present a fully compelling case against the 12 defendants. Police did not conduct thorough investigations, and prosecutors did not call key eyewitnesses to the attack. The prosecutors also sought reduced sentences, contending that the Ahmadiyah provoked the attack.

In August the Serang court convicted one of the Ahmadiyah members seriously injured in the attack, Deden Sudjana, for assault and disobeying police orders, sentencing him to six months imprisonment.

In 2011 Islamist mobs attacked Ahmadiyah communities and mosques in various places, including West Java, Banten, and South Sulawesi. In August in Makassar, South Sulawesi, a lawyer who represented the Ahmadiyah was assaulted.

In April an Islamist suicide bomber attacked a police mosque in Cirebon, West Java, killing himself and injuring at least 28 people. The bomber had previously been involved in violent protests over a blasphemy trial and an anti-Ahmadiyah attack in Cirebon in 2010. In September another Islamist suicide bomber attacked a church in Solo, Central Java, killing himself and wounding 14 churchgoers.

In February Islamists also attacked three churches in Temanggung, Central Java, after the district court convicted controversial preacher Antonius Bawareng of blasphemy. The court sentenced him to five years in jail, the maximum penalty for blasphemy, but Islamists called for him to be executed. The Semarang district court later convicted eight of the Islamists involved in the attack, sentencing them to between five months and one year imprisonment.

Minority congregations reported that local government officials arbitrarily refused to issue them permits required, under a 2006 decree, for building houses of worship. Those who attempted to worship without a permit faced harassment and violence.

In January the Supreme Court ordered the reopening of a Presbyterian church known locally as GKI Yasmin, overturning the Bogor administration's ruling which had revoked the church's building permit. However, Bogor Mayor Diani Budiarto refused to comply. Government ministers offered the church "relocation." In October an Islamist organization began to harass churchgoers who were holding Sunday services on a sidewalk outside the sealed church.

Senior government officials—including Minister of Religious Affairs Suryadharma Ali, Home Affairs Minister Gamawan Fauzi, and Minister of Human Rights and Law Patrialis Akbar—continued to justify restrictions on religious freedom in the name of public order.

Papua/West Papua

In August internal military documents—mainly from Kopassus, Indonesia's special forces—were made public, exposing how the Indonesian military monitors peaceful activists, politicians, and religious clergy in Papua. The documents show the deep military paranoia in Papua that conflates peaceful political expression with criminal activity. Several of those named in the documents as targets have faced arrest, imprisonment, harassment, or other forms of violence.

Access to Papua in 2011 remained tightly controlled. Few foreign journalists and human rights researchers can visit independently without close monitoring of their activities. Since October the vice president's office has set up the Unit to Accelerate Development in Papua and West Papua, which is focused on economic development. Its board members include some veterans of peace talk over Aceh.

In July over 500 representatives of Papuan civil society met at a peace conference in Jayapura, organized by a government-funded peace-initiative network.

Violence in Papua worsened in July and August with several unrelated attacks in which more than two dozen people were killed or seriously injured. Seventeen people were killed in Puncak Jaya in July when two rival political camps clashed in an election dispute.

In Puncak Jaya there has been a long insurgency between the Free Papua Organization (OPM) and the Indonesian military. The OPM commander in Puncak Jaya claimed responsibility for several attacks against the Indonesian military in July, including one in which an Indonesian military chopper was shot down, injuring seven soldiers and killing one.

In October security forces used excessive violence when arresting more than 300 Papuans involved in a three-day Papuan Congress. At least three men were killed and more than 90 were injured. Six Papuan leaders were charged with treason.

Aceh

Aceh's provincial government continued to implement a repressive Sharia-inspired dress code with disregard for women's agency and a law on "seclusion," banning association between unmarried men and women in "isolated" places. The provisions are enforced primarily through a Sharia police force that harasses, intimidates, and arbitrarily arrests and detains children, women, and men. Local community groups also forcibly enter homes and assault and publicly humiliate couples they suspect are committing "seclusion." Police make little effort to deter and prosecute such assaults. In April two couples were publicly caned under the "seclusion" law.

At this writing it was unclear what effect a decision by Partai Aceh, the main party of the former rebels, to boycott December 2011 local elections would have. The party claimed that Jakarta-sponsored election regulations were not in line with the 2005 Helsinki peace agreement that ended the decades-long conflict in Aceh.

Migrant Domestic Workers

Migrant domestic workers continue to face abuses both during the recruitment process in Indonesia and while employed abroad. The government has failed to stop local recruiters from charging prospective migrants exorbitant fees that leave them highly indebted, which contributes to situations of forced labor abroad.

In May Indonesia and Malaysia signed a new Memorandum of Understanding on Indonesian domestic workers traveling to Malaysia. The revised agreement includes some improved benefits for migrant domestic workers, allowing them to keep their passports instead of having to surrender them to their employers, and guarantees them a weekly day off. But the agreement does not set a minimum wage, as Indonesia had wanted, and perpetuates recruitment fee structures that leave workers indebted.

In June the Saudi government executed Ruyati binti Sapubi, a 54-year-old domestic worker from western Java. She was convicted of murdering her Saudi employer, who she claimed was abusing her.

Child Domestic Workers

Hundreds of thousands of girls in Indonesia are employed as domestic workers. Many work long hours, with no day off, and are forbidden from leaving the house where they work. In the worst cases, girls are physically, psychologically, and sexually abused by their employers. Despite supporting the landmark International Labour Organization convention in June that extended key labor protections to domestic workers, Indonesia's domestic laws exclude all domestic workers from the basic labor rights afforded to formal workers. A domestic workers law that was introduced in 2010 has since stalled in parliament.

Key International Actors

Indonesia assumed the chairmanship of the Association of Southeast Asia Nations (ASEAN) in 2011, holding an ASEAN summit in Jakarta in May and Bali in November. In May Indonesia committed to "uphold the highest standards in the promotion and protection of human rights" when it was elected by the General Assembly to become a member of the United Nations Human Rights Council, but left unaddressed which concrete steps would be taken to fulfill pledges on key issues like freedom of religion and expression, and accountability of abuses by military forces.

The United States continued to provide extensive military assistance to Indonesia. In July US Secretary of State Hillary Clinton and Indonesia Foreign Minister Marty Natalegawa co-chaired the second annual Joint Commission of the US-Indonesia Comprehensive Partnership. In November President Barack Obama visited Indonesia as part of the ASEAN Summit in Bali.

The US also continued to reengage with Kopassus, and provide significant support to Detachment 88, Indonesia's counterterrorism police. Similarly, the Australian government continued cooperation with both units.

In July the European Parliament issued a resolution on human rights in Indonesia, condemning recent attacks on Christians and Ahmadiyah properties.

MALAYSIA

Despite government promises of reform and relaxation of controls in some areas, human rights in Malaysia remain tightly constrained.

On September 15, 2011, Prime Minister Seri Najib Tun Razak announced the government's intention to repeal the Internal Security Act (ISA), revoke three emergency proclamations that underpin many of Malaysia's most repressive laws, and review the Restricted Residence Act. In the same speech, however, he committed to introducing two new laws under article 149 ("Special Laws against Subversion") of the Federal Constitution, which allows parliament to enact sweeping security provisions that deny basic freedoms.

On July 9, police in Kuala Lumpur, the capital, broke up a peaceful rally organized by Bersih 2.0, the Coalition for Clean and Fair Elections, arresting nearly 1,700 demonstrators demanding electoral reforms. Police fired teargas at close range at protesters in an underground tunnel, injuring several, and into the Tung Shin and Chinese Maternity hospital courtyard.

Detention without Charge or Trial

The ISA permits indefinite detention without charge or trial of any person that officials deem a threat to national security or public order. While use of the ISA has declined over the years, government figures released in connection with Najib's speech said 37 people were in ISA detention. The government continues to detain thousands under the Emergency (Public Order and Crime Prevention) Ordinance (EO) and the Dangerous Drugs (Special Preventive Measures) Act. However, in October parliament repealed the Restricted Residence Act and 125 people previously confined under the act were released.

The United Nations Working Group on Arbitrary Detention singled out the EO for criticism in its February 2011 report, noting the law permits indefinite detention "without the need to sustain evidence or probe penal responsibility."

Malaysian authorities arbitrarily applied the ISA in October 2010 against immigration officers allegedly involved in human trafficking despite the availability of Malaysia's Anti-Trafficking in Persons Act, but abruptly released all but one of the accused in August 2011. The last detainee was released on November 10. On July 2, police used the EO to detain six leaders of the Parti Sosialis Malaysia (PSM) on the bogus charge that they were responsible for planning the Bersih rally and, until their July 29 release, subjected them to lengthy interrogations, isolation, and blindfolding.

Freedom of Expression, Assembly, and Association

Rights of expression, peaceful public assembly, and association —guaranteed in Malaysia's Constitution—continued to be violated in 2011. On May 21 Bersih announced a July 9 "Walk for Democracy" to call for reform of the electoral system. In mid-June the police announced that no police permit, required by section 27 of the Police Act, would be issued for the march. Inspector-General of Police Tan Sri Ismail Omar threatened that "stern action" would be taken against anyone involved in an "illegal rally."

Throughout June police mounted repeated shows of force, arresting activists distributing leaflets, wearing yellow Bersih shirts, or coordinating gatherings to promote the rally. On June 29 a plainclothes police unit without a warrant raided Bersih's secretariat, confiscating Bersih materials and detaining some of those present for questioning; on July 1 the Home Ministry declared Bersih an illegal organization under the Societies Act. On the day before the march police obtained a court order prohibiting 91 rally leaders from entering downtown Kuala Lumpur. Although the thousands who eluded police blockades were peaceful and well-disciplined, but police broke up the rally using baton charges, chemically infused water cannons, and teargas barrages. Nearly 1,700 people were arrested. Journalists and ordinary citizens released photographs and video documenting much of the abuse.

On June 25, police stopped a bus carrying PSM activists to a planned rally, detaining 30 on suspicion of "preparing to wage war against the king." They were released from pre-trial detention on July 2, but police immediately re-detained six of their leaders under the EO. All 30 were charged under the Societies Act and a section of the ISA outlawing possession of subversive documents. On September 19 the attorney general released them and on October 10, a court affirmed the release as a "discharge not amounting to an acquittal," which makes them subject to future prosecution. On October 28, six PSM leaders were granted the same discharge

Media Censorship

With nearly all mainstream newspapers and television and radio stations controlled by media companies close to political parties in the government coalition, social media usage has expanded rapidly, joining popular online news portals as alternative sources for news and information. The internet remains uncensored but the Home Ministry in 2011 again refused the Malaysiakini website's application to publish a daily print version, saying that a publishing permit is "a privilege," not a right. Malaysiakini has challenged the Home Ministry's decision; at this writing the High Court was set to review the challenge on December 8, 2011. Online news portals critical of the government also came under repeated cyber-attacks by unknown assailants at key news junctures, such as the Sarawak elections in April and the Bersih rally in July.

In his September speech, Prime Minister Najib promised to amend the Printing Presses and Publications Act but only to end the mandatory annual licensing requirement. The minister of home affairs would retain broad authority, without judicial review, to refuse permission to publish anything he determines "likely to be prejudicial to public order, morality, security ... or national interest."

On July 14 the High Court in Kuala Lumpur upheld the ban on seven books by Malaysiakini cartoonist Zunar and threatened revocation of printers' licenses if they produced his books.

In September the Malaysian Communications and Multimedia Commission ordered broadcasters not to show a non-partisan voter education public service announcement created by well-known film producer and musician Peter Teo.

Trial of Anwar Ibrahim

The trial of Anwar Ibrahim, parliamentary leader of Malaysia's political opposition, has raised serious human rights concerns. Anwar is charged with "sodomy" for allegedly engaging in consensual homosexual conduct on June 26, 2008.

Court rulings have denied Anwar's legal team access to the prosecution's witness list, critical forensic samples needed for independent examination, and medical examiners' notes from hospital examinations of the accuser, in violation of international fair trial standards.

In a September 23, 2011, affidavit to the court, Prime Minister Najib affirmed he had met Saiful, the accuser, two days before the alleged incident of sodomy.

Migrant Workers, Refugees, Asylum Seekers, and Trafficking Victims

The Malaysian Immigration Act 1959/1963 fails to differentiate between refugees, asylum seekers, trafficking victims, and undocumented migrants. The government is not a party to the 1951 Refugee Convention and lacks domestic refugee law and asylum procedures.

On July 25 Australia and Malaysia signed a "refugee swap" deal that would have permitted Australia to send 800 asylum seekers to Malaysia for refugee screening in exchange for receiving 4,000 refugees registered by the Office of the UN High Commissioner for Refugees. On August 31 the Australia High Court struck down the agreement after determining that it did not legally bind Malaysia to protect the rights of transferred asylum seekers.

Malaysia has made little progress in ensuring respect for human rights in its anti-human trafficking efforts. The Anti-Trafficking in Persons Act conflates the crimes of trafficking and smuggling, thereby reducing protections for both groups of victims, and making it less likely that trafficking victims will cooperate in identifying and prosecuting perpetrators.

A 2011 program to register all migrant workers lacked transparency regarding which migrant workers will be permitted to remain in Malaysia.

Some 300,000 migrant domestic workers are excluded from key protections under Malaysia's Employment Act, including limits on working hours, a mandatory day off per week, annual and sick leave, maternity protections, and fair termination of contracts. NGOs and embassies of labor-sending countries handle hundreds of complaints involving unpaid wages, physical and sexual abuse, and forced confinement. Indonesia and Malaysia signed a Memorandum of Understanding that guarantees a weekly day off and allows domestic workers to keep their passports rather than surrendering them to employers. However, the agreement perpetuates recruitment fee structures that leave workers deeply indebted. Malaysia is one of only nine states that did not vote for International Labour Organization Convention No. 189 on Decent Work for Domestic Workers.

Drug Policy

The National Anti-Drugs Agency maintains over 20 *Puspens* (drug retention centers) where detainees are held a minimum of two years. Although rates of relapse to drug use have been estimated in Malaysia at 70 to 90 percent, people who are re-arrested as users face long prison terms and caning.

Sexual Orientation and Gender Identity

The government refuses to consider repeal of article 377B of the penal code, which criminalizes consensual "carnal intercourse against the order of nature," or to replace article 377C on non-consensual sexual acts with a modern, gender-neutral law on rape.

In July the high court refused to permit Aleesha Farhnan Abdul Aziz, a transgender individual, to change her registered name and gender from male to female. In April Malaysian authorities sent 66 allegedly effeminate schoolboys to camp "to guide them back to the right path."

On November 3 police banned Seksualiti Merdeka, a festival held annually since 2008 to celebrate the rights of people of diverse sexual orientations and gender identities, as a threat to public order.

Freedom of Religion

Malaysia's constitution affirms the country is a secular state that protects religious freedom for all, but treatment of religious minorities continues to raise concerns. On August 3, 2011, Selangor state religious authorities raided a Methodist church where an annual charity dinner was being held. The authorities alleged that there had been unlawful proselytization of the Muslims present at the event but presented no evidence to support their allegations.

Nazri Aziz, de facto law minister, said that since Islam allows underage marriage, the government "can't legislate against it."

Key International Actors

The United States continues to exercise significant influence in Malaysia through expanding links in trade and investment, military-to-military ties, and cooperation in regional security. When Deputy Prime Minister Tan Sri Muhyiddin Yassim visited Washington in January 2011, US Secretary of State Hillary Clinton emphasized the "positive track" of the growing bilateral relationship and suggested the possibility of a US presidential visit. She also urged a fair trial for Anwar Ibrahim.

Malaysia continued to have close ties with China and agreed to a request by Beijing in August to summarily return to China a group of ethnic Uighurs in Malaysia despite the likelihood that they would face torture and ill-treatment. Eleven were sent back while five remain in Malaysia.

Malaysia continued to lead efforts to stymie the efforts of the Association of Southeast Asian Nations Committee on Migrant Workers to negotiate a legally binding instrument for the protection and promotion of the rights of migrant workers.

NEPAL

Nepal's political and peace processes remained stalled in 2011, resulting in instability; weak governance; and no progress on accountability for the killings, enforced disappearances of civilians, and other abuses that accompanied Nepal's civil war between 1996 and 2006.

Prime Minister Jhala Nath Khanal resigned on August 14, citing his failure to resolve the constitutional stalemate and his desire to make way for a consensus government. On August 28, days before the expiration of the mandate of the Constituent Assembly, Baburam Bhattarai, a senior member of the United Communist Party of Nepal-Maoist (UCPN-M), was elected prime minister. He became the second member of his party to head the government since the 2008 elections.

In a last minute deal political parties extended the term of the Constituent Assembly by three months until the end of November. Next steps were not clear at this writing: the Supreme Court ruled in November 2010 that the Constituent Assembly mandate could not be extended by more than six months absent exceptional circumstances and the declaration of a state of emergency, although the court has subsequently backed away from this position.

On November 1 the parties announced an all-party agreement laying out the terms for integration of Maoist combatants into the Nepal Army and for the rehabilitation of others, an issue that has long been at the core of the stalled peace process.

The government has made little progress in realizing economic, social, and cultural rights, and reports of lawlessness persist in many parts of the country, especially in the Terai and eastern hills. Armed groups and ethnic organizations have been involved in killings and extortion with impunity.

Accountability for Past Abuses

The government and political parties have consistently failed to muster the will to establish accountability for even egregious wartime human rights violations.

Not one person has been held criminally responsible for such crimes. In many cases, those accused of violations actively receive protection from security forces or political parties.

In August Prime Minister Bhattarai announced that the government was willing to offer amnesties for rebels and government soldiers alike. A formal agreement between the UCPN-M and its coalition partner, the United Democratic Madhesi Front (UDMF), called for the withdrawal of criminal cases against individuals affiliated with the Maoist party and with the Madhesi, Janajati, Tharuhat, Dalit, and Pichadabarga movements. It also declared a general amnesty that could include serious crimes and human rights abuses. The Maoist party's "Commitments and Proposal Concerning Government, the Peace Process, and the Constitution," made public on August 25, contained a near identical provision. Although the prime minister subsequently backed away slightly, saying he only intended to withdraw "politically motivated" cases, he failed to state what exactly that means or who would make the determination. The November 1 all-party agreement is vague on what will happen to wartime cases.

Previous governments have expressed a similar desire to withdraw such cases. Then-Home Minister Krishna Bahadur Mahara indicated in May 2011 that he was inclined to withdraw the case against UCPN-M Central Committee member Agni Sapkota. Sapkota, a Constituent Assembly member, was a cabinet minister from May to August 2011 even while he was under investigation for the April 2005 abduction and killing of Arjun Lama.

On October 2, in what is feared will be the first in a string of amnesties, the cabinet pardoned Balkrishna Dhungel, a Constituent Assembly member whose conviction for the 1998 murder of Ujjwal Kumar Shrestha was confirmed by the Supreme Court in January 2011. The UCPN-M protested the conviction, claiming that the case was counter to the spirit of the Comprehensive Peace Agreement and the interim constitution.

Draft bills to establish a Truth and Reconciliation Commission and a Disappearances Commission have been tabled in parliament but await debate by the Statute Committee. While the bills are a step towards ensuring justice for war victims, several of their provisions are inconsistent with international law.

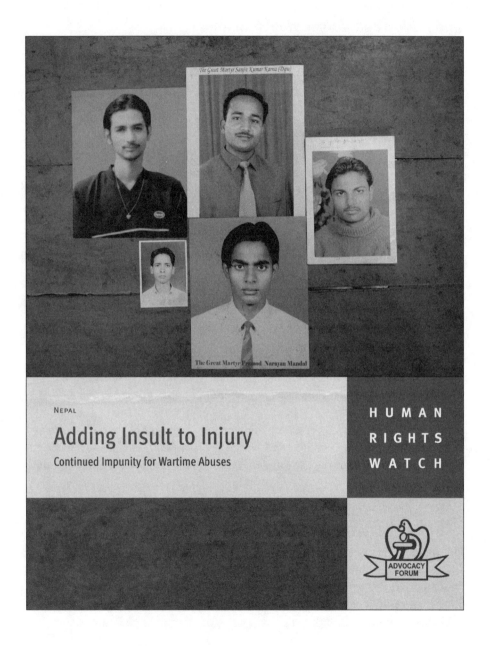

The Great Martyr Sanju Kumar Karna (Dipu)

The Great Martyr Pramod Narayan Mandal

NEPAL

Adding Insult to Injury

Continued Impunity for Wartime Abuses

HUMAN
RIGHTS
WATCH

ADVOCACY
FORUM

Integration of Maoist Combatants

For more than four years, 19,602 former Maoist combatants have been held in United Nations-monitored cantonment sites. In January 2010 the process began to discharge a further 2,973 individuals recruited as children and 1,035 recruited near the end of the civil war.

A UN monitoring mechanism was formed in 2011 to scrutinize UCPN-M compliance with the terms of a 2009 action plan it agreed to with government and UN representatives, including a ban on recruitment of children.

A special committee established in mid-2009 to address the integration of Maoist combatants into the security forces was unable to function for several months due to the continuous absence of UCPN-M representatives from meetings. The November 1, 2011, agreement calls for the establishment of a new special committee to oversee the integration of 6,500 Maoist combatants into the Nepal Army in non-combat roles. The remaining combatants, who have chosen not to join the Nepal Army, will receive compensation and rehabilitation.

Dalits

Dalits ("untouchables") suffer from endemic discrimination, especially in the economic, social, and cultural spheres. In September 2009 Nepal announced its support for UN-endorsed guidelines on the elimination of caste discrimination. However, Nepal has yet to implement recommendations made in 2004 by the Committee on the Elimination of Racial Discrimination, including the adoption of legislation enabling the National Dalit Commission—a state agency—to fulfill its mandate.

Sexual Orientation and Gender Identity

The Nepal government has made significant strides towards ensuring equality for lesbian, gay, bisexual, transgender, and intersex people (LGBTI) in recent years. Yet progress remains tenuous. The draft fundamental rights chapter of the constitution includes LGBTI rights but draft civil and criminal codes are extremely regressive and threaten to negate constitutional guarantees.

Nepal

Indifference to Duty

Impunity for Crimes Committed in Nepal

HUMAN RIGHTS WATCH

ADVOCACY FORUM

According to local NGOs, Nepal has 280 discriminatory legal provisions affecting the LGBTI community.

The government's promise that the 2011 national census would allow citizens to identify themselves as male, female, or transgender was a largely superficial gesture. Social prejudice and stigma, including on the part of census takers, resulted in gross undercounting of third gender individuals. And although individuals could identify as third gender on the census household survey, they could not do so on other census forms and almost no data was gathered on such individuals.

Another challenge is the ability of third gender individuals to have identity documents that accurately reflect their self-identified gender. Despite a 2007 Supreme Court ruling requiring that they be supplied with such documents—allowing them full access to state protections and benefits—only a handful of people have received updated cards. In September the prime minister and home minister promised to start issuing third gender citizenship identity cards, but no progress had been made at this writing.

Women's Rights

While women have constitutional guarantees of equality and strong representation in the Constituent Assembly, women and girls continue to face widespread discrimination. Trafficking, domestic violence, dowry-related violence, rape, and sexual assault remain serious problems. Sexual violence cases are often settled in private and, even when complaints are filed, police rarely carry out effective investigations. Women in the Constituent Assembly have formed a caucus to push for greater focus on women's concerns.

The millions of Nepalis who have migrated to the Middle East in recent years risk abuse at every step of the migration process, including imposed debts and deception during recruitment, labor exploitation and abuse abroad, and limited access to redress. The number of women migrating as domestic workers has significantly increased since a ban on such migration was lifted in 2010, and they face especially high risks given their exclusion from labor laws abroad. The government failed to comply with a requirement under the Foreign Employment

Act of 2008 to place labor attaches in destination countries with a significant number of Nepali workers.

Tibetan Refugees

Tibetan refugees have faced increasing harassment as Nepali authorities grow increasingly responsive to pressures from China. Arrests, criminalization of entry, arbitrary detention, and forced return of refugees to China were reported in 2011. In March the government banned Tibetans from celebrating during the Tibetan New Year. In August police arrested and briefly detained Thiley Lama, the Dalai Lama's envoy to Nepal, and his assistant after they publicly asked for the inclusion of refugee rights in Nepal's new constitution and the issuance of identity cards for Tibetans in Nepal.

In September Nepali authorities arrested more than 20 Tibetan refugees, including several children, for illegal entry. Pursuant to a "gentleman's agreement" between the government and the UN High Commissioner for Refugees (UNHCR), authorities are to immediately hand over such refugees to UNHCR which is then to facilitate their onward progress to India. But these refugees were transferred to UNHCR only after a court intervened more than a week later.

Disability Rights

Children with disabilities in Nepal face diverse and imposing barriers to obtaining a basic education. Schools are physically inaccessible, teachers are inadequately trained, and some children are denied admission to neighborhood schools. Some also experience abuse and neglect at home and in their communities. These barriers result in low attendance and high dropout rates for children with disabilities compared with their non-disabled peers.

Key International Actors

After years of heavy dependency on India, Nepal increasingly has attempted to strengthen ties with China, its other powerful neighbor. In March China provided military aid of about US$19.8 million, and helped build military medical facilities.

India played a positive role in bringing about the Comprehensive Peace Agreement that ended Nepal's 10-year civil war but was subsequently accused of meddling in Nepal's selection of a prime minister, adding to political instability. The Indian government maintained an overt distance from Nepal's political turmoil in 2011.

Nepal is dependent on aid and relies heavily on its traditional donors, such as Japan, the United States, the United Kingdom, India, and the European Union. The US and UK provide significant military assistance to Nepal, though US aid continues to be restricted on human rights grounds. Resumption of full US military aid is contingent on Nepali military cooperation with civilian investigation and prosecution of security force abuses. The UCPN-M remains on the US list of banned terrorist organizations.

Nepal continues to be a major troop contributor to UN peacekeeping missions. The UN announced in July that the Office of the High Commissioner for Human Rights (OHCHR) field office in Kathmandu, the capital, would close as of December 2011. The status of the office has been in dispute since 2009, with the government whittling down its terms of reference and extending the UN in-country presence on only a six monthly basis. At this writing it remained unclear whether OHCHR will pull out or seek a timed phase-out contingent on the government meeting required benchmarks.

Futures Stolen

Barriers to Education for Children with Disabilities in Nepal

HUMAN
RIGHTS
WATCH

NORTH KOREA

The Democratic People's Republic of Korea (North Korea) systematically violates the basic rights of its population. Although it has signed four key international human rights treaties and includes rights protections in its constitution, it allows no organized political opposition, free media, functioning civil society, or religious freedom. Arbitrary arrest, detention, lack of due process, and torture and ill-treatment of detainees remain serious and endemic problems. North Korea also practices collective punishment for various anti-state offenses, for which it enslaves hundreds of thousands of citizens in prison camps, including children. The government periodically publicly executes citizens for stealing state property, hoarding food, and other "anti-socialist" crimes.

During 2011 observers increasingly concluded that Kim Jong-Il, North Korean leader and chairman of the National Defense Commission (NDC), has selected his youngest son, Kim Jong-un, to continue the Kim family's dynastic rule of the country. In February 2011 Jong-un was appointed vice-chairman of NDC, reinforcing his earlier appointments in September 2010 to the Central Committee of the Ruling Workers Party and the Central Military Commission.

The new International Coalition to Stop Crimes against Humanity in North Korea (ICNK), comprised of 41 international NGOs, was launched in September to advocate for the establishment of a United Nations commission of inquiry on North Korea.

Food Shortages and Famine

In March 2011 a joint UN survey estimated that over six million vulnerable persons in North Korea urgently required international food assistance to avoid famine. As estimated food shortages reached more than one million metric tons, the World Food Programme called it the worst famine in a decade, and South Korea-based NGOs and media with informants inside North Korea reported hunger-related deaths. Causes include dismal harvests resulting from floods and an extremely harsh winter; economic mismanagement of a monetary devaluation scheme in November 2009 that wiped out many peoples' savings and heavily damaged informal food markets; and the government's blatantly discriminatory food policies that favor the military, government officials, and other loyal groups. North Korea's two largest food donors, the United States and South Korea, refused to provide food aid until North Korea apologizes for the sinking of the South Korean warship *Cheonan* and shelling of Yeonpyeong Island in 2010.

Torture and Inhumane Treatment

Testimony from escaped North Koreans indicates that individuals arrested on criminal charges often face torture by officials aiming to enforce obedience and extract bribes and information. Common forms of torture include sleep deprivation, beatings with iron rods or sticks, kicking and slapping, and enforced sitting or standing for hours. Detainees are subject to so-called pigeon torture, in which they are forced to cross their arms behind their back, are handcuffed, hung in the air tied to a pole, and beaten with a club. Guards also rape female detainees. One study done in 2010 found that 60 percent of refugee respondents who had been incarcerated witnessed a death due to beating or torture.

Executions

North Korea's Criminal Code stipulates that the death penalty can be applied only for a small set of crimes, but these include vaguely defined offenses such as "crimes against the state" and "crimes against the people" that can be and are applied broadly. In addition, scholars and NGOs monitoring conditions in North Korea say that a December 2007 amendment to the penal code extended the death penalty to many more crimes, including non-violent offenses such as fraud and smuggling.

Forced Labor Camps

Testimony from escapees has established that persons accused of political offenses are usually sent to forced labor camps, known as *gwalliso*, operated by the National Security Agency.

The government practices collective punishment, sending to forced labor camps not only the offender but also his or her parents, spouse, children, and

357

even grandchildren. These camps are notorious for abysmal living conditions and abuse, including severe food shortages, little or no medical care, lack of proper housing and clothes, mistreatment and torture by guards, and executions. Forced labor at the *gwalliso* often involves difficult physical labor such as mining, logging, and agricultural work, all done with rudimentary tools in dangerous and harsh conditions. Death rates in these camps are reportedly extremely high.

North Korea has never acknowledged that these camps exist, but US and South Korean officials estimate some 200,000 people may be imprisoned in them, including in camp No. 14 in Kaechun, No. 15 in Yodok, No. 16 in Hwasung, No. 22 in Hoeryung, and No. 25 in Chungjin.

Refugees and Asylum Seekers

North Korea criminalizes leaving the country without state permission. Those who leave—most often by crossing the country's northern border into China—face harsh punishment upon repatriation, including interrogation, torture, and punishments depend on North Korean authorities' assessments of what the returnee did while in China. Those suspected of simple commerce or other money-making schemes are usually sent to work in forced labor brigades. Others suspected of religious or political activities, including contact with South Koreans, are given lengthier terms in horrendous detention facilities or forced labor camps with chronic food and medicine shortages, harsh working conditions, and mistreatment by guards.

Hundreds of thousands of North Koreans have fled since the 1990s, and some have settled in China's Yanbian Korean Autonomous Prefecture. Beijing categorically labels North Koreans in China "illegal" economic migrants and routinely repatriates them, despite its obligation to offer protection to refugees under both customary international law and the Refugee Convention of 1951 and its 1967 protocol, to which China is a state party.

Many North Korean women in China live with local men in de facto marriages. Even if they have lived there for years, they are not entitled to legal residence and face the risk of arrest and repatriation. Some North Korean women and girls are trafficked into marriage or prostitution in China. Many children of such unrecognized marriages are forced to live without a legal identity or access to elementary education because their parents fear that if they register the children the mother will be identified by Chinese authorities and forcibly repatriated to North Korea.

Government-Controlled Judiciary

North Korea's judiciary is neither transparent nor independent. All personnel involved in the judiciary—including judges, prosecutors, lawyers, court clerks, and jury members—are appointed and tightly controlled by the ruling Workers' Party of Korea. In cases designated as political crimes, suspects are not even sent through a nominal judicial process; after interrogation they are either executed or sent to a forced labor camp, often with their entire families.

Labor Rights

North Korea is one of the few nations in the world that is not a member of the International Labour Organization (ILO). The ruling Korean Workers' Party firmly controls the only authorized trade union organization, the General Federation of Trade Unions of Korea. South Korean companies employ some 44,000 North Korean workers in the Kaesong Industrial Complex (KIC), where the law governing working conditions falls far short of international standards on freedom of association, the right to collective bargaining, and protection from gender discrimination and sexual harassment.

Freedom of Association, Information, and Movement

The government uses fear—generated mainly by threats of forced labor and public executions—to prevent dissent, and imposes harsh restrictions on freedom of information, association, assembly, and travel.

North Korea operates a vast network of informants to monitor and punish persons for subversive behavior. All media and publications are state-controlled, and unauthorized access to non-state radio or TV broadcasts is severely punished. The government periodically investigates the "political background" of its citizens to assess their loyalty to the ruling party, and forces Pyongyang residents who fail such assessments to leave the capital.

Key International Actors

The North Korean government continues to refuse to recognize the mandate of the UN special rapporteur on the situation of human rights in the DPRK or extend any modicum of cooperation to him. However, the government did permit a visit in May 2011 by Robert King, US special envoy for North Korean human rights issues, and during the visit released US citizen Eddie Jun after holding him for more than a year.

In March the UN General Assembly adopted a resolution against North Korea for the sixth straight year, citing member states' serious concerns about continuing reports of "systemic, widespread, and grave violations of civil, political, economic, social, and cultural rights" and concerns about "all-pervasive and severe restrictions on the freedoms of thought, conscience, religion, opinion and expression, peaceful assembly and association." In the same month, the UN Human Rights Council (HRC) adopted a resolution against North Korea for the fourth year in a row for abysmal, systematic human rights violations. Both resolutions condemned North Korea's failure to state whether it accepted any of the 167 recommendations that it took under advisement from a HRC Universal Periodic Review session of its record in December 2009.

In July 2010 the European Parliament adopted a resolution calling for the European Union to sponsor a resolution to establish a UN commission of inquiry to assess past and present human rights violations in North Korea.

The six-party talks on denuclearizing the Korean peninsula—involving North and South Korea, China, Japan, Russia, and the US—remain stalled. The US and South Korea demanded that North Korea halt its uranium-enrichment program, freeze nuclear and missile tests, and allow international nuclear inspectors back into the country before talks could start, while North Korea insisted there be no pre-conditions to resumption of talks.

North Korean leader Kim Jong Il visited Chinese leaders in Beijing in May 2011 to discuss economic cooperation and security issues and met with Russian President Dmitry Medvedev in August.

North Korea's relations with Japan remain frosty, largely due to a dispute over abductees. North Korea admitted in 2002 that its agents had abducted 13 Japanese citizens in the 1970s and 1980s for use in training North Korean spies. It returned five to Japan, but claimed the other eight had died. Japan insists the number of abductees is higher. No legal means of immigration between the two countries exists; of the nearly 100,000 migrants from Japan to North Korea between 1959 and 1984, only 200 have been able to return to Japan by escaping clandestinely.

PAKISTAN

Pakistan had a disastrous year in 2011, with increasing attacks on civilians by militant groups, skyrocketing food and fuel prices, and the assumption of near-total control of foreign and security policy by a military that operated with complete impunity. Religious minorities faced unprecedented insecurity and persecution. Freedom of belief and expression came under severe threat as Islamist militant groups murdered Punjab Governor Salmaan Taseer and Federal Minorities' Minister Shahbaz Bhatti over their public support for amending the country's often abused blasphemy laws. Pakistan's elected government notably failed to provide protection to those threatened by extremists, or to hold the extremists accountable.

In August and September the southern province of Sindh experienced massive flooding for the second year running, displacing some 700,000 people. Pakistan's largest city, Karachi, suffered from hundreds of targeted killings perpetrated by armed groups who are patronized by political parties.

Security continued to deteriorate in 2011, with militant and sectarian groups carrying out suicide bombings and targeted killings across the country. The Taliban and affiliated groups targeted civilians and public spaces, including marketplaces and religious processions. Ongoing rights concerns include the breakdown of law enforcement in the face of terror attacks, a dramatic increase in killings across the southwestern province of Balochistan, continuing torture and ill-treatment of criminal suspects, and unresolved enforced disappearances of terrorism suspects and opponents of the military. Abuses by Pakistani police, including extrajudicial killings, also continued to be reported throughout the country in 2011.

Relations between Pakistan and the United States—Pakistan's most significant ally and its largest donor of civilian and military aid—deteriorated markedly in 2011, fueled by a diplomatic crisis over a CIA contractor killing two men at a Lahore traffic junction and the US's killing of al Qaeda leader Osama bin Laden.

PAKISTAN

"We Can Torture, Kill, or Keep You for Years"

Enforced Disappearances by Pakistan Security Forces in Balochistan

HUMAN
RIGHTS
WATCH

Balochistan

Conditions markedly deteriorated in the mineral-rich province of Balochistan. Human Rights Watch documented continued "disappearances" and an upsurge in killings of suspected Baloch militants and opposition activists by the military, intelligence agencies, and the paramilitary Frontier Corps. Baloch nationalists and other militant groups also stepped up attacks on non-Baloch civilians, teachers, and education facilities, as well as against security forces in the province. Pakistan's military continued to publicly resist government reconciliation efforts and attempts to locate ethnic Baloch who had been subject to "disappearances." The government appeared powerless to rein in the military's abuses.

Human Rights Watch recorded the killing of at least 200 Baloch nationalist activists during the year, as well as dozens of new cases of disappearances. The dead included Abdul Ghaffar Lango, a prominent Baloch nationalist activist, and Hanif Baloch, an activist with the Baloch Students Organisation (Azad).

Since the beginning of 2011, human rights activists and academics critical of the military have also been killed in the province. They include Siddique Eido, a coordinator for the nongovernmental Human Rights Commission of Pakistan (HRCP); Saba Dashtiyari, a professor at the University of Balochistan and an acclaimed Baloch writer and poet; and Baloch politician Abdul Salam. Three employees of the BGP Oil and Gas company were killed and four injured in an attack in eastern Balochistan in September; the Baloch Liberation Army, a militant group, claimed responsibility for the attack.

Religious Minorities

Across Pakistan attacks took place against Shia and other vulnerable groups. Sunni militant groups, such as the supposedly banned Lashkar-e Jhangvi, operated with impunity even in areas where state authority is well established, such as the Punjab province and Karachi. On September 19, 26 members of the Hazara community travelling by bus to Iran to visit Shia holy sites were forced to disembark by gunmen near the town of Mastung and shot dead. Three others were killed as they took the injured to a hospital. Lashkar-e-Jhangvi claimed responsibility. On October 4, gunmen riding on motorbikes stopped a bus carrying mostly Hazara Shia Muslims who were headed to work at a vegetable market on the outskirts of Quetta, Balochistan's capital. The attackers forced the passengers off the bus, made them stand in a row, and opened fire, killing 13 and wounding 6.

In 2001 Aasia Bibi, a Christian from Punjab province, became the first woman in the country's history to be sentenced to death for blasphemy. She continued to languish in prison after the Lahore High Court, in a controversial move, prevented President Asif Ali Zardari from granting her a pardon in November 2010. High-ranking officials of the ruling Pakistan People's Party (PPP) called for her release and the amendment of section 295(C) of Pakistan's penal code, otherwise known as the blasphemy law. However, the government succumbed to pressure from extremist groups and dropped the proposed amendment.

Ruling party legislator Sherry Rehman, who tabled the amendment, received multiple public death threats in the face of government inaction. On January 4 Punjab Governor Salmaan Taseer was assassinated by a member of his security detail for supporting the amendment. On March 2 Federal Minister for Minorities Shahbaz Bhatti was shot dead for the same reason. While Taseer's alleged assassin was arrested on the spot, the government reacted to the murders by seeking to appease extremists rather than hold them accountable. Emboldened extremists exploited the government's passivity by intimidating minorities further, and the year saw an upsurge of blasphemy cases and allegations. Minorities, Muslims, children, and persons with mental disabilities have all been charged under the law.

Members of the Ahmadi religious community also continue to be a major target for blasphemy prosecutions and are subjected to specific anti-Ahmadi laws across Pakistan. They also face increasing social discrimination, as illustrated by the October expulsion of 10 students from a school in Hafizabad, Punjab province, for being Ahmadi. In November, four Hindus, three of them doctors, were killed in an attack by religious extremists in the town of Shikarpur in Sindh province, sending shockwaves through the minority community.

Women's Rights

Mistreatment of women and girls—including rape, domestic violence, and forced marriage—remains a serious problem. Public intimidation of, and threats to, women and girls by religious extremists increased in major cities in 2011.

In a disappointing development, the government failed to honor its commitment to reintroduce the Domestic Violence (Prevention and Protection) Bill, unanimously passed by the National Assembly in August 2009, but lapsed after the Senate failed to pass it within three months as required under Pakistan's constitution. In April the Supreme Court upheld a 2005 ruling by the provincial Lahore High Court acquitting five of the six men accused of the gang-rape of Mukhtar Mai, a villager from Muzaffargarh district in Punjab province, who was raped on the orders of a village council in 2002.

Militant Attacks and Counterterrorism

Suicide bombings, armed attacks, and killings by the Taliban, al Qaeda, and their affiliates targeted nearly every sector of Pakistani society, including journalists and religious minorities, resulting in hundreds of deaths. The US and others alleged that the military and Inter Services Intelligence (ISI) were complicit with these networks, claims the military and government adamantly denied.

Security forces routinely violate basic rights in the course of counterterrorism operations. Suspects are frequently detained without charge or are convicted without a fair trial. Thousands of suspected members of al Qaeda, the Taliban, and other armed groups—who were rounded up in a country-wide crackdown that began in 2009 in Swat and the Federally Administered Tribal Areas— remain in illegal military detention; few have been prosecuted or produced before the courts. The army continues to deny lawyers, relatives, independent monitors, and humanitarian agency staff access to persons detained in the course of military operations.

Aerial drone strikes by the US on suspected members of al Qaeda and the Taliban in northern Pakistan continued in 2011, with some 70 strikes taking place through early November. As in previous years these strikes were often accompanied by claims of large numbers of civilian casualties, but lack of access to the conflict areas has prevented independent verification.

Karachi

Karachi experienced an exceptionally high level of violence during the year, with some 800 persons killed. The killings were perpetrated by armed groups patronized by all political parties with a presence in the city. The Muttaheda Qaumi Movement (MQM), Karachi's largest political party, with heavily armed cadres and a well-documented history of human rights abuse and political violence, was widely viewed as the major perpetrator of targeted killings. The Awami National Party (ANP) and PPP-backed Aman (Peace) Committee killed MQM activists. Despite an October 6 Pakistan Supreme Court ruling calling for an end to the violence, authorities took no meaningful measures to hold perpetrators accountable.

Freedom of Media

At least six journalists were killed in Pakistan during the year. Saleeem Shahzad, a reporter for the Hong Kong-based Asia Times Online and the Italian news agency Adnkronos International, disappeared from central Islamabad, the capital, on the evening of May 29, 2011. Shahzad had received repeated and direct threats from the military's dreaded ISI agency. Shahzad's body, bearing visible signs of torture, was discovered two days later on May 31, near Mandi Bahauddin, 80 miles southeast of Islamabad. Following an international and domestic furor caused by the murder, a judicial commission was formed within days to probe allegations of ISI complicity. On August 9 Human Rights Watch testified before the commission. At this writing the commission had not announced its findings.

Earlier, on January 13, Geo TV reporter Wali Khan Babar was shot and killed in Karachi shortly after covering gang violence in the city. On May 10 Tribal Union of Journalists President Nasrullah Khan Afridi was killed when his car blew up in Peshawar; the provincial information minister described the act as a "targeted killing by the Taliban." On August 14 thugs killed online news agency reporter Munir Ahmed Shakir after he covered a demonstration by Baloch nationalists in the Khuzdar district, Balochistan. On November 5 the body of Javed Naseer Rind, a sub-editor with the Urdu-language *Daily Tawar,* was found with torture marks and gunshot wounds in the town of Khuzdar in Balochistan province. He had been missing since September 9.

A climate of fear impedes media coverage of military and militant groups. Journalists rarely report on human rights abuses by the military in counterterrorism operations, and the Taliban and other armed groups regularly threaten media outlets over their coverage.

Chief Justice Iftikhar Chaudhry and the provincial high courts effectively muzzled media criticism of the judiciary in 2011 through threats of contempt of court proceedings, as has been the case since Pakistan's independent judiciary was restored to office in 2009. In a positive development, journalists vocally critical of the government experienced less interference from elected officials than in previous years.

Key International Actors

The US remained Pakistan's most significant ally and was the largest donor of civilian and military aid to Pakistan, but relations deteriorated markedly in 2011. A major diplomatic crisis erupted on January 27 when Raymond Davis, a CIA contractor, shot two men dead at a Lahore traffic junction. While the US maintained that Davis had diplomatic immunity, Pakistan's Foreign Ministry disputed the claim. Davis was released on March 16 after US$2.4 million was paid in "blood money" compensation to the victims' families under the country's controversial Islamic law.

Further strains developed after a successful US operation in the city of Abbotabad killed al Qaeda leader Osama bin Laden. In July the US announced it was withholding some $800 million in military aid to Pakistan. Relations deteriorated still further over Pakistan's allegedly persistent support for "Haqqani network" militants, a group US officials accused of targeting the US Embassy and US troops in Afghanistan.

In October 2010 the US sanctioned six units of the Pakistani military operating in the Swat valley under the Leahy Law. That law requires the US State

Department to certify that no military unit receiving US aid is involved in gross human rights abuses and, when such abuses are found, they are to be thoroughly and properly investigated. Despite pledges, Pakistan did not take any action in 2011 to hold perpetrators of abuse accountable as required under the law. In several instances in Swat, Balochistan, and the tribal areas, US aid to Pakistan appeared to continue to contravene the Leahy Law.

As tensions increased between the US and Pakistan, neighboring China repeatedly expressed support for Pakistan. Relations between Pakistan and nuclear rival India remained tense, although in a significant move Pakistan granted its larger neighbor "Most Favored Nation" trade status in November.

PAPUA NEW GUINEA

Papua New Guinea has abundant natural resources, but poor governance and corruption have prevented ordinary citizens from benefitting from this wealth. The government has failed to safeguard environmental concerns in mining operations, and the continued dumping of mine waste into rivers poses potentially severe health risks.

The government has not taken concrete steps to address pervasive abuses by the police force that are committed with impunity, as documented in a February report by the United Nations special rapporteur on torture. Violence against women is widespread, buttressed by limited social services and a weak justice system.

Dysfunctional government institutions continue to paralyze the country. In August Peter O'Neill, the former treasurer, was elected prime minister after opposition leaders persuaded parliament to declare the prime minister's office vacant while sitting Prime Minister Michael Somare received medical treatment overseas. In September the National Court referred Somare's bid to hold his seat in parliament to the Supreme Court. Somare has been the country's dominant political figure for more than 40 years. Some have expressed cautious optimism that new leadership could herald a more transparent and accountable government.

Extractive Industries

Extractive industries are the main engine of the economy, but the government has long failed to adequately regulate them, with devastating consequences to the environment. Papua New Guinea's sprawling Porgera gold mine, 95 percent owned by Canadian company Barrick Gold, has produced more than 16 million ounces of gold since opening in 1990, worth more than US$20 billion today. The mine dumps 16,000 tons of liquid waste into the Porgera River every day, a controversial practice that is out of line with current industry standards. Critics worry it could pose serious health risks to communities downstream.

PAPUA NEW GUINEA

Gold's Costly Dividend

Human Rights Impacts of Papua New Guinea's
Porgera Gold Mine

HUMAN
RIGHTS
WATCH

A protracted legal battle over the Ramu Nickel mine, set to begin operations in late 2011, involves Ramu Nico Management (MCC), the Chinese company that owns the majority of the mine, and landowners raising compensation discrepancies and environmental concerns. In July the National Court dismissed an application that landowners had brought for a permanent injunction preventing the mine from dumping waste into the sea. The Supreme Court was hearing an appeal at this writing.

Exploration drilling as part of a projected $15 billion Liquid Natural Gas (LNG) project is set to expand at the end of the year. Disputes between local landowners and LNG contractors have been common since the project was sanctioned in 2009, and unresolved disputes over compensation for landowners, outstanding business development grants, and inadequate benefits for employees continue to generate protests and occasional violence. In August local villagers attacked two employees at the LNG site in Komo, a proposed airfield, forcing Exxon Mobile to temporarily halt operations.

Torture and Other Police Abuse

Human Rights Watch has previously documented widespread abuse by Papua New Guinea's police, including use of excessive force against demonstrators, torture, and sexual violence, including against children.

In February the UN special rapporteur on torture released a report on Papua New Guinea documenting routine beatings of criminal suspects that often rise to the level of torture, extortion of sex from female detainees, corruption, and other abuses. Conditions in correctional institutions were "poor," and "appalling" in police lockups, where children are regularly detained with adults. The report outlined measures to address corruption and impunity in the police force, including ratifying the Convention against Torture and amending domestic legislation. At this writing the government had taken no substantive measures to address widespread abuses documented in the report.

Violence against Women

Violence, including sexual violence, against women and girls is rampant in Papua New Guinea. Support services such as shelters and emergency health care are grossly inadequate. Victims face formidable barriers to obtaining redress through the justice system, including lack of information, limited legal aid, and geographic distance. Many village courts rely on customary laws that do not protect women's rights. The system often leaves perpetrators unpunished, a problem exacerbated by the propensity of some police to engage in sexual violence.

Private security personnel employed at the Porgera gold mine have been implicated in alleged gang rapes and other violent crimes. Following publication in February of *Gold's Costly Dividend*, Human Rights Watch's report on this issue, Barrick Gold and police uncovered additional cases of alleged abuse. Barrick fired six employees for involvement in, or failure to report, alleged sexual violence. Police arrested three current and former Porgera Joint Venture employees in January. Two were charged with rape and the third with inflicting grievous bodily harm. Barrick has committed to improve oversight and accountability mechanisms in order to prevent future abuse. At this writing it was working to establish a compensation mechanism for victims.

Corruption

The government has regularly been embroiled in corruption scandals. In Transparency International's 2010 Corruption Percentage Index, which evaluates and ranks public sector corruption in countries all over the world, Papua New Guinea ranked 154 out of 178 countries surveyed.

After taking office Prime Minister O'Neill called for establishing an independent commission against corruption and initiated a corruption investigation task force. In August the prime minister announced an investigation of the National Planning and Monitoring Department after revelations that $850 million in development funds had allegedly been inappropriately distributed to companies and individuals. Despite public commitments to tackle the corruption crisis, the new government's rhetoric must be matched by action to address the government's systemic culture of graft.

Health and Education

Papua New Guinea performs poorly on most indicators of economic and social well-being. Rates of maternal and child mortality are among the region's highest. The closure of rural aid posts and health centers, and the shortage of drugs, medical equipment, and trained health professionals all limit access to quality health care.

The country has the highest prevalence of HIV/AIDS among the Pacific islands. According to the most recent health data, around 34,100 people live with the disease (0.92 percent of adults in 2010), with young women most likely to be diagnosed. Gender inequality; sexual violence; inadequate HIV-prevention information, including opposition to condom promotion; and poor access to health care fuels the virus's spread. People living with HIV/AIDS often face violence and discrimination.

Primary education remains neither free nor compulsory. According to AusAID, the net enrollment in primary education was 63 percent of school-age children in 2009. Barriers include long distances to schools, a shortage of upper secondary placements, high school fees, and school closures due to insecurity. The new government has committed to fully subsidize education up to grade 10 beginning in January 2012, though similar pledges have been made in the past with few results.

Key International Actors

Australia, Papua New Guinea's former colonial ruler, is the country's most important international partner, providing some $498 million in annual assistance.

In August Australia and Papua New Guinea agreed to reopen a processing center on Manus Island for asylum seekers who arrive in Australia by boat. However, the issue has been deferred indefinitely after the Australian High

Court's September ruling that overseas detention and processing of asylum seekers was unlawful. Despite Australia's apparent agreement to process asylum claims on Manus Island, Papua New Guinea remains responsible as a party to the 1951 Refugee Convention for ensuring a fair refugee status determination process and respect for the principle of nonrefoulement ("non-return" to persecution), as well as being responsible for humane treatment of migrants and durable solutions for refugees. The center has yet to officially open.

In 2011 the UN Human Rights Council examined Papua New Guinea's rights record through the Universal Periodic Review process. Addressing the recommendations of states, Papua New Guinea acknowledged a wide range of human rights concerns, but failed to offer clear steps to combat such issues. For instance, in addressing questions about the special rapporteur's report on police abuse and torture, Papua New Guinea offered what is now a familiar response: the recommendations, it said, were "under review."

THE PHILIPPINES

The Philippines is a multiparty democracy with an elected president and legislature, a thriving civil society sector, and a vibrant media. Several key institutions, including the judiciary and law enforcement agencies, remain weak and the military and police still commit human rights violations with impunity. Armed opposition forces, including the communist New People's Army (NPA) and various Islamist Moro groups, also commit abuses against civilians.

President Benigno Aquino III maintains that the government is "working overtime" to prevent new cases of human rights violations and to resolve previous cases, and has pleaded for patience. Yet despite promises of reform, his administration has made little progress in addressing impunity. Extrajudicial killings of leftist activists and petty criminals continue, with the government failing to acknowledge and address involvement by the security forces and local officials.

Extrajudicial Killings and Enforced Disappearances

Hundreds of leftist politicians and political activists, journalists, and outspoken clergy have been killed or abducted since 2001. The government has largely failed to prosecute military personnel implicated in such killings, even though strong evidence exists in many cases. Only seven cases of extrajudicial killings from the past decade have been successfully prosecuted, none of which were in 2011 or involved active duty military personnel.

Politically motivated killings have continued despite President Aquino's pledges to address the problem. Human Rights Watch has documented at least seven extrajudicial killings and three enforced disappearances for which there is strong evidence of military involvement since Aquino took office in June 2010.

On February 27, unidentified assailants shot and killed Rudy Dejos, a tribal chieftan and local human rights officer, and his son Rudyric. The elder Dejos's body showed signs of torture. Prior to the killing, according to Dejos's wife, Philippine army soldiers had threatened him on several occasions. The police

blamed the NPA for the killing before gathering any evidence, and have now filed charges against an alleged NPA member. The family does not believe the NPA is behind the killing.

A landmark Supreme Court decision in May and a National Commission on Human Rights report in March said military officers were behind the "disappearance" of four leftist activists in 2006 and 2007; Sherlyn Cadapan, Karen Empeño, Manuel Merino, and Jonas Burgos. The government still has not brought charges against the implicated officers; faced with this inaction, the families themselves have filed cases against the officers.

Private Armies

Aquino campaigned on promises to dismantle the "private armies" of politicians and wealthy landowners, which have long been responsible for serious abuses. While Interior Secretary Jesse Robredo has claimed the Aquino administration has dismantled almost half of the private armies in the southern island of Mindanao, he has not presented any evidence. Promises to revoke Executive Order 546, which local officials cite to justify the provision of arms to their personal forces, also have not come to fruition. Aquino still defends the use of poorly trained and abusive paramilitary forces to fight NPA insurgents and Islamist armed groups. In October Aquino announced the deployment of additional paramilitary personnel to provide security to mining companies.

The trial of senior members of the Ampatuan family for the November 23, 2009 massacre of 58 political opponents and others, including more than 30 media workers, in Maguindanao in Mindanao, is ongoing.

Torture

The police and the military were implicated in numerous incidents of torture in 2011. While several investigations are ongoing, the rigor of investigations varies and at this writing no one had been convicted under the 2009 Anti-Torture Act.

In September the Department of Justice filed charges of torture against a Manila precinct chief, Senior Inspector Joselito Binayug, and six others, including one of his superiors, after a cell phone video was circulated in March 2010 showing Binayug pulling on a rope tied around a criminal suspect's genitals and beating him during the interrogation. The whereabouts of the victim, Darius Evangelista, remain unknown.

On July 23 in Sumisip, Basilan army scout rangers arrested 39-year-old baker Abdul-Khan Balinting Ajid as an alleged member of the Abu Sayyaf armed group. Soldiers allegedly stripped him naked, sexually assaulted him, and set him on fire. While the military said several soldiers involved had been relocated to Manila, the capital, and restricted to barracks, at this writing no criminal charges had been filed against them.

Targeted Killings of Petty Criminals and Street Youths

So-called death squads operating in Davao City, Tagum City, and other cities continue to target alleged petty criminals, drug dealers, gang members, and street children. Aquino's administration has not acted to dismantle such groups, end local anti-crime campaigns that promote or encourage unlawful use of force, or prosecute government officials complicit in such activities. At this writing the National Commission on Human Rights had still not reported on the outcome of multi-agency task force investigations into summary killings in Davao City in 2009.

Conflict in Mindanao

A ceasefire remains in place between the Philippine government and the Moro Islamic Liberation Front, and peace talks are ongoing. The army continues to fight Abu Sayyaf, an armed group implicated in numerous attacks on and abductions of civilians, particularly in Sulu and Basilan.

Conflict with the New People's Army

Military clashes continue between government forces and the NPA, especially in the Eastern Visayas, Negros, and parts of Mindanao.

The NPA has unlawfully killed and detained civilians and extorted "taxes" from individuals and businesses. NPA leaders have often sought to justify targeted killings by noting that "people's courts" earlier condemned those killed for "crimes against the people." For instance, the NPA killed Raymundo Agaze in Kabankalan City, Negros Occidental on August 19, and Ramelito Gonzaga in Mindanao on September 2 following "people's court" rulings. Philip Alston, former United Nations special rapporteur on extrajudicial executions, concluded that the NPA's court system "is either deeply flawed or simply a sham."

The Philippine army fabricated stories that several children taken into military custody were NPA rebels. In several cases investigated by Human Rights Watch, the army paraded the children in front of the media, publicly branding them rebels despite conclusive contrary evidence. In two of the cases, the army detained the children for several days.

The UN Children's Fund has documented the use of children in armed conflict by the NPA and the Moro Islamic Liberation Front, as well as by government forces. The UN has reported a rising trend of government security forces using schools as barracks and bases in contravention of national legislation prohibiting such practice.

Reproductive Rights

Contraceptives, including condoms, are restricted in parts of the Philippines, which prohibits and criminally punishes abortion without exception. The law leaves open the possibility that a serious threat to a pregnant woman's life could be classified as a justifying circumstance barring criminal prosecution. However, the Philippine Supreme Court has yet to adjudicate this possibility, which does little to mitigate the serious consequences of criminalizing abortion for women's health and lives.

Despite vehement opposition from the Catholic Bishops' Conference of the Philippines, Aquino has remained publicly committed to a reproductive health bill that aims to provide universal access to contraception and maternal health care. The bill goes some way toward enhancing protection of sexual and reproductive rights and the right to the highest obtainable standard of health, but still makes abortion a criminal offense. At this writing it remained before Congress.

Philippine Workers Abroad

Approximately two million Filipinos work abroad, and in the first nine months of 2011 sent home an estimated US$13 billion. Hundreds of thousands of women work in Southeast Asia and the Middle East as domestic workers, where they are typically excluded from labor laws and are often subject to abuses including unpaid wages, food deprivation, forced confinement in the workplace, and physical and sexual abuse. In 2011 the Philippine government either proposed or implemented bans on sending workers to countries with high incidences of abuse. These bans have largely been ineffective, with host countries turning to other labor sources instead. The Philippines has yet to extend labor protections to household workers domestically, but played a key role globally by chairing negotiations for the International Labour Organization Convention on Decent Work for Domestic Workers, adopted on June 16, 2011.

Key International Actors

The United States is the Philippines's most influential ally and, together with Australia and Japan, among the country's largest bilateral donors. The US military has access to Philippine territory and seas under a Visiting Forces Agreement, and the two militaries hold annual joint exercises. In fiscal year 2011-2012 the US government appropriated $12 million to the Philippines under Foreign Military Financing for procurement of US military equipment, services, and training. Of this sum, $3 million is contingent upon the Philippine government showing progress in addressing human rights violations, including ending extrajudicial killings. US Ambassador Harry Thomas, Jr. has publicly called on the Philippine government to do more to end impunity for extrajudicial killings.

The European Union's 2009 to 2011 €3.9 million ($5.3 million) program to address extrajudicial killings and strengthen the criminal justice system concluded in April.

In May UN member states elected the Philippines to the UN Human Rights Council.

SINGAPORE

Singapore's People's Action Party (PAP), in power since 1959, garnered its low-est-ever winning margin in May 2011 elections, losing six parliamentary seats to the opposition Workers' Party. The government's relaxation of prohibitions on campaign rallies and online electioneering were improvements, but the government continued to effectively control television and print media.

During the May 2011 review of its human rights record at the United Nations Human Rights Council (HRC), Singapore rejected many of the member states' suggestions for human rights improvements, including ratification of core UN conventions.

Freedoms of Expression, Assembly, and Association

Singapore's constitution guarantees rights to freedom of expression, peaceful assembly, and association. However, it also permits broadly interpreted restrictions not only for security, public order, and morality, but also for parliamentary privilege and racial and religious harmony. These restrictions facilitate censorship of broadcast and electronic media, films, video, music, sound recordings, and computer games. The Newspaper and Printing Presses Act requires yearly renewal of registration and allows government officials to limit circulation of foreign newspapers they deem "engage in the domestic politics of Singapore." Two corporations dominate the media in Singapore. MediaCorp is wholly owned by a government investment company; Singapore Press Holdings Limited (SPH) is a private company, but the government must approve and can remove shareholders, who have the authority to hire and fire all directors and staff.

Although Singapore loosened some limitations on free speech, association, and assembly in mid-March 2011, it maintained or tightened other restrictions. Blogs, podcasts, and social networking sites were permitted to be used for internet election advertising as long as they did not contain recorded messages that were "dramatized" or "out of context." Candidates were also required to announce within 12 hours of the start of campaigning all new media content they planned to use.

Government officials continue to maintain that religious and ethnic differences have "the potential to cause friction and divide Singaporeans" and therefore necessitate restrictions on free speech. Outdoor gatherings of five or more persons require police permits.

On December 10, 2010, police refused to grant Singaporeans for Democracy (SFD) a permit to hold an International Human Rights Day parade. In February 2011 Chee Soon Juan, secretary general of the Singapore Democratic Party, paid a heavy fine for "speaking without a permit" during the 2006 general election campaign to avoid a prison term of 20 weeks.

In January 2011 the government ordered The Online Citizen (TOC), a popular blog site, to register as a political association. According to the Prime Minister's Office, "TOC has the potential to influence the opinions of their readership and shape political outcomes in Singapore. It has been gazetted to ensure that it is not funded by foreign elements or sources."

A police investigation is underway to determine if a SFD invitation-only event in September 2011 should be considered a public event held without a permit. The Public Order Act 2009 mandates that permits for indoor assemblies are needed if, as was the case here, all speakers are not citizens of Singapore. Police raised concerns that invitations issued through a Facebook events page and by email compromised the forum's private status.

Police were also investigating a public forum of former Internal Security Act detainees organized by the opposition Singapore Democracy Party (SDP) in September. According to the Ministry of Foreign Affairs, the SDP "arranged for a fugitive from justice, Francis Seow [speaking online from Boston], and a foreign national, Ms. Tang Fong Harr [speaking from Hong Kong] to participate in a discussion on Singapore's domestic politics."

All associations of 10 or more members must seek approval, which can be denied by the Registrar of Societies if deemed "prejudicial to public peace, welfare or good order."

Singapore also resorts to charges of contempt of court, criminal and civil defamation, and sedition to rein in its critics. On June 1, 2011, British author

Alan Shadrake began serving a six-week prison term for contempt of court for "scandalizing the judiciary" by alleging in his book, *Once a Jolly Hangman: Singapore Justice in the Dock*, that Singapore's justice system permits interference by the People's Action Party with court decisions relating to capital punishment. At his trial, the prosecution cited 11 specific statements, including the book title, to argue that Shadrake's allegations and insinuations "muzzle confidence in the courts' impartiality, integrity and independence." Shadrake was immediately deported upon release.

Criminal Justice System

Singapore's Internal Security Act (ISA) and Criminal Law (Temporary Provisions) Act permit arrest and virtually unlimited detention of suspects without charge or judicial review. As the Ministry of Home Affairs explained in September 2011, threats such as subversion, espionage, and terrorism keep ISA "relevant." At least three suspected terrorists were detained in 2011.

The Misuse of Drugs Act permits confinement of suspected drug users in "rehabilitation" centers for up to three years without trial. Second-time offenders face prison terms and may be caned.

Singapore continued to implement mandatory death sentences for some 20 drug-related offenses in the face of repeated criticism by UN human rights bodies and experts.

Judicial caning, an inherently cruel punishment, is a mandatory additional punishment for medically fit males between 16 and 50-years-old who have been sentenced to prison for a range of crimes including drug trafficking, rape, and immigration offenses. A sentencing official may also, at his discretion, order caning in cases involving some 30 other violent and non-violent crimes. The maximum number of strokes at any one time is 24. The United States State Department reported that in 2010, "3,170 convicted persons were sentenced to judicial caning, and 98.7 percent of caning sentences were carried out." During its HRC Universal Periodic Review (UPR), Singapore rejected all recommendations designed to eliminate caning.

Sexual Orientation and Gender Identity

Penal Code section 377A criminalizes sexual acts between consenting adult men. Sexual acts between women are not criminalized.

The Board of Film Censors gave its strictest classification, R21, to "The Kids are All Right," a film depicting a lesbian-headed household. The classification prevents advertising and home video release of the film, and restricts viewers to persons over 21-years-old. Only one print of the film was authorized to be released, significantly limiting public showings.

Migrant Domestic Workers and Trafficking

Singapore continues to improve rights protections and working conditions for some 196,000 foreign domestic workers through vigorous prosecution of employers and recruiters who physically abuse workers, fail to pay wages, or subject workers to dangerous conditions. Effective April 1 it amended the Employment Agencies Act to cap recruitment fees at two months salary for workers on two-year contracts but exempted substantial training and travel costs from the cap.

The government also refuses to include domestic workers under the Employment Act, and uses a sponsorship system that ties a domestic worker to a specific employer who, in turn, retains the right to cancel the migrant worker's contract, making her subject to immediate deportation. Unscrupulous employers often use the threat of contract cancellation to intimidate workers into accepting unlawful work conditions, restricting their movements, and preventing them from filing complaints.

A government-mandated standard contract for migrant workers does not address issues such as long work hours, poor living conditions, and enforced confinement. Instead of guaranteeing one day off per month and a set number of rest hours per day, it makes such breaks a matter of negotiation between employer and employee. It also fails to provide protections against denial of annual or medical leave, requires immediate deportation of pregnant workers, and stipulates that no foreign domestic workers may marry a Singaporean.

Singapore is one of only nine states that did not vote for passage of International Labour Organization (ILO) Convention No. 189 on Decent Work for Domestic Workers.

At this writing Singapore had not ratified the Protocol to Prevent, Suppress and Punish Trafficking in Persons.

Human Rights Defenders

Human rights defenders in Singapore risk being fined, jailed, bankrupted, and forbidden from traveling outside the country without government approval. At its UPR review, Singapore rejected the suggestion that it accept a visit by the UN special rapporteur on the situation of human rights defenders.

Key International Actors

Maritime security, counterterrorism, trade, and investment dominated relations between Singapore and the US, one of its most important allies, with both parties eager to expand already robust military ties in the region, preserve open shipping lanes in the South China Sea, and impede terrorist financing. Singapore and the US are in talks about establishing a permanent Singapore base for an advanced US littoral combat ship.

The US continued to be restrained in its criticism of Singapore's human rights record. It was silent, for example, during the May 2011 review of Singapore's record as part of the UPR process.

Singapore continued to play a leading role in the Association of Southeast Asian Nations (ASEAN) yet did little to ensure that the human rights principles contained in the ASEAN Charter were applied to member countries like Burma, Cambodia, Laos, and Vietnam, where human rights abuses are systemic.

SRI LANKA

The aftermath of Sri Lanka's quarter century-long civil war, which ended in May 2009 with the defeat of the separatist Liberation Tigers of Tamil Eelam (LTTE), continued to dominate events in 2011. In April United Nations Secretary-General Ban Ki-moon released a report by a panel of experts that concluded that both government forces and the LTTE conducted military operations "with flagrant disregard for the protection, rights, welfare and lives of civilians and failed to respect the norms of international law." The panel recommended the establishment of an international investigative mechanism. Sri Lankan officials responded by vilifying the report and the panel members.

The government has failed to conduct credible investigations into alleged war crimes by security forces, dismissing the overwhelming body of evidence as LTTE propaganda. The government's Lessons Learnt and Reconciliation Commission (LLRC), characterized as a national accountability mechanism, is deeply flawed, does not meet international standards for such commissions, and has failed to systematically inquire into alleged abuses.

In August the government allowed emergency regulations in place for nearly three decades to lapse, but overbroad detention powers remained in place under other laws and new regulations. Several thousand detainees continue to be held without trial, in violation of international law.

Accountability

Sri Lanka has made no progress toward justice for the extensive laws of war violations committed by both sides during the long civil war, including the government's indiscriminate shelling of civilians and the LTTE's use of thousands of civilians as "human shields" in the final months of the conflict. Since the war ended the government has not launched a single credible investigation into alleged abuses. The lack of investigation was especially conspicuous with regard to several incidents featured in a June 2011 program on the British television station Channel 4, showing gruesome images of what appear to be summary executions of captured and bound combatants. Incredibly, the government repeatedly has dismissed the footage as fabricated despite several independent expert reports finding it authentic.

In May the Sri Lankan Defense Ministry held an international conference in Colombo, the capital, on defeating terrorism that gave scant attention to government abuses. In August the Defense Ministry issued its own report, conceding for the first time that government forces caused civilian deaths in the final months of the conflict, but taking no responsibility for laws of war violations and concluding peremptorily without further investigation that the deaths were the unfortunate collateral damage of war.

Impunity for serious violations also continues for older cases. Despite strong evidence of involvement by government forces in the execution-style slayings of 17 aid workers and five students in separate incidents in 2006, government inquiries continue to languish and no one has been arrested for the crimes.

The government has repeatedly extended the deadline for the LLRC. The LLRC's mandate focuses on the breakdown of the 2002 ceasefire between the government and the LTTE, and does not explicitly require it to investigate alleged war crimes during the conflict. The LLRC heard testimony but undertook no investigations into such allegations. The LLRC was due to submit its report to President Mahinda Rajapaksa on November 15. The government has stated that the report will be made public but has not indicated when it will do so. The government has not acted on the LLRC's preliminary recommendations.

Torture, Enforced Disappearances, and Arbitrary Detention

While the government allowed longstanding emergency regulations to lapse in August, it failed to rescind other legislation granting police and other security forces overbroad detention powers and it adopted new regulations that in effect continue several of the emergency provisions. The president continues to issue monthly decrees granting the armed forces search and detention powers.

Despite the end of the formal state of emergency, the government also continues to hold several thousand people initially detained under the emergency regulations. Many have been held for years without trial, in violation of international law. The government has so far refused to even publish lists of those detained.

The government has gradually released many, but not all, of the more than 11,000 suspected LTTE members detained at the end of the war and sent to so-called rehabilitation centers. The government denied detainees important due process guarantees, such as access to legal counsel, and thousands spent two years or more in detention. There are reports that some people released from the rehabilitation centers were harassed by security forces after they returned home.

In 2011, new reports of "disappearances" and abductions in the north and the east emerged, some linked to political parties and others to criminal gangs. The government has lifted its restriction on travel to parts of the north, although it maintains a very high security presence. Violence, including sexual assault, by so-called grease devils, some of whom could allegedly be traced to military camps, highlighted insecurity in the north and east.

The Prevention of Terrorism Act gives police broad powers over suspects in custody. Sri Lanka has a long history of torture by the police forces, at times resulting in death.

Civil Society and Opposition Members

Free expression remained under assault in 2011. Gnanasundaram Kuhanathan, editor of a Jaffna-based newspaper, was beaten with iron bars by a group of unidentified youths in late July. He was severely injured and required hospitalization. In July a team of Radio Netherlands journalists were harassed by police and later robbed and attacked at gunpoint by a gang in a white van, a notorious symbol of terror in Sri Lanka. Lal Wickrematunge, chairman of the *Sunday Leader* and brother of Lasantha Wickrematunge (who was gunned down in 2009), received a phone call from President Rajapaksa in response to an article on high-level corruption in which the president said to Wickrematunge, "You are writing lies, outrageous lies! You can attack me politically, but if you attack me personally, I will know how to attack you personally too."

There have been no further developments regarding the killing of Lasantha Wickrematunge or the disappearance of Prageeth Ekneligoda, a contributor to Lanka e-news, who has been missing since January 24, 2010.

Members and supporters of the Tamil National Alliance (TNA), campaigning ahead of local elections in Jaffna in June, were attacked by army personnel wielding rods, batons, and sticks. Among the injured were TNA members and police officers assigned to provide security to the parliamentarians. The results of an investigation into the incident ordered by the secretary of defense are not known.

In November the government blocked at least six news websites claiming that they had maligned the character of the president and other top government officials.

Reconciliation Efforts

Reconciliation efforts, meant to address longstanding grievances of the ethnic Tamil population, have been slow at best. Local elections in March, July, and October further consolidated the hold of Rajapaksa's ruling alliance, although the TNA garnered significant victories in the north. The TNA and the government have been in negotiations to deal with, among other matters, devolution of powers to the provinces, a key issue underpinning the civil war. The talks have been rife with tension, with the TNA accusing the government of deceitful and facetious behavior, and the government accusing the TNA of issuing LTTE-type ultimatums as a result of its electoral victory in the north. The TNA left talks with the government in August but has since returned.

In September the TNA reacted angrily to government statements at the UN Human Rights Council (HRC) in Geneva, saying government claims that reconciliation efforts have been predicated on "building trust and amity" between the communities is not supported by the experience of the Tamil people.

Internally Displaced Persons

The vast majority of the nearly 300,000 civilians illegally confined in military-controlled detention centers after the war have moved out of the centers back into communities, although not necessarily into their original homes. About 110,000 persons still live with host families or in camps and several thousand are not able to return because their home areas have not been demined. The government has still not granted international demining agencies access to several areas.

Key International Actors

Pressure on accountability from key international actors mounted following the April release of a damning panel report commissioned by the UN secretary-general. Several countries—including Britain, Canada, Australia, and the United States—called on Sri Lanka to investigate the allegations contained in the report. The European Parliament adopted a resolution in May urging Sri Lanka to immediately investigate the allegations and the European Union to "support further efforts to strengthen the accountability process in Sri Lanka and to support the UN report." Even India, which had largely stayed silent on alleged abuses in Sri Lanka, added to the pressure in May when it called for investigations. Also in May the UN special rapporteur on extrajudicial, summary, or arbitrary executions called on the government to investigate "textbook examples of extrajudicial executions" in Sri Lanka following a review of evidence related to government execution of prisoners.

In September UN Secretary-General Ban Ki-moon submitted the panel report on the war to the president of the HRC and, acting on one of the report's recommendations, announced that the UN would undertake a separate inquiry into the its own actions in Sri Lanka during the final months of the war.

While several countries called for accountability for laws of war violations during the September HRC session, the Council failed to act following Ban's transmission of the panel report and has not yet taken steps towards establishing an international accountability mechanism, the main recommendation in the report.

Several governments indicated that they will support an international accountability mechanism if the LLRC report fails to properly address accountability issues. US Assistant Secretary of State Robert Blake said during a trip to Sri Lanka in September that unless there is a full, credible, and independent accounting, "there will be pressure for some sort of alternative mechanism." The UK has likewise said that it will "support the international community in revisiting all options" unless the Sri Lankan government demonstrates progress by the end of 2011.

US legislation restricts military aid to Sri Lanka, subject to strict conditions regarding progress on accountability and human rights.

At a Commonwealth summit in October, Canadian Prime Minister Stephen Harper called for a boycott of a planned Commonwealth heads of government summit in Sri Lanka in 2013, should Sri Lanka fail to improve its human rights record by that time.

THAILAND

Yingluck Shinawatra, younger sister of exiled former Prime Minister Thaksin Shinawatra, won a landslide victory in July 2011 elections, offering what was hoped would be political stability in Thailand after several years of political upheaval. The new government has not yet fulfilled early promises to give priority to Thailand's many human rights problems. In October and November Bangkok—the capital—and 23 other provinces were severely affected by the worst flooding in decades, which displaced hundreds of thousands people and massively devastated livelihood and economy.

Accountability for Political Violence

At least 90 people died and more than 2,000 were injured during violent political confrontations from March to May 2010. The loss of life resulted from the unnecessary use of lethal force by Thai security forces, attacks by armed elements operating in tandem with the United Front for Democracy against Dictatorship (UDD), known as the "Red Shirts," and incitement to violence by some UDD leaders.

In January 2011 the Justice Ministry's Department of Special Investigation (DSI) announced the results of preliminary investigations into the violence. The DSI implicated soldiers in 13 deaths, and armed UUD elements in another 12 deaths. But lack of police cooperation stalled efforts to initiate post-mortem inquests and prosecutions. Prime Minister Yingluck vowed to end these delays after appointing Gen. Priewpan Damapong,Thaksin's brother-in-law, as national police chief in September.

The status of investigations into alleged crimes by UDD "Black Shirt" militants remained unclear, with the Yingluck government denying the group's existence. A number of those accused of deadly attacks against soldiers, police officers, and anti-UDD groups were released on bail. The election of 12 senior UDD leaders as ruling Pheu Thai Party members of parliament raised serious concerns that they would be able to use their political influence and parliamentary immunity to evade accountability for their role in the 2010 violence.

THAILAND

Descent into Chaos

Thailand's 2010 Red Shirt Protests and
the Government Crackdown

HUMAN
RIGHTS
WATCH

Yingluck promised full support for the work of the Truth for Reconciliation Commission of Thailand (TRCT), established by the government of Abhisit Vejjajiva to look into the political violence, but has yet to grant the TRCT subpoena power, rendering it unable to obtain complete information about security force deployment plans and operations, autopsy reports, witness testimony, photos, and military and police video footage.

In its initial work, the TRCT found that the Abhisit government had pressured law enforcement officials to charge hundreds of ordinary UDD protesters with serious criminal offenses and hold them in pre-trial detention for months without the possibility of bail. The government announced in September that it would review the charges against those protesters and ensure they are treated in accordance with due process and human rights guarantees. The TRCT also recommended that a special mechanism be established to provide fair compensation and other remedies to all victims of abuse and political violence.

Progress in investigating criminal offenses committed by members of the People's Alliance for Democracy (PAD), known as the "Yellow Shirts," during protests in 2008 has also been slow. Additionally, the police officers and politicians believed responsible for the excessive use of force against PAD protesters rallying in front of the parliament on October 7, 2008, continue to enjoy impunity.

Freedom of Expression and Freedom of Media

From 2008 to 2011 the Abhisit government oversaw the closure of more than 1,000 websites, a satellite television station, online television channels, printed publications, and more than 40 community radio stations for allegedly threatening national security or broadcasting material deemed offensive to the monarchy.

Thai authorities continue to use the Computer Crimes Act and article 112 of the penal code, lese majeste (insulting the monarchy), to enforce censorship and persecute dissidents. The National Human Rights Commission estimates that more than 400 lese majeste cases were sent to trial in 2010 and 2011. Persons charged with lese majeste offenses are frequently denied bail and remain in prison for months awaiting trial. In most cases, the trials are closed to the public. In March a court sentenced Tanthawut Taweewarodomkul to 13 years in prison for posting material on the anti-monarchy website Nor Por Chor USA. Lese majeste prosecutions in 2011 also targeted webmasters and editors, such as Chiranuch Premchaiporn, webmaster and director of Prachatai.com, and Somyos Pruksakasemsuk, editor of *Red Power* magazine.

New Deputy Prime Minister Chalerm Yubumrung told parliament on August 26 that lese majeste offenses would not be tolerated. The government established a "war room" at national police headquarters to monitor the internet and lead the crackdown on websites deemed critical of the monarchy. On September 1, police arrested Surapak Phuchaisaeng in Bangkok for allegedly posting pictures, audio clips, and messages deemed insulting to the royal family on Facebook. It was the first lese majeste arrest under Yingluck's government.

Critics of Yingluck and the Pheu Thai Party, such as Jermsak Pinthong and T-News group, lost contracts with the government-controlled National Broadcasting Services of Thailand (NBT) to produce television and radio news analysis programs broadcast nationally.

Violence and Human Rights Abuses in Southern Border Provinces

Separatist insurgents in the loose National Revolution Front-Coordinate (BRN-Coordinate) network continue to attack civilians in the southern border provinces. Car bombs and motorcycle bombs killed six and wounded 118 in the September 16 attacks in the Su Ngai Kolok district, Narathiwat province. Insurgents have planted landmines in rubber plantations to spread terror among the ethnic Thai Buddhist population and force them to relinquish ownership of the plantations.

Insurgent groups continue to target teachers in government-run schools, whom they see as symbols of state efforts to undermine ethnic Malay Muslim identity. On September 6, insurgents fatally shot teacher Kanit Lamnui in Yala province's Raman district, poured gasoline over his body, and set it ablaze. Since 2004, insurgents have killed at least 148 teachers and educational officials.

Government security forces frequently use schools for barracks and bases, endangering students and teachers, and impairing education.

Although Fourth Region Army commander Lt. Gen. Udomchai Thammasarorat vowed that the ethnic Malay Muslim population would see justice done for abuses against them, Thai security forces still face little or no consequences for extrajudicial killings, torture, enforced disappearances, and other abuses. After a sharp decline since 2007, new cases of "disappearances" increased in 2011.

Anti-Narcotics Policy

Deputy Prime Minister Chalerm announced in September that the government would respect human rights and due process when implementing anti-narcotics policy, but flatly denied any official involvement in the more than 2,800 extrajudicial killings that accompanied then Prime Minister Thaksin's 2003 "war on drugs."

Starting in September the Yingluck government set a target to "rehabilitate" 400,000 drug users within one year. There was little change in the government practice of arbitrarily arresting drug users and detaining them in compulsory drug "rehabilitation" centers, mostly run by the military and the Interior Ministry, where the ostensible treatment is based on military-style physical exercise. Routinely detained in prison prior to compulsory rehabilitation, detainees get little or no medical assistance for drug withdrawal symptoms.

Human Rights Defenders

Gunmen shot dead environmentalist Thongnak Sawekchinda in Samut Sakhon province on July 28, allegedly in retaliation for his campaign against local coal industry pollution. Since 2001 more than 20 environmentalists and human rights defenders have been killed in Thailand. Investigations into the killings have frequently suffered from inconsistent and shoddy detective work, the failure of the Justice Ministry to provide adequate protection for witnesses, and political interference in law enforcement efforts.

Refugees, Asylum Seekers, and Migrant Workers

Thai authorities continue to return refugees and asylum seekers to countries where they are likely to face persecution. Nur Muhammed, an ethnic Uighur, was arrested on August 6 and taken to the Bangkok Immigration Detention Center (IDC), where he was charged under the Immigration Act with illegal entry. Instead of being brought to a court, as stipulated by Thai law, he was handed directly into the custody of Chinese government officials and has since disappeared. China's record of arbitrary detention and torture of ethnic Uighurs places Muhammed at grave risk of abuse.

Thai authorities at least twice "pushed back" boats carrying ethnic Rohingyas from Burma and Bangladesh in 2011 despite allegations that such practices led to hundreds of deaths in 2008 and 2009. After providing basic supplies of food and water, Thai authorities towed the boats far out into international waters before cutting the boats adrift. One boat of 91 Rohingya was stopped in Trang province on January 22 and pushed back out to sea, ultimately landing in India's Andaman and Nicobar Islands. A second boat, with 129 Rohingya on board, was pushed back on the high seas and drifted to Aceh, Indonesia.

Thailand is not a party to the 1951 Refugee Convention and has no law that recognizes refugee status. Asylum seekers and refugees who are arrested often face long periods of detention until they are accepted for resettlement or agree to be sent back to their own country. In some cases, Sri Lankan, Nepalese, and Rohingya refugees have been held for more than two years. On June 6, 94 refugees and two asylum seekers from Pakistan's persecuted Ahmadiyah community were released on bail; some had been detained for nearly six months.

Thai labor laws provide little protection to migrant workers from Burma, Cambodia, and Laos who have been abused by police, civil servants, employers, and criminal elements. A migrant worker registry and "nationality verification" scheme provides legal documentation for workers, but does little to counter the impunity with which employers violate such workers' rights. Migrant workers remain extremely vulnerable to exploitation, with female migrants enduring sexual violence and labor trafficking, and male migrants facing extreme labor exploitation, including being trafficked onto fishing boats. In October NGOs and the media documented that migrant workers fleeing

Thailand's flooding, which affected millions of people, were being targeted by police for arrest, extortion, and abuse.

Key International Actors

The United Nations, United States, Australia, European Union, Switzerland, and Norway expressed strong support for political reconciliation and greater human rights protections in Thailand in 2011, urging the government and all other conflicting political factions to engage in dialogue and refrain from using violence. Switzerland provided training and technical assistance to the TRCT.

Thailand made many human rights pledges in its successful 2010 campaign to join the UN Human Rights Council, but few have been implemented. In September Foreign Minister Surapong Tovichakchaikul said Thailand would seek to renew its seat at the council for another term and also bid for a non-permanent seat at the UN Security Council.

The Cluster Munitions Coalition strongly criticized Thailand for using cluster munitions in a border conflict with Cambodia in February 2011. In June the Thai ambassador to the UN in Geneva informed the first intersessional meeting of the Convention on Cluster Munitions that Thailand hoped to ratify the convention in "the near future."

VIETNAM

The Vietnamese government systematically suppresses freedom of expression, association, and peaceful assembly. Independent writers, bloggers, and rights activists who question government policies, expose official corruption, or call for democratic alternatives to one-party rule are routinely subject to police harassment and intrusive surveillance, detained incommunicado for long periods of time without access to legal counsel, and sentenced to increasingly long terms in prison for violating vague national security laws.

Police frequently torture suspects to elicit confessions and, in several cases, have responded to public protests over evictions, confiscation of land, and police brutality with excessive use of force. Anti-China protests in Hanoi and Ho Chi Minh City in 2011 were dispersed and protesters were intimidated, harassed, and in some cases detained for several days.

The 11th Vietnam Communist Party Congress in January 2011 and the stage-managed National Assembly election in May determined the leadership of the party and government for the next five years. During both, there was no sign of any serious commitment to improve Vietnam's abysmal human rights record. Prime Minister Nguyen Tan Dung began his second term in July, enjoying strong support from the Ministry of Public Security and other hard-liners.

Repression of Dissent

2011 saw a steady stream of political trials and arrests, likely spurred in part by Vietnamese government concerns that pro-democracy Arab Spring movement might reach Asia.

During the first 10 months of 2011, the authorities sent at least 24 rights activists to prison. All but one were convicted of "conducting propaganda against the state" (penal code article 88), "undermining national unity" (article 87), or "subversion of the administration" (article 79). These three vaguely defined articles have been employed to imprison hundreds of peaceful activists in the last decade. In addition, the police arrested at least 27 political and religious advocates in 2011. Blogger Nguyen Van Hai, known by his pen name Dieu

Cay, has been held incommunicado since October 2010. Two other pro-democracy internet writers, Nguyen Ba Dang and Phan Thanh Hai, have been detained since 2010 without trial.

In a major trial in April 2011, prominent legal activist Dr. Cu Huy Ha Vu was convicted of conducting propaganda against the state and sentenced to seven years in prison. The sentence was upheld on appeal.

In May the People's Court of Ben Tre convicted seven peaceful land rights activists, including Mennonite pastor Duong Kim Khai and Hoa Hao Buddhist member Tran Thi Thuy, for subversion and sentenced them to long prison terms.

Authorities continue to harass, interrogate, and in some cases detain and imprison online critics. In January 2011 police arrested human rights blogger Ho Thi Bich Khuong. In May democracy advocate Nguyen Kim Nhan was arrested for allegedly conducting propaganda against the state, five months after he was released from prison on the same charge. In August blogger Lu Van Bay was sentenced to four years for his pro-democracy articles published on the Internet. Also in August blogger Pham Minh Hoang was sentenced to three years for subversion.

Ethnic minority activists also face arrest and imprisonment. In January the Lang Son provincial court sentenced blogger Vi Duc Hoi, an ethnic Tay, on charges of conducting propaganda against the state to eight years in prison, reduced to five years on appeal in April. In March land rights activist Chau Heng, a member of the Khmer Krom minority group, was sentenced to two years in prison in An Giang on charges of "destruction of property" and "causing public disorder." The People's Court of Gia Lai imprisoned eight Montagnard Protestants in April to sentences between eight to twelve years for violating article 87 of the penal code, which outlaws "undermining unity policy."

Freedom of Expression, Assembly, and Information

The government does not allow independent or privately-owned domestic media to operate and exerts strict control over the press and internet. Criminal penalties apply to authors, publications, websites, and internet users who disseminate materials deemed to oppose the government, threaten national secu-

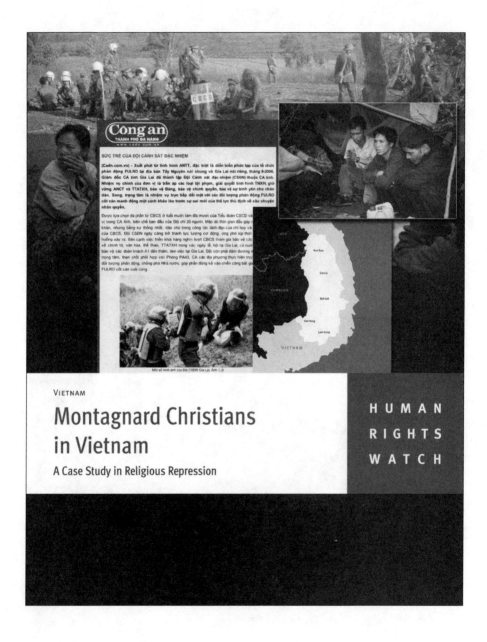

VIETNAM

Montagnard Christians in Vietnam

A Case Study in Religious Repression

HUMAN
RIGHTS
WATCH

rity, reveal state secrets, or promote "reactionary" ideas. The government blocks access to politically sensitive websites, requires internet cafe owners to monitor and store information about users' online activities, and subjects independent bloggers and online critics to harassment and pressure.

In August anti-China protests in Hanoi were dispersed with force. Protesters were intimidated, harassed, and detained for peacefully marching near the Embassy of China and around Hoan Kiem lake. Government media, including newspapers and television stations, continually cast negative images of protesters and labeled them "reactionary."

Freedom of Religion

The government restricts religious practices through legislation, registration requirements, and harassment and surveillance. Religious groups are required to register with the government and operate under government-controlled management boards. Despite allowing many government-affiliated churches and pagodas to hold worship services, the government bans any religious activity that it arbitrarily deems to oppose "national interests," harm national unity, cause public disorder, or "sow divisions."

Local police continue to prohibit unsanctioned Buddhist Hoa Hao groups from commemorating the anniversary of the death of Hoa Hao founder Huynh Phu So. During Buddhist festivals in May and August, Da Nang police blocked access to Giac Minh and An Cu pagodas and intimidated Buddhist followers. Both pagodas are affiliated with the un-sanctioned Unified Buddhist Church of Vietnam.

Protestant pastor Nguyen Trung Ton was arrested in January on unknown charges. Three Catholic Ha Mon Montagnard activists—Blei, Phoi, and Dinh Pset—were arrested in March. Two Cao Dai activists, Nguyen Van Lia and Tran Hoai An, were arrested in April and July. Also in April Protestant pastor Nguyen Cong Chinh was arrested and charged with "undermining national unity." At least 15 Catholics affiliated with Redemptorist churches in Hanoi and Ho Chi Minh City, including bloggers Le Van Son and Ta Phong Tan, were arrested in July, August, and September.

In July prominent religious and democracy campaigner Father Nguyen Van Ly was sent back to prison after approximately 16 months of medical parole/house arrest. Father Ly suffers from partial paralysis resulting from strokes previously suffered in prison and there continue to be serious concerns for his health.

Criminal Justice System

Police brutality, including torture and fatal beatings, continues to be reported in all regions of the country. At least 13 people died in police custody within the first 10 months of 2011.

Political and religious detainees and others whose cases are considered sensitive are frequently tortured during interrogation, held incommunicado prior to trial, and denied family visits and access to lawyers. Vietnamese courts remain under the firm control of the government and the Vietnam Communist party, and lack independence and impartiality. Political and religious dissidents are often tried without the assistance of legal counsel in proceedings that fail to meet international fair trial standards. Defense lawyers who take on politically sensitive cases are intimidated, harassed, debarred, and imprisoned.

Vietnamese law continues to authorize arbitrary "administrative detention" without trial. Under Ordinance 44 (2002) and Decree 76 (2003), peaceful dissidents and others deemed threats to national security or public order can be involuntarily committed to mental institutions, placed under house arrest, or detained in state-run "rehabilitation" or "re-education" centers.

People dependent on illegal drugs can be held in government detention centers where they are subjected to "labor therapy," the mainstay of Vietnam's approach to drug treatment. In early 2011 there were 123 centers across the country holding some 40,000 people, including children as young as 12. Their detention is not subject to any form of due process or judicial oversight and routinely lasts for as long as four years. Infringement of center rules—including the work requirement—is punished by beatings with truncheons, shocks with electrical batons, and being locked in disciplinary rooms where detainees are deprived of food and water. Former detainees report being forced to work in

VIETNAM

The Rehab Archipelago

Forced Labor and Other Abuses in Drug Detention Centers
in Southern Vietnam

HUMAN
RIGHTS
WATCH

*"Those who refused to work were beaten
by the guards and then put into the disciplinary
room. In the end they agreed to work."*
QUY HOP, FORMER DETAINEE OF BINH DUC CENTER

cashew processing and other forms of agricultural production, including potato or coffee farming; construction work; and garment manufacturing and other forms of manufacturing, such as making bamboo and rattan products. Under Vietnamese law, companies who source products from these centres are eligible for tax exemptions. Some products produced as a result of this forced labor made their way into the supply chain of companies who sell goods abroad, including to the United States and Europe.

Key International Actors

Vietnam's complicated relationship with China plays a key role in both domestic and foreign affairs. Domestically, the government has been increasingly criticized on nationalist grounds by many activists and some retired military officials for weak responses to what is widely seen in Vietnam as China's aggressive behavior in the disputed Spratly and Paracel Islands. The government in 2011 worked to silence this increasingly public and audible anti-China chorus.

Internationally, the government has attempted to increase cooperation with the US, India, Japan, and neighboring Association of Southeast Asian Nations countries as a regional counter-balance China's influence.

Despite Japan's considerable leverage as Vietnam's largest bilateral donor, it has repeatedly failed to publicly comment on Vietnam's deteriorating rights record.

The relationship between Vietnam and the US continues to grow closer. In September Vietnam opened a new consulate in New York, and the US Consulate in Ho Chi Minh City expanded with the opening of an American Center. The US and Vietnam are also among those currently negotiating to join the Trans-Pacific Partnership, a multilateral free trade agreement.

In January and May United Nations independent experts who had visited Vietnam in 2010 published their findings. The UN special rapporteur on human rights and extreme poverty issued a broadly positive report but urged the government to ratify and implement major human rights treaties, including the Convention against Torture and Other Cruel, Inhuman or Degrading Treatment. The UN special rapporteur on minority issues issued a more critical report, acknowledging some progress but raising concerns about the potential denial of religious freedom and "other serious violations of civil rights." The rapporteur also pointedly noted that obstacles during her visit "impeded her ability to obtain perspectives other than those in consonance with official Government positions."

EUROPEAN UNION

Human Rights in the European Union

Excerpt from Human Rights Watch World Report 2011

HUMAN
RIGHTS
WATCH

HUMAN
RIGHTS
WATCH

WORLD REPORT

2012

EUROPE
AND CENTRAL ASIA

ARMENIA

More than three years after deadly street clashes between police and opposition protesters left 10 individuals dead, there has been no meaningful accountability for the excessive use of force by law enforcement. The government decriminalized libel, but drastically increased financial penalties in civil libel suits. Authorities continue to restrict freedom of assembly. Torture and ill-treatment in police custody persist and the government has failed to effectively investigate a troubling number of deaths in custody and non-combat deaths in the military.

Armenia's international partners have not fully leveraged their influence to improve the human rights situation.

Lack of Accountability for Excessive Use of Force

In April 2011 President Serge Sargsyan ordered efforts to intensify investigations into the role of security forces in the March 1, 2008 clashes with opposition protestors in Yerevan, the capital, which resulted in the deaths of 10 people, including two police. Four officers were convicted in December 2009 but immediately amnestied. Under a May 2011 general amnesty all civilians remaining in custody on charges related to the clashes, including two prominent opposition politicians, Sasun Mikaelian and Nikol Pashinian, were released.

Freedom of Assembly

In April 2011, Yerevan officials allowed the opposition Armenian National Congress (ANC) to demonstrate in Freedom Square for the first time since the March 2008 clashes. However, opposition activists allege that the authorities prevented demonstrators from traveling from other cities to participate in subsequent large opposition rallies.

In October police arrested Vartgen Gaspari outside the prime minister's office as he participated in a peaceful demonstration of a few dozen parents of military personnel and activists protesting the large number of military non-combatant deaths. Gaspari was charged with hooliganism and resisting police and released on bail two days later.

In December 2010 a court imposed a two-year suspended sentences on opposition activists Sargis Gevorgian and Davit Kiramijyan for hooliganism and assaulting police when police tried to prevent demonstrators from entering Freedom Square in March 2010.

Torture and Ill-Treatment

Local and international human rights organizations reported ill-treatment of detained persons in police custody. In August the Council of Europe's Committee for the Prevention of Torture (CPT) made public the report on its 2010 visit, which documented a "significant number of credible and consistent allegations of physical ill-treatment of detained persons," as well as torture of detainees, allegedly in order to secure confessions and other information.

In August police beat and detained seven ANC activists after they intervened in what they believed was an illegal police stop and search of another man in a Yerevan park. Medics diagnosed the activists with concussions. Police charged all seven with hooliganism and assaulting an official. A court remanded one activist, Tigran Arakelian, to four months of pre-trial detention. At this writing there had been no investigation into the police's actions.

In June two plainclothes Yerevan police officers shot and killed robbery suspect Arman Yengibaryan. Police justified the use of force by saying Yengibaryan fired a gas pistol at police while fleeing. Local human rights groups contend police actions were excessive. Yengibaryan's gun had no live ammunition and gunshot wounds to his head and abdomen suggest police did not try to minimize recourse to lethal force. An initial criminal investigation concluded the police actions were lawful, but Yengibaryan's family is challenging that outcome on the basis that the investigation was not effective, as required by international law, and in particular because they, as the family of the deceased, had no access to the investigation.

Despite a May amnesty releasing 590 prisoners, prison overcrowding persists, leading to violations in detention conditions and standards of treatment, such as unhygienic conditions, inadequate medical care, and lack of exercise. Overcrowding is mainly due to courts improper overuse of pre-trial detentions.

Deaths in Custody

Unexplained deaths in custody also mar Armenia's human rights record. In October 2010 Slavik Voskanyan died in pre-trial detention in Vanadzor two weeks after his detention on murder charges involving a police officer's mother. According to his family, Voskanyan died from gangrene, which developed after a wound sustained in custody became infected and was not properly treated. A criminal investigation was closed after it concluded that the prison doctor's negligence was not responsible for Voskanyan's death. The investigation never examined how Voskanyan sustained the wounds that lead to his death.

In November 2010 a court convicted Ashot Harutyunyan, former head of the Charentsavan Police Investigative Department, to eight years for abuse of authority and incitement to suicide with respect to Vahan Khalafyan, who died from knife wounds in police custody in April 2010. Local human rights groups and Khalafyan's family believe he was stabbed to death.

In May 2011 a court overturned prosecutors' March 2011 decision to terminate the investigation into the 2007 death of Levon Gulyan. Officials claim Gulyan jumped from the second story of a police station while trying to escape. Gulyan's relatives insist he was tortured.

Army Abuses

Local human rights groups report ill-treatment, hazing, and an alarming number of non-combat deaths in the army. The Helsinki Citizens' Assembly's Vanadzor Office reported at least 17 non-combat deaths through October 2011. For example, Torgom Sarukhanyan, 21, died in February, allegedly of a self-inflicted gunshot. Ministry of Defense investigators arrested three servicemen on charges of incitement to suicide. Sarukhanyan's family claims that he was murdered and that his body bore signs of beatings.

In December 2010 a court sentenced Maj. Sasun Galstyan to three years imprisonment for abuse of authority. A video of Galstyan beating and humiliating two conscripts appeared on YouTube in September 2010.

Freedom of Media

In May 2010 Armenia decriminalized libel. However, amendments to the civil code introduced high monetary fines for libel and defamation and led to an increase in lawsuits against newspapers, particularly by public officials. In some cases courts' disproportionately large damage awards threaten the survival of newspapers. Journalists and editors report the chilling effect of large fines.

In February 2011 a court ordered the pro-opposition daily *Haykakan Zhamanak* to pay three government-connected businesspeople approximately US$16,500 in damages and retract allegations that they were implicated in criminal activities (the average monthly salary in Armenia is $90). The newspaper has sought donations from its readers to pay the fine and keep publishing.

In June a court ordered the opposition newspaper *Zhamanak* to pay former President Robert Kocharyan approximately $8,250 for having published allegations implicating him in corrupt business deals during and after his presidency, placing *Zhamanak* in serious financial straits. In another defamation suit brought by Kocharyan, a court in June froze the daily newspaper *Hraparak's* bank accounts pending a verdict.

In a separate case, in September a Yerevan court froze approximately $8,000 of *Hraparak's* assets and prohibited the newspaper from writing about a libel lawsuit filed against the paper by the head of the state body responsible for judicial supervision.

In February a court ordered the daily *Yerkir* to pay approximately $800 to pro-government parliamentarian Tigran Arzakantsyan in a spurious suit after the newspaper called Arzakantsyan a "dandy" in an article.

Lack of media pluralism remains a problem. In December 2010 the National Commission on Television and Radio, responsible for broadcasting licenses, denied independent television station A1+ a license for the 13th time, despite a 2008 European Court of Human Rights (ECtHR) judgment that Armenia had violated freedom of expression by repeatedly and arbitrarily denying the station a license.

The authorities also refused to grant digital broadcast licenses to ALM television, whose owner has expressed political ambitions, and to the Gyumri-based GALA TV, although GALA can broadcast on analogue frequencies until 2015 with its existing license. Since 2007 GALA has been subject to apparently politically motivated court cases and harassment by state agencies, seemingly in retaliation for the station's coverage of opposition party activities.

Human Rights Defenders

In August a court heard a defamation suit Lernapat Mayor Vano Yeghiazaryan filed against Artur Sakunts, head of Helsinki Citizens' Assembly's Vanadzor Office, after Sakunts accused Yeghiazaryan in a newspaper interview of embezzlement and abuse of power, and criticized the authorities' unwillingness to investigate the allegations. The trial is ongoing.

Key International Actors

Several of Armenia's international partners limited their criticism of the government's human rights record.

In its May European Neighborhood Policy progress report, the European Union highlighted Armenia's lack of judicial independence, limited media pluralism, poor prison conditions, and inadequate investigations into ill-treatment, but stopped short of articulating concrete human rights improvements required as part of its engagement with Armenia's government.

In an October 2011 resolution on Armenia's fulfillment of its obligations as a Council of Europe member, the organization's Parliamentary Assembly gave the government undue credit by stating, "the chapter on the March 2008 events can finally be considered closed." The resolution nevertheless reiterated concerns about the lack of accountability for the 10 deaths during the clashes.

In a May report on Armenia, Thomas Hammarberg, Council of Europe commissioner for human rights, focused on freedom of expression, assembly, and association, and abuses in the army. He urged the authorities hold accountable those responsible for excessive use of force in the March 2008 clashes.

In its April concluding observations, the United Nations Committee on the Elimination of Racial Discrimination urged the authorities to, among other things, do more to combat manifestations of discrimination against individuals and groups.

AZERBAIJAN

Azerbaijan's human rights record deteriorated in 2011. The government cracked down on all forms of protest and imprisoned dozens of youth activists after sham trials. Although the number of government-initiated criminal and civil libel cases against journalists decreased, the atmosphere for journalists and other critics remained hostile. The government's so-called beautification campaign in central Baku, the capital, resulted in forced evictions and illegal demolitions. Restrictions on freedom of religion and torture and ill-treatment in custody also persisted.

Azerbaijan continued to deny access to the country for the Council of Europe Parliamentary Assembly rapporteur on political prisoners in Azerbaijan.

Freedom of Media

The Institute for Reporters' Freedom and Safety, a local media monitoring organization, reported that more than 50 domestic and foreign journalists were harassed or attacked in 2011. In March six masked men abducted and beat Seymur Haziyev, a journalist for the pro-opposition daily *Azadlig*, warning him to stop writing articles criticizing the authorities. In April, three unidentified assailants kidnapped *Azadlig* reporter Ramin Deko, held him for eight hours, and warned him against using social media to criticize the government. Police failed to effectively investigate the attacks.

In October a court remanded *Khural* newspaper editor-in-chief Avaz Zeinalli to three months pre-trial custody on dubious extortion charges. Earlier in October a court ordered the seizure of Khural's office equipment to pay fines imposed in three defamation cases brought by the head of the presidential administration and other officials against the newspaper in 2009.

In April police prevented a Swedish television crew from covering a protest by taking their cameras and deleting all footage. In July officials deported Bloomberg Markets photographer Diana Markosian from the Baku airport. In June four men assaulted American freelance writer Amanda Erickson and British human rights activist Celia Davies, breaking Davies's arm. Two alleged assailants now face criminal charges.

Despite repeated calls from Azerbaijan's international partners for the government to decriminalize libel and refrain from using criminal and civil libel charges against critical voices, officials initiated seven libel cases against journalists and others in the first half of 2011; at least two resulted in imprisonment.

In May the authorities released Eynulla Fatullayev, a prominent editor and government critic, who was imprisoned in 2007 on politically motivated charges, and whose release the European Court of Human Rights had ordered in April 2010.

Freedom of Assembly

The government severely restricted freedom of assembly. Officials did not authorize any demonstrations in central Baku and police quickly and often violently dispersed unauthorized protests.

The government cracked down on a series of protests inspired by the pro-democracy Arab Spring movements. Police detained more than 50 activists in March after a two-day protest. The courts tried dozens in closed late night trials, sentencing activists for up to 10 days.

In an unauthorized rally on April 2, police physically obstructed protesters from gathering and detained over 200 people—including public figures, journalists, and opposition activists—fourteen of whom were sentenced in unfair trials to up to three years imprisonment. On April 17, police again forced demonstrators away from a protest site, detained more than 100 people and prosecuted dozens on misdemeanor charges.

Political Prisoners

Imprisonment on politically motivated charges is a continuing problem. In the first six months of 2011, local human rights activists counted between 23 and

45 political prisoners, including several activists involved in the March and April protests.

In March police detained youth activist Bakhtyar Hajiyev, 29, in advance of a protest planned for March 11, which he had promoted through social media. In a politically motivated trial, Hajiyev was sentenced to two years in prison for military draft evasion, although he had asked to perform alternative service, as permitted by law.

Also in March social media activist and opposition Popular Front party member Jabbar Savalanli, 20, was sentenced to two-and-a-half years in prison on bogus drug possession charges. In the days leading up to his arrest he had posted comments online criticizing the government.

The authorities still refuse to grant a visa to the Council of Europe Parliamentary Assembly's rapporteur on political prisoners in Azerbaijan, who has never been allowed to visit Azerbaijan since being appointed in March 2009.

Ill-Treatment and Deaths in Custody

Torture and ill-treatment continue with impunity and two men died in police custody in 2011. In the first half of 2011 the Azerbaijan Committee against Torture, an independent prison monitoring group, received 89 complaints alleging ill-treatment in custody.

In January Elvin Askerov, 31, died following a police chase and his subsequent detention. Police allege he was bruised during the chase. Askerov's family believes he was beaten in Baku's Nizami District police station. Despite the family's request, no investigation followed.

Turac Zeynalov, 31, was detained on August 24 on espionage charges and later died in the custody of the Ministry of National Security of the Nakhichevan Autonomous Republic. Relatives who visited Zeynalov the day after his detention stated that he appeared to have been beaten and could not move. He died three days later. Officials claim that he died of skin cancer. The authorities opened an investigation. In September security ministry officials detained and deported a Radio Free Europe Azerbaijani Service correspondent investigating

Zeynalov's death.

Forced Evictions and Illegal Demolitions

Since 2009, citing city "beautification," the Baku mayor's office has evicted hundreds of residents—sometimes using force—and demolished their homes. Homeowners often receive compensation well below market value and have few options for legal recourse.

Evictions were also used to harass human rights defenders. On August 11, violating a court injunction, the authorities demolished without warning a building owned by human rights defender Leyla Yunus that served as an office for Yunus's Institute for Peace and Democracy, the Azerbaijani Campaign to Ban Landmines, and the only women's crisis center in Baku. Yunus had repeatedly criticized the government's demolition campaign.

Freedom of Religion

The government tightened restrictions on all religious groups, dramatically increasing fines for unauthorized religious activity and requiring all religious groups to seek prior authorization from the government to gather after the June 2010 amendments.

In June police dissolved a private meeting of 40 Jehovah's Witnesses in Ganja, detaining and questioning attendees for up to 10 hours. A court fined three for violating regulations on religious meetings. The same day police raided the Baptist congregation in Sumgait, warning the leader not to meet for worship without state permission. The Ganja community of Jehovah's Witnesses has unsuccessfully attempted to register at least twice since June 2010.

In December 2010 the government banned women from wearing head scarves in schools and universities, leading thousands to drop out. In October a court convicted five people of organizing unsanctioned protests and resisting police during a May demonstration against the head scarves ban, imprisoning them to up to two-and-a-half years.

In January 2011, officials arrested Movsum Samadov, leader of an outlawed Islamic party, after a speech was posted on YouTube in which he denounced President Ilham Aliyev. In October he was convicted to 12 years imprisonment for an attempted coup.

Human Rights Defenders

In August a court sentenced Vidadi Isganderov, head of the human rights organization Support for Protection of Democracy, to three years in prison on dubious charges of interference with the November 2010 parliamentary elections. The authorities charged Isganderov a few months after he filed a complaint alleging vote rigging in the district in which he ran for parliament. Isganderov also served short sentences in April after two arrests for participating in unsanctioned rallies.

Several human rights lawyers faced politically motivated disciplinary and criminal actions and the government interfered with the work of human rights groups. In August, following a complaint by a police chief, Azerbaijan's Bar Association suspended Khalid Bagirov, who represented the family of Elvin Askerov who died in police custody in January. Another lawyer, Elchin Namazov, was permanently disbarred and faces criminal sanctions.

In March the Justice Ministry suspended the Azerbaijan Human Rights House, a member of the International Human Rights House Network and a registered organization that served as a training and resource center and conference venue for local groups. Also in March the ministry ordered the National Democratic Institute (NDI) to suspend activities in Azerbaijan pending registration. Since 2006, authorities have denied NDI's repeated registration attempts.

The Ministry of Justice again refused registration to the Media Monitoring Institute, which has unsuccessfully attempted to register six times since 2009.

In March in Ganja, Azerbaijan's second largest city, local officials and police, without explanation, evicted from their offices three NGOs: the Regional Center for Development of Democratic Education, Demos, and the Election Monitoring and Democracy Studies Center.

Key International Actors

While the European Union, United States, and other international and regional institutions and partners criticized Azerbaijan's human rights record, they failed to condition their engagement on concrete human rights improvements.

The EU, the Organization for Security and Co-operation in Europe (OSCE), and the US Embassy in Baku all expressed concern over the arrests of youth activists.

In May the European Parliament adopted a resolution expressing "deep concern at the increasing number of incidents of harassment, attacks and violence against civil society and social network activists and journalists in Azerbaijan." The same month Catherine Ashton, EU High representative for foreign affairs and security policy/ vice-president of the European Commission, issued a statement expressing concern about the convictions of Jabbar Savalanli and Bakhtyar Hajiyev.

On August 16 the UN high commissioner for human rights criticized the destruction of Leyla Yunus's property and called on the government to ensure safe working conditions for human rights defenders. The EU and the US Mission to the OSCE also objected to the demolition.

In a September observation on human rights in Azerbaijan, Thomas Hammarberg, Council of Europe commissioner for human rights, criticized the authorities for failure to adequately protect freedom of expression, association, and assembly.

BELARUS

The December 2010 presidential election resulted in victory for Alyaksandr Lukashenka, who has ruled the country for the last 16 years. The Organization for Security and Co-operation in Europe (OSCE) found the election to be flawed, crushing hopes for democratic progress in Belarus. On election night riot police beat and arrested hundreds of largely peaceful protesters. Over 40 were imprisoned, although in apparent response to international pressure the government released many throughout the year.

In the following months the authorities unleashed a harassment campaign, targeting human rights defenders, political activists, journalists, and lawyers. Severe restrictions on freedoms of association, assembly, and media remain and the level of repression is unprecedented.

In August 2011 prominent Belarusian human rights defender Ales Bialiatski was arrested on politically motivated charges of tax evasion.

December 2010 Post-Election Unrest and Political Prisoners

On the night of December 19, tens of thousands of demonstrators took to the streets of Minsk, the capital, protesting what they felt was another stolen election. Riot police violently dispersed the largely peaceful demonstration, beating everyone within reach. They arrested more than 700 protesters, including dozens of journalists and seven presidential candidates. Hundreds served up to 15 days in detention for misdemeanor charges of "hooliganism." A coalition of independent human rights NGOs in Minsk who documented the crackdown found that hundreds of detainees alleged abuse while in police custody, including beatings, no access to food and water, and being forced to sign police reports containing false information about the circumstances of their arrest.

Trials were held behind closed doors and marred by multiple due process violations. Most defendants had no access to defense counsel and were not allowed to call witnesses. There were no acquittals.

BELARUS

Shattering Hopes

Post-Election Crackdown in Belarus

HUMAN
RIGHTS
WATCH

Belarusian authorities sought to portray the December unrest as an attempt, planned by the opposition and foreign states, to overthrow the government.

More than 40 persons—including journalists, civil society leaders, and five former presidential candidates—were sentenced to up to six years of imprisonment on trumped-up rioting charges. The NGO coalition found that detainees were held in poor detention conditions, in virtual isolation from the outside world, and had severely restricted access to legal counsel at all stages of detention and trial. Human rights monitors reported that those accused of rioting or public disorder were convicted despite lack of evidence of engaging in or inciting violence.

There continue to be allegations of serious psychological and physical abuse and due process rights violations of political prisoners who remain in custody. Many are routinely denied meetings with their lawyers. They often do not receive correspondences and are prohibited from family visits. Some are repeatedly placed in solitary confinement or punishment cells without justification and some are denied medical care.

Human Rights Defenders, Civil Society Groups, and Lawyers

In the weeks following the December protests, state security forces repeatedly raided offices of human rights groups, confiscating equipment, interrogating staff, and arresting those suspected of participating in pro-democracy protests. Human rights NGOs report several cases of politically motivated expulsions from universities and dismissals from public sector jobs.

Involvement in an unregistered organization constitutes a criminal offense under Belarusian law. The authorities continue to routinely deny registration to most civil society groups for arbitrary reasons, making activists constantly vulnerable to prosecution.

In January and June 2011 the Belarusian Helsinki Committee, Belarus's only nationally registered human rights group, received two politically motivated warnings from the Ministry of Justice. Under Belarusian law, two official warnings may lead to suspension of an organization's activities.

In August Ales Bialiatski, vice-president of the International Federation for Human Rights (FIDH)and head of the Human Rights Centre Viasna (Viasna), an independent human rights group, was arrested on criminal charges of large-scale tax evasion, after Lithuanian and Polish authorities released details of his personal bank accounts to Belarusian authorities. Viasna used the funds, received from international donors, for legal and financial assistance for political prisoners and their families in Belarus.

Authorities withdrew Viasna's registration in 2003 and have since routinely denied it registration. As a result, Viasna cannot open a bank account in Belarus.

In 2011, authorities expelled or banned from entering Belarus an unprecedented 13 foreign human rights defenders, seriously impeding independent monitoring of the human rights situation in the country.

The authorities consistently targeted lawyers representing clients charged in connection with the December events. The Ministry of Justice arbitrarily disbarred or revoked the licenses of seven lawyers, a clear warning to lawyers against taking on "political" cases. Lawyers who represent political prisoners continue to face difficulties accessing their clients, resulting in some individuals being left without legal counsel.

Freedom of Peaceful Assembly

Belarusian authorities continue to severely curtail the right to assemble peacefully. In 2011 the political opposition held "silent" demonstrations to protest Lukashenka's government or express support for political prisoners. Police disperse, sometimes harshly, protesters who do nothing more than stroll silently or clap their hands. Many were sentenced to up to 15 days of administrative detention for "hooliganism." In October the Belarusian parliament adopted restrictive amendments to a number of laws that seemed aimed at banning silent demonstrations. The amendments included restrictions on where demonstrations can be held, and introduced a more complicated procedure for obtaining permits for public gatherings. Also according to the new legislation, actions directed at spreading or sharing information about a planned gathering may constitute an offense unless the gathering had already been approved by the authorities.

Freedom of Media

The government continued to severely restrict freedom of media. The authorities routinely threatened the independent print media, and on several occasions blocked social media and other websites. Police arrested dozens of journalists covering pro-democracy protests in December and the later "silent" protests. For example, in May 2011 a court handed independent journalist Iryna Khalip a two-year suspended sentence on trumped-up riot charges in connection with the December protests. In May the authorities initiated closure proceedings for the independent newspapers *Nasha Niva* and *Narodnaya Vola*. Although legal proceedings were discontinued in August, both newspapers received fines for trumped-up violations of media law. In July a court convicted Andrzej Poczobut, a correspondent for the Polish newspaper *Gazeta Wyborcza*, for defaming Lukashenka. In his articles Poczobut called President Lukashenka a dictator. He was handed a three-year suspended sentence. In September a higher court upheld the conviction.

Death Penalty

In July 2011 Belarusian authorities executed two individuals, despite the United Nations Human Rights Committee's request to not carry out the executions pending the committee's review of their cases. Both men, convicted of murder, admitted their guilt but alleged they were tortured during interrogations. The committee deplored their executions, stating that Belarus violated its international obligations by imposing death sentences on individuals whose right to fair trial may have been violated.

Key International Actors

Many foreign governments and international organizations condemned the post-election crackdown and expressed concern over the deepening human rights crisis in Belarus.

In December 2010 Hillary Clinton, United States secretary of state, and Catherine Ashton, European Union representative for foreign affairs and security policy/ vice-president of the European Commission, issued a joint statement calling the election "an unfortunate step backwards" in the democratic development of Belarus. In January 2011 the foreign ministers of Germany, Sweden, Poland, and the Czech Republic issued a joint statement condemning the post-election crackdown.

In January the EU and the US imposed new financial and travel sanctions against the Belarusian government. The US significantly extended the list of Belarusian top-ranking officials subject to visa bans and travel restrictions, but did not specify how many officials were affected by the limitations. In August the US imposed new economic sanctions against four major state-owned Belarusian companies.

In 2011 the European Parliament adopted four resolutions on the human rights situation in Belarus. In its resolution on Belarus adopted in January, the European Parliament expressed its dismay at the "unprecedented wave of violence, intimidation, mass arrests, and prosecution of political opponents."

In February 2011 UN Secretary-General Ban Ki-moon expressed concern about "reports of harassment and continued detention of journalists, civil society activists and opposition candidates" and called for their release.

In June 2011 the UN Human Rights Council adopted a resolution condemning violations in Belarus, and called on the high commissioner for human rights to monitor the human rights situation and report to the Council during the following sessions. The resolution also encouraged relevant UN thematic special procedures mandate holders to pay particular attention to the human rights situation in Belarus.

During her speech at the Eastern Partnership summit in September, German Chancellor Angela Merkel called the government's actions against opposition "unacceptable."

In contrast, Russia has condemned international sanctions against Belarus, calling them "counterproductive." In August 2011 Russian Prime Minister

Vladimir Putin announced that in 2012 Russia will supply gas to Belarus at a discount price as a sign of support.

In response to international pressure, Lukashenka's government gradually released some political prisoners. In January 2011 Belarusian authorities released several of the detainees facing riot charges and transferred several others to house arrest. In March they re-classified riot charges against six detainees to less serious offences. Between June and August the authorities pardoned 13 individuals who were convicted in relation to December events; most, however, had to admit guilt as a condition of their release.

In an unexpected public statement in August, Lukashenka called on opposition leaders to join him in a strategic discussion on leading Belarus out of political and economic crises. In September, 11 more political prisoners were released after being granted a presidential pardon.

Meanwhile the Belarusian government ignored international requests to restore the OSCE mandate in Belarus, which it discontinued in January, following the organization's critical assessment of the December election. Lukashenka's government also refused to cooperate with the Moscow Mechanism, the OSCE's only existing monitoring mechanism that does not require consensus. The OSCE imposed the procedure in April.

Bosnia and Herzegovina

The continuing political crisis in Bosnia and Herzegovina impeded necessary human rights reforms, including the constitutional changes needed to end discriminatory restrictions on Jews and Roma holding political office. Roma in particular remain extremely vulnerable and subject to widespread discrimination. More than 15 years after being indicted for the 1995 Srebrenica genocide, Bosnian Serb wartime commander Ratko Mladic faced trial in the Hague. Returns of refugees and displaced persons continued to dwindle with little or no progress on durable solutions, including for Roma refugees from Kosovo.

Ethnic and Religious Discrimination

Bosnia again failed to implement a 2009 European Court of Human Rights (ECtHR) ruling (the *Sejdic and Finci v. Bosnia and Herzegovina* case) ordering the country to amend its constitution to eliminate ethnic discrimination in the national tri-partite presidency and House of Peoples. Currently only members of the three main ethnic groups (Bosniaks, Serbs, and Croats) may stand for election. Political gridlock, including failure to form a national government one year after general elections, meant the parliamentary body charged with proposing constitutional amendments had to yet to be formed and a similar ministerial-level body had yet to meet at this writing.

Although more Roma children were enrolled in primary and secondary education in 2011, they still attend school at lower rates than their peers. In addition, the 99 percent unemployment rate for Roma in Bosnia in 2011 meant even those who completed school had virtually no chance of finding work. According to the Office of the United Nations High Commissioner for Refugees (UNHCR), up to 10 percent of Roma are not on the public registry in Bosnia, impeding their access to public services. Many Roma remained unable to access needed health care services due to registration restrictions, and most Roma remained in informal settlements with poor housing.

More than 100 Roma in Mostar, many elderly or children, faced imminent forced eviction in November from their homes in a settlement to make room for a housing project sponsored by the city and the Ministry of Human Rights for 18 other Roma families. At this writing the authorities had failed to identify alternative housing for those facing eviction, some of whom were moved in late 2010 from another location in Mostar.

War Crimes Accountability

On May 31, 2011, Bosnian Serb army commander Ratko Mladic was extradited to the International Criminal Tribunal for the Former Yugoslavia (ICTY) (see Serbia chapter). Mladic made his first appearance in court in June, pleading not guilty to 11 counts of genocide, crimes against humanity, and war crimes, including the massacre of up to 8,000 Bosnian men and boys from Srebrenica in July 1995 and the siege of Sarajevo from 1992 to 1995. In October the trial member rejected a request from the prosecutor to split the charges into two trials and proceed with the Srebrenica charges first to ensure efficiency and justice for victims. The trial member concluded the request would "prejudice the accused and render the trials less manageable."

The trial of Bosnian Serb wartime president Radovan Karadzic, charged with many of the same crimes as Mladic, continued at the ICTY in 2011, with some delays due to disputes between his legal team and the prosecutor's office about delayed disclosure of evidence to the defense.

In September Momcilo Perisic, former Yugoslav army chief of staff, was convicted at the ICTY of war crimes committed in Bosnia and Herzegovina and Croatia, including involvement in the Srebrenica massacre. He was sentenced to 27 years in prison.

Between September 2010 and 2011, the domestic War Crimes Chamber in Bosnia reached final verdicts in 24 cases, raising the total number of completed cases to 75.

Refugees and Internally Displaced Persons

The adoption of a revised strategy in 2010 to support the return of refugees and internally displaced persons (IDPs) did little to arrest the declining number of such returns. According to UNHCR only 146 refugees and 177 IDPs returned to their areas of origin in the first six months of 2011. As of mid-2011, there were 113,188 registered IDPs (including about 7,000 in collective centers), according to UNHCR, with 48,583 in the Federation, 64,359 in Republika Srpska, and 246 in Brcko District. Impediments to return remained similar to previous years: lack of economic opportunity in Bosnia, inadequate housing, and reluctance to return to areas where residents would be an ethnic minority.

Bosnia continued to host Roma, Ashkali, and Egyptians from Kosovo under temporary protected status, many of whom had lived in the country for over a decade. As of June 2011, UNHCR reported that there were 152 Kosovo Roma in Bosnia, up from previous years.

National Security and Human Rights

In June Ahmed el-Farahat, an Egyptian national arrested and detained at Lukavica immigration detention center in October 2010 under national security legislation, was deported to Egypt without criminal charges being filed against him or the opportunity to examine evidence and appeal his deportation. El-Farahat, who had gone on hunger strike earlier in the year to protest his indefinite detention, had lived in Bosnia with legal permanent resident status since the early 1990s.Five other national security suspects were detained without charge at Lukavica, including three with cases pending before the ECtHR.

In March Thomas Hammarberg, Council of Europe commissioner of human rights, condemned Bosnia's failure to implement recommendations, made after his 2007 visit to the country, on improved safeguards for national security suspects, including a judicial remedy for long-term detainees at Lukavica detention center and suspending deportations for those at risk of torture or ill-treatment in the countries of return.

In February the Court of Bosnia and Herzegovina began the trial of six defendants charged with the 2010 bombing of a police station in the town of Bugojno, which killed one police officer. Three of the six defendants pleaded not guilty, while two defendants refused to enter pleas and one did not attend the hearing. At this writing only two defendants had attended the two hearings of the trial.

Freedom of Media

In August journalist Omer Hasanovic and cameraman Emir Hrncic of the Federation Radio-Television were attacked in Zivinice by 10 men who confiscated their equipment. They were reporting on Mehmed Butkovic's activities during his suspension as the head imam of the Islamic community in Zivinice. Witnesses claimed that the assailants were Butkovic and his followers. There were no arrests in the case at this writing.

There were no significant developments in investigating threats made in 2010 against TV editor Bakir Hadziomerovic and an assault on TV journalist Osman Drina the same year. Hadziomerovic continued to receive death threats—the latest in February 2011—but no arrests had been made at this writing. Hadziomerovic has been living under police protection since 2009.

Key International Actors

The European Union played an increasingly significant role in Bosnia in 2011, opening a new office in Sarajevo to house both the EU Special Representative in Bosnia and an increasing number of staff working towards EU integration. Peter Sorensen, the new head of the EU Delegation to Bosnia and Herzegovina (BiH) and EU special representative (EUSR), was appointed in 2011 and took office in September.

Catherine Ashton, the EU high representative for foreign affairs and security policy/ vice-president of the European Commission, assumed the main role in defusing tensions with Republika Srpska leader Milorad Dodik after he called for an RS referendum on national government institutions, including the war crimes tribunals, which was seen as a precursor for eventual referendum on Republika Srpska's secession from Bosnia.

The European Commission's annual progress report on Bosnia and Herzegovina in October identified the continued failure to form a state-level government as a key obstacle to reform, including implementation of the *Sejdic and Finci* ruling. The report also highlighted ongoing discrimination against Roma (despite some moves to implement the Roma strategy), political pressure on the media and intimidation of journalists, segregated education, and little progress on rule of law.

In his March report released following his visit to Bosnia, Hammarberg under-lined the need to enhance protection of Roma, including the Kosovo Roma, under temporary protected status, end ethnic segregation in public schools, and to find a durable solution for refugees and IDPs.

In February the Council of Europe's European Commission against Racism and Intolerance (ECRI) criticized lack of progress on implementing the *Sejdic and Finci* ruling, while highlighting the continued marginalization of minority groups, particularly Roma.

In a joint opinion issued in June, United States Secretary of State Hillary Clinton and United Kingdom Foreign Affairs Minister William Hague expressed disap-pointment at the protracted institutional gridlock in Bosnia that was preventing needed reforms, including ending ethnic discrimination in politics. During a visit to Bosnia the same month, US Assistant Secretary of State Philip H. Gordon stated the country had made little political progress since 2006-2007 and called on Bosnian politicians to form a government and stop stoking ethnic tensions.

CROATIA

As Croatia closed membership negotiations and received a tentative date (July 2013) to join the European Union, its progress on human rights lagged behind its commitments. The government's reaction to the international war crimes conviction of a Croatian general and its domestic handling of war crimes revealed continuing difficulties in coming to terms with the past. Croatia released a long-promised plan for deinstitutionalizing persons with intellectual or mental disabilities, but took little action to implement it. Despite the announcement of a plan to compensate Croatian Serbs stripped of property rights during the war from 1991 to 1995, Serbs faced continued obstacles reintegrating back into Croatia.

War Crimes Accountability

In April the International Criminal Tribunal for the Former Yugoslavia (ICTY) found former generals Ante Gotovina and Ivan Cermak guilty of war crimes and crimes against humanity committed against Serbs in 1995. A third defendant, Mladen Markac, was acquitted. The convictions of the generals led to days of protests by veterans' groups and others opposed to the ruling, and condemnation from political leaders in Croatia, including Prime Minister Jadranka Kosor and President Ivo Josipovic.

On July 20, 2011, the remaining fugitive wanted by the ICTY, Goran Hadzic, was arrested in Serbia and extradited to The Hague two days later (see Serbia chapter). Hadzic, president of rebel Serb-controlled territory in Croatia in 1992 and 1993, is charged with ordering the killing of hundreds and the deportation of thousands of Croats and other non-Serbs between 1991 and 1993. In August he pled not guilty to 14 counts of war crimes and crimes against humanity.

In the first eight months of 2011, 20 individuals were indicted for war crimes in domestic courts: 11 Serbs and 9 members of the Croatian army and police. The most prominent of the nine, Tomislav Mercep, is accused of having command responsibility for—and in some cases ordering—the illegal detention, torture, and killing of 53 Yugoslav Army soldiers in 1991.

The number of war crimes trials conducted in absentia increased in 2011, particularly in cases in which the defendant was a Serb. An ongoing plan by the Chief State Attorney's Office to revise past convictions rendered in absentia fails to address the continuing problem of conducting trials in absentia. In the first eight months of 2011, 20 of the 33 active war crimes trials took place at least partially in absentia, and of the 20 newly-indicted individuals in 2011, 10 were indicted in absentia, primarily Serbs. Suspects continued to face trial in regular district courts rather than the four courts specially designated for war crimes trials.

Disability Rights

In March—five years after pledging with the EU to move people with disabilities out of institutions and into the community—Croatia published a five-year plan for deinstitutionalization. The plan pledges to move 30 percent of people with intellectual disabilities out of institutions by 2016 and 20 percent of people with mental disabilities by 2017, while developing community-based support for these populations, such as organized housing.

However, the plan continued to consider smaller institutions as adequate community living options and did little to define criteria for community-based support. At this writing the government had yet to provide increased funding to community support programs for people with intellectual or mental disabilities, according to disability groups in Croatia.

More than 17,000 people in Croatia remain deprived of their legal capacity, stripping them of the opportunity to exercise basic legal rights and putting them at risk of arbitrary detention in institutions. Despite commitments by Croatia at the Universal Periodic Review before the United Nations Human Rights Council in November 2010, including to abolish guardianship laws, there has been no progress in reforming the system.

Return and Reintegration of Serbs

Four hundred seventy-nine refugees—all Serbs—returned to Croatia in the last six months of 2010 and the first six months of 2011, according to the Office of the UN High Commissioner for Refugees (UNHCR), down slightly from the same period twelve months earlier. Only two Serb internally displaced persons (IDPs) returned to their homes in Croatia in the first six months of 2011. As of the end of June there were 2,084 IDPs in Croatia, 1,636 of them Serbs.

Croatian authorities began to implement a September 2010 decision to permit Serbs stripped of the tenancy rights during the 1991-1995 war to buy apartments at discounts of up to 70 percent, a key impediment to Serb returns in urban areas. Out of the 1,140 households eligible for this program and contacted by Croatian authorities, 610 had submitted applications to purchase homes as of September 2011. However, according to official data, as of mid-year none of the apartments had been sold because of delays in legal registration of the state entity in charge of selling the apartments.

There were ongoing delays in government-sponsored housing programs for returnees. Only 286 applications were approved from June 2010 to June 2011, bringing overall approvals to 7,742, of which 60 percent were from Serb families.

There was some progress in processing Serb's pension eligibility claims for recognition of wartime work in formerly rebel-held areas. According to UNHCR, as of the end of June, 23,568 of 24,901 requests had been processed, although only 57 percent were resolved positively, with ongoing problems about admissible evidence. There were only minor increases in positive decisions in regions where recognition had been as low as 30 percent in previous years, continuing to compromise the financial security of returnees to those regions.

Asylum and Migration

Asylum applications rose to 392 in the first seven months of the year compared to 290 in all of 2010. Problems with processing asylum applications remained, including lack of access to a state-funded lawyer at first instance and for those seeking to challenge their detention. The recognition rate for asylum applications in 2011 decreased to about 3 percent, with 7 individuals recognized as refugees in the first 7 months of 2011 and 2 granted subsidiary protection.

Croatia addressed overcrowding at its asylum reception center in Kutina by securing a temporary facility with similar conditions that can accommodate 150 more individuals.

Despite increasing arrivals of unaccompanied migrant children (213 in 2010), Croatia continued to lack an adequate infrastructure to protect them. Although guardians are appointed to all unaccompanied migrant children upon arrival in Croatia, they lack capacity and guidance on how to secure the best interests of their wards, with no provision for interpreters, legal assistance (other than for asylum appeals), or a tracking system, despite UNHCR reports that about 90 percent leave Croatia before their asylum procedure is completed.

Freedom of Media

Concerns over freedom of media, particularly for journalists reporting on corruption and organized crime, prompted a visit in January of the civil society organization Southeast European Media Organization (SEEMO). Croatian parliamentarian Josip Djakic filed defamation suits against Aleksandra Stankovic from the public television station HTV in July and Goran Gazdek, journalist and editor of *Virovitica.net*, in September, following their critical reporting on alleged corruption in the Association for Croatian War Veterans.

In October a judge ruled that Gazdek had not committed defamation, stating that Gazdek's reporting on the association was truthful, and that he was not required to reveal his sources. First hearings in the case against Stankovic were held in Zagreb in October.

In December 2010, 12 individuals were arrested in the June 2008 attack of Dusan Miljus, an investigative journalist for *Jutarnji List* newspaper covering corruption. However, the state attorney dropped charges against suspects in June, citing insufficient evidence. No other suspects have been arrested in the case.

Human Rights Defenders

In October the Croatian parliament passed a law merging all five of its national human rights institutions into one central body, citing the need for cost-saving and efficiency. The merger affects the Human Rights Center as well as the four ombudsperson offices (the General People's Ombudsperson and the Ombudspeople for Disabilities, Children, and Gender Equality). The ombudsperson offices had opposed the change, arguing it would overstretch the capacity of one office to deal with all these human rights issues. The law will go into effect in July 2012.

Key International Actors

At the end of June Croatia closed negotiations for entry into the EU. Despite ongoing concerns about corruption, war crimes accountability, and freedom of expression, amongst other human rights issues, Croatia received a tentative entry date of July 2013 but will continue to be monitored by the EU until that time to ensure compliance with membership requirements.

In November the EU progress report on Croatia cited progress on tackling war crimes impunity and corruption but expressed concern at the limited progress in investigating prior cases of intimidation of journalists, slow progress on deinstitutionalizing people with disabilities, and ongoing discrimination against Roma.

EUROPEAN UNION

Even as the EU and member states proclaimed the importance of human rights in the pro-democracy Arab Spring movements, they remained unwilling to prioritize human rights at home. Policy responses to migration from North Africa— including calls to limit free movement inside EU internal borders, disputes over rescuing boat migrants in peril, and reluctance to resettle refugees from Libya— exemplified this negative approach.

The European Commission failed to pursue vigorously its duty to enforce fundamental rights, dropping proceedings against Hungary over its media law and France over Roma expulsions, and suspending proceedings against Greece on its dysfunctional asylum and migration system despite continuing problems. The commission's first annual report on rights inside the EU shied away from criticizing members states, with Fundamental Rights Commissioner Viviane Reding emphasizing that the Charter for Fundamental Rights was a "compass" rather than a "stick."

Populist extremist parties remained strong across the EU, corroding mainstream politics especially on issues related to Roma, Muslims, and migrants. Governments frequently responded by echoing these parties' criticism of minorities and pursuing policies that infringed human rights.

Common EU Asylum and Migration Policy

Upheaval in North Africa brought thousands of migrants and asylum seekers to European shores. The United Nations estimated that at least 1,400 people died crossing the Mediterranean in the first seven months of 2011, most as they tried to flee Libya. While rescue efforts—particularly by Italy and Malta—saved countless lives, poor coordination and disputes over where to disembark rescued migrants endangered others.

The Council of Europe (CoE) Parliamentary Assembly (PACE) initiated an inquiry in June into the deaths of boat migrants in the Mediterranean since January, following allegations that European and NATO warships ignored the plight of a boat in distress in late March or early April, leading to 63 deaths.

One hundred migrants rescued by a Spanish NATO warship spent five days at sea in July as Spain, Italy, and Malta refused to take them (Tunisia agreed). The dispute prompted concerns that NATO ships would be more reluctant to rescue migrants in the future. In August Italy accused NATO of forcing Italian coast guards to assist a boat in distress despite a NATO ship's greater proximity.

With Tunisia and Egypt hosting hundreds of thousands displaced by the Libyan conflict, EU countries remained reluctant to help. As of September eight EU states had agreed to resettle fewer than 700 UN-recognized refugees from North Africa.

In June the European Commission presented proposals to revise the Reception Directive, which covers assistance to asylum seekers, and the Procedures Directive, which deals with asylum procedures. The proposals—which include broad grounds for detention, low standards on access to social assistance and healthcare, and expanded use of fast-track asylum procedures—remained subject to negotiation with the EU's council and parliament at this writing. Amendments to the Qualification Directive, approved by the European Parliament in October, improved protection for victims of gender-related persecution and children. At this writing the council had yet to adopt the modified directive.

Legal proceedings in 2011 highlighted structural defects with the Dublin II Regulation, which generally requires that asylum claims be heard in the first EU state entered. Opposition from a majority of EU states blocked efforts to reform the regulation, which places a disproportionate burden on countries at the EU's external borders.

In January the European Court of Human Rights (ECtHR) Grand Chamber ruled in *MSS v. Belgium and Greece* that Belgium's transfer of an Afghan asylum seeker to Greece under the regulation exposed him to abusive detention conditions in Greece and denied him the chance to seek asylum. An advocate general of the Court of Justice of the European Union (CJEU) said in September, in another case involving a transfer to Greece, that an EU country must examine an asylum claim if return to the first country of entry would expose the individual to rights violations. The CJEU had not ruled on the case at this writing.

Also at this writing at least eight EU states were processing claims from asylum seekers who passed through Greece and a larger number had suspended Ireland's returns to Greece.

The debate about whether to reinstitute internal border controls in the Schengen area—a free movement zone comprising 25 EU and other countries—sparked in part by a dispute between France and Italy over Tunisian migrants, raised concerns that EU member states might restore checks in a discriminatory way. France intensified document checks at and around the border with Italy in an apparent effort to identify Tunisian migrants coming from Italy. A police union revealed that an official notice in the Cannes central police station in February calling on officers to target Tunisians for such checks had been removed following protests.

Changes to the regulations governing Frontex, the EU's external border agency, adopted in September and October made more explicit its duty to respect human rights in its operations, and established a rights officer post and a forum to consult civil society, but failed to create a mechanism to hold Frontex accountable for rights violations. Frontex border guards on the Greece-Turkey border were complicit in exposing migrants to abusive conditions in Greek detention centers.

The CJEU ruled in March that undocumented parents of children who themselves are EU citizens are entitled to reside and work in the EU. The court ruled in April that member states cannot impose prison terms on undocumented migrants for failing to leave the country when ordered.

Discrimination and Intolerance

The horrific terrorist attacks in Norway (not an EU state) in July underscored growing intolerance in Europe. One man killed 77 people—almost half of them children—and injured over 150 in two separate attacks on the same day. His writings betrayed extremist, xenophobic, and anti-Muslim views, echoing what has increasingly become mainstream debate in Europe.

In February United Kingdom Prime Minister David Cameron and French President Nicolas Sarkozy separately declared multiculturalism a failed policy.

The CoE's European Commission against Racism and Intolerance (ECRI) warned in June against rising racism with hateful discourse, discrimination against Muslims, and violence targeting migrants, refugees, and asylum seekers, calling anti-Roma sentiment one of the most acute problems in many European societies.

Laws banning women and girls from wearing full-face veils entered into force in France (April) and Belgium (July) amid criticism from Thomas Hammarberg, the CoE Commissioner for Human Rights, and human rights groups that these bans violate women's rights, non-discrimination, personal autonomy, and freedom of religion and expression. The first two women to receive fines, in September, for violating the ban in France announced they would appeal. Italy moved closer to adopting similar nationwide legislation when a parliamentary committee endorsed a bill in August, while the Netherlands's government proposed to adopt a ban on face-covering veils by 2013.

A June report by Hammarberg's office found that homophobic and transphobic biases persist in public opinion, policies, and laws. The UK announced it would lift its lifetime ban on gay men donating blood. Only three other EU member states allow gay men to donate (Italy, Portugal, and Sweden). Germany's Constitutional Court ruled in January that requiring transgender people to undergo sex reassignment surgery and irreversible sterilization to legally change their gender was unconstitutional. At least sixteen EU countries, including the Netherlands, have such requirements. The Dutch government submitted draft legislation in September to eliminate the requirement.

Eleven EU countries were among the first to sign a CoE convention on preventing and combating violence against women and domestic violence adopted in May. The convention requires measures to prevent violence, protect victims regardless of legal status in the country, and prosecute perpetrators.

In June the CoE Venice Commission rejected proposals to amend its official position on the political participation of persons with intellectual or mental disabilities by removing undue restrictions on their right to vote. This position violates the binding UN Convention on the Rights of Persons with Disabilities, which has been ratified by 17 EU member states and the EU itself.

Counterterrorism Measures and Human Rights

Accountability remained elusive for complicity by EU countries in CIA rendition and secret prison programs. In January Lithuania's prosecutor general closed the investigation into secret CIA prisons in that country, one year after it began. In September Hammarberg criticized continuing failure to determine responsibilities in Romania, Poland, and Lithuania. In a resolution adopted in October PACE expressed concern about the use of state secrecy doctrine to undermine or impede appropriate parliamentary oversight of intelligence services and investigations into unlawful acts.

Human Rights Concerns in Select EU Member States

France

Expulsions of Eastern European Roma continued, with a June immigration law increasing certain procedural safeguards while also allowing expulsions for "abusing" the right to short-term stay as EU citizens. Despite evidence of continued discriminatory targeting of Roma, the European Commission said in August it was satisfied with France's response to its concerns.

In April France's Council of State (highest administrative court) ruled that an August 2010 Ministry of Interior circular (later withdrawn) telling police to prioritize the dismantling of unlawful Roma settlements was discriminatory.

The June immigration law weakened the rights of migrants and asylum seekers, expanding the use of so-called transit zones—where they have fewer rights and can be easily deported—to detain individuals. The maximum detention period pending deportation was increased to 45 days, with judicial review delayed for five days after placement in detention.

The same law allowed the government to detain foreign terrorism suspects for up to six months, including in cases where deportation is blocked because of the risk of torture or ill-treatment upon return. The Constitutional Council struck down the government's attempt to increase such detention to up to 18 months.

The ECtHR ruled in September that France could not deport an Algerian to his home country because of the risk he faced of torture or ill-treatment.

Following civil society pressure and several binding court rulings, legal changes enacted in April increased safeguards in police custody, including notification of the right to remain silent and to have a lawyer present during questioning. However private client-lawyer conferences are still limited to 30 minutes, and authorities can still delay the presence of a lawyer in certain circumstances. The changes left in place exceptional rules for terrorism and organized crime suspects, who can be held for up to 72 hours without access to a lawyer.

Germany

In August Rheinland-Pfalz became the sixth state to grant freedom of movement to asylum seekers. In the 10 other states asylum seekers must stay within a circumscribed geographic area, with violation punishable by fines or prison. The UN Committee on Economic, Social and Cultural Rights (CESCR) expressed concern in July over inadequate social benefits, housing, access to employment, and healthcare for asylum seekers.

In September the parliament adopted a law exempting school personnel from the obligation to report undocumented migrants. Efforts by opposition parties to extend the exemption to health care and labor court personnel failed. In July the CESCR urged Germany to strengthen efforts to address obstacles facing people with a migration background in education and employment.

In October parliament renewed counterterrorism legislation for another four years and established an independent monitoring commission. The legislation permits extensive surveillance and data mining. In December 2010 a Cologne court dismissed Khaled el-Masri's case against the German government for failing to pursue the extradition of 13 United States citizens allegedly involved in his rendition to Afghanistan in 2004.

In October the UN Working Group on Arbitrary Detention expressed concern over the preventive detention of individuals deemed dangerous, a regime the German Constitutional Court ruled unconstitutional in May. Germany faced questions in November from the UN Committee against Torture (CAT) on the use of diplomatic assurances and the deportation of unaccompanied migrant children.

Greece

Critical problems with the asylum system persisted, despite an official increase in the refugee recognition rate to 12.35 percent (including appeals) in the first seven months of the year. Access to asylum and review of claims at first instance remained problematic, with the new asylum service—created in a January law—expected to become fully operational only in 2012. Organizational and technical problems hampered the work of appeals committees established to tackle the backlog, which the government calculated in September at 38,000.

Migrants and asylum seekers, including women and families with children, continued to be detained in inhumane conditions. There was a chorus of criticism of migrant detention conditions in Greece, including in March by the EU Fundamental Rights Agency, the CoE Committee for the Prevention of Torture (CPT), and CoE Secretary General Thorbørn Jagland.

Numerous countries expressed concern about the situation of migrants, refugees, and asylum seekers in Greece during its Universal Periodic Review at the UN Human Rights Council (HRC) in May and urged Greece to take effective measures, including prosecution against discrimination, racism, and xenophobia.

Racist violence in Athens was a serious problem. The Pakistani Community of Greece documented attacks on 60 Pakistani men in the first three months of 2011. Far-right extremists rampaged through immigrant neighborhoods in May, leaving at least 25 people hospitalized with stab wounds or severe beatings. Two men and one woman were due to stand trial in December for the September assault and serious injury of a 24-year-old asylum seeker.

There were frequent demonstrations and strikes against austerity measures during the year, with fears that cuts to wages, pensions, and social spending are disproportionately affecting the poor, persons with disabilities, the elderly, migrants, and ethnic minorities.

The Athens prosecutor's office opened an investigation in July into allegations of excessive and indiscriminate police use of force, including tear gas, during a June protest. The investigation was ongoing at this writing. A police officer was arrested in October for assaulting a news photographer at an anti-austerity rally the same month.

In March the Ombuds Institute published a damning report on abuses against children with disabilities at the Children's Care Center of Lechaina, including the use of cage beds, tying children to their beds, and routine sedation. As of September the number of staff at the center had increased, but concerns persisted about conditions and treatment.

Roma continued to face systemic discrimination in housing and education. In March the ECtHR agreed to examine a school segregation case brought by 140 Roma children and parents. Greek authorities failed to implement a 2008 ECtHR ruling on school segregation involving the same families.

Hungary

A widely criticized media law, which undermines freedom of expression entered into force on January 1, the day Hungary assumed the EU presidency. Amendments adopted in March left in place the most significant problems, including overly broad and vague restrictions on media reporting with violations punishable by large fines, and regulatory powers in the hands of government-appointed bodies.

A new constitution was adopted in April. Drafted by the ruling Fidesz party, it contains provisions that discriminate against women; lesbian, gay, bisexual, and transgender (LGBT) people; and people with disabilities. In June the CoE's Venice Commission criticized the lack of consultation with civil society and recommended amendments. The constitution goes into effect in January 2012.

Migrants from third countries entering Hungary through Ukraine continued to be returned across the border despite evidence of ill-treatment in Ukraine, in some cases after their pleas to seek asylum in Hungary were allegedly ignored. Legislation adopted in December 2010 increased maximum immigration detention to twelve months, and permitted extended detention for asylum seekers.

GREECE

The EU's Dirty Hands

Frontex Involvement in Ill-Treatment of Migrant Detainees
in Greece

HUMAN
RIGHTS
WATCH

Roma faced harassment and threats from vigilante groups in rural areas. In April the Hungarian Red Cross evacuated 277 Roma from a settlement after an anti-Roma vigilante group threatened to conduct "military" training nearby. Four men stood trial in March for killing six Roma and injuring ten others during attacks between July 2008 and August 2009. The verdict was pending at this writing.

During Hungary's Universal Periodic Review at the HRC in May, numerous countries recommended action against discrimination based on gender and sexual orientation, and to improve minority rights, in particular of Roma, including by combating hate crimes.

Italy

Over 55,000 boat migrants, including at least 3,700 unaccompanied children, reached Lampedusa, a small Italian island in the Mediterranean, from North Africa in the first seven months of the year. Reception centers on Lampedusa were periodically overwhelmed, with enduring concerns about the procession of asylum claims and conditions there and elsewhere in Italy, including for women and unaccompanied children. A fire allegedly set by Tunisians destroyed most of a detention center on the island in September, leading the government to declare Lampedusa an unsafe port. International and national organizations, including the Office of the UN High Commissioner for Refugees (UNHCR) and PACE, expressed concern that this could delay rescue operations.

As many as 12,000 Tunisians who arrived before April 5, when Italy signed a bilateral agreement with the new Tunisian government, received temporary visas. Those who arrived later were detained, pending deportation, in poor conditions following procedures that lacked sufficient safeguards.

Hundreds spent up to five days in detention on boats after the fire at the Lampedusa center before being transferred to other detention facilities or deported. In August an Italian navy ship intercepted around 100 migrants in international waters and transferred them to a Tunisian vessel, in what appeared to be an unlawful pushback.

ITALY

Everyday Intolerance

Racist and Xenophobic Violence in Italy

HUMAN
RIGHTS
WATCH

All those arriving from Libya, primarily sub-Saharan Africans, applied for asylum, with many placed in specially created reception centers. In August the Italian interior minister estimated that 35 to 40 percent would be granted asylum, with the rest ordered to leave Italy or forcibly removed.

Italy signed an immigration cooperation agreement with the Libyan National Transitional Council in June, including the repatriation of undocumented migrants. At this writing there had been no returns to Libya in 2011. In June the Grand Chamber of the ECtHR heard a case involving the pushback by Italy of 24 Africans to Libya in May 2009, but had yet to rule at this writing.

In September an appeals court acquitted two Tunisian boat captains of charges stemming from their 2007 rescue and transfer to Lampedusa of 44 boat migrants in defiance of Italian authorities.

The ECtHR ruled in April that Italy's 2009 expulsion of Ali Ben Sassi Toumi to Tunisia, in breach of its order to suspend removal, had violated the ban on returns to risk of torture, rejecting Italy's argument that diplomatic assurances from Tunisia mitigated the risk.

In July the lower house of parliament rejected draft legislation that would have extended hate crime provisions to protect LGBT persons.

The UN Committee on the Elimination of Discrimination against Women communicated in July its deep concern about a range of issues affecting women in Italy, including multiple forms of discrimination and vulnerability to violence facing migrant and Roma women in particular. In September Hammarberg expressed concern about racist and xenophobic political discourse, particularly targeting Roma and Sinti, and called on Italian authorities to improve their response to racist violence. He criticized ongoing emergency powers leading to serial evictions of Roma camps.

In October the UN Committee on the Rights of the Child expressed concern about discrimination against Roma children in enjoyment of the rights to health, education, and an adequate standard of living, as well as reports of overrepresentation of Roma and foreign children in the juvenile justice system.

The Netherlands

In February the government narrowed the right of some asylum seekers to a suspensive appeal. In July it announced that rejected asylum seekers and irregular migrants should be forced to bear all costs for their forced return and narrowed the right to a suspensive appeal in certain cases.

In August an appeals court reaffirmed that Turkish nationals should be exempt from the in-country integration test required for long-term residency. In September the government said that Turkish migrants are no longer required to pass integration tests before immigrating to the Netherlands.

In September the Dutch government announced plans to introduce stricter requirements for family reunification, impose fines or prison for unauthorized stay, and make it easier to deport non-EU foreigners who commit a crime. In a move that could discourage domestic violence victims from reporting abuse, the plans also increase from three to five years the period women migrants must remain with their husbands before they can seek residency independently. Under the proposals family members of recognized refugees would be exempt from having to claim asylum. At this writing the measures had yet to be presented to parliament.

While NGOs applauded a March central government decision to end detention of unaccompanied migrant children, local authorities criticized a separate central government decision, effective in July, to sever all financial and housing support once they turn 18-years-old.

Geert Wilders, leader of the Freedom Party, was acquitted in June of charges of inciting hostility or discrimination against Muslims, non-Western immigrants, and Moroccans. The prosecutor had recommended the charges be dismissed on free expression grounds. But the finding of the Dutch court that, as a politician, Wilders had greater latitude than members of the public to express inflammatory ideas appeared at odds with ECtHR jurisprudence on free speech.

Poland

In May the prosecutor general replaced the lead prosecutor investigating allegations of Polish government complicity in CIA secret detention on Polish soil. A leading newspaper alleged that the replacement had political motivations. An investigation was ongoing at this writing.

New anti-discrimination legislation went into effect in January, despite criticism from civil society that it offers inadequate protection for sexual orientation, gender identity, and disability. A cut in the budget of the office of the ombudsperson for civil rights, whose mandate is expanded by the new law, prompted it to call for the law to be suspended on the grounds that it cannot perform its new functions with reduced resources.

Poland continued to have one of the most restrictive abortion laws in Europe. In May the ECtHR ruled in the case *RR v. Poland* that the denial of access to genetic pre-natal testing and a legal abortion amounted to a violation of the prohibition on cruel and inhuman treatment, as well as a violation of the right to privacy and family life. Draft legislation to impose a total ban on abortions was narrowly defeated in parliament in August.

Spain

Widespread protests against austerity measures began in May, with occupations of squares in several cities. There were credible reports of excessive use of force by police in dispersal operations in Madrid and elsewhere between May and August. Accusations of excessive force also marred a protest against the Pope's visit to Madrid in mid-August.

New immigration regulations in June ensured that undocumented migrant women who report domestic violence do not risk immediate expulsion. The rules make it easier for parents of children with Spanish citizenship to obtain residency permits, facilitate residency for unaccompanied migrant children at 18-years-old, and create a presumption in age-dispute cases that the individual is a child. The Ombuds Institute nonetheless criticized age-determination practices in September and recommended procedural reforms.

In February ECRI expressed continuing concerns about insufficient application of criminal provisions to combat racially motivated crimes, inadequate data collection on racism and discrimination, and ethnic profiling of migrants by police. The UN Committee on the Elimination of Racial Discrimination (CERD) echoed these concerns in April. A comprehensive government-proposed non-discrimination bill was before parliament at this writing.

In March the CPT repeated its call for reform of incommunicado detention for suspects of serious crimes such as terrorism, including access to a lawyer from the outset of detention and the right to examination by a doctor of choice. In July the Ombuds Institute also recommended improving safeguards in incommunicado detention.

Spain extradited Belgian-Moroccan citizen Ali Aarrass to Morocco in December 2010 to face terrorism charges, despite a binding order from the CAT in November to suspend extradition while it examined the case.

In October 2011 the violent Basque separatist group ETA announced it would give up its 43-year armed struggle.

United Kingdom

Rioting in early August in London, Manchester, Liverpool, and elsewhere across the UK, triggered by death of a man in north London shot by the police, led to five deaths and over 3,000 arrests, including hundreds of children. An investigation into the shooting was ongoing at this writing.

Penal reform groups and a former chief prosecutor expressed concern about the severity of sentencing in some riot-related cases, including of children. In October an appeals court upheld seven riot sentences, including the widely criticized four-year terms for inciting riot on Facebook, and reduced three others.

CERD urged the government in October to thoroughly investigate the underlying causes of the rioting, and ensure that policy responses do not disproportionately affect minorities.

A commission appointed in May to review the domestic Human Rights Act had yet to report at this writing. The act faced renewed criticism from the prime minister and home secretary.

Correspondence between the government of former Libyan leader Muammar Gaddafi and British intelligence discovered in Libya in September indicated British involvement in rendition to Libya, underscoring the need for an effective inquiry into UK complicity in rendition and overseas torture.

In August NGOs and victims' lawyers withdrew their cooperation with the government-established inquiry set up for that purpose on the grounds that government-imposed conditions announced in July, including limits on questioning witnesses and government control over disclosure, made an effective process impossible. At this writing the inquiry had yet to begin.

In July the ECtHR affirmed the extra-territorial application of the European Convention on Human Rights, ruling that the UK had both arbitrarily detained an Iraqi civilian for over three years in a British-run detention center in Iraq, and had failed to conduct independent and effective investigations into the deaths of five Iraqis apparently killed by British soldiers in Iraq.

In September a three-year public inquiry found a British military regiment responsible for the 2003 death in custody of Iraqi civilian Baha Mousa after being subject to inhuman and degrading treatment and sustaining multiple injuries. The inquiry recommended comprehensive steps against hooding and stress techniques in detention, as well as independent inspection of battlefield detention centers. Another inquiry into allegations that up to 20 men were tortured and murdered in British custody in southern Iraq in 2004 had yet to begin at this writing.

Four counterterrorism bills that the government tabled in February, May, and September were under parliamentary scrutiny at this writing. Terrorism pre-charge detention limits would be reduced from 28 to 14 days, but with the option of a new 28-day emergency power, drawing criticism from the parliamentary human rights committee.

Control orders would also be limited in severity and duration, but again with the option of restoration in exceptional circumstances. Inadequate judicial safeguards and the use of secret evidence remained. Terrorism stop and search without suspicion will also be permanently limited, although the risk of misuse remains.

Children continued to be detained with family members pending deportation despite a 2010 government pledge to end the practice.

GEORGIA

Georgia's human rights record remained uneven in 2011. The government used excessive force to disperse anti-government protests in Tbilisi, the capital, in May, and prosecuted dozens in misdemeanor trials without full respect for due process rights. The authorities failed to effectively investigate these events and past instances of excessive use of force. Other concerns include restrictions on freedom of association and media, as well as forced evictions of internally displaced persons (IDPs) living in state-owned temporary housing.

The United States and the European Union deepened their political and economic ties with Georgia but failed to use their leverage to secure human rights improvements.

Freedom of Assembly and Police Violence

As in past years, the authorities interfered with freedom of assembly. On May 26, 2011, police used water cannons, tear gas, and rubber bullets to disperse anti-government protests in Tbilisi, 15 minutes after the rally permit expired. Police pursued fleeing demonstrators, detaining some 160, and beating many, including those who offered no resistance. Police also interfered with the work of Georgian and foreign journalists, verbally and physically assaulting at least ten and detaining two. Police also took some journalists' press cards and damaged or confiscated several reporters' equipment.

In summary trials the Tbilisi city court convicted over 90 of the protestors detained on May 26 of disobeying police orders, sentencing them to up to 30 days administrative detention. In most cases, the court relied exclusively on police testimonies to convict demonstrators and did not take any action in response to defendants' visible injuries.

In July a closed Ministry of Interior internal investigation into the May 26 events led to administrative punishments for 16 police officers including dismissal of four for excessive use of force. The authorities did not investigate allegations of ill-treatment by police.

Authorities' failure to fully address excessive use of force by police was further
tainted by the continued lack of effective investigations into past instances of
abuse, including the events of November 7, 2007, when police used excessive
force against largely peaceful protestors in Tbilisi, injuring at least 500, and the
June 15, 2009 police attack against 50 opposition supporters outside police
headquarters, in which at least 17 demonstrators were injured.

Administrative (Misdemeanor) Detentions

In 2010 the government increased the maximum misdemeanor sentence from
30 to 90 days. Although the sentence is equivalent to a criminal penalty,
detainees do not have access to full due process rights. Although defense
counsel is permitted, some detainees had difficulties accessing a lawyer in part
because they are not allowed to inform their families of their detention. Lawyers
who act for those facing administrative charges have inadequate time (sometimes as little as 10 to 15 minutes) to prepare a defense. Defendants also often
cannot present evidence or call witnesses in court. In 2010 the authorities
decreased the appeal period for administrative sentences from ten to two days,
although court records become available only three days after a trial.

Administrative detainees stay in Ministry of Interior holding cells, which are
unsuitable for detention over 72 hours, with inadequate access to exercise and
hygienic and medical care.

Forced Evictions of Internally Displaced People

Beginning in June 2010 the authorities evicted thousands of IDPs from state-
owned temporary collective centers in Tbilisi, supposedly to provide them with
durable housing solutions. The authorities failed to respect international standards regarding evictions: they did not engage in genuine consultation with
IDPs and failed to agree on adequate alternative housing or compensation prior
to eviction. Georgia has some 246,000 IDPs as a legacy of conflicts in the
1990s and in 2008.

In late 2010, in consultation with the Office of the United Nations High
Commissioner for Refugees, the government adopted guidelines on eviction

procedures, which resulted in some improvements, but the process still failed to meet international standards.

The authorities evicted hundreds of families in February and August 2011. Many families refused resettlement to remote areas, fearing limited employment opportunities, but were still forced out of collective centers.

Labor Rights Violations

In August 2011, 147 workers of the Kutaisi Hercules Steel plant, a Georgian-Indian joint venture in western Georgia, formed a trade union and elected union representatives. On September 13 the union launched a strike to demand better working conditions and higher salaries. Although the strike was in accordance with Georgian law, two days later police detained over a dozen strikers demonstrating near the front of the plant. Police released the strikers several hours later, but some reported being forced to sign a statement that they would not participate in further protests.

On September 18, police stopped three union members in various parts of the city and insisted that they each take a drug or alcohol test. The men refused, were arrested for disobeying police orders, and sentenced to 10 days administrative detention. The workers believe the charges were an attempt to intimidate them and other workers.

The government abolished the labor inspectorate in 2006, apparently to limit government interference with business, and no other supervisory agency has been created to ensure compliance with labor laws.

Lack of Accountability for Laws of War Violations

Over three years after the Georgian-Russian conflict over South Ossetia, Georgian authorities have yet to ensure a comprehensive investigation into, and accountability for, international human rights and humanitarian law violations by their forces. During the war the Georgian military used indiscriminate force including firing multiple rocket launchers, an indiscriminate weapon that should not be used in civilian areas.

The Office of the Prosecutor at the International Criminal Court—to which Georgia is a party—continued with its preliminary examination of the situation.

Freedom of Media

The media environment remains mixed, print media is diverse, but nationwide television broadcasting is limited to the state-owned Public Broadcaster and pro-government Rustavi 2 and Imedi stations. In a positive step, parliament passed a bill in April mandating that broadcasting companies make ownership information public.

In July police arrested four photo journalists—Zurab Kurtsikidze, a European Press Agency photographer; Giorgi Abdaladze, a contract photographer with the Ministry of Foreign Affairs; Irakli Gedenidze, President Mikhail Saakashvili's personal photographer; and Gedenidze's wife Natia—on espionage charges related to passing sensitive information to Russia. The case was classified as "secret" and the evidence never declassified. Local and international groups considered the charges politically motivated, allegedly in retribution for coverage of the May 26 events. Two weeks later a court released the journalists on conditional sentences of up to three years, in plea bargain deals with prosecutors.

In June the Ministry of Finance started simultaneous unannounced tax audits of several firms owned by Georgia's largest media group, Media Palitra, which also owns numerous newspapers, including the popular weekly *Kviris Palitra,* a radio station, eleven magazines, the news agency Interpressnews and the online Palitra TV. Media and civil society groups believed the audits were designed to harass Media Palitra in retaliation for its media outlets' extensive coverage of the May 26 crackdown. In August the audit was suspended indefinitely.

Criminal Justice System

Overcrowding in prisons remains a problem, leading to poor prison conditions. The Ombudsman's Office documented numerous cases of ill-treatment in prisons. In prison No. 2 in Kutaisi, inmates are forced to spend up to 24 hours in an empty two to three square meter cell wearing only their underwear as punishment for prison rules violations. The ombudsman called on the prosecutor's office to investigate.

In a June report, Thomas Hammarberg, Council of Europe commissioner for human rights, welcomed the government's efforts to reform the justice system, but urged the authorities to adopt a more human rights oriented criminal justice policy.

Key International Actors

The US and the EU deepened their engagement and economic ties with Georgia. While both actors raised human rights concerns, neither used the process toward upgraded relations to secure concrete human rights improvements.

The US, the EU, the Parliamentary Assembly of the Council of Europe (PACE), and other governments and institutions called on the Georgian authorities to investigate police conduct during the May 26 protests.

Dunja Mijatovic, the Organization for Security and Co-operation in Europe representative on freedom of the media, expressed concern about abuse, detention, and questioning of journalists during the May protests.

The Democracy Working Group of the US-Georgia Charter on Strategic Partnership met in Tbilisi in April to discuss progress and cooperation on democratic reforms in Georgia. The US committed over US$90 million to support democracy and good governance in Georgia.

In an April resolution on Georgia's fulfillment of its obligations as a Council of Europe member, PACE welcomed the "significant progress" Georgia had made to meet its obligations, but expressed concern about the administration of justice and fair trial norms.

In its May European Neighborhood Policy progress report, the EU commended Georgia for judicial reforms, but expressed concerns about failures to guarantee political and media pluralism and protection of labor rights and freedom of association.

In July the European Commission adopted the Annual Action Programme for Georgia, committing over € 50 million ($ 70 million) to support the country's criminal justice system, conflict resolution efforts, and IDPs.

Kazakhstan

Kazakhstan failed to carry out long-promised human rights reforms in the year following its chairmanship of the Organization for Security and Co-operation in Europe (OSCE). Instead, its rights record suffered further setbacks. Control of the penitentiary systems moved from the Ministry of Justice to the Ministry of Internal Affairs, putting prisons back in police control, and a new restrictive religion law was adopted. Websites were blocked and legal amendments limiting media freedoms remained. A union lawyer was imprisoned for six years for speaking out on workers' rights. The government continued to punish activists for breaking restrictive rules on freedom of assembly and Kazakhstan's leading human rights defender, Evgeniy Zhovtis, remains in prison.

National Referendum and Presidential Elections

In January 2011 parliament voted in favor of holding a national referendum to extend President Nursultan Nazarbaev's term in office. The European Union and United States sharply criticized the proposal, with the US calling it a "setback for democracy in Kazakhstan."

President Nazarbaev vetoed the referendum, but called for early presidential elections, which took place on April 3. According to the Central Election Committee, the incumbent received 95.55 percent of the vote with an 89.99 percent turnout. The OSCE's Office for Democratic Institutions and Human Rights (ODIHR) concluded that "serious irregularities" marred the poll, and the US Mission to the OSCE warned that "such irregularities are not in keeping with Kazakhstan's OSCE commitments ... to hold elections that meet OSCE standards." Opposition groups criticized the early election and urged citizens to boycott the poll.

Freedom of Expression

The environment for freedom of expression remains restrictive and marked by government loyalists dominating broadcast media outlets, harassment of independent journalists, prohibitive penalties for civil defamation, and criminal penalties for libel. Local human rights groups voiced concern over a draft broadcast bill that would limit independent media broadcasting if adopted.

Media watch dog Adil Soz reported that seven journalists were physically attacked in the first half of 2011. They included Daniyar Moldashev, director of the Almaty publishing house that prints the *Respublika* and *Golos Respubliki* opposition newspapers, who was beaten and robbed by unknown individuals on March 25. In late October, two Stan.TV journalists were attacked with a baseball bat and shot with rubber bullets by four unknown assailants while covering the oil strikes in Aktau, western Kazakhstan. *Adil Soz* reported that another 12 journalists were accused of criminal libel in the same period, although in August an Aktobe court dismissed a libel suit against Alima Abdirova, a human rights activist and journalist.

On August 19 the authorities blocked the popular Russian-language blogging platform *Livejournal* after an Astana city prosecutor claimed the site distributed information of a religious extremist and terrorist nature. In June authorities temporarily blocked *Wordpress.com* alleging its publications contain illegal information. Other popular independent websites, including that of the independent weekly *Respublika*, remain blocked.

On August 16 the authorities denied parole for the fourth time to imprisoned journalist Ramazan Yesergepov, editor of the *Alma-Ata Info* newspaper, but permitted him to spend a week with his ill mother in September. In a 2009 closed trial marred by due process violations, Yesergepov was sentenced to three years in prison for disclosing state secrets.

Freedom of Assembly

Kazakh authorities maintain restrictive rules on freedom of assembly and detained and fined activists and other individuals for organizing and/or participating in unsanctioned protests and pickets. Work on a draft law on peaceful assembly remained suspended.

In two separate incidents in January small groups of activists in Almaty and Urals were detained and fined for protesting against the proposed referendum to extend President Nazarbaev's rule. In August three activists of the Socialist

Movement of Kazakhstan were sentenced to short term administrative sen-tences after staging a protest in support of the striking oil workers outside the Nur-Otan party office in Almaty.

In mid-May workers in the oil sector in western Kazakhstan staged strikes and labor protests demanding higher wages, revised collective agreements, and non-interference in union work. On June 5, police dispersed several hundred workers who tried to protest outside the regional mayor's office in Aktau, and temporarily detained and fined several dozen. On July 8 riot police dispersed oil workers on strike in Zhanaozen, and the following night used force to round-up workers who remained on a hunger strike. In mid-August Akzhanat Aminov, an oil worker, was given a two-year suspended sentence for allegedly organizing an illegal strike.

There was an increased number of protests over housing issues, after the finan-cial crisis left many unable to pay back home loans. On March 16 an Astana Court sentenced Esenbek Ukteshbayev, chairman of the unregistered union *Zhanartu* and leader of the Almaty-based movement Leave Peoples' Homes Alone, to 15 days administrative detention, a day after he participated in a peaceful rally of estate investors and mortgage holders.

Detention of Activists

On August 8 union lawyer Natalia Sokolova was sentenced to six years in prison and banned from civil work for three years on charges of "inciting social dis-cord" for addressing workers about wage disparity and "actively participating in illegal gatherings" at an oil company in western Kazakhstan. On September 26 her sentence was upheld on appeal, endorsing the government's violations of her right to free expression and association.

On August 19 a prison appeals commission rejected political activist Aidos Sadykov's latest request to be transferred from prison to a settlement colony, a penal establishment that allows for more freedoms than an ordinary prison. He was imprisoned for two years in July 2010 for "hooliganism accompanied by resistance to the police" in what appears to be a politically motivated set up.

On August 2 Evgeniy Zhovtis, Kazakhstan's most prominent human rights defender and head of the Kazakh International Bureau for Human Rights and the Rule of Law, was denied early release for the second time. On September 3, 2009, Zhovtis was found guilty of vehicular manslaughter, following an unfair trial marred by serious procedural flaws that effectively denied him the right to present a defense. Zhovtis was sentenced to four years in a settlement colony.

Risk of Refoulement

On June 9, in blatant violation of international human rights law and the non-refoulement principle, Kazakh authorities extradited to Uzbekistan at least 28 men whom Uzbek authorities wanted on various anti-state and religion-related charges, despite interim measures from the United Nations Committee Against Torture (CAT) directing the suspension of extraditions, and significant and credible evidence the men risked being tortured if returned. The men had been detained a year earlier and were subsequently denied refugee status by Kazakh authorities. Serious due process violations marred judicial review of their refugee claims and extradition orders.

On May 30, Kazakh authorities extradited Ershidin Israil to China, despite the clear risk of torture he faced if returned. Israil, an Uighur refugee who had fled to Kazakhstan after the July 2009 Urumqi riots, was denied refugee status by Kazakh authorities.

Labor Abuses and Child Labor in Agriculture

Philip Morris Kazakhstan (PMK), a subsidiary of Philip Morris International, increased protections for migrant workers on tobacco farms by requiring written contracts to ensure migrant workers receive regular payments and other protections. PMK expanded trainings regarding labor rights and child labor and increased monitoring to prevent abuses frequent in past years such as hazardous child labor, forced labor, and passport confiscation. The government continues to prevent migrant workers' children from accessing education by blocking them from registering in schools.

Freedom of Religion

In a clear setback for religious freedom, on October 13 President Nazarbaev signed a restrictive new law, "On Religious Activities and Religious Associations." According to Forum 18, an independent international religious freedom group, the new law "severely restrict[s] freedom of religion and belief" and "imposes a complex four-tier registration system, bans unregistered religious activity, imposes compulsory religious censorship and require both central and local government approval to build or open new places of worship."

Key International Actors

Kazakhstan's controversial OSCE chairmanship culminated in a summit in December 2010 in Astana. NGOs held a parallel OSCE civil society conference and adopted recommendations to strengthen OSCE states' implementation of human dimension commitments and improve cooperation with civil society. On the eve of the summit, US Secretary of State Hillary Clinton held a town hall meeting with civil society organizations, stressing that fundamental freedoms such as expression, association, and religion are "are absolutely critical to the building of sustainable societies." Clinton honored several Kazakh human rights groups, including the Almaty Helsinki Committee and the Kazakhstan Bureau for Human Rights and Rule of Law.

A July 2011 review by the UN Human Rights Committee criticized the use of child labor in tobacco and cotton fields and undue restrictions on freedom of association and assembly. The committee noted "concern at reports that threats, assaults, harassment and intimidation of journalists and human rights defenders have severely reduced the exercise of freedom of expression," and called on Kazakhstan to "fully comply with the principle of non-refoulement."

In July Catherine Ashton, EU high representative for foreign affairs and security policy/vice president of the European Commission, welcomed the launch of negotiations for a new "enhanced partnership" between the EU and Kazakhstan, which began in October, stressing that "the successful conclusion of the negotiations will be influenced by the advancement of democratic reforms."

In September the US ambassador to the OSCE and the EU issued critical statements reacting to developments in Kazakhstan, including Sokolova's imprisonment and the transfer of penitentiary control to the Ministry of Internal Affairs. However, such public criticism by the EU and US of human rights violations by the Kazakhstan government is muted.

Kyrgyzstan

In 2011 Kyrgyzstan continued to grapple with the consequences of the June 2010 violence that erupted between ethnic Kyrgyz and Uzbeks in the country's south, killing more than 400 people. Four commissions of inquiry were completed and thousands of criminal investigations continued in 2011, with the justice process skewed to scapegoat ethnic Uzbeks for the violence.

Torture and arbitrary detentions in the context of investigations into the June 2010 violence are rampant and go largely unpunished. Ethnic Uzbeks in the south are particularly vulnerable to police torture. Violations of international fair trial standards plagued the administration of justice in the south.

While the climate for freedom of media generally improved in 2011, the authorities made several attempts to limit freedom of expression.

Kyrgyzstan's presidential elections took place on October 30, 2011.

Skewed Justice

In May 2011 the Kyrgyzstan Inquiry Commission (KIC)—commissioned by President Roza Otunbayeva in 2010 and headed by Kimmo Kiljunen, a member of the Parliamentary Assembly of the Organization for Security and Co-operation in Europe (OSCE)—published its findings that the government failed to prevent and stop the June 2010 violence. The KIC also found that some military personnel participated in attacks on Uzbek neighborhoods, and that some crimes committed during the June 2010 violence might amount to crimes against humanity if proven in court.

However, official commissions published three reports in 2011 that did not acknowledge the role that military and security personnel played, and generally failed to recognize the systematic nature of attacks on Uzbek neighborhoods.

The authorities opened more than 5,000 criminal cases into the June 2010 violence. Although most of those killed were ethnic Uzbek, 83 percent of those facing prosecution for homicide were also ethnic Uzbek.

In 2011 trials in connection with the June 2010 violence continued to be held with violations of international fair trial standards. Defendants, mostly ethnic Uzbeks, are found guilty and sentenced to prison terms ranging from several years to life primarily based on confessions that many allege were coerced under torture.

The Kyrgyz Supreme Court routinely upholds these court verdicts, leaving the accused with no other national recourse to justice. In one of the few exceptions, in April 2011 the Supreme Court returned a ruling against an ethnic Uzbek sentenced to 15 years imprisonment for re-examination after finding inconsistencies in the evidence against him. A judge at the Osh city court paid little attention to the recommendations from Bishkek and after yet another biased trial added a year to the initial verdict, sentencing the Uzbek man to 16 years in prison.

The hostile and violent environment in which trials occurred undermined defendants' fair trial rights. Lawyers in southern Kyrgyzstan who defend ethnic Uzbek clients continue to be harassed and physically attacked. Although court staff and police officers often witness such attacks, no one has been held accountable for violence against lawyers.

Torture and Arbitrary Detentions

While local human rights NGOs report that incidents of arbitrary detentions and torture in police custody decreased in 2011 in the south, these abuses remain rampant and unpunished, particularly in the context of investigations into the June 2010 violence. Most judges in such cases dismiss, ignore, or fail to order investigations into torture allegations. In at least nine cases police also arbitrarily detained and tortured ethnic Uzbek men and threatened to charge them in relation to the June 2010 violence if they did not pay large sums.

Human Rights Watch research found at least two ethnic Uzbeks died in 2011 due to injuries sustained when detained in police extortion schemes. Given the routine use of torture by the country's law enforcement officials, efforts by the prosecutor's office to investigate allegations of torture were inadequate. The prosecutor general's office stated it had launched 34 criminal investigations into torture allegations between January and July 2011. However, only three law enforcement officials have been convicted in just two cases. At this writing six more cases had been sent to a court.

Freedom of Expression

While the climate for media freedoms has generally improved since President Kurmanbek Bakiev's fall in April 2010, there were several attacks on journalists in 2011, and parliament adopted two resolutions curbing freedom of expression regarding the 2010 events.

In 2011 several reporters were physically or verbally attacked while performing journalism work. In May supporters of the Asaba nationalist political party verbally threatened non-ethnic Kyrgyz staff of the Bishkek-based online news agency www.24.kg. The agency plans to appeal in court the prosecutor's decision not to investigate these threats.

On June 20 in Osh a group of Ata-Jurt political party supporters attacked and beat a cameraman for NTS, a Bishkek-based television channel. Local media reported that law enforcement officials did not intervene. Instead of investigating the attack, they later accused the journalist of unprofessional behavior and provoking the fight.

In a May 2011 resolution the Kyrgyz parliament barred KIC Chair Kiljunen from entering the country, alleging he had provided partial information about the June 2010 violence. In a June 16 resolution, parliament instructed government agencies to "take measures to block the site Ferghana.ru," an independent Central Asian news website. Although the site is still accessible in Kyrgyzstan, the move clearly reflected parliament's intent to silence those who do not adhere to the official version of the June events.

In July 2011 the Kyrgyz government decriminalized libel. However, "insult" and "insult of a public official" remain criminal offenses.

KYRGYZSTAN

Distorted Justice

Kyrgyzstan's Flawed Investigations and Trials
of the June 2010 Violence

**HUMAN
RIGHTS
WATCH**

Human Rights Defenders

Azimjon Askarov, a human rights defender who has worked on documenting police treatment of detainees, remains in a prison facility in Bishkek, the capital, awaiting the Supreme Court hearing of his appeal. After a trial marred with violations and allegations of torture, he was sentenced to life for "organizing mass disorders," "inciting ethnic hatred," and taking part in killing a police officer on June 13, 2010.

Human rights activists who have exposed violations following the June 2010 violence face hostility, particularly among nationalist groups.

In June 2011 the Bishkek-based Kyrgyz-language newspaper *Alibi* published an article that accused two prominent human rights defenders, Toleikan Ismailova and Aziza Abdirasulova, of being "traitors" and betraying Kyrgyzstan's interests in exchange for grants from foreign donors. On September 20 in Bishkek, Abdirasulova's son was arbitrarily detained and beaten by plainclothes operatives and prevented from consulting his lawyer for several hours, actions that Abdirasulova believes were due to her human rights work.

Elections

In July 2011 the CEC accredited mass media for involvement in, and coverage of, the presidential election campaign. However, it denied accreditation to online news agencies, significantly limiting their campaign coverage.

On October 30 the country elected its new president. Prime Minister Almazbek Atambaev received 62.52 percent of the votes in the first round of the elections. The OSCE's Office for Democratic Institutes and Human Rights monitoring mission noted that the elections were "peaceful, but shortcomings underscore need to improve integrity of process" referring to reports of flawed lists of voters and tabulation processes. The post-election period was calm despite warnings from two nationalist presidential candidates that they would contest the election results if they lost.

Key International Actors

At the June 2011 session of the United Nations Human Rights Council the UN high commissioner for human rights presented a report on Kyrgyzstan that acknowledged cooperation between the Kyrgyz government and her office and exposed the authorities' failure to protect victims of the June 2010 violence. Also in June 2011 the Council passed a resolution calling Kyrgyzstan to improve its record in the areas of administration of justice, torture, arbitrary detention, and press freedom, and renewing its mandate in Kyrgyzstan.

On September 21, 2011, Kyrgyzstan signed the UN Convention on the Rights of Persons with Disabilities that the UN General Assembly adopted in December 2006.

During a May 2011 visit to Kyrgyzstan the OSCE representative on freedom of the media met in Kyrgyzstan with government officials and the media community. She praised the government's efforts to implement media reforms and noted the situation regarding freedom of the media in the country had improved since 2010. She emphasized the authorities' responsibility to ensure journalists' safety so they can work without fear of retaliation.

In January 2011 a small group of OSCE police consultants was deployed to southern Kyrgyzstan after lengthy negotiations between the OSCE and the government, which in July 2010 had requested an OSCE police presence but subsequently opposed a mandate authorizing the police group to do anything more than consult with local law enforcement. The restrictive mandate significantly curbed the OSCE police advisory group's ability to help protect rights in the region.

On June 9 and 10, 2011, the United States-Kyrgyzstan Annual Bilateral Consultations took place in Washington, with an agenda that included discussion of US support for Kyrgyzstan's parliamentary democracy, judicial and legal reform, human rights, regional stability, and security.

The European Union issued several public statements throughout the year responding to human rights developments in the country. An August statement by the EU Delegation in Bishkek, for example, welcomed the decriminalization of libel, expressing hope that the reform would contribute to "greater respect" for freedom of media in the country. In May Catherine Ashton, EU high representative for foreign affairs and security policy/vice-president of the European Commission, called on the Kyrgyz authorities to implement the recommendations forwarded by the KIC, noting that some of them "meet priorities of the EU assistance programmes, especially on reform of the judiciary."

In August 2011 the World Bank approved a US$30 million loan for Kyrgyzstan to finance social programs for the poor and improve "accountability and transparency in government processes" in Osh and Jalal-Abad provinces.

RUSSIA

The announcement in September that Prime Minister Vladimir Putin would run for president in 2012 led most analysts to believe that his election is a foregone conclusion, and cast a shadow over the prospect of much-needed political reform. Harassment of human rights defenders continues and the working climate for civil society organizations and activists remains hostile. Impunity for past abuses and murders of activists in the North Caucasus is rampant. Russia's cooperation with international institutions on human rights appears perfunctory. Several positive developments pertaining to freedom of expression were offset by detrimental legislative initiatives in other areas.

Human Rights Defenders

Human rights defenders are vulnerable to harassment and violent attack, and those working in the North Caucasus are especially at risk.

In Chechnya the 2009 murders of three activists—Natalya Estemirova, Zarema Saidulaeva, and Alik Dzhabrailov—remain unpunished. Impunity for these murders has had a chilling effect on Chechen activists. In at least two cases in 2011, activists were subjected to severe harassment by officials, but made no official complaints for fear of retribution.

One activist who spoke out about threats was Supyan Baskhanov, a Chechen lawyer who runs the Grozny office of the Committee against Torture, a Russian NGO. In June 2011 Baskhanov helped organize a small, peaceful, anti-torture rally in Grozny, the Chechen capital. Police dispersed the demonstration, detained Baskhanov and his colleague, and threatened them with reprisals if they persevered in efforts to hold police accountable.

Human Rights Watch documented five incidents in 2010 of law enforcement physically attacking and harassing Dagestani lawyers. In 2011 the authorities failed to conduct effective investigations into these attacks, despite pledges to the contrary. Indeed, instead of holding accountable police who beat human rights lawyer Sapiyat Magomedova in 2010, the authorities charged Magomedova with using violence against state officials and insulting police officers on duty. Magomedova's indictment appears to be in retaliation for her work.

Activists from other Russian regions also faced serious problems. The day before a civil society forum held in conjunction with the June 2011 European Union-Russia summit in Nizhny Novgorod, the conference venue suddenly, and without proper explanation, refused to host the event. It took place elsewhere. Before the summit, law enforcement officials warned at least 10 local activists against holding public rallies.

In June 2011 two unidentified men severely beat Bakhrom Hamroev—Central Asia expert with Memorial Human Rights Center (Memorial), a leading Russian human rights group—in his Moscow apartment building. It was the second such beating he had endured in less than six months. Both attacks remain unpunished.

One positive development was the June 2011 acquittal of Oleg Orlov, head of Memorial, on criminal slander charges. The case stemmed from Orlov's 2009 statement suggesting that Chechnya's leader, Ramzan Kadyrov, was responsible for the murder of Natalya Estemirova. The court's decision was appealed a week later and appeal hearings started in October.

A month before the ruling, President Dmitry Medvedev introduced amendments to Russia's criminal code that would decriminalize libel and make it an administrative offense. The amendments are pending in the Duma and will advance free speech protections in Russia if passed into law.

Killings of Whistleblowers

There was some progress in the investigation of the 2006 murder of journalist Anna Politkovskaya. In August 2011 a police official was arrested on suspicion of organizing the murder. However, there is no official information indicating who ordered Politkovskaya's murder. Other investigations into attacks on independent journalists have been largely ineffective.

In 2011 an ad-hoc working group under Medvedev's Council on Civil Society conducted the first independent public inquiry into the death of Sergei

Magnitsky. Magnitsky, an anti-corruption lawyer who had alleged wide-scale tax fraud, was prosecuted on trumped-up charges and died in pre-trial custody in 2009. His death generated massive international attention. The working group's report appeared to prod the authorities to reactivate the investigation into the case, which had previously been closed.

Hate Crimes

In May 2011 two ultra-nationalists, Nikita Tikhonov and Evgenia Khassis, were convicted and sentenced to life in prison and 18 years respectively for the 2009 murders of human rights lawyer Stanislav Markelov and journalist Anastasiya Baburova.

This unique example of an effective and prompt investigation into the killing of civil activists appears to be part of a police campaign against neo-Nazism. In 2010, 329 ultra-nationalists were convicted for hate crimes, twice as many as in 2009. This trend continued in 2011, resulting in a gradual fall in violent hate crimes, especially murders. However, aggressive racism and xenophobia continue to rise, as evidenced nationalist riots that took place in the December 2010.

Freedom of Assembly

The right to freedom of assembly remains problematic in Russia, where police frequently disperse public rallies held by civil society activists and the political opposition. Police use excessive force and arbitrarily detain peaceful protesters. Courts fine protesters or sentence them to administrative detention.

While Moscow authorities generally permitted the now-traditional freedom of assembly rallies on the 31st day of each month that has 31 days, similar demonstrations were rarely allowed in other cities. For example, the authorities in Nizhny Novgorod dispersed a peaceful rally on March 31 and detained over 20 activists.

May saw a series of violent attacks by private security agents, at times aided by unidentified men, against individuals protesting the construction of a highway between Moscow and St. Petersburg through the Khimki forest. Police refused to investigate the attacks. The protesters informed Human Rights Watch of several cases of excessive use of force against them by police, including the violent dispersal of a peaceful rally and a beating in police custody.

In October 2010 the European Court of Human Rights (ECtHR), in the *Alexeev v. Russia* ruling, found Russia in violation of freedom of assembly for denying activists the right to hold gay pride marches. Despite this legally binding ruling, the May 2011 gay pride gathering in central Moscow was once again dispersed. Police used excessive force and failed to protect peaceful protesters from homophobic violence. One assailant delivered a heavy blow to the head of *Novaya Gazeta* journalist Elena Kostyuchenko. She had to be hospitalized.

Elections

With Russian parliamentary elections scheduled for December 4, 2011, the government's refusal to register new political parties became a particular concern. No independent party founded in 2010—Parnas, Other Russia, RotFront, Motherland-Common Sense—was granted registration. In April 2011 the ECtHR ruled that the 2006 de-registration of the Republican Party of Russia violated the European Convention on Human Rights. The court found party registration requirements were unmanageable for small parties.

In June 2011, in what appeared to be a sudden move towards liberalization, Medvedev introduced legislation lowering the threshold of votes that parties must garner to secure a Duma seat from 7 to 5 percent, starting with the 2016 election. However in 2011, as in previous election periods, pro-government parties benefitted from disproportionate access to media and abuse of administrative resources, resulting again in an uncompetitive electoral environment.

The Russian government allowed the Organization for Security and Co-operation in Europe to carry out only limited-scale monitoring of the vote (200 monitors).

In May 2011 Russia's Central Election Committee adopted a resolution strictly limiting the activities of election observers, including forbidding Russian citizens to be members of international monitoring missions. Legislative restrictions make it nearly impossible for Russian NGOs to observe elections.

North Caucasus

According to official statements, the number of insurgent attacks in the North Caucasus doubled in 2010 compared to 2009. In 2011 the Islamist insurgency remained on the rise, especially in the Republic of Dagestan. In January a suicide bomber from the North Caucasus killed 37 people and wounded over 120 at a Moscow airport. The February killing of three tourists in Kabardino-Balkaria, allegedly by insurgents, prompted the authorities to close ski resorts there.

The authorities' use of torture, abduction-style detentions, enforced disappearances, and extrajudicial killings in the course of their counterinsurgency campaign, coupled with impunity for these abuses, antagonized the population of the North Caucasus.

Dagestan's president appeared to seek social consensus and stability, but the republic had the highest number of documented abductions, according to Memorial. Between January and September 2011, 28 people were abducted and nine subsequently "disappeared." Salafi Muslims remained especially vulnerable to persecution.

In Ingushetia, 12 local residents were abducted, seven of whom "disappeared" between January and September, according to Memorial.

Chechen law enforcement and security agencies under Ramzan Kadyrov's de facto control continued to resort to collective punishment against relatives and suspected supporters of alleged insurgents. Memorial documented 11 abductions of local residents by security forces between January and September 2011. Five of the abducted subsequently "disappeared."

Increasingly, victims refuse to speak about violations due to fear of official retribution.

In a letter to a Russian NGO in March 2011 federal authorities stated that police in the Chechen Republic sabotaged investigations into abductions of local residents and sometimes covered up for perpetrators. The letter marked the first public acknowledgement of the impotence of federal investigative authorities in investigating abuses in Chechnya.

Police in Austria gathered evidence of a link between the 2009 murder of a Chechen refugee, Umar Israilov, and the Chechen leadership, but in 2011 the Russian authorities ignored judicial requests to question key witnesses in Russia, including Kadyrov. Israilov had filed a complaint with the ECtHR in 2006 alleging Kadyrov had tortured him. In June 2011 a court in Vienna handed down sentences ranging from 16 years to life to three men accused of organizing the murder.

There were no further reports of attacks on women and girls in Chechnya who refuse to wear headscarves, although those who do not cannot work in the public sector or attend schools and universities.

Cooperation with the European Court of Human Rights

In June the Duma received draft legislation to allow Russia's Constitutional Court to override certain ECtHR judgements. If adopted, this initiative would impede implementation of ECtHR rulings, place Russia in violation of its international legal obligations, and obstruct access to justice for Russians.

At this writing the ECtHR had issued more than 210 judgments holding Russia responsible for grave human rights violations in Chechnya. Russia continues to pay the required monetary compensation to victims. But it fails to meaningfully implement the core of the judgments, chiefly because it does not conduct effective investigations and hold perpetrators accountable.

Health Issues and Palliative Care

Access to quality healthcare remains a serious problem in Russia. Ill-advised government policies around drug treatment and HIV prevention continued to undermine Russia's battle against the HIV epidemic, leading to significant numbers of preventable new infections and deaths. Although over 300,000 Russians die of cancer each year, with many facing severe pain, available palliative care services remained limited. As a result, hundreds of thousands of patients die in avoidable agony each year. In much of the country, the government does not make oral morphine available through the public healthcare system, or adequately train healthcare workers on modern pain treatment methods. Existing drug regulations are excessively restrictive and limit appropriate morphine use for pain relief.

Migrant Worker Rights

Russia hosts between 4 and 9 million migrant workers who come overwhelmingly from states of the former Soviet Union. Thousands are employed in building sports venues and other infrastructure necessary for Russia to host the 2014 Winter Olympic Games in Sochi. Some workers reported employers' failure to provide contracts, adequate housing, or payments in full or on time. In October 2010, numerous migrant workers in Sochi protested non-payment of wages; some employers retaliated against workers with irregular work status by denouncing them to the authorities. Several of these workers were deported.

Property Expropriation and Evictions before the 2014 Olympics

To make way for venues for the 2014 Winter Olympics, hundreds of families living in the Adler region of Sochi have lost their property through state expropriations. The regional government provided most homeowners with compensation, but in many cases these amounts and expropriation procedures were neither fair nor transparent.

Key International Actors

The EU's human rights consultations with Russia continued to be an ineffective tool for advancing human rights. At the June EU-Russia summit, Herman Van Rompuy, European Council president, noted "strong concerns" about human rights and stressed the importance of "respect for the international obligations and political pluralism" in the context of upcoming elections. Additionally, the European Parliament adopted three critical resolutions on Russia that have addressed the human rights situation.

Widespread public outcry, including by German politicians, forced the German nonprofit group Quadriga to reverse a decision to award a prestigious prize to Vladimir Putin. The Quadriga Prize invokes the "moral courage of the civil movement" that brought the fall of the Berlin Wall.

The Civil Society Working Group under the United States-Russia Bilateral Presidential Commission continued its work and discussed issues such as child protection, migration, prison reform, and corruption.

In July the US State Department imposed a visa ban on around 60 Russian officials implicated in the death of Sergei Magnitsky. In July 2011 the Dutch parliament unanimously endorsed a Magnitsky-like bill, and the European parliament in December 2010 adopted a resolution recommending similar sanctions to countries in Europe. In response Medvedev ordered the government to develop similar measures against US citizens.

SERBIA

Serbia made little discernible progress on human rights issues in 2011, despite the European Parliament in January ratifying the European Union's Stabilization and Association Agreement with Serbia, and the arrests of Ratko Mladic and Goran Hadzic, the two remaining fugitives wanted by the International Criminal Tribunal for the former Yugoslavia (ICTY). The situation of ethnic minorities remains concerning, independent journalists face threats and violence, and the weak asylum system needs reform. Rising tensions with Kosovo have exacerbated Serbia's dialogue with the EU.

In late July the Kosovo government sent armored units to Kosovo's northern border, populated by Kosovo Serbs, in an unsuccessful attempt to seize control of two crossing points. Local Serbs erected roadblocks to stop them and a shootout erupted, killing one Kosovo policeman. In late August German Chancellor Angela Merkel visited Belgrade and warned Serbian authorities they must normalize relations with Kosovo for Serbia to move closer to EU membership.

War Crimes Accountability

In May and July, respectively, the two remaining ICTY war crimes suspects Ratko Mladic, wartime Bosnian Serb military commander, and Goran Hadzic, wartime leader of the Croatian Serb separatist forces, were arrested on Serbian soil, ending the long period of impunity for war crimes committed in Bosnia and Herzegovina and Croatia. In his visit to Serbia in September, ICTY Chief Prosecutor Serge Brammertz commended the Serbian government for arresting Mladic and Hadzic, but also stressed the importance of Serbia's technical cooperation with the tribunal regarding ongoing trials. Additionally, he underlined the importance of regional cooperation in prosecuting war criminals.

Domestic war crimes prosecutions have proceeded steadily, although the Serbian War Crimes Chamber has faced increasing criticism for limited progress in domestic war-related criminal proceedings, and for indictments of individuals for war crimes that were eventually dropped due to lack of evidence.

In March Jovan Divjak, a Bosnian army wartime general, was arrested by
Austrian police under a Serbian arrest warrant in Austria over charges that he
committed war crimes in 1991 against Yugoslav People's Army (JNA) troops on
Dobrovoljacka Street in Sarajevo. Many NGOs and NGO spokespeople, including the president of the Helsinki Committee of Serbia, condemned the indictment as shameful and provocative, especially because Divjak is an active member of the NGO community. The Korneuburg District Court in Austria declined
Serbia's request for extradition, and Divjak was released in July. There have
been several other high-profile indictments and arrests for war crimes against
the JNA—including against Ejup Ganic, former de facto Bosnian vice-president
during the war, and Ilija Jurisic, former wartime high ranking official in the
Ministry of Interior—all of which were eventually dropped due to lack of evidence and pressure from NGOs and government officials.

Freedom of Media

Hostile acts against independent media outlets and journalists remained a serious problem. Milan Savatovic was sentenced to 10 months of house arrest in
May, three years after the 2008 brutal attack on Bosko Brankovic, a cameraman
with the B92 media company, during a protest against Radovan Karadzic's
arrest. Savatovic's two accomplices received suspended sentences. Journalistic
associations criticized the light sentences, arguing that Serbian law does not
adequately protect journalists.

In January and February the *Insider* television show reported in a series entitled
"Fraud of the Century" on alleged financial abuses in the mining basin of
Kolubara, near the town of Lazarevac. In an apparent act of intimidation after
the report, unknown perpetrators in Lazarevac put up posters "announcing" the
death of *Insider* journalists.

Danilo Zuza and Milos Mladenovic, who are believed to be associated with
extremist nationalist groups, were arrested for the July 2010 beating of Teofil
Pancic, a political commentator. In September 2010 they were sentenced to
three months in prison, although the legally proscribed penalty for the crime is
six months to five years. However, due to their lack of previous criminal records
and their ages (both 20-years-old) they were sentenced below the legal mini-

mum. Pancic appealed the low sentences. In November the Court of Appeals in Belgrade sentenced Mladenovic and Zuza to seven additional months.

Serbia's government is currently examining a long-awaited draft law on media strategy forwarded by the Ministry of Culture. Journalist NGOs and associations in Serbia have criticized the draft for allowing continued state ownership of media and for what they say are inadequate safeguards against political interference regarding media content.

Treatment of Minorities

Roma continue to suffer discrimination and attacks. In March a Roma boy was repeatedly verbally insulted and beaten outside his high school; the young men responsible were arrested but have not yet been charged. In a similar incident in May three individuals beat a young Roma adult in a Belgrade bus. They have been arrested but not yet charged.

Roma families living in informal settlements in Belgrade face forced evictions with little access to alternative housing. Twelve Roma families were evicted from their homes under Pancevo Bridge in June without notice. Police escorted them to the outskirts of Belgrade to live in metal containers without sanitation or electricity. Five families were evicted from their homes in Skadarska Street, Belgrade, and spent the next night sleeping in city parks, despite a coalition of 22 NGOs urging the authorities to provide alternative housing.

Human Rights Defenders

A gay rights pride parade set for October 2 was cancelled over fears of mass violence. Police security assessments showed there could have been riots and clashes between extremist right-wing groups and marchers. Many local and international NGOs accused the authorities of giving into threats and for not adequately tackling hate speech. In her statement, Antje Rothemund, head of the Council of Europe Office in Belgrade, said she was deeply concerned about the degree of hatred and violence in Serbian society that led to the event's cancellation.

In April 2011 a Serbian court sentenced far right leader Mladen Obradovic to two years in prison for inciting violence during the 2010 gay pride march. Belgrade's Higher Court ruled that Obradovic, leader of extremist group Honor, used violence to disrupt the gathering in order to incite hatred and discrimination. The court sentenced 13 others to prison terms of 8 to 18 months. Gay activists and liberals said the sentences were important as the first ever in Serbia for discrimination against gays, but complained they were too lenient.

Asylum Seekers and Internally Displaced Persons

Serbia's law on asylum went into effect in April 2008, transferring the power for making asylum decisions from the Office of the United Nations High Commissioner for Refugees (UNHCR) to the Serbian asylum office. According to Ministry of Interior figures, 2,134 asylum seekers were registered in Serbia between the start of January and end of August, a striking jump from 522 in 2010. The rise appears to be due to an influx of migrants through Greece, Turkey, and Macedonia. There are currently two centers for asylum seekers in Banja Koviljaca and Bogovadja in Serbia; the one in Bogovadja opened in June and is already at capacity. There have been no reports of poor treatment or abuse so far, but UNHCR reports that overcrowding is likely.

In March the Serbian Commissariat for Refugees and Internally Displaced People (IDP), in cooperation with UNHCR, published an IDP vulnerability assessment. It showed there were 73,358 refugees in Serbia, most of them of Croatian origin, and 97,286 persons from Kosovo with displacement-related needs in Serbia.

UNHCR reported in March that Serbia (including Kosovo) sent 28,900 asylum seekers to Europe and North America in 2010. The largest group of asylum seekers in the world in 2010 were from Serbia (including Kosovo), according to UNHCR. According to Serbia's minister of interior, 95 percent of Serbian asylum applicants in Western European countries belong to ethnic minorities, many of them Roma of Serbian and Kosovo origin.

Key International Actors

The European Parliament's ratification of the EU's Stabilisation and Association Agreement with Serbia marked a key step toward the latter's membership in the union. The resolution particularly underlined the importance of eliminating parallel structures in the north of Kosovo and the need to improve treatment of minorities.

In October the European Commission recommended that Serbia become a candidate to join the EU "on the understanding that Serbia reengages on the dialogue with Kosovo ." The accompanying progress report commended Serbia's judicial reform efforts and improved legal and policy frameworks for human rights protection, but called for greater efforts to counter threats and violence against journalists and the media and to improve the status of Roma.

Following a review in March the UN Committee on the Elimination of Racial Discrimination urged Serbian authorities to halt forced evictions for Roma and improve their access to education and registration. In a September report on Serbia Thomas Hammarberg, Council of Europe commissioner for human rights, stressed the need to counter hate speech by extreme right groups, ensure protection of journalists, and improve human rights for Roma.

Kosovo

Kosovo's human rights situation improved little in 2011, amid faltering negotiations with Serbia and tensions between Serbs and Albanians at the northern border that sometimes led to violence. The justice system remained weak, despite efforts to prosecute individuals for corruption and war crimes. Kosovo's Roma, Ashkali, and Egyptian (an Albanian speaking group with supposed origins in Egypt) remained marginalized and vulnerable to discrimination. General elections in December 2010 occurred without violence, but were marred by irregularities that international observers said called the results into question.

Protection of Minorities

Roma, Ashkali, and Egyptians continued to face persistent discrimination—particularly in housing and access to public services—and the highest unemployment, school dropout, and mortality rates in Kosovo.

Following an accidental fire in January in their social housing apartments in Plementina, approximately 250 Roma, Ashkali, and Egyptians were forced to move to a makeshift camp in town without electricity and consistent access to running water. During the summer there was a water shortage at the camp. At this writing repairs to their apartments had yet to be completed and they remained in the temporary camp.

Tensions between Serbs and Albanians in northern Kosovo intensified in August, after Kosovo authorities occupied border stations on the Serbia border. Serbs in northern Kosovo held blockades and protests that persisted until November, with one fatality, a Kosovo police officer killed by Serb protestors in a border skirmish in late July. In September sixteen Serbs and four peacekeepers from the NATO-led Kosovo Force (KFOR) were injured in a confrontation over Serb blockades near border crossings.

Local prosecutors received reports of 60 inter-ethnic incidents during the first nine months of 2011, according to the Kosovo prosecutor's office. Reports from the UN Mission in Kosovo indicated that although most were low-level incidents, including vandalism at religious sites in January and February, they included a number of serious assaults and murders.

A Serb man was shot dead and his son wounded in a village in Orahovac municipality in October. At this writing the police had yet to make arrests. A Serb man was shot dead and three Serbs, including a police officer, were injured in an incident in Mitrovica in November. Police were investigating at this writing.

In October the Organization for Security and Co-operation in Europe (OSCE) called on Kosovo authorities to do more to protect Serb returnees to a village in Ferizaj municipality after an arson attack on an Orthodox cemetery in October and a spate of burglary and looting since August.

Return of Refugees and Internally Displaced Persons

In March UNHCR reported that Serbia and Kosovo produced the highest number of asylum applicants in "industrialized" countries in 2010. The trend was attributed to the EU visa liberalization with Serbia and the economic problems and discrimination that minorities face in Kosovo. Most claims were lodged in Europe. According to UNHCR, many claimants were Roma, Ashkali, and Egyptians from Kosovo. Almost all were rejected.

UNHCR Kosovo registered a total of 695 voluntary minority returns in the first seven months of the year, a decline from the peak in 2010: 237 Serb, 76 Roma, 187 Ashkali and Egyptian, 36 Bosniak, 68 Gorani, 12 Albanian (to Serbian majority areas, mainly Mitrovica), and 7 Montenegrins.

Deportations of Kosovars from Western Europe continued, with little assistance for returnees once in Kosovo. According to UNHCR, 1,334 Kosovars were deported from Western Europe during the first seven months of 2011, including 336 people to areas where they were in a minority: 168 Roma, 76 Ashkali, 5 Egyptians, 22 Bosniaks, 8 Gorani, 3 Turks, 16 Albanians, and 38 Serbs.

Deportations continued to disproportionately impact Roma, Ashkali, and Egyptian communities, with most returnees living in informal settlements and lacking basic utilities such as running water and electricity. The UN Children's Fund reported in August that most Roma, Ashkali, and Egyptian children returned to Kosovo were now on the national registry, giving them a legal right to access education and other social services. Three-quarters still do not attend school due to poverty, curriculum differences, and language barriers.

The state of North Rhine-Westphalia, which hosts the largest number of Kosovo Roma, Ashkali, and Egyptians in Germany, suspended forced returns of Roma, Ashkali, and Egyptians for the winter months of 2010 and 2011, due to concerns about their safety in Kosovo. Forced returns from North Rhine-Westphalia resumed in April 2011, although more nuanced assessments introduced in September 2010 meant that school-age children were less likely to be deported.

Activists and Roma leaders voiced concerns in March and April 2011 about lack of treatment for poisoning for most former inhabitants of a lead-contaminated camp in Mitrovica that closed in October 2010. A similar lead-contaminated camp at Osterode remained open as approximately 20 families remaining there feared violence and discrimination if they returned to their former homes in southern Mitrovica. In July 2011 the authorities in north Mitrovica reached an agreement with Mercy Corps and the European Commission to provide land for homes for these families.

Impunity, Accountability, and Access to Justice

The partial retrial at the ICTY of Ramush Haradinaj, former Kosovo prime minister, and Idriz Balaj and Lahi Brahimaj, Kosovo Liberation Army (KLA) commanders, began in August on charges related to wartime prisoner abuse at a KLA detention facility. A key prosecution witness who had declined to testify in the first trial again refused to give evidence citing fears over his safety, reawakening concerns over witness security that the ICTY appeals chamber had cited when ordering the retrial.

In January the Parliamentary Assembly of the Council of Europe adopted a report by Swiss parliamentarian Dick Marty, alleging that some KLA members, including current senior officials in Kosovo, had participated in the post-war abductions, enforced disappearances, and killing of Serbs, as well as alleged organ trafficking and organized crime including weapons and drug smuggling. In May the EU approved a special task force in its Rule of Law and Police Mission in Kosovo (EULEX) to investigate the allegations. In August EULEX appointed an experienced American prosecutor to head the investigation.

In October the trial of seven Kosovoar Albanians accused of separate allegations of organ trafficking and human trafficking, known as the Medicus case, opened in Pristina. The defendants are accused of luring donors from poor countries to Kosovo with false promises of high payments for their kidneys.

During the period from July 2010 to June 2011, EULEX completed five war crime cases, with three more ongoing and 67 in pre-trial stages.

The war crimes prosecution of Fatmir Limaj, a Kosovo member of parliament in the ruling party, was delayed from March until September because of confusion about whether he had parliamentary immunity from prosecution. In September the Constitutional Court of Kosovo ruled that lawmakers are not immune from prosecution and a district court ordered him placed under house arrest. Limaj is accused of torturing and killing Serbian and Albanian prisoners in the town of Klecka in 1999.

The impending trial faced a setback in late September when a key witness under witness protection, Agim Zogaj, was found dead in a park in Germany. While German police investigations indicated suicide, Zogaj's family criticized the protection offered to him by EULEX and said Zogaj had been under intense pressure. The Office of the UN High Commissioner for Human Rights noted that the case highlighted the wider challenge of effective witness protection in Kosovo.

Freedom of Media

In an open letter in February Christopher Dell, the United States ambassador to Kosovo, accused three media outlets—Koha Ditore, Koha Vision TV, and Express—of illegal conduct after they obtained and reported on text messages and a tape recorded conversation between Ambassador Dell and Kosovo politicians during that month's presidential elections. The Independent Media Commission in Kosovo cleared the three publications of wrongdoing the same month. In March Reporters without Borders criticized Dell's intervention as "unacceptable harassment."

In August EULEX issued indictments against Rexhep Hoti and four other staff at the Kosovo daily *Infopress* after threats made in the paper in May and June 2009 against a prominent journalist, Jeta Xharra. The threats followed Xharra's reporting on threats to media freedom in Kosovo. The indicted individuals could face up to five years in prison if convicted.

Human Rights Defenders

The EULEX Human Rights Review Panel (HRRP), an advisory body that adjudicates claims brought by individuals against EULEX, issued its first decision in April (an employment case) and a second in June (non-implementation of a court judgment) finding that EULEX had breached property rights in both and the right to fair hearing in the second.

Key International Actors

In February the head of the UN Mission in Kosovo, Lamberto Zannier, highlighted before the Security Council the need for a speedy investigation into war crimes and organ trafficking allegations in the Council of Europe report. He also noted "widespread irregularities and manipulation of votes" during the December 2010 elections. Election irregularities were also criticized in January by Ulrike Lunacek, the European Parliament rapporteur on Kosovo.

The Committee for the Prevention of Torture, a Council of Europe body, released a report in October after a July visit that found persistent ill-treatment in Kosovo police custody and lack of legal safeguards for those forcibly placed in psychiatric facilities.

In October the European Commission's annual progress report highlighted "serious shortcomings" in the December 2010 elections and the need for greater efforts to tackle organized crime, citing "weak" witness protection as a particular obstacle. The report noted lack of progress on refugees and IDP returns, and difficult conditions for displaced persons. It called on the authorities to do more to tackle access to "education, healthcare, housing and social protection" for Roma, Ashkali, and Egyptians.

TAJIKISTAN

The human rights situation in Tajikistan remains poor. The government persisted with enforcing a repressive law on religion and introduced new legislation further restricting religious expression and education. Authorities continued to restrict media freedoms and journalists—including BBC correspondent Urunboy Usmonov—were targeted for their work. Domestic violence against women remains a serious problem in Tajik society. The judiciary is neither independent nor effective.

In August President Emomali Rahmon signed a wide-ranging amnesty into law to mark the 20th anniversary of Tajikistan's independence. Approximately 15,000 prisoners are reported to be covered under its terms, including alleged members of banned religious and political groups; several thousand prisoners are expected to be released in 2011.

Institutional Human Rights Reform

In May the Office of the Ombudsman presented its first human rights report since Zarif Alizoda, the president's former legal adviser, was appointed ombudsman in May 2009. The report covers the office's work from September 2009 to December 2010, and provides an overview of various human rights concerns in Tajikistan, including torture, freedom of speech, housing, and children's rights. Some local human rights groups have criticized the office for lacking political will to effectively respond to human rights violations.

Criminal Justice and Torture

Torture remains an enduring problem within Tajikistan's penitentiary system and is used to extract confessions from defendants, who are often denied access to family and legal counsel during initial detention. Despite discussions with the International Committee of the Red Cross (ICRC) in August, authorities have not granted ICRC access to places of detention. With rare exceptions, human rights groups are also denied access.

While torture is practiced with near impunity, authorities took a few small steps to hold perpetrators accountable. In an unprecedented ruling in September two law enforcement officers were sentenced to eight years in prison (reduced to six years under amnesty) on charges of "deliberate infliction of bodily harm carelessly resulting in the death of a victim" and "abuse of powers," after Ismoil Bachajonov, 31, died in police custody in Dushanbe, the capital, in January. A third officer was sentenced to three years in prison on charges of "negligence," but was released under amnesty.

NGOs and local media also reported on the deaths of Safarali Sangov, 37, who was detained on March 1 on alleged drug-related charges and died in a hospital several days later, and of Bahromiddin Shodiev, 28, who was detained on October 14 and died in a hospital on October 30. Police claim that Sangov and Shodiev each tried to commit suicide at the police station, but their respective families insist that each died after sustaining injuries during beatings while in custody. In early November a Ministry of Internal Affairs spokesperson announced that there would be a "thorough investigation" into Shodiev's death and that three officers had been dismissed. Following Sangov's death two policemen were charged with "negligence." Soon after the trial began in September the judge ordered that the case undergo further investigation.

In July Ilhom Ismanov and 52 other defendants were put on trial in Khujand for alleged membership in the Islamic Movement of Uzbekistan. Amnesty International reported that during a pre-trial detention hearing on November 12, 2010, the judge ignored Ismanov's testimony that he had been tortured, including with electric shocks and boiling water, and that other defendants have since made similar allegations of torture and ill-treatment in pre-trial detention.

Freedom of Media

The clampdown on Tajikistan's media continued in 2011. Government officials continued to file debilitating defamation civil suits that seem aimed at muffling media. Reporters Without Borders said in February that Tajik authorities "are using a range of methods in an attempt to control the media, including informal and financial pressure, an increase in the number of defamation suits and arbitrary arrest." According to media watchdog Article 19, a new draft mass media law needs further amendments before it complies with international standards on freedom of expression.

In January then-chief of the Sughd Regional Department of Fighting Organized Crime (UBOP) filed a lawsuit against the weekly *Asia Plus* for 1 million somoni (US$210,000) in moral damages, after a December 2010 article described alleged torture and ill-treatment by UBOP officers in the Sughd region. In April, authorities confiscated equipment from *Paykon* newspaper in connection with a 2010 libel suit. In May, after a Dushanbe court granted the Ministry of Justice's petition to liquidate *Paykon*'s founding organization for alleged violations, printing houses refused to print the paper, forcing it to close.

In October Mukhamadyusuf Ismoilov, a journalist detained in the Sughd region on November 23, 2010, was convicted and fined 35,000 somoni ($7,300) on charges of inciting national, racial, local, or religious hostility; defamation; insult; and extortion. He was released under amnesty, but banned from journalism for three years. His colleagues believe his arrest and prosecution are retribution for his critical articles, including in *Nuri Zindagi*, an independent weekly in Dushanbe.

On February 7 Khikmatullo Saifullozoda, the editor of opposition Islamic Renaissance Party of Tajikistan newspaper *Nadjot*, was beaten outside his home in Dushanbe by unidentified assailants and was hospitalized. The United States and European Union "strongly condemn[ed]" the attack. Authorities opened a criminal investigation but no one has been held accountable.

On June 13 veteran BBC journalist Usmonov was detained on charges of membership to the banned religious organization Hizb ut-Tahrir, but released on bail after an international outcry. Authorities persisted in prosecuting Usmonov on charges of complicity in the activities of a banned religious extremist organization, and on October 14 he was sentenced to three years in prison, but released under amnesty. At his trial, Usmonov testified that he had been tortured in pretrial detention. He denied the charges against him, explaining that his contact with the group was part of his work.

Freedom of Religion

Tajik authorities further tightened restrictions on religious freedoms, and pursuant to newly adopted legislation, the government now extends far reaching controls over religious education and worship. According to a June statement by Forum 18, authorities continue "to try to suppress unregistered Muslim education throughout the country" and "have brought administrative charges against at least fifteen Muslim teachers in three different regions." Authorities have also closed unregistered mosques.

On August 2 President Rahmon signed the highly controversial Parental Responsibility Law, stipulating that parents must prevent their children from participating in religious activity, except for state-sanctioned religious education, until they reach 18-years-old. Human rights groups, religious groups, and international bodies criticized the adoption of the law. In June the government passed amendments to the already restrictive 2009 religion law requiring students who wish to study at religious institutions abroad to first obtain state permission.

Under the pretext of combating extremist threats, Tajikistan continues to ban several peaceful minority Muslim groups. Christian minority denominations, such as Jehovah's Witnesses, are similarly banned. Local media continued to report on prosecutions of alleged members of Hizb ut-Tahrir and the Jamaat Tabligh movement.

Women's Rights

Women and girls in Tajikistan continue to face gender-based discrimination and domestic violence; violence in the home impacts women and children alike. On July 28 the United Nations Women Office in Tajikistan hosted National Public Hearings with various stakeholders on the draft law on domestic violence, which has been under discussion for many years. At the hearing, participants raised concerns about the growing number of domestic violence cases in Tajikistan, and stated their plan to submit recommendations to further strengthen the law, according to news reports.

Key International Actors

The UN Human Rights Council's first Universal Periodic Review of Tajikistan took place in October and resulted in a number of key recommendations. Tajikistan committed to combat domestic violence, prevent abusive child labor, bring the definition of torture in line with the Convention Against Torture, and prevent and investigate alleged cases of torture. However, Tajikistan rejected key recommendations on religious freedom, such as revising the new Parental Responsibility Law, and left those related to media freedom pending until March 2012.

During a European tour in June, President Rahmon met with EU officials to discuss investment and bilateral cooperation in key areas including energy and security. Human rights concerns were featured in some of the meetings, including with Council of Europe Secretary General Thorbjorn Jagland and then-chairwoman of the European Parliament's Human Rights Subcommittee Heidi Hautala.

 The EU held human rights dialogues with Tajikistan in February and October, but per established practice, did not make public any concrete results yielding from these exchanges, stating only that it had discussed human rights developments and recommendations on the right to a fair trial, judicial independence, and women's rights. A July civil society seminar organized by the EU in Dushanbe focused on labor migrants' rights and resulted in recommendations submitted to the Tajik government.

The US held its second Annual Bilateral Consultations with Tajikistan in April. According to a US embassy statement, Assistant Secretary of State Robert Blake raised human rights and freedom of media concerns during a meeting with President Rahmon, and met with representatives of political parties and civil society. The US made a number of critical statements on media and religious freedoms in Tajikistan over the year, including by US Secretary of State Hillary Clinton during an October visit to Dushanbe. On March 3, US Ambassador to the OSCE Ian Kelly identified Tajikistan as a government that "cite[s] concerns about political security as a basis to repress peaceful religious practice."

TURKEY

As the Justice and Development Party (AKP) government focused on promoting Turkey's regional interests in response to the pro-democracy Arab Spring movements, human rights suffered setbacks at home. The government has not prioritized human rights reforms since 2005, and freedom of expression and association have both been damaged by the ongoing prosecution and incarceration of journalists, writers, and hundreds of Kurdish political activists.

After winning a third term in office with a historic 50 percent of the vote in the June 12 general election, Recep Tayyip Erdoğan's AKP government again pledged to embark on a complete revision of the 1982 constitution. Rewriting the constitution to further human rights has been a recurring political discussion since the 2007 general election.

The government's "democratic opening," announced in summer 2009 to address the minority rights of Kurds in Turkey, did not progress. Ground-breaking negotiations between the state and the armed, outlawed Kurdistan Workers' Party (PKK) to reach a settlement to end the ongoing conflict collapsed. In July violence escalated with the PKK stepping up attacks on the military and police, and the Turkish government in August launching the first aerial bombardment of PKK bases in Iraqi Kurdistan since 2008. Among a rising number of attacks on civilians were two on September 2: an Ankara bombing by the Kurdistan Freedom Falcons (TAK)—a PKK-linked group—which killed three, and a PKK attack on a car that killed four women in Siirt.

The non-resolution of the Kurdish issue remains the single greatest obstacle to progress on human rights in Turkey.

Turkey provided camps for around 7,500 Syrian refugees who had fled the Syrian government's crackdown on demonstrators. Access to camp residents was restricted, as was the residents' movement.

Freedom of Expression, Association, and Assembly

While the last decade has demonstrated momentum in Turkey for increasingly open debate on even controversial issues, Turkey's laws, prosecutors, judges, and politicians still lag behind. Turkey's overbroad definition of terrorism still allows for arbitrary imposition of the harshest terrorism charges against individuals about whom there is little evidence of logistical or material support for terrorism or of involvement in plotting violent activities. Prosecutors frequently prosecute individuals for non-violent speeches and writings. Politicians sue their critics for criminal defamation. Courts convict with insufficient consideration for the obligation to protect freedom of expression. A comprehensive review of all existing laws that restrict freedom of expression is overdue.

Particularly concerning was the March arrest and imprisonment on terrorism charges of two journalists, Ahmet Şık and Nedim Şener, and of academic Büşra Ersanlı and publisher Ragip Zarakolu in October. Şık and Şener are charged with aiding and abetting the Ergenekon organization, a criminal gang charged with coup-plotting against the AKP government. The sole evidence against Şık and Şener is their non-violent writing, in Şık's case consisting of an unpublished manuscript. At this writing the two had spent eight months in pre-trial detention, awaiting their November trial.

Ersanlı and Zarakolu will face trial in 2012 for alleged links with the Union of Kurdistan Communities (KCK/TM), a body associated with the PKK leadership. They were arrested during a clamp-down on the pro-Kurdish Peace and Democracy Party's (BDP) legal political activity, which began in April 2009 and intensified in 2011. Hundreds remain in pre-trial detention and thousands are on trial on terrorism charges after waves of arrests of officials and activist members of the BDP (which won 36 independent seats in the June 2011 general election) for alleged KCK links.

There was little progress in the main Diyarbakir KCK trial of 153 defendants, which included six BDP mayors and a human rights defender held in pre-trial detention for 22 months. Defendants insisted on conducting their defence in Kurdish but this was rejected by the court.

In August the government revised a plan to impose obligatory filtering packages on all internet users and delayed implementation of optional filtering packages, following forceful public opposition in Turkey and by international bodies, including the OSCE and the Council of Europe. However, the practice of blocking an estimated 15,000 websites in Turkey—most of which have pornographic content but some of which are restricted for pro-Kurdish or other political content by order of the Telecommunications Ministry and court decisions—raises concerns about restrictions on the right to freedom of expression and access to information.

Violence against Women

In May Turkey took the important step to uphold women's rights in the international arena by becoming the first signatory to the Council of Europe Convention against Domestic Violence and Violence against Women. However, there remains a pressing need to address the domestic rights deficit for women in Turkey. Violence in the home is endemic, and police and courts regularly fail to protect women who have applied for protection orders under the Family Protection Law. Reports of spouses and family members killing women rose in 2011.

Torture, Ill-Treatment, and Lethal Force by Security Forces

Police violence against demonstrators is still a serious problem in Turkey, requiring more resolute action from the government. Too often the authorities mask the problem by investigating demonstrators for resisting police dispersal, joining unlawful demonstrations, or terrorist propaganda, rather than investigating allegations of police abuse or investivating senior officers for the conduct of officers under their authority. In 2011 there were also reports that police beat detainees during arrest.

During an anti-AKP government demonstration in the Black Sea town of Hopa on May 31, retired teacher Metin Lokumcu died of a heart attack after excessive tear gas exposure. Doctors documented injuries on individuals who reported being beaten and ill-treated by police during the demonstration's dispersal and in detention. Some police officers also sustained injuries. Five demonstrators are on trial for participating in an unlawful demonstration, resisting police, and damaging public property. Seven were acquitted of terrorist propaganda in September. The investigation into police ill-treatment is ongoing.

Use of firearms by police and the gendarmerie remains a matter of concern, particularly against unarmed suspects. There was no progress on tightening rules governing use of force.

Combating Impunity

Increasing public discussion of the past and emerging new information on past crimes means there are opportunities for criminal investigations into human rights abuses by state actors in the 1980s and 1990s. The government needs to support the process, take steps to reform deficits in Turkey's criminal justice system, and strengthen fair trial standards. Great obstacles remain to securing justice for victims of abuses by police, military, and state officials.

The most significant attempt to bring justice to the state perpetrators of extrajudicial killings and enforced disappearances continued with the ongoing trial in Diyarbakır involving a now-retired colonel, village guards, and informers for the murder of 20 individuals in Cizre, Şırnak, between 1993 and 1995.

In March former police officer Ayhan Çarkın spoke publicly for the first time and later testified before a prosecutor about his involvement in a special operations unit committing political assassinations of named Kurds and leftists in the 1990s. Çarkın alleged the unit acted under government orders and with its collusion. In June he was remanded to prison pending trial after claiming involvement in four killings; the prosecutor's investigation continued at this writing.

In September Mehmet Ağar—a former police chief, interior minister, and parliamentarian implicated in Çarkın's testimony—received a five-year prison sentence for forming an armed criminal gang involving state actors and mafia. Proceedings against Ağar began with the evidence of state-mafia activities, which were revealed after a 1996 traffic accident near Susurluk, western Turkey. Until 2007 Ağar was protected from prosecution by parliamentary immunity. He has appealed the conviction and remains at liberty.

TURKEY, EUROPE AND CENTRAL ASIA

"He Loves You, He Beats You"

Family Violence in Turkey and Access to Protection

HUMAN
RIGHTS
WATCH

Trials continued of alleged anti-AKP coup plotters, made up of senior retired military, police, mafia, journalists, and academics, and know as the "Ergenekon" gang. One of the most important advances in 2011 was circumstantial evidence pointing to Ergenekon gang involvement in the 2007 murder of three Christians in Malatya. However, the prolonged pre-trial detention of some Ergenekon defendants, and the prosecution of Şık and Şener risk undermining this important effort to combat impunity.

There was no progress in uncovering the full plot behind the January 2007 murder of journalist Hrant Dink, although in September the prosecutor suggested that the main suspects—who face possible life imprisonment—may have Ergenekon gang connections. In July the gunman Ogün Samast, who was 17-years-old at the time of the murder, received a 23-year prison sentence.

Key International Actors

There was little progress in Turkey's bid for European Union membership in 2011. Accession negotiations remained stalled over Cyprus, the Turkish government's undertaking of too few reforms, the lack of opening a new chapter in the negotiations in 2011, and leading EU member states continued hostility towards Turkey's accession. The AKP focused more on building a dynamic regional foreign policy. The European Commission, in its annual progress report, highlighted flaws in Turkey's criminal justice system, fair trial issues, and restrictions on freedom of expression and media; emphasized that "promoting gender equality and combatting violence against women remain major challenges"; and deemed the wide definition of terrorism in Turkish law a "serious concern."

The United States government remains an important influence on Turkey, sharing military intelligence on PKK movements in northern Iraq. The US has raised particular concerns over Turkey's record regarding freedom of media and expression.

Following its November 2010 review of Turkey, the United Nations Committee against Torture voiced concerns about the failure to investigate "numerous, ongoing and consistent allegations concerning the use of torture" and asked Turkey to report again in a year regarding steps taken to address the problems identified. In September Turkey ratified the Optional Protocol to the UN Convention against Torture.

In a July report the Council of Europe commissioner for human rights termed the situation in Turkey with respect to freedom of expression and media freedom "particularly worrying."

TURKMENISTAN

With presidential elections in Turkmenistan scheduled for February 2012, President Gurbanguly Berdymukhamedov's authoritarian rule remains entrenched, highlighting Turkmenistan's status as one of the world's most repressive countries.

The country remains closed to independent scrutiny, media and religious freedoms are subject to draconian restrictions, and human rights defenders face constant threat of government reprisal. The United Nations Human Rights Committee expressed concern about allegations of widespread torture and ill-treatment, and of enforced disappearances in custody.

Turkmenistan continued to expand relations with foreign governments and international organizations, but with no meaningful outcomes for human rights.

Cult of Personality and Presidential Elections

Five years after the death of dictator Saparmurad Niyazov, President Berdymukhamedov, his relatives, and associates enjoy unlimited power and total control over all aspects of public life in Turkmenistan. In 2010 and 2011 newspapers and other publications began to bestow on Berdymukhamedov the honorific title *arkadag* (patron), symbolizing the strengthening of his cult of personality.

The only political party in Turkmenistan is the Democratic Party of Turkmenistan, led by Berdymukhamedov, and the president did not fulfill his pledge to ensure adoption of a new law on political parties.

In June 2011 Berdymukhamedov invited exiled political opposition leaders to return to Turkmenistan to run in the presidential election and promised to guarantee their safety. It is not clear whether this pledge would be honored, since key exiled leaders were convicted in absentia in closed trials years ago on embezzlement and treason charges.

Civil Society

The repressive atmosphere in Turkmenistan makes it extremely difficult for independent NGOs to operate. Activists and journalists in Turkmenistan, and in exile, face constant threat of government reprisal. The security services frequently warn activists not to meet with visiting foreign delegations.

In April, on the eve of the arrival of a delegation from the European Parliament to examine the country's human rights situation, the security services arrested Bisengul Begdesenov, who had previously tried unsuccessfully to register an ethnic Kazakh cultural center in Ashgabat, the capital. According to Begdesenov's family, officials searched his apartment without a warrant and confiscated computers and other materials. In May a court handed him a suspended nine-year sentence for swindling and abetting bribery.

Freedom of Media and Information

All print and electronic media are state-controlled. It is very difficult for foreign media outlets to cover Turkmenistan because they often cannot access the country.

Internet access remains limited and heavily controlled by the state. The country's only internet service provider is state-operated, and political opposition websites are blocked. Internet cafes require visitors to present their passports. The government is known to monitor electronic and telephone communications.

In August 2011 Berdymukhamedov ordered that cable television replace satellite dishes. If enforced, the order would significantly curtail viewers' access to information, especially foreign programming, since the government could at any point interfere with cable television broadcasts. Berdymukhamedov's attempt in 2007 to dismantle satellite dishes failed due to an international outcry.

Freedom of Movement

Turkmenistan's government continues to restrict peoples' right to travel freely internationally by means of an informal and arbitrary system of travel bans commonly imposed on, but not limited to, civil society activists and relatives of exiled dissidents. Such a ban can be arbitrarily imposed on anyone, including students studying in foreign universities or citizens traveling abroad for business.

According to the Turkmen Initiative for Human Rights (TIHR)—a Vienna-based exiled human rights group—Turkmen migration services on April 6, 2011, stopped health officials at passport control, preventing them from traveling to the United States for an exchange program. The authorities claimed the officials had unlawfully brought medicines into Turkmenistan, although no charges have been brought against them.

TIHR further reported that 1,600 Turkmen students were banned without explanation from departing to study to Tajikistan in September 2011. Berdymukhamedov also banned, without explanation, government officials from travelling to Iran for medical treatment.

Freedom of Religion

The right to freedom of thought, conscience, and religion is heavily restricted in Turkmenistan, where no congregations of unregistered religious groups or communities are allowed. Religious communities have been unable to register for years.

Ilmurad Nurliev, a Pentecostal pastor sentenced in October 2010 to four years in prison on what appear to be bogus swindling charges, continues to serve his sentence. According to Forum 18, an independent international religious freedom group, in January 2011 two Jehovah's Witnesses, who are conscientious objectors, were handed 18-month prison sentences for evading military service. At this writing there were seven such prisoners.

Forum 18 also reported that local officials harassed and insulted about 40 members of a Baptist church vacationing together on the Caspian Sea, causing them to leave the area.

Political Prisoners, Enforced Disappearances

Unknown numbers of individuals continue to languish in Turkmen prisons on what appear to be politically motivated charges. The justice system lacks transparency, trials are closed in political cases, and the overall level of repression precludes any independent human rights monitoring. The government has persistently denied access to the country for independent human rights monitors, including the International Committee of the Red Cross, NGOs, and 10 UN special procedures whose requests for visits have not been answered.

The government ignored calls by the UN Committee against Torture and the Working Group on Arbitrary Detention to release well-known political prisoners Annakurban Amanklychev and Sapardurdy Khajiev, who had worked with human rights organizations prior to their imprisonment in 2006. Political dissident Gulgeldy Annaniazov, arrested in 2008, also remains imprisoned.

In October 2011 a court sentenced Radio Free Europe/Radio Liberty (RFE/RL) correspondent Dovlet Yazkuliev to five years imprisonment on bogus charges of urging a relative to commit suicide. The charges appeared to be brought in retribution for Yazkuliev's work. In July the security services questioned and warned Yazkuliev that he could face criminal slander charges for his reporting on the July 2011 explosions in Abadan (see below). In late Octover Yazkuliev was released under a presidential prison amnesty.

Another RFE/RL contributor, Amangelen Shapudakov, 80, was detained on March 7, 2011, and forcibly confined in a psychiatric facility for 43 days. Police previously detained Shapudakov in February 2011, after he complained to international organizations about official harassment. According to RFE/RL, Shapudakov had also been banned from leaving his home district.

In March Jumageldi Mulkiyev was dismissed from his position as editor-in-chief of the magazine *Turkmen World* and forcibly confined for eight days in a psychiatric hospital after his return from holiday in Iran.

In April 2011 the security services imprisoned Bazargeldy and Ayjemal Berdyev, who have sought redress for more than a decade for their alleged torture in custody and the arbitrary seizure of their property in the 1990s. The arrests occurred on the eve of the European Parliament's visit. Human Rights Watch does not know their current whereabouts.

Approximately 50 prisoners convicted in relation to the November 2002 alleged assassination attempt on Saparmurat Niyazov—including former Foreign Minister Boris Shikhmuradov and Turkmenistan's former ambassador to the Operation for Security and Co-operation in Europe, Batyr Berdiev—remain the victims of enforced disappearances. Their fate is unknown, and their whereabouts not disclosed even to their families. Human Rights Watch is aware of unconfirmed reports that several defendants in the 2002 plot case have died in detention.

Illegal House Evictions in Ashgabat

In 2011 local authorities in Ashgabat and the surrounding area continued to evict, expropriate, and demolish homes of residents without a court ruling or providing adequate compensation, alternative accommodations, or notice. The demolitions make way for construction as part of a massive urban renewal project initiated in the late 1990s. While official statistics are not published, Human Rights Watch estimates that in the past decade the projects have displaced thousands of residents.

On June 8, 2011, police in Ashgabat broke up a small and peaceful demonstration of evictees protesting their difficulties receiving alternative accommodation.

Explosion in Abadan

On July 7, 2011, high temperatures caused a huge explosion of ammunition in the city of Abadan, resulting in dozens of civilian deaths. The government concealed information about the explosion, sealed the city, and shut down mobile and internet lines, hindering people's efforts to locate loved ones and concealing the extent of destruction.

Key International Actors

Several international actors continue to seek to leverage Turkmenistan's energy wealth, pushing aside concerns about the government's human rights record. The European Union in particular continues to press forward with a Partnership and Cooperation Agreement (PCA) with Turkmenistan, frozen since 1998 over human rights concerns, without requiring any human rights reforms in exchange. Throughout 2011 the European Parliament continued to hold up approval of the PCA over human rights concerns. At this writing the PCA was pending European Parliament approval.

Two national parliaments—in France and the United Kingdom—have yet to ratify the PCA. Human rights conditions for ratification that the French parliament set in 2010 remain in place. The UK Foreign Commonwealth Office's annual report on human rights failed to convey the severity of Turkmen government abuses and suggested that UK companies could support the government's efforts to build new prisons.

The UN Committee against Torture reviewed Turkmenistan in May 2011 and found "numerous and consistent allegations about the widespread practice of torture and ill-treatment." It voiced concern about enforced disappearances and incommunicado detention and requested that the Turkmen government report back within one year on measures taken to address these and other concerns.

UKRAINE

In 2011 Ukraine adopted reforms to facilitate closer association with the European Union and adopted new laws on access to information and refugee protection.

The conviction of former Prime Minister Yulia Tymoshenko and the arrest and trial of other former government officials undermined confidence in the judiciary's independence, media faced increasing pressure, and corruption continued to plague public and private institutions. Violations of the rights of migrants and asylum seekers remain serious concerns. Regarding the right to health, in 2011 the government's record was uneven on HIV/AIDS prevention and poor on access to pain relief.

Migration and Asylum

On August 4, 2011, a new law on refugees came into force that expands the grounds for recognizing refugee status, provides for temporary and complementary forms of protection, automatically grants minors refugee status when parents receive it, and ensures better access to education for children of refugees by simplifying school registration procedures.

Unlike EU standards, the law does not provide complementary protection to those facing indiscriminate violence. At this writing local migration service offices often refused applications for temporary and complementary protection while they awaited implementing instructions on the new law from the Cabinet of Ministers. Asylum seekers remain vulnerable to arbitrary detention, police harassment, and torture. There is no standard procedure for determining the age of refugees and asylum-seeking children.

In March 2011 the State Border Guard Service forcibly deported at least 10 asylum seekers and migrants back to Afghanistan before some could appeal the rejection of their asylum status. Members of the group did not have access to adequate legal representation or interpreters during their asylum and deportation hearings.

The 10 were part of a larger group of 14 asylum seekers who were held in custody at the Borispyl airport. Border guards allegedly handcuffed some detainees for more than a day, and at least three border guards allegedly punched, kicked, and verbally abused group members.

Rule of Law

In 2011 several ministers who served under former President Yushchenko were tried on criminal charges of "abuse of office" as part of President Viktor Yanukovych's anti-corruption campaign. In October a Ukrainian court convicted and sentenced Tymoshenko to seven years imprisonment for signing a gas contract with Russia allegedly without approval from the Cabinet of Ministers. The contract significantly increased the price of natural gas. Other officials facing prosecution include former acting Minister of Defense Valeriy Ivashchenko, former Interior Minister Yuri Lutsenko, and former First Deputy Justice Minister Yevhen Korniychuk, some of whom are also prominent opposition leaders. The EU, United States, and Russia expressed concern that the allegations against the former officials did not constitute crimes and that the charges are politically motivated.

Although international observers declared the 2010 presidential elections generally in accordance with international standards, OPORA, an independent NGO, reported procedural violations in the November 2010 local elections.

Hate Crimes and Discrimination

In 2010 the number of reported violent and apparently racially motivated attacks fell to fewer than 15 from its peak of over 80 attacks per year in 2007 and 2008, but by July 2011 there were already 13. Police and prosecutors remain reluctant to classify attacks as racially motivated. Racial profiling, nonviolent harassment by police, and hate crimes against persons of non-Slavic appearance and ethnic and religious minorities persist. Crimean Tatars and Roma continue to face discrimination and problems integrating into society, including lack of education in their native languages.

Civil Society

Despite legislative reforms, the situation for journalists and media outlets deteriorated in 2011, and civil society activists faced official threats that appeared to be retaliation for their work. In January 2011 the government passed the Law on Access to Public Information, which provides for the protection of journalists and, with the exception of confidential information, mandates the release of government information about the use of public property and funds.

Attacks on journalists, while not pervasive, often occur with impunity. On July 13, unidentified gunmen shot through the car windshield of *Obozrebatel* reporter Anatoly Shariya as he drove home. Although Shariya, who covers gambling, was not injured, Yanukovych ordered an investigation into the attack. The same month arsonists barricaded the door to *Novosti Donbasu* editor Aleksiy Matsuka's apartment with cement bags, put a funeral wreath with a threatening message outside the apartment, and set the door on fire. Matsuka, who was not home at the time, requested on August 8 that authorities reclassify the current "hooliganism" charges as an "attempted murder" investigation connected to his work. In response to Matsuka's request, on September 9 the Ministry of Internal Affairs added article 129 "threat of homicide" to the criminal investigation.

The national investigation into the August 2010 disappearance of Vasyl Klymentyev, *Noviy Stil* editor-in-chief, remains open. In August former Gen. Oleksiy Pukach confessed to the 2000 murder of investigative journalist Georgy Gongadze and implicated former President Leonid Kuchma and current Parliament Speaker Volodomyr Lytvyn in the crime. The proceedings remain closed, although the Gongadze family's lawyer made three separate appeals to the court to have the murder trial public.

In July ATN TV's provider unexpectedly and without explanation dropped ATN's signal, and local authorities ordered the termination of ATN's broadcasting due to a lack of a valid Sanitary and Epidemiological Service permit. ATN, the only independent Kharkiv news program, wrote an open letter to Yanukovych on September 13 alleging that the measures were politically motivated. The next day Fora and A/TVK, two other channels that broadcast ATN news and have valid broadcasting licenses, were unexpectedly removed from the air without a clear or official explanation. An opaque August 2011 bidding process for digital television frequencies resulted in several regional stations, including 9 Kanal, Chornomorska TV, and 3 Studia losing their frequency.

In December 2010 Vinnytsya Human Rights Group (VHRG) coordinator Dmytro Groisman was charged with disseminating pornography and desecrating state symbols. At the time VHRG was documenting asylum seekers who claim that the Vinnytsya police regularly extorted them. Authorities confiscated VHRG's documents and equipment in January in connection with Groisman's case, but returned all the materials on March 25, 2011. At this writing Groisman could not legally travel outside the Vinnytsya city limits due to his pending case. International pressure prevented human rights activist Andrei Bondarenko from undergoing a groundless, compulsory psychiatric examination in December 2010.

Health

Ukraine took several positive steps to fight the HIV/AIDS epidemic. On January 15, 2011, the government enacted a national law on HIV/AIDS that for the first time identifies substitution treatment and needle exchange as essential elements of Ukraine's national HIV prevention strategy. Ukraine also expanded the number of people with opioid drug dependence receiving opiate substitution treatment from none in 2004 to 6,390 in September 2011.

Developments early in 2011 threatened this progress. On January 18 the Ministry of Interior issued an order to collect personal data of patients enrolled in opiate substitution programs across Ukraine. Police pursued patients at clinics and at home to obtain this data and denied them access to services if they did not provide confidential information, including their HIV status and criminal record. NGOs working on HIV prevention and treatment were also ordered to surrender project documents, effectively paralyzing essential HIV prevention and outreach programs for drug users. In October 2010 the government recriminalized small amounts of narcotic drugs, resulting in decreased use of needle exchange programs and a 15 percent rise in drug possession arrests in the first quarter of 2011.

Tens of thousands of patients with advanced cancer in Ukraine unnecessarily suffer from severe pain every year because pain treatment is often inaccessible, best practices for palliative care are ignored, and anti-drug abuse regulations hamstring healthcare workers' ability to deliver evidence-based care. Those healthcare workers who try to provide the most effective pain treatment possible often have no choice but to act, as one oncologist said, "on the edge of the law." The situation is particularly devastating in rural areas—home to about one-third of Ukraine's population of 46 million—where strong opioid analgesics are often hard to access or simply unavailable.

Key International Actors

In August Yanukovych reaffirmed that "Ukraine's future lies with Europe" and declined to join a customs union with Russia, Belarus, and Kazakhstan. However, Tymoshenko's conviction jeopardized Ukraine's prospects of concluding an EU Association Agreement, which was being finalized at this writing. The agreement, which includes a free trade agreement, would bring closer economic and political integration with the EU.

Rising oil prices and Ukraine's rejection of Russia's customs union have led to mounting tensions between the two countries. Despite expressing concern over the prosecution of opposition leaders, the US continues to provide economic aid to Ukraine.

The Parliamentary Assembly of the Council of Europe's standing rapporteur for media freedom voiced concern over the deteriorating situation for media freedom in Ukraine.

The United Nations Committee on the Rights of the Child reviewed Ukraine in January, expressing concern over the overall lack of data on children at risk of torture, domestic violence, and other forms of ill-treatment. In its August review the UN Committee on the Elimination of Racial Discrimination welcomed Ukraine's new refugee law, but expressed concern that several government bodies working on discrimination ceased work in 2010.

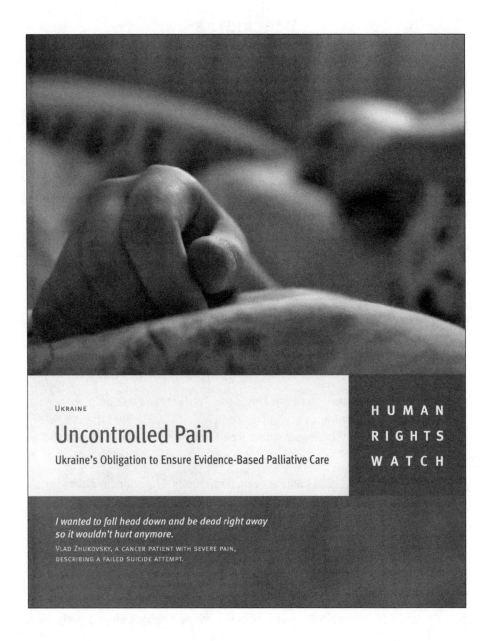

UKRAINE

Uncontrolled Pain

Ukraine's Obligation to Ensure Evidence-Based Palliative Care

HUMAN
RIGHTS
WATCH

*I wanted to fall head down and be dead right away
so it wouldn't hurt anymore.*
VLAD ZHUKOVSKY, A CANCER PATIENT WITH SEVERE PAIN,
DESCRIBING A FAILED SUICIDE ATTEMPT.

UZBEKISTAN

Uzbekistan's human rights record remains appalling, with no meaningful improvements in 2011. Torture remains endemic in the criminal justice system. Authorities continue to target civil society activists, opposition members, and journalists, and to persecute religious believers who worship outside strict state controls.

Freedom of expression remains severely limited. Government-sponsored forced child labor during the cotton harvest continues. Authorities continued to deny justice for the 2005 Andijan massacre in which government forces shot and killed hundreds of protestors, most of them unarmed.

Reacting to the pro-democracy Arab Spring movements, the Uzbek government increased the presence of security forces across the country and widened its already-tight control over the internet. Despite the government's persistent refusal to address concerns about its abysmal record, the United States and European Union continued to advance closer relations with the Uzbek government in 2011, seeking cooperation in the war in Afghanistan.

Human Rights Defenders and Independent Journalists

Uzbek authorities regularly threaten, imprison, ill-treat, and torture human rights defenders and other peaceful civil society activists. In 2011 the Uzbek government continued to harass activists and interfere with independent civil society.

The Uzbek government holds at least 13 human rights defenders in prison, and has brought charges against others, because of their human rights work. They are: Solijon Abdurakhmanov, Azam Formonov, Nosim Isakov, Gaibullo Jalilov, Alisher Karamatov, Jamshid Karimov, Norboi Kholjigitov, Abdurasul Khudainasarov, Ganihon Mamatkhanov, Habibulla Okpulatov, Yuldash Rasulov, Dilmurod Saidov, and Akzam Turgunov.

Several are in very poor health and at least seven have been ill-treated or tortured in custody. For example, relatives of imprisoned rights defender Gaibullo

Jalilov reported after a January 2011 visit that he had been repeatedly tortured, including being beaten with a stick that left him nearly deaf in both ears.

Other activists, including independent journalists and opposition figures, remain imprisoned on politically motivated charges. While authorities released the poet Yusuf Jumaev and three activists, Farkhad Mukhtarov, Norboi Kholjigitov, and Maksim Popov, the government did not ease its overall campaign to crush its critics.

Members of the Human Rights Alliance, an Uzbek human rights group, were regularly subjected to arbitrary detention and de facto house arrest for their activism. On April 24 a Russian television program exploring conditions for ethnic Russians in Central Asia interviewed Alliance members Elena Urlaeva, Viktoriya Bazhenova, and Tatyana Dovlatova. The next night assailants accosted the activists in their homes, screaming insults and threatening violence.

Following the airing of the program, Dovlatova was sued for defamation, a case that appears to have been orchestrated by authorities. Police later raided her home and she lost badly needed disability benefits.

In June Uzbekistan's Supreme Court granted a Justice Ministry petition to "liquidate" Human Rights Watch's Tashkent office. The ruling followed years of the Uzbek government obstructing Human Rights Watch's access to the country, including denying visas and staff member accreditation, most recently in December 2010. The obstruction and legal ruling led to the organization's expulsion from Uzbekistan after 15 years in the country.

In July, in a development that appears designed to discourage diplomats from engaging with independent activists, authorities brought administrative charges against a local British Embassy employee, Press Secretary Leonid Kudryavtsev, for holding "unauthorized meetings" with human rights defenders.

On August 10 Dovlatova and activist Abdullo Tojiboy-ugli were attacked by assailants in separate incidents that appear to have been instigated by authorities.

On August 22 journalist Elena Bondar was detained at Tashkent airport after returning from a journalism course abroad. Security agents confiscated her flash drives, interrogated her, and sent the confiscated items for "analysis" to the Center for Monitoring of the Uzbek Information Agency, which has been involved in trumping up cases against journalists.

Also in August Urlaeva was detained and beaten when she went to investigate a case of three TV journalists, whom authorities had charged with extortion in Namangan.

The Andijan Massacre

Six years later, the government continues to refuse an independent investigation into the 2005 massacre of hundreds of citizens in Andijan, denying justice to victims and failing to bring to account those responsible. Authorities continue to persecute anyone suspected of having participated in, or witnessed, the atrocities.

The Uzbek government also continued to intimidate families of Andijan survivors who have sought refuge abroad. Police subject them to constant surveillance, call them for questioning, and threaten them with criminal charges or home confiscation.

Torture, Ill-Treatment, and Criminal Justice

Torture remains rampant in Uzbekistan and continues to occur with near-total impunity. Rights of detainees are violated at each stage of investigations and trials, despite habeas corpus amendments that went into effect in 2008. The Uzbek government has persistently failed to meaningfully implement steps to combat torture that the United Nations special rapporteur in 2003 and other international bodies have recommended.

Suspects are not permitted access to lawyers, a critical safeguard against torture in pre-trial detention. Police use torture to coerce confessions from detainees. Authorities routinely refuse to investigate allegations of abuse.

In July authorities arrested Said Ashurov, a Tajik national who worked for the British company Oxus Gold, which the government had forced to close earlier in the year. A military court sentenced Ashurov to 12 years in prison for "possession of state secrets" after a closed trial. Witnesses who testified against him reported to Human Rights Watch that they were beaten in detention to procure their testimony. Prison authorities have denied Ashurov, who suffers from chronic hepatitis B, access to adequate medical treatment, resulting in a serious deterioration of his health.

Human Rights Watch continues to receive regular, credible reports of torture and ill-treatment in pre-trial and post-conviction detention.

Freedom of Religion

Although Uzbekistan's Constitution ensures freedom of religion, Uzbek authorities continued their unrelenting, multi-year campaign of arbitrary detention, arrest, and torture of Muslims who practice their faith outside state controls. Over 100 were arrested or convicted in 2011 on charges related to religious extremism.

Continuing a trend that began in 2008, followers of the late Turkish Muslim theologian Said Nursi continued to be prosecuted for religious extremism. Dozens of Nursi followers were arrested or imprisoned in 2011.

Authorities also continue to impose short-term prison sentences and fines on Christians and members of other minority religions conducting peaceful religious activities for administrative offenses, such as illegal religious teaching. On February 4 the Supreme Court again dismissed an appeal by Tohar Haydarov, a Baptist sentenced to 10 years on allegedly fabricated drug-related charges. In July a Protestant couple in Fergana, Muradiljon Umurzakov and Dilorom Mamasadikova, were physically abused and threatened with charges after police raided their home and found a Bible.

Authorities continue to extend sentences of religious prisoners for alleged violations of prison regulations. Such extensions occur without due process and can add years to a prisoner's sentence.

In November relatives of Muslim religious prisoners serving sentences at Jaslyk colony, Uzbekistan's most notorious prison, told Human Rights Watch that following a hunger strike, prison authorities tortured several inmates, including by undressing them naked in front of other inmates, beating, and subjecting them to sexual humiliation.

Forced Child Labor

Forced child labor in the cotton fields remains a serious concern. The government took no meaningful steps to implement the two International Labour Organization (ILO) conventions on child labor, which it ratified in March 2008. Despite repeated requests, it continued to refuse ILO access to monitor the harvest.

The government continues to force 1.5 to 2 million schoolchildren as young as nine-years-old to help with the cotton harvest for two months a year. They live in filthy conditions, contract illnesses, miss school, and work daily from early morning until evening for little to no pay. Hunger, exhaustion, and heat stroke are common.

Human Rights Watch is aware of several cases of authorities harassing activists who tried to document forced child labor. In September authorities detained activists Gulshan Karaeva and Nodir Akhatov while they photographed children forced to pick cotton in the Kashkadarya region.

Also in September, responding to concerns from Human Rights Watch and other groups, the organizers of New York Fashion Week cancelled a show by the president's daughter, Gulnara Karimova, who serves as Uzbekistan's permanent representative to the UN and its ambassador to Spain.

Key International Actors

The Uzbek government continued to refuse to cooperate with international institutions but faced virtually no consequences for this intransigence. It continues to deny access to all eight UN special procedures that have requested invitations, has failed to comply with recommendations made by various expert bodies, and blocks the ILO from sending independent observers to monitor compliance with the prohibition of forced child labor in the cotton industry.

The EU's position on human rights remained disappointingly weak, with virtually no public expressions of concern about Uzbekistan's deteriorating record. In January the European Commission president, Jose Manuel Barroso, received President Islam Karimov in Brussels, a highly controversial visit that marked Karimov's first to Europe since the Andijan massacre. The EU's eagerness to deepen its relationship with Uzbekistan without requiring improvements contrasted with its recent re-thinking of its relationships with autocratic governments in the Middle East. The annual human rights dialogue between the EU and Uzbekistan, held in May, again yielded no known results and appeared to have no bearing on the broader relationship.

In 2011 the US deepened its policy of re-engagement with Uzbekistan. Since 2004 Congress had expressly restricted assistance to Uzbekistan based on its deplorable rights record and further tightened restrictions following the Andijan massacre. However, in a particularly troubling move, and despite no meaningful improvements, the Obama administration sought to re-start assistance and provide military aid to Uzbekistan.

Uzbekistan is seen as a critical stop in the Northern Distribution Network, through which the US has sent non-lethal supplies to Afghanistan since 2009 as an alternative to what are viewed as unstable supply lines through Pakistan. US military contracts with Uzbeks as part of this supply chain are potentially lucrative for persons close to the Uzbek government. Despite the State Department's re-designation in September of Uzbekistan as a "Country of Particular Concern" for systematic violations of religious freedom, the US government retained a waiver on the sanctions outlined in the designation.

SYRIA

"We've Never Seen Such Horror"

Crimes against Humanity by Syrian Security Forces

HUMAN
RIGHTS
WATCH

WORLD REPORT

2012

MIDDLE EAST
AND NORTH AFRICA

ALGERIA

President Abdelaziz Bouteflika lifted Algeria's 19-year state of emergency in February and announced legal and political reforms amidst increasing economic unrest, pro-reform street protests, and worker strikes. However, at this writing these measures had not given Algerians the freedom to exercise their rights of expression, assembly, and association.

Security forces and armed groups continued to enjoy broad impunity for atrocities committed during the civil war of the 1990s. The state offered compensation to families of persons forcibly disappeared in the 1990s, but not answers about their fate. Armed groups continued to carry out deadly attacks, mostly targeting state security forces.

Freedom of Assembly

January 2011 saw several days of violent protests and rioting in several cities, triggered by price hikes on basic food items. As the riots subsided, Algerians— inspired by the stirrings in Tunisia and Egypt—on January 22 began attempting to hold weekly peaceful pro-reform demonstrations in Algiers, the capital. Large deployments of police were usually on hand and either prevented the protests from getting started or confined them to small spaces. Larger-scale labor protests also took place, including a march by thousands of communal guards in Algiers on March 7 demanding more pay.

On February 24 President Bouteflika ended the state of emergency. The emergency decree had given the Interior Ministry sweeping powers to administratively detain persons deemed to endanger "public order," close down meeting places, and ban gatherings. However many restrictions on civil liberties imposed during the state of emergency continued, as authorities drew on other repressive laws and regulations. For example, an indefinite ban imposed in 2001 on demonstrations in Algiers remained in effect. Outside the capital, a 1991 decree-law required prior approval for public gatherings. While authorities tolerated some demonstrations critical of the government outside of Algiers, these remained more the exception than the rule.

On March 16 in the city of Mostaganem authorities arrested and held overnight Dalila Touat of the unrecognized National Committee to Defend the Rights of the Unemployed for handing out leaflets and charged her with violating article 100 of the criminal code, which prohibits "any direct instigation ... by distributing written matter, of an unarmed gathering." A court in Mostaganem acquitted her on April 28. Authorities also subjected leaders of Algeria's several independent and legally unrecognized labor unions to various forms of harassment.

Freedom of Expression and Association

The state controls all domestic broadcast media, which provide live telecasts of parliamentary sessions but air almost no critical coverage of government policies. Privately-owned newspapers enjoy a freer scope, but repressive press laws and dependence on revenues from public sector advertising limit their freedom to criticize the government and the military. Authorities barred Al Jazeera television from maintaining a bureau in the country.

In July parliament revised two articles of the press code to eliminate prison terms—but not fines—as punishment for the offense of defaming or showing contempt for the president, state institutions, or courts. In September the Council of Ministers approved a draft press code that, if adopted, would eliminate prison as a punishment for speech offenses; however prison sentences for speech offenses remain present in the penal code.

The Council of Ministers on September 12 adopted a draft law on associations that allows authorities to oppose the creation of an association they deem to be contrary to "the public order" or "good morals." It also makes it easier for authorities to dissolve an association without a court order and harder for an association to receive funding from abroad. Under the proposed law, administering an "unapproved" association would remain a crime.

Authorities required organizations to obtain authorization from the local governor before holding indoor public meetings. The government in June banned two events organized by the Algerian League for the Defense of Human Rights: a conference on the occasion of the Day of the Child scheduled for June 1 in the *wilaya* (governorate) of el-Taref and one to be held in Algiers on June 10 about corruption in the Arab world.

Freedom of Religion

Algeria's constitution defines the state religion as Islam and requires that the president to be Muslim. A 2006 law criminalizes proselytizing Muslims by non-Muslims, but not the reverse, and forbids non-Muslims from worshiping except in state-approved locations. In practice authorities rarely authorized Algerian Protestant groups to use buildings for worship. In May the governor of the *wilaya* of Béjaia ordered the Protestant Church of Algeria (EPA) to shut seven "unauthorized" places of worship operating in the *wilaya*. EPA President Moustapha Krim said in October that the churches continued to operate while the EPA appealed the order in the courts. On May 25 an Oran court convicted Abdelkarim Siaghi, a convert to Christianity, of "offending" the Prophet Muhammad under the penal code and sentenced him to five years in prison and a fine. He was freed pending an appeal scheduled for November 2011.

Impunity for Past Abuses

Over 100,000 Algerians died during the political strife of the 1990s. Thousands more were subjected to enforced disappearances by security forces or abducted by armed groups fighting the government and never found. The 2006 Law on Peace and National Reconciliation provides a legal framework for the continued impunity enjoyed by perpetrators of atrocities during this era. The law also makes it a crime to denigrate state institutions or security forces for the way they conducted themselves during the political strife, thus potentially penalizing those who allege that the security forces perpetrated human rights violations.

The law promises compensation to families of "disappeared" persons. But organizations representing families of the "disappeared" criticized the state for its failure to provide a detailed account of the fate of their missing relatives, and for the pressure they said is applied to the families to accept compensation and abandon demands to learn the truth.

Algerian courts pronounced many death sentences during 2011 but observed a de facto moratorium on executions since 1993.

Women's Rights

Algerian women face discrimination under the code of personal status. A man has the right to divorce his wife without cause, but a woman can file for divorce only on specific grounds, such as abandonment. *Khul'a* (a no-fault divorce) is the only option for women who wish to file for a divorce without invoking the accepted reasons, but in so doing they forfeit any financial claims.

Terrorism and Counterterrorism

Attacks by armed groups were down dramatically compared to the mid-1990s, but al Qaeda in the Islamic Maghreb (AQIM) continued to launch fatal attacks, directed mostly—but not exclusively—at military and police targets.

On February 24, the same day the president lifted the state of emergency, President Bouteflika issued a decree authorizing the Algerian army to conduct counterterrorism operations, a role it had played during the state of emergency. A branch of the military, the Department of Intelligence and Security (DRS), was implicated in some of the worst abuses perpetrated during counterterrorism operations since the 1990s.

Also on February 24, Bouteflika promulgated article 125 bis of the code of criminal procedure, allowing judges to place suspects in "protected residence." The law allows this form of custody to take place in a secret location and authorizes prosecution for revealing its whereabouts. "Protected residence" replaced "assigned residence," practiced during the state of emergency against a small number of suspected terrorists. "Assigned residence" involved removing these individuals from the judicial system and detaining them indefinitely in an undisclosed location, cut off from contact with families and lawyers.

After the lifting of the state of emergency the detainees who had been in "assigned residence" were presented in court and transferred to official places of detention. However authorities continued to prevent some from appearing at trials. For example, lawyers for accused terrorists Omar Ferrah and Yacine Aïssani withdrew from the courtroom in protest when the court failed to produce the accused mens' co-defendant and alleged leader, Amar Saïfi, at several sessions of their trial between March and June, prompting the adjournment of the trial until November.

In one case dating to the 1990s, Malik Mejnoun and Abdelkader Chenoui were brought to trial on July 18 for the 1999 assassination of Kabyle (Berber) singer-activist Lounes Matoub after they had spent 12 years in pre-trial detention. Both men claimed they were innocent and said they were tortured while in incommunicado detention. The court convicted them and sentenced them to 12 years in prison.

Key International Actors

Algeria and the European Union have an association agreement and signed an agreement that provides Algeria €172 million (approximately US$234 million) in aid between 2011 and 2013. In September there was a meeting of the subcommittee of the bilateral Association Council on "political dialogue, security and human rights."

According to the United States government, Algeria "is a major partner in combating extremism and terrorist networks such as al Qaeda and is our second-largest trading partner in the Arab world." The US provides almost no financial aid to Algeria, but is the leading customer of its exports, primarily gas and oil. US President Barack Obama also congratulated the government on February 24 for lifting the state of emergency, noting that "we look forward to additional steps by the government that enable the Algerian people to fully exercise their universal rights, including freedom of expression, association and assembly."

Algeria in 2011 continued to fail to invite five of the special procedures of the United Nations Human Rights Council that had requested to visit the country, including the Working Group on Enforced or Involuntary Disappearances and the special rapporteurs on torture and on human rights while countering terrorism. Algeria hosted a visit by the special rapporteur on the right to adequate housing.

BAHRAIN

In mid-February Bahraini authorities used lethal force to suppress peaceful anti-government and pro-democracy protests, killing seven and wounding many more.

The crackdown resumed in mid-March, after troops from Saudi Arabia entered Bahrain and Bahraini military and security forces launched a systematic campaign of retribution, arresting thousands of demonstrators or individuals who supported the protests. Authorities fired hundreds of public sector employees suspected of supporting the protests, as did large private firms in which the state had a substantial stake.

Security forces' use of birdshot pellets, rubber bullets, and tear gas as well as live ammunition caused most of the deaths and injuries of protesters and bystanders. Attacks against protesters continued after authorities formally lifted the "state of national safety" on June 1. At this writing more than 40 persons had been killed in connection with suppression of protests, including four who died in custody in April from torture or medical neglect, and several members of security forces.

Right to Assembly

During the early morning hours of February 17, security forces attacked peaceful demonstrators at the Pearl Roundabout in Manama, the capital. Many were sleeping. The assault left four protesters dead and hundreds injured. On February 18, security forces and the Bahrain Defense Force (BDF) fired live ammunition and rubber bullets at peaceful protesters marching towards the Pearl Roundabout—then occupied by BDF tanks, armored vehicles and police units—mortally wounding Abd al-Ridha Bu Hameed.

On February 19, authorities ordered security and military forces to withdraw and protesters reoccupied the Pearl Roundabout. For four weeks protesters gathered at the roundabout and other areas to voice opposition to the government and ruling Al Khalifa family. Crown Prince Salma bin Hamad bin Isa Al Khalifa appeared on national television and guaranteed that protesters would be free to demonstrate at the Pearl Roundabout without facing arrest or attack by government forces.

On March 16—a day after King Hamad declared a "state of national safety," akin to a state of emergency—security and military forces forcibly cleared the Pearl Roundabout, the center of anti-government protests. The same day, forces dispersed protesters in villages outside Manama and surrounded the Salmaniya Medical Complex, the country's largest public hospital, preventing patients and medical staff from entering or leaving the hospital. At least six people were killed during clashes on March 16, including two police officers.

After lifting the state of emergency on June 1, authorities permitted Al Wefaq, the largest opposition political society, to hold several rallies, which remained peaceful, but clashes with security forces regularly broke out when protesters held demonstrations in Shia villages. At least eleven protesters and bystanders, including two children under age 18, had been killed as a result of protest-related injuries between June 1 and this writing.

Arbitrary Arrests and Detentions

Since mid-March security forces have arrested over 1,600 people who participated in, or were suspected of supporting, the anti-government demonstrations. Some of those arrested and detained were children. In many cases armed masked men, some in uniforms and others in civilian clothes, pulled people out of their homes in pre-dawn raids and transferred them to unknown locations. Others were arrested at work or pulled out of cars at checkpoints. Authorities held most detainees in incommunicado detention for weeks, in some cases months. Detainees had little or no contact with lawyers or family except when they were presented before a special military court.

Those held incommunicado included doctors, teachers, students, athletes, a prominent defense lawyer, and leaders of legally recognized opposition political societies. Ibrahim Sharif, a Sunni who heads the secularist National Democratic Action Society, was one of the first arrested, in a pre-dawn raid on March 17. Matar Ibrahim Matar and Jawad Fairouz—who represented Al Wefaq, the largest opposition bloc in parliament before its members resigned in protest in February—were seized on May 2. Authorities released Matar and Fairouz in August but they still face charges related to their political activities.

Dozens remained in pre-trial detention as of October, in addition to the more than 250 who were convicted and sentenced by special military courts. The government provided little information about the number of people arrested and typically gave reasons for arrest only when detainees were charged before special military courts.

Torture, Ill-Treatment, and Abuse

In April four people died in custody, apparently as a result of torture and medical neglect. The body of one—Ali Isa Ibrahim Saqer, arrested in connection with the deaths of two police officers—bore unmistakable signs of torture on his body. On April 28 Bahrain TV broadcast Saqer's purported confession in connection with the trial of his co-defendants, although authorities notified Saqer's family of his death on April 9.

Abdulhadi al-Khawaja, a leading human rights and political activist, appeared before a special military court on May 8 with facial fractures and head injuries, apparently the result of severe beatings he sustained when authorities detained him on April 9. Several other co-defendants showed signs of possible abuse or ill-treatment. Since mid-February dozens of released detainees, including doctors, nurses, and paramedics arrested in March and April, have alleged they were abused or tortured during detention, often to coerce confessions.

On February 23, authorities released from prison 23 opposition leaders and activists arrested between mid-August and early September 2010 for alleged terrorist offenses. Several in the group described lengthy interrogation sessions during which they were blindfolded and subjected to both physical and psychological abuse, some of which amounted to torture. The abuse included threats, humiliation, solitary confinement, beatings to the head, chest, and other sensitive areas, beatings on the soles of feet with sticks or hoses, sleep deprivation, denying access to the bathroom, and electric shocks. Some said they were sexually harassed or assaulted. Most of the defendants have since been rearrested.

Authorities denied requests for visits to detention facilities by independent human rights and humanitarian organizations as well as United Nations human rights mechanisms.

Unfair Trials in Special Military Courts

On March 15 King Hamad established by decree special military courts, called the "Courts of National Safety," to try protesters and people perceived as supporting the street protests. BDF Commander-in-Chief Field Marshal Khalifa bin Ahmed Al Khalifa appointed the military judge who presides over the court, along with two civilian judges, and the military public prosecutor who prosecuted the cases.

Since March, authorities have tried several hundred defendants before military courts and have convicted and sentenced more than 300 persons.

Among those the special military court sentenced to prison terms ranging from five years to life were Sharif al-Khawaja, and 19 other protest leaders, seven of them in absentia, on June 22. The charges against them ranged from calling for a change of government, leading "illegal" demonstrations, "spreading false news," and "harming the reputation" of the country. The trial record cited no evidence linking any of the accused to acts of violence or other recognizable criminal offenses. An appeals court upheld their convictions and sentences on September 28.

On April 28 the special military court sentenced four defendants to death and three others to life in prison for their alleged involvement in the murder of two police officers. Two of the death sentences were upheld by the Appeals Court of National Safety, while the other two were changed to life imprisonment. On September 29 the special military court sentenced another defendant to death for the alleged murder of a third police officer.

Lawyers defending suspects before the special military court had extremely limited access to their clients and were unable to adequately prepare their clients' defenses. In many cases convictions were based solely on secret evidence that the military prosecution provided, the testimony of interrogators, and confessions that defendants claimed were coerced.

The special military courts ended their operation on October 7, more than four months after a June 29 decree by King Hamad that supposedly transferred all protest-related cases to civilian courts.

Attacks on Doctors and Other Health Care Staff

Since the outbreak of anti-government protests in mid-February, Human Rights Watch documented restrictions on provision of emergency care at temporary health posts, sieges at hospitals and clinics by security forces, arrests and beatings of people with protest-related injuries, and arrests of doctors and other health care staff who had criticized these actions.

Police attacked a volunteer medical tent in the February 17 raid on Pearl Roundabout, beating and arresting nurses and doctors as well as protesters. In response to this attack and to allegations that authorities prevented the dispatch of ambulances to attend to wounded protesters, demonstrators gathered outside the emergency facilities of Salmaniya hospital, with the support of some of the health care staff. For several weeks the grounds outside the complex became a staging ground for anti-government demonstrations, with posters, tents, photos of wounded protesters, and speeches by opposition leaders.

The BDF took over Salmaniya hospital on March 16 and restricted entry to and exit from the complex. Hospital staff and protesters being treated for injuries inside the hospital were subjected to harassment, beatings that sometimes rose to the level of torture, and arrest. Security forces also raided health care facilities elsewhere, where they interrogated and arrested medical staff.

On September 29 the special military court sentenced 20 doctors and other health care staff charged with serious crimes, including kidnapping and storing weapons at Salmaniya hospital, and terms of imprisonment ranging from 5 to 15 years. The court denied the doctors and other health care staff a fair trial by relying on tainted or questionable evidence including coerced confessions,

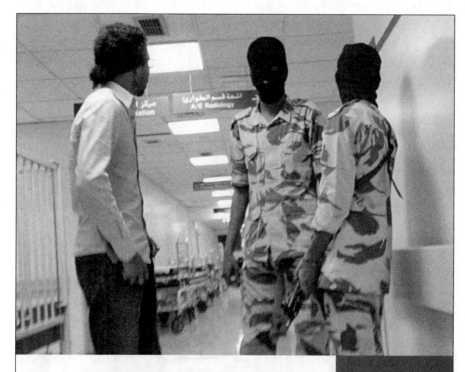

BAHRAIN

Targets of Retribution

Attacks against Medics, Injured Protesters,
and Health Facilities

HUMAN
RIGHTS
WATCH

hearsay, and "secret evidence" submitted by interrogators, who often served as the prosecutor's main witness. Judges also prevented the doctors and other health care staff from testifying in their own defense. At this writing a civilian court was scheduled to hear the doctors and health care staff's appeal on November 28.

Twenty-eight other doctors and health care staff faced misdemeanor charges before a civil court.

Summary Workplace and University Dismissals

According to the General Federation of Bahraini Trade Unions, ministries, other official bodies, and private companies in which the state held a substantial interest dismissed more than 2,500 employees in the first half of the year.

In most cases the stated reason for dismissal was absence from work during and immediately after street protests, but the dismissals appear to have been arbitrary and carried out in violation of Bahraini law.

On April 19 the Bahrain News Agency (BNA) reported that the University of Bahrain had dismissed 200 students, academics, and other employees in connection with protests and clashes on the campus in March. On May 25, according to the BNA, Education Minister Majid al-Nuaimi confirmed that some students in Bahrain and abroad who participated in anti-government protests lost their government scholarships. The University of Bahrain required all students to sign a loyalty pledge to the ruling family before they could re-enroll when the university reopened in early May and again in September.

Women's Rights

Unlike for Sunnis, there is no codified personal status law dealing with marriage, divorce, guardianship and child custody, and inheritance for Shias. Such matters are left to the judge's discretion in Shia courts. The penal code does not adequately deal with violence against women as there are no comprehensive provisions on sexual harassment or domestic abuse. Rape can be punished with life in prison, but marital rape is not recognized as a crime.

Migrant Workers

More than 460,000 migrant workers, primarily from Asia, work in Bahrain on temporary contracts in construction, domestic work, and other services. Abuses such as unpaid wages, passport confiscation, unsafe housing, excessive work hours, and physical abuse are common. A 2009 reform allowing workers to change jobs more freely has yet to be publicized widely and does not apply to domestic workers, who are also excluded from protection under the labor law. Bahrain voted to adopt the International Labour Organization Convention on Domestic Work, but has yet to ratify it or to pass draft national legislation on domestic work.

Key International Actors

Troops primarily from Saudi Arabia and the United Arab Emirates entered Bahrain on March 14 to support Bahrain's crackdown against largely peaceful protests.

Bahrain hosts the United States Navy's Fifth Fleet, and the US sells military equipment to Bahrain, a "major non-NATO ally." After the February attacks on demonstrators the United Kingdom and France announced they would cut off security and military sales and assistance to Bahrain, and the US announced it would "review" such sales. In September the US Department of Defense formally notified Congress of a proposed the sale of US$53 million in armored Humvees and other equipment to the BDF as well as $15 million in Foreign Military Financing for Bahrain.

US President Barack Obama telephoned King Hamad on February 18 after Bahraini forces fired on demonstrators and, according to a White House statement, "reiterated his condemnation of the violence used against peaceful protesters," and in a speech on May 19 criticized the government's "mass arrests and brute force." For the most part, however, Bahrain's major western allies—the US and the European Union and its member states—were muted in their public criticism of Bahrain's serious human rights violations in a manner that contrasted sharply with their public statements concerning other governments

BAHRAIN

For A Better Life

Migrant Worker Abuse in Bahrain
and the Government Reform Agenda

HUMAN
RIGHTS
WATCH

engaged in similar abuses in the region. They also failed to prompt any action at the UN Human Rights Council.

On June 29 King Hamad issued a decree establishing the Bahrain Independent Commission of Investigation (BICI) headed by M. Cherif Bassiouni and four other internationally recognized human rights experts. The commission's mandate is to investigate "the events occurring in Bahrain February/March 2011, and any consequences arising out of the aforementioned events." The commission was scheduled to issue its findings on November 23.

The Office of the UN High Commissioner for Human Rights and the UN secretary-general welcomed the establishment of the BICI. The US government has said it will wait for the commission's final report and the government's response before deciding on the $53 million arms sales.

After the March crackdown the government sharply restricted access to the country by independent journalists and international rights organizations, including Human Rights Watch.

EGYPT

Egyptians took to the streets starting on January 25 to protest peacefully against President Hosni Mubarak's 30-year rule, calling for social justice, democracy, and an end to police brutality. Police violence against protesters, especially on January 28, only hardened the protesters' determination. On February 11 Mubarak was forced to resign and the Supreme Council of the Armed Forces (SCAF), composed of leading army figures, took over, assuming full legislative and executive powers two days later. In March voters approved constitutional amendments in a referendum, and the SCAF issued a Constitutional Declaration setting out a roadmap for holding parliamentary and presidential elections.

Overall, there was no improvement in human rights protections in Egypt. On assuming power the SCAF ordered the release of all detainees held under the Emergency Law (Law No. 162 of 1958)—numbering several thousand at the end of 2010 according to estimates by human rights groups—and promised to end the State of Emergency. However, the SCAF has continued to use special courts under the Emergency Law and has referred more than 12,000 civilians to military tribunals since January, more than the total number of civilians tried by military courts during the 30-year-long Mubarak presidency. Those referred to military tribunals have included children as young as 15, even though international law discourages trials of children in military proceedings. Furthermore, on September 10 the SCAF announced that it was expanding the scope of the Emergency Law's application, and that it would remain in force through May 2012.

Throughout the year the military used excessive force to break up demonstrations and torture detainees. Despite official recognition of the need to rebuild public confidence in the police, no process of security sector reform was initiated. There has been no comprehensive investigation into systematic acts of torture and ill-treatment practiced in recent years by Egyptian police, and in particular the State Security Investigations (SSI) agency.

On August 3 the trial began of Mubarak and former Minister of Interior Habib al-Adly, as well as 11 other police officials around the country. They were charged with the killing of protestors and corruption. Their trials were still in progress at this writing.

Police Violence and Killing of Unarmed Protesters

On January 28, tens of thousands of demonstrators took to the streets of Alexandria, Suez, and Cairo, the capital. Police responded with tear gas, water cannons, rubber bullets, and live ammunition in an effort to prevent protesters from advancing towards the central squares of those cities. The Ministry of Health said 846 persons died during the protests in January and February. Most of these were killed on January 28 and 29. On February 2 and 3, armed men in plainclothes—some mounted on camels and horses—attacked protesters in Tahrir Square, injuring several hundred; on those two days at least eight people died of gunshot wounds.

Torture and Excessive Use of Force by Military and Police Officers

The military arbitrarily arrested scores of journalists while they were covering the protests in January, in addition to hundreds of peaceful protesters. The journalists were released within a few days of their arrests, but military courts sentenced many protesters to imprisonment. For example, authorities filed dubious charges of "thuggery" against peaceful protester Amr Beheiry, arrested during a protest in Tahrir Square on February 26. Military courts convicted and sentenced him to five years in prison. Beheiry remained in prison at this writing. Authorities also detained children, who faced physical abuse and torture. Street children were particularly vulnerable to arrest and abuse.

Torture by military personnel was first reported on February 2, shortly after the army took over law enforcement duties from the police. On March 9 the military broke up a peaceful sit-in in Tahrir Square, arrested at least 174 protesters, and beat, kicked, whipped, and applied electric shocks to them on the grounds of the nearby Egyptian Museum. The military brought these protesters before military courts, which sentenced 134 of them to three to five years in prison on charges of "thuggery," but released all of them in May after two months of public campaigning on their behalf.

EGYPT

"Work on Him until He Confesses"

Impunity for Torture in Egypt

HUMAN
RIGHTS
WATCH

The military used excessive force and carried out arbitrary mass arrests in various cities to disperse demonstrations and sit-ins on numerous occasions—February 25, March 9, March 23, May 16, July 22, and August 1—beating and tasering those arrested. On April 9, military officers used rubber bullets and live ammunition to break up a sit-in opposing SCAF's rule, wounding at least 71 protesters, one fatally. On October 9, during the dispersal by military police and riot police of a protest of Coptic Christians in front of the state TV building in Cairo, at least two military vehicles ran over and killed 13 protesters and a further 24 were killed by live ammunition. Military prosecutors are overseeing the investigation into the incident, a conflict of interest likely to reinforce military impunity.

Central Security Forces, Egypt's riot police, continued to use excessive force when policing demonstrations. On June 28 and 29, riot police clashed with protesters outside the ministry of interior for 16 hours. The police fired tear gas into the crowd and used rubber bullets and pellet guns, injuring 1,114 persons according to the Ministry of Health. After the removal of Mubarak, police continued to use torture in police stations, detention centers, and at points of arrest. In June bus driver Mohamed Sabah Nasr died in custody in Azbakeya police station in Cairo after police arrested him along with seven others for "disrupting traffic." Those detained with Nasr said that they saw the police beating him. The Ministry of Interior said that it is investigating his death but they have yet to make a report public.

Freedom of Expression and Association

News media enjoyed greater freedom in the aftermath of the ouster of Mubarak on all issues except those concerning the military. As of September the military prosecutor under the SCAF had summoned at least nine activists and journalists for questioning on charges of "insulting the military," but released most without charge. An exception was blogger Maikel Nabil, whom a military tribunal in April sentenced to three years imprisonment for "insulting the military" and "spreading false information" on his blog. At this writing Nabil remained in prison while awaiting his retrial, scheduled for November 27.

On September 7, Minister of Information Osama Heikal said that due to the current "media chaos" he would no longer issue broadcasting licenses for new satellite TV stations. Four days later police raided the offices of Al Jazeera Live Egypt, the station that had provided the most detailed coverage of anti-SCAF protests over the preceding weeks, and ordered it to stop broadcasting from Egypt. The station continued to broadcast from Qatar. On October 30 a military prosecutor detained blogger Alaa Abdel Fattah, one of the most vocal critics of the military, for 30 days on charges of inciting the October 9 demonstration at Maspero and assaulting military officers, charges for which the prosecutor provided no evidence. Abdel Fattah remained in detention at this writing.

In March the SCAF amended the Political Parties Law to make it easier for new political parties to form by enabling them to register as long as they meet the requirements set out in the law. Under Mubarak, applications to register new parties were usually rejected. However, there was no move to amend the Associations Law, which allows for excessive government interference in associations. In July the state security prosecutor announced that he would investigate possible "treason" charges against NGOs that were not registered under the Associations Law and that received foreign funding. In November a Cairo criminal court ordered banks to report on all transactions on the private accounts of 63 human rights defenders and organizations.

Freedom of Religion and Sectarian Violence

Incidents of sectarian violence continued throughout 2011. In the early hours of January 1, 2011, a bomb went off in a church in Alexandria, killing 23 people. The prosecutor opened an investigation but had not charged anyone in connection with the attack at this writing. On March 8, Christians in the eastern Cairo suburb of Muqattam protested the burning of a church four days earlier in Atfih, 13 miles south of Cairo, and clashed with Muslims. Twelve people died in the ensuing violence and shootings, and several Christian homes and businesses were torched. The prosecutor has yet to investigate the incident.

In May sectarian violence outside a church in Imbaba, a neighborhood of Cairo, left 12 dead. On July 3, the trial of those arrested in connection with the violence opened before an Emergency State Security Court. On September 30, a mob burnt down the Mar Girgis church in Marinab, in Aswan, but local authorities and prosecutors failed to investigate instead insisting on a settlement. The prime minister ordered an acceleration of the drafting of a new law to facilitate the renovation and construction of churches, a long-standing demand of Christians, who face discrimination in this respect.

Refugee and Migrants' Rights

Egyptian border police continued to shoot at unarmed African migrants who attempted to cross the Sinai border into Israel, killing at least 22 since January. Police arrested hundreds of irregular migrants, primarily Eritreans, Ethiopians, and Sudanese, and detained them in police stations and prisons in Sinai and Upper Egypt without access to the Office of the United Nations High Commissioner for Refugees, thereby denying them the right to make an asylum claim.

In October immigration officials forcibly deported three Eritreans. Prison officials in Shallal gave Eritrean embassy officials access to 118 detained Eritrean men who were asylum seekers and beat them to force them to sign paperwork agreeing to return to Eritrea. Egyptian authorities announced they would deport the group to Eritrea.

Migrants reported beatings and rape at the hands of traffickers operating in the Sinai. In September traffickers detained a group of 120 Eritreans, including 6 women, and threatened to detain and abuse them until they or their families paid US$3,000 each to allow them to continue their journey to Israel. The Egyptian authorities failed to conduct any investigations into this organized trafficking or to arrest anyone in connection with it.

Labor Rights

Strikes, sit-ins, and labor protests increased in number compared to previous years and spread to new sectors. In April the SCAF passed Law 34 criminalizing strikes that involve "the disruption of the work of public institutions or public or private work." Military police used excessive force on at least 11 occasions to disperse labor protests and sit-ins. In June military police arrested five workers demonstrating outside the Ministry of Petroleum and a military court sentenced them to a one-year suspended sentence for participating in the strike. In March the minister of labor and manpower recognized the right of independent trade unions to be established through a simple formality of declaration—pending adoption of a draft law—prepared by the cabinet, that would ease registration procedures. At least 70 new independent trade unions have declared their establishment since March.

Women's Rights

On March 9, military police arrested 20 women as they broke up a sit-in in Tahrir Square and then beat them on the grounds of the nearby Egyptian Museum. Military officers took 17 of the group to a military prison and the next day conducted virginity tests on seven of the women who identified themselves as unmarried. In response to the public outcry, the SCAF said that it would "look into the truth of the matter," but at this writing there had been no progress in investigating or prosecuting those officers involved.

In May the SCAF amended the Political Rights Law, canceling the women's quota of 64 seats in the People's Assembly that was first used in the November 2010 parliamentary elections, and replacing it with a requirement that each party must nominate at least one female candidate on its list, a formula likely to lead to a sharp drop in the number of women deputies.

Egypt's Sharia-based Personal Status Law—which discriminates against women in family affairs—applies only to Muslims, while Copts are governed by church regulations that prohibit them from divorcing, except in cases of adultery. Some Copts grew more vocal in their demand for a civil law that would give them the right to divorce.

Key International Actors

When protests broke out in January United States and European Union officials initially voiced cautious support of the protesters' right to freedom of assembly and expression and criticized police violence. As the protests grew, their support for protesters' demands became stronger and eventually they called upon President Mubarak to step down.

The US announced in March that it had earmarked $65 million for democracy and human rights funding in Egypt for 2011, as well as $100 million for economic development in addition to the roughly $250 million of economic and $1.3 billion in military aid that it had provided in previous years. In May the US also laid out plans for debt relief. The US Agency for International Development quietly removed its requirement that local organizations applying for funding be registered under Egypt's restrictive Associations Law, provoking criticism from the Egyptian government. In October US President Barack Obama spoke to Field Marshall Mohamed Hussein Tantawy, head of the SCAF, and urged him to lift the Emergency Law and end trials of civilians before military courts.

IRAN

In 2011 Iranian authorities refused to allow government critics to engage in peaceful demonstrations. In February, March, April, and September security forces broke up large-scale protests in several major cities. In mid-April security forces reportedly shot and killed dozens of protesters in Iran's Arab-majority Khuzestan province. There was a sharp increase in the use of the death penalty. The government continued targeting civil society activists, especially lawyers, rights activists, students, and journalists. In July 2011 the government announced it would not cooperate with, or allow access to, the United Nations special rapporteur on Iran, appointed in March 2011 in response to the worsening rights situation.

Freedom of Assembly and Association

In February and March thousands of demonstrators took to the streets of Tehran, the capital, and several other major cities to support pro-democracy protests in neighboring Arab countries and protest the detention of Iranian opposition leaders. The authorities' violent response led to at least three deaths and hundreds of arrests.

In response to calls by former presidential candidates and opposition leaders Mir Hossein Mousavi and Mehdi Karroubi for mass protests in February, security forces arbitrarily arrested dozens of political opposition members in Tehran and several other cities beginning on February 8. Several days later they placed both Mousavi and Karroubi under house arrest, where they remained at this writing.

In April Iran's parliament passed several articles of a draft bill which severely limits the independence of civil society organizations, and creates a Supreme Committee Supervising NGO Activities chaired by ministry officials and members of the security forces. Authorities had already banned or severely restricted the independence of several professional organizations not covered by the draft bill, including the Journalists' Association and the Bar Association. Dozens of activists affiliated with banned opposition political parties or student groups are currently serving time in prison.

Death Penalty

In 2010 Iranian authorities recorded 252 executions, but rights groups believe many more were executed without official acknowledgement. Most of those executed had been convicted of drug-related offenses following flawed trials in revolutionary courts. The number of executions increased even further following the entry into force in late December 2010 of an amended anti-narcotics law, drafted by the Expediency Council and approved by Supreme Leader Ayatollah Ali Khamenei. Since then Iran has executed more than 400 prisoners—including 67 drug offenders in January 2011 alone—according to rights groups. Authorities have refused to acknowledge more than half these executions.

Crimes punishable by death include murder, rape, trafficking and possessing drugs, armed robbery, espionage, sodomy, adultery, and apostasy. On September 3 the semi-official Iranian Students News Agency announced the execution of six men in the southwestern city of Ahvaz. Three of the men were convicted under Iran's anti-sodomy laws.

Iran leads the world in the execution of juvenile offenders, individuals who committed a crime before turning 18-years-old. The Iranian state executed at least three children in 2011, one of them in public. Iranian law allows capital punishment for persons who have reached puberty, defined as nine-years-old for girls and fifteen for boys. There are currently more than a hundred juvenile offenders on death row.

Authorities have executed at least 30 individuals on the charge of *moharebeh* ("enmity against God") since January 2010, allegedly for their ties to armed or terrorist groups. During the early morning hours of January 24, 2011, authorities in Tehran's Evin prison hanged Jafar Kazemi and Mohammad Ali Haj-Aghai for their alleged ties to the banned Mojahedin-e Khalq (MEK) opposition group. Ali Saremi, who admitted to sympathizing with the MEK's ideological aspirations, was also hanged in Evin prison on December 28, 2010, for the crime of *moharebeh*.

As of October 2011 at least 16 Kurds were on death row, many of them for alleged national security crimes and *moharebeh*.

Freedom of Expression

Authorities continue to shut down newspapers and target journalists and blog-gers. On September 5 the Ministry of Islamic Culture and Guidance's Press Supervisory Board shut down the weekly *Shahrvand* (Citizen) and daily *Ruzegar* (Time) for insulting the authorities and "propaganda against the state," among other crimes. On September 5 and 6, Intelligence Ministry forces raided the offices of Majzooban-e Noor, a website affiliated with the Nematollahi Gonabadi Sufi order, and arrested at least 11 members of its editorial staff on unknown charges.

According to Reporters Without Borders, there were 49 journalists and bloggers in Iran's prisons as of October 2011. The judiciary sentenced Vahid Asghari, a 24 year-old blogger, to death for his alleged involvement in "running obscene websites," according to rights groups.

The Ministry of Science, backed by the Supreme Council of the Cultural Revolution, implemented regulations to limit social science course offerings at various universities as part of an Islamicization program. Authorities also issued restrictive quotas to limit the courses and majors that women students could take at certain universities. State universities prevented some politically active students from registering for graduate programs despite test scores that should have guaranteed them access.

The government systematically blocked websites that carry political news and analysis, slowed down internet speeds, and jammed foreign satellite broad-casts.

Human Rights Defenders and Lawyers

Authorities have imprisoned, prosecuted, or harassed dozens of defense lawyers since June 2009. In August 2011 Nobel Peace Laureate Shirin Ebadi said at least 42 lawyers had faced government persecution since June 2009. In January a revolutionary court convicted Nasrin Sotoudeh, a prominent rights lawyer, of "acting against the national security" and "propaganda against the regime" and sentenced her to 11 years in prison. Authorities also barred

Sotoudeh from practicing law and from leaving the country for 20 years. In September the judiciary reduced her sentence to six years imprisonment.

In February a revolutionary court sentenced rights lawyer Khalil Bahramian to 18 months in prison and imposed a 10-year ban on his practicing law. In July the judiciary sentenced Mohammad Ali Dadkhah, a prominent lawyer and co-founder (with Ebadi) of the Center for Defenders of Human Rights (CDHR), to nine years in prison and a 10-year ban from teaching and legal practice. On September 10 security forces arrested Abdolfattah Soltani, another CDHR co-founder. On September 27 a revolutionary court in Tehran sentenced Narges Mohammadi, an executive member of the CDHR, to 11 years imprisonment for acting against the national security and membership in an illegal organization.

Also on September 27, security forces raided the home of Masoud Shafiee, the lawyer who represented three American hikers detained in Iran since July 31, 2009, and interrogated him for several hours. On October 2 they prevented him from leaving the country. Authorities had earlier released one of the hikers, Sarah Shourd, on September 14, 2010, and the two others, Shane Bauer and Josh Fattal, on September 21.

Few if any independent rights organizations can openly operate in the country in the current political climate.

Women's Rights

Iranian women are discriminated against in personal status matters related to marriage, divorce, inheritance, and child custody. A woman requires her male guardian's approval for marriage regardless of her age. An Iranian woman cannot pass on her nationality to her foreign-born spouse or their children. A woman may not obtain a passport or travel outside the country without her husband's written permission.

Treatment of Minorities

The government denies freedom of religion to adherents of the Baha'i faith, Iran's largest non-Muslim religious minority. On May 21, security forces arrested

IRAN

We are a Buried Generation

Discrimination and Violence Against Sexual Minorities in Iran

HUMAN
RIGHTS
WATCH

at least 30 Baha'is in a series of coordinated raids in several major cities. At this writing authorities were still holding the defendants without charge. All those arrested were affiliated with the Baha'i Institute for Higher Education, a correspondence university established in 1987 in response to the government's policy of depriving Baha'i students of the right to pursue higher education. According to the Baha'i International Community, there were 100 Baha'is detained in Iran's prisons as of October.

Authorities discriminate against Muslim minorities, including Sunnis who account for about 10 percent of the population, in political participation and employment. They also prevent Sunni Iranians from constructing mosques in major cities. In recent years officials have repeatedly prevented Sunnis from conducting separate Eid prayers in Tehran and other cities. On September 5, in Fars province, paramilitary Basij militia attacked members of Iran's largest Sufi sect, the Nematollahi Gonabadi order, killing one. The authorities then launched a campaign of arrests against members of the group in several cities.

Authorities also targeted converts to Christianity. In September a revolutionary court convicted six members of the evangelical Church of Iran to one year prison terms on charges of "propaganda against the state," allegedly for prose-lytizing. On September 25, authorities summoned Yousef Nadarkhani, the pas-tor of a 400-member Church of Iran congregation in northern Iran, to court and told him he had three opportunities to renounce his faith and embrace Islam. Nadarkhani refused to recant and faced possible execution as of this writing. In 2010 the judiciary had sentenced Nadarkhani to death for "apostasy from Islam" despite the fact that no such crime exists under Iran's penal code.

The government restricted cultural and political activities among the country's Azeri, Kurdish, Arab, and Baluch minorities, including organizations that focus on social issues. In April security forces reportedly killed several dozen protest-ers, most of them ethnic Arabs, in Iran's southwestern province of Khuzestan. Authorities arrested dozens and executed nine men allegedly connected to protests on May 9. Security forces also arrested hundreds in Iran's Azerbaijan region following large-scale protests in August and September, part of a pattern of harassment against environmental and Azeri civil society activists.

Key International Actors

In March the UN Human Rights Council appointed a special rapporteur for Iran. In July 2011 the Iranian government announced it would not cooperate with or allow the special rapporteur access. On September 23 the special rapporteur submitted his first report on Iran in which he highlighted a "pattern of systematic violations of … human rights" and repeated his call on the government to allow him to visit the country.

Iran continued to refuse access to UN special procedures, despite their long-standing and repeated requests for invitations to visit. No special rapporteurs have visited the country since 2005.

On September 15 the UN secretary-general submitted a report to the UN General Assembly in which he said he was "deeply troubled by reports of increased numbers of executions, amputations, arbitrary arrest and detention, unfair trials, torture and ill-treatment" and bemoaned "the crackdown on human rights activists, lawyers, journalists and opposition activists." On November 3 the UN Human Rights Committee issued its concluding observations following its review of Iran's implementation of the International Covenant on Civil and Political Rights. The committee concluded "that the status of international human rights treaties in domestic law is not specified in the legal system, which hinders the full implementation of the rights contained in the Covenant."

On April 14 the European Union imposed asset freezes and travel bans on 32 Iranian officials, including members of Iran's judiciary, who have committed rights abuses. In June the United States extended individuals sanctions against additional members of the Revolutionary Guards, the Basij militia, and Iran's security forces involved in rights violations. Later that month the US sanctioned companies with ties to the Revolutionary Guards and military.

Iranian and Turkish cross-border military operations against Kurdish rebels in Iraqi Kurdistan, which began in mid-June, killed at least 10, injured dozens, and displaced hundreds of civilians.

IRAQ

Human rights conditions in Iraq remained extremely poor, especially for journalists, detainees, and opposition activists. In part inspired by peaceful uprisings elsewhere in the region, thousands of Iraqis demonstrated in the streets to demand better services and an end to corruption. Security forces and gangs responded with violence and threats.

Reports continued of torture of detainees unlawfully held outside the custody of the Justice Ministry. In late June or early July United States forces handed over the last of the 192 detainees in Iraq who were still under US control at the end of 2010, including some former members of Saddam Hussein's government. Attacks by armed groups killed hundreds of civilians as well as police. The US continued to withdraw troops as part of a 2008 agreement that calls for a complete US withdrawal by the end of 2011.

Freedom of Assembly

After thousands took to the streets in February to protest widespread corruption and demand greater civil and political rights, federal Iraqi authorities and Kurdistan Regional Government (KRG) authorities both responded with violence.

On February 21, Iraqi police stood by as dozens of assailants, some wielding knives and clubs, stabbed and beat at least 20 protesters intending to camp in Tahrir Square in Baghdad, the capital. During nationwide demonstrations on February 25, security forces killed at least 12 protesters across the country and injured more than 100. Baghdad security forces beat unarmed journalists and protesters that day, smashing cameras and confiscating memory cards.

Anti-government protests started in Kurdistan on February 17. At this writing security forces had killed at least 10 protesters and bystanders and injured more than 250.On March 6, masked assailants attacked demonstrators in Sara Square—the center of daily protests in Sulaimaniya—and set the demonstrators' tents on fire, but failed to evict the demonstrators from the site. On April 18, security forces seized control of Sara Square to prevent further demonstrations. On April 27 the KRG released a 19-page report that determined that both security forces and protesters were responsible for violence, and that security forces "were not prepared to control the situation."

On June 10 in Baghdad government-backed thugs armed with wooden planks, knives, iron pipes, and other weapons beat and stabbed peaceful protesters and sexually molested female demonstrators as security forces stood by and watched, sometimes laughing at the victims.

Authorities also used legal means to curtail protests. On April 13, Iraqi officials issued new regulations barring street protests and allowing them only at three soccer (football) stadiums, although they have not enforced the regulations. In May the Council of Ministers approved a "Law on the Freedom of Expression of Opinion, Assembly, and Peaceful Demonstration" that authorizes officials to restrict freedom of assembly to protect "the public interest" and in the interest of "general order or public morals." At this writing the law still awaited parliamentary approval.

Freedom of Expression

In 2011 Iraq remained one of the most dangerous countries in the world to work as a journalist. Armed groups and unknown assailants killed at least five journalists and one media worker, according to the New York-based Committee to Protect Journalists. Journalists also contended with emboldened Iraqi and KRG security forces.

On February 20, dozens of masked men attacked the private Nalia Radio and Television (NRT) station in Sulaimaniya. They shot up broadcasting equipment and wounded one guard. They then doused the premises with gasoline and set fire to the building, according to the station's staff. NRT had begun its inaugural broadcasts of footage of the protests only two days before the attack.

On February 23 security forces in Baghdad raided the office of the Journalistic Freedoms Observatory, a press freedom group. Their destructive search lasted more than an hour and they seized computers, external hard drives, cameras, cell phones, computer disks, and documents as well as flak jackets and helmets marked "Press."

More than 20 journalists covering protests in Kurdistan said that security forces and their proxies routinely threatened journalists, subjected them to arbitrary arrest, beatings, and harassment, and confiscated or destroyed their equipment. After quashing the daily protests in Sulaimaniya in April, KRG officials and security forces expanded their suppression of journalists through libel suits, beatings, detentions, and death threats. The threat of attacks and arrests sent some journalists into hiding.

On September 8 an unknown assailant shot to death Hadi al-Mahdi, a popular radio journalist often critical of government corruption and social inequality, at his Baghdad home. The Ministry of Interior said it would investigate his death, but at this writing no one had been charged. Immediately prior to his death al-Mahdi received several phone and text message threats not to return to Tahrir Square. Earlier, after attending the February 25 "Day of Anger" mass demonstration in Baghdad, security forces arrested, blindfolded, and severely beat him along with three other journalists during their subsequent interrogation.

In April Iraq's parliament approved a Journalists' Protection Law, intended to protect media workers and compensate them for injuries sustained while working. Critics say the law does not do enough to ensure proper protections for journalists.

In May the Council of Ministers approved a draft of the "Law on Freedom of Expression of Opinion, Assembly, and Peaceful Demonstration," which contains provisions that would criminalize speech, with penalties of up to 10 years in prison. Under article 13, anyone who "attacks a belief of any religious sect or shows contempt for its rites", or publicly insults a "symbol, or person who is held sacred, exalted, or venerated by a religious sect" would face up to one year in jail and fines of up to 10 million Iraqi dinars (US$8,600). The law provides no guidance about what might constitute an unlawful insult.

Secret Prisons and Torture

In February Human Rights Watch uncovered, within the Camp Justice military base in Baghdad, a secret detention facility controlled by elite security forces who report to the military office of Prime Minister Nuri al-Maliki. Beginning on

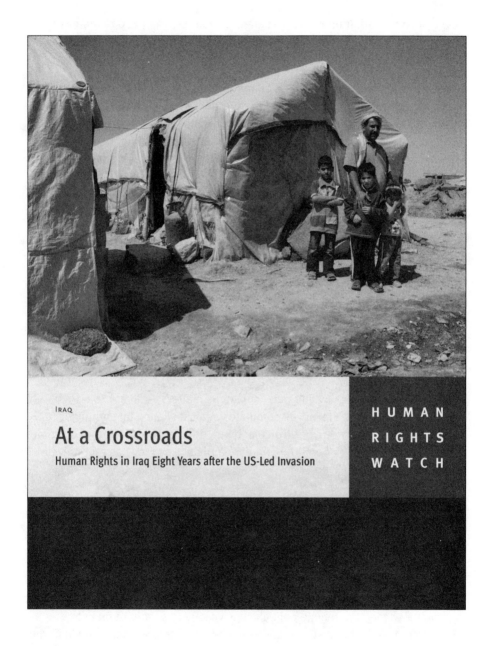

IRAQ

At a Crossroads

Human Rights in Iraq Eight Years after the US-Led Invasion

HUMAN
RIGHTS
WATCH

November 23, 2010, Iraqi authorities transferred more than 280 detainees to the facility, which was controlled by the Army's 56th Brigade and the Counter-Terrorism Service.

The same elite divisions controlled Camp Honor, a separate facility in Baghdad where detainees were tortured with impunity. More than a dozen former Camp Honor detainees told Human Rights Watch how detainees were held incommunicado and in inhumane conditions, many for months at a time. Detainees said interrogators beat them; hung them upside down for hours at a time; administered electric shocks to various body parts, including the genitals; and repeatedly put plastic bags over their heads until they passed out from asphyxiation. On March 14 the Justice Ministry announced that it would close Camp Honor after a parliamentary investigative committee found evidence of torture during a spot inspection of the facility. Human Rights Watch has since received credible information that elite forces may still hold and interrogate detainees at Camp Honor.

At this writing the authorities had not prosecuted any officials responsible for torture at Camp Honor.

Women's and Girls' Rights and Gender-Based Violence

Iraq adjudicates family law and personal status matters pursuant to a 1959 Personal Status Code. The law discriminates against women by granting men privileged status in matters of divorce and inheritance. The law further discriminates against women by permitting Iraqi men to have as many as four polygamous marriages.

On October 6 Iraq's parliament passed legislation to lift Iraq's reservation to article 9 of the Convention on the Elimination of All Forms of Discrimination against Women. Article 9 grants women equal rights with men to acquire, change, or retain their nationality and pass on their nationality to their children.

Violence against women and girls continued to be a serious problem across Iraq. Women's rights activists said they remained at risk of attack from extremists, who also targeted female politicians, civil servants, and journalists. "Honor" crimes and domestic abuse remained a threat to women and girls, who were also vulnerable to trafficking for sexual exploitation and forced prostitution due to insecurity, displacement, financial hardship, social disintegration, and the dissolution of rule of law and state authority.

Female genital mutilation (FGM) is practiced mainly in Kurdish areas of northern Iraq and several official and non-governmental studies estimate that the prevalence of FGM among girls and women in Kurdistan is at least 40 percent. On June 21 Kurdistan's parliament passed the Family Violence Bill, which includes several provisions criminalizing the practice, as well as forced and child marriages, and verbal, physical, and psychological abuse of girls and women.

Attacks on Civilians

Attacks by armed groups killed hundreds of civilians and security forces. Assailants targeted provincial councils and government officials, checkpoints, markets, and mosques. In one of the worst attacks, a string of over 40 coordinated assaults in 17 cities on August 15 killed more than 90 people, including many unarmed civilians and members of the security forces.

The ongoing attacks, along with injuries from abandoned landmines and cluster munitions, have created a disproportionately high number of persons with physical and mental disabilities, many of whom have not received rehabilitation or support for re-integration into their communities. On August 17 Iraq's parliament held a second reading of a resolution to ratify the Convention on the Rights of Persons with Disabilities (CRPD). Two draft disability laws under consideration would create a national body to oversee disability issues. But the proposed laws have several deficiencies including language that is incompatible with the CRPD.

Key International Actors

The European Court of Human Rights issued two landmark judgments on July 7, 2011, which ruled that the United Kingdom's human rights obligations apply to British acts in Iraq, and that the UK had violated the European Convention on Human Rights by failing to adequately investigate the killings of five Iraqis by its forces there, and that its internment of Iraqis had amounted to arbitrary detention.

On September 8 a three-year UK inquiry into the death of Baha Mousa, a hotel receptionist who died in British custody following serious abuse by British soldiers, condemned inadequate detention procedures, leadership failures, poor training, a loss of discipline, and a lack of "moral courage" among soldiers to report abuse. Only one British soldier was convicted of any crime in connection with this killing, and he was sentenced to only one year in prison.

In September Wikileaks released thousands of classified cables from the US embassy in Baghdad, one of which called into question the results of a US military investigation of a 2006 incident in which US soldiers may have handcuffed and executed at least 10 Iraqi civilians.

In July the United Nations Security Council voted to extend the mandate of the UN Assistance Mission for Iraq (UNAMI) for another year. UNAMI's 2010 Report on Human Rights in Iraq, released in August 2011, found that "significant problems remain with law enforcement and the administration of justice, especially in relation to the provision and respect for due process and fair trial rights," and that "incidents of abuse and torture remain widely reported."

ISRAEL/OCCUPIED PALESTINIAN TERRITORIES

Serious human rights violations continued in 2011 in the Occupied Palestinian Territories (OPT). Israeli soldiers used unnecessary lethal force against demonstrators in the Israeli-occupied Golan Heights and across the border in Lebanon. Israeli military attacks in Gaza and policing operations in the West Bank resulted in the deaths of at least 37 civilians.

Israel continued to block exports from, and many imports to, the Gaza Strip, hindering the rebuilding of Gaza's devastated economy. In the West Bank, including East Jerusalem, Israel demolished a record number of Palestinian homes under discriminatory practices, imposed severe restrictions on Palestinian freedom of movement, continued to build unlawful settlements, and arbitrarily detained peaceful protesters, including children.

Palestinian armed groups in Gaza launched hundreds of rocket attacks at Israeli population centers in 2011, killing two civilians and seriously injuring at least nine others; indiscriminate mortar attacks seriously injured at least four civilians in Israel. Another attack fatally injured an Israeli youth in a school bus. Egyptian attackers whom Israel claimed operated in coordination with armed groups in Gaza crossed the Egyptian border and killed six Israeli civilians.

Hamas authorities carried out three judicial executions in 2011 after unfair military trials, and allegedly tortured scores of detainees, some of whom died in custody.

The Palestinian Authority's (PA) security services arbitrarily detained hundreds of Hamas supporters as well as politically unaffiliated protesters who supported the pro-democracy Arab Spring movements and reconciliation between Hamas and Fatah. The PA also arrested journalists who were critical of the authorities. Credible allegations of torture by the PA's security services continued.

Gaza Strip

Israel

Israel Defense Forces (IDF) conducted attacks on Gaza, including against smuggling tunnels and in response to rocket attacks, that killed 32 Palestinian civilians as of October, the Israeli rights group B'Tselem reported. The cases included civilians killed during aerial and artillery attacks, as well as IDF shootings of Palestinian civilians in the "no-go" zone along Gaza's northern and eastern borders. In April one Israeli aerial attack apparently targeted a Palestinian ambulance, while another aerial attack killed a mother and daughter in an area where no members of armed groups were present. In August an Israeli aerial attack on a sports club that witnesses said was not used for military purposes killed two civilians.

There were no further convictions for laws of war violations during "Operation Cast Lead," which ended in January 2009, despite individual IDF soldiers having allegedly intentionally killed civilians and the widespread, wanton destruction of civilian property. Israel previously convicted only three soldiers for crimes during the conflict, and only one received a prison sentence, for stealing a credit card. Hamas has prosecuted no one for indiscriminate attacks on Israel.

Blockade

Israel's punitive closure of the Gaza Strip, tightened after Hamas's takeover of Gaza in June 2007, continued to have severe humanitarian and economic consequences for the civilian population.

Gaza's economy grew rapidly, but the World Bank said the growth depended on international assistance. The economy had not returned to pre-closure levels; daily wages, for instance, had declined 23 percent since 2007. Israel's near-total restrictions on exports from Gaza hindered economic recovery. Due to low per capita income, 51 percent of the population was unable to buy sufficient food, according to UN aid agencies.

OCCUPIED PALESTINIAN TERRITORIES

No News is Good News

Abuses against Journalists by Palestinian Security Forces

HUMAN RIGHTS WATCH

Israel allowed imports to Gaza that amounted to around 40 percent of pre-closure levels, the UN reported. Israel continued to bar construction materials, like cement, which it said had "dual use" civilian and military applications. Israel allowed shipments of construction materials for projects operated by international organizations, but as of September Gaza still had an estimated shortage of some 250 schools and 100,000 homes.

A report requested by the UN secretary-general found in September 2011 that Israeli commandos used excessive force in the killing of nine participants in the 2009 "Gaza Flotilla." The report found that Israel's naval blockade of Gaza was lawful, but did not address the human rights implications of Israel's broader closure policy. Israeli officials had justified the closure in part as a means to pressure Hamas to release soldier Gilad Shalit, who was captured in 2006 and was released in October 2011 (see below).

Egypt shared responsibility for the closure of Gaza by restricting the movement of goods and people at the Rafah crossing on Gaza's southern border. In late May Egypt announced it would allow up to 400 Gaza residents to enter Egypt per day. By August more than 920 people per day crossed Rafah in both directions, compared to 1,320 people per day when the crossing was last fully operational in 2006. However, Egyptian border authorities continued to require Palestinians to present official identification cards, which cannot be issued without Israeli approval, even for Gaza residents. Egypt did not permit regular imports or exports through Rafah; in 2005 up to 8,600 truckloads of goods per month entered Gaza from Egypt.

"No-Go" Zone

Israeli forces regularly shot at Gaza residents up to 1.5 kilometers from the armistice line between Gaza and Israel, creating a "no-go" zone that comprises 35 percent of Gaza's agricultural land, according to the UN. The Israeli navy shot at and confiscated Palestinian fishing boats that sailed more than two nautical miles from the coast, prohibiting access to some 85 percent of Gaza's maritime area. In August Israel notified Gaza fishermen that they could retrieve dozens of confiscated boats at the Kerem Shalom land crossing, but delivered the boats without their equipment and demanded payment for transporting them; the fishermen refused.

Hamas

Palestinian armed groups launched 316 rockets at Israeli population centers in 2011, as of November 8, up from 236 rockets in all of 2010. In April Hamas's armed wing claimed responsibility for an attack, which Israel said involved an antitank missile, on an Israeli school bus, fatally injuring a 16-year-old boy. In August armed groups launched scores of rocket attacks that seriously injured at least five people and killed a man in Beer Sheva. An Ashkelon man was killed by shrapnel from a rocket in October.

The Hamas Interior Ministry carried out three judicial death sentences. Hamas executed, by hanging, a father and son convicted of murder and collaboration with Israel. Abd al-Karim Shrair was executed by firing squad, following an unfair military court trial for collaboration that did not address evidence that security forces had tortured him.

The internal security service of the Interior Ministry and Hamas police in Gaza allegedly tortured 102 people as of September, according to complaints received by the Independent Commission for Human Rights (ICHR), a Palestinian rights body. In April Hamas authorities arrested 'Adel Razeq, 52, without a warrant, denied his family access to him in detention, and allegedly tortured him to death. The ICHR received 163 complaints of arbitrary arrest by Hamas security forces.

On October 18 Hamas released Israeli soldier Gilad Shalit in exchange for 477 Palestinian prisoners, many of whom had been convicted for attacks on Israeli civilians. Hamas had subjected Shalit to cruel and inhuman treatment that may amount to torture by having refused to allow him to communicate with his family or receive visits by the International Committee of the Red Cross.

Hamas police and internal security forces assaulted, arbitrarily detained, and allegedly tortured civil society activists and peaceful protesters who had sought to demonstrate in solidarity with Egyptian and Syrian protesters and had called for an end to the political split between Hamas and its rival, Fatah.

Hamas's Interior Ministry closed several NGOs in Gaza, including the Sharek Youth Forum. In August the Education Ministry banned eight secondary-school students from traveling to the United States, where they had won scholarships. Hamas banned three newspapers printed in the West Bank from distribution in Gaza. Police harassed people for so-called morality offenses, including male hairdressers who cut women's hair, and confiscated "immoral" novels.

West Bank

Palestinian Authority

Complaints of torture committed by West Bank PA security services decreased slightly compared to the same period last year, with the ICHR receiving 91 complaints as of September. PA courts have not found any security officers responsible for torture, arbitrary detention, or prior cases of unlawful deaths in custody. The ICHR received 479 complaints of arbitrary arrests by PA security forces. In a positive development, PA military courts implemented a January decision to stop exercising jurisdiction over civilians.

The PA's security services, and men in civilian clothes whom witnesses identified as security employees, arbitrarily prevented or violently dispersed numerous nonviolent protests during the year and assaulted and arbitrarily detained journalists covering the incidents. PA security officials also arbitrarily arrested and detained, confiscated equipment from, and physically abused journalists perceived to be critical of the PA or supportive of Hamas. In several cases, security officials ignored court orders to release detained journalists.

Palestinian civilians injured 29 settlers in the West Bank and killed seven as of November, the UN reported. In September Israeli police concluded that a father and son from the settlement of Kiryat Arba died in a car crash because Palestinians had thrown rocks at their car. In August an Israeli military court convicted a Palestinian man for killing five members of the Fogel family in the Itamar settlement in March; a second man plead guilty to murder charges in the case in October.

Israel

Israeli forces in the West Bank killed at least five Palestinian civilians as of October. After the end of an arrest operation, soldiers fatally shot two men while they were standing with a group of demonstrators who were throwing stones, B'Tselem reported. In another case, a soldier shot and killed an unarmed resident of Qusra who was protesting against settler incursions on village lands. Soldiers shot and killed an unarmed 66-year-old man in his bed after mistakenly entering his home in search of a suspected Hamas member, according to Palestinian rights groups and international media reports.

The Israeli government generally took no action against Israeli settlers who destroyed or damaged mosques, homes, olive trees, cars, and other Palestinian property, or physically assaulted Palestinians. In January a settler shot and killed a 15-year-old boy near the Palestinian village of Safa; in September a settler killed an 8-year-old Palestinian boy in a hit-and-run incident near Hebron. As of October 31 the UN reported 377 attacks by settlers that damaged Palestinian property, including almost 10,000 olive trees, and injured 167 Palestinians. On average Israeli authorities indict only nine percent of the settlers whom police investigate for attacking Palestinians or damaging Palestinian property, according to the Israeli rights group Yesh Din.

Settlement Building, Discriminatory Home Demolitions, and Evacuations

As of November 1, Israeli authorities had demolished 467 Palestinian homes and other buildings in the West Bank (including East Jerusalem), displacing 869 people, a rate that means Israel will have forcibly displaced more West Bank Palestinians in 2011 than during any year since the UN started collecting cumulative figures in 2006.

Israel usually carries out demolitions on the grounds that the structures were built without permits, but in practice such permits are almost impossible for Palestinians to obtain in Israeli-controlled areas, whereas a separate planning process available only to settlers grants new construction permits much more readily.

The Israeli NGO Peace Now reported that from October 2010, when Israel ended its temporary settlement "building freeze," to July 2011 construction began on 2,598 new settlement homes, and another 2,149 new homes were completed.

Settlers also continued to take over Palestinian homes in East Jerusalem, based in part on laws that recognize Jewish ownership claims there from before 1948 but bar Palestinian ownership claims from that period in West Jerusalem.

Freedom of Movement

Israel maintained onerous restrictions on the movement of Palestinians in the West Bank, especially in "Area C," which is under exclusive Israeli control. It maintained more than 520 checkpoints and other closure obstacles as of July.

Israel continued construction of the wall or separation barrier around East Jerusalem. Some 85 percent of the barrier's route falls within the West Bank, placing many settlements on the "Israeli" side of the barrier. The barrier led to the confiscation of private land and separated many Palestinian farmers and pastoralists from their lands.

Arbitrary Detention and Detention of Children

Israeli military justice authorities arbitrarily detained Palestinians who advocated non-violent protest against Israeli settlements and the route of the separation barrier. In January a military appeals court increased the prison sentence of Abdallah Abu Rahme, from the village of Bil'in, to 16 months in prison on charges of inciting violence and organizing illegal demonstrations, largely on the basis of coerced statements of children.

In a positive development, in September the Israeli military issued an order raising the age of majority for Palestinians to 18 years; previously 16 and 17-year-olds had been treated as adults under the security regime. Human rights groups reported, however, that Israeli authorities continued to sentence Palestinians according to their age at the time of sentencing even if they were children at the time of the offense, and documented cases in which Israeli authorities arrested children in their homes at night, at gunpoint, questioned them without a family member or a lawyer, and coerced them to sign confessions in Hebrew, which they did not understand.

As of September 31 Israel detained 164 Palestinian children under 18-years-old, and also held 272 Palestinians in administrative detention without charge; Israel released at least 9 administrative detainees, but no children, in the prisoner exchange.

Israel

In May and June Israeli forces used lethal force against demonstrators, reportedly killing 35, across the northern border in Lebanon and in the Israeli-occupied Golan Heights. Protesters threw rocks over a high border fence in Lebanon, and some protesters entered the Israeli-occupied Golan, but witnesses said the demonstrators posed no threat to the soldiers' lives.

The Israeli parliament passed legislation penalizing calls for boycotts of Israeli settlements. Another new law allows "admissions committees" to screen applicants who wish to move to small communities on the basis of vague "suitability" criteria; the law circumvents a Supreme Court prohibition on housing discrimination against Palestinian citizens of Israel. A third new law penalizes cultural, academic, or other institutions or municipalities that commemorate the *Nakba* (catastrophe), the Palestinian term for the dispossession and flight of Palestinians around Israel's founding.

Bedouin citizens of Israel suffered discriminatory home demolitions. The Israel Land Administration repeatedly demolished dwellings in the Bedouin village of Al-Araqib, and confiscated the personal belongings of residents who attempted to hide in a cemetery. At the time residents were contesting in court the state's claims that they had never owned lands in the area. Some 90,000 Bedouin live in "unrecognized" villages with no basic services and at risk of demolitions. In September the Israeli government adopted a plan that reportedly recommended the transfer of up to 30,000 Bedouin from the "unrecognized" villages to other townships. Israel has retroactively legalized large, Jewish-owned, private farms in the area.

There are an estimated 200,000 migrant workers in Israel; employers' withholding of wages and underpayment is reportedly common. Most workers are

indebted to recruiting agencies, beholden to a single employer for their livelihood, and are unable to transfer their employment without their employer's
consent. Government policies restrict migrant workers from forming families,
deporting migrant workers and their children born in Israel.

Israel continued to deny asylum seekers who entered the country irregularly
from Egypt the right to a fair asylum process. According to affidavits by soldiers
and asylum seekers filed to Israel's Supreme Court in April and August, Israeli
forces continued to forcibly return people to Egypt, which is known to return
refugees to countries where they could face persecution and torture. Israeli
NGOs said the government failed to ensure access to health screening in detention or upon release for border-crossers, many of whom alleged they were tortured and raped by traffickers in Egypt's Sinai peninsula.

Key International Actors

Israel has been the largest overall recipient of foreign aid from the US since
World War II, receiving US$3 billion in military aid in 2011. In February the US
vetoed a United Nations Security Council resolution that sought to reaffirm that
Israeli settlements are illegal under international law, even though the US and
virtually every other government has found such illegality.

The US continued to train and equip Palestinian security forces and provided
$200 million to the PA in budgetary support. In response to the PA's bid for
statehood at the UN in September, as of October the US Congress was blocking
$150 million in funding for PA security assistance and $192 million in humanitarian assistance to the West Bank and Gaza. The EU allocated €295 million
($405 million) to the PA for 2011, including for projects in Gaza, as well as €125
million ($172million) to the UN Relief and Works Agency for Palestine Refugees
in the Near East (UNRWA).

ISRAEL/OCCUPIED PALESTINIAN TERRITORIES

Separate and Unequal

Israel's Discriminatory Treatment of Palestinians
in the Occupied Palestinian Territories

HUMAN
RIGHTS
WATCH

JORDAN

International observers considered voting in the November 2010 parliamentary elections a "clear improvement" over the 2007 elections, which were widely characterized as fraudulent. The elections were held under an amended voting system that continues to under-represent Jordanians of Palestinian origin.

On February 1, after demonstrators inspired by events in Tunisia and Egypt took to the streets in January to protest the slow pace of political reform and continued corruption, King Abdullah II replaced the prime minister after only three months in office, and again in October.

The king ordered Marouf al-Bakhit, the newly appointed prime minister in February, to implement political and economic reforms as protests spread. Reform initiatives included convening a national dialogue committee in March, and appointing a royal committee to revise the constitution in April. The committees proposed modest reforms to the electoral system, and significant reforms to the constitution, though they left out guarantees for gender equality. Parliament rejected proposed constitutional restrictions on the military-dominated State Security Court's powers to try civilians.

The General Intelligence Department affirmed in May that its agents were no longer present on university campuses, in response to the king's directives.

A committee established in April to restore nationality to Jordanians of Palestinian origin, from whom officials had previously arbitrarily withdrawn nationality, benefited only around 50 persons according to the National Center for Human Rights.

Enforcement of legal protections for approximately 70,000 migrant domestic workers in the country—including limits to working hours, a weekly day off, and criminalization of traffickers—remains negligible.

Freedom of Expression

Jordan criminalizes speech critical of the king, government officials and institutions, Islam, and speech deemed insulting to other persons. In 2010 a revision of the penal code increased penalties for some speech offenses, and the 2010 Law on Information System Crimes extended these provisions to online expression. Following the protest resignation in June of government spokesperson Taher 'Udwan the government withdrew controversial proposed amendments to the Press and Publications Law, which would have allowed for the banning of local and foreign publications that violate the law. In September the government amended a draft anti-corruption commission law, replacing a six-month prison sentence on anyone who accused others of corruption without justification with a hefty fine.

In 2011 the legal aid unit of the Amman-based Center for Defending Freedom of Journalists assisted journalists with 70 ongoing criminal cases for speech in violation of articles 5 and 7 of the Press and Publications Law requiring journalists to be objective.

Attacks against journalists increased in 2011. In February unknown assailants attacked Basil al-'Ukur, and threatened Samir al-Hiyari, executives at online Ammonnews. In March Sami Zubaidi of the online Ammanpost said a prominent member of parliament threatened him with physical harm. In April relatives of Khalid al-Sarayira, retired armed forces chief of staff, ransacked the office of journalist Jihad Abu Baidar and threatened to kill him. Yahya Sa'ud, a member of parliament, led protesters who ransacked the Amman bureau of Agence France Presse on June 15, demanding that bureau chief Randa Habib be tried in the State Security Court over what Sa'ud claimed were false reports of attacks on the king's convoy. On July 15, police attacked 19 journalists covering a demonstration in downtown Amman, the capital. Despite recommendations for a police investigation to prosecute officers involved, this did not occur.

Freedom of Assembly

In March an amended Public Gatherings Law, which no longer required government permission to hold public meetings or demonstrations, took effect.

Since January hundreds of protests demanding political and economic reforms have taken place. Almost all remained peaceful. In February pro-government protestors in downtown Amman attacked peaceful opposition demonstrators with clubs, unhindered by nearby police. There was no investigation into police conduct. On March 25, pro-government protestors approached Amman's Interior Circle, a busy roundabout opposition protesters had occupied, and attacked the protesters. Police at one point formed a protective cordon around the opposition demonstrators, but also allowed pro-government protesters free access to the area and later joined pro-government protesters in beating the opposition demonstrators, one of whom died as a result. No investigation of police conduct has taken place.

On April 15 several hundred persons demonstrated in Zarqa for the application of Islamic law and the release of prisoners. In an ensuing brawl with government supporters, in which police participated, numerous police and demonstrators were injured. The police arrested around 100 demonstrators and charged 150 others, though no government supporters or police, with "carrying out terrorist acts," "assault," "rioting," and "unlawful gathering." No evidence of terrorist acts beyond the brawl was presented at the State Security Court.

On July 15, police attacked opposition protesters in Amman, including journalists wearing distinctive media vests.

Labor Rights

Hundreds of migrant workers working in the Qualified Industrial Zones, agriculture, and domestic work complained about labor violations, including unpaid salaries, confiscation of passports, and forced labor. In July the government mandated that migrant domestic workers' salaries be paid directly into verifiable bank accounts and in September proposed lifting restrictions on the freedom of movement of migrant domestic workers. A Ministry of Labor committee charged with solving labor disputes failed consistently to secure unpaid salaries of domestic workers, or to adequately protect workers from working long hours and from remaining trapped in abusive households. Jordan has no shelter for domestic workers who escape abusive conditions.

NGOs repeatedly presented domestic workers who had suffered a range of abuses to investigators who almost never classified them as trafficking victims, sometimes even detaining them for "escaping" employers.

Domestic Plight

How Jordanian Law, Officials, Employers, and Recruiters
Fail Abused Migrant Domestic Workers

HUMAN
RIGHTS
WATCH

Tamkeen

Tamkeen Center for Legal aid and Human Rights

Women's and Girls' Rights

In September the Royal Committee on Constitutional Review proposed amendments to Jordan's constitution, including an amendment (to article 6) which prohibits discrimination based on race, language, or religion. The Royal Committee promised women's rights activists that it would include the term "gender" in the new revised article. The final draft handed to King 'Abdallah did not include this.

Article 9 of Jordan's nationality law denies women married to foreign-born spouses to pass on their nationality to their husbands and children. Women's rights activists called on the government to amend the law in accordance with its obligations to the Convention on the Elimination of All Forms of Discrimination Against Women.

There were four reported "honor" crimes in 2011. In June a court sentenced a father who murdered his daughter to 15 years in prison, later reduced to 10 years because her husband dropped private claims against him. A February 2011 study by the National Council for Family Affairs concluded that perpetrators in 50 "honor" crimes between 2000 and 2011 received reduced sentences because of dropped private claims.

Jordan's personal status code remains discriminatory despite a 2010 amendment. A Muslim woman is forbidden from marrying a non-Muslim. A non-Muslim mother forfeits her custodial rights after the child reaches seven-years-old.

Torture, Arbitrary Detention, and Administrative Detention

Perpetrators of torture enjoy near-total impunity. The redress process begins with a deficient complaint mechanism, continues with lackluster investigations and prosecutions, and ends in police court, where two of three judges are police-appointed police officers.

In April officers of a special unit arrested scores of suspected participants in a demonstration in the town of Zarqa, northeast of Amman, and beat them for hours before delivering them to Amman's criminal investigation unit. No investigation into the police abuse took place. At the demonstrators' trial , police witnesses testified that they "did not remember" whether a demonstrator complained about ill-treatment, although at least one had been brought to custody from a hospital for injuries sustained during police beatings, defense lawyers claimed. The Public Security Directorate did not respond to a request submitted in August under the Law on the Right to Freedom of Information for the number of deaths in custody, their reasons, and results of any investigations.

Interior Minister Mazin al-Sakit in September recommended changes in the Crime Prevention Law, under which provincial governors can detain people administratively. The suggested changes, if approved by the Council of Ministers and parliament, would restrict administrative detention to a non-renewable 15-day period, require the detainee's release or referral to the judiciary thereafter, and prohibit use of administrative detention for "protective custody" of women whose family members threaten them with violence.

Key International Actors

Saudi Arabia was Jordan's largest donor in 2011, announcing a grant of US$400 million in January, and a further $1 billion in July. Saudi Arabia also supported the initiative by the Gulf Cooperation Council to invite Jordan and Morocco to join, in what analysts described as an exchange of Gulf financial support for Jordanian military expertise and manpower.

The United States has a memorandum of understanding, going into effect in 2010, to provide Jordan with a minimum of $360 million in economic assistance, and $300 million in foreign military financing annually. In October 2010 the US Millennium Challenge Corporation committed $275 million to Jordan over the coming five years.

The European Union in October 2010 upgraded its relations with Jordan to "advanced status," indicating closer ties in all areas, as well as more funding. The EU will provide Jordan with a €223 million ($310 million) aid package over three years until 2013. The EU was developing a three-year plan designed to provide more support for human rights reform.

KUWAIT

Hundreds of stateless people in Kuwait, known as Bidun, took to the streets in early 2011 demanding citizenship and other rights. The government violently dispersed the protests, but later promised to restore to the Bidun social benefits, including government-issued documentation and free education and health care. However, Bidun claims to Kuwaiti citizenship remained unresolved.

Kuwaiti authorities continued to restrict free expression, increasing internet surveillance and arresting individuals for criticizing the government.

Migrant workers in Kuwait, who comprise 80 percent of the country's workforce, continued to face exploitation and abuse under the sponsorship system. Although Minister of Labor Mohammad al-'Afasi announced that the government would abolish the sponsorship system in February 2011, the government made no major sponsorship reforms during the year.

In May Kuwait won election to its first term on the United Nations Human Rights Council, stepping in after Syria withdrew its bid.

Bidun

At least 106,000 stateless persons, known as Bidun, live in Kuwait. After an initial registration period for citizenship ended in 1960, authorities shifted Bidun citizenship applications to a series of administrative committees that have avoided resolving their claims.

While maintaining that most Bidun are "illegal residents" who deliberately destroyed evidence of other nationality, the government has not provided individualized review of Bidun citizenship claims. Kuwaiti law bans courts from ruling on citizenship claims.

The Bidun cannot freely leave and return to Kuwait. The government issues them temporary passports at its discretion, mostly valid for only one journey. As "illegal residents," the Bidun cannot legally hold most public and private sector jobs, and Bidun children may not enroll in free government schools. Unregistered Bidun, whose citizenship applications the authorities have either

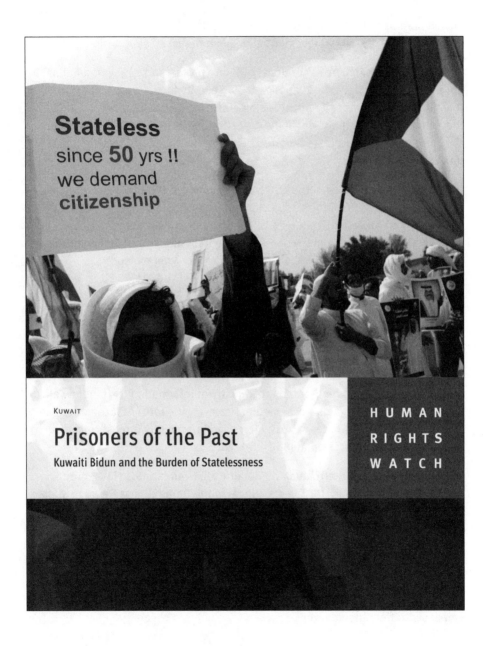

Stateless
since **50** yrs !!
we demand
citizenship

KUWAIT

Prisoners of the Past
Kuwaiti Bidun and the Burden of Statelessness

H U M A N
R I G H T S
W A T C H

closed or refused to register, are even more vulnerable than others, with restrictions on their freedom of movement and constant fear of deportation.

In February and March 2011 hundreds of Bidun protested the government's failure to act on their citizenship applications. Security forces used water cannons, tear gas, smoke bombs, and concussion grenades (sound bombs) to break up the demonstrations; they beat some protestors, and detained dozens. Bidun detained during the protests reported beatings and physical abuse in detention.

In response to the protests, the government promised benefits, including free health care; free education at private schools that primarily serve Bidun children; birth, marriage, and death certificate; and improved access to jobs. Bidun have confirmed receiving many of these benefits, but continue to cite problems accessing employment and increased difficulty receiving passports.

Freedom of Expression and Assembly

While 2011 saw some gains for free expression, authorities increased internet surveillance, and continued to detain and criminally prosecute individuals based on nonviolent political speech, including web commentary.

In early February the emir ordered the Ministry of Information to withdraw all lawsuits it had filed against local media. However, the local Al Jazeera bureau, closed by government order in 2010 after covering security forces' crackdown on a peaceful gathering, remained shuttered.

In June the government arrested and detained for four months Nasser Abul, a 26-year-old Kuwaiti man, for Tweets critical of the Bahraini and Saudi royal families. According to his lawyer, state security officers beat and insulted Abul in detention. Kuwait continued to crack down on public gatherings and demonstrations. In addition to violently dispersing Bidun protests in February and April, authorities repeatedly warned foreign nationals not to participate in public demonstrations and threatened to deport them. In August police officers turned non-Kuwaitis away from protests calling for the expulsion of Syria's ambassador from the country.

Migrant Worker Rights

In June the government voted to adopt the International Labour Organization's Convention on Decent Work for Domestic Workers, which establishes the first global labor standards on domestic work.

The government passed a new private sector labor law in February 2010 that set maximum working hours, required a weekly rest day and annual leave, and set end-of-service bonuses. However, the law excluded migrant domestic workers, who come chiefly from South and Southeast Asia and work and live inside employers' homes in Kuwait. Many domestic workers complain of confinement in the house; long work hours without rest; months or years of unpaid wages; and verbal, physical, and sexual abuse.

A major barrier to redressing labor abuses is the *kafala* (sponsorship) system, which ties a migrant worker's legal residence to a "sponsoring" employer. Migrant workers who have worked for their sponsor less than three years can only transfer with their sponsor's consent (migrant domestic workers always require consent). If a worker leaves their sponsoring employer, including when fleeing abuse, the employer must register the worker as "absconding." This can lead to detention and deportation. In September 2010 the government announced that it would abolish the sponsorship system in February 2011, but made no major sponsorship reforms during the year.

Few perpetrators of abuse are investigated and prosecuted. In November 2010 doctors in Sri Lanka removed 14 nails from the body of V.R. Lechchami, a domestic worker recently returned from Kuwait. The government failed to properly investigate Lechchami's allegations that her employers inserted these objects after she asked for six months of unpaid salary.

Women's Rights

Kuwait's nationality law denies Kuwaiti women married to non-Kuwaiti men the right to pass their nationality on to their children and spouses, a right enjoyed by Kuwaiti men married to foreign spouses. The law also discriminates against women in residency rights, allowing the spouses of Kuwaiti men but not of Kuwaiti women to be in Kuwait without employment and to qualify for citizenship after 10 years of marriage. In June 2011 Kuwaiti women were granted the right to sponsor their foreign husbands and children. However, this privilege is not extended to women who were previously naturalized, if they are widowed or divorced.

In 2005 Kuwaiti women won the right to vote and to run in elections, and in May 2009 voters elected four women to parliament. However, courts have denied women the right to become public prosecutors and judges.

Kuwait adjudicates family law and personal status matters for Sunni and Shia Muslims pursuant to interpretations of Islamic law, with no option to seek adjudication pursuant to a civil code. The law in particular discriminates against women in matters of divorce, inheritance, and child custody, granting men privileged status in these matters.

Kuwait has no laws prohibiting domestic violence, sexual harassment, or marital rape.

Sexual Orientation and Gender Identity

In 2007 Kuwait passed an amendment to article 198 of the penal code, which criminalized "imitating the appearance of the opposite sex," imposing arbitrary restrictions upon individuals' rights to privacy and free expression.

Police have since arrested scores of transgender women (persons designated male at birth but who identify and present themselves as female) under this law. Human Rights Watch has documented multiple arrests of 33 transgender women, many of whom have reported ill-treatment in detention, torture, sexual harassment, and assault. Victims say they rarely report police abuse due to fear of retaliation and police threats of rearrest.

Key International Actors

The United States, in its 2010 State Department Trafficking in Persons report, classified Kuwait as Tier 3—among the most problematic countries—for the fifth year in a row. The report cited Kuwait's failure to enact comprehensive anti-trafficking legislation, provide a large-capacity shelter for trafficking victims, and pass a law on domestic work.

LEBANON

2011 was mostly a year of political paralysis for Lebanon. The country had no government for the first six months, and while political life resumed in July following the formation of a new government, there was no progress on draft laws to prevent torture, improve the treatment of migrant domestic workers, and protect women from domestic violence.

Following multiple riots by inmates demanding better conditions, parliament approved in September the building of additional prisons to reduce overcrowding, but failed to tackle the underlying causes of lengthy pre-trial detention. Activists and artists who usually operate freely faced increased harassment for criticizing the army and certain high-ranking officials.

Torture, Ill-Treatment, and Prison Conditions

Despite repeated pledges by the Lebanese government to prevent torture, accountability for acts of torture remains elusive. A number of detainees, especially suspected spies for Israel and armed Jihadists, told Human Rights Watch that their interrogators tortured them in detention facilities, including in the Ministry of Defense and the Information Branch of the Internal Security Forces. Lebanon has not yet established a national preventive mechanism to visit and monitor places of detention, as required under the Optional Protocol to the Convention against Torture, which it ratified in 2008.

Conditions in prisons remain poor, with overcrowding and lack of proper medical care a persistent problem. In April the Interior Ministry stated that the country's main prison in Roumieh, a facility built for 1,500 inmates, held 3,700. Of those, 2,757 were awaiting trial. Prisoners rioted on multiple occasions to protest their conditions of detention. On April 6, security forces killed two inmates during a raid to end a four-day riot. In September parliament approved the building of additional prisons to reduce overcrowding in prisons, but failed to tackle the reasons behind lengthy pre-trial detention periods.

According to the Internal Security Forces, around 13 percent of detainees in Lebanese prisons were foreigners who had finished serving their sentences. The group included asylum seekers and refugees who cannot safely return to their countries.

Lebanon maintained its de facto moratorium on executions, but military tribunals passed at least three death sentences in 2011 against men suspected of spying for Israel.

Freedom of Expression

2011 saw increased harassment of activists, bloggers, and artists who criticized the army and certain high-ranking officials. In March the general prosecutor opened a criminal investigation against the Lebanese Center for Human Rights (CLDH) after Amal, a leading political party, filed a complaint against CLDH for alleging that some detainees reported being tortured by members affiliated with Amal. In July Military Intelligence summoned Saadeddine Shatila of the international human rights group Alkarama for his work documenting torture by security forces and detained him for seven hours. At this writing a military investigative judge was investigating Shatila for "publishing information harmful to the reputation of the Lebanese Military." Also in July Lebanese judicial authorities detained musician Zeid Hamdan for several hours based on an accusation that he had defamed the Lebanese president in a song calling on the president to "go home."

Refugees

Since April Lebanon has witnessed an influx of Syrians escaping the crisis in their country. While many subsequently returned to Syria, by mid-October there were 3,149 Syrian refugees registered with the Office of the United Nations High Commissioner for Refugees (UNHCR) and Lebanon's High Relief Commission. Most of the Syrians reside with host families, often in difficult circumstances. Lebanese authorities have provided some material assistance: around 200 refugees are accommodated in two schools in northern

Lebanon. In May security forces detained at least 15 Syrian refugees for cross-ing illegally into Lebanon, but subsequently released them.

The estimated 300,000 Palestinian refugees in Lebanon live in appalling social and economic conditions. 2011 saw no improvement in their access to the labor market, despite a labor law amendment in 2010 that was supposed to ease such access. The main reason was the government's failure to implement the amendment. Lebanese laws and decrees still bar Palestinians from working in at least 25 professions requiring syndicate membership, including law, medi-cine, and engineering. Palestinian refugees are still subject to a discriminatory law introduced in 2001 preventing them from registering property. In September, after repeated delays, authorities completed the reconstruction of a first batch of houses in the Nahr al-Bared refugee camp, which was destroyed in the 2007 battle between Lebanon's army and the armed Fatah al-Islam group. The new houses can accommodate 317 families; at least 8,000 Palestinians from the camp remain displaced.

As of September 30 there were 11,295 non-Palestinian refugees and asylum seekers registered with the UNHCR, more than 80 percent of them from Iraq. Since Lebanon has not ratified the 1951 Refugee Convention, it does not give legal effect to UNHCR's recognition of refugees and generally treats most as ille-gal immigrants subject to arrest; 17 recognized refugees or asylum seekers were in detention solely for illegal entry.

Migrant Workers' Rights

Following a visit to Lebanon in October, the UN special rapporteur on contem-porary forms of slavery urged the government to enact laws to protect the esti-mated 200,000 migrant domestic workers who face exploitation and abuse by employers, including excessive work hours, non-payment of wages, confine-ment in the workplace, and in some cases, physical and sexual abuse.

The minister of labor had proposed a draft law to regulate the work of migrant domestic workers in February but no steps have been taken since. Migrant domestic workers suing their employers for abuse face legal obstacles and risk imprisonment and deportation due to the restrictive visa system.

In August the Lebanese parliament enacted an anti-trafficking law strengthening legal protections for victims of trafficking. It enacted the measure after the United States government downgraded Lebanon to tier 3, the worst possible level, in its 2011 report on trafficking in persons.

Male migrant workers—mostly from Syria and Egypt—working in construction and other manual jobs face hazardous working conditions and are regular targets for robbery and violent attack. State authorities have not made any concerted effort to protect them or bring perpetrators to justice.

Women's and Girls' Rights

In August parliament annulled a provision of the criminal code that had mitigated sentences for so-called honor crimes. However, parliament has yet to consider a bill referred to it by the government in April 2010 that would protect women from domestic violence. The bill requires anyone who witnesses domestic violence to report it, and obliges perpetrators to provide the plaintiff with alternative living arrangements, an allowance, and medical expenses. Both Dar al-Fatwa, the country's highest Sunni Muslim authority, and the Higher Shia Islamic Council, oppose the draft bill, and it is feared that their opposition has paralyzed parliamentary action.

Discriminatory provisions that significantly harm and disadvantage women continue to exist in personal status laws, determined by an individual's religious affiliation, in matters pertaining to marriage, divorce, child custody and guardianship, and inheritance, as well as in nationality laws and penal laws relating to violence in the family. In September the minister of labor introduced a regulation to exempt foreign husbands of Lebanese women and their children from many restrictions placed on foreign workers, but Lebanese women, unlike Lebanese men, still cannot pass their nationality to foreign husbands and children.

Legacy of Past Conflicts and Wars

In March, as part of the UN Human Rights Council's Universal Periodic Review process, the government pledged to establish a national commission to investigate the fate of the Lebanese and other nationals who "disappeared" during and after the 1975 to 1990 Lebanese civil war and to ratify the International Convention for the Protection of all Persons from Enforced Disappearances. However, the government took no steps to fulfill these pledges.

An official joint Syrian-Lebanese committee established in May 2005 to investigate cases of Lebanese who "disappeared" at the hands of Syrian security forces had not published any findings at this writing. In February three Syrian brothers from the Jasem family were kidnapped in Lebanon. Military Intelligence had detained one of them two days earlier for distributing flyers calling for reform in Syria. The Lebanese judicial investigation stalled despite a leaked report showing that the Internal Security Forces had information linking the kidnapping to a Lebanese security official working at the Syrian embassy. In May Shibli Aisamy, an 86-year-old Syrian dissident, was abducted in the mountain town of Aley; at this writing there was no information regarding his whereabouts.

Hariri Tribunal

In June the UN's special tribunal for Lebanon indicted four members of Hezbollah for the killing of former Prime Minister Rafik Hariri in 2005. The four have not been arrested, and the pre-trial chamber is seeking to initiate in absentia proceedings. The government's ongoing support for the tribunal was in doubt as leading parliamentary blocs, including Hezbollah and the Free Patriotic Movement, criticized the tribunal.

Key International Actors

Multiple international and regional actors compete for influence in Lebanon. Regionally, Syria, Iran, and Saudi Arabia maintain a strong influence on Lebanese politics through their local allies.

France, the US, and the European Union provide assistance for a wide range of programs, including military training, seminars on torture prevention, and civil society activities. However, these countries have not fully used their leverage to push Lebanon to adopt concrete measures to improve its human rights record, such as investigating specific allegations of torture or adopting laws that respect the rights of refugees or migrant workers.

The UN deploys over 12,000 peacekeepers at Lebanon's volatile southern border with Israel as part of its 33-year-old peacekeeping force in the country.

LIBYA

2011 was a dramatic year for Libya. A popular uprising and government crackdown led to an armed revolt, NATO intervention, and the death of a dictator who had amassed a deplorable human rights record over 42 years. At this writing Libya's new interim leadership, the National Transitional Council (NTC), was struggling to rein in the many militias and local security forces across the country, secure unguarded weapons, and build a new Libya based on independent institutions and the rule of law. A weak criminal justice system, torture and mistreatment of detainees, and revenge attacks against Gaddafi officials and supporters were pressing concerns, as was the apparent execution of Libyan leader Muammar Gaddafi, his son Muatassim, and dozens of his supporters.

The Uprising

On February 15, 2011, anti-government protests began in Libya's second-largest city, Benghazi, following popular uprisings in neighboring Tunisia and Egypt. The protests were triggered by the arrests of government critics, including a lawyer representing the families of an estimated 1,200 prisoners who had been killed at Tripoli's Abu Salim prison in 1996.

Government forces responded by arresting and attacking peaceful demonstrators in Benghazi and other eastern cities. The government used excessive force when protests spread to the western cities of Tripoli, the capital, Misrata, Zawiya, Zuwara, and Zintan. Human Rights Watch documented the government's lethal use of live fire on peaceful protesters, as well as the arrest and disappearance of hundreds of people suspected of involvement in anti-government demonstrations.

The international response to Gaddafi's crackdown was swift. On February 25 the United Nation Human Rights Council condemned "gross and systematic" violations in Libya and called for the creation of a commission of inquiry. The next day the UN Security Council unanimously passed Resolution 1970, imposing an arms embargo, sanctions on Gaddafi and key members of his family and government, and referring the situation in Libya to the International Criminal Court (ICC). The resolution gave the ICC jurisdiction over war crimes and crimes against humanity committed in Libya from February 15. In June ICC judges authorized arrest warrants for crimes against humanity against three suspects: Muammar Gaddafi, his son Saif al-Islam, and Gaddafi's intelligence chief and brother-in-law Abdullah Sanussi. Muammar Gaddafi died on October 20, but at this writing the other two suspects remained at large.

Faced with violent government repression, the uprising rapidly evolved into an armed conflict, especially after opposition forces seized arms from abandoned government military depots in eastern Libya. On March 17, as Gaddafi's military forces closed in on Benghazi, the key opposition stronghold, the UN Security Council passed Resolution 1973 imposing a no-fly zone over Libya and authorizing the use of "all necessary measures"—with the exception of an occupation force—to protect civilians. This led to NATO's Operation Unified Protector, with a mandate to protect civilians, which prevented Gaddafi forces from retaking Benghazi and eastern Libya. The NATO mission expanded over time beyond its mandate to give air support for anti-Gaddafi forces. France, Qatar, the United Arab Emirates, and possibly other governments provided weapons and training to opposition fighters. Qatar later said it had deployed hundreds of its own forces on the ground.

The Armed Conflict

From February until August, when Tripoli fell, Gaddafi forces arrested thousands, if not tens of thousands, of people across the country, including anti-government protesters, suspected government critics, and people alleged to have provided information to international media and human rights organizations. Many of those arrested were fighters, but many others were civilians, including doctors, journalists, and people caught in areas where fighting took place. The Gaddafi government provided no information regarding how many people it had arrested, where they were being held, or the charges they faced. Detainees who were released from government custody during and after the conflict reported frequent torture, including beatings with wooden sticks and plastic pipes, and the use of electric shock. Some prisoners apparently died from the abuse or the subsequent lack of medical care.

In the fighting, government forces repeatedly launched indiscriminate attacks with mortars and GRAD rockets into civilian-inhabited areas, especially in Misrata and towns of the western mountains. The coastal city of Misrata suffered a two-month siege with near daily attacks that killed scores of civilians and for a while blocked delivery of humanitarian aid. Human Rights Watch confirmed the government's use in Misrata of mortar-fired cluster munitions in residential areas, and the use of "parachute" antivehicle mines fired by GRAD rockets.

The government laid thousands, perhaps tens of thousands, of antipersonnel and antivehicle landmines in various parts of Libya, including in Ajdabiya, Brega, Misrata and the western mountains. Human Rights Watch confirmed the use of five types of landmines in six separate locations, which will likely endanger civilians for many years. The Brazilian T-AB-1 antipersonnel landmine appears to have been the most frequently used mine; its low metal content makes the mine more difficult to detect and clear.

Human Rights Watch documented 10 cases of apparent gang rape and sexual assault of men and women by Gaddafi forces during the conflict, including of detainees in custody. The extent of sexual violence during the conflict remains unknown, due in part to the stigma surrounding rape in Libya and the dangers that survivors may face when they publicize such crimes.

During the conflict, and especially just before the fall of Tripoli, Gaddafi forces executed prisoners in their custody. Members of the Khamis Brigade, a powerful military force run by Gaddafi's son Khamis, appear to have summarily executed at least 45 detainees in a warehouse in Tripoli in August. Thirty-four bodies exhumed from a mass grave near the town of al-Qawalish in western Libya in August seemed to be those of men detained by Gaddafi forces in early June. In September the bodies of 18 detainees, who died by suffocation when detained by Gaddafi forces in June in al-Khoms, were discovered buried in western Libya. In May security forces apparently executed 10 antigovernment protesters in Bani Walid.

At this writing Libya was still dealing with the problem of missing persons from the conflict. The number of missing and dead remains unclear. Mass graves continued to be discovered, but the lack of forensic expertise complicated the identification process.

Rebel forces also committed human rights and humanitarian law violations during the armed conflict. The most significant documented case came in October, when militias from Misrata appeared to have executed 53 Gaddafi supporters in Sirte.

In areas of eastern Libya under NTC control since late February and early March, volunteer security groups arbitrarily arrested dozens of suspected Gaddafi loyalists. This led to serious abuses, including torture. Human Rights Watch documented one apparent death in custody by a local security group in Baida, and heard credible reports of other such deaths. At least 10 former Gaddafi security officials were found dead in Benghazi and Derna in what appear to be revenge killings.

When the Gaddafi government retreated from the east, tens of thousands of sub-Saharan African foreign workers came under threat of violence and arbitrary arrest, forcing thousands to flee. These migrants, along with dark-skinned Libyans, were widely accused without evidence of having fought as mercenaries for Gaddafi, although mercenaries from some countries did come to fight.

In July the commander of the opposition forces, Gen. Abdul Fatah Younes, was killed with two aides in unclear circumstances. Despite promises, the authorities appear not to have conducted an independent investigation.

In the western mountains, rebel forces engaged in revenge attacks in some towns they captured, including looting, arson, and some physical violence.

As NTC forces took control of western Libya in late August, local militias arbitrarily arrested hundreds, if not thousands, more sub-Saharan migrant workers and dark-skinned Libyans from the south, accusing them of being mercenaries. In some cases, the militias subjected these detainees to physical abuse and forced labor in detention. Thousands of African migrants sought shelter in makeshift camps with very poor living conditions and security.

Prison conditions in post-Gaddafi western Libya were sub-standard, with over-crowding, inadequate food and water, and consistent reports of abuse, including beatings and some use of electric shock. The NTC has failed to provide most detainees with prompt judicial reviews, let alone access to a lawyer.

A key problem was the large number of local security forces in Tripoli and other cities and towns, many of which maintained their own makeshift detention facilities. At this writing the NTC was struggling to bring these disparate forces under a unified civilian command.

Revenge attacks against populations deemed to have supported Gaddafi also grew in September and October. In particular, militias from Misrata prevented about 30,000 people from returning to their homes in Tawergha, a town near Misrata, because they accused them of having committed atrocities in Misrata together with Gaddafi forces. Displaced Tawerghans were subject to arbitrary arrests and torture in detention, in some cases leading to death. Members of the Mesheshiya tribe in the western mountains, accused of past loyalty to Gaddafi, also reported harassment and revenge attacks.

On October 20, after weeks of fierce fighting in Sirte, NTC forces captured Muammar Gaddafi and his son Muatassim. Video footage strongly suggests that they were executed in custody. The NTC said it will form a commission of inquiry to examine the deaths.

Three days after Gaddafi's death, Human Rights Watch found 53 bodies of apparent Gaddafi supporters outside the Mahari Hotel in Sirte, where rebel forces from Misrata had been based. Some victims had their hands bound behind their backs; they all seemed to have been shot at that location. The NTC said it will investigate.

Despite promises, the NTC had failed through October to secure some of the military weapons and munitions depots abandoned by Gaddafi forces. These stockpiles included unsecured surface-to-air missiles (SAMs) and vast amounts of explosive weapons. Many of these sites were extensively looted by civilians and armed groups.

The NTC responded positively to some requests from human rights organizations during and after the conflict, for instance by granting Human Rights Watch and other groups unrestricted access to their detention facilities. The NTC publicly promised to respect the laws of war and to cooperate with the ICC, and political leaders repeatedly condemned revenge attacks. On April 28 the NTC officially pledged not to use antipersonnel and antivehicle landmines, and to destroy all mines in its forces' possession. At the same time, NTC leaders said they had limited control over the many local militias and brigades who had committed abuses during and after the fighting.

NATO forces led by the French and British, with significant support from the United States, launched thousands of air strikes on government targets during the conflict, some of which killed civilians. Based on a partial Human Rights Watch investigation, the number of civilian deaths appeared far lower than claimed by the Gaddafi government, but higher than acknowledged by NATO.

In early August Human Rights Watch investigated four sites in Gaddafi government-held territory of western Libya in which about 50 people appear to have died, some of them clearly civilians. It was not possible under the circumstances to determine at any of the sites whether these civilians had died in an unlawful NATO attack. NATO has failed to provide detailed information about these targets and the reasons for the civilian casualties. NATO forces were also accused of failing to rescue African migrants at sea who were fleeing the conflict, on one occasion leading to 63 deaths.

Key International Actors

Many countries played crucial roles in Libya in 2011, especially those who participated in the NATO campaign. Qatar and the United Arab Emirates provided significant support to the anti-Gaddafi opposition, and then to some post-Gaddafi groups. All these countries, and the European Union, have a major stake in seeing that future Libyan governments respect human rights and the rule of law. A UN mission is tasked with assisting Libya's transition, especially democratic elections and transitional justice.

Libya's new leaders face an enormous challenge: to build a country based on the rule of law after 42 years of one-family rule, while preventing revenge attacks, ensuring accountability for abuses by all parties to the conflict, and promoting reconciliation. All these processes will take time and will require outside assistance. But the events of 2011 have given Libyans the opportunity to begin this arduous process.

Morocco and Western Sahara

Responding to the pro-democracy Arab Spring movements and to pro-reform demonstrations in Morocco, King Mohammed VI proposed in June constitutional amendments with substantial human rights guarantees but few significant curbs on the monarch's own powers. The electorate voted the amendments into law in July.

The new constitution recognizes Amazigh, the Berber language, as an official language and prohibits torture, inhuman, and degrading treatment; arbitrary detention; and enforced disappearances. It also requires any person who is arrested to be informed "immediately" of the reason for his arrest, and to enjoy the presumption of innocence and the right to a fair trial. However at this writing the amendments had yet to transform Morocco's decidedly mixed human rights performance.

Freedom of Assembly, Association, and Expression

Inspired by popular protests elsewhere in the region, Moroccans began marching on February 20 to demand sweeping political reforms. The marches—usually spearheaded by the youthful, loosely-organized February 20 Movement for Change and backed by other political and civil society forces, including the powerful Islamist Justice and Spirituality movement—sometimes exceeded 10,000 participants and were staged in several cities simultaneously. The police tolerated some of the protests, but on some occasions attacked and beat protesters severely. Some of the harshest police violence occurred at peaceful protests in Casablanca, Kenitra, and Rabat, the captial, during the weeks prior to the king's much-anticipated speech in June outlining constitutional reforms.

On May 29, security forces in the town of Safi beat Kamal Ammari, a 30-year old protester. He died on June 2. The Office of the Prosecutor announced that forensic doctors concluded that Ammari died from a pre-existing condition that was "aggravated" by "a simple blow to the torso that would normally have been benign." The case remains under investigation.

Terrorism and Counterterrorism

On April 28, a bomb exploded in a Marrakesh cafe frequented by foreign tourists, killing 17 persons and wounding dozens. No group claimed responsibility for what was the deadliest terrorist attack in Morocco since 2003. The special terrorism chamber of the Rabat Court of Appeals on October 28 convicted nine suspected Islamist militants in the attack and sentenced one to death and the others to prison. Moroccan courts continue to impose the death penalty but Morocco has not executed anyone since the early 1990s.

Hundreds of suspected Islamist extremists arrested in the aftermath of the Casablanca bombings of May 2003 remain in prison. Many were convicted in unfair trials after being held in secret detention and subjected to mistreatment and sometimes torture. Since further terrorist attacks in 2007, police have arrested hundreds more suspected militants, many of whom were convicted and imprisoned, not for having committed acts of terrorism, but for belonging to a "terrorist network" or preparing to join "the jihad" in Iraq or elsewhere.

There were fewer reports than in previous years of intelligence agencies interrogating terrorism suspects at unacknowledged detention centers and holding them in pre-charge custody for longer than the 12-day maximum period the law allows for terrorism cases. In May delegations from parliament and the new National Human Rights Council (NHRC), which the king established in March to replace his Advisory Council on Human Rights, visited the reported site of the most notorious of these detention centers, the headquarters of the General Directorate for the Surveillance of the Territory in Témara, near Rabat. They reported finding no evidence during their visit of a detention facility operating there.

Police Conduct and the Criminal Justice System

Courts seldom provide fair trials in cases with political overtones. Judges routinely ignore requests for medical examinations from defendants who claim to have been tortured, refuse to summon exculpatory witnesses, and convict defendants based on apparently coerced confessions.

The minister of justice in August 2010 suspended Judge Jaâfar Hassoun from his post as president of the Marrakesh Administrative Court. Then in December 2010 Hassoun was ousted from his membership in the High Council of the Magistrature (HCM). Authorities accused Hassoun of disclosing confidential deliberations of the HCM to *Essabah* newspaper. Hassoun said he was innocent and the authorities were persecuting him for his judicial independence, such as his 2009 ruling that invalidated a Marrakesh mayoral election won by a candidate from a pro-palace party. In January the king signed an order expelling Hassoun from the judiciary.

In January an appeals court upheld the conviction and imprisonment of champion boxer Zakaria Moumni for fraud after trials at which the complainants never appeared and a confession allegedly coerced by torture was used as evidence. Moumni, who was being retried at this writing, contends that his prosecution is politically motivated and stems from his persistent and public lobbying of the palace for government benefits to which he says he is entitled.

In March Mohammed VI pardoned and freed retired Maj.-Col. Kaddour Terhzaz. In November 2008 a military court convicted Terhzaz of disclosing "national defense secrets" based on a 2005 letter he wrote to the king criticizing what he saw as Morocco's bad treatment of its pilots whom the Polisario had imprisoned for a quarter century.

In April the king also pardoned five political figures convicted in the mass "Belliraj" trial on charges of mounting a terrorist plot. In 2010 an appeals court had upheld the guilty verdict against all 35 defendants even though most had repudiated their confessions. The court refused to investigate the defendants' allegations of torture, detention in secret jails, and the falsification of confessions. Twenty-nine other defendants in the case continued to serve their prison terms, which included a life term for alleged ringleader Abdelkader Belliraj. Another defendant had already been freed in 2010 after serving a two-year term.

A Casablanca court on April 14 provisionally released prominent, non-violent, pro-independence, Sahrawi activists Ali Salem Tamek, Brahim Dahane, and Ahmed Naciri, after 18 months of pre-trial detention. The police had arrested them and four other activists in October 2009 upon their return from a visit to the Polisario-run refugee camps in Algeria. The trial of the seven, on charges of "harming [Morocco's] internal security," started in October 2010, but was postponed repeatedly. At this writing it had not resumed.

Twenty-three Sahrawi civilians remained in pre-trial detention before a military court for their alleged role in clashes in and around El-Ayoun in November 2010 between security forces and Sahrawis that caused fatalities on both sides. Another 120 Sahrawis were bailed and faced less serious charges before a civilian court for their role in the clashes. One year after they occurred, no trials had begun.

Freedom of Association

Morocco boasts of thousands of independent associations, but government officials arbitrarily impede the legalization of many, undermining their freedom to operate. Groups affected include some that defend the rights of Sahrawis, Amazighs (Berbers), sub-Saharan immigrants, and unemployed university graduates, as well as charitable, cultural, and educational associations whose leadership includes members of Justice and Spirituality, a well-entrenched, nationwide movement that advocates for an Islamic state and questions the king's spiritual authority. The government, which does not recognize Justice and Spirituality as a legal association, tolerated many of its activities but prevented others.

Local and international human rights organizations operate with few impediments in the major cities, but individual activists sometimes pay a heavy price for whistle-blowing. Chekib el-Khayari, president of the Association for Human Rights in the Rif, served two years of a three-year term for "gravely insulting state institutions" and minor currency violations, before the king pardoned him in April. The authorities jailed el-Khayari after he accused certain Moroccan officials of complicity in narcotics trafficking.

Women's Rights

The new constitution guarantees equality for women, "while respecting the provisions of the Constitution, and the laws and permanent characteristics of the Kingdom." Major reforms to the Family Code in 2004 raised the age of marriage and improved women's rights in divorce and child custody. However, the new code preserved discriminatory provisions with regards to inheritance and the right of husbands to unilaterally repudiate their wives.

On April 8 Morocco withdrew its reservations to articles 9(2) and 16 of the Convention on the Elimination of All Forms of Discrimination against Women, while maintaining other reservations. The withdrawal signaled a commitment to eliminate gender discrimination in marital rights and responsibilities and in the right of spouses to confer Moroccan nationality on their children when the other spouse is non-Moroccan. In its first national study on violence against women the Haut Commissariat au Plan, a government agency tasked with compiling national statistics, found that 55 percent of Moroccan women surveyed between 18 and 64-years-old experienced domestic violence during 2009; 15 percent reported suffering physical violence and 48 percent emotional violence.

Domestic Workers

In July an employer allegedly beat to death an 11-year-old domestic worker in el-Jadida. The case drew attention to the tens of thousands of Moroccan children employed as live-in household workers, and the abusive conditions to which they are often subjected. The case was still in court at this writing. Morocco approved a draft law in October that, if approved by parliament, would toughen sanctions on persons who violate the prohibition on employing children under 15 and would tighten conditions for employing persons aged 15 to 18 in households.

Freedom of Media

Morocco's independent print and online media investigate and criticize government officials and policies, but face prosecution and harassment when they cross certain lines. The press law includes prison terms for "maliciously" spreading "false information" likely to disturb the public order or for speech that is defamatory, offensive to members of the royal family, or that undermines "Islam, the institution of the monarchy, or territorial integrity," that is, Morocco's claim on Western Sahara.

Moroccan state television provides some room for investigative reporting but little for direct criticism of the government, or dissent on key issues. Hundreds of journalists who work for state-controlled media, notably the television channels and the state news agency, held protests on March 25 to demand, among other things, more editorial independence.

In April authorities arrested Rachid Nini, a popular columnist and editor of *al-Masa'* daily. In June a Casablanca Court of First Instance convicted him of attempting to influence judicial decisions, showing contempt for judicial decisions, and falsely accusing public officials of crimes. The court gave him a one-year prison term and refused to free him provisionally pending appeal. The evidence against him consisted of articles he wrote that criticized Morocco's intelligence agencies and accused persons close to the royal palace of corruption. An appeals court confirmed the verdict and sentence on October 24.

Morocco revoked or delayed renewal of accreditation of some journalists working for foreign media. Voicing its displeasure with Al Jazeera's coverage of the Western Sahara conflict, the government closed the station's news bureau in Morocco in 2010.

Key International Actors

In 2008 the European Union gave Morocco "advanced status," placing it a notch above other members of the EU's "neighbourhood policy." Morocco is the biggest Middle Eastern beneficiary of EU aid after the Occupied Palestinian Territories, with €580 million (US$808 million) earmarked for 2011 to 2013.

France is Morocco's leading trade partner and source of public development aid and private investment. France increased its Overseas Development Assistance to €600 million ($810 million) for 2010 to 2012. France rarely publicly criticized Morocco's human rights practices and openly supported its autonomy plan for Western Sahara. On July 18 the French presidency of the G8 praised the results of the constitutional referendum and pledged the G8 countries' "concrete support" for "the full and swift implementation of Morocco's reform agenda."

The United States provides financial aid to Morocco, a close ally, including a five-year $697 million grant beginning in 2008 from the Millennium Challenge Corporation to reduce poverty and stimulate economic growth. On human rights, the US continued to publicly praise Morocco's reform efforts and advances made by women. However, US Deputy Assistant of State Tamara Wittes, on a visit to Morocco in June, said that US officials had voiced concerns to the Moroccan government about police violence when handling peaceful demonstrations.

The 2011 United Nations Security Council resolution renewing the mandate of the peacekeeping force for Western Sahara (MINURSO) contained human rights language more explicit than in previous years but did not enlarge the MINURSO mandate to include human rights monitoring, an enlargement that the Polisario supports and Morocco opposes. MINURSO is the only peacekeeping operation created since 1990 that has no human rights monitoring component. Resolution 1979 encouraged "the parties to work with the international community to develop and implement independent and credible measures to ensure full respect for human rights." It welcomed "the commitment of Morocco to ensure unqualified and unimpeded access to all Special Procedures of the United Nations Human Rights Council."

OMAN

Oman's 3.5 million citizens have little opportunity to change their government or affect its policies. All legislation and regulations are promulgated by royal decree.

Omani authorities generally respected the right to freedom of expression, though public criticism of Sultan Qaboos bin Sa'id and his family remains off-limits. On several occasions in 2011 authorities arrested journalists who wrote articles supportive of large-scale protests calling for reforms.

Authorities placed restrictions on the freedoms of association and assembly, both in law and in practice, but tolerated spontaneous peaceful sit-ins and informal gatherings from late February to May 2011.

Freedom of Assembly

Beginning in February thousands of Omanis took to the streets in cities throughout the country to demand jobs, an end to corruption, and the dismissal of senior officials perceived to be corrupt. Though police and security forces initially tolerated the largely peaceful protests, on February 27 they used tear gas, rubber bullets, and live ammunition against several thousand protesters who attacked and burned a police station in the northern coastal town of Sohar. The clashes led to dozens of injuries, and police shot dead protester Abdullah al-Ghimlasi. On April 1, police and army units fired tear gas and rubber bullets at stone-throwing protesters. Khalifa al-Alawi, 22, was killed by a rubber bullet that struck him in the face.

In a coordinated move on May 13 and 14, riot police assisted by regular army units used tear gas and police batons to disperse peaceful sit-ins in the northern cities of Muscat, the capital, and Sur, as well as in the southern city of Salalah. Following the May 13 dispersal of the Muscat sit-in in front of the Shura council building, authorities arrested at least seven activists who attempted to return to the site the next day. They charged Basma al-Kayoumi with "illegal gathering" and released the others without charge.

Also on May 13, police broke up a sit-in in front of the governor's office in the southern city of Salalah, detaining several hundred protesters for 24 hours before releasing all but a few. Authorities transferred at least eight demonstrators from Salalah to Sama'il Central Prison, outside Muscat, where they were held for 54 days without charge, including 13 days in solitary confinement. The public prosecutor initially charged at least one of them with "dishonoring the sultan," though eventually the charges were dropped and all eight released.

On June 28 the Misdemeanor Court of First Instance in Muscat handed down sentences in a group trial ranging from six months to five years imprisonment. Authorities charged 15 demonstrators from Sohar with "shutting down work at a government organization," "blocking roads," and "humiliating on-duty civil servants."

To Human Rights Watch's knowledge, authorities have not investigated or held accountable any officials in connection with the protest-related deaths, injuries, or arbitrary arrests and detentions carried out by Omani security forces during the protests.

Freedom of Expression

Omani authorities generally respected the right to freedom of expression and allowed several independent publications in the capital to operate freely, some of which regularly published articles criticizing official corruption as well as crackdowns on protesters.

Some journalists, however, claimed that officials retaliated against them for their reporting. At 3 a.m. on March 29, security forces raided the home of Ahmed al-Shezawi, head of the press relations department at the government-owned daily *al-Shabiba*, after he published stories on the Sohar demonstration; he is a relative of one of the protest leaders. Authorities held him for several days before releasing him without charge. One week later the Ministry of Information revoked his journalism license and his newspaper fired him.

On September 21 a lower court in Muscat convicted journalist Yusif al-Haj, a reporter at the independent newspaper *Azzamn*, and Ibrahim al-Ma'mari, his editor, of defaming and insulting the Minister of Justice and his deputy in an article alleging that they had improperly intervened in an employment dispute. The judge sentenced al-Haj and al-Ma'mari to five months in prison and ordered the newspaper to close for a month. Al-Haj has been a prominent voice for reform and was an active participant in the Muscat sit-in.

Pro-Reform Activists

Several pro-reform activists reported threats, intimidation, and physical abuse by unknown assailants and security forces.

On April 8, masked plainclothes men abducted Said al-Hashemi and Bassima al-Rajhi, two activists involved with the Muscat sit-in, and drove them deep into the desert, where they beat them, subjected them to mock executions, and abandoned them. Al-Hashemi said that the men behaved in a manner reflecting they were subject to a clear chain of command, and that the black clothes and boots that several wore were typically associated with security services. He said that the van used to transport him and al-Rajhi into the desert was identical to the well-equipped GMC vans known to be used by security services. At this writing authorities have released no information regarding the investigation they said they had opened into this case.

Human rights activist and blogger Salem Al Towayyah reported receiving emails and chat messages from anonymous sources threatening him with retribution for criticizing government officials and calling for a constitutional monarchy on a March 9 show that aired on al-Hurra television. On April 1 a representative of the Royal Oman Police called a member of Al Towayyah's family to ask about his activities and threatened to charge him with "inciting" people if he did not discontinue his pro-reform activities.

Naming Issues

The Ministry of Interior's Committee for the Correction of Tribal Names and Titles continued to regulate and arbitrarily change tribal surnames, effectively assimilating members of one tribe into another. Despite numerous court decisions against ministry orders compelling members of the Al Towayyah and al-Khalifin tribes to change their surnames to names of other tribes, ministry officials continued to challenge the names of individuals when they attempted to renew identification documents.

In 2011 the Directorate General of Civil Status, a branch of the Royal Oman Police, continued its policy of restricting names permitted to newborns to those found on a civil registry database and rejecting names not in the database. Any newborn whose name was rejected could not get a birth certificate until the parents submitted an acceptable name. Activists reported that the appeals process was lengthy and unclear.

Women's Rights

Article 17 of Oman's Basic Law officially bans discrimination on the basis of gender, and authorities have made efforts to ensure that women are visibly represented at the highest levels of government and society.

Oman adjudicates family law and personal status matters in religious courts in which judges base rulings on their interpretations of Islamic law. Individuals have no option to seek adjudication pursuant to a civil code. Family law as generally interpreted discriminates against women in matters of divorce, inheritance, child custody, and legal guardianship, granting men privileged status in these matters.

Key International Actors

Oman, as well as Bahrain, received a US$20 billion development grant from wealthier Gulf Cooperation Council (GCC) states in 2011, reportedly in order to counter popular uprisings in the two countries.

Oman is one of the few GCC members that maintains friendly relations with Iran. On September 21 Sultan Qaboos helped negotiate the release of two detained American hikers imprisoned in Iran for 26 months.

Both the United States US and United Kingdom provide significant economic and military aid to the sultanate and maintain military bases there.

QATAR

Qatar has the highest ratio of migrants to citizens in the world, with only 225,000 citizens in a population of 1.7 million. Yet the country has some of the most restrictive sponsorship laws in the Persian Gulf region, leaving migrant workers vulnerable to exploitation and abuse. Forced labor and human trafficking remain serious problems.

While the constitution protects freedom of expression "in accordance with the conditions and circumstances set forth in the law," in practice Qatar restricts freedom of speech and the press. Local media tend to self-censor, and the law permits criminal penalties, including jail terms, for defamation.

Qatar currently holds a seat on the United Nations Human Rights Council, winning an election to its second consecutive term in May 2010. In June the government voted to adopt the International Labour Organization's Convention on Decent Work for Domestic Workers, which establishes the first global labor standards on domestic work.

Migrant Workers

More than 1.2 million migrant workers—mostly from India, Pakistan, Sri Lanka, the Philippines, Nepal, and Bangladesh—live and work in Qatar. The largest sector, construction, employs 506,000 migrants.

Law 14 of 2004—governing labor in the private sector—limits working hours, requires paid annual leave, sets requirements on health and safety, and requires on-time wages each month. Neither the law nor supporting legislation set a minimum wage. The law allows Qatari workers to form unions, and permits strikes with prior government approval. Migrant workers have no right to unionize or strike, though they make up 99 percent of the private sector workforce.

The labor law excludes approximately 132,000 migrant domestic workers. While the Advisory Council, a 35-member appointed legislative body, approved a separate law covering domestic work in 2010, at this writing the law awaited the approval of Emir Sheikh Hamad bin Khalifa Al Thani.

Migrant workers reported extensive labor law violations. Common complaints included late or unpaid wages and employers' failure to procure work permits that proved workers' legal residence in the country. Many workers said they received false information about their jobs and salaries before arriving and signed contracts in Qatar under coercive circumstances. Some lived in overcrowded and unsanitary labor camps, and lacked access to potable water.

Qatar employs only 150 labor inspectors to monitor compliance with the labor law, and inspections do not include worker interviews.

A major barrier to redressing labor abuses is the *kafala* (sponsorship) system, which ties a migrant worker's legal residence to his or her employer, or "sponsor." Migrant workers cannot change jobs without their sponsoring employer's consent, except in exceptional cases with permission from the Interior Ministry. If a worker leaves his or her sponsoring employer, even if fleeing abuse, the employer can report the worker as "absconding," leading to detention and deportation. In order to leave Qatar, migrants must obtain an exit visa from their sponsor, and some said sponsors denied them these visas. Workers widely reported that sponsors confiscated their passports, in violation of the Sponsorship Law.

In October 2011 Qatar passed new legislation to combat human trafficking, using the definition of trafficking provided in the UN Trafficking Protocol. Those who commit offenses specified in the law could face up to fifteen years in prison.

Statelessness

Between 1,200 and 1,500 stateless Bidun, who claim they have a right to Qatari citizenship, live in Qatar. The 2005 Nationality Law allows individuals to apply for citizenship after living in Qatar for 25 years, but limits naturalization to only 50 people per year. Bidun cannot register for education or health benefits, or legally hold employment. The government does not register the birth of Bidun children.

In 2004 and 2005 the government stripped more than 5,000 Qataris from the al-Murra tribe of citizenship as delayed punishment for some members' participation in a 1996 coup attempt against the current emir. In 2006 the Qatari government officially reinstated the citizenship of most of this group, but an estimated 200 remain stateless. They cannot legally work in the country and report economic hardship.

Women's Rights

Both women and men vote in municipal elections, though representatives have limited power. Qatari women do not have the same rights as Qatari men to obtain nationality for their spouses and children. In 2010 Qatar appointed its first female judge.

Qatar has no law specifically criminalizing domestic violence, and the government currently publishes no data on incidents of domestic violence. Representatives of the Qatar Foundation for the Protection of Women and Children, a government-funded charitable institution, told local media that domestic violence continued to be a problem, based on their work with women and children who sought assistance.

Qatar adjudicates family law and personal status matters in religious courts in which judges base rulings on their interpretations of Islamic law. People have no option to seek adjudication pursuant to a civil code. Family law as generally interpreted discriminates against women in matters of divorce, inheritance, and child custody, granting men privileged status in these matters.

Freedom of Expression

On March 2, plainclothes individuals believed to be state security agents took into custody Sultan al-Khalaifi, a Qatari blogger and former secretary general of Alkarama, a Geneva-based NGO monitoring human rights in the Arab world. They searched his home for two hours and confiscated possessions, including al-Khalaifi's laptop. Authorities released him a month later without charge.

In June Qatar's Advisory Council approved a new media law that allows for criminal penalties against journalists who write critically on "friendly countries" or matters pertaining to national security, but arrests require a court order. The emir had not approved the law at this writing. Under the media law still in effect, journalists may be arrested without a court order. In April police arrested two Swiss sports journalists for Radio Television Suisse (RTS) and interrogated them for several hours. The journalists had been filming a segment on soccer (football) in Qatar after the country won its bid to host the 2022 soccer World Cup. An RTS statement said a judge ordered them to pay a fine, and that authorities prevented them from leaving the country for 13 days.

Al Jazeera, the international news agency broadcasting in both Arabic and English, is headquartered in Doha, the capital, and funded by the Qatari government. While the station covers regional and international news, and played an important role in reporting the pro-democracy Arab Spring movements, few stories report on Qatar.

Key International Actors

On December 2, 2010, the Fédération Internationale de Football Association selected Qatar to host the 2022 World Cup. Qatar's winning bid included commitments to build nine new stadiums, a new airport, metro and rail systems, a bridge to Bahrain, 54 team base camps, and significant new hotel stock, at a total estimated cost of US$80 to 100 billion. Local media estimated that these projects would require recruitment of hundreds of thousands of new workers from abroad.

In March Qatar was among the first countries to recognize Libya's National Transitional Council, and was the first Arab country to contribute to NATO's enforcement of a no-fly zone over Libya. On June 2 the Qatari government forcibly returned to eastern Libya Eman al-'Obeidi, a refugee recognized by UN high commissioner for refugees, who said that forces loyal to the government headed by Muammar Gaddafi gang-raped her in Tripoli.

SAUDI ARABIA

Saudi Arabia responded with unflinching repression to demands by citizens for greater democracy in the wake of the pro-democracy Arab Spring movements. King Abdullah bin Abd al-'Aziz Al Saud announced economic benefits worth over US$130 billion, but authorities continued to jail Saudis for peaceful dissent. New laws introduced or proposed in 2011 criminalize the exercise of basic human rights such as freedom of expression, assembly, and association.

Authorities continue to suppress or fail to protect the rights of 9 million Saudi women and girls, 8 million foreign workers, and some 2 million Shia citizens. Each year thousands of people receive unfair trials or are subject to arbitrary detention.

In March Saudi troops helped quell Bahrain's pro-democracy protests. Saudi Arabia reacted with dismay to the toppling of Egypt's President Hosni Mubarak, but supported a transition of power, at least in public, in Yemen and Libya and urged Syria to stop internal repression. At Saudi urging, the Gulf Cooperation Council invited Arab monarchies Jordan and Morocco to join the council, and provided Jordan, Bahrain, Oman, Egypt, and Yemen with substantial financial aid.

Women's and Girls' Rights

The Saudi guardianship system continues to treat women as minors. Under this discriminatory system, girls and women of all ages are forbidden from traveling, studying, or working without permission from their male guardians. In 2009 the Ministry of Commerce, though not other ministries, stopped requiring women to conduct ministerial business through a male representative.

On September 25 King Abdullah announced that women will be able to vote in municipal elections in 2015. The government continued to exclude women as voters or candidates in the September 2011 municipal elections, despite a two-year delay to allow for logistical preparations to include women. In March 2011 women activists launched the Baladi (My Country) campaign in protest, trying—unsuccessfully—to register to vote. In the first municipal elections in 2005, authorities said that election workers could not verify a woman's identity since many did not have identity cards. However, the Interior Ministry began issuing identity cards to women over 22 years old in 2000. The king also promised to appoint women as full members of the Shura Council.

On May 22, Saudi authorities arrested Manal al-Sharif after she defied the kingdom's de facto ban on women driving. Al-Sharif appeared in a video showing herself behind the wheel. Prosecutors charged her with "tarnishing the kingdom's reputation abroad" and "stirring up public opinion," according to Saudi press reports. On May 30, Khobar police released al-Sharif from prison after she appealed to King Abdullah.

On June 17 around 40 women with international drivers' licenses participated in a "women2drive" campaign. No law bars women from driving, but senior government clerics have ruled against the practice. Saudi Arabia is the only country in the world to prohibit women from driving.

Migrant Worker Rights

Over 8 million migrant workers fill manual, clerical, and service jobs, constituting more than half the national workforce. Many suffer multiple abuses and labor exploitation, sometimes amounting to slavery-like conditions.

The *kafala* (sponsorship) system ties migrant workers' residency permits to their "sponsoring" employers, whose written consent is required for workers to change employers or exit the country. Employers abuse this power to confiscate passports, withhold wages, and force migrants to work against their will.

In August Jadawel International, owned by Saudi Arabia's third richest man, Shaikh Muhammad bin Issa Al Jaber, was six months in arrears with salary payments, as in previous years, and managers threatened workers not to pursue complaints in labor court.

Some 1.5 million migrant domestic workers remain excluded from the 2005 Labor Law. As in years past, Asian embassies reported thousands of complaints from domestic workers forced to work 15 to 20 hours a day, seven days a week, and denied their salaries. Domestic workers, most of whom are women, frequently endure forced confinement, food deprivation, and severe psychological, physical, and sexual abuse.

In December 2010, authorities made no attempts to rescue an Indonesian migrant domestic worker who had worked for 10 years without pay and whose sponsors were "renting" her out to other houses, according to one Saudi woman who informed authorities. In November 2010, authorities in Abha, southern Saudi Arabia, recovered the body of Kikim Komalasari, a 36-year-old Indonesian domestic worker, bearing signs of extensive physical abuse. In September an appeals court overturned a three-year prison sentence for the employer found guilty of severely assaulting Sumiati Mustapa, her Indonesian domestic worker. In June the government beheaded Ruyati binti Sapubi, an Indonesian domestic worker convicted of murdering her employer who allegedly refused to allow binti Sapubi to return home. Courts sentenced another Indonesian domestic worker to death for killing her employer after he allegedly tried to rape her.

Saudi Arabia continued to deport hundreds of Somalis to Mogadishu, Somalia's capital, according to the Office of the United Nations High Commissioner for Refugees, despite the acute violence there.

Criminal Justice and Torture

Detainees, including children, commonly face systematic violations of due process and fair trial rights, including arbitrary arrest and torture and ill-treatment in detention. Saudi judges routinely sentence defendants to thousands of lashes.

Judges can order arrest and detention, including of children, at their discretion. Children can be tried and sentenced as adults if physical signs of puberty exist. The Interior Ministry said it had executed Bandar al-Luhaibi, a child, in October for killing his grandmother.

Authorities rarely inform suspects of the crime with which they are charged, or of supporting evidence. Saudi Arabia has no penal code, so prosecutors and judges largely define criminal offenses at their discretion. Lawyers do not assist suspects during interrogation and face difficulty examining witnesses or pre-senting evidence at trial.

From January to October 2011 Saudi Arabia had executed at least 61 persons, including two women and one child, mostly for murder or drugs offenses, but also a Sudanese man, Abd al-Hamid al-Fakki, for "sorcery."

In March a court, after only two sessions, sentenced four Iraqis and two Syrians to the amputation of one foot and one hand each for stealing money from a supermarket. One of the Iraqis told Human Rights Watch that interrogators physically tortured him for eight days into a signing, unread, a prepared confes-sion.

Secret police detained without trial or access to lawyers, in many cases for years, thousands of persons suspected of sympathies for or involvement with armed groups, or for their peaceful political views.

In July the government proposed a counterterrorism law that would criminalize "infringing upon the interests of the kingdom" or "describing the king—or the crown prince—as an unbeliever, doubting his integrity, defaming his honesty, breaking the [oath of] loyalty [to him], or inciting such [acts]."

Prisoners and detainees in several facilities described inhumane conditions. On January 3 Mikhlif al-Shammari, a rights advocate detained in Dammam prison since June 2010, alleged that guards beat inmates. According to his family, guards assaulted al-Shammari in July for his criticisms by putting a chemical agent in his mouth.

Freedom of Expression, Belief, and Assembly

Authorities further tightened the space for public criticism of officials or govern-ment policies in the wake of the pro-democracy Arab Spring movements. The Ministry of Culture and Information heavily censored print and broadcast media. Internet critics crossing vague "red lines" faced arrest.

In October 2010 the General Court in Qubba, in northern Saudi Arabia, sen-tenced to lashes Fahd al-Jukhaidib, a local journalist and teacher who reported on a rare protest against the local electricity company. In December authorities detained incommunicado for three months Muhammad al-'Abd al-Karim, a professor of Islamic jurisprudence, for an online article speculating whether Saudi Arabia would survive as a political entity without the ruling Saudi royal family.

In July the authorities arrested prominent cleric Dr. Yusuf al-Ahmad, one day after he criticized the Interior Ministry's policy of long-term detention without charge or trial.

In January Minister of Culture and Information Abd al-'Aziz Khuja issued the Executive Regulation for Electronic Publishing Activity, which subjects virtually all news and commentary distributed electronically to the country's press law, including the requirement for a press license.

In April King Abdullah amended the 2000 Press and Publications Law to further prohibit speech that "contradicts rulings of the Islamic Sharia [law] or regulations in force," or "call[s] for disturbing the country's security, or its public order, or ... caus[es] sectarianism or ... damage[s] public affairs in the country." New restrictions also include a prohibition on damaging the reputation of the chief mufti, members of the Council of Senior Religious Scholars, or any other government official or government institution.

Saudi Arabia does not tolerate public worship by adherents of religions other than Islam and systematically discriminates against its religious minorities, in particular Shia and Ismailis (a distinct branch of Shiism). Official discrimination against Shia encompasses religious practices, education, and the justice system. Government officials exclude Shia from certain public jobs and policy questions and publicly disparage their faith.

This discrimination sometimes amounts to persecution. Professing Shia beliefs in private or in public, in particular at holy sites in Mecca and Medina, may lead to arrest and detention. In October the Interior Ministry said that it would pursue what it called "radicalized or hired instigators" among the Shia with an "iron fist."

Prince Badr bin Jilawi, governor of Ahsa' province, repeatedly had Shia citizens detained, in violation of Saudi criminal procedure law, for private prayer or public display of Shia banners or slogans. The domestic intelligence agency in February summoned and then arrested Shia cleric Tawfiq al-'Amir after he had called for a constitutional monarchy and equal rights for Shia in his Friday sermon.

On March 5 the Interior Ministry categorically prohibited public protests "because they contradict the principles of the Islamic Shari'a and the values and customs of Saudi society." The royally appointed Council of Senior Religious Scholars, whose interpretation of religious law is binding, seconded the ban, and intelligence forces in March arrested Muhammad al-Wad'ani, and Khalid al-Juhani for advocating protests for political change.

Small, peaceful protests by Shia took place since late February in the Eastern Province, demanding the release of nine "forgotten" Shia detained for over 13 years without charge or trial on suspicion of involvement in a 1996 attack on a United States military installation in Khobar, which killed 19. Saudi authorities detained 160 protesters until May, and at least 40 remained in detention at this writing.

In March a small group of Sunni Saudis demonstrated in Riyadh, the capital, calling for the release of thousands of people detained for years without charge or trial on suspicion of involvement in militant activity. Police arrested several, including three women as well as lawyer Mubarak bin Zu'air and rights activist Muhammad Bajadi, both of who remain in detention. In August Judge Abd al-Latif al-'Abd al-Latif prohibited defense lawyers for Bajadi from attending a trial session in a secret location of the Specialized Criminal Court, a state security tribunal for terrorism cases, where Bajadi faced charges of "insurrection against the ruler," "instigating demonstrations," and "speaking with foreign [media] channels."

Police in October arrested human rights activist Fadhil al-Manasif after he complained about the police seizing two elderly citizens in order to pressure their sons to give themselves up. The sons were wanted in connection with peaceful demonstrations in the Eastern Province. Al-Manasif, who was detained from May until August for peaceful protest, remains in incommunicado detention. A judge in September charged rights activist Walid Abu al-Khair with "offending the judiciary," "asking for a constitutional monarchy," and "participating in media [programs] to distort the reputation of the country."

Saudi Arabia does not allow political or human rights associations. In February intelligence forces arrested six persons who planned to found the kingdom's first political party.

Key International Actors

Saudi Arabia is a key ally of the US and European countries. The US failed to publicly criticize Saudi human rights violations or its role in putting down pro-democracy protests in neighboring Bahrain. US President Barack Obama failed to mention Saudi Arabia in a major speech on the Arab uprisings and continued to pursue a $60 billion arms sale to Saudi Arabia, the biggest-ever US arms sale.

In June Germany proposed to sell the kingdom over 200 tanks, worth $5 billion.

UN High Commissioner for Human Rights Navenathem Pillay criticized a spate of executions in October. Indonesia's President Susilo Bambang Yudhoyono in July publicly criticized treatment of Indonesian workers in Saudi Arabia, as did a fact-finding delegation of Philippines lawmakers in a report issued in January.

SYRIA

Syria, a repressive police state ruled under an emergency law since 1963, did not prove immune in 2011 to the pro-democracy Arab Spring movements. Anti-government protests erupted in the southern governorate of Daraa in mid-March and quickly spread to other parts of the country. Security forces responded brutally, killing at least 3,500 protesters and arbitrarily detaining thousands, including children under age 18, holding most of them incommunicado and subjecting many to torture. The security forces also launched large-scale military operations in restive towns nationwide.

In parallel, Syria's government enacted a number of reforms in an unsuccessful effort to quell the protest movement, lifting the state of emergency, introducing a new media law, and granting citizenship to stateless Kurds. But at this writing the ongoing bloody repression signaled the government's determination to crush dissent and reject reforms that might undermine its authority.

Killings of Protesters and Bystanders

Security forces and government-supported armed groups used violence, often lethal, to attack and disperse overwhelmingly peaceful anti-government protesters from mid-March onwards. The exact number of dead is impossible to verify due to restrictions on access, but local groups documented 3,500 civilian dead as of November 15.

Many of the killings took place during shootings on protesters and funeral processions, such as the April killings in the central city of Homs of at least 15 people at the New Clock Tower Square when protesters tried to organize a sit-in, and in the southern town of Izraa of at least 34 protesters. While in some cases security forces initially used tear gas or fired in the air to disperse the crowds, in many others, they fired directly at protesters without advance warning. Many victims sustained head, neck, and chest wounds, suggesting they were deliberately targeted. In several cases, security forces chased and continued to shoot at protesters as they ran away.

SYRIA

"We Live as in War"

Crackdown on Protesters in the Governorate of Homs

HUMAN
RIGHTS
WATCH

Syrian authorities repeatedly claimed that security forces were responding to armed attacks by terrorist gangs. In most cases that Human Rights Watch documented, witnesses insisted that those killed and injured were unarmed and posed no lethal threat. Instances where protesters used lethal force against Syrian security forces were limited, and often came in response to lethal force by security forces.

Violations during Large-Scale Military Operations

Security forces conducted several large-scale military operations in restive towns and cities, resulting in mass killings, arrests, and detentions as well as the use of torture. In April tanks and armored personnel carriers imposed a siege on the city of Daraa for 11 days, killing at least 115 residents according to local activists. Daraa residents told Human Rights Watch that security forces occupied all neighborhoods, placed snipers on roofs of buildings across the city, and prevented any movement of residents by firing on those who tried to leave their homes. Security forces launched a massive arrest campaign, arbitrarily detaining hundreds. Released detainees said that security forces subjected them, as well as hundreds of others they saw in detention, to various forms of torture and degrading treatment.

In May security forces attacked the coastal city of Banyas, using the town's sports stadium as a detention facility, and the town of Tal Kalakh, near the Lebanese border, forcing more than 3,000 Syrians to flee over the border to Lebanon. In June security forces sent tanks into the northern town of Jisr al-Shughur following armed confrontations between locally posted security forces and residents. In July security forces stormed Hama, which had witnessed the largest anti-government protests in Syria, killing at least 200 residents in four days, according to lists of the names of those killed provided by local activists. In August tanks and armored vehicles entered al-Ramel neighborhood in the coastal town of Latakia. Security forces also stormed the neighborhoods of Bab Sba, Bab Amro, and Bayyada in Homs on multiple occasions between May and September.

Arbitrary Arrests, Enforced Disappearances, and Torture

Security forces subjected thousands of people to arbitrary arrests and wide-spread torture in detention. The exact numbers are impossible to verify but information that Human Rights Watch collected suggests that security forces detained more than 20,000 people between March and September. Many detainees were young men in their 20s or 30s; but children, women, and elderly people were also included. While the government appears to have released most after several days or weeks in detention, several hundred remained missing at this writing.

According to released detainees, the methods of torture included prolonged beatings with sticks, twisted wires, and other devices; electric shocks; use of improvised metal and wooden "racks"; and, in at least one case, the rape of a male detainee with a baton. The interrogators and guards also subjected detainees to various forms of humiliating treatment, such as making them kiss their shoes and declare that President Bashar al-Assad was their god. Several detainees said their captors repeatedly threatened them with imminent execution, and all described appalling detention conditions, with overcrowded cells in which at times detainees could only sleep in turns.

At least 105 detainees died in custody in 2011, according to local activists. In cases of custodial death reviewed by Human Rights Watch, the bodies bore unmistakable marks of torture including bruises, cuts, and burns. The authorities provided the families with no information on the circumstances surrounding the deaths and, to Human Rights Watch's knowledge, no investigation has been launched. In some cases, families of dead detainees had to sign statements that "armed gangs" had killed their relatives and promise not to hold public funerals as a condition to receiving the bodies. Some of those who died in detention were prominent protest leaders like Ghiyath Mattar, a 26-year-old community organizer from Daraya—a Damascus suburb—whose body security forces returned to his family four days after detaining him in September.

Denial of Medical Assistance

Syrian authorities in many cases denied wounded protesters access to medical assistance. On several occasions security forces prevented ambulances from reaching the wounded and, in at least three instances that Human Rights Watch documented, opened fire on medical personnel, in one case killing a doctor and a nurse in Daraa in March.

Security forces also arrested many injured protesters at hospitals, forcing many wounded to instead seek treatment in makeshift field hospitals—set up in private homes or mosques—for fear of arrest. In September hospital workers told Human Rights Watch that security forces forcibly removed 18 wounded persons from al-Barr hospital in Homs, including five who were still in the operating room.

Arrest of Activists and Journalists

The Syrian security forces have arrested hundreds of activists since protests erupted in mid-March, often merely for communicating with media or helping to organize protests. In April security forces detained Rasem al-Atassi, 66, former president of the Arab Organization for Human Rights in Syria, and a board member of the regional Arab Organization for Human Rights. A military investigative judge ordered his detention for 15 days to investigate his role in supporting protests. In May security forces detained Mohammed Najati Tayyara, a human rights activist from Homs who had spoken to international media about the government's crackdown. He remained in detention at this writing.

Women activists were also targeted. In May security forces detained journalist and activist Dana al-Jawabra from outside her house in Damascus. Al-Jawabra, who hails from Daraa, was active in attempts to break the siege of the town by attempting to arrange a relief convoy. Also in May security forces detained human rights lawyer Catherine al-Talli, 32, in Damascus and held her incommunicado for two days.

In some instances, when the security forces were unable to locate the activist they were seeking, they detained family members. In May security forces detained Wael Hamadeh, a political activist and husband of prominent rights advocate Razan Zeitouneh, from his office. The security forces had gone to the couple's house on April 30 searching for them but instead detained Hamadeh's younger brother, Abdel Rahman, 20, when they could not find them. Security forces released Wael and Abdel Rahman months later.

The Syrian government also detained journalists trying to report on Syria's crackdown. In March Syrian security services detained Reuters journalist Suleiman al-Khalidi, a Jordanian national, for reporting on the violence in Daraa. They expelled him from the country after holding him incommunicado for four days. In April security services detained Khaled Sid Mohand, a Franco-Algerian freelance journalist, and held him incommunicado for almost one month. Security services also detained Dorothy Parvaz—a national of the United States, Canada, and Iran—upon her arrival in Syria in April and held her incommunicado for six days, and detained Ghadi Frances and Ghassan Saoud, two Lebanese journalists, for short periods of time.

Reforms

In an attempt to quell the protests, Syrian authorities enacted a number of reforms, but the ongoing repression undermined their impact and made it impossible to assess the government's intent to implement them. On April 4 President Assad enacted a decree that would grant citizenship to a number of Syria-born stateless Kurds. On April 21 he lifted the state of emergency in place since 1963 and abolished the State Security Court, an exceptional court with almost no procedural guarantees. In May and June Assad also issued two general amnesties, which benefited a small group of political prisoners.

The Syrian authorities also enacted a number of reforms that they say will open up the political system in Syria and increase freedom of media. On July 28 Assad issued a decree approving a new political parties law. In August Assad issues a decree for a General Elections Law and approved a new media law meant to uphold freedom of expression, although the law still requires media to "respect this freedom of expression" by "practicing it with awareness and responsibility."

Women's and Girls' Rights

Syria's constitution guarantees gender equality, and many women are active in public life. However personal status laws and the penal code contain provisions that discriminate against women and girls, particularly in marriage, divorce, child custody, and inheritance. While the penal code no longer fully exonerates perpetrators of so-called honor crimes, it still gives judges options for reduced sentences if a crime was committed with "honorable" intent. The nationality law of 1969 prevents Syrian women married to foreign spouses the right to pass on their citizenship to their children or spouses.

Key International Actors

In response to the crackdown, the US and European Union imposed sanctions against individuals and entities, including travel bans and asset freezes against senior officials in the government and security forces, business officials who benefited from and/or aided government oppression and a host of entities. Both the US and the EU froze the assets of Syrian companies and banks tied to the government or its supporters, and the US government prohibited US entities and citizens from doing business with those companies and banks. In September the EU, which buys 95 percent of Syria's oil exports, prohibited the purchase of Syrian oil and banned EU companies from investing in Syria's oil sector.

A number of Arab states joined together in condemning Syria's crackdown. In August Saudi Arabia, Bahrain, Kuwait, and Tunisia withdrew their ambassadors from Damascus for consultations. In November the Arab League voted to suspend Syria's membership after Syria failed to implement an agreed-to plan to end to the violence.

Turkey, until recently a close ally and major trade partner, repeatedly condemned the Syrian crackdown and stopped at least two weapons shipments to Syria. It also hosted a number of meetings for Syria's opposition.

In August the United Nations Security Council unanimously adopted a presidential statement condemning 'the widespread violations of human rights and the use of force against civilians by the Syrian authorities." However, in October

Russia and China, as well as India, Brazil, and South Africa, refused to support a Security Council resolution applying significant pressure on the Syrian government.

In April the UN Human Rights Council "unequivocally condemned the use of lethal violence against peaceful protesters." In August a report from the Office of the UN High Commissioner for Human Rights "found a pattern of human rights violations ... which may amount to crimes against humanity," and the council again condemned the "grave and systematic human rights violations by the Syrian authorities" and established "an independent international commission of inquiry to investigate all alleged violations since March 2011." The commission was appointed in September and was due to issue its report in late November, but had not been granted access to Syria at this writing. Navi Pillay, the UN high commissioner for human rights, recommended in a briefing to the Security Council in August that it refer Syria to the International Criminal Court.

TUNISIA

Tunisia experienced historic changes in 2011. Street protests triggered by the self-immolation of Mohamed Bouazizi, a street vendor in Sidi Bouzid, on December 17, 2010, spread from city to city. The protests persisted, despite police using live ammunition against mostly peaceful demonstrators until President Zine el-Abidine Ben Ali fled the country on January 14. The protests were fuelled by long-simmering grievances against a government that had relentlessly stifled dissent and meaningful pluralism, and whose repressive laws suffocated Tunisians' freedom of expression, association, and assembly.

Human rights advanced during the year, most significantly with the adoption of the pluralist electoral law for choosing the Constituent Assembly; ratifying the Rome Statute, and thereby becoming a member of the International Criminal Court; the lifting of most of Tunisia's reservations on the Convention on the Elimination of All Forms of Discrimination against Women; and adoption of a new press code and decree laws on political parties and associations. Tunisians were allowed to demonstrate, express themselves, and form parties and associations to an extent unmatched since independence in 1956.

However, the consolidation of human rights protection in the post-Ben Ali era was hampered by the police resorting to excessive force against continuing protests, delays in adopting decisive reforms toward a more independent judiciary, and challenges to freedom of expression that the interim government did not properly address.

Key Political Developments

Two interim governments quickly succeeded one another after Ben Ali's ouster in January. After large-scale protests in Tunis, the capital, a third interim government formed on March 7 that pledged to organize the free and transparent election of a Constituent Assembly tasked with writing a new constitution. Elections for the assembly occurred on October 23.

More than 106 parties were legalized in the wake of the uprising, including the Islamist an-Nahdha party and the Tunisian Communist Workers Party, both of which had been illegal and the targets of repression during Ben Ali's presidency. Similarly, many associations considered illegal under Ben Ali, such as the International Association in Support of Political Prisoners and the Tunisian Association to Combat Torture, received their official authorization soon after Ben Ali's departure.

The interim government dissolved the Democratic Constitutional Rally, Ben Ali's ruling party, and announced the dismantling of the so-called political police, whose ubiquitous plainclothes agents had monitored and harassed dissident activists.

On February 19 the interim government adopted a general amnesty law for political prisoners, which allowed for the release of the more than 500 remaining prisoners being held for political offenses. Most of these had been convicted or were facing charges under the counterterrorism law.

The interim government also ratified the International Convention for the Protection of All Persons from Enforced Disappearance and joined the Optional Protocol to the Convention against Torture and other Cruel, Inhuman or Degrading Treatment or Punishment, which establishes monitoring mechanisms to fight torture, as well as the Second Optional Protocol to the International Covenant on Civil and Political Rights, which requires the state to abolish the death penalty.

Accountability for Past Crimes and Reform of the Judiciary

The interim government took some positive steps in order to investigate crimes committed during the uprising and compensate those who were injured or who lost family members. The first interim government established a national commission to investigate abuses committed during the protests, which made public its preliminary conclusions on the abuses committed between December 17, 2010, and the end of January.

The commission identified 240 civilians killed during the uprising in towns and cities around the country, most of them by police gunfire. In addition, it found that 1,464 were injured in the month-long protests, and scores of inmates perished in prison mutinies and fires between January 13 and 16. On October 24 the government promulgated a decree-law on the reparation for the victims of the uprising that provides for a monthly allocation and free access to public medical care and free public transport for them and/or their families.

On September 14 the office of the military prosecutor announced the filing of charges against Ben Ali, the two ministers of interior who held office at the time of the uprising, and 40 other high officers within the state security apparatus for committing intentional homicide during the uprising. At this writing no one had been held accountable for most killings committed by security force members, although several trials of policemen were underway in civilian and military courts.

In the first of several trials initiated, the former president, his wife Leila Trabelsi, members of their families, and close allies of the couple were convicted of embezzlement and sentenced in absentia to 35 years in prison.

While the interim authorities improved the military justice system, most importantly by adding the possibility of appellate review, they have been slow to put in place long-needed reforms of the judiciary, which played a repressive role under Ben Ali.

Freedom of Expression, Press, and Association

The arsenal of repression under the rule of Ben Ali included a wide range of laws crafted and then abusively interpreted by courts to suppress the expression of dissent. The High Commission for the Protection of the Objectives of the Revolution Political Reform and Democratic Transition approved new laws that were then promulgated by the acting president.

The decree-law on associations, promulgated on September 24, eliminates the crime of "membership in" or "providing services to" an unrecognized organization, a provision that had been used to imprison thousands of opposition party activists. The decree-law on political parties eliminated an article stating that a party may not base its principles, activities, and programs on a religion, language, race, sex, or region, a provision used in the past to restrict the basis upon which Tunisians could found parties.

Penal code, article 121(3)

The distribution, putting up for sale, public display,
possession with the intent to distribute, sell or display
for propaganda purposes, of tracts...that can harm
public order or good morals, is prohibited.
Any infraction...can bring about, in addition to
immediate confiscation, a prison term of six months
to five years and a fine of 120 to 1200 dinars.

Mohamed Abbou, imprisoned
by the Ben Ali government in 2005
pursuant to article 121(3)

Samir Feriani, detained by
the interim government in 2011
pursuant to article 121(3)

TUNISIA

Tunisia's Repressive Laws
The Reform Agenda

HUMAN
RIGHTS
WATCH

Similarly, the new press code is significantly more liberal as it eliminates criminalization of defamation against state institutions, and of "offending" the president of the republic. However, it maintains defamation as a criminal offense, although it eliminates prison terms as a punishment for it while preserving fines. It also maintains the criminal offense of defaming religions "whose practice is permitted" as well as the offense of "distributing false information," a concept that the Ben Ali government used to prosecute many dissidents and human rights activists.

On occasion the interim government availed itself of these repressive provisions. For example, on May 29 authorities detained high-ranking police officer Samir Feriani on charges under the penal code of "harming the external security of the state" and distributing information "likely to harm public order" because he wrote a letter to the interior minister that accused current high-level ministry officials of responsibility for killing protesters during the Tunisian revolution. He also accused ministry officials of destroying classified documents showing collaboration between the Ben Ali administration and Israel's secret service.

The Tunis military court provisionally released Feriani on September 22, and acquitted him one week later of the charge of harming the external security of the state. However, the charge of distributing false information was still pending at this writing.

The interim government failed at times to respond forcefully to assaults on free speech. On October 9, hundreds of protesters rallied against the decision by the private television station Nessma to broadcast the animated feature film *Persepolis,* which tells the story of a girl living in post-revolution Iran. One scene was perceived by some as violating the Islamic precept of prohibiting images personifying God. Two days later a prosecutor in Tunis announced that it would open an investigation in response to a complaint filed against the TV owners on the basis of press and penal code articles criminalizing defamation of religion and assaults on public decency.

On June 29 several dozen protesters forced their way into the screening in Tunis of a film on atheism in Tunisia. Although a police station is located close to the cinema and the organizers of the screening had already contacted the police to ask for protection, the security forces remained idle in the face of the attack.

Women's Rights

Tunisia, long viewed as the most progressive Arab country with respect to women's rights, marked additional advances in this field. The adoption of a gender parity requirement in the Constituent Assembly electoral law required political parties to alternate between males and females on each of their lists of candidates. However, few parties put women in the first place on many of the lists, with the result that only 49 women were elected to the Constituent Assembly out of 217 seats.

On August 16 the Council of Ministers adopted a draft decree to lift Tunisia's reservations to the Convention on the Elimination of All Forms of Discrimination against Women. However, the government maintained "a general declaration" suggesting that it might not implement reforms that conflict with Islam.

The Tunisian personal status code outlaws polygamy and repudiation, the practice by which a man can divorce his wife merely by declaring his decision to do so. The code gives men and women equal rights to divorce and requires they go through the courts to obtain a divorce. The code establishes 18 as the minimum age for marriage for both sexes. A 1993 amendment to the law granted women the right to pass their name and nationality to her children. However discrimination still exists in matters of inheritance and child custody.

Abuses against Protesters

Following Bouazizi's self-immolation, thousands of Tunisians took to the streets to protest against the government. The protesters were mostly peaceful, although some threw rocks and in some cases Molotov cocktails. They braved the deadly force of the security forces, who killed more than 200 by firing into crowds, with high numbers of deaths sustained in Tunis and the inland cities of Kasserine, Thala, and Regueb.

Police violence against protesters continued after the ouster of Ben Ali, especially on January 29, February 27 and 28, and again at the beginning of May, when the police assaulted several demonstrators and bystanders, arbitrarily arrested them, and subjected them to harsh treatment that may amount to torture. This came as a disturbing reminder that, while Tunisians enjoy the right to demonstrate to a far greater degree than in the past, the security apparatus continues to rely on its violent methods of the past and has yet to implement crowd control techniques aimed at minimizing the use of force.

Refugees and Migrants

Since late February 2011, in the wake of the Libyan uprising, Tunisia has been confronted by a humanitarian crisis due to the influx of refugees and migrants crossing the borders from Libya. Tunisia hosted at least 195,241 third-country nationals as of June 30. Overall, the military authorities—aided by Tunisian civil society, international organizations, and volunteers—made significant efforts to respond to the humanitarian needs. However, in May several violent incidents took place in the refugee camps near Ras Jedir that left at least six migrants dead and parts of the camp destroyed by fire. The Tunisian military, which provided security at the camp, failed to prevent the violence and may have taken part in some attacks on camp residents.

Key International Actors

France has continued to be the closest European partner of Tunisia, although the relations between the two countries suffered during the uprising, when the French authorities showed reluctance to denounce the crackdown on the demonstrators. In January the European Union decided to freeze the assets of 46 allies and relatives of Ben Ali and his wife.

The interim authorities welcomed the visits of the United Nations special rapporteurs on torture and on counterterrorism and granted them access to detention facilities, which the International Committee of the Red Cross continued to visit on a regular basis. The interim authorities also legalized branch offices of various international human rights organizations, including Human Rights Watch, and allowed the UN Office of the High Commissioner for Human Rights to open an office in the country.

United Arab Emirates

The human rights situation in the United Arab Emirates (UAE) worsened in 2011, as authorities cracked down on peaceful dissent by arresting activists, disbanding the elected boards of civil society organizations, and preventing peaceful demonstrations. Despite some progress in addressing violations of migrant workers' rights in Saadiyat Island, a high profile development and construction zone, the issue remained a source of concern.

Freedom of Association and Expression

Human rights defenders and government critics face harassment, imprisonment, and criminal prosecution. The UAE's penal code criminalizes speech based on broad content-based restrictions, allowing the government to prosecute people for speech critical of the government, in contravention of international standards.

In April UAE security forces arrested Ahmed Mansoor, a prominent blogger and a member of Human Rights Watch's Middle East and North Africa Advisory Committee. For at least seven days authorities held him in solitary confinement and refused him access to his lawyer and family. His arrest followed a campaign of harassment against him and other activists after they, and dozens of other UAE nationals, signed a petition in March demanding constitutional and parliamentary reforms. Prior to his arrest Mansoor, a prominent reformer, received six death threats and was the target of an online smear campaign.

In April security forces also detained Nasser bin Ghaith, an economics lecturer at the Abu Dhabi branch of Paris's Sorbonne University. Bin Ghaith had criticized the government's failure to undertake significant political reforms. Authorities also arrested three other online activists: Fahad Salim Dalk, Hassan Ali al-Khamis, and Ahmed Abdul Khaleq. The government formally charged the activists under article 176 of the penal code, which makes it a crime to publicly insult the country's top officials. Authorities additionally charged Mansoor with inciting others to break the law by calling for an election boycott and demonstrations.

The Supreme Court said it would issue a verdict in the largely closed-door trial on November 27. There is no right of appeal.

UAE authorities widened their clampdown on freedom of expression by disbanding the elected boards of the Jurists Association and the Teachers' Association after they and two other NGOs co-signed a public appeal in April calling for greater democracy in the country. Social Affairs Minister Mariam Mohammed Khalfan Al Roumi issued decrees to replace the two boards with state appointees.

According to the decrees, the associations violated section 16 of the UAE's 2008 Law on Associations, which prohibits NGOs and their members from interfering "in politics or in matters that impair state security and its ruling regime." The Law on Associations tightly controls NGOs permitted to operate in the UAE.

On September 24 the UAE held national elections for the Federal National Council (FNC), a government advisory board without legislative powers. The UAE authorities increased the number of eligible voters to 129,000, from about 7,000 in the previous election in 2006. Voters chose only 20 of the 40 FNC seats; the rulers of the seven emirates appointed the other half.

Migrant Worker Rights

According to the latest statistics, foreigners account for more than 88.5 percent of UAE residents, many of them poor migrant workers. Immigration sponsorship laws grant employers extraordinary power over the lives of these workers. They have no right to organize or bargain collectively and face penalties for going on strike. Employment protections laid out in the Labor Law of 1980 do not extend to domestic migrant workers employed in private households. Although the law calls for a minimum wage, the Ministry of Labor has yet to implement it.

Across the country, abuses include unsafe work environments, the withholding of travel documents, and low and nonpayment of wages, despite a mandatory electronic payment system introduced in 2009.

In May Athiraman Kannan, a 32-year-old Indian foreman, jumped to his death from the 147th floor of the Burj Khalifa, the world's tallest building. Local media reports said that Kannan jumped after his employer denied granting him leave to go home. His death was the 26th known suicide by an Indian worker in the country in 2011.

In January more than 3,000 workers employed by Arabtec went on a two week strike to demand a wage increase. The workers had been making between 650 and 800 dirhams (US$175 and $220) a month. Some alleged that they had not been paid for overtime work. UAE authorities deported 71 Bangladeshi nationals for their alleged role in instigating the strike. According to the government, the UAE saw 34 worker protests in the first three months of 2011, less than half the number from the same period a year ago. The protests were related to delayed payment of salaries, non-payment of overtime, or demands for pay increases, the government said.

The year 2011 saw some positive developments for migrant workers, particularly on Saadiyat Island, the site of a major development and construction project. In March New York University (NYU) announced that it would be hiring the United Kingdom construction firm Mott MacDonald to monitor labor conditions on its Abu Dhabi campuses, while in May the Abu Dhabi Tourism Development and Investment Company (TDIC), a government entity that is the largest developer in Abu Dhabi, announced its appointment of international auditing firm, PwC, to monitor workers' conditions on Saadiyat Island. Both firms will publish yearly reports on their findings. However, neither NYU nor TDIC have released comprehensive information about the terms of reference and monitoring methodology of their new independent monitors.

In March TDIC also amended its Employment Practices Policy to require contractors to reimburse their employees for any recruitment costs or fees associated with their employment on Saadiyat Island. This followed new labor regulations issued by the UAE government in January to curb exploitative recruiting agents who entrap foreign workers with recruiting fees and false contracts. The new regulations explicitly prohibit UAE recruitment agencies from imposing recruitment fees on workers or intermediaries. If a worker is found to have paid a fee to anyone associated with an Emirati recruitment agency either inside or outside the UAE, the Labor Ministry may compel the agency to reimburse the worker. The regulations also hold recruitment agencies partly liable if they place the worker with an employer who subsequently does not pay the workers, and ban recruiters from placing workers with companies involved in collective labor disputes. Recruiters will have to put down a Dh 300,000 ($81,000) minimum deposit, which will be available to pay workers' salaries if the company fails to do so. Additionally, agencies must pay Dh 2,000 ($540) per worker for insurance.

Many female domestic workers in the UAE suffer unpaid wages, food deprivation, long working hours, forced confinement, and physical and sexual abuse. The standard contract for domestic workers introduced in April 2007 calls for "adequate breaks" but does not limit working hours or provide for a weekly rest day, overtime pay, or workers' compensation.

In June the UAE, along with other governments, trade unions, and employers' organizations, voted to adopt an International Labour Organization (ILO) treaty that extends key labor protections to domestic workers. The ILO Convention on Decent Work for Domestic Workers, which establishes the first global standards for domestic workers worldwide, addresses their routine exclusion from labor protections guaranteed to other workers, such as weekly days off, limits to hours of work, and a minimum wage.

Women's Rights

The UAE adjudicates family law and personal status matters for Muslims pursuant to interpretations of Islamic law, with no option to seek adjudication pursuant to a civil code. The law in particular discriminates against women by granting men privileged status in matters of divorce, inheritance, and child custody. Emirati women can obtain a divorce through *khul'a* (a no-fault divorce) thereby losing their financial rights. They may only ask for a divorce in exceptional circumstances. Females can only inherit one-third of assets while men are entitled to inherit two-thirds.

The law further discriminates against women by permitting Emirati men, but not women, to have as many as four polygamous marriages and forbidding Muslim women, but not men, from marrying non-Muslims. Emirati women married to non-citizens do not automatically pass citizenship to their children, a right enjoyed by Emirati men married to foreign spouses.

Despite the existence of shelters and hotlines to help protect women, domestic violence remains a pervasive problem. The penal code gives men the legal right to discipline their wives and children, including through the use of physical violence. The Federal Supreme Court has upheld a husband's right to "chastise" his wife and children with physical abuse.

In the September elections 85 women out of 450 ran for 20 FNC seats. Only one woman was voted into office.

YEMEN

Human rights violations increased significantly in Yemen in 2011, as authorities sought to quash largely peaceful demonstrations challenging the 33-year rule of President Ali Abdullah Saleh. State security forces, often acting together with armed plainclothes assailants, responded to anti-government protests with excessive and deadly force, killing at least 250 people and wounding more than 1,000.

Clashes on several fronts between government forces and various armed groups killed scores more civilians and displaced more than 100,000 others. State security forces, opposition tribal fighters, and Islamist militants may have committed laws of war violations during some of these confrontations.

Attacks on Protesters

In January, inspired by popular uprisings in Tunisia and Egypt, thousands of Yemenis began protests in major cities to force President Saleh's resignation. Popular discontent, fueled by widespread unemployment and government corruption, soared in late 2010 after the ruling party proposed to amend electoral laws and the constitution so that Saleh could stand for re-election when his seventh term expires in 2013.

Security forces responded to the largely peaceful demonstrations with excessive force, often firing live ammunition directly at unarmed protesters. These forces include Central Security, a paramilitary unit commanded by President Saleh's nephew, Yahya Saleh; the Republican Guard, an elite army unit led by the president's son, Ahmed Saleh; and General Security. Central Security includes a counterterrorism unit that receives United States training, but Human Rights Watch was unable to verify allegations that the unit participated in the attacks on protests. The security forces sometimes attacked protesters together with armed assailants in civilian clothing, or stood by during attacks by armed gangs.

At least 250 civilians and bystanders died in these attacks, most in Sanaa, the capital, as well as in Taizz, and Aden. At least 35 of those killed were children.

YEMEN

Days of Bloodshed in Aden

HUMAN
RIGHTS
WATCH

On March 18, snipers firing on a protest in Sanaa killed at least 45 people. Between May 29 and June 3, security forces killed at least 22 people in Taizz and razed a protest encampment. On September 18 and 19, Central Security and other government forces shot directly at rock-throwing protesters in Sanaa, killing about 30. In the following days security forces killed dozens more protesters and other civilians with gunfire, rocket-propelled grenades, and mortar rounds.

In Sanaa, Aden, and Taizz, security forces blocked wounded protesters' access to medical care. They also raided and looted hospitals, and threatened, detained, or beat medical workers who sought to treat wounded protesters. In June Republican Guard forces began occupying al-Thawrah Hospital in Taizz and using it as a base to shell opposition neighborhoods. In September Central Security forces attacked opposition forces from Sanaa's Jumhuri hospital. In November a government shell struck al-Rawdha Hospital, killing at least one patient.

A September report from the Office of the United Nations High Commissioner for Human Rights (OHCHR) found that elements "seeking to achieve or retain power" were "collectively punishing" the population by curtailing access to electricity, fuel, and water.

Authorities failed to prosecute any members of the security forces for serious human rights violations.

Armed Clashes

In May, after Saleh reneged for a third time on signing a Gulf Cooperation Council-brokered agreement to cede power, dozens of civilians were killed in fighting between government forces and various armed factions.

In May and June fighters of the opposition al-Ahmar clan skirmished with government forces in Sanaa. On June 3, an explosion in the mosque of the presidential palace in Sanaa killed 11 people, and gravely wounded Saleh and several high-ranking officials. Saleh spent three months in Saudi Arabia for medical treatment.

In mid-2011 government forces began fighting with tribal opposition fighters in Arhab, outside Sanaa, and in Taizz. In September Central Security and Republican Guards in Sanaa began clashes with fighters of the al-Ahmar clan and with soldiers from the First Armored Division, a military unit led by Gen. Ali Mohsen al-Ahmar—no relation to the al-Ahmar clan—who defected to the opposition in March.

During these armed confrontations there were credible reports of extrajudicial killings and indiscriminate attacks by security forces on densely populated areas. On June 22, at al-Buraihi checkpoint outside Taizz, a soldier of the Republican Guard fired on a minibus that his unit had just searched and authorized to proceed, killing a 15-year-old boy.

In May the government also launched a military campaign in Abyan province against Ansar al-Sharia (Partisans of Islamic Law), an armed group reportedly backed by Yemen-based al Qaeda in the Arabian Peninsula (AQAP). Ansar al-Sharia had previously captured two provincial cities, Zinjibar and Jaar. On May 20, Central Security forces opened fire with assault rifles in a crowded market in Zinjibar, killing six merchants and shoppers and wounding three dozen others. The forces opened fire after a car bomb nearby killed four members of Central Security, but there were no reports of militants or other suspects inside the market.

Witnesses said that opposition fighters repeatedly deployed in densely populated neighborhoods in Taizz, and that Islamist forces did the same in Abyan, potentially placing civilians at unnecessary risk of attack. Both government and opposition forces deployed children to patrol streets and guard checkpoints.

Freedom of Expression and Opinion

Government forces and armed gangs attacked, harassed, or threatened scores of Yemeni journalists and human rights activists, many for reporting on or denouncing attacks on protesters.

Two journalists were killed covering protests in Sanaa. Jamal al-Sharabi, a photojournalist for the independent weekly al-Masdar, was killed during the March 18 attack. Hassan al-Wadhaf of the Arabic Media Agency died five days after being hit in the face by sniper fire on September 19; he filmed his own shooting.

At a protest in Sanaa on February 18, men armed with sticks beat Al-Arabiya's bureau chief, Hamoud Munasser, and his cameraman, then attacked his car in front of the director of Yemen's US-funded Counterterrorism Unit and a Central Investigation Department official, both of whom failed to intervene.

Authorities expelled several foreign journalists and confiscated press runs of independent Yemeni print media, including *Al-Yaqeen,* that contained reports on security force attacks on Saleh's opponents.

On May 25, pro-Saleh forces fired machineguns and mortar rounds at the satellite TV station Suhail, owned by the opposition al-Ahmar clan. On August 12, government forces arrested Ahmed Firas, a Suhail TV cameraman, as he left Arhab and confiscated his equipment. At this writing he remained detained without charge.

Authorities continued to prosecute journalists in specialized criminal courts that failed to meet international standards of due process. On January 18 the Specialized Criminal Court in Sanaa sentenced Abdulelah Haidar Shae' of the state-run Saba New Agency to five years imprisonment after convicting him of membership of a terrorist group in a trial fraught with procedural irregularities. Shae' had criticized government approaches to fighting al Qaeda.

Scores of human rights defenders were beaten or received frequent anonymous threats. In January some human rights defenders who were active in protests were briefly detained, including Tawakkol Karman of Women Journalists Without Chains and human rights lawyer Khaled al-Anisi. On February 24, five armed assailants repeatedly stabbed a guard at the Sanaa offices of the Yemen Observatory for Human Rights following anonymous threats against the group for releasing information on attacks on protestors.

Internally Displaced People

Armed clashes displaced about 100,000 people, mostly from Abyan to Aden. Approximately 300,000 had already been displaced during the intermittent six-year armed conflict in the north between government forces and Huthi rebels, who despite a ceasefire recaptured Sa'da governate in March. Up to 100,000 of these displaced people reportedly returned home. Aaid agencies were unable to access many displaced people due to insecurity, inadequate funding, and a lack of government permission.

Terrorism and Counterterrorism

US officials in 2011 designated AQAP as a greater threat to its security than the core al Qaeda group in Pakistan.

AQAP claimed responsibility for placing bombs aboard two US-bound cargo planes in October 2010. The group also reportedly provided support to Ansar al-Sharia, the armed group that captured Jaar and Zinjibar in Abyan. Dozens of civilians were killed during clashes between government forces and Ansar al-Sharia in Abyan.

The US reportedly conducted more than a dozen drone strikes and piloted air attacks on alleged AQAP militants in Yemen, including one in September that killed the cleric Anwar al-Awlaki, and Samir Khan, editor of AQAP's English-language magazine *Inspire*. Another suspected drone strike in October killed nine people including al-Awlaki's 16-year-old son, Abderrahman. Both Awlakis and Samir were US citizens. US President Barack Obama called Awlaki the "leader of external operations" for AQAP, but the killing of three Americans outside a traditional battlefield heightened a controversy over the US targeted killing program.

Unnamed US and Yemeni officials said the drones and other air strikes killed dozens of militants. Local officials reported some civilian casualties but lack of access to the targeted areas prevented independent verification.

Campaign against Southern Separatists

Security forces targeted activists of the Southern Movement, an umbrella group seeking independence or greater autonomy for southern Yemen, a separate state until 1990. After the Southern Movement joined anti-Saleh protests in

February, security forces briefly detained dozens of its members and forcibly disappeared at least eight of them for days or weeks. The eight who were "disappeared" included a leader of the Southern Movement, Hassan Baoum, 68, and his son Fawaz, 34. Masked security forces kidnapped the pair on February 20 from an Aden hospital where the elder Baoum was receiving medical treatment. They were held incommunicado until July and at this writing remained detained without charge.

In June soldiers in Aden killed Jiyab Ali Muhammad al-Saadi, 35, the son of a Southern Movement leader, when he asked them to stop blocking a burial procession for Ahmad al-Darwish, whom local activists alleged was tortured to death in police custody in 2010. Authorities transferred Aden's Chief of General Security Abdullah Qairan to Taizz in March after a local court accused him in connection with al-Darwish's death.

Women's and Girls' Rights

Women in Yemen generally have low social status and are excluded from public life.

Child marriages and forced marriages remain widespread, exposing young girls to domestic violence and maternal mortality and truncating their education. Judges are not obliged to ensure a girl's free consent before notarizing a marriage contract. In August a 12-year-old bride from Hudeida was reportedly injured after being drugged and raped by her 50-year-old husband. Despite such cases, conservatives have stalled a draft law that would set the minimum age for marriage at 17.

Women played an important role in anti-Saleh protests, despite beatings, harassment, and, in some cases, shame from relatives. In April Saleh admonished women demonstrators, saying "divine law does not allow" public intermingling of the sexes. Women responded with further protests. Karman was named a co-recipient of the Nobel Peace Prize in October for her role in the protests.

Yemen has a high maternal mortality rate of 370 deaths per 100,000 live births. Approximately seven to eight women die each day from childbirth complications.

Key International Actors

Saudi Arabia, Qatar, and other Gulf states provided substantial assistance to the Yemen government, tribal leaders, and religious institutions. The US was the largest donor outside the region. European Union states also provided humanitarian and development aid.

A Gulf Cooperation Council initiative, supported by the UN Security Council, offered immunity to Saleh and top officials in return for Saleh relinquishing power.

By May most Western and Gulf states had withdrawn public support for Saleh and informally suspended military assistance and arms sales, but ignored calls to freeze the president's assets abroad. The US delayed counterterrorism assistance to Yemen because of political unrest after providing an estimated US$172 million in fiscal year 2010.

In September the UN Human Rights Council condemned human rights violations in Yemen, but failed to authorize an international, independent investigation into them or to establish an OHCHR field office in the country, despite calls for these actions from the OHCHR.

In October, for the second consecutive year, President Obama issued a waiver allowing Yemen to receive military assistance prohibited by the Child Soldiers Prevention Act of 2008, despite documented use of child soldiers by government forces and militias allied to the government.

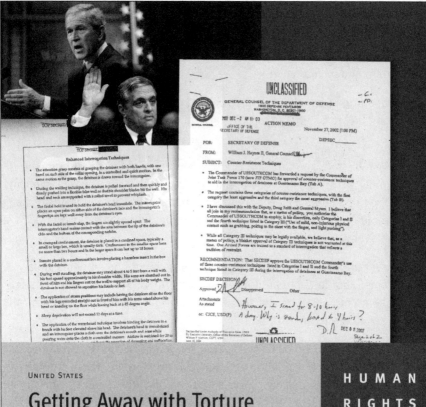

UNITED STATES

Getting Away with Torture

The Bush Administration and Mistreatment of Detainees

HUMAN

RIGHTS

WATCH

WORLD REPORT

2012

UNITED STATES

UNITED STATES

The US incarcerates more people than any other country in the world, some-times imposing very long sentences marred by racial disparities. Increasing numbers of non-citizens—363,000 in 2010—are held in immigration detention facilities, although many are not dangerous or at risk of absconding from immi-gration proceedings.

The federal government continues abusive counterterrorism policies, including detentions without charge at Guantanamo Bay, Cuba; fundamentally flawed military commissions; and effectively blocking lawsuits seeking redress for tor-ture victims.

The US Census reported in 2011 that 46 million people live in poverty, the largest number in the 52 years for which poverty estimates have been pub-lished. Widespread poverty, its many intersections with racial and gender inequalities, and its disproportionate impact upon children and the elderly, raises serious human rights concerns.

Death Penalty and Extreme Criminal Punishments

In 2011 the state of Illinois joined 15 other states in abolishing the death penal-ty. Thirty-four states continue to allow its imposition. At this writing 39 people have been executed in 2011, continuing a downward trend from 2009, when 52 people were executed.

The state of Georgia executed Troy Davis on September 21, 2011, despite signif-icant doubts about his guilt. Davis, who was sentenced to death for the 1989 murder of off-duty police officer Mark MacPhail, maintained his innocence until the last moment. The prosecution's case rested almost entirely on testimony from eyewitnesses, but seven of the nine who testified against Davis at his trial recanted and said they were no longer sure who shot MacPhail, and another three people said that another man confessed to the crime.

While the US Supreme Court held in 2010 that youth offenders under age 18 convicted of non-homicide crimes could not be sentenced to life without the possibility of parole, about 2,600 youth offenders continue to serve such a sentence for homicide-related crimes. State-level efforts continue to reform life without parole when sentencing youth. For example, California is slated in early 2012 to vote on a bill to allow reconsideration and resentencing of youth offenders serving life without parole.

Youth convicted of sex offenses in adult and juvenile courts also met with harsh treatment. July 2011 marked the deadline for all states and other jurisdictions to comply with the Adam Walsh Child Protection and Safety Act. The act requires jurisdictions to register people aged 14 and up convicted of certain sexual offenses on a national, publicly accessible, online registry. In some cases youth will be registered for life. The Department of Justice (DOJ) says 14 states have now substantially implemented the act.

Prison Conditions

The US continued to have the world's largest incarcerated population at 2.3 million, and the world's highest per capita incarceration rate at 752 inmates per 100,000 residents.

In December 2010 Human Rights Watch reported on the unnecessary pre-trial detention of thousands of people accused of minor crimes in New York City due to their inability to pay even small amounts of bail. Almost 90 percent of those arrested in 2008 for non-felony crimes who had bail set at US$1,000 or less were incarcerated pre-trial solely because they could not post bail.

The US Supreme Court decided in May that the state of California must reduce prison overcrowding. California prisons have failed to provide adequate medical and mental health care for decades, and a lower court panel found that prison under-staffing and severe overcrowding had led to such substandard care. The panel directed the state to significantly cut its prison population to improve care; the US Supreme Court agreed.

In February 2011 the DOJ issued its long-overdue proposed standards to implement the Prison Rape Elimination Act (PREA). While some standards meet the 2009 PREA Commission recommendations, several proposed standards are significantly weaker. For example, the proposed DOJ standards do not clearly require facilities to be staffed sufficiently to prevent, detect, and respond to the sexual abuse of prisoners. The standards would leave survivors of sexual assault without legal remedy because they were unable to comply with unduly strict internal grievance procedures. The proposed standards also explicitly exclude immigration detention facilities from coverage. At this writing the final PREA standards have not been issued.

This year Nevada, Hawaii, Idaho, and Rhode Island enacted laws restricting the shackling of pregnant prisoners, bringing the number of states with such laws to 14.

Racial Disparities in the Criminal Justice System

Racial and ethnic minorities continue to be disproportionately represented in the criminal justice system. Whites and African Americans engage in drug offenses at roughly equivalent rates, and African Americans account for only about 13 percent of the US population, yet African Americans comprised about 33 percent of all drug arrests in 2009. Not surprisingly, higher arrest rates lead to higher incarceration rates. For example, 45 percent of inmates in state prisons for drug offenses in 2009 were African American; only 27 percent were white.

Persons of color comprise 77 percent of all youth serving life without parole sentences. And for the first time in the country's history in 2011, people of Latin American origin made up the majority of federal prisoners in the US, due to the federal government's increased focus on prosecuting unauthorized immigrants.

African Americans have historically borne the burden of far harsher federal sentences for crack cocaine offenses compared to powder cocaine offenses. The Fair Sentencing Act, passed in August 2010, partially reduced these sentencing disparities. However the act was not explicitly retroactive. In June 2011 the US Sentencing Commission voted to make the new sentencing guidelines retroactive, so that 12,040 offenders are now eligible for reduced sentences.

Non-Citizens' Rights

There are approximately 25.3 million non-citizens in the US, of which the government estimates 10.8 million are without authorization. Sixty-one percent of these unauthorized immigrants have lived in the US for 10 years or more.

In fiscal year 2010 US Immigration and Customs Enforcement (ICE) deported 387,242 non-citizens—over twice as many as in fiscal year 2000—and detained over 363,000 persons in immigration detention facilities, an increase of over 50 percent since fiscal year 2005. The unchecked expansion of immigration detention in the US over the past two decades has led to a nationwide detention system comprised of over 300 facilities, from small local jails to large, dedicated immigration detention facilities.

In June Human Rights Watch documented the vast numbers of detainees who are subjected to chaotic, frequent, and recurrent transfers between facilities. Between 1998 and 2010 there were over two million detainee transfers. Two hundred thousand detainees were transferred three or more times. On average, detainees were moved 370 miles between facilities, while a common transfer route between Pennsylvania and Texas covered 1,600 miles. The frequent transfers interfere with detainees' access to counsel, witnesses, evidence, and family support.

In August the Department of Homeland Security (DHS) declared a fingerprint-sharing program mandatory, reversing prior policy. The Secure Communities program requires local law enforcement to share fingerprints with DHS, which claims that Secure Communities is used to identify and remove non-citizens convicted of serious crimes. However, 59 percent of those removed under the program between October 2008 and July 2011 had no criminal convictions or had convictions only for minor offenses, including traffic offenses. Several local law enforcement agencies and community groups across the country have vigorously opposed Secure Communities, arguing it impedes community policing and encourages racial profiling. DHS plans nationwide implementation by 2013.

In one of the few rights-protective immigration reforms in 2011, DHS announced that it will undertake case-by-case reviews of over 300,000 pending deportation cases and cases deemed to be low-priority will be administratively closed, allowing some potential deportees to remain in the country with temporary legal status. In identifying low-priority cases DHS will weigh non-citizens' family and community ties, military service, and whether they arrived in the US as children.

Congress criticized the flaws in the country's immigration system but failed to act. The Senate held a hearing in June on the DREAM Act, a bill that would grant legal status to non-citizens brought to the US as children, but it took no further action. The House of Representatives held several hearings on bills that would tighten border and visa security, require the detention of certain immigrants, and reduce both unauthorized and authorized immigration, but voted on none of these measures.

In April the Ninth Circuit Court of Appeals partially enjoined Arizona's Senate Bill 1070 from going into effect. Governor Jan Brewer has appealed the decision to the US Supreme Court. Alabama surpassed Arizona in mid-2011 by passing what is likely the country's strictest state-level immigration measure. The law criminalizes transporting or renting to an unauthorized immigrant and requires public schools to document their students' immigration status, among other measures. The Alabama law has also been temporarily partially enjoined, as have similarly problematic laws in Utah, Indiana, and Georgia. Nevertheless, appeals courts allowed several problematic provisions in the Alabama law to go into effect.

Labor Rights

US workers continue to face severe obstacles in forming and joining trade unions, and the federal government and many state governments are failing to meet their international obligations to protect the free exercise of these rights. Several states—including Arizona, Indiana, Michigan, New Hampshire, Ohio, Oklahoma, and Wisconsin—placed severe restrictions in 2011 on workers' rights to bargain collectively.

Hundreds of thousands of children work on US farms. The 1938 Fair Labor Standards Act specifically exempts farmworker children from the minimum age and maximum hour requirements that apply to all other working children,

exposing them to work at younger ages, for longer hours, and under more hazardous conditions. As a result, child farmworkers, most of who are of Latin American descent, often work 10 or more hours a day and risk pesticide poisoning, heat illness, injuries, life-long disabilities, and death. More than half of all working children who suffered fatal occupational injuries in 2010 worked in crop production, up from previous years. Many child farmworkers drop out of school, and girls are sometimes subjected to sexual harassment. Federal protections that do exist are often not enforced: agricultural inspections and child labor law violations declined in 2010. Notably, in August the Department of Labor proposed to expand the list of hazardous agricultural tasks prohibited for children under age 16. (Outside agriculture federal law bans hazardous work for children under age 18).

Millions of US workers, including parents of infants, are harmed by weak or non-existent laws on paid leave, breastfeeding accommodation, and discrimination against workers with family responsibilities. A February 2011 Human Rights Watch report showed that having scarce or no paid leave contributed to delaying babies' immunizations, postpartum depression, and other health problems, and caused mothers to stop breastfeeding early.

Health Policy

HIV infections in the US continued to rise at an alarming rate in 2011, particularly in minority communities. Many states continue to undermine human rights and public health with restrictions on sex education, inadequate legal protections for HIV-positive persons, resistance to harm-reduction programs such as syringe exchanges, and failure to fund HIV prevention and care. Human Rights Watch reported in 2011 on state laws and policies that are blocking access to HIV treatment and services in Mississippi, where half of those testing positive for HIV are not in care and the death rate from AIDS is 60 percent higher than the national average. Human Rights Watch also highlighted the struggle to expand syringe access to injection drug users in North Carolina, where laws criminalizing syringe possession are forcing exchange programs to operate underground and advocates to risk arrest on a daily basis.

UNITED STATES

We Know What to Do

Harm Reduction and Human Rights in North Carolina

HUMAN
RIGHTS
WATCH

Women's and Girls' Rights

In a 2011 decision the Inter-American Commission on Human Rights ruled that the US violated the American Declaration of the Rights and Duties of Man when the government failed to enforce a restraining order obtained by a wife against an abusive husband who abducted the couple's daughters in Colorado in 1999. The commission recommended that the US make enforcement of protection orders mandatory, adopt protection measures for children in domestic violence situations, and better train officials on domestic violence prevention and response.

The US Supreme Court ruled in June 2011 that 1.5 million women employees of Walmart could not constitute a class for a class action suit against the corporation for discrimination in pay and advancement opportunities. The decision calls into question the viability of large-scale gender discrimination suits in the US, where women earn an average of 77 cents for every dollar earned by men.

Rights relating to abortion access continued to be heavily contested in 2011, with fights at the state and national levels over insurance coverage for abortion and over patients' rights to information and services. Federal judges ruled against laws in Baltimore and New York City that would have required "crisis pregnancy centers" to inform clients that they do not provide abortions or certain methods of contraception.

Sexual Orientation and Gender Identity

US law offers no protection against discrimination based on sexual orientation or gender identity. In December 2010 President Barack Obama signed the "Don't Ask, Don't Tell Repeal Act of 2010," which repealed the discriminatory policy barring gays and lesbians from serving openly in the US military, pending military review. The repeal went into effect in September 2011.

The Defense of Marriage Act continues to bar recognition of same-sex marriage at the federal level. However, in February the DOJ informed Congress that it would not continue defending in the courts the constitutionality of the provision that defines "marriage" as a legal union between one man and one woman.

Same-sex marriages are not recognized or performed in forty-one states. In June New York state passed the Marriage Equality Act, becoming the sixth and largest state (Washington, DC, is the seventh jurisdiction) to grant these marriage licenses. At this writing the California Supreme Court was considering jurisdictional questions raised by a challenge to a district court decision that California's 2008 same-sex marriage ban (Proposition 8) was unconstitutional.

Hawaii, Connecticut, and Nevada passed measures to ban employment discrimination based on sexual orientation or gender identity. In August a federal appeals court upheld a lower court's decision that declared unconstitutional a Wisconsin law barring transgender inmates from receiving hormone therapy or sex reassignment surgery, even when medically necessary.

Disability Rights

According to the US government, persons with disabilities are almost twice as likely as those without disabilities to be victims of violence. While the 2009 Matthew Shepard and James Byrd Hate Crime Prevention Act increased awareness of hate crimes against people with disabilities, underreporting of these crimes remains a concern.

Counterterrorism

Despite overwhelming evidence that senior Bush administration officials approved illegal interrogation methods involving torture and other ill-treatment after September 11, 2001, the Obama administration failed to criminally investigate high-level officials or to establish a commission of inquiry.

A long-awaited investigation by Special Prosecutor John Durham concluded that further criminal investigation was warranted only with respect to the deaths in custody of two detainees, but there have been no investigations into hundreds of other instances of detainee abuse. The Obama administration continued to invoke an overly broad interpretation of the "state secrets" privilege in civil suits brought by current and former detainees alleging abuse, further limiting a possible avenue for redress for victims of torture and other ill-treatment.

In December 2010 Congress enacted funding restrictions limiting the administration's ability to repatriate and resettle Guantanamo detainees. The only detainee transferred in 2011 was sent against his will to Algeria where he feared he would be tortured. While Human Rights Watch has not received reports of abuse since his return, the US refused to allow an independent arbiter to review his claim of fear of torture.

In March 2011 Obama signed an executive order establishing a periodic administrative review system for detainees currently held at Guantanamo and either designated for indefinite detention, or for trial but not yet facing charges. At this writing no implementing regulations have been issued.

Proposed legislation in Congress seeks to expand US domestic authority to detain alleged terrorism suspects indefinitely without charge and to mandate military detention for a certain category of terrorism suspects. In February a detainee pled guilty before a military commission and was sentenced to 34 months, conditioned upon his continued cooperation with the government, or 14 years otherwise.

The military commission appellate court ruled in two cases that military commissions have jurisdiction over conspiracy and material support for terrorism, crimes that have never previously been considered as war crimes under international law. In April 2011 Attorney General Eric Holder announced that he had reversed his earlier decision to prosecute the five men accused of plotting the 9/11 attacks in federal court and would instead try them before a military commission. Charges were sworn against the five men. Charges were also referred against the man accused of plotting the bombing of the *USS Cole* in Yemen in October 2000; he was arraigned in November before a military commission.

The Obama administration announced in July 2011 that it had captured a terrorism suspect off the coast of Somalia and detained him on a ship for nearly two months before the International Committee of the Red Cross was allowed to visit him in detention. He was later transferred to New York for prosecution in federal court.

In May 2011 a team of US Navy SEALS killed al Qaeda leader Osama bin Laden in Abbotabad, Pakistan. In September Anwar al Awlaki, a cleric with US citizenship who Obama described as the "leader of external operations" for al Qaeda in the Arabian Peninsula (AQAP), was killed by a US-operated drone strike in Yemen. Another US citizen, Samir Khan, who was the editor of AQAP's online magazine Inspire, was killed in the same strike. In October a drone attack killed Awlaki's 16-year-old son, along with several others; the US has said the son was not the target. Despite calls for greater transparency, the US continues to be vague about the legal justifications for these killings and about who can be targeted, when, and under what conditions.

In September Human Rights Watch uncovered a cache of documents in Tripoli that detailed the CIA's role in the rendition of terrorism suspects to Libya, as well as its role in questioning those suspects once in Libya. The CIA participated in these actions despite overwhelming evidence at the time that the suspects would likely face torture.

INTERNATIONAL JUSTICE

Course Correction

Recommendations to the ICC Prosecutor for a
More Effective Approach to "Situations under Analysis"

HUMAN
RIGHTS
WATCH

WORLD REPORT
2012

2011
HUMAN RIGHTS WATCH
PUBLICATIONS

BY COUNTRY

Afghanistan

"Just Don't Call It a Militia": Impunity, Militias, and the "Afghan Local Police", September 2011, 102 pp.

Bahrain

"Targets of Retribution": Attacks against Medics, Injured Protesters, and Health Facilities, July 2011, 54 pp.

Bangladesh

"Crossfire": Continued Human Rights Abuses by Bangladesh's Rapid Action Battalion, May 2011, 53 pp.

Belarus

"Shattering Hopes": Post-Election Crackdown in Belarus, March 2011, 31 pp.

Burma

"Dead Men Walking": Convict Porters on the Front Lines in Eastern Burma, July 2011, 70 pp.

Cambodia

"They Deceived Us at Every Step": Abuse of Cambodian Domestic Workers Migrating to Malaysia, October 2011, 105 pp.

China

"My Children Have Been Poisoned": A Public Health Crisis in Four Chinese Provinces, June 2011, 75 pp.

"Promises Unfulfilled": An Assessment of China's National Human Rights Action Plan, January 2011, 67 pp.

Côte d'Ivoire

"They Killed Them Like It Was Nothing": The Need for Justice for Côte d'Ivoire's Post-Election Crimes, October 2011, 130 pp.

Egypt

"Work on Him Until He Confesses" : Impunity for Torture in Egypt, January 2011, 95 pp.

Eritrea

"Ten Long Years": A Briefing on Eritrea's Missing Political Prisoners, September 2011, 46 pp.

Georgia

"Living in Limbo": Rights of Ethnic Georgians Returnees to the Gali District of Abkhazia, July 2011, 71 pp.

Greece

"The EU's Dirty Hands": Frontex Involvement in Ill-Treatment of Migrant Detainees in Greece, September 2011, 62 pp.

Guinea

"We Have Lived in Darkness": A Human Rights Agenda for Guinea's New Government, May 2011, 68 pp.

Haiti

"Nobody Remembers Us": Failure to Protect Women's and Girls' Right to Health and Security in Post-Earthquake Haiti, August 2011, 78 pp.

"Haiti's Rendezvous with History": The Case of Jean-Claude Duvalier, April 2011, 47 pp.

India

"The "Anti-Nationals": Arbitrary Detention and Torture of Terrorism Suspects in India, February 2011, 106 pp.

Iraq

"At a Crossroads": Human Rights in Iraq Eight Years after the US-Led Invasion , February 2011, 102 pp.

Israel and the Occupied Territories

"No News is Good News": Abuses against Journalists by Palestinian Security Forces, April 2011, 35 pp.

"Separate and Unequal": Israel's Discriminatory Treatment of Palestinians in the Occupied Palestinian Territories, December 2010, 164 pp.

Italy

"Everyday Intolerance": Racist and Xenophobic Violence in Italy, March 2011, 71 pp.

Jordan

"Domestic Plight": How Jordanian Laws, Officials, Employers, and Recruiters Fail Abused Migrant Domestic Workers, September 2011, 111 pp.

Kenya

"Hold Your Heart": Waiting for Justice in Kenya's Mt. Elgon Region, October 2011, 48 pp.

"Turning Pebbles": Evading Accountability for Post-Election Violence in Kenya, December 2011, 95 pp.

Kuwait

"Prisoners of the Past": Kuwaiti Bidun and the Burden of Statelessness, June 2011, 63 pp.

Kyrgyzstan

"Distorted Justice": Kyrgyzstan's Flawed Investigations and Trials on the 2010 Violence, June 2011, 86 pp.

Laos

"Somsanga's Secrets": Arbitrary Detention, Physical Abuse, and Suicide inside a Lao Drug Detention Center, October 2011, 76 pp.

Mali

"A Poisonous Mix": Child Labor, Mercury, and Gold Mining in Mali, November 2011, 101 pp.

Mexico

"Neither Rights Nor Security": Killings, Torture, and Disappearances in Mexico's "War on Drugs," November 2011, 212 pp.

Nepal

"Futures Stolen": Barriers to Education for Children with Disabilities in Nepal, August 2011, 76 pp.

"Adding Insult to Injury": Continued Impunity for Wartime Abuses, December 2011, 49 pp.

The Netherlands

"Controlling Bodies, Denying Identities": Human Rights Violations against Trans People in the Netherlands, September 2011, 85 pp.

Nigeria

"Corruption on Trial?": The Record of Nigeria's Economic and Financial Crimes Commission, August 2011, 65 pp.

Pakistan

"We Can Torture, Kill, or Keep You for Years": Enforced Disappearances by Pakistan Security Forces in Balochistan, July 2011, 132 pp.

Papua New Guinea

"Gold's Costly Dividend": Human Rights Impacts of Papua New Guinea's Porgera Gold Mine, February 2011, 94 pp.

Philippines

"No Justice Just Adds to the Pain": Killings, Disappearances, and Impunity in the Philippines, July 2011, 96 pp.

Russia

"You Dress According to Their Rules": Enforcement of an Islamic Dress Code for Women in Chechnya, March 2011, 40 pp.

669

Rwanda

"Justice Compromised": The Legacy of Rwanda's Community-Based Gacaca Courts, May 2011, 144 pp.

Somalia

"You Don't Know Who to Blame": War Crimes in Somalia, August 2011, 58 pp.

South Africa

"We'll Show You You're a Woman": Violence and Discrimination against Black Lesbians and Transgender Men in South Africa, December 2011, 93 pp.

"Ripe with Abuse": Human Rights Conditions in South Africa's Fruit and Wine Industries, August 2011, 96 pp.

"Stop Making Excuses": Accountability for Maternal Health Care in South Africa, August 2011, 66 pp.

Sudan

"Darfur in the Shadows": The Sudanese Government's Ongoing Attacks on Civilians and Human Rights, June 2011, 28 pp.

Syria

"We Live as in War": Crackdown on Protestors in the Governorate of Homs, November 2011, 139 pp.

Thailand

"Descent into Chaos": Thailand's 2010 Red Shirt Protests and the Government Crackdown, May 2011, 139 pp.

Turkey

"He Loves You, He Beats You": Family Violence in Turkey and Access to Protection, May 2011, 58 pp.

Uganda

"Righting Military Injustice": Addressing Uganda's Unlawful Prosecutions of Civilians in Military Courts, July 2011, 27 pp.

"Even Dead Bodies Must Work": Health, Hard Labor, and Abuse in Ugandan Prisons, July 2011, 80 pp.

"Violence Instead of Vigilance": Torture and Illegal Detention by Uganda's Rapid Response Unit, March 2011, 59 pp.

United States

"Getting Away with Torture": The Bush Administration and Mistreatment of Detainees, July 2011, 107 pp.

"A Costly Move": Far and Frequent Transfers Impede Hearings for Immigrant Detainees in the United States, June 2011, 35 pp.

"Rights at Risk": State Response to HIV in Mississippi, March 2011, 59 pp.

"Failing its Families": Lack of Paid Leave and Work-Family Supports in the US, February 2011, 90 pp.

"No Way to Live": Alabama's Immigrant Law, December 2011, 52 pp.

Ukraine

"Uncontrolled Pain": Ukraine's Obligation to Ensure Evidence-Based Palliative Care, May 2011, 93 pp.

Uzbekistan

"No One Left to Witness": Torture, the Failure of Habeas Corpus, and the Silencing of Lawyers in Uzbekistan, December 2011, 104 pp.

Yemen

"How Come You Allow Little Girls To Get Married?": Child Marriage in Yemen, December 2011, 52 pp.

Vietnam

"The Rehab Archipelago": Forced Labor and Other Abuses in Drug Detention Centers in Southern Vietnam, September 2011, 121 pp.

The Party vs. Legal Activist Cu Huy Ha Vu, May 2011, 56 pp.

"Montagnard Christians in Vietnam": A Case Study in Religious Repression, March 2011, 46 pp.

Zambia

"You'll Be Fired if You Refuse": Labor Abuses in Zambia's Chinese State-Owned Copper Mines, November 2011, 122 pp.

Zimbabwe

"Perpetual Fear": Impunity and Cycles of Violence in Zimbabwe, March 2011, 40 pp.

BY THEME

Business and Human Rights

"A Poisonous Mix": Child Labor, Mercury, and Gold Mining in Mali, November 2011, 101 pp.

"You'll Be Fired if You Refuse": Labor Abuses in Zambia's Chinese State-Owned Copper Mines, November 2011, 122 pp.

"Corruption on Trial?": The Record of Nigeria's Economic and Financial Crimes Commission, August 2011, 65 pp.

"Ripe with Abuse": Human Rights Conditions in South Africa's Fruit and Wine Industries, August 2011, 96 pp.

"Gold's Costly Dividend": Human Rights Impacts of Papua New Guinea's Porgera Gold Mine, February 2011, 94 pp

Children's Rights

"A Poisonous Mix": Child Labor, Mercury, and Gold Mining in Mali, November 2011, 101 pp.

"Futures Stolen": Barriers to Education for Children with Disabilities in Nepal, August 2011, 76 pp.

"Schools and Armed Conflict": A Global Survey of Domestic Laws and State Practice Protecting Schools from Attack and Military Use, July 2011, 162 pp.

"My Children Have Been Poisoned": A Public Health Crisis in Four Chinese Provinces, June 2011, 75 pp.

Counterterrorism

"Ten Long Years": A Briefing on Eritrea's Missing Political Prisoners, September 2011, 46 pp.

"We Can Torture, Kill, or Keep You for Years": Enforced Disappearances by Pakistan Security Forces in Balochistan, July 2011, 132 pp.

"Getting Away with Torture": The Bush Administration and Mistreatment of Detainees, July 2011, 107 pp.

"The "Anti-Nationals"": Arbitrary Detention and Torture of Terrorism Suspects in India, February 2011, 106 pp.

Disability Rights

"Futures Stolen": Barriers to Education for Children with Disabilities in Nepal, August 2011, 76 pp.

"My Children Have Been Poisoned": A Public Health Crisis in Four Chinese Provinces, June 2011, 75 pp.

Environment

"My Children Have Been Poisoned": A Public Health Crisis in Four Chinese Provinces, June 2011, 75 pp.

"Gold's Costly Dividend": Human Rights Impacts of Papua New Guinea's Porgera Gold Mine, February 2011, 94 pp.

Economic, Social, and Cultural Rights

"Promises Unfulfilled": An Assessment of China's National Human Rights Action Plan, January 2011, 67 pp.

"Separate and Unequal": Israel's Discriminatory Treatment of Palestinians in the Occupied Palestinian Territories, December 2010, 164 pp.

Health and Human Rights

"A Poisonous Mix": Child Labor, Mercury, and Gold Mining in Mali, November 2011, pp. 101.

"Somsanga's Secrets": Arbitrary Detention, Physical Abuse, and Suicide inside a Lao Drug Detention Center, October 2011, 76 pp.

"The Rehab Archipelago": Forced Labor and Other Abuses in Drug Detention Centers in Southern Vietnam, September 2011, 121 pp.

"Nobody Remembers Us": Failure to Protect Women's and Girls' Right to Health and Security in Post-Earthquake Haiti, August 2011, 78 pp.

"Stop Making Excuses": Accountability for Maternal Health Care in South Africa, August 2011, 66 pp.

"Targets of Retribution": Attacks against Medics, Injured Protesters, and Health Facilities, July 2011, 54 pp.

"Even Dead Bodies Must Work": Health, Hard Labor, and Abuse in Ugandan Prisons, July 2011, 80 pp.

"Dead Men Walking": Convict Porters on the Front Lines in Eastern Burma, July 2011, 70 pp.

"My Children Have Been Poisoned": A Public Health Crisis in Four Chinese Provinces, June 2011, 75 pp.

"Prisoners of the Past": Kuwaiti Bidun and the Burden of Statelessness, June 2011, 63 pp.

"Global State of Pain Treatment": Access to Medicines and Palliative Care, June 2011, 128 pp.

"Uncontrolled Pain": Ukraine's Obligation to Ensure Evidence-Based Palliative Care, May 2011, 93 pp.

"Rights at Risk": State Response to HIV in Mississippi, March 2011, 59 pp.

International Justice

"Unfinished Business": Closing Gaps in the Selection of ICC Cases, September 2011, 55 pp.

"Corruption on Trial?": The Record of Nigeria's Economic and Financial Crimes Commission, August 2011, 65 pp.

"No Justice Just Adds to the Pain": Killings, Disappearances, and Impunity in the Philippines, July 2011, 96 pp.

"Justice Compromised": The Legacy of Rwanda's Community-Based Gacaca Courts, May 2011, 144 pp.

"Haiti's Rendezvous with History": The Case of Jean-Claude Duvalier, April 2011, 47 pp.

"Adding Insult to Injury": Continued Impunity for Wartime Abuses, December 2011, 49 pp.

Schools and Armed Conflict

A Global Survey of Domestic Laws and State Practice
Protecting Schools from Attack and Military Use

HUMAN
RIGHTS
WATCH

Keeping the Momentum

One Year in the Life of the UN Human Rights Council

HUMAN
RIGHTS
WATCH

LGBT Rights

"We'll Show You You're a Woman": Violence and Discrimination against Black Lesbians and Transgender Men in South Africa, December 2011, 93 pp.

"Controlling Bodies, Denying Identities": Human Rights Violations against Trans People in the Netherlands, September 2011, 85 pp.

"Rights at Risk": State Response to HIV in Mississippi, March 2011, 59 pp.

Migrant Workers

"You'll Be Fired if You Refuse": Labor Abuses in Zambia's Chinese State-Owned Copper Mines, November 2011, 122 pp.

"They Deceived Us at Every Step": Abuse of Cambodian Domestic Workers Migrating to Malaysia, November 2011, 105 pp.

"Domestic Plight": How Jordanian Laws, Officials, Employers, and Recruiters Fail Abused Migrant Domestic Workers, September 2011, 111 pp.

"The EU's Dirty Hands": Frontex Involvement in Ill-Treatment of Migrant Detainees in Greece, September 2011, 62 pp.

"A Costly Move": Far and Frequent Transfers Impede Hearings for Immigrant Detainees in the United States, June 2011, 35 pp.

"Everyday Intolerance": Racist and Xenophobic Violence in Italy, March 2011, 71 pp.

"At a Crossroads": Human Rights in Iraq Eight Years after the US-Led Invasion, February 2011, 102 pp.

Media Freedom

"Ten Long Years": A Briefing on Eritrea's Missing Political Prisoners, September 2011, 46 pp.

"Haiti's Rendezvous with History": The Case of Jean-Claude Duvalier, April 2011, 47 pp.

"No News is Good News": Abuses against Journalists by Palestinian Security Forces, April 2011, 35 pp.

Refugees/Displaced Persons

"Domestic Plight": How Jordanian Laws, Officials, Employers, and Recruiters Fail Abused Migrant Domestic Workers, September 2011, 111 pp.

"The EU's Dirty Hands": Frontex Involvement in Ill-Treatment of Migrant Detainees in Greece, September 2011, 62 pp.

"Living in Limbo": Rights of Ethnic Georgians Returnees to the Gali District of Abkhazia, July 2011, 71 pp.

"A Costly Move": Far and Frequent Transfers Impede Hearings for Immigrant Detainees in the United States, June 2011, 35 pp.

"Everyday Intolerance": Racist and Xenophobic Violence in Italy, March 2011, 71 pp.

Terrorism and Counterterrorism

"Ten Long Years": A Briefing on Eritrea's Missing Political Prisoners, September 2011, 46 pp.

"Getting Away with Torture": The Bush Administration and Mistreatment of Detainees, July 2011, 107 pp.

Torture

"We Can Torture, Kill, or Keep You for Years": Enforced Disappearances by Pakistan Security Forces in Balochistan, July 2011, 132 pp.

"No Justice Just Adds to the Pain": Killings, Disappearances, and Impunity in the Philippines, July 2011, 96 pp.

"Getting Away with Torture": The Bush Administration and Mistreatment of Detainees, July 2011, 107 pp.

"Crossfire": Continued Human Rights Abuses by Bangladesh's Rapid Action Battalion, May 2011, 53 pp.

"Haiti's Rendezvous with History": The Case of Jean-Claude Duvalier, April 2011, 47 pp.

"Violence Instead of Vigilance": Torture and Illegal Detention by Uganda's Rapid Response Unit, March 2011, 59 pp.

"Perpetual Fear": Impunity and Cycles of Violence in Zimbabwe, March 2011, 40 pp.

"At a Crossroads": Human Rights in Iraq Eight Years after the US-Led Invasion, February 2011, 102 pp.

"The "Anti-Nationals": Arbitrary Detention and Torture of Terrorism Suspects in India, February 2011, 106 pp.

United Nations

"Keeping the Momentum": One Year in the Life of the UN Human Rights Council, September 2011, 69 pp.

Women's Rights

"We'll Show You You're a Woman": Violence and Discrimination against Black Lesbians and Transgender Men in South Africa, December 2011, 93 pp.

"They Deceived Us at Every Step": Abuse of Cambodian Domestic Workers Migrating to Malaysia, November 2011, 105 pp.

"Nobody Remembers Us": Failure to Protect Women's and Girls' Right to Health and Security in Post-Earthquake Haiti, August 2011, 78 pp.

"Stop Making Excuses": Accountability for Maternal Health Care in South Africa, August 2011, 66 pp.

"Prisoners of the Past": Kuwaiti Bidun and the Burden of Statelessness, June 2011, 63 pp.

"He Loves You, He Beats You": Family Violence in Turkey and Access to Protection, May 2011, 58 pp.

"Haiti's Rendezvous with History": The Case of Jean-Claude Duvalier, April 2011, 47 pp.

"You Dress According to Their Rules": Enforcement of an Islamic Dress Code for Women in Chechnya, March 2011, 40 pp.

"Failing its Families": Lack of Paid Leave and Work-Family Supports in the US, February 2011, 90 pp.

"At a Crossroads": Human Rights in Iraq Eight Years after the US-Led Invasion , February 2011, 102 pp.

"How Come You Allow Little Girls To Get Married?": Child Marriage in Yemen, December 2011, 52 pp.

All reports can be accessed online and ordered at www.hrw.org/en/publications.